The Samuel Gompers Papers

THE
Samuel Gompers
PAPERS

VOLUME
13
Cumulative
Index

Editors
Peter J. Albert
Grace Palladino

Assistant Editors
Christina G. Larocco
Katarina Keane

UNIVERSITY OF ILLINOIS PRESS
Urbana, Chicago, and Springfield

Major funding of the publication costs of this volume
was provided by the Department of History and the
Division of Research at the University of Maryland.

*The paper in this book meets the guidelines for permanence and
durability of the Committee on Production Guidelines for
Book Longevity of the Council on Library Resources.*
∞ This book is printed on acid-free paper.

Library of Congress Cataloging-in-Publication Data
The Samuel Gompers Papers
Includes bibliographies and indexes.
Contents: v. 1. The making of a union leader, 1850–86 — v. 2. The early
years of the American Federation of Labor, 1887–90 — v. 3. Unrest and
depression, 1891–94 — v. 4. A national labor movement takes shape,
1895–98 — v. 5. An expanding movement at the turn of the century,
1898–1902 — v. 6. The American Federation of Labor and the rise of
progressivism, 1902–6 — v. 7. The American Federation of Labor under
siege, 1906–9 — v. 8. Progress and reaction in the age of reform, 1909–13
— v. 9. The American Federation of Labor at the height of progressivism,
1913–17 —v. 10. The American Federation of Labor and the Great War,
1917–18— v. 11. The postwar years, 1918–21 — v. 12. The last years,
1922–24— v. 13. Cumulative Index.
1. Gompers, Samuel, 1850–1924—Archives.
2. Trade-unions—United States—History—Sources.
3. Labor movement—United States—History—Sources.
I. Gompers, Samuel, 1850–1924.
HD6508.S218   2003
331.88í32í902   84–2469
ISBN-10 0-252-01138-4 (alk. paper: set)
ISBN-13 978-0-252-01138-2 (alk. paper: set)
ISBN-10 0-252-03742-1 (alk. paper: v. 13)
ISBN-13 978-0-252-03742-9 (alk. paper: v. 13)

If the unexamined life is not worth living,
the unexamined past is not worth possessing. It bears
fruit only by being held continuously up to the light.
—BRENDAN GILL

CONTENTS

INTRODUCTION

Publication of this cumulative index completes the work of the Samuel Gompers Project, to collect and publish the voluminous papers of the first president of the American Federation of Labor.

It would be impossible to thank all the individuals and organizations that have supported the Samuel Gompers Project over the years, but we want to mention some of them. First, we want to acknowledge the great debt we owe our friend and colleague Stuart Kaufman, who envisioned this documentary record of workers in America in the half-century between 1875 and 1925, launched the Gompers Project, and saw our first volumes and our microfilm into publication before his untimely death in 1997.

And we want to thank the Gompers family, particularly Samuel Gompers' granddaughter Florence Gompers MacKay, for their permission to publish these records.

The AFL-CIO gave its official consent to publish these papers, and the AFL-CIO and the many unions that date back to the Gompers era opened their archives to us, making a wealth of documents available for our research.

We also want to express our appreciation for long-term financial support to the Samuel Gompers Project from the National Historical Publications and Records Commission, the National Endowment for the Humanities, and the University of Maryland, as well as major grants from the AFL-CIO and constituent unions, the George Meany Memorial Archives, the Joseph Anthony Beirne Memorial Foundation of the Communications Workers of America, the Ford Foundation, and the Stiftung Volkswagenwerk. Without this partnership of financial support, the Project would not have been possible.

We deeply appreciate the ongoing day-to-day support the Samuel Gompers Project has received from so many individuals here at the University of Maryland, College Park, particularly our colleagues in the History Department and our generous hosts in McKeldin Library, where our offices are located and where we have worked for so many

years. In addition, we want to thank the many other libraries and archives whose ongoing assistance to our research has been so crucial to our work.

We are indebted to the members of our advisory board, who gave each of our volumes a careful reading while still in manuscript and improved them with helpful suggestions and penetrating criticism. We deeply appreciate how generously they contributed their valuable time and considered judgment.

And we want to acknowledge our debt to the editorial staff of our publisher, the University of Illinois Press, for their indefatigable support and cooperation through these many years.

Finally, we want to thank the many colleagues who have worked with us on the Samuel Gompers Project—nearly sixty of them over the years, editors and researchers, annotators and translators, transcribers and proofreaders, indexers and fact checkers—an ongoing community of scholarship. We are indebted to them for their resourcefulness and skill, their commitment and collegiality, their thoughtful judgment and common sense, their patience and good humor. They have made these volumes better in countless ways.

CUMULATIVE INDEX

Volume numbers in this index appear in **boldface** type. An "n" following a page number indicates a subject is mentioned in a note. For example, the entry

Abrahams, Albert, **8:**140–41, 141n

indicates that Albert Abrahams appears in volume 8 on pages 140–41 and in a note on page 141.

Volumes with glossary entries for specific individuals or organizations are designated with an asterisk. For example, the entries **7:***, **8:***, **9:***, **10:***, and **12:*** under John Alpine indicate that volumes 7, 8, 9, 10, and 12 contain glossary entries for Alpine.

References to substantive annotations in notes appear in *italic* type. For example, the entry

Abbett, Leon, **2:**137, *138n*

indicates there is a substantive annotation of Leon Abbett in volume 2 in a note on page 138.

Abbett, Leon, **2:**137, *138n*
Abern, Martin, **12:**275–77, 277–*78n*
Abrahams, Albert, **8:**140–41, 141n
Abrahams, Henry, **2:***, 198–99, *198–99n*, 407, 410, **12:**91n
Abrams, Jessie E., **10:**99, 102n
Abrams, L. N., *10:69n; letter from,* **10:**67–69
Acme Press Brick Co., **5:**504, 505n
Acornley, A. H., **5:**240, 243–44n
Acquisitive Society, The (Tawney), **12:**191, *192n*
Acton, Harry H., **4:**236–37, *238n*, 239
Actors' National Protective Union, **6:***, 517, 518n, **7:***, 41n
—local: local 14 (New York City), **6:**517–18n
—strike/lockout: 1906 (New York City), **6:**516–17, *517–18n*
Adair, John A. M., *7:99n,* **8:**342; *letter from,* **7:**99

Adames, William J., **8:**258, *259n*
Adams, Alva, **2:**82, *88n,* **4:**266
Adams, Charles, **4:**249n
Adams, Charles Francis, **5:**464n, *496–97n; letter from,* **5:**494–96
Adams, Elijah J., **3:**139, *140n*
Adams, Emmet L., **11:**456, *459n,* 525–26
Adams, Frederick U., **3:**85, *86n*
Adams, John Quincy, **7:**88
Adams, Norman, **11:**122
Adams, Oswin T., **11:**190, *191n*
Adamski, Albert, **9:**406, *406n,* **12:**550
Adamson, William C., **9:**450n, **10:**15, 16–*17n*
Addams, Jane, **4:**45n, *9:231–32n,* 274n, **12:**427n; *letter to,* **9:**231
Address, An. To the Western Federation of Miners, in Convention Assembled, Salt Lake City, Utah (AFL), **5:**150, *151n*
Adkins et al. v. Children's Hospital of

1

D.C., **12:**227, *228n,* 230, 244, 246, 248–50, 370
Adler, C. N., **3:**378, 381, *382n*
Adler, Felix, **2:***, 94, *94n,* **5:**352
Adler and Landauer, **1:**112, *115n*
Advance (Detroit labor journal), **2:**97
Afel (cargo ship), **11:**97, *97n*
AFL. *See* American Federation of Labor (AFL)
"A.F. of L. Campaign Programme," **7:**20, 21n, 60–64, 64n, 65–67, 95
Agard, Edgar A., **5:**441–42, *444n,* **6:**55, *57n,* 59–61, 67–68, 205, 206n
Agricultural Labourers' Union, National, **1:***, 340, 353n, **3:**145–46, 146n
Agricultural Wheel, **3:**24n
Aguilar Vargas, Cándido, **9:**306, *307n*
Aguinaldo, Emilio, **5:**64n
Ahearn (meatpacker), **10:**285n
Ailes, Milton E., **5:**411, *411n*
airplanes, transatlantic crossings by, **11:**90, 92n
Aishton, Richard, **9:**312n
Alabama, disfranchisement of blacks in, **6:**106, 107n
Alabama Drydock and Shipbuilding Co., strike/lockout, 1920–21, **11:**484–85, *486n*
Alabama State Federation of Labor, **6:**106, *107n,* 108
—convention: 1903 (Bessemer), **6:**109, *110n*
Alameda County (Calif.), Federated Trades of, **8:**414, *414n*
Albany (N.Y.) Central Federation of Labor, **5:**361n
Albert I, **10:**563, *567n,* **11:**56
Albright, Albion D., **12:**276, *278n*
Albright, Jacob, **2:**319n
alcohol, consumption of. *See* drinking; Prohibition; temperance movement
Alcorn, Robert H., **12:**345, *348n*
Aldrich, William F., **7:**80, *90n*
Aldridge, G. W., **4:**333n
Aldridge, William, **7:**130, 142n
Ale and Porter Brewery Union 1 (Albany, N.Y.), **4:**222, 223n
Alexander, D. L., **3:***, *24n; letter from,* **3:**23–24

Alexander, DeAlva, **9:**200n
Alexander, George, **8:**248, *249n,* 291
Alexander, H. M., **6:**39, *40n*
Alexander, John, **5:***, *413n; letter from,* **5:**412–13
Alexander, Joshua, **10:**213n
Alexander, Magnus W., **11:**287–88, *289n*
Alexander II, assassination of, **6:**321, 326n
Alger, George W., **8:**489, *493n,* **12:**74n
Alger, Russell A., **5:**151n, **6:**243, *244n*
Alifas, Nels P., **10:**19, *21n,* **12:**345–47
All-American Conference, 1924 (Washington, D.C.), **12:**452, *452n*
Alleged Shortage of Labor, The (AFL), **10:**240n
Allegheny Coal and Coke Co.: organization of, attempted, **11:**121, 123n; strike/lockout, 1919, **11:**121–22, *123n*
Allegheny County, Pa., breweries, boycott, 1896, *4:145n*
Allen, Amos L., **7:**80, 89–*90n*
Allen, Andrew J., **12:**364, *364n*
Allen, Clay, **10:**398–99, *400n*
Allen, Colonel. *See* Mulhall, Martin M.
Allen, Florence, **12:**427n
Allen, Ford A., **5:**125, *127n*
Allen, Henry J., **11:**289–90, *290n,* **12:**169; SG debate with, **11:**289–90, 290n, 298–99, 304–8, 320n
Allen, Henry T., *12:435n; letter to,* **12:**435
Allen, Jacob S., **8:**184, *185n,* 493n, 498, **10:**103n; *letter to,* **8:**496–97
Allen, John W., and Sons, **7:**461n
Allen, Joseph B., **3:**661, *664n,* **6:**174, *175n*
Allen, L. B., *letter from,* **6:**115–16
Allen, Louis L., **7:**301, *302n*
Allen, Mary E., **8:**497, *497n*
Allen, Noah, **11:**326n
Allen, Norman M., **1:**261, *263n*
Allen, Thomas, **3:**77, *78n*
Allen, William O., **1:**283, 285n
Allen, William V., **4:**324n
Aller, Juan, **5:**185, *188n,* 232
Allgemeiner Deutscher Arbeiterverein, **1:**23, 32, *43n,* **2:**159n

Allgemeiner Deutscher Gewerk-
schaftsbund, **12:**368; and women
workers, **12:**361n
Allied Freight Transportation Coun-
cil, **5:**497n
Allied Trades and Labor Association
(Ottawa, Ont.), **6:**156, *158n*
allied union label councils, **5:**519
Allimon, Walter D., **6:**293, *294n*
Allis-Chalmers Co., **5:**334n
All-Russian Congress of the Russian
Communist Youth League, Fifth,
1922 (Moscow), **12:**293, 294n
All-Russian Council of Workers' and
Soldiers' Deputies, **10:**90n
Alma, Juan, **5:**180
Alonso, José G., **9:**429n, 467, *468n*
Alonso, Manuel, **5:**180, *188n*
Alonso, Rafael, **6:**253, 258n, *7:53n,*
9:533
Alpert, Nathan, *9:405n; letter to,*
9:403–5
Alpine, John R., **7:***, *442n,* 453n, **8:***,
125n, 159, 402, 500–501, **9:***, *14n,*
74n, 274n, **10:***, 104, *105n,* 421,
519n, 546n, **11:**40n, **12:***, 550, *553n;*
at AFL Executive Council meetings,
8:503–4, **9:**270–71, 436; and Cantonment Adjustment Commission,
10:114, 204; election of, as AFL
vice-president, **7:**427n, **8:**18n, 295,
9:38n, 226n, 348n, **10:**475; *letters
from,* **10:**544–48; *letter to,* **10:**520–23;
and Liberty Loan drive, **10:**543;
and Norfolk Navy Yard strike, 1917,
10:223n
Alsbury, John, **3:**364
Alschuler, Samuel, **10:**280n, *304n,*
11:453n, **12:**154
Alt, Charles, **1:**413, *414n*
Altgeld, John P., **2:***, 53, 301, *304n,*
3:*, *350n,* 358, 359n, 523, 559,
4:377, 379n, **5:**414–15, 415n; *letters
to,* **3:**350, **5:**87–88
Alton (Ill.) Trades and Labor Assembly, **6:**186–89, *189n*
Altschuler, Modest, **10:**130, *134n*
Altvater (carpenter?), **2:**129
Aluminum Castings Co., **10:**365
Aluminum Ore Co., **10:**152–53n

Alvord, Thomas G., **1:**208, *210n*
*Amalgamated Association of Street and
Electric Railway Employes of America,
Local Union No. 497 v. Joplin and
Pittsburg Railway Co.,* **11:**408, *409n*
Amalgamated Copper Co., **6:**284,
285n, **9:**270–71, 275n
Amalgamated Labor Union, **1:**160
Amalgamated Trades and Labor
Union of New York and Vicinity,
1:96, 98, *101n,* 151–52, 238; found-
ing of, **1:**84; journal, official, of,
1:268n; and political action, **1:**248,
379n
American Academy of Political and
Social Science:
—conventions: 1902 (Philadelphia),
5:505–10, *510n;* 1911 (Philadelphia), *8:203n;* 1912, **8:**203n
American Agents Association, **4:***,
502, 502n
American Alliance for Labor and
Democracy, **9:**383n, *10:160n,*
227, 228n, 236–38, 357; and AFL,
10:258–62, 262n, 264; and *American Labor's Position in Peace or in
War,* **10:**212, 263n; and Bastille Day,
10:495, 496n; and Committee on
Public Information, **10:**160–61n,
161–62, 313n, 382–83, 495–96, 496–
97n, 499n; declarations of, **10:**192,
210–13, 261, 263n; founding of,
10:159–60, 160n, 206, 226; and Labor Loyalty Week, **10:**311, *312–13n,*
324, 330n; mission of, to Russia,
10:237, 238n; office, publications,
and staff of, **10:**161–62, 162–63n;
revenue of, **10:**240–41, 241n; and
sedition, **10:**211–12, 259; and Washington's Birthday, **10:**313n, 363n
—convention: 1917 (Minneapolis),
10:192, *194n,* 206, 236–37, 240–
41n, 260
American Ambulance in Russia,
10:129, *134n*
*American and English Encyclopaedia of
Law,* **7:**468n
American Anti-Boycott Association,
7:245, *246n,* **8:**198, 204n, 319,
9:285n, **11:**408

American Anti-Saloon League,
  12:429, *430n*
American Association for Labor Leg-
  islation, **9:**276–77, *277n;* and AFL
  Permanent Conference for Aboli-
  tion of Child Labor, **12:**82n
American Association of University
  Professors, **9:**429, *430n*
American Association of University
  Women, and AFL Permanent Con-
  ference for Abolition of Child La-
  bor, **12:**82n
American Bicycle Co., **5:**157, 158n
American Boom and Timber Co.,
  strike/lockout, 1908, **7:**378–80
American Bridge Co., *6:515n,* **8:**227n,
  272, 434; strike/lockout, 1905–?,
  6:514–15, *515–16n,* **7:**12–13
American Can Co., antitrust case
  against, **10:**322, 323n
American Cigar and Tobacco Work-
  ers' Association, *1:274n*
American Cigar Co., **6:**31n
American Civil Liberties Union,
  10:485n, **12:**263–64, 265n, 309,
  311n
American Committee for Relief of
  German Children, **12:**435, *435n*
American Committee for the Encour-
  agement of Democratic Government in Russia, **10:**89–90n
American Conference on International Arbitration, *6:378n,* 381,
  381n
American District Telegraph Co.,
  1:306
American Express Co., **6:**287
American Federationist (AFL journal),
  3:474–75, 483, 549n, **6:**161, **12:**277;
  advertising in, **4:**394–95, 395n, 412;
  and AFL Political Program, **3:**419–
  21, 502–3; and Buck's Stove injunction, **7:**249n, 263; circulation of,
  4:xiv, **5:**xiv; criticism of, **3:**478–81,
  7:425, 427n; printer of, **1:**167n
  —extra numbers of: 1902, *6:307–8n;*
  1904, **6:**300–307, *307–8n*
American Federation of Labor (AFL):
  accounts, audit of, **9:**478–79, 479n;
  affiliates, autonomy of, **2:**76–77,
  119, 122, 131, 139, 215, 262, 362,

3:100, 135, 166, 280, 406, 467, 518–
  19, 572–73, 655, **4:**120, 212–14, 245,
  12:87n, 88, 89n; charters issued by,
  2:95, **6:**318, 321–22, 326n, 493–96,
  501, 502–3n; constitution of,
  1:224, 240, 348, **2:**78, **7:**319, 320n;
  description of, **1:**387, **4:**119–20,
  7:476; dual organizations in, **4:**83,
  84n, **12:**400–401, 401n; funds of,
  2:134, **5:**xiii, xxn, 432, 432n, **6:**409,
  12:242–43; industrial divisions in,
  2:95, 175, 175n, **7:**367 (*see also AFL
  departments;* American Federation
  of Labor [AFL]: Scranton Declaration); journal, official, of, **2:**25, 26n,
  27, 37, 422, 425, **3:**402, 403n (see
  also *American Federationist; Union Advocate*); legal proceedings, financial
  support of, **3:**125–27, 128n, 129–31,
  139–40, 147–48, 148n, 186, 214–
  15n, 221–22, 250–53, 263–66, 266n,
  294, 297–98, 298n, 453–54, 454n,
  562–63, 567 (*see also specific court
  cases*; American Federation of Labor
  [AFL]: Legal Department; American Federation of Labor [AFL]: Legal Information Bureau); lobbying
  committee of, **2:**410–11, 418, 422,
  424 (*see also* American Federation
  of Labor [AFL]: Legislative Committee); membership of, **2:**90, 128,
  134, **3:**49, 93, 603–4, **4:**xiii, xxn, 60,
  160, 419, 492, **5:**xiii, xix–xxn, 73n,
  119, 431, 432n, **6:**xiv–xv, **7:**456–57,
  8:352–53, **12:**276; and military intelligence, **10:**434–36, 436n; and per
  capita tax, **2:**38, 39n, 77, 95–96, 134,
  141, 165, **4:**215–16, 279, **5:**57–58,
  58n, 447, 448n, **8:**145, 354, 355n,
  9:30; postwar reconstruction program of, **10:**356–57, 357–58n, 471–
  72, 472n, **11:**7, 7–8n, 33, 53, 54n;
  powers of, **8:**185–87 (*see also specific
  jurisdictional disputes*); president of,
  term of office of, **2:**411; quarterly financial report of, **2:**75, 93–94, 94n,
  120, 158, 187, 203; Scranton Declaration, **5:**443–44, 444n, **8:**105, *106n,*
  407–8, 408n, **12:**102, 102n, 126;
  sinking fund of (*see* American Federation of Labor [AFL]: Defense

Fund); state branches of, **2:**95–96 (*see also specific state branches*); strike fund of (*see* American Federation of Labor [AFL]: Defense Fund); and transfer of union members without new initiation fees, **12:**86, 87n
—Board of Mediation and Conciliation, **9:**224–25, 225n
—Building Trades Department, *6:175n,* 492, **7:**447, 481, **8:**367, **9:**503, **10:**452, **11:**271, **12:**155n; and Carpenters, **8:**149–50, 151n, 295, **9:**70, 73n, **11:**544–45, 545n, **12:**163n, 399–401, 401n; and Chicago building trades, **9:**261n; and Glass Workers, **7:**449–50, 451n; and Hartford, Conn., building trades, **7:**459–60, 461n; and Hod Carriers, **7:**443–44, 445–46n; and McNamara case, **8:**234–38, 238n, 355n; and National Board for Jurisdictional Awards, **11:**21–22, 22–23n, 545n; and New York City building trades, **11:**352, 445, 467, 467n; organization of, **7:**275–76, 276n, 277–79, 365–68, 368n; and Plumbers, **8:**151n, 296; and Sheet Metal Workers, **8:**151n, 295, **9:**70, 73n, **11:**545n, **12:**163n; and Steam, Hot Water, and Power Pipe Fitters, **6:**343n, **8:**149–50, 151n, 296
—Building Trades Department, conventions: 1908 (Denver), **7:**443, *445n;* 1908 (Washington, D.C.), **7:**312, *313n;* 1909 (Tampa, Fla.), **7:**445n, **8:**151n; 1910 (St. Louis), **7:**451n, **8:**149–50, *150–*51n; 1913, **9:**347n; 1915 (San Francisco), **9:**355n; 1919, **11:**23n; 1920 (Montreal), **11:**378, *379n;* 1921, **11:**468n; 1924 (El Paso, Tex.), **12:**518, *520n*
—Commission of Progress and Co-operation (proposed), **12:**141–46, 146n
—Conference Committee of Trade Union Legislative Representatives in Washington, D.C., **11:**465–66, 467n, **12:**35, 37–38, 343–47
—conventions: building trades, committee on, **6:**205–6, 206n, **7:**275–76, 276n, 277–79; date of, **3:**203, **4:**248;

5:440–41, **8:**146, 146n, **10:**257–58, 258n; proceedings of, **7:**405–6, 406–7n; quorum at, **6:**209–10; representation at, **3:**595, 597n; voting at, **5:**397, **6:**225–26
—conventions, specific: 1886 (Columbus, Ohio), **1:**167, 168n, *387,* 437, 450–52, **2:**15, 21, 23n, 261, **3:**13, *14n,* **12:**521–22; 1887 (Baltimore), **2:**18, *64n,* 105, 189, **3:**567, *580n,* **7:**211, *214n;* 1888 (St. Louis), **2:**105, 155, *156n,* 174, 376, **3:**567, *580n,* **5:**259, *260n,* **7:**367, *368n;* 1889 (Boston), **2:**231, *232n,* 249n, 255–56, 293, 294n, 346n, **3:**71, *75n;* 1890 (Detroit), *2:378n,* 430, **3:**6, *6n,* 30, 72, 91–92, **4:**368, *368n,* **6:**300, *308n,* **10:**260, *263n,* **11:**65, *66n,* **12:**374, *375n;* 1891 (Birmingham, Ala.), **3:**13, *14n,* 70n, 83n, 105, 109n, 162, 164n, 226, 264, 269n, 288–89, **10:**346, *350n;* 1892 (Philadelphia), **2:**346n, **3:**185, 214, *214–15n,* 242, 245, 245n, 246, 265, 276, 345n, 348–49, 401, 428, 635, **4:**141n; 1893 (Chicago), **3:**4, 268n, 371, *371n,* 403n, 412n, 414n, 415, 415n, 441, 467, 470, 475, 499, 511, 650, **4:**46, *49n,* **6:**35, *37n,* **11:**32, *34n,* **12:**374, *375n;* 1894 (Denver), *3:437n,* 589n, 590, 596, *4:9n,* 10–12, 21n, 44, 96, 98n, 341, 389; 1895 (New York City), **3:**421, *4:9n,* 21n, 53, 341, **12:**516, *516n;* 1896 (Cincinnati), *4:124n,* 255–56, **5:**85, *85n;* 1897 (Nashville, Tenn.), *4:355n,* 389, *5:268n,* **7:**60, *64n,* **9:**103n, **11:**65, *66n;* 1898 (Kansas City, Mo.), **4:**416, *417n,* **5:**14, *15n,* 20n, 68, 77, 79n, 104n, 142n, 169, 221n, 232n, 235n, 236; 1899 (Detroit), *5:48n,* 104–5n, 119n, 121n, 140n, 142n, 179, 203, 221n, 231, 232n, 235n, 236–37, **7:**170, *177n;* 1900 (Louisville, Ky.), **5:**xiv, 172n, 176, *177n,* 216n, 221n, 256n, 262n, 298, 328n, 333n, 342n, 344, 414, 460, 503n, 515, **6:**365, *368n,* 496n, **11:**66, *66n;* 1901 (Scranton, Pa.), **5:**xiv, 104n, 287n, 294, *294n,* 342n, 366n, 397, 398n, 416n, 446–47, 447–48n, 456, 470n,

503n, 515, **6:**9, *11n,* 52–53n, 65, 67n, 109, 128n, 308n, **8:**105, *106n,* 407, **11:**42, *46n,* 66, **12:**102, *102n;* 1902 (New Orleans), **5:**445, *445n,* 503n, **6:**10, *11n,* 38, 41–43, 44–45n, 71n, 128n, 133–34, 165, 171, 201, 206n, 208, 224, 231, 308n, 317, 324, 326n, 343n, 356, 373, **7:**37n, *56n,* 243n; 1903 (Boston), **6:**53n, 126, *128n,* 136n, 183n, 191, 214–15, 224, 226–27, 231, 275, 282n, 311–12, 312n, 326n, 342, 343n, 356–57, 373–74, 396, 462, 507, *7:56n,* 268n, **8:**173, *173n,* **11:**260–61, *262n,* 444, 444n; 1904 (San Francisco), **6:**209, *210n,* 271–73, 340–41, 341n, 351, 377–78, 378n, 483, 484n, 486n, 502–3n, **7:**34, *36n,* 486n, **9:**9n; 1905 (Pittsburgh), **6:**343n, 381n, 476, *476n,* 483, 484n, 485, 486n, 511, 512n, 515n, 546, **7:**33, *36n,* 130, 201n; 1906 (Minneapolis), **6:**381n, 509n, **7:**37n, *113n,* 143–44, 146n, 148–50, 151n, 153, 156–57, 168n, 172, 175, 178, 180n, 182, 185, 186n, 199–200, 201–2n, 214–16, 235, 272–73, 274n, 317, 346n, 389–90, 408n, 424n, 450, **9:**424, *424n,* 472; 1907 (Norfolk, Va.), **7:**216, *217n,* 223n, 258n, 286n, 288, 290, 297, 298n, 301, 317–18, 365–68, 389–90, 401n, 470n, *8:52n,* 122, 123n; 1908 (Denver), **7:**269, *269n,* 276n, 281n, 395, 400, 401n, 428, 441, 452, 457, 470n, **8:**16, 16n, 78, *79n,* **9:**276n, 423–24, 471–72, 472n, **12:**215; 1909 (Toronto), **7:**426, 427n, 445n, 461n, 471n, 473n, 486n, 491, *8:6n,* 137–38, 139n, **10:**250, *251n,* **12:**217, *218n;* 1910 (St. Louis), **7:**446n, 473n, **8:**18n, 107, *108n,* 128–30, 130n, 133, 240, **9:**145n; 1911 (Atlanta), **8:**144, *146n,* 151n, 352, 400, **9:**145n, **11:**532; 1912 (Rochester, N.Y.), **6:**343n, *8:286n,* 295, 456, **9:**19, *21n;* 1913 (Seattle), **8:**414–15, *416n, 9:21n,* **10:**535, 538n, **12:**249; 1914 (Philadelphia), **9:**25, *28n,* **10:**538n; 1915 (San Francisco), **9:**106n, *107n,* 340, 355n, 363; 1916 (Baltimore), **9:**348, *348n,* 476, 487,

10:9, 11, *13n;* 1917 (Buffalo, N.Y.), **9:**526n, *10:148n,* 255, 255n, 283, 309, 346–47, 350n, 353, 422, 473, **11:**66, *66n,* 210; 1918 (St. Paul, Minn.), *10:357n,* 430, 431–32n, 463n, 477–78, 518n, **11:**27n, 66, *66n;* 1919 (Atlantic City, N.J.), **10:**438n, 475, *475n,* **11:**63–64, *64n,* 67n, 69, 70n, 98, 108, 110, 111n, 114, 116, 117n, 130, 131n, 146n, 150, 243, 271, 367, **12:**270, *271n;* 1920 (Montreal), **11:**270, *281n,* 325–26, 328–29, 346, 370–71, 392, 393n, 394–95, 397–98, 434, 436, 438, 441–42, 462, 463n, 469, 478n, **12:**269; 1921 (Denver), **11:**400, *400n,* 417, 420n, 485, 488, 491n, 492, 493–94n, 497, 504n, 506, 507n, 534–35, 541–42, 543n, 555, 559, **12:**4, *6n,* 8n; 1922 (Cincinnati), **11:**60n, 482, *482n,* 507n, **12:**43, *43n,* 100–102, 102n, 111, 115, 126–27, 137–39, 150, 158, 208, 217, 218n, 230, 313–14, 352n; 1923 (Portland, Ore.), **12:**262, *263n,* 281n, 319n, 321, 321n, 326, 338–39, 343, 346, 348n, 350, 352, 352n, 356–57, 360, 361n, 370, 380, 382–83n, 395–97, 398n, 403–4, 407, 409, 410n, 421–22, 446n; 1924 (El Paso, Tex.), **12:**338, *338n,* 362n, 449n, 466, 468n, 518, 520n, 534, 535n; 1925 (Atlantic City, N.J.), **12:**555, *562n*
—conventions, specific, *accounts of:* 1886 (Columbus, Ohio), **1:**456–58, 460–61, 463, 465–70; 1887 (Baltimore), **2:**64–79; 1888 (St. Louis), **2:**165–72; 1889 (Boston), **2:**258–75; 1890 (Detroit), **2:**383–416; 1891 (Birmingham, Ala.), **3:**125–38; 1892 (Philadelphia), **3:**249–60; 1893 (Chicago), **3:**423–40; 1894 (Denver), **3:**607–58, 661–64; 1895 (New York City), **4:**80–102; 1896 (Cincinnati), **4:**268–84; 1897 (Nashville, Tenn.), **4:**405–16; 1898 (Kansas City, Mo.), **5:**35–58; 1899 (Detroit), **5:**158–76; 1900 (Louisville, Ky.), **5:**278–94; 1901 (Scranton, Pa.), **5:**430–45; 1902 (New Orleans), **6:**50–70; 1903 (Boston),

6:196–212; 1904 (San Francisco), 6:354–76; 1905 (Pittsburgh), 6:491–508; 1906 (Minneapolis), 7:126–41; 1907 (Norfolk, Va.), 7:267–81; 1908 (Denver), 7:418–26; 1909 (Toronto), 8:3–18; 1910 (St. Louis), 8:136–46; 1911 (Atlanta), 8:282–301; 1912 (Rochester, N.Y.), 8:399–416; 1913 (Seattle), 9:19–21, 23–38; 1914 (Philadelphia), 9:210–26; 1915 (San Francisco), 9:343–50; 1916 (Baltimore), 9:517–29; 1917 (Buffalo, N.Y.), 10:257–67; 1918 (St. Paul, Minn.), 10:463–75; 1919 (Atlantic City, N.J.), 11:79–91, 93–94; 1920 (Montreal), 11:313–23; 1921 (Denver), 11:472–82; 1922 (Cincinnati), 12:86–98; 1923 (Portland, Ore.), 12:327–38; 1924 (El Paso, Tex.), 12:520–32

—Defense Fund, 3:149, 257–58, 351–53, 353n, 470, 4:300, 5:235n, 431, 439–40, 6:126–27, 128n, 134, 136n, 243–44, 244n, 310, 400n, 489, 489n, 7:52n, 123–24, 427n, 455n, 8:3–6, 145, 9:29–33, 33n, 156–57, 157n, 268, 11:478n, 556–58, 558n, 565–70

—Education, Committee on, 12:191

—Education Department, *12:157n*

—Eight-hour Advisory Board, 4:321, *323n*, 327

—Executive Council, 3:6, 108, 346n, 361n, 551–52, 655, 6:162, 9:42–43n, 362, 363n, 11:331; *circulars of,* 2:112–15, 117–19, 121–22, 299–301, 3:71–74, 206–8, 4:383–85, 6:273–75, 279–81, 7:3–6, 6n, 60–64, 64n, 95, 389–93, 440–42, 8:146–48, 9:11–13, 12:113–17, 118n, 453–55, 457, 458n; circulars of, mentioned, 5:66–67, 266, 267n, 7:268n, 336n, 372, 372n, 389, 8:29, 31n, 76n, 214n, 236–37, 238n, 9:38n, 65, 191n; and election of 1906, 7:60–64, 64n, 65–67, 126–41; and election of 1920, 11:239–40, 264; and election of 1922, 12:162; and election of 1924, 12:453–57, 458n, 462, 465, 474, 475n, 480–81, 483n, 486–94, 494n, 498–99; *letters from,* 2:152–54, 4:325–29, 8:123–25, 10:121–22, 11:436–39;

letters to, 2:26, 92–94, 110–12, 127, 157–58, 206–7, 223–24, 3:30, 175–77, 182, 182n, 188, 263–64, 283–84, 297–98, 342–45, 351–53, 360–61, 411–12, 453–54, 460–61, 490–97, 590–91, 4:66, 123–24, 176–77, 259, 331–33, 337–38, 364–66, 385–86, 429–30, 452, 471, 476–78, 486–87, 5:76–78, 105–9, 155–56, 210–11, 250, 393–95, 423–25, 456–58, 6:111–12, 173–74, 228–32, 241–44, 315, 384, 387–88, 487–89, 525–29, 7:17, 32–35, 109–10, 143–46, 152, 223, 266, 287, 289–90, 295–96, 309, 312–13, 318–20, 348, 356–57, 451–53, 457–58, 493–97, 8:100–101, 107–8, 152–54, 158, 213, 216–17, 335, 424–25, 453–54, 469–71, 498–99, 9:63–67, 140–41, 175–76, 197–98, 418–19, 10:3–4, 13–14, 17–20, 104–5, 407, 503–4, 544–46, 11:112–13, 119–20, 132–34, 213–14, 223–24, 227–28, 401–3, 406–7, 410, 505–6, 507n, 12:127–28, 221–22, 229, 311–15, 351, 356–59, 367–69, 455–57, 461–62, 503–4, 538–39; meetings with Mexican labor representatives, 9:426–27n, 436–42, 443n, 10:10; meetings with U.S. government officials, 3:292, 292n, 342, 343n, 404, 4:321–22, 5:325–26, 327n, 9:9, 10n, 396, 396n, 10:31–34; number of members of, 2:411–13, 5:56, 6:205–6, 206n, 207; salaries of, 2:29, 72, 75, 77, 158, 228, 414, 429, 430n, 7:463, 464n, 9:213, 214n, 11:395, 397n, 12:323, 328; statement of, mentioned, 12:146–47; *statements of,* 10:352–55, 11:208–11, 211n, 213n, 12:560–62; *wire to,* 12:539

—Executive Council, election of members of, 8:282–85, 286n, 397; in 1887, 2:72, 79; in 1888, 2:165; in 1889, 2:226; in 1891, 3:117, 127–28, 133, 135; in 1893, 3:429, 437–38, 464; in 1894, 3:609–11, 661–65, 4:9, 78, 389; in 1895, 4:6–7, 9, 78–79, 82, 94–99, 134; in 1896, 4:278, 278n; in 1897, 4:389–91, 413, 414n; in 1898, 5:57n; in 1899,

5:176, 177n; in 1900, **5:**294n; in
1901, **5:**445; in 1903, **6:**208–9, 210n;
in 1904, **6:**376n; in 1905, **6:**509n; in
1907, **7:**280, 281n; in 1908, **7:**425,
427n; in 1909, **8:**17–18, 18n; in
1910, **8:**144; in 1911, **8:**295; in 1912,
8:414–15, 416n, **9:**348, 349n; in
1913, **9:**37, 38n; in 1914, **9:**225–26,
226n; in 1915, **9:**348, 348n; in 1917,
10:266–67; in 1918, **10:**475; in 1919,
11:91, 93n; in 1920, **11:**321, 321n;
in 1921, **11:**480–82; in 1922, **12:**95,
97n; in 1923, **12:**337, 338n; in 1924,
12:554–60
—Executive Council, meetings: Dec.
1891, **3:**123; Apr. 1894, **3:**460, 460n;
Aug. 1894, **3:**552; Jan. 1895, **3:**667;
Oct. 1898, **5:**19, *20n;* Oct. 1899,
5:151n; Dec. 1899, **5:**157, *158n;*
Mar. 1900, **5:**199, *199n;* July 1900,
5:256n, 266; Feb. 1901, *5:327n;*
Sept. 1901, *5:396n;* Apr. 1902,
5:503, *503n,* 516–18; July 1902,
5:469, *470n,* **6:***23n;* Oct. 1902, **6:**41,
42n; Apr. 1903, **6:**109, *110n,* 126;
June 1903, **6:**151n; Sept. 1903,
6:177, *178n,* 183, **7:**451n; Apr. 1904,
6:239, *240n,* 260n, 282n, 315, 326n,
353, 354n; Sept. 1904, **6:**312n, 316,
317n, 342–43; Mar. 1905, **6:**405;
June 1905, **6:**430–31, *432n,* 440,
485; Sept. 1905, **6:**432n, 486, *486n,*
487; Mar. 1906, **6:**528, *529n,* 531,
531n, 535, 546n, **7:**32–33, *36n;* June
1906, **7:**37n; Nov. 1906, *7:113n,*
152n, 157, 178; Mar. 1907, **7:**154n,
158n, 194n, *201n,* 216–17; Aug.
1907, **7:**195n, 223n, 242n, 252n,
286n; Jan. 1908, **7:**274n, 309, *310n;*
Mar. 1908, **7:**307, *308n,* 311n, 315n,
319, 320n; Apr. 1908, **7:**470n; June
1908, **7:**308n, 310n, 315n, 342n,
347, *347n;* July 1908, **7:**310n, 350n;
Sept. 1908, **7:**383n, 387, *388n,* 389,
399; Jan. 1909, **7:**443; Apr. 1909,
7:451n, 457, *457n,* 458; June 1909,
7:470, 470–*71n,* 496, 498n; Oct.
1909, **7:**471n, 491, *492n;* Jan. 1910,
8:9n; Mar. 1910, **8:**76n, *79n,* 86;
June 1910, **8:**62n, 86–87, *87n,* 126,
338; Jan. 1911, **8:**49n, 106n, 169–

70, *170n,* 175n, 188n; June 1911,
7:451n, **8:**151n, 193n, *238n,* 351;
Oct. 1911, *8:279*–80n; Jan. 1912,
8:299, *301n,* 311, 346n, 400; May
1912, *8:380n;* Aug. 1912, **8:**386n,
393, *394n;* Nov. 1912, *8:425n;*
Jan. 1913, **8:**443, *448n;* July 1913,
8:501, *501n,* 503–4, **9:**143, 146n,
169, 169n; Sept. 1913, *9:10n;* Jan.
1914, **9:**41, *42n,* 47, 48n, 62, 63n,
65, *68n,* 89, 234; May 1914, **9:**106,
107n, 140; July 1914, **9:**143, *145n,*
158, 163; Oct. 1914, **9:**191, *191n;*
Nov. 1914, **9:**209n; Jan. 1915, **9:**234,
235n; Apr. 1915, **9:**234, *235n,* 260,
261n, 326; Sept. 1915, **9:**326, *328n,*
443n; Feb. 1916, **9:**365–66, *366n,*
396, 401, 443n, 461n; June–July
1916, *9:367n;* July 1916, **9:**460,
461n, 463; Oct. 1916, **9:**477, *478n,*
485; Jan. 1917, **9:**526n, 529–30n;
Mar. 1917, **10:**20, *22n,* 39, 44n; Apr.
1917, *10:81n;* Oct. 1917, *10:255n;*
Feb. 1918, *10:331n;* May 1918,
10:430, *431n;* July 1918, **10:**498,
499n; Nov. 1918, **10:**545, *546n,* 547,
568; Dec. 1918, **11:**25n; May 1919,
11:60, *61n,* 63, 67n; June 1919,
11:110, *111n;* Aug. 1919, *11:125n,*
130, 131n, 134, 135n; Oct. 1919,
11:152n, 213, *214n;* Nov. 1919,
11:208, *211n,* 213–14, 214n; Dec.
1919, *11:240n;* Feb.–Mar. 1920,
11:265n; May 1920, *11:294n;* June
1920, **11:**326, *326n,* 328, 359; Aug.
1920, **11:**345, *345n;* Nov. 1920,
11:395, *396n,* 401; Feb.–Mar. 1921,
11:407, *408n,* 436, 468, 470; June
1921, *11:471n,* 492, 493n, 517; Aug.
1921, **11:**513, *514n,* 517–18; Nov.
1921, **11:**515, *515n;* June 1922,
12:150, *152n;* Sept. 1922, **12:**133,
136, *137n;* Feb. 1923, *12:206n,* 223,
225n, 229, 243; May 1923, **12:**229,
229n, 244, 262, 263n, 271n; Aug.–
Sept. 1923, **12:**263n, 274n, 298,
299n; Sept.–Oct. 1923, *12:319n,*
324, 326n; Feb. 1924, **12:**340n, 351,
352n; May 1924, **12:**340n, *442n,*
456, 457n, 458, 458n; Aug. 1924,
12:391n, 457n, 462, *462n,* 465, 478,

481, 494n, 499–500, 502–3, 503n, 504, 514; Oct. 1924, *12:514n;* Dec. 1924, *12:562n*
—Executive Council, meetings, *minutes or news accounts of:* Apr. 1887, **2:**36–37; Feb. 1890, **2:**282–83; May 1892, **3:**162–63; Oct. 1896, **4:**239–41; Dec. 1896, **4:**266–67; Apr. 1897, **4:**321–23; Mar. 1900, **5:**209–10; July 1900, **5:**255–56; Feb. 1901, **5:**325–27; Apr. 1902, **5:**514–15; Apr. 1903, **6:**133–35; Mar. 1907, **7:**199–201; Mar. 1910, **8:**77–78; June 1911, **8:**234–38; May 1912, **8:**370–80; Sept. 1913, **9:**9; May 1914, **9:**111; Apr. 1915, **9:**269–74; June–July 1916, **9:**435–42; Oct. 1916, **9:**508–10; Mar. 1917, **10:**23–38; Apr. 1917, **10:**80–81; Feb. 1918, **10:**345–50, 352–55; Aug. 1919, **11:**124–25; Oct. 1919, **11:**151–52; Dec. 1919, **11:**239–40; Feb.–Mar. 1920, **11:**271–74; June 1920, **11:**310–13; Nov. 1920, **11:**384–90; Feb.–Mar. 1921, **11:**426–31, 433–34; June 1921, **11:**468–71; Sept. 1922, **12:**140–46; Feb. 1923, **12:**202–5; Sept.–Oct. 1923, **12:**339; May 1924, **12:**438–42; Aug. 1924, **12:**486–94; Oct. 1924, **12:**514; Dec. 1924, **12:**554–60
—federal labor unions (FLUs), **1:**469, **2:**95, 128, 128n, **3:**170, 592, **5:**440, **9:**503; FLU 2479 (Birmingham, Ala.), *2:103n;* FLU 2703 (Chicago), **2:**176, *176–77n;* FLU 2705 (Sturgeon Bay, Wis.), **2:**137, *138n;* FLU 3792 (Pittsburgh), **2:**235, 235n; FLU 3873 (Boston), **3:**12, 14n; FLU 4013 (New York City), *3:14n;* FLU 5327 (Hot Springs, Ark.), **3:**69, 70n; FLU 5335 (Cincinnati), **4:**123–24, *124n;* FLU 6617 (Nashville, Tenn.), **4:**180–81, *182n;* FLU 6898 (Chattanooga, Tenn.), **4:**334, *334n;* FLU 6964 (Ouray, Colo.), **5:**89, *92n;* FLU 7010 (Owensboro, Ky.), *5:38n;* FLU 7087 (Belleville, Ill.), *10:110n;* FLU 7204 (Carbondale, Pa.), **5:**484–85, *485n;* FLU 7295 (Knoxville, Tenn.), *6:119n;* FLU 7591 (Pana, Ill.), **5:**402–3,

404n; FLU 8083 (Springfield, Ill.), **5:**178–79, *179n;* FLU 8276 (DeSoto, Ill.), **5:**336–37, *337–*38n; FLU 8393 (Brunswick, Ga.), **7:**187, *190n;* FLU 8875 (Scranton, Pa.), **5:**331, *332n;* FLU 8892 (Waco, Tex.), **6:**194, *194n;* FLU 8921 (San Pedro, Calif.), **6:**243, *244n;* FLU 9985 (Midvale, Ohio), **6:**244, *244n;* FLU 9989 (Bedford, Ill.), **6:**244, *245n;* FLU 10,554 (Peru, Ind.), *6:141n;* FLU 10,722 (Poplar Bluff, Mo.), *6:223n;* FLU 10,917 (Fort Bragg, Calif.), **6:**241, 244n; FLU 11,478 (Girard, Kans.), **6:**221, *222n;* FLU 11,747 (Walnut, N.C.), **7:**205, *205n;* FLU 12,050 (Lexington, Ky.), *7:22n;* FLU 12,362 (Galeton, Pa.), *8:35n;* FLU 12,495 (Tell City, Ind.), *7:229n;* FLU 12,776 (Washington, D.C.), **10:**229, *231n;* FLU 12,985 (Butte, Mont.), **9:**183n; FLU 13,153 (Alamosa, Colo.), **9:**456, *457n;* FLU 14,365 (Big Springs, Tex.), **9:**43, *43n;* FLU 14,592 (Trois-Rivières, Que.), **9:**15, *16n;* FLU 14,949 (New York City), **9:**323, *324n;* FLU 16,354 (Boston), *10:542n;* in Montgomery, Ala., **4:**29; in Muncie, Ind., **3:**359, *360n*
—federal labor unions (FLUs), strikes/lockouts: 1900–1903 (FLU 7295, Knoxville, Tenn.), **6:**118, *119n;* 1903 (FLU 8393, Brunswick, Ga.), **7:**187, *190n;* 1903–4 (FLU 10,722, Poplar Bluff, Mo.), **6:**222, *223n;* 1903–4 (FLU 10,723, Poplar Bluff, Mo.), **6:**222, *223n;* 1903–6? (FLU 10,917, Fort Bragg, Calif.), **6:**170, *171n,* 241–44, 244n; 1904 (FLU 9985, Midvale, Ohio), *6:245n;* 1907 (FLU 12,495, Tell City, Ind.), **7:**227–29, *229n,* 234–35; 1909–10 (FLU 12,362, Galeton, Pa.), **8:**33–35, *35n;* AFL financial support of, **6:**243–44, 244n, **8:**33–35, 35n
—Information and Education Bureau (proposed), **11:**402–3
—Information and Publicity Service, **12:**229, 433n, 461n, 467n; and AFL Permanent Conference for Aboli-

tion of Child Labor, **12**:82n; *bulletin of,* **12**:540–41
—Labor Representation Committee, **7**:63, *110n,* 135, 376–77, **8**:100–101, 124, **9**:488n; *report of,* **7**:389–92
—Legal Bureau of Information, *9:530n*
—Legal Department, **9**:528, *529–30n,* **10**:47
—Legal Information Bureau, **12**:91, *93n*
—Legislative Committee, **4**:112, *113n,* **5**:362, 456–58, **6**:211–12, 232, 369–73, 373n, 393, 451, **7**:191, 346–47, 457, 458n, **8**:372, 376, 379–80, 386, 425n, **9**:7–8, 40, 68n, 91, 141, 153, **11**:294n, 329, 407, 465, 502, **12**:35, 190, 343; and AFL Permanent Conference for Abolition of Child Labor, **12**:82n; and election of 1924, **12**:433n, 461n, 462, 467n; *letter from,* **6**:48; *letter to,* **5**:455–56; and railroad shopmen's strike, 1922–?, **12**:106n, 155n; reports of, mentioned, **7**:141n, 371n, 372, 389, **8**:370, 386n, **12**:165, 166n
—local unions (LUs), directly affiliated, **2**:74, 95, 263–64, 268n, **8**:36–37, 38n; LU 2709 (spinners, cotton, Kearney, N.J.), **2**:221, *222n;* LU 2711 (marble, slate workers, and tile layers, Pittsburgh and Allegheny, Pa.), **2**:217n; LU 3696 (electrical workers, Pittsburgh), *2:223n;* LU 3702 (metal polishers, Plymouth, Mich.), **3**:89; LU 3723 (granite polishers, Barre, Vt.), **2**:215, *217n,* 282n; LU 3849 (laborers, Rochester, N.Y.), **2**:251–52; LU 3873 (conductors and motormen, Boston), **4**:189–91, *191n;* LU 4007 (tackmakers, Boston), **3**:12, *14n;* LU 5041 (plate printers, Washington, D.C.), *3:120n;* LU 5043 (architectural iron workers, Indianapolis), **3**:68; LU 5105 (ice drivers and helpers, Pittsburgh), *2:315n;* LU 5150 (sash, door, and blind workers, Chicago), **3**:150, *153n;* LU 5162 (car drivers, Indianapolis), **3**:174, 175n; LU 5180 (plumbers, Columbus, Ohio), *2:366n;* LU 5254 (laundry workers, Indianapolis), *3:161n;* LU 5337 (teamsters, Columbus, Ohio), **3**:167–68; LU 5358 (laundry workers, Troy, N.Y.), **3**:164, *165n;* LU 5391 (street car employees, Detroit), **3**:175n; LU 5464 (marine firemen, St. Louis), **3**:163, *163n,* 350; LU 5467 (hod carriers, East St. Louis, Ill.), **3**:80, 80n; LU 5490 (car drivers, New Orleans), **3**:170, 172; LU 5491 (hod carriers, East St. Louis, Ill.), **3**:80, *80n;* LU 5504 (watchmakers, Elgin, Ill.), **3**:347–48; LU 5533 (musicians, Butte, Mont.), **4**:289–90, *291n;* LU 5550 (street car employees, Youngstown, Ohio), **3**:228, *229n;* LU 5577 (collar, cuff, and shirt starchers, Troy, N.Y.), **3**:108, *109n,* 164–65n, 176, 177n; LU 5579 (musicians, St. Louis), **4**:123n; LU 5611 (pavers and rammermen, New York City), **3**:165, 166n; LU 5616 (stair builders, New York City), **3**:150, *153n;* LU 5626 (marine firemen, St. Louis), **3**:350; LU 5635 (carriage and wagon laborers, South Bend, Ind.), **3**:149; LU 5637 (teamsters and draymen, South Bend, Ind.), **3**:149, 247; LU 5658 (stationary engineers, St. Louis), **3**:462, 463n; LU 5707 (marine and stationary firemen, New Orleans), **3**:171, *171n,* 172, 178; LU 5778 (tobacco workers, St. Louis), **3**:343–44, *345n;* LU 5800 (warehousemen and packers, New Orleans), **3**:243n; LU 5809 (Britannia metal workers, Meriden, Conn.), **4**:239, *241n;* LU 5813 (teamsters and loaders, New Orleans), **3**:243n; LU 5869 (scalesmen, New Orleans), **3**:243n; LU 5873 (farm laborers, Bellaire, Ohio), **3**:260, *260n;* LU 6042 (tobacco boxmakers, St. Louis), **3**:462, *463n,* **4**:147, 148n; LU 6049 (rail mill helpers, New Albany, Ind.), **3**:357; LU 6087 (sprinkler fitters, Chicago), *5:39n;* LU 6146 (sheep butchers, Kansas City, Mo.), **4**:286–

87, *287n;* LU 6237 (hod carriers, Belleville, Ill.), **3:**409, *410n;* LU 6321 (fishermen, Astoria, Ore.), *4:342n,* 363–64; LU 6349 (musicians, St. Louis), **3:**486, *486n;* LU 6352 (musicians, New York City), **4:**56, *57n,* 397–98, 399n; LU 6356 (water department workers, Boston), **5:**76–78, *79n;* LU 6408 (musicians, Milwaukee), **3:**496, *498n;* LU 6423 (pork butchers, Kansas City, Kans.), **4:**286–87, *287n;* LU 6468 (tobacco factory laborers, St. Louis), **4:**130, *131n;* LU 6496 (beef butchers, Kansas City, Kans.), **4:**286–87, *287n;* LU 6574 (mattress makers, Piqua, Ohio), **4:**139–40, *140n;* LU 6619 (textile workers, Fort Wayne, Ind.), *4:128n;* LU 6636 (bricklayers and stonemasons, Chicago), **4:**157, *158–59n,* 162, 162n; LU 6647 (cattle butchers, New York City), **4:**229–30, *230n;* LU 6745 (stationary engineers, etc., Leadville, Colo.), **4:**259, *259n,* 297; LU 6751 (paving department workers, Boston), **5:**79n; LU 6836 (liquor bottlers, New York City), *4:218n;* LU 6852 (coal handlers, Lynn, Mass.), **4:**188, *189n;* LU 6861 (button workers, Muscatine, Iowa), *4:314n;* LU 6869 (laborers, Ludington, Mich.), **4:**336–37, *337n;* LU 6899 (mattress makers, Chicago), *5:102n;* LU 6961 (watch workers, Elgin, Ill.), **5:**30–31, *32n,* 392; LU 7033 (tube workers, Ellwood City, Pa.), **4:**483–85, *485n;* LU 7073 (horse nail makers, New Brighton, Pa.), *5:17n;* LU 7362 (foundry laborers, Buffalo, N.Y.), *5:209n;* LU 7413 (architectural foundry workers, St. Louis), **6:**244, *245n;* LU 7417 (house shorers and movers, New York City), **11:**467, *467n;* LU 7437 (farmers, Lentner, Mo.), **5:**120–21, *121n;* LU 7471 (building laborers, Birmingham, Ala.), *6:107n;* LU 7483 (coal employees, London, Ont.), *5:401n;* LU 8014 (glass packers, Bridgeton, N.J.), **5:**200–201, *201n;* LU 8104 (black laborers, Fort Worth, Tex.), **5:**221, *222n;* LU 8145 (mosaic marble workers, Philadelphia), *5:281n;* LU 8156 (tobacco strippers, Boston), **7:**306, *308–*9n, 365, 461–62, **9:**492n, *11:420n;* LU 8178 (quarrymen, Lithonia, Ga.), **6:**116n, 120, *121n,* 147n; LU 8193 (plate printers' assistants, Washington, D.C.), **5:**199; LU 8324 (laundry workers, Denison, Tex.), **5:**264, *264n;* LU 8990 (paving cutters, Lithonia, Ga.), **6:**120, *121n;* LU 9001 (black electrical workers and linemen, Jacksonville, Fla.), **5:**327, *327–28n;* LU 9039 (glove workers, Chicago), **5:**373, *374n;* LU 9077 (newsboys, Boston), **5:**475–77, *477n;* LU 9323 (freight handlers, Nashua, N.H.), *5:400n;* LU 9363 (hod carriers, Stockton, Calif.), **6:**39, *40n;* LU 9560 (suspender makers, New York City), *6:310n;* LU 9840 (gas workers, San Francisco), **6:**101–2, *102–*3n; LU 9891 (shingle weavers, Tacoma, Wash.), *6:45n;* LU 9914 (telephone operators, Washington, D.C.), **6:**32–33, *33n;* LU 10,227 (tobacco strippers, Hartford, Conn.), *11:420n;* LU 10,315 (riggers, Boston), **6:**210, *211n;* LU 10,422 (tobacco strippers, Denver), *11:478n;* LU 10,535 (bottle caners, San Francisco), **7:**219–20, *220n;* LU 10,584 (women can workers, Maywood, Ill.), **6:**244, *245n;* LU 10,618 (wine and liquor workers, San Francisco), *6:219n;* LU 10,630 (excavators, New York City), **7:**149, *150n;* LU 10,631 (rockmen, New York City), **7:**149, *150n;* LU 10,851 (gill net stringers and helpers, Cleveland), **6:**153–54, *154n;* LU 11,102 (laborers, Jackson, Miss.), **6:**181, *182n;* LU 11,103 (street laborers, Chicago), **6:**283, *285n;* LU 11,121 (sugar beet and farm laborers, Oxnard, Calif.), **6:**149–50, *150n;* LU 11,594 (hat trimmers, Wabash, Ind.), **7:**197–99, *199n, letter to,* **7:**230–31; LU 11,744 (truckers and stock movers, Dayton,

Ohio), **6**:489, *489n;* LU 11,754 (lime workers, Rockland, Maine), **6**:399n, 435, *439n;* LU 11,773 (stenographers and clerks, Washington, D.C.), **6**:411, *412n*, **8**:56–61, 62n, 125–26, **9**:537, 539n; LU 11,835 (lime trimmers, Rockland, Maine), **6**:397–98, *399n*, 435, 439n; LU 11,843 (lobster fishermen, Vinalhaven, Maine), **6**:403, *404n;* LU 11,927 (barbers, Rockland, Maine), **6**:404, *405n;* LU 12,046 (tobacco strippers, New Haven, Conn.), *11:420n;* LU 12,283 (moccasin and moccasin slipper workers, Bangor, Maine), *7:126n;* LU 12,429 (dock builders, New York City), **9**:292n, 311n; LU 12,442 (laborers, Goldfield, Nev.), **7**:283, *286n;* LU 12,542 (chair plaiters, Tell City, Ind.), **7**:234–35, *236n;* LU 12,647 (marine sack sewers and cargo repairers, New Orleans), *7:225n;* LU 12,675 (ladies' hat makers, Chicago), **9**:107, *110n;* LU 12,755 (stenographers and typists, Chicago), **9**:235n, *10:82n*, **12**:275, *278n;* LU 12,766 (newspaper solicitors, San Francisco), **8**:142–43, *144n;* LU 12,821 (laborers, Woodward, Okla.), **8**:46, *46n;* LU 12,952 (machinists' helpers and laborers, Pocatello, Idaho), *8:156n;* LU 12,971 (tobacco strippers, Manchester, N.H.), *11:420n;* LU 14,204 (cork and seal operatives, Baltimore), **9**:333n; LU 14,268 (stenographers and typists, Kansas City, Kans.), *10:64n, wire from,* **10**:62–63; LU 14,332 (flat janitors, Chicago), **11**:450, *450n;* LU 14,440 (ladies' hat makers, Chicago), **9**:1.10n; LU 14,451 (crane followers and platform workers, Schenectady, N.Y.), **11**:411–12, *412n;* LU 14,569 (hat trimmers, New York City), **9**:108, *110n,* **10**:468n; LU 14,596 (school custodians and janitors, Washington, D.C.), **9**:267–68, *268n;* LU 14,790 (dye house workers, Chicago), **9**:354, *356n;* LU 15,155 (office janitors, Chicago), **10**:215–17,

218n; LU 15,277 (coal trimmers, Sewell's Point and Norfolk County, Va.), **10**:177, *177n;* LU 15,298 (porters and bootblacks, Granite City, Madison, and Venice, Ill.), **10**:134–35, *136n;* LU 15,403 (cereal mill employees, Cedar Rapids, Iowa), **10**:368, *369n;* LU 15,842 (railroad helpers and laborers, Spencer, N.C.), *12:342n;* LU 15,850 (hat trimmers, Newark, N.J.), *10:468n;* LU 15,899 (railroad helpers and laborers, Hamlet, N.C.), *10:494n;* LU 15,900 (railroad helpers and laborers, Raleigh, N.C.), *12:342n;* LU 15,920 (railroad helpers and laborers, Grand Junction, Colo.), **10**:505, *505n;* LU 16,088 (railway coach cleaners, St. Louis), **11**:119–20, *120–*21n; LU 16,199 (boilermakers', blacksmiths', and machinists' helpers, Mobile, Ala.), **11**:484–85, *486n;* LU 16,220 (freight handlers, Richmond, Va.), **11**:314, *317n;* LU 16,304 (stenographers, typewriters, bookkeepers, and assistants, Seattle), **12**:274–75, *275n;* LU 16,313 (watchmen and transportation workers, Lynn, Mass.), **11**:186–87, *187n;* LU 16,381 (freight handlers, Baltimore), *11:492n;* LU 16,406 (freight handlers, Little Rock, Ark.), **11**:183, *183n;* LU 16,488 (cigar factory employees, Manchester, N.H.), **11**:417–18, *420n;* LU 16,685 (railway coach and station cleaners and porters, Cleveland), **11**:325, *326n;* LU 16,718 (city policemen, Washington, D.C.), *11:146n;* LU 16,807 (city policemen, Boston), **11**:145, *146n;* LU 16,982 (freight handlers, Winston-Salem, N.C.), *11:492n;* LU 17,196 (freight handlers, Columbia, S.C.), *11:492n;* LU 17,300 (railroad shop helpers, Fitzgerald, Ga.), *12:342n;* LU 17,306 (baggage and mail handlers, Washington, D.C.), *11:492n;* LU 17,362 (railroad mechanics' helpers, Americus, Ga.), *12:342n;* LU 17,417 (railway coach and car

cleaners, Waco, Tex.), *11:565n;* LU
17,430 (boilermakers' helpers, Columbia, S.C.), *12:342n;* LU 17,456
(machinists' helpers, Columbia,
S.C.), *12:342n;* LU 17,490 (horse
nail makers, Buffalo, N.Y.), **12:**220,
221n; LU 17,535 (railroad laborers,
Tampa, Fla.), *12:342n;* LU 17,545
(freight handlers, Newport News,
Va.), **12:**129–30, *130n;* LU 17,597
(mechanics' helpers, Savannah,
Ga.), *12:342n;* LU 17,603 (boilermakers', pipe fitters', and machinists' helpers, Jacksonville, Fla.),
12:342n; coach cleaners, **11:**478n,
564–65, 565n; in Pittsburgh, **2:**234,
234n; railroad helpers and laborers,
10:427, 431n
—local unions(LUs), directly affiliated, strikes/lockouts: 1889 (LU
2709, spinners, cotton, Kearney,
N.J.), *2:222n;* 1890 (LU 3723, granite polishers, Barre, Vt.), **2:**281–82,
282n; 1891–92 (LU 5577, collar,
cuff, and shirt starchers, Troy,
N.Y.), **3:**109, *109n;* 1896 (LU 6321,
fishermen, Astoria, Ore.), **4:**364,
364n; 1896–98 (LU 6146, sheep
butchers, Kansas City, Mo.), **4:**286,
287n; 1898–99 (LU 6869, laborers,
Ludington, Mich.), **5:**58–59, *59n,*
60–61; 1900 (LU 8248, freight handlers, Buffalo, N.Y.), **5:**247, *247n;*
1901 (LU 8360, blast furnace workers, Buffalo, N.Y.), **5:**383, *383–84n;*
1904 (LU 7413, architectural
foundry workers, St. Louis), **6:**244,
245n; 1904 (LU 9560, suspender
makers, New York City), **6:**310,
310n; 1904 (LU 10,584, women can
workers, Maywood, Ill.), *6:245n;*
1908 (LU 8156, tobacco strippers,
Boston), *7:308–9n,* 365, 461–62;
1911–12 (LU 12,854, button workers, Muscatine, Iowa), **8:**297–98,
298n; 1917 (LU 15,403, cereal mill
employees, Cedar Rapids, Iowa),
10:369n; AFL financial support of,
3:149, **6:**310, 489, 489n, **7:**51, 52–
53n, **8:**298n
—Metal Trades Department, **5:**287n,

6:492, **7:**365–68, *368n,* 447, **8:**237,
238n, 367, **9:**503, **10:**207n, **11:**62,
76n, 271, **12:**155n; and railroad
shopmen's strike, 1922-?, **12:**106n;
and Street Railway Employes,
9:388–90, 390n
—Metal Trades Department, conventions: 1923 (Portland, Ore.),
12:341, *343n;* 1924 (El Paso, Tex.),
12:518, *520n*
—Mining Department, **8:**367, *368n,*
9:271, 351–52, 503, **10:**374, **11:**271,
12:151; and railroad shopmen's
strike, 1922-?, **12:**106n
—missions to Europe: 1895, **4:**50,
50n, 52–53, 55–63, 66, 85–91, 193,
11:10–11; 1909, **7:**472, *473–74n,*
474–81, 483–85, 487–91, 492n,
8:241, **10:**563; spring 1918, **10:**332,
333n, 356n, 445–46, 463–66, 468–
69, 471n, 504; fall 1918, **10:**468,
470n, 492–93, 503–4, 504n, 506,
520–23, 525–27, 529–37, 537n, 540,
541n, 543, 546n, 549–54, 554–55n,
557–58, 560–65; spring 1919, **11:**25,
25n, 37–40, *40n,* 46–48, 52–59, 62n,
63–64; summer 1919, **11:**110, *111n,*
113n, 118, 119n, 460n
—missions to Mexico: 1918, **10:**498,
499n; 1921, **11:**402, *404n,* 407;
1924, **12:**518, *520n,* 534–35, *536n*
—National Non-Partisan Political
Campaign Committee, **11:**279,
301, 377, 382, **12:**34–35, 37, *38n,*
160–62, 163–64n, 170, 172n; circulars of, mentioned, **12:**434n, 494n;
and election of 1922, **12:**162, 164n,
186–87, 189, 436; and election of
1924, **12:**433–34n, 456, 461n, 462,
465, 472n, 481, 486–94, 494n, 500–
501; financial appeal of, **11:**272,
274, 275n; members of, **11:**240n,
272, 275n; report of, mentioned,
12:186–87, 189; *reports of,* **11:**271–
74, **12:**486–94
—Needle Trades Department (proposed), **10:**373–74, *374n,* 379–80
—newsletter, **7:**426, 427n, **11:**403. *See
also* American Federation of Labor
(AFL): *Weekly News Service*
—office, **3:**667, **6:**47, 160–62, **8:**338;

hours of, **6:**411, **8:**58–59, 62n, 126;
location of, **2:**81, 81n, 275, **3:**429,
438–39, 543, 661, 664n, **4:**xiv, 133,
248, 281–82, 284, 288, **5:**xiv, **7:**446–
47; office boy in, **2:**26, 26n, 30,
9:308; staff of, **5:**xiv, **6:**161, 237–38,
411, **8:**56–61, 62n, 125–26; and
typewriters, **2:**223
—office building, **7:**426, 427n, 446,
9:275–76, *276n,* 308, 366, 508–10;
cornerstone of, **9:**276n, 308, 367–
70, 370n; dedication of, **9:**276n,
436, 443–48, 448n; groundbreaking
for, **9:**276n
—organizers, **5:**141, 450, **6:**15–17,
223n, 351, 352n, 416n, 530, **7:**156–
58, 225–26, **8:**36–37, 47n, 280n,
342, **9:**32, **11:**480; assessments for,
5:49n, **8:**122, 123n, **9:**38, 38n; black,
5:439, 439n, **6:**107n, 108–9, **10:**176–
77, 347, 350n, 424, 426, 430–31,
462, **11:**83–84n, 317n, 325–26, 464
(*see also* Brown, James; Clay, W.
H.; Clemmons, Ralph; Goode, Armistead; Hale, William W.; Jones,
James E.; Norton, George L.; Porter, James E.; Rice, Garrett; Riley,
John; Saul, A.; Worthey, James W.);
cost of, **5:**xiii, xxn, 49n, 57, 432n,
446, **6:**410n, **7:**165, 191, 231–32,
8:356, **9:**38, 38n, **11:**396n, **12:**242–
43, 276; and election campaigns
(*see under* elections in United
States, national); female (*see* Colby,
Josephine; Conboy, Sara A.; Fitzgerald, Anna; Kelleher, Mary J.; Kenney, Mary E.; Lanphere, Emma; Mahoney, Nellie; Neary, Anna; Nestor,
Agnes; O'Sullivan, Mary Kenney;
Scott, Melinda; Scully, Mary P.; Sullivan, Dora; Thorne, Florence C.;
Valesh, Eva McDonald; Williams,
Isabel); female, AFL conventions
and, **3:**133, 136; layoffs of, **5:**254,
6:315, 409–10, 410n, **11:**395–96,
396n, 517, **12:**242; *letters to,* **5:**268,
9:141–42, 153–54, 194, 246–51,
510–11, **11:**509, 554–56, 556n (*see
also* specific organizers); letters to,
mentioned, **5:**330, 331–32n, **6:**533n,
9:145n, 154n, 236n, 443n, **10:**491–

92, **11:**509, 509n, 524n, **12:**161 (*see
also* specific organizers); number
of, **5:**xiii, 143, 329, 343, 361, **6:**xv,
12:277; political activities of, **3:**136–
38, **4:**239–41, 268–72, 272n, **6:**439n;
salaries of, **11:**395, 397n; for South,
AFL conventions and, **5:**43, 46–47,
48–49n, 278–79, 279n, **6:**107n; for
West, AFL conventions and, **5:**48–
49n, 278–79, 279n. *See also* Adams,
Emmet L.; Alexander, H. M.; Allen,
Joseph B.; Alonso, Rafael; Ander-
son, Edward E.; Applehagen, Emil;
Askew, Robert; Bailey, Robert D.;
Baker, D. C.; Ball, Elmer E.; Ban-
ford, Lawrence H.; Bannister, E. M.;
Barrett, James F.; Barrett, John H.;
Bauer, Joseph A.; Bean, John H.;
Beckler, George H.; Belk, Mason S.;
Bennett, George; Berger, Frederick
L.; Bert, George; Bestel, Charles F.;
Bettenhausen, George A.; Billings,
Hollis C.; Bodine, George C.; Bo-
gert, John N.; Boyd, David A.; Bre-
idenbach, Elias; Brown, Fred W.;
Brown, James; Brown, Jay G.; Bru-
net, G. R.; Brunson, Hartwell L.;
Burns, Patrick J.; Burt, Joseph H.;
Byrne, Joseph F.; Caldwell, Howard
H.; Callaghan, John M.; Canfield,
F. A.; Cardinale, Giuseppe; Car-
ney, William A.; Cattermull, Alfred
C.; Chance, George; Cherry, Ed-
ward H.; Claherty, Coleman; Clay,
W. H.; Clemmons, Ralph; Colby,
Josephine; Collins, William; Con-
boy, Sara A.; Conboy, Thomas J.;
Cosgrove, Joseph T.; Covert, Clair;
Crough, Edward; Crowley, Timothy
M.; Davidson, Emmett; Dean, John
J.; DeNedrey, Samuel; Dennis, Jere;
Dietrich, Charles E.; Doane, Lester
B.; Donegan, Edward J.; Downey,
Patrick J.; Doyle, Charles W.; Doyle,
Peter F.; Drain, Parda D.; Driscoll,
Dennis D.; Duncan, James; Eber-
hardt, William F.; Eichelberger,
Harry L.; Estes, Fred J.; Euphrat,
Charles; Evans, Christopher; Evans,
Newton W.; Fahey, Charles P.; Farn-
ham, Milton G.; Fennessey, Thomas

D.; Fitzgerald, Anna; Fitzgerald, Frank A.; Fitzgibbon, James H.; Fitzpatrick, John J.; Flaherty, Martin D.; Flett, John A.; Flood, Emmet T.; Flynn, Thomas H.; Ford, Cornelius; Franklin, Joseph A.; Frayne, Hugh; Freeman, William E.; Frey, John P.; Friedman, Julius; Galley, Alford A.; Garfield, Alex H.; Gill, Frank H.; Golden, John; Goldwater, Samuel; Goode, Armistead; Gordon, F. G. R.; Grace, Lawrence A.; Gray, James A.; Greene, Prince W.; Grimes, James F.; Griscom, William S.; Grossman, Herman; Gruelle, Thomas M.; Hale, William W.; Hamilton, M. Grant; Hamlin, Frank D.; Harper, Robert L.; Harriman, Charles A.; Harris, George W.; Harry, George Y.; Hartmann, Louis; Hartwig, Otto R.; Hay, Arthur A.; Hayes, John; Heimerdinger, David S.; Henderson, James "Pitchfork"; Hickey, John H.; Hilfers, Henry F.; Himmelsbach, Henry; Holder, Arthur E.; Howard, Robert; Hushing, William C.; Idar, Clemente N.; Iglesias Pantín, Santiago; Ireland, Arthur E.; Ives, Harry M.; Jensen, Sofus; Johnson, Jesse; Johnson, Robert C.; Jones, A. W. "Puggy"; Jones, James E.; Jones, Jerome; Keegan, John J.; Kelleher, Mary J.; Kelly, José W.; Kennedy, Frederick E.; Kenney, Mary E.; Kidd, Thomas I.; Kirby, John; Kirchner, John S.; Kissinger, William B.; Kline, James W.; Kreyling, David J.; Lake, Emmett J.; Lanphere, Emma; Leitch, Andrew S.; Lennon, John B.; Leonard, James; Levi, Isaac M.; Lewis, John L.; Lord, James; Lynch, M. W.; MacArthur, Walter; Madsen, John A.; Mahon, William D.; Mahoney, Nellie; Manee, James T.; McCarthy, Frank H.; McGrady, Edward F.; McGuigan, Bernard; McKinney, William H.; McKinstry, William H.; McLean, Robert E.; McMahon, James; McMahon, Thomas F.; McSorley, William J.; Menche, Adam; Merritt, Harry D.; Metzger, Martin; Miles, Charles A.; Modie, Frank E.; Moffitt, John A.; Monck, Richard S.; Montgomery, William H.; Mullen, William H.; Neary, Anna; Nestor, Agnes; Nockels, Edward N.; Noonan, Martin J.; Norton, George L.; Notton, Frank M.; Oakes, John; O'Brien, John; O'Connell, James; O'Fallon, Daniel W.; Ogg, Robert Y.; O'Sullivan, John F.; O'Sullivan, Mary Kenney; Pacelli, Tito; Parker, William N.; Peetz, Charles; Penning, George C.; Perkins, Edgar A.; Perry, John B.; Petry, Charles W.; Pettipiece, Richard P.; Pierce, Jefferson D.; Pinard, William O.; Pomeroy, William C.; Porter, James E.; Prince, Samuel; Randall, Harvey N.; Reid, Stuart; Reuter, M. P.; Reynolds, Louis; Rice, Garrett; Richie, Joseph; Riley, John; Rist, Frank L.; Roach, James E.; Roberts, Flournoy C.; Roberts, James C.; Roberts, William C.; Robinson, Herman; Rocker, Charles; Rogers, Louis W.; Rosemund, Charles L.; Rosenberg, Edward; Ross, Samuel; Ruiz, Rufus M.; Ryan, William D.; Samuels, Arthur S.; Saul, A.; Sauls, Thomas C.; Schamel, Harvey; Schelling, Henry; Schlesinger, Benjamin; Schrader, Levi P.; Scott, Melinda; Scully, Mary P.; Sexton, Sehon Rollin "Rolla"; Shanessy, James C.; Sheehan, John F.; Sherman, Charles O.; Sherman, W. T.; Short, James A.; Shurtleff, Wade; Smith, J. E.; Smith, Oliver P.; Smith, Paul J.; Smith, William S.; Smyth, Arthur B.; Sontheimer, Solomon; Spencer, William J.; Stillman, Charles B.; Strasser, Adolf; Streifler, Henry E.; Suchanek, Joseph; Sullivan, Charles A.; Sullivan, Dora; Sullivan, James H.; Sullivan, Jere L.; Swift, John; Taylor, Charles P.; Tazelaar, Jacob; Terry, William E.; Theis, Edward H.; Thomas, Harry D.; Thorne, Florence C.; Tobin, John F.; Todtenhausen, August A.; Tossy, L. E.; Tracy,

Thomas F.; Tucker, Edward L.;
Urick, Ambrose L.; Valesh, Eva Mc-
Donald; Varley, William; Wagner,
Karl H.; Walker, Henry M.; Walker,
Robert W.; Wallace, Edgar; Weber,
Frank J.; Weeks, Louis W.; Wheeler,
Fred C.; White, Frank A.; Whitney,
F. Stacy; Williams, Isabel; Winn, Wil-
liam H.; Wilson, William B.; Wood,
Francis N.; Woodman, Con W.;
Worthey, James W.; Wright, Edwin
R.; Wyatt, Calvin; Young, Charles O.
—Permanent Conference for the Abolition of Child Labor, **12:**81, *82n,*
346, 348n
—Permanent Conference for the Protection of the Rights and Interests
of Women Wage Earners, **12:**246–47
—Political Program, **3:**366, 419–21,
442–45, **4:**10–12, 44, 96–97, 98n;
content of, **3:**421, 422n, 435, 443,
616–17, 659n; debate on, **3:**419–21,
421n, 435–37, 437n, 459, 479, 502–
3, 611–13, 616–58, 659n; Plank 8,
3:630–31, 644; Plank 9, **3:**630–31,
644; Plank 10, **3:**419–21, 444, 503,
611, 618, 627–58; preamble of,
3:421, 611, 619–27; SG and, **3:**419,
421, 444–45, 585, 596, 606–7, 611–
13, 624–26
—Printing Trades Department, **6:**492
—Publicity Department, *11:426n,*
12:162; and railroad shopmen's
strike, 1922-?, **12:**106n, 155n
—Railroad (Railway) Employes'
Department, **8:**35n, 252, *253n,*
323n, 367, **9:**50n, 343n, 503, **10:**18,
11:271, **12:**10, 20, 21n, 158–59,
160n; and railroad shopmen's
strike, 1919 (threatened), **11:**120n
—Railroad (Railway) Employes' Department, conventions: 1922 (Chicago), **12:**53–54, *54*–55n, 66, 66n;
1924, **12:**518, *520n*
—Research Department, and AFL
Permanent Conference for Abolition of Child Labor, **12:**82n
—Secret Service Bureau, **6:**430–32
—Union Label Trades Department,
7:457n, **8:**237, 238n, 367, 475,
9:503, **11:**271, **12:**155n, 247n, 444,
461n
—Union Label Trades Department,
conventions: 1909 (Washington,
D.C.), **7:**456, *457n;* 1924 (El Paso,
Tex.), **12:**518, *520n*
—*Weekly News Service,* **12:**106n, 204,
206n, 277; and AFL Permanent
Conference for Abolition of Child
Labor, **12:**82n
—Women's Department, consider-
ation of, **12:**277, 360–61, 361–62n,
408n, 446–47n, 448–49, 449n,
450–51
—Women's Department, meetings regarding: Feb. 1924, **12:**361n, 408n;
Mar. 1924, **12:**361n, 408n, 417,
418n; Apr. 1924, **12:**361n, 417–18,
418n; May 1924, **12:**362n, 408n,
445–46n, 448, 449n, 450, 451n
—Women's Department, meetings
regarding, *minutes of:* Mar. 1924,
12:404–7; May 1924, **12:**443–45
American Federation of Labor et al. v.
Buck's Stove and Range Co., **7:***249–
50n. See also* Buck's Stove and Range
Co. cases: injunction case
*American Federation of Labor Reconstruc-
tion Program* (AFL), *10:358n,* **11:**7,
7–*8n,* 33, 53, 54n
American Fire Engine Co., **6:**151
American Friends Service Committee,
12:435n
American Fund for Public Service
(Garland Fund), **12:**226, *227n,* 257,
264
American Individualism (Hoover),
12:191, *192n*
American Industrial Union, **9:**118n,
507n
American Industries (periodical), **3:**342,
343n, **10:**390
American Institute of Architects,
11:23n
American Iron and Steel Institute,
12:281n
American Labor Alliance, **11:**549n
*American Labor Movement, The: Its
Makeup, Achievements, and Aspira-
tions* (SG), *9:224n*

American Labor Union, *4:453n,* **6:**17n, 191; and AFL, **4:**453n, **6:**37, 37n, 202–3, 224; in Butte, Mont., **6:**284, 285n; in California, **6:**17; in Chicago, **6:**283, 285n; in Colorado, **6:**15; in Denver, **6:**85–86, 87n; and IWW, **4:**453n, **6:**443–44, 447, 461–63, 468; in San Francisco, **6:**233–34; and socialists, **6:**203, 395–96, **10:**260, 264; in Texas, **6:**264. *See also* Western Labor Union
—locals: local 127 (bartenders, Butte, Mont.), **6:**285n; local 158 (firemen's and engineers' helpers, Denver), **6:**131n; local 188 (paper mill workers, Denver), **6:**131n; local 261 (grain counter workers, Lynn, Mass.), **5:**492n; local 263 (heel makers, Lynn, Mass.), **5:**492n; local 423 (street laborers, Chicago), **6:**283, 285n, 463; local 435 (musicians, San Francisco), **6:**233, 234n; local 474 (actors, San Francisco), **6:**234, 234n
—strike/lockout: 1903 (Denver), *6:131n*
"American Labor's Political Strategy—A Failure" (West), **12:**41
American Labor's Position in Peace or in War (AFL), **10:**22n, 39–44, 44n, 203, 212, 226, 263–64n, 283, 560, **11:**521n
American Land League, *1:286n*
American League (baseball), **9:**237n
American League to Aid and Cooperate with Russia, *10:313n*
—conference: 1918 (New York City), **10:**507–12
American Legion, **11:**217n
—conference: 1924 (Washington, D.C.; All-American Conference), **12:**452, *452n*
—convention: 1922 (New Orleans), **12:**158, *159n,* 162
American Lithographic Co. v. *Castro,* **12:**302, *303n*
American Mason (periodical), **11:**374, *376n*
American Masters of Sculpture (Caffin), **7:**442, *443n*

American Newspaper Publishers' Association, **8:**142–43
American Peace Society, **7:**214n
"American Plan," **12:**396, 451n. *See also* open shop
American Protective Association, **3:**652, *660n,* **4:**97, 190, 260–61, **12:**352, 352n
American Railroad Executives' Association, **12:**203–4
American Railway Union, **3:***, 512, 512n, 568, 587, 592, 622, **4:***, 82n, **6:***, 36, 37n, **7:***, 402–4, 405n, **8:***, 253n, **11:***, 259n; injunctions against, **3:**523–25, 526n, 530, 531n, 537, 547n, 559, 561n, 563n, 576, 632–33, **7:**402; and Pullman strike, 1894, **3:**186, 521–25, 526n, 527, 529, 534–35, 537–38, **7:**403, **8:**251, **11:**250–51
—conventions: 1894 (Chicago), **3:**522, 529, *532n;* 1897 (Chicago), **4:**324n, 341, *342n*
—strike/lockout: 1894 (Great Northern Railroad), **3:**521, 544, *547n. See also* Pullman strike, 1894
American Red Cross, **10:**383–84, 384n
American Revolution, **9:**290
American Sheet and Tin Plate Co., **10:**69–70n; strike/lockout, 1909–10, **7:**472, *473n,* 480, **8:**7, 9n, 12, 12n, 27–30, 54–55
American Sheet Steel Co., strike/lockout, 1901, *5:384n*
American Smelting and Refining Co.: strike/lockout, 1899, *5:115n;* strike/lockout, 1903–4, *6:282n*
American Socialist Society, **8:**398n
American Social Science Association:
—convention: 1891 (Saratoga Springs, N.Y.), **3:**83, 85n, 95–102, *102n*
American Society of Equity, **7:**234, *236n,* 268, 301
—conventions (state): Kentucky, 1908 (Henderson), **7:**301, *302n;* Minnesota, 1908 (St. Paul), **7:**301, *302n;* Wisconsin, 1908 (Eau Claire), **7:**301, *302n*
American Society of Mechanical Engineers:

—conference: 1920 (New York City),
  12:142, *146n*
American Steel and Wire Co., strikes,
  1913, **8**:391n, 453, *455n*
American Steel Foundries, **10**:152n;
  injunction, **10**:252, *253n*
American Steel Foundries v. *Tri-City Central Trades Council et al.,* **10**:252,
  253n, **12**:93n, 302
American Steel Hoop Co., strike/
  lockout, 1901, *5:384n*
American Telephone and Telegraph
  Co., strike/lockout, 1919, **11**:93,
  94–95n, 102–4, 104n
American Tin Plate Co., **5**:79; strike/
  lockout, 1901, *5:384n*
American Tobacco Co., **4**:116, **5**:117,
  119n, **6**:401, *402n,* **7**:473n, **8**:153,
  154n, **9**:481; boycott, 1895, **4**:117n;
  boycott, 1899, *5:119n*
American Tobacco Co. v. *U.S.,* **8**:153, *154n*
American Union against Militarism,
  9:430–31, *433n,* **10**:485n
American Vocational Association,
  9:353n
American Woolen Co., **8**:326n, **11**:352n
American Workingman's Protective
  Association, *5:417n*
Ames, Charles B., **11**:202, *203n*
Ames, Walter, **8**:232–34, *234n*
Ammon, Charles G., **9**:*, 353, *355n*
Ammons, Elias, **9**:24n, 95n
Anaconda Copper Mining Co., **9**:275n
anarchists, **1**:386, 444, **5**:404. *See also*
  Haymarket: defendants
Ancona, Mary D., **1**:17–18, *18n,* **9**:538,
  539n
Anderson, Albert B., **8**:238n, 413,
  414n, 434, **9**:206–7, 208n, 220,
  11:196n, 209, 220, **12**:22, 24n
Anderson, Carl C., **8**:100, *101n*
Anderson, Edward E., **9**:*, 457, *457n,*
  10:*, *58n; wire from,* **10**:57–58; *wire
  to,* **10**:58
Anderson, George M., *12:174n; letter
  to,* **12**:173–74
Anderson, John F., **10**:19, *21n*
Anderson, Mary, *10:82n,* **11**:18–20,
  132, 134, **12**:446n; *letters from,*
  10:482–83, **12**:450–51; *wire from,*
  10:81–82

Anderson, Sydney, **11**:332n
Anderson, Thomas H., **7**:357, *357n*
Andersonville Prison, *5:138n*
Andrews, Elisha B., **4**:435, *435n*
Andrews, George P., **5**:244n
Andrews, John B., *9:277n; letter to,*
  9:276–77
Andrews, William S., **3**:384, *385n*
Angel, Moses, **1**:11, *12n*
Angelo, Julius, **3**:174, *174n*
Anglo-Soviet Trade Agreement, 1921,
  12:15n
Anheuser-Busch Brewing Co., **4**:329–
  30, 330n; *letter to,* **5**:332–33
Anniston (Ala.) Trades and Labor
  Council, **6**:106, *107n*
Ansley, Hubert M., **6**:183n
Ansonia case, **10**:281, *284n*
Anthony, Benjamin M., **5**:160n
Anthony, Daniel R., Jr., **12**:346, *349n*
Anthony, Elizabeth S. Cole, **5**:159,
  160n
Anthony, Susan B., *5:140n,* 160n,
  6:482n, 512n; *address by,* **5**:158–60;
  letter from, **6**:511–12; *letter to,* **5**:139–
  40
Anthracite Coal Strike Commission,
  6:14n, 45–46, 46n, 103–4, 104n,
  334, **9**:86–87, 88n, 323
Anti-Corn Law League, **1**:32, *44n*
Anti-Imperialist League, **5**:xv
Anti-Militarism Committee, **9**:433n
Anti-Preparedness Committee, **9**:433n
Anti-Saloon League of America,
  12:429, *430n*
anti-tenement campaign, **1**:47, 50, 58,
  67, 79, 102–3, 119, 124–27, 129–31,
  151–52, 169–210, 230, 242, 250–51,
  260–62, 292–93, 448; and doctors,
  1:201–6, **2**:216; opposition by manufacturers, **1**:260–62; SG and, **1**:125,
  130–31, 151–52, 169–210, 262, 291–
  93. *See also under* legislation, states
  and territories: New York
Antonini, Luigi, **11**:318n, **12**:91n, 550,
  553n
Appel, George W., **1**:*, 457, *459n,* **2**:*,
  110, *111n; letter to,* **2**:115–16
Appel, Jacob S., **3**:34, *41n*
Applehagen, Emil, **2**:169, 172, *173n,*
  356; *letter to,* **2**:182–83

Appleton, William A., **7:***, 489, *490n,*
8:*, 518, *519n,* **9:***, 174, *175n,*
385, 385n, 485, 487, **10:***, *294n,*
521–22, 537, **11:***, 28, *30n; cable to,*
10:309; and British labor mission to
United States, 1918, **10:**309, 309n;
and International Federation of
Trade Unions, **9:**265, 289n, **11:**223,
437; *letters from,* **9:**192–93, 238–39,
288–89, **10:**292–94, 445–46, 492–93;
letter to, **11:**117–19; and postwar labor conference, AFL proposal for,
9:468, 469n, 474
apprentices, **12:**6; legislation regarding, demand for, **1:**225, 467 (*see also
under* legislation, states and territories: New Jersey); limitation of number of, **12:**69, 71–72
Arabic pledge, *9:287n*
Arago case. See *Robertson* v. *Baldwin*
Aragon mine (Norway, Mich.), **4:**165n
A. R. Barnes and Co. et al. v. *Chicago Typographical Union No. 16,* **7:**12n
Arbeiter-Stimme (New York City socialist
journal), **1:**97
Arbeiter Union, *1:21*
arbitration, **1:**37, 42, 100, 287, **3:**303–
4; Boot and Shoe Workers' Union
and, **7:**37, 39–40n; in "Coke region"
dispute, **2:**31–32, *32n;* in *Morgen
Journal* dispute, **2:**371–74; in *Philadelphia Tageblatt* dispute, **2:**25, *26n,*
37; SG and, **1:**349–50, **2:**87–88,
4:291–92, 303, **6:**542. *See also* conciliation; meatpacking arbitration,
1918–21; mediation of industrial
disputes
—compulsory, **3:**192, 258–60, 303–4,
426–28, 545–46, 575–76, 601–2,
4:111–12, **5:**291–92, 296, 298–304,
306, 307–8n, 310, 328, 508–9,
8:56n, 115n, 198, 199n, 277n, 409,
453n, **9:**56n, 85–86, 212, 312–13,
408–9, 449–50, 450n, 463, 527,
529n, **10:**15, **12:**3
—international, **6:**377–78, 378n,
7:179–80, 180n, 206, 211, 214n,
8:205–8
—voluntary, **4:**112, **5:**299–302, 304,
306, 307–8n, **9:**55–56, 57n, 85, 449,
457n, **12:**3, 6

arbitration boards, **4:**69, **7:**300, 300n,
9:55–56, 56n
arbitration treaty, Anglo-American:
1887 (proposed), **2:**63, *64n;* 1897,
4:301, 303, *304n*
Arcand, Narcisse, **9:**15, 15–*16n*
Arch, Joseph, **1:***, 340, *353n,* **3:**146n
Archibald, James P., **2:***, 120, *120n,*
191, 257, 332, **3:***, 62n, 298, *300n,*
4:*, 18, *19n,* 56
Archie, David, **2:**172, *173n*
Architectural Iron Workers' Industry
of North America, International
Union of the, **3:***, 68, 69n
—convention: 1891 (Indianapolis),
3:68, *69n*
Architectural Sheet Iron Cornice
Workers' Union of Philadelphia,
2:110–11, *111n,* 115–16
Arena (periodical), **3:**468, *469n*
Argentina, **9:**363n, **10:**10, **12:**386
Argo, George W., **3:**265, *266n*
Argyle, duke of (George Douglas
Campbell), **1:**344, *354n*
Aristotle, **5:**6
Arizona, copper miners' strikes in:
1903, **7:**24, *25n;* 1915–16, **9:**351–52,
352n, 425; 1917, **10:**125, *126n,*
148–49, 167–68, 259, 262, 301, 321,
323–24n, 336–39
Arizona, labor party in, **8:**283–84
Arizona Copper Co., strike/lockout,
1915–16, **9:**351–52, *352n,* 425
Arizona State Federation of Labor,
9:352n, *468n,* **10:**265, **11:**340–41
—convention: 1917 (Clifton), **10:**172–
74, *175n*
Arkwright Club, **4:**435, *435n*
Armaments, General Committee on
Limitation of (AFL), **11:**547, *548n,*
12:310, 311n
Armas, Francisco de, **5:**185, 188n
Armenia, workers from, **8:**115
Armistice Day disarmament demonstrations, 1921, **11:**523–24, 524–
25n, 533–34, 534n
Armour, Mr. (owner of meatpacking
firm), **10:**285n
Armour meatpacking company,
10:152n; boycott, 1886, *1:467n;*
boycott, 1896–?, **4:**286; strike/lock-

out, 1896–98, **4:**286, *287n;* strike/
lockout, 1904, **6:**313–14, 314–15n;
strike/lockout, 1921–22, *11:571n*
Armstrong, Hamilton, **3:**40, *41n,* 439,
440n, **4:**196, 205
Armstrong, J. B., *letter to,* **5:**140–42
Arnold, Benedict, **5:**97, *99n,* **11:**368
Arnold, Emil, **7:**427n, **9:**31, *34n*
Arnold, Frank W., **3:***, *533n; wire from,*
3:532–33
Arnold, Matthew, **1:**10, *12n*
Arrandale, Matthew, **6:**62n
Arras, battle of, **11:**57, 58n
Arrington, Louis, **1:**455, *455n,* 460
Arthur, Chester A., **3:**200, *204n*
Arthur, Peter M., **1:***, 390, *390n,* **2:***,
148n, 181, 323–24, 335, **3:***, 294n,
414n, 467, **4:***, 104, *106n; letters to,*
2:146–48, **3:**413–14
Arundel, Ernest J., **1:**414, *414n,* **3:**141
Aschermann, Edward, **1:**297–98, *327n*
Aschermann and Co., **1:**297–99, 301,
327n
Ash, Louis, **1:**195, *198n,* 199
Ashbridge, Samuel H., **6:**6, *8n*
Ashby, Irene M., *5:315–16n,* 340–41,
342n, 348–49; *letter to,* **5:**314–15. *See
also* Ashby-Macfadyen, Irene M.
Ashby-Macfadyen, Irene M.: article by,
5:465, 465n; *letter to,* **5:**465. *See also*
Ashby, Irene M.
Ashe, Robert, **4:**79, *79n,* 98–99, 99n,
270, 272n, 280, 284
Ashley, Alfred, **2:**305–6, **3:**342, *343n*
Ashley, Henry W., **3:**330–31, *340n*
Ashley, William F., Jr., **11:**353n, 378,
379n, 460
Ashton, Thomas, **8:***, 116, *117n*
Ashton, William, **11:**459n
Asian workers: competition from,
5:309; immigration of, **7:**477, **8:**340,
9:100–101, **12:**416n; organization
of, **8:**145, **10:**266n. *See also specific
nationalities*
Asiatic Exclusion League, **7:**147, 148n
Askew, Robert, **4:***, *165n,* 221, 222n,
5:*, 148, *151n;* at AFL conventions,
4:271, 272n, 410, 411n; *letter to,*
4:162–64; and miners' strike, 1897,
4:348, 350, 357, 359n, 366, 378
assembly, freedom of, **9:**124, **11:**8,

18n, 70n, 159, 163, 176, 247, 311,
12:454, 487, 510
Associated Press, **7:**406n
Associated Waist and Dress Manufac-
turers, **8:**40n
association, freedom of, **8:**68, 318–20,
11:8n, 11, 70–71n, 100, **12:**454
Association for National Service,
9:451n
Association of American Agricultural
Colleges and Experimental Sta-
tions, **8:**398–99, 399n
Association of Master Painters and
Decorators of New York City, strike/
lockout, 1920–21, *11:358n*
Association of United Workers of
America, *1:84n*
assumption of risk, **8:**32, 181, 317–18,
9:7, 9n, **12:**4
Astor, John Jacob, **8:**274, *277n*
Atchison, Topeka, and Santa Fe Rail-
road, **3:**282n; strike/lockout, 1900,
5:295–96, *307n*
*Atchison, Topeka, and Santa Fe Railroad
Co. v. Matthews,* **8:**479, *492n*
*Atchison, Topeka, and Santa Fé Railway
Co. v. Gee et al.,* *11:458n*
Atkins, Milton W., **11:**95n, 103, *104n*
Atkinson, Alatau L. C., **6:**472, *473n*
Atkinson, Edward, **4:**446n
Atkinson, George W., **4:**360n, *363n,*
365; *letter to,* **4:**362–63
Atkinson, Thomas, **6:***, 176n, *220n;
letter to,* **6:**219–20
Atl, Dr. *See* Murillo, Gerardo
Atlanta Federation of Trades, *4:24n,*
427n, **11:**66
Atlantic Coast Seamen's Union:
—local: local 56 (Philadelphia),
5:387n
Atlas Cement Works, **7:**45
Atterbury, William W., **12:**103, *106n,*
114
"At the Needle," **2:**80, *80n*
*Attorney General ex rel. Prendergast et al.
v. Bedard et al.,* *8:502n*
Aubrey, James L., **1:***, 266, *267n*
Auburn (Maine) Shoe Manufactur-
ers' Association: injunction, **3:**412n;
strike/lockout, 1893–94, **3:**411,
412n, 460–61

Auerbach, Julius, **12:**456, *457n*, 542
Auger and Simon Works, strike/lock-
out, 1902, **6:**29n
Augusta (Ga.) Trades Council, *7:59n*
Aull, Richard F., *1:448n; statement of,*
1:446–47
Ault, Erwin B. "Harry," **11:**217, *217–
18n,* **12:**274n, 324
Austin, John, *7:468n*
Austin Trades Council, **5:**413–14,
414n
Austria, and International Labor Con-
ference, 1919, **11:**136–37, 137–38n
Austria-Hungary, **10:**559, 568n; condi-
tions in, **10:**342; and outbreak of
World War I, **9:**160n, 163n; peace
proposal of, **10:**564, 567n
authority, SG on respect for, **9:**451
Avanti! (Italian socialist journal),
10:551, *555n,* 561–62
Aveling, Eleanor Marx, **3:***, *33–*34n;
letter to, **3:**32–33
Averill, John W., **6:**153, 154n
Avery, Martha Moore, **6:**117, *118n*
Avery (mill superintendent), **4:**483,
485
"Away" (Riley), **12:**550, 552n
Axe and Edge Tool Makers' National
Union of America, **3:***, 24n
Aylsworth, Ira B., **1:***, 403, *404n,* **2:**39n

Bablitz, August A., **9:**244, *244n*
Babson, Roger W., **10:**496, *496–97n*
Bache-Denman Coal Co., **10:**323n
Bachelder, Nahum J., **8:**45, *45n*
Bäcker-Zeitung, Deutsch-Amerikanische
(trade union journal), *3:114n*
Backus, Josephus R., **1:**165, *166n*
Bacon, Abraham, **6:**277, *278n*
Bacon, Augustus O., **8:**373–74, 380–
81n, **9:**10n
Bacon, Henry J., **2:***, *140n; letter to,*
2:140
Bacon, Robert, **6:**490, *490n*
Baden, Max von, **10:**543n
Badgett, Harry, **11:**84n
Baer, Frederick W., **11:***, 434, *435n*
Baer, George, **6:**14n
Baer, Henry, **1:**68, *69n,* 83, **12:**393,
394n
Baer, John, **12:**433n

Baer, Louis, **1:**73, *74n,* **12:***394n; letter
from,* **12:**393; *letter to,* **12:**399
Baglin, Mrs. Thomas, *letter to,* **5:**178–
79
Bailey, Ernest, *letter to,* **12:**129–30
Bailey, George S., **2:**181, *182n,* 219
Bailey, Joseph W., **11:**339, *342n,* 375
Bailey (professor), **3:**656
Bailey, Robert D., **5:**462–63, *463n*
Bailey, William, **2:**60, *63n*
Bailey, William B., **12:**324, *326n*
Bailey, William H., **1:***, *401n,* 466,
2:*, 18, 24n, 32n, 49, *50n,* 340,
343n; *letter from,* **1:**409–11; *report of,*
1:399–401
Bailey, Willis J., **7:**80, *90n*
*Bailey v. Drexel Furniture Co., 10:499n,
11:514n,* **12:**82n, 84–85, 93n, 227,
230, 250
Bailey v. George, 11:514n
Bailin, Albert, **12:**132, *132n*
Bailor, W. J., **4:**351–52, *352n*
Bainbridge, Alexander G., **6:**114, *115n*
Baine, Charles L., **7:***, *39n,* **8:***, *416n,*
9:*, *460n,* **10:***, 470n, 547, *548n,*
549–50, **11:***, *560n,* **12:***, 406, *408n,*
550; at AFL conventions, **8:**415,
12:97n; *letter from,* **7:**37–39; *letters to,*
9:458–59, **11:**559–60
Baker, D. C., *letter to,* **12:**421–22
Baker, Francis E., **12:**154, *155n*
Baker, Horace, **11:**538, 539–*40n*
Baker, Newton D., **9:***512n,* 524, 525n,
10:116, 245, 274, 285n, **11:**191,
206n, 259n, 393n, **12:**183n; and
Cantonment Construction Agreement, **10:**114, 115n, 171–72n, 204;
and clothing workers, **10:**151n,
204, 335; and Houston mutineers,
10:327n; *letter from,* **11:**116; *letters
to,* **9:**511, **10:**182–84, 363–65, 450,
12:174–83; and meatpackers' strike,
1917 (threatened), **10:**280n, 442;
and President's Mediation Commission, **10:**194–95; and Puerto Rico,
conditions in, **10:**438n; and "Work
or Fight" draft provision, **10:**451n,
514n, 539, 540n
Baker, William T., **3:**151, *153n*
Bakers' and Confectioners' International Union of America, Journey-

men, **1**:*, **2**:*, 417n, **3**:*, 27n, 65–66, 270, 270n, 353, 621, **4**:*, 82n, 99, **6**:*, **9**:*; AFL financial support of, **3**:470, 471n; boycott, **2**:417–18n, **3**:270, 270n; executive council of, **2**:396; journal, official, of, **3**:114n; and KOL, **3**:105, 105n, 270, 270n
—locals: local 1 (New York City), **3**:379, 382n; local 7 (New York City), **3**:114n; local 17 (Mobile, Ala.), **3**:105, 105n; local 24 (San Francisco), **3**:27, 27n; local 35 (New Orleans), **5**:377, 379n; local 51 (San Francisco), **3**:27, 27n; local 73 (Birmingham, Ala.), **3**:105, 105n; local 93 (New York City), **3**:111, 114n
—strike/lockout: 1891 (Rochester, N.Y.), *3:105n*
Bakers' Association of New York and Vicinity, **2**:240–41, 242n; boycott, 1889–93, **2**:242, 242n, 417n
Bakers' Journal (trade union journal), **2**:241, 242n, *3:114n; letter to,* **2**:214–15
Bakers' Journal and Deutsch-Amerikanische Bäcker-Zeitung (trade union journal), *3:114n*
Bakers' local 1 (Chicago; independent), **2**:202, 202n
Bakers' National Union of the U.S., Journeymen, **1**:*, 457, 458n, **2**:*, 201, 202n, 235, **3**:*, **4**:*, **6**:*, **9**:*; boycott, **2**:242, 242n; executive council of, **2**:241
—convention: 1886 (Pittsburgh), **2**:241, *242n*
—local: local 49 (Chicago), **2**:202, 202n
—strike/lockout: 1889 (New York City and Brooklyn, N.Y.), **2**:240–41, *242n*, 417n
Bakery and Confectionery Workers' International Union of America, **1**:*, **2**:*, **3**:*, **4**:*, **6**:*, 393n, **8**:344, **9**:*, 34n, 191n; and black workers, **11**:84n; and industrial unionism, **9**:148–49; jurisdiction of, **9**:143, 145n, 147–49
—local: local 48 (Montreal), **6**:447, 449n
—strike/lockout: 1923–24, **12**:406, *408n*

Bakhmeteff, Boris A., **10**:128n, 129–30, 133, *134n*
Bakunin, Mikhail, **1**:22n
Balanoff, Albert (alias Albert Bailin), **12**:132, *132n*
Balboa (Canal Zone) Central Labor Union, **11**:391, *393n*
Balch, Emily Greene, **4**:193, *195n*, *10:94n; wire from,* **10**:93
Balcomb, E. E., **8**:80n
Baldwin, Roger N., **12**:132n, 226, *227n; letter to,* **12**:263–64
Baldwin-Felts detectives, **9**:24n, **11**:296n
Baldwin Locomotive Works, **5**:194, 198n; organization of, **8**:228–29, 230n; strike/lockout, 1911, **8**:228–29, *230n*
Balfour, Arthur J., **10**:72n, **11**:69, *71n*
Ball (delegate), **4**:12, 15
Ball, Elmer E., **10**:404, *404n*
Ball, William, **2**:384, *385n*
Ballard, Everett G., **8**:53, *54n*
Ballard, S. Thruston, **9**:139, *139n*, 312n
Ballard, Samuel T., **10**:94, *96n*
Balloch, Edward A., **5**:155, 156n, 157
Baltic Mining Co. et al. v. *Houghton Circuit Judge, 9:13n*
"Baltimore Agreement," *12:87n*, 204, 206n
Baltimore and Ohio Railroad, **9**:516, **12**:383n, 412–13; dynamiting of, **8**:232–34, 234n
Baltimore Federals (baseball team), **9**:237–38n
Baltimore Federation of Labor, *2:68n*, 188–89, 189n, 226, 228n, 388, **4**:482, 483n, **7**:120n
Baltz, J. & P., Brewing Co., boycott, 1906 (threatened), **7**:33
Bandlow, Robert, **2**:*, 407, *409n*, **3**:*, 253, *253n*, 260, **4**:45n, 449, 451n; *letter to,* **3**:598–99
Banford, Lawrence H., **2**:*, *138n; letter to,* **2**:138
Bankhead, John, **10**:288n
banks, **4**:326; labor, **12**:401–3; savings, **4**:92, 424–25
Banner, Louis, **3**:141, *142n*
Banner, Louisa, **3**:141, 142n
Banner, Rose, **3**:140, *141n*

Bannister, E. M., **4:**453n
barbers: Japanese local of, in Seattle, **12:**336; strike/lockout: 1913 (New York City), **8:**501–2, *503n*
Barbers' International Union of America, Journeymen, **2:***, 35, **3:***, 154, 154n, **4:***, 82n, 99, **5:***, 169n, **6:***, 20n, **8:***, 302n, 502, 503n, **9:**222, **10:***, 475n, **11:***, 317n, **12:***, 241n; and black workers, **4:**220, **11:**84n; jurisdiction of, **12:**334–37; and women barbers, **12:**237–39, 241n, 267–68, 334–37, 476–78, 478n
—convention: 1924 (Indianapolis), **12:**476, *478n*
—locals: local 166 (Denison, Tex.), **6:**19–20, 20n; local 195 (Seattle), **12:**239; local 205 (Denver), **5:**393, 395, 395n, **7:**8, 9n; local 395 (Denison, Tex.), **6:**20, 20n
Barbers' National Union, Journeymen, **1:**459n, **2:***, 98n, **3:***, **4:***, **5:***, **6:***, **8:***, **10:***, **11:***, **12:***
Barbers' Protective Association of Chicago, **4:**80, *82n*
Barbers' Protective Union of New York, Journeymen, **1:**457, *459n*
Barbier v. Connolly, **8:**479, *492n*
Barbosa, José Celso, **8:**88, *89n*
Barbour, E. T., **11:**286n
Barend, Simon, **2:**66, *68n*
Barker, Allan E., **11:***, 59–60, *60n*
Barlow, Lester P., **11:**277–78, *278n*
Barnaby, C., **5:**321, *322n*
Barnard, George G., **7:**442, *443n*
Barnes, George N., **10:***, 520, *524n*, **11:***, *70n*, 136, 137n; *letter from*, **11:**69–70
Barnes, J. Mahlon, **3:***, 234, *235n*, 403, 403n, **4:***, 78, *79n*, 103, 118, **5:***, *441n*, **6:***, *70n*, **7:***, *141n*, 144, 427n, **8:***, *6n*, 172, **9:***, 339, *341n*, **10:***, 261, *262n*, **11:***, 478n; at AFL conventions, **3:**627–28, 643, 645, 659n, **4:**93, 95–96, 99, **5:**398n, 439, 441n, **6:**69, 70n, 202, 204n, 211–12, 212n, 363, 365n, 369–70, 372, 507–8, 509n, **7:**129, 141n, **8:**3, 6n, 405–6, 406n, 415, 416n, **9:**9n, 348–49, 349n, 350, **10:**258, 262n, 263–64, **11:**93n, 477; at Cigar Makers' 1896 convention, **4:**236–37, 239

Barnett, Augustus E., *8:442n; letter to*, **8:**440–41
Barnett, Cicero M., *7:329n*
Barney, H. S., and Co.: boycott, 1903–4, **6:**176, *176n*, 179; *letter from*, **6:**175–76; strike/lockout, 1903, **6:**175–76
Barnum, Gertrude, *6:483–*84n; *letter from*, **6:**482–83; *letter to*, **6:**520
Baroff, Abraham, **10:***, *62n*, **12:***, *416n*, 444–45, 448; *letter from*, **10:**61–62; *letter to*, **12:**414–16
Baron de Hirsch Trade School, **3:**375, *376n*
Barondess, Joseph, **3:***, *123n*, 364, 367, 377, 380–82, **10:**156–57n; *letter to*, **3:**123
Barr, Frank, *7:408n; letter from*, **7:**407
Barr, Matthew, **2:***, 55, *55n*
Barr, William H., **12:**261, *263n*
Barrett, Charles S., **7:**59, *59n*, **8:**10n, 45, 45n
Barrett, George C., **3:**295n, 302
Barrett, James F., **11:***, 510–11, *512n*, 526, **12:***, *252n; letter from*, **12:**251–52
Barrett, James J., **10:**242, *243n*
Barrett, John H., **4:***, 454–55, *456n*
Barrett, Patrick A., **4:**263, 264n
Barrett, William H., **2:**209, *210n*
Barrie, James L., **3:**51, *55n*
Barry, James L., **6:***, 517, *518n*
Barry, Robert A., **1:**204–5, *206n*
Barry, Thomas B., **1:***, *401n*, 426, 466, 467n, **2:**18–19; *letter from*, **1:**409–11; *report of*, **1:**399–401
Barry, William J. (painter), **1:**361, *362n*
Barry, William J. (pilot), **2:**332, *337n*
Barter, Henry C., **4:**479n, **5:***, 59n, 249, *249n*, 283, 286n, *417n*, **6:***, 499, *499n; letter to*, **5:**416–17
Barthelmy, F., **3:**400–401, *401n*
Bartholomay Brewing Co., **4:**332
Bartholomee, Robert H., **3:**15, *18n*
Bartlett, Adolphus C., **5:**311, *311n*, 369n
Bartlett, Charles L., **8:**374–75, *381n*, **9:**10n
Barton, Alexander, **3:**51, *55n*
Barton, Bruce, *9:17n; letter to*, **9:**16–17
Barton, Dante, **9:**422n

Barton, Robert, **11:**538, 539n
Barton, William E., strike/lockout,
  1895, **2:**12, *13n,* 340
Bartow, C. J., *letter to,* **2:**102–3
Baruch, Bernard M., **10:**21n, 137,
  137–*38n,* 412, **11:**167, 172, 176–77,
  523n, **12:**424n, 550; *letter to,* **12:**422–
  24
baseball disputes, **9:**237, 237–38n
Bass, Robert P., *10:476n; wire to,*
  10:476
Bates, Edward A., **8:**327, *327n,* 472n,
  10:328; *letter to,* **12:**169–70
Bath Iron Co., **4:**499n
Batt, Dennis, **11:**488n
Battle, C. M., **10:**372n
Battle Creek Breakfast Food Co., Ltd.,
  7:302–4, 304n
Baudot, Marien, **4:**77n
Bauer, Ernest, **5:**269–70, *271n*
Bauer, Joseph, **3:**21, *23n*
Bauer, Joseph A., *11:343n; letter to,*
  11:342–43
Baum, Jacob D., **10:**273, *278n*
Baum, L., and Co., strike/lockout,
  1904, **6:**310, *310n*
Baumeister, Albert, **8:***, 241, *242n,*
  412n, 518, **9:***, 107, *107n; letter from,*
  9:173–74
Baur, Thomas, **2:**245
Bausch, Jacob E., **4:**57, *57–58n,* 249n
Baustian, Charles A., **3:***, *509n; letter
  from,* **3:**509; *letter to,* **3:**510–11; *wire
  from,* **3:**532–33
Bayard, Thomas F., **2:**156, *157n*
Bay City (Mich.), Greater, Central
  Trades Council, *5:330n*
Bayne, Harry, **3:**236, *240n*
Beach, John K., *8:42n,* 78, 194n
Beale, W. N. R., **8:**154n
Beales, Edmund V., **3:**34, *41n*
Beall, Edmond, **6:**186–89, *189n*
Beall Bros., **6:**186–89, 189n
Beam, Andrew, **4:**501–2, *502n*
Bean, J. C., *3:273n; letter to,* **3:**272–73
Bean, John H., *6:106–7n; letter from,*
  6:106
Beard, Butler, **8:**48, *49n*
Beattie, Samuel G., **9:**27, *28n*
Beattie, William W., **7:***, 250, *252n*
Beatty, James H., **6:**442n

Beaumont, Ralph, **2:***, 324, *325n,* **3:**3
Bebel, August, **1:**43n, **2:**159n, **3:**639,
  660n, **4:**68
Becerril, Joaquín A., **6:**252–53, *258n*
Bechtold, Charles F., **2:***, 397, *408n,*
  3:*, *533n,* **4:***, *330n,* **5:***, 219, *221n,*
  257–58; *letter from,* **4:**329–30; *letter to,*
  5:244–45; *wire from,* **3:**532–33
Bechtold, George, **7:***, *154n,* **8:***, 200,
  202n; letter from, **7:**153–54
Beck, Jacob, *4:399n*
Beck, James M., **7:**250n, **8:**217, *217n,*
  12:152–53, 155, 155n
Beck, Joseph, **12:**433n
Becker, De Los Isaac, **12:**552, *554n*
Beckler, George H., **2:***, 202, *202n*
Beckly, Mr. (Democratic campaign op-
  erative), *letter to,* **4:**233–34
Bedard, Joseph, **8:**502n
Beddall, Joseph, *6:104n*
Bedford Cut Stone Co., injunction,
  12:398n
*Bedford Cut Stone Co. et al. v. Journey-
  men Stone Cutters' Association of North
  America et al.,* **12:**398n
Beecher, Henry Ward, **1:**98–100, *101–
  2n,* **12:**135
Beeks, Gertrude B., **6:**386, *387n,*
  7:244, **10:**52n, 73, *74n,* 141. *See also*
  Easley, Gertrude Beeks
Behnke, Edward, **4:**72, *75n*
Behrens, Jacob, **3:**157, *158n*
Beifeld, Joseph, **5:**101–2
Beifeld, Joseph, and Co., strike/lock-
  out, 1898, **5:**101, *102n*
Beinke, George, **5:**170, *172n,* 292n
Belanger, John N., **12:**324, *326n*
Belcher, George W., **9:**480, *480n*
Belcher, Park, and Co., **1:**113, *115n*
Belgian Federation of Labor, meet-
  ings with AFL peace delegation,
  11:55–56
Belgium, **10:**112; commission of, to
  United States, **10:**72n; German
  atrocities in, **9:**192, 193–94n, 195;
  German invasion of, **9:**163n, 193n,
  295, 296, 364, **10:**559; indemnity
  imposed on, by Germany, **10:**88;
  labor representatives of, at Leeds
  (England) conference, 1916,
  9:470n; and neutrality treaty, **9:**295,

296n, 373, **10:**192, 200–201, 220,
564; socialists in, **10:**356n; workers
from, **8:**115
Belinski, Konstany, **10:**216, *218n*
Belk, Mason S., **5:**370, *371n, 6:48n; letter to,* **6:**47–48
Bell, Alexander Graham, bust of,
12:533n
Bell, Charles K., **7:**160–61, *161n*
Bell, George W., **6:**101, *102n,* **7:**383,
385n
Bell, Henry C., **7:**348–50, *350n,* 357–
60, 377; *letter to,* **7:**348–50
Bell, John, **2:**332, *337n*
Bell, John E., **4:**41, *42n*
Bell, Samuel H., *3:402n; letter to,*
3:401–2
Bell, Stephen, **4:**57, *57n*
Bell, Theodore A., **7:**117, *118n,* 384
Bell, William H., **5:**160n
Bellaire, Arthur, **10:**460n; *letter from,*
10:459–60
Bellamy, Albert, **10:***, 522, *524n*
Bellamy, Edward, **2:**288n, **3:**355n,
4:305, *307n,* **6:**397n
Belleau Wood, battle of, **11:**47, *49n,*
56, 118
Belleville (Ill.) Trades and Labor Assembly, **6:**369n
Bell Telephone Co., strike/lockout,
1904, **6:**265–66
Belmont, August, *6:380n,* **8:**288; as
president of Interborough Rapid
Transit Co., **6:**475–76, 521–22n,
7:69–70, 70n; as president of National Civic Federation, **6:**236n,
379–80, 381n, 417, 423n, 521
Bemis, Edward W., *3:376n,* 656, **6:**235,
236n; letter to, **3:**375–76
Bence, George, **1:**118, *118n,* 175–77,
177n, 178, 199, 260, 262
Benditt, Morris, **4:**236, *238n*
Benedict, M. S., Manufacturing Co.,
5:376, *377n; letter to,* **5:**376–77
Bengough, Herbert H., **1:**214, *216–17n,* 217, 235
Benjamin, Alfred, and Co., boycott,
1890, **2:**348, *349n*
Benjamin, Philip P., **2:**245, 245n
Benner, Lafayette, **7:**76, *90n*
Bennet, John B., **5:**95, *98n,* 134

Bennett, Albert W., **9:**29, 31, 33–*34n*
Bennett, George, **4:**432n
Bennett, J. S., **7:**104, *105n*
Bennett, Samuel L., **5:***, 124–26, *126n*
Bensley, Martha, **6:**484n, **7:**46, *47n*
Benson, Allan L., **9:**462, *462n*
Bereutz, E., **3:**141
Berg, Benita, *letter to,* **11:**244
Bergdoll, Louis, Brewing Co., **6:**503n
Berger, Frederick L., **2:**98, *98n*
Berger, Victor L., **3:***, 492, *497*–98n,
6:*, *62n,* 445, **7:***, *141–42n,* **8:***,
376–80, *381n,* 518, 519n, **9:***, 80–
82, 82–*83n,* 353, 355, 383n, **10:**90n,
11:*, 248, *248–49n,* **12:***, *123n,* 149,
452n; at AFL conventions, **6:**58,
357–60, 360n, 361–63, 491–92,
493n, 501, **7:**129–31, 137–39, 142n,
269, 269n, 270, 274, 280; *editorial by,*
12:121–23
Berger et al. v. U.S., *11:249n*
Bergh, Henry, **1:**99, *101n*
Bergoff Detective Bureau, **8:**50
Berk, Edward, *letter to,* **2:**365–66
Berkman, Alexander, **3:**211n, 238,
5:84–85, *85n*
Berlin, N.H., Central Labor Union,
12:90, *90n*
Berliner, Louis, **1:***, 73, *74n,* 83, 85,
87–89, 94, 108, 130, 255n, **12:**393,
394n; letter from, **1:**86–87; *letters to,*
4:224–25, 234–35, 461–62
Berlyn, Bernard, **7:**363, *364n*
Bernard, Thomas, *statement of,* **1:**446–
47
Berner, Edmund, **7:**130, 142n
Bernhardi, Friedrich von, **9:**192, *193n*
Bernstorff, Johann H. von, **9:**287n,
10:274, *278n*
Berres, Albert J., **8:***, 158, *159n,* 228,
237, 257, **9:***, 91, *94n,* 157n, **10:***,
19, *21n,* 53, 221, 361, **11:***, *76n,*
401, *403n,* 434, 560n, **12:***, 345,
348n, 383n, 445n, 543; *letter from,*
10:86–87; *letter to,* **10:**360–62; *wire to,*
10:360
Berry, David, **10:**156–57n
Berry, Edward, **6:**215n
Berry, George L., **7:***, 337, *338n,*
9:*, *36n,* 410n, **10:***, *262n,* 333n,
12:*, 51, *52n;* at AFL conventions,

9:34–36, 36n, 347, 350, **10:**259, 261, 262n; and election of 1924, **12:**468, 468n, 474; *letter to,* **9:**409–10
Berry, Thomas, **1:**360, *362n*
Berry, Thomas F., **5:***, *81n; letter to,* **5:**79–81
Bert, George, **7:**48, 48n
Bessette, Edward, **6:**56, *57n*
Best, George S., injunction against, **5:**123
Bestel, Charles F., *letter to,* **3:**359–60
Bethell, Union N., *6:33n; letter to,* **6:**32–33
Bethlehem Iron Co., **4:**500; strike/lockout, 1883, **4:**490–91, *499n*
Bethlehem Steel Co., **5:**207n, **8:**331, 345, 459–60, **11:**399n; strike/lockout, 1910, **8:**43, *44n;* strike/lockout, 1919, **11:**126n
Bethmann-Hollweg (German chancellor), **9:**296n
Bettenhausen, George A., *4:307n; letter to,* **4:**305–7
Beutler, Otto G., **8:**198, *199n*
Beveridge, Albert J., **12:**169, *171n*
Bevin, Ernest, **9:***, 353, *355n,* **10:***, 445, *447n*
Bibb Manufacturing Co., **11:**76n
Bibliography of Industrial and Labour Questions in Soviet Russia (International Labor Organization), **12:**231–32, *232–33n*
Bice, William F., *5:59n; letter from,* **5:**59–61; *letter to,* **5:**58–59
Bichler, William, **1:**103–6, *106n*
Bicycle Workers, International Union of, **4:***, 460n, **5:***, **6:***
—local: local 23 (Dayton, Ohio), **4:**459–60, 461n
—strike/lockout: 1898 (Dayton, Ohio), **4:**457–60, *460n*
Bielaski, A. Bruce, *10:243n,* 298n, 480, *481n,* **12:***101n*
Bier and Co., **1:**196, 199
Billings, Edward C., **3:**293, 294n, 302
Billings, Frank, **10:**310, *312n*
Billings, Hollis C., *7:59n; letter from,* **7:**58–59
Billings, John S., **2:**239, *240n*
Billings, Warren, **9:**517–18n, **11:**87n, 541, **12:**90, 91n

Bimetallic League, **4:**508, *509n*
Bimetallic League of Shelby County, Tenn., Central, **4:**40–41
Binder, Charles A., **1:**446, *447n*
Binghamton (N.Y.) Cigar Manufacturers' Association, **3:**26n; injunction, **3:**26, 26n, 148n
Birch, Nathan P., **11:**80, *82n*
Bird (federal labor union president), **5:**402–3
Bird, Joseph, **6:**6, *8n*
Birkenhauer, George, *1:369n; report of,* **1:**368–69
Birmingham, John, Jr., **8:**249n
Birmingham (Ala.), United Labor League of, *6:193n*
Birmingham (Ala.) Metal Trades Council:
—strike/lockout: 1918, **10:**376–77, *378n,* 385–86, 440–44, 516–18, 518n
Birmingham (Ala.) Trades Council, **2:**355n, **5:**316n, **6:**193n, *10:518n*
Birth Control Conference, American, 1921 (New York City), **11:**540, 540n
Bisbee (Ariz.), deportations from, **10:**126n, 148–49, 150n, 168, 172–75, 175–76n, 183, 224, 248, 321, 323–24n, 336–39
Bisbing, Ingham W., **1:**359, *359n*
Bischoff, John W., **6:**12, *14n*
Bishop, Michael J., **3:***, 268–69, *269n,* 270
Bismarck, Otto von, **4:**68, *70n,* **11:**10
Bissell, Wilson S., **3:**413, *414n,* 560
Bissolati, Leonida, **10:**552, *556n*
Bittner, Van Amberg, **8:***, 475, *476n,* **9:**38n
Bjork, Daniel, **4:**194, *195n*
Black, David, **4:**273–74, *275n,* **5:**57, 58n, **6:**147, 147n
Black, J. J., **1:**458
Black, Robert J., **7:**121, *122n*
Black, Thomas, **10:**265, 266n
Black, William P., **2:**62n
Black and Tans, **11:**452–53, *454n*
Black Hand Society, **7:**393
Blackman, William, **4:***, *463n,* **7:***, 108, *109n,* **10:***, 318n, 361, *363n*
Blackmore, Henry H., **2:**169, 172, *172n*
Blacksmiths, Drop Forgers, and Help-

ers, International Brotherhood of,
3:*, **5:***, **6:***, **8:***, **10:***, **11:***, 27–28n,
85n, 344, 362, 475n, **12:***, 113n,
238, 241n, 267; and black work-
ers, **11:**84n, 284, **12:**148, 343n; injunctions against, **12:**9n, 267; and
railroad shopmen's strike, 1919
(threatened), **11:**120n
—locals: local 211 (Seattle), **12:**237–
38, 241n, 267; local 422 (Mobile,
Ala.), **11:**486n
—strikes/lockouts: 1920–21 (Mobile,
Ala.), **11:**484–85, *486n;* 1920–21
(Springfield, Mass.), **12:**8–9, *9n*
Blacksmiths, International Brotherhood of, **3:***, 346n, **4:**127n, **5:***,
162n, 285, **6:***, **8:***, **10:***, **11:***, **12:***;
jurisdiction of, **5:**161, 162n, 516,
517n
—convention: 1893 (Philadelphia),
3:345
—local: local 104 (Philadelphia),
5:126n
—strike/lockout: 1899–1900 (Philadelphia), **5:**124, *126n,* 205–6
Blacksmiths and Helpers, International Brotherhood of, **3:***, **5:***,
6:*, 186–89, 189n, **8:***, 189n, 323n,
10:*, 21n, 502n, **11:***, **12:***; jurisdiction of, **9:**347, 347–48n; label of,
6:188–89
—locals: local 179 (Alton, Ill.), **6:**186–
89, 189n; local 287 (Galeton, Pa.),
8:35n
—strike/lockout: 1909–10 (Galeton,
Pa.), *8:35n*
Blackstone, William, **3:**560, 561n,
4:40, *7:468n*
Blackwell, Alice Stone, **12:**427n
Blackwell, Jerome E., *11:197n; letter
from,* **11:**196–97
black workers, **2:**152, **3:**62–63, 133,
167, 235, 284–85, 357, **4:**26, 220,
430–31, **5:**xiv, 342–46, **6:**31n, 121n,
181–82, 182n, 223n, 401, **7:**21–22,
228, 234, **8:**46, 137, 139n, 145,
146n, **9:**161n, 267–68, **10:**109–10,
134–35, 136n, 215–17, 218n, 327n,
372n, 494, **11:**42–46, 46n, 82, 121n,
143n, 148–49, 189n, 197n, 243n,
349–50, 366n, 506, 529n, 565n,

12:289, 305; AFL conventions and,
4:406–8, 408–9n, **5:**xiv, 47, 430–31,
432n, 438–39, 439n, 440, **6:**106,
107n, **10:**350n, 358–59, 431–32n,
463n, **11:**65–66, 66n, 82–83, 83–
84n, 313–16, 316–17n, 325–26, 476–
78, 478n; AFL local unions of, num-
ber of, **10:**427, **11:**349, 464, **12:**111;
Bakery Workers and, **11:**84n;
Barbers and, **4:**220, **11:**84n; Blacksmiths and, **11:**84n, 284, **12:**148,
343n; Boiler Makers and, **10:**541–
42, 542n, **11:**106, 107n, 478n, 484–
85, 486n, **12:**148, 341, 343n; Boot
and Shoe Workers and, **11:**84n;
Brewery Workers and, **11:**84n; Brick
and Clay Workers and, **11:**84n;
Bricklayers and, **11:**84n, 529n; Carpenters and, **6:**114, 115n, **8:**278,
279n, **11:**84n, 366n; in central bodies, **5:**221–22, 261, 262n, 413–14,
430–31, 432n, 439n, 440, 460–62,
6:19–20, 20n, 39, 91n, 108–9, 533–
34, **8:**336–37, **9:**268, **10:**347; Cigar
Makers and, **1:**48, **6:**293, 293n,
11:84n; conferences with, **9:**169n,
10:330–31, 331n, 345–50, 350–51n,
421–31, 431–32n, 461–63, 463n,
11:189n, 488–91, 491–92n; DuBois
and, **6:**90–91, 91n; Electrical Workers and, **5:**327, 327–28n, **12:**148,
343n; as farmers, **12:**425; Federal
Employees and, **11:**84n; Firemen
and Oilers and, **11:**84n, **12:**299–
300, 341–42, 342–43n; Fur Workers and, **11:**84n; Granite Cutters
and, **6:**115–16, 116n, 146–47, 147n;
Hod Carriers and, **3:**80, 409, **9:**480,
480n, **10:**135, **11:**84n; Hotel and
Restaurant Employees and, **10:**180,
11:42–46, 84n; housing of, in Washington, D.C., **7:**255; Iron Molders
and, **4:**314–17, 317n, 318, 324, 334,
11:84n, 284; Ladies' Garment Workers and, **11:**84n; Laundry Workers
and, **5:**264, **8:**47, **11:**84n; Leather
Workers and, **11:**84n; Letter Carriers and, **11:**84n; Locomotive Firemen and, **4:**125–26, 213, **8:**250,
253n, **10:**249; Longshoremen and,
7:187–89, 190n, 224–25, 225n,

9:83n, 10:459–60, 460n, 11:84n; Machinists and, 2:296–97, 297n, 409–11, 3:62, 124, 135, 166–67, 167n, 343, 405–7, 4:4, 7n, 130, 213, 11:36–37, 37n, 148–49, 149n, 285, 12:148, 341, 342–43n; Maintenance of Way Employes and, 11:46n, 84n; McGuire and, 4:407, 408–9n, 430; Meat Cutters and, 11:84n; migration of, 9:481, 510–11, 516, 10:103–4, 109, 131, 133n, 152–53n, 216, 12:282–83, 419; military service of, 12:282; Mine, Mill, and Smelter Workers and, 11:84n; and miners' strike, 1897, 4:351–52; Mine Workers, United, and, 10:347, 11:84n; Morrison and, 9:282n, 10:371, 372n, 421, 423–24, 427–28, 430–31, 12:341–42, 342–43n; Musicians and, 3:486, 9:168–69, 169–70n, 11:84n; National Committee for Organizing Iron and Steel Workers and, 11:283–86, 286n; O'Connell and, 4:4, 407, 10:421, 424–27; organization of, 6:106, 107n, 108–9, 113–15, 115n, 214, 8:504, 10:176–77, 177n, 358–59, 463n, 11:82–83, 83–84n, 325–26, 12:111–12, 112n, 148, 282, 289, 299–300 (*see also* American Federation of Labor [AFL]: organizers, black); Painters and, 6:113–14, 115n, 8:278–79, 279n, 11:84n; Paving Cutters and, 6:115–16, 116n, 120–21, 146, 147n; Plasterers and, 11:84n; Post Office Clerks and, 11:84n; Quarry Workers and, 11:84n; Railroad Telegraphers and, 9:342, 11:315; Railroad Trainmen and, 8:244, 244–45n, 11:42–43, 286, 393–94, 394n, 400, 400n; Railway Carmen and, 11:46n, 119–20, 478n, 564–65, 565n, 12:148, 343n; Railway Clerks and, 11:46n, 83n, 182–83, 313–16, 316–17n, 488–91, 491–92n, 501–2, 502n, 550–52, 552n, 12:111–12, 112n, 129–30; Seamen and, 11:84n; Sheet Metal Workers and, 12:148, 343n; Steam and Operating Engineers and, 9:281, 282n, 497, 497n, 11:84n; and steel strike, 1919–20, 11:196–97, 283–86, 286n;

Stereotypers and, 11:84n; Street and Electric Railway Employes and, 11:84n; as strikebreakers, 5:30n, 44, 322n, 10:109, 12:289; Switchmen and, 8:244, 244–45n, 246–47, 247n, 10:491–92, 492n; Tailors and, 11:84n; Teachers and, 11:84n; Textile Workers and, 4:427n, 11:84n; Theatrical Stage Employes and, 11:546, 547n; Timber Workers and, 11:366n; Typographical Union and, 11:84n; Upholsterers and, 11:84n; Washington and, 4:406, 8:165, 166n, 336–37, 337n, 10:348. *See also specific unions*

Blaete, Henry, 4:57

Blain, W. J., 5:51–52, *53n*

Blaine, Elbert F., 10:398, *400n*

Blaine, James G., 2:170, *173n,* 3:119, *120n,* 7:88, 9:88n

Blair, George, 1:*, 361, *362n; statement of,* 1:446–47

Blair, Henry W., 1:287, 289–356 passim, *326–27n,* 2:123, 268n, 278n, 3:245, 245n, 405n, 590–91; *letters to,* 2:366, 3:230–31, 465–66

Blanck, Max, 8:297n

Bland, Lawrence D., 9:208n, 255, *255–56n,* 11:447

Blandy, Graham F., 12:284, *285n*

Blanton, Thomas L., 10:454n, 459n, 11:65, 66n, 245, 245n, 12:366; *letter from,* 10:453–54; *letter to,* 10:456–59

Blaskopf, Hermann, and Co., 1:174–75, 199, 262

Blaskovec, Henry, *letter to,* 2:207–8

Blast Furnace Workers and Smelters of America, National Association of: —local: local 2 (Buffalo, N.Y.), 6:168, 168n, 169 —strike/lockout: 1903 (Buffalo, N.Y.), 6:168, *168n,* 169, *169n,* 170, 170n

Blatch, Harriot Stanton, 9:187n

Blend, Fred, 1:*, 157–58, *158n,* 257n; *letter from,* 1:263–64

Blermstrong, John, *letter to,* 9:50–51

Blick, Edward H., 3:141, *142n*

Blick, Mrs. Edward H., 3:141

Bliss, Cornelius N., 6:236, *236n*

Bliss, E. W., and Co., 5:207n

Bliss, Tasker H., 11:41n, 48, *49n,* 58n

Bliss, William D. P., **4:**50n
Blissert, Robert, **1:***, 100, *102n*, 151, **5:***, 34, *35n*
Bloch, Alexander, **7:**469, *471n*
Bloch, H. S., and Co.: boycott, 1896–97, **4:**340, *340n;* strike/lockout, 1896–97, **4:**340, *340n*
Bloch, Henry S., **4:**340, *340n*
Block, George G., **1:***, 457, *458n*, 460, **2:***, 194, *194n*, 241, **3:***, 141, *142n*, **4:***, 152, *155n*
Block, Mary, **3:**141, 142n
Blodgett, Rufus, **2:**137, *138n*
Bloete, Charles G., **1:***, *171n*, **3:***, 141, *143n; letter from,* **1:**171
Bloete, Fred, **1:**71, 83
Blood, D. H., **4:**481
Bloodgood, Rufus, **12:**367n
Bloom, Evelyn Hechheimer, **11:**53, 54n
Bloom, Jacob E., **5:**180, *188n; letter to,* **5:**231–32
Bloom, Sol, **11:**53, *54n*
Bloor, Ella Reeve, **12:**48, *49n*
Bloor, Richard, **12:**49n
Blount, Henry P., *4:24n; letter to,* **4:**23–24
Blue Label Pacific Coast Boycotter (trade union journal), **1:**393
Blum, Nicholas, **4:**238, *239n*
Blumenberg, Robert, **2:**367, *371n*
Blunt, Stanhope, **6:**216n
Board of Adjustment of the Railway and Steamship Freight Handlers and Station Employes of the Southern Railway, **11:**550–51, *551n*, 552–54, 559
Board of Control of Labor Standards in Army Clothing, **10:**139n, *151n*, 335, 336n
board of labor adjustment (proposed), **10:**74–75, 75n, 80–81, 81n
Board of Railroad Wages and Working Conditions, **10:**320n, 382n, **11:**157n
Bock, Charles, **7:**116, *118n*
Bock, Gustavo, **5:**181, *188n; letter from,* **5:**182
Boddy, Samuel L., **11:**62, 63n
Boden, J., **4:**57
Bodine, George C., *7:498n; letter from,* **7:**493–97

Bodine, Lester, **3:**34, *41n*
Boehne, John W., *8:246n; letter to,* **8:**245–46
Boer War, **5:**122, *122n*, **10:**200, 526
Boese, Thomas, **1:**19, *20n*
Bogert, John N., **4:**56, *57n*
Bohemia, workers from, **1:**46–47, 50–51, 53, 57, 66, 77, 96, 102–3, 107, 110
Bohm, Ernest, **2:***, 192, *195n*, 387, 393–95, **3:***, 8, *10n*, **4:***, *16n*, 102, **5:***, *287n*, **6:**90n, **8:**232n, **9:***, *291n*, **10:***, 127, *127–28n*, 156–57n, **11:***, 263, *265n;* at AFL conventions, **2:**384–85, 390, 397, **5:**286, 287n; *letters from,* **3:**11–14, **4:**16, **10:**127; *letters to,* **2:**195, 358–59, 362–63, 377–78, **4:**17–18, **9:**290–91, 303–4, **10:**392–95; *wire to,* **10:**392
Bohn, Frank, **11:**401, *403–4n*, **12:**392; *letter to,* **12:**160–63
Bohnen, George J., **6:**65, *67n*, 207, 207n
"Bohunks," **12:**210
Boies, William D., *11:302n; letter to,* **11:**300–302
Boiler Makers, International Brotherhood of, **2:***, 173n, 235, **4:***, **5:***, **7:***, **8:***, **10:***, **11:***, **12:***
Boiler Makers, Iron Ship Builders, and Helpers of America, International Brotherhood of, **2:***, **4:***, **5:***, **7:***, 89n, 178n, **8:***, 82n, **10:***, 21n, 170n, 502n, **11:***, 28n, 85n, 106n, 131n, 318n, 344, 475n, **12:***, 49n; and black workers, **10:**429, 541–42, 542n, **11:**106, 107n, 478n, 484–85, 486n, **12:**148, 341, 343n; jurisdiction of, **10:**406n; and railroad shopmen's strike, 1919 (threatened), **11:**120n
—conventions: 1906 (Kansas City, Kans.), **7:**75, *89*–90n; 1920, **11:**107n
—locals: local 33 (Quincy, Mass.), **10:**541, 542n; local 40 (Louisville, Ky.), **7:**233–34, 235n; local 112 (Mobile, Ala.), **11:**486n; local 168 (Bath, Maine), **7:**76, 90n; local 298 (Portsmouth, Va.), **10:**177n; local 438 (Galeton, Pa.), **8:**35n
—strikes/lockouts: 1909–10 (Galeton,

Pa.), *8:35n;* 1920–21 (Mobile, Ala.),
11:484–85, *486n*
Boilermakers and Iron Shipbuilders,
United Society of (Great Britain),
3:640, *660n*
Boiler Makers and Iron Ship Builders'
Helpers, Heaters, and Holders-on
of America, International Brotherhood of, 7:177n
Boiler Makers and Iron Ship Builders of America, Brotherhood of,
2:*, 4:*, 127n, 177n, 5:*, 164, 168n,
285, 7:*, 176, 177n, 8:*, 10:*, 11:*,
12:*
—convention: 1896 (Cleveland),
4:177, *177n,* 179n
Boiler Makers and Iron Ship Builders
of North America, United, 7:176,
178n
Bolander, Carl N., 9:260, *261n*
Bolivia, and civil war in Mexico,
9:363n
Bollenbacher, Peter, 11:87n
Bolsheviks, 10:275, 279n, 342–44,
507–10, 512n, 561, 563, 11:150, 318
"Bolshevism" in United States: accusations of, 10:435, 11:6, 51, 81,
157, 355, 357, 421, 12:64, 133, 135,
309–10, 333, 447; AFL and, 11:150,
371, 389, 425, 442, 12:255–56; and
Prohibition, 11:81, 184; and steel
strike, 1919–20, 11:123n, 163, 165,
194. *See also* communism: in United
States, accusations of
Bolte, Friedrich, 12:393, *394n*
Bomeisl, Bernard, 4:461, *462n*
Bonaparte, Charles J., 5:464n, *484n,*
7:196–97, 197n, 8:204n
Boncer, William, 11:83n
Bondy, Charles, and Co., 1:56, *58n*
Bondy, Isaac, 2:365n
Bondy and Lederer, 1:196, *198n,* 199
Bondy and Schwartzkopf, 1:184–85,
188n, 199
Bonfield, John, 2:57, *58n*
Bonillas, Ignacio, 9:498–500, *500n*
Bonney, Richard W., *6:39n; letter to,*
6:38–39
Bonsall, A. M., 4:374
Booher, Charles, 8:332n
Bookbinders, International Brother-

hood of, 3:*, 169, 169n, 8:302n,
12:446n
—locals: local 29 (Denver), 5:395,
396n; local 58 (Denver), 5:395, 396n
Boot and Shoe Manufacturers' Association, Rochester (N.Y.), 2:427n
Boot and Shoe Workers' International
Union of America, 2:*, 18, 3:*, 22n,
139, 140n, 155, 155n, 269n, 411–12,
4:*, 5:*, 6:*, 7:*, 8:*, 9:*, 10:*, 11:*;
AFL financial support of, 3:20–22,
23n, 461, 461n; injunctions against,
3:21, 26, 26n, 412n; and KOL,
2:208–9, 209n, 212
—conventions: 1889 (Boston), 2:209,
209n, 212, 213n; 1890 (Rochester,
N.Y.), 3:20, *23n;* 1891 (Boston),
3:75, *76n;* 1892 (Philadelphia),
3:180, *181n*
—locals: local 21 (Auburn, Maine),
3:411, 412n, 460–61; local 117 (New
York City), 2:371n, 3:111, 115n
—strikes/lockouts: 1890–91 (Fairport
and Rochester, N.Y.), 2:423, *427–
28n,* 3:20–21, 26; 1892 (Chicago),
3:155, *155n;* 1893–94 (Auburn,
Maine), 3:411, *412n,* 460–61
Boot and Shoe Workers' Union, 2:*,
3:*, 4:*, 97n, 5:*, 111–12n, 6:*, 16,
17n, 357, 7:*, 39n, 8:*, 103n, 9:*,
452, 452n, 10:*, 82n, 374, 11:*,
135n, 287–88, 12:446n; and American Labor Union, 6:203, 395; and
arbitration, 7:37, 39–40n; benefits
of, 5:110–11, 112n; and black workers, 11:84n; and Douglas, W. L.,
Shoe Co., 7:399, 400n; dues of,
5:110–11, 112n, 9:452; financial
condition of, 7:38–39; Joint Council 1 of (Brockton, Mass.), *5:111n,*
112n; jurisdiction of, 5:491, 492n;
and KOL, 4:187–88, 7:39; label of,
5:112n, 6:203, 395; and socialists,
4:95, 99, 185–88, 340–41
—conference: 1906 (Boston), 7:38,
40n
—conventions: 1896 (Boston), 4:185,
188n; 1897 (Boston), 4:340–41,
342n; 1899 (Rochester, N.Y.),
5:110–11, *111–12n,* 7:40n; 1906
(Milwaukee), 7:39, *40n*

—locals: local 32 (Lynn, Mass.), **7**:50; local 94 (Chicago), **9**:302, 303n; local 159 (Syracuse, N.Y.), **7**:185, 186n, 339–40, 340n, **8**:157; local 192 (Brockton, Mass.), **7**:37, 39n; local 216 (San Francisco), **8**:175n; local 339 (San Francisco), **8**:174, 175n, 185

—strikes/lockouts: 1905 (Brockton, Mass.), **7**:37, *39n;* 1906–7 (Syracuse, N.Y.), **7**:185, *186n,* 339

bootblacks, **1**:307–8

Bope, George W., *11:245n; letter to,* **11**:245

Borah, William E., **8**:332n, 372, 374–75, *380n,* 395–96, **10**:310, 507

Borden, Robert L., **11**:69, *71n,* 91, 92–93n, 101

Bordson, Alfred B., **12**:326, *327n*

"boring from within," **12**:403, 438

Borland, William P., *10:454n*

Boseen, Aaron, **1**:8

Boshman, A. J., **3**:403, *403n*

Bossert, Louis, and Son, injunction, **10**:253, *254n*

Bossie, Levie, **1**:68, *68n*

Boston Bridge Co., **6**:515n

Boston Building Trades Council, **9**:268n

Boston Central Labor Union, **4**:144, 144–45n, 148, 169, 189–91, 216, **5**:77–78, **7**:313, **9**:492n, **10**:155n, **11**:146n

Boston Central Trades and Labor Union, *1:166n,* **2**:101n, 157

Boston Elevated Railway Co., **9**:390n

Boston Globe, **3**:415, 415n

Boston police strike, 1919, **11**:145–46, *146–47n,* 318, 319n

Boston Post, letter to, **10**:444–45

Boston Workingmen's Central Union, *1:166n*

Bottomley, Charles M., *10:209n; wire to,* **10**:208–9

Boulware, Joseph, **11**:478n

"Bourbons," **6**:29, 125, **8**:511, **11**:171, **12**:116

Bourse du travail (Paris), **3**:369, *370n,* **4**:63, 68–69, 90, **5**:87–88

Bousfield, Harry, *7:69n; letter from,* **7**:69; *letter to,* **7**:94–95

Bouvé, Crawford, and Co., boycott, 1891–95, *3:269n,* 270

Bowen, Anna T., *7:365n; letter from,* **7**:365

Bowen, George W., **4**:175, *175n*

Bowen, William J., **10**:*, 470n, 503, *504n,* 562, **11**:529n, **12**:*, 550, *553n*

Bower, Robert, **2**:172, *173n*

Bowerman, Charles W., **8**:*, 518, *519n,* **9**:*, *105n,* 385n, 474, 485, 487, **10**:*, 71, *72n,* 497, **11**:*, 12, *17n,* 28, 30n, 38; *letters to,* **9**:105, 162–63, 384–85

Bowers, Lloyd, **7**:473n

Bowersock, Justin D., **7**:94, *95n*

Bowles, Francis T., **10**:452, *453n*

Bowman, James H., **5**:*, 340, *342n,* 437

Boyard, A. F., **3**:404n

Boyce, Edward, **4**:*, *192n,* 323, 463n, **5**:*, 90–91, *93n,* 464n, 469, **6**:*, 36, *37n;* and Leadville, Colo., strike, 1896–97, **4**:254–56, 258n, 266; *letters from,* **4**:192, 304–5, 313; *letters to,* **4**:297–99, 308–12, **5**:100–101; and sectional division of American labor movement, **4**:304–5, 313, 385–86; and Wardner, Idaho, strike, 1899, **5**:101n, 114, 138n, 148–50, 151n; and Western Labor Union, **4**:257, 452, 452n, 462

Boyce, Tully, **3**:47, *48n*

boycotts, **2**:76–77, 107–8, **4**:84, **5**:210, 210n, **6**:333, 423n, **8**:13–14, 64–65, 348–49, 481, 483, 486–87, 491, **11**:422, **12**:4; and AFL locals, directly affiliated, **8**:144n; and central bodies, **5**:209–10, **8**:142–43, 144n; KOL and, **1**:365, 467n, **2**:77; secondary boycotts, **8**:152, 167, **11**:406–7. *See also under* legislation, states and territories; "We Don't Patronize List" (AFL)

—in specific labor disputes: Allegheny County, Pa., breweries, 1896, *4:145n;* American Tobacco Co., 1895, **4**:117n; American Tobacco Co., 1899, *5:119n;* Armour and Co., 1886, *1:467n;* Armour and Co., 1896–?, **4**:286; Bakers' Association of New York and Vicinity, 1889–93, **2**:242, 242n, 417n; Baltz, J. & P.,

Brewing Co., 1906 (threatened), 7:33; Barney, H. S., and Co., 1903–4, 6:176, *176n,* 179; Benjamin, Alfred, and Co., 1890, 2:348, *349n;* Bloch, H. S., and Co., 1896–97, 4:340, *340n;* Bouvé, Crawford, and Co., 1891–95, *3:269n,* 270; Brewers' Board of Trade of New York and Vicinity, Lager Beer, 1888–1902, 2:100–101, *101n,* 107, 341, 6:89n; Brown and Williamson Tobacco Co., 1905, 6:401; Brown Tobacco Co., 1898, 4:394, *395n;* Buck's Stove and Range Co., 1906-?, 7:153–54, *154n,* 249n, 263, 287, 289, 295–96, 296n, 430, 434–35, 8:271; Carnegie Steel Co., 1892 (threatened), 3:232–34, 235n; Cheyenne Street Railway Co., 1911–12, 8:269, *277n; Chicago Daily News,* 1898–1903, 5:340, 341n, *342n; Chicago Record,* 1898–1903, 5:340, 341–*42n;* Cincinnati Brewers' Exchange, 1902, *5:503n, 516n;* Cincinnati Brewing Co., 1897, 4:402–4; Cincinnati Brewing Co., 1898, 4:404n; Clark's O. N. T. Cotton Thread Co., 1891, 3:53, *56n;* clothing cutters, 1893 (New York City), 3:295, 295n, 296, *296n;* Cluett, Peabody, and Co., 1905–6, 6:484n; coal, West Virginia, 1898, 4:345n, 503, *505n;* Continental Tobacco Co., 1899-?, *5:119n;* Contractors' and Material Men's Association, 1902, *6:18n;* Dayton Manufacturing Co., 1899–1900, 7:194n; Denver building contractors, 1902, *6:18n;* Denver newspapers, 1903 (threatened), 6:131, *131n,* 132, 132n; Detroit Stove Works, 1896, 4:227–29, *229n;* Drummond Tobacco Co., 1893, 3:344, *345–46n;* Duryea Starch Co., 1882, 1:438n; Eastmans Co., 1896, 4:231n; *Elizabeth* (N.J.) *Daily Journal,* 1908, 7:337–38, 338n; Fauber, W. H., Co., 1898, 4:500, *501n;* Fleischmann and Co., 1889–93, *2:417–18n,* 3:270, *270n;* Franklin Brewing Co., 1907, 7:209–10; Fuller, Warren, and Co., 1884–86, 1886-?, *1:402n,* 2:8; Ganter, Francis X., 1899–1900, 5:107, *108n,* 271n; Hackett, Carhart, and Co., 1894–95, 4:20, *21n;* Houston Ice and Brewing Co., 1907, 7:222; Jacksonville, Fla., newspapers, 1886, *2:343n;* Kimble, Andrew, 1899-?, 5:107, *108n;* Knoxville Woolen Mills, 1900–1903, 6:118–19, *119n;* Kuppenheimer, B., and Co., 1907-?, 7:178–79, *179n;* La Kurba Cigar Co., 1917, 12:133n; Lippmann, L., and Sons, 1891–92, 3:107, *108n;* Loewe, D. E., and Co., 1902, *6:177–78n,* 440–42; Los Angeles breweries, 1910-?, 8:148n; *Los Angeles Times,* 1893-?, 6:212–13, *213n,* 417n; Ludlow Valve Co., 1906 (threatened), 7:53–54, 54n; Merritt Expanded Metal Fireproofing Co., 1903–6, *6:292n;* Miller, Hall, and Hartwell, 1891–92, *3:109n,* 164, *164–65n,* 176; National Cash Register Co., 1901–2, *5:366n,* 460n, 6:240n; National Cash Register Co., 1907 (threatened), 7:167–68, 168n, 193, 194–95n; Nettleton, A. E., Co., 1907, *7:186n;* New York City breweries, 1888–1902, 2:100–101, *101n,* 107, 341, 6:89n; New York City breweries, 1902, 6:89, 90n; *New Yorker Staats-Zeitung,* 1892, *3:486n; New York Sun,* 1899–1902, *5:236n,* 477, 477n; Northwestern Brewers' Association, 1905, *6:442n;* Pabst Brewing Co., 1899, 5:106–7, *107n,* 108–9, 110n; Palmers Manufacturing Co., 1903–5, *6:223n;* Peoples' Street Railway Co., 1901–4, *5:379n,* 6:142–44, *145n; Philadelphia Tageblatt,* 1886–87, *2:25–26n;* Plymouth Rock Pants Co., 1892, 3:179, *180n;* Poth, F. A., and Sons, 1902–3, *6:44–45n;* Pray, Small, and Co., 1894, *3:412n;* Pullman Palace Car Co., 1894 (*see* Pullman strike, 1894); Rochester, N.Y., clothing manufacturers, 1903–8, 6:297n; Rucker and Witten Tobacco Co., 1903, 6:214, 214–15n; *San Francisco Call,* 1909, 8:142–43, *144n;* San Francisco minor league baseball team, 1901, *5:339n;* Schultz, Otto B., 1905–6,

7:158n; Shelby Steel Tube Co., 1898–99, *4:485n;* Star and Western breweries, 1904-?, **6:**369n; Straiton and Storm, 1885, **1:**365; Theiss Music Hall, 1886, *1:430n;* Todd, Sullivan, and Baldwin, 1891, **3:**107, *108n;* Toledo, Ann Arbor, and Northern Michigan Railroad, 1893, *3:294n;* Washburn-Crosby Milling Co., 1905?, **6:**430n; Wellington collieries, 1891, **3:**53, 56n; Western Wheel Co., 1893, **3:**356n; Williams Cooperage Co., 1903–5, *6:223n*
Boyd, David A., **5:***, *324n; letter to,* **5:**322–24
Boyd, James E., **7:**186n, **11:**512–14, *514n*
Boyd, William, *11:96n; letter from,* **11:**96
Boyer, C. S., **9:**496, *497n*
Boyer, David P., **1:***, 386, *396n,* 460, 463, **2:***, *144n; letter from,* **1:**395–96; *letter to,* **2:**143–44
Boyer, William, **5:**453n
Boyer, William C., **3:**131, *132n*
Boyle, Christopher J., **3:**47, *48n*
Boyle, J. P., **2:**66–67, *69n*
Boynton, Charles A., **5:**424, *425n*
Boynton, Henry B., *6:268n; letter to,* **6:**267–68
boys: bootblacks, **1:**307–8; breaker boys, **11:**305, **12:**179; education of, **11:**221–23; glassworkers, **5:**246; messenger boys, **1:**306–7; newsboys, **1:**307–8, **5:**475–77, 477n
Bracken, Edward J., **5:***, 282, *286n*
Brackenridge, Pa., murders in, **11:**121–23, 123n
Braddock wire mill, strike/lockout, 1913, **8:**391n, 453, *455n*
Bradley, John, **4:**294n
Bradley, W. J., **6:**459, *460n*
Brady, George, **11:**447n
Brady, Peter J., *9:153n,* **11:**354–55, **12:**461n, 550; *letter to,* **9:**152–53
Braff, Bernard, **6:***, 276–77, *278n*
Brailsford, Henry N., **12:**231, *232n*
Brais, Eugene J., **8:***, *38n,* **9:***, 71, *74n,* 236, 236n
Bramley, Fred, *12:377n; letter to,* **12:**376

Bramwood, John W., **3:***, *659n,* **4:***, 195, *196n,* 205, **5:***, *113n,* 510–11; at AFL conventions, **3:**618, 641, 659n, **5:**288
Branch, Christopher, **1:**414
Brand, Charles, **3:**141
Brand, Herman, **3:**141
Brand, Mrs. Charles, **3:**141
Brand, Mrs. Herman, **3:**141
Brand, Mrs. Sigmund, **3:**141
Brand, Sigmund, **3:**141
Brandeis, Elizabeth, **12:**250n, *250n*
Brandeis, Louis D., *6:83n,* **7:**186n, 245, 339–40, 400n, **8:**110–12, 114n, 202, **9:**409–10, 410n, **10:**144, 512n, **12:**250, 250n; debate with SG, **6:**71–83
Brandenburg, Broughton, **7:**257–58n, 269, *270n,* 271, **8:**52n
Branstetter, Otto F., **11:**427, *432n*
Brant, Lyman A., **1:***, *166n;* and calling of FOTLU convention, **1:**161, 165; at FOTLU convention, **1:**211, 214, 216, 222, 227–28, 230, 242
Branting, Karl H., **7:**484, *486n,* **10:**90n
Brass Finishers' and Molders' Protective Union 1 (Detroit), **1:**231, 232n
Brass Moulders' International Union of North America, **6:***, 446n
Brauer Zeitung (trade union journal), **7:**215, 217n
Braunschweig, Richard, **2:**384–85, *385n,* 421
Bray, George L., **4:**188, *189n*
Brazil, and civil war in Mexico, **9:**363n
breaker boys, **11:**305, **12:**179
Breckon (typographer), **6:**221
Breen, J. L., **6:**142
Breen, John, **7:**445n
Breen, Michael, **12:**550
Breen, Peter, *3:294n; letter to,* **3:**293–94
Breidenbach, Elias, **6:**143, *145n*
Bremer, Alexander H. W., **4:***, 397–98, *399n*
Brennan, John, **3:**21, 23n
Brennan, Redmond S., **11:**451, *453n*
Brennan, Thomas S., **3:**384, *385n*
Brennan, Walter A., **4:**39, *42n*
Brennen, William J., **1:**222, 226, *229n*
Brennock, James, **4:**415, *416n*
Brentano, Lujo, **1:**24, 34, *43n*

Brer Rabbit, **11:**68, *68n*
Brest Litovsk, treaty of, **10:**344–45n, 353, *355n,* 564
Brettell, James, **3:***, 427, *429n,* 532, 615, 616n, 646–47, 662
Brewer, David J., **6:**340n
Brewers' Association, Philadelphia Lager Beer, **2:**38, 42
Brewers' Association, U.S., **2:**101n, 112–14, *115n,* 203
Brewers' Board of Trade of New York and Vicinity, Lager Beer, boycott, 1888–1902, **2:**100–101, *101n,* 107, 341, **6:**89n
Brewers' Exchange, Buffalo (N.Y.), **5:**221n
Brewers' Exchange, Cincinnati, **5:**375, 375n, 503, 503–4n; boycott, 1902, *5:503n, 516n;* injunction, **5:**516n; strike/lockout, 1902, *5:503n,* 516n
Brewers' Exchange, New Orleans, **7:**494–95, 497
Brewers' National Union, **2:***, 38, 38–39n, 42, **3:***, **4:***, **5:***, **6:***, **7:***, **8:***, **9:***, **12:***
Brewers' Protective Union, Ale and Porter, *2:337n*
Brewers' union (Detroit), **2:**418
Brewers' union (St. Louis), **1:**457
Brewers' Union of New York, Journeymen, **3:**113, *115n*
Brewery, Flour, Cereal, and Soft Drink Workers of America, International Union of United, **2:***, **3:***, **4:***, **5:***, **6:***, **7:***, **8:***, **9:***, **11:**81n, **12:***, 66n; and black workers, **11:**84n; and industrial unionism, **12:**62
brewery workers, **2:**100–101, 101n, 113–14
Brewery Workers of America, United, **7:**498n; jurisdiction of, **7:**498n
Brewery Workmen of America, International Union of the United, **2:***, **3:***, **4:***, **5:***, **6:***, 10n, 384, **7:***, 36n, **8:***, 92n, **9:***, 34n, 181, **12:***; charter, restoration of, **7:**272–74, 274n, 317–18; charter, revocation of, **6:**318, 321–22, 326n, 501, **7:**33–35, 36–37n, 199–201, 201–2n, 215–17, 223, 223n, 317; and industrial unionism, **5:**433–34, **8:**406,

9:148–49, 502; injunctions against, **6:**226, 228n, 442n; and IWW, **6:**487, **7:**8, 34, **9:**30; jurisdiction of, **6:**9–10, 10–11n, 88–89, 89–90n, 133–34, 135–36n, 208, 223–28, 228n, 317–26, 326–27n, 365–67, 367–68n, 452, 453n, 500–502, 502–3n, **7:**32–35, 36–37n, 152, 152–53n, 199–201, 201–2n, 208–10, 210–11n, 221–22, 222n, 272–74, 274n, 317–18, 451–52, 493–97, **9:**143–45, 146n, 148; label of, **5:**375n, **6:**88–89, 90n, 503n, **7:**36–37n, 201, 494; *letter to,* **7:**317–18; and Western Labor Union, **6:**9
—conventions: 1903 (Cincinnati), **6:**90n, *135n;* 1908 (New York City), **7:**495, *498n*
—locals: local 28 (Belleville, Ill.), **6:**369n; local 31 (New York City), **6:**89, 90n; local 44 (Denver), **7:**8, 9n; local 56 (Denver), **7:**8, 9n; local 58 (Denver), **7:**8, 9n; local 59 (New York City), **6:**89, 90n; local 80 (Columbus, Ohio), **7:**152n; local 111 (Houston), **7:**221, 222n; local 161 (New Orleans), **7:**498n; local 215 (New Orleans), **7:**495–96, 498n; local 223 (Indianapolis), **6:**226, 228n; local 246 (St. Louis), **6:**369n; local 285 (Philadelphia), **6:**503n; local 289 (Philadelphia), **6:**503n; locals in San Francisco, **6:**442n
—strikes/lockouts: 1905 (Seattle), *6:442n;* 1907 (Columbus, Ohio), **7:**209–10, *210n;* 1907–8 (New Orleans), *7:498n;* 1910–11 (Los Angeles), **8:**147, *148n*
Brewery Workmen of the U.S., National Union of the United, **2:***, 235, **3:***, 14n, 30, 261–62, 344, 353, **4:***, 80, 82n, 99, **5:***, 162n, 210n, **6:***, **7:***, **8:***, **9:***, **12:***; AFL financial support of, **2:**114–15, 203, 203n; and Brewery Workmen's Union of the Pacific Coast, **3:**30–31n, 43, 81–82, 87–88; injunction, **6:**90n; jurisdiction of, **4:**329–30, 403–4, **5:**161, 162n, 169–71, 172n, 219–20, 221n, 257–60, 260n, 288, 290, 292n, 374–75, 375n, 433–34, 503, 503–4n, 514–15, 515–16n; and KOL, **4:**83,

144, 145n, 222–23, 331–32, **5:**244–
45, 245n; national executive committee of, **2:**397
—conventions: 1889 (Cincinnati),
2:384, *385n;* 1891 (St. Louis), **3:**87–
88, *88n;* 1892 (Buffalo, N.Y.), **3:**89n
—locals: local 1 (New York City),
3:112–13, 115n, **5:**244–45; local 6
(St. Louis), **2:**408n, **3:**346n; local
12 (Cincinnati), **5:**501–3, 503n,
514–15; local 16 (San Francisco),
3:30, 30n, 81, 88; local 19 (Albany,
N.Y.), **4:**222–23, 223n; local 22 (Allegheny County, Pa.), **4:**145n; local
33 (New York City), **2:**408n; local
34 (Troy, N.Y.), **4:**222–23, 223n;
local 44 (Denver), **5:**393, 396n; local 46 (Kansas City, Mo.), **5:**260n;
local 56 (Denver), **5:**393, 396n; local 58 (Denver), **5:**393, 396n; local
59 (New York City), **2:**337n, **5:**245,
245n; local 83 (Hamilton, Ohio),
4:399–400, 400n, 401–4, 404n; local 129 (Albany, N.Y.), **4:**223n; local
269 (Cincinnati), **5:**374–75, 375n,
516n; local in Portland, Ore., **3:**81,
83n
—strikes/lockouts: 1888–1902 (New
York City), **2:**100–101, *101n,* 107,
113–15, 203n, 341; 1900 (Kansas
City, Mo.), **5:**260n; 1902 (Cincinnati), *5:503n,* 516n
Brewery Workmen's Union of the Pacific Coast, United, **3:**30–31n, 43,
81–82, 87–88
—branch: branch 8 (Portland, Ore.),
3:82n
Brewster, Thomas T., **11:**204, *205n*
Briceville (Tenn.) mines, **3:**215n
Brick, Tile, and Terra Cotta Workers'
Alliance, International, **5:***, 462,
463n, **9:***, 74n, 205n, **12:***
Brick and Clay Workers of America,
United, **5:***, **9:***, 203, 205n, **11:**28n,
85n, **12:***, 353–55, 355n, 446n; and
black workers, **11:**84n; wages of,
12:353–55
—strike/lockout: 1914 (Chicago),
12:353, *355–56n*
Bricklayers', Masons', and Plasterers'
International Union of America,

3:*, **6:***, **7:***, **8:***, 150, 151n, 302n,
344, **9:***, 70, 73n, **10:***, 567n,
11:28n, 85n, **12:***, 80n, 223, 223n;
and black workers, **11:**84n, 529n; jurisdiction of, **9:**73n
—convention: 1914 (Houston), **9:**70,
73n
—locals: local 8 (So. Bethlehem, Pa.),
8:43, 44n; local 34 (So. Bethlehem,
Pa.), **8:**43, 44n; local 60 (New York
City), **12:**80, 80–81n
Bricklayers' and Masons' International Union of America, **1:***,
385–86, 390, 390n, **2:***, 139, 235,
3:*, 145n, **6:***, 173–74, 175n, **7:***,
281–82, 282n, **8:***, **9:***, **10:***, **12:***;
executive board of, **2:**139n; jurisdiction of, **2:**131, 131n
—conventions: 1886 (St. Louis),
2:139n; 1888, **2:**139n; 1908 (Detroit), **7:**282n
—locals: local 1 (Washington, D.C.),
2:70, 71n; local 2 (Jacksonville,
Fla.), **7:**354–55, 356n; local 4 (Reading, Pa.), **2:**138–39, 139n; local 5
(Cleveland), **7:**282, 282n; local 7
(Milwaukee), **3:**494, 497, 498n; local 21 (Chicago), **4:**159n; Jewish
union in Cleveland, **7:**281–82, 282n
Bricklayers and Stonemasons, United
Order of American, **4:**157, *158–59n,*
162, 162n
Bridge, Structural, and Ornamental
Iron Workers, International As-
sociation of, **6:***, **7:***, **8:***, **9:***, **10:***,
170n, 266n, 502n, **11:***, 28n, 85n,
362, 365n, **12:***, 223, 223n; jurisdiction of, **10:**171, 171–72n, 405, 406n
Bridge, Structural, and Ornamental
Iron Workers and Pile Drivers, International Association of, **6:***, **7:***,
8:*, **9:***, 191n, 300, 302n, **10:***, **11:***,
12:*; jurisdiction of, **9:**305n
—strike/lockout: 1915 (Bridgeport,
Conn.), **9:**304, *305n*
Bridge and Beach Manufacturing Co.,
8:201
Bridge and Structural Iron Workers,
International Association of, **6:***,
173–74, 175, **7:***, 13n, **8:***, 209n,
213, 214n, 227n, 236–37, 432–34,

436–37, 475, **9**:*, **10**:*, **11**:*, **12**:*;
AFL financial support of, **7**:12–13;
jurisdiction of, **6**:210, 211n
—conventions: 1905 (Philadelphia),
6:514, 515–*16n;* 1913 (Indianapolis), **8**:470, *471n*
—locals: local 15 (New Haven,
Conn.), **6**:514, 515n; local 40 (New
York City), **8**:231n
—strikes/lockouts: 1905-?, **6**:514–15,
515–16n, **7**:12–13; 1905-? (New Haven, Conn.), **6**:514, 515n; 1906-?
(New York City), **6**:515n
Bridgman, Mich., Communist party
meeting at, 1922, **12**:132, 132n, 338,
338n; raid on, **12**:131–32, *132n*
Briegel, Joseph A., **12**:56, *61n*
Briggs, Riley R., **10**:187, *189n*
Brindell, Robert P., **9**:290, *292n,* 311n,
10:360, **11**:324, 324–25n, 352–53,
355–56, 378–79, 467, 467n, **12**:75–
76; conviction of, **11**:445, 446n
Brine, R. S., Transportation Co.:
strike/lockout, 1902, *5:496–97n;*
strike injunction, **5**:497n
Brinkman, John, **7**:246n
Brinkmann, William, **1**:250, *251n*
Brisbane, Arthur, **3**:387, *388n,* **6**:522n
British Columbia Loggers' Union,
12:442n
Broadhurst, Henry, **1**:*, 211, 212n,
3:*, 516, *517n,* **9**:337
Broadway and Seventh Ave. Railroad
Co., **1**:433n
Broadway Surface Railroad Co.,
1:433n, 444
Brock, James F., **9**:*, 148, *149n,*
10:470n, **11**:*, 477, *478n*
Brockhausen, Frederick, *7:67n,* 130,
142n, **8**:409, 412n; *letters from,* **7**:64–
67, 157
Brockmeyer, Herman F., **2**:*, *346n; let-
ter to,* **2**:346
Brockton (Mass.) City Council, **7**:400n
Brockton (Mass.) Joint Shoe Council,
7:37, 39n
Brockton (Mass.) Shoe Manufactur-
ers' Assn., **7**:37, 39n, 400n
Broekmay, H. H., **2**:245
Bromley, Owen, **5**:86, *87n*
Brookhart, Smith W., **12**:170, *171n,*
348n

Brooklyn (N.Y.) Central Labor Federation, **3**:83–84, *85n,* 112–13
Brooklyn (N.Y.) Central Labor Union,
2:67, *68n,* 177–78, **3**:471, **9**:62, *63n,*
11:358n
Brooklyn Labor Lyceum, **3**:484–85,
485–86n; strike/lockout, 1893,
3:485n
Brooklyn Navy Yard, wage rates at,
10:52–53, 54n, 86–87, 87n
Brooklyn Rapid Transit Co., strike/
lockout, 1920, **11**:356, *358n*
Broom Makers' Union, International,
3:*, 346n
—convention: 1893 (Chicago), **3**:344,
346n
—local: local 40 (Denver), **5**:393, 395,
396n
Brophy, John (mine worker),
12:296n
Brophy, John (stove mounter), **2**:12–
13, *13n,* 14
Brounstein, Abraham A., **6**:276–77,
278n
Browder, Earl, **10**:64n, **11**:561n,
12:48n
Browder, Marguerite, *10:64n; letter to,*
10:62–63
Browder, Ralph, **10**:64n
Browder, William, **10**:64n
Brower, William L., **4**:102, *106n*
Brown, Arthur L., *7:186n*
Brown, Ashmun N., **10**:154, *154n*
Brown, E. Gerry, **7**:141n
Brown, Edward M., **6**:43–44, *45n*
Brown, Elon, **10**:77n
Brown, Francis Shunk, **6**:6, 8n
Brown, Fred W., **10**:149; *letter from,*
10:223–25
Brown, George R., **10**:304, **11**:389,
391n
Brown, George W., *9:50n*
Brown, J. C., **4**:166, 166n
Brown, J. F., *letter to,* **4**:130
Brown, James, *4:131n,* **5**:439n, 460–
61, 461n, 462, **6**:400–401, **11**:326,
327n
Brown, Jay G., **9**:*, 221, 223–*24n,* **10**:*,
245, *246n,* 259, 262n, 266n, **11**:*,
360, 365n; *letter to,* **10**:252–53
Brown, John, **3**:630–31, 641, **6**:331
Brown, John W., **12**:357, *360n*

Brown, Lathrop, **11:**158, *160n*

Brown, Mabel Elizabeth, **11:**460, *460n,* **12:***554n*

Brown, Morris, **3:**141, *143n,* **4:**57, **5:**101n, *6:364n,* 396n; at AFL conventions, **6:**361–62, 364n, **9:**23, 24–25n; *letter to,* **7:**254–55

Brown, Rome G., **9:**316, *318n*

Brown, W. Sprigg, **6:**223n

Brown, William L., *3:159n; letter to,* **3:**159

Brown, William S., **11:***,* 434, *435n*

Brown and Earle, strike/lockout, 1886, **1:**379, 381–82, 392

Brown and Williamson Tobacco Co.: boycott, 1905, **6:**401; *letter from,* **6:**400–402

Browne, Carl, *3:482n; letter to,* **6:**35–37

Browne, Edward B. M., **3:**424, *426n*

Browne, Lennox D., *6:293n; letter from,* **6:**293

Brown Hoisting and Conveying Machine Co., strike/lockout, 1896, **4:**177, *178n*

Brown Tobacco Co., boycott, 1898, **4:**394, *395n*

Brückmann, Englebert, **1:**250, *251n,* **4:**72, *75n*

Bruère, Robert W., **10:**112, *114n,* 116; *letter from,* **10:**411–12

Brumbaugh, Martin G., **10:**99, *102n,* 124, 125n, 204

Brumm, Charles N., *7:336n; letter to,* **7:**334–36

Bruner, John E., **6:***,* 352n, 384, *384n*

Bruner, Mary, **7:**231, 231n

Brunet, G. R., **9:**15, *15–16n*

Brunson, Hartwell L., **12:**388, *389n*

Brussels, German occupation of, **9:**195, 197n

Brussels (steamship), attack on, by German submarines, **9:**475, 477n

Bryan, Charles W., *12:467n;* and election of 1924, **12:**463–64, 467–68n, 492–93

Bryan, William E., **10:***,* 281, *285n,* **11:***,* 103, *104n; letter from,* **11:**556–58, 558n; *letter to,* **11:**565–70

Bryan, William Jennings, **4:**179n, 185n, 233–34, *234n,* 235, 249n, **7:**300n, 387, 387n, 404, **8:**90, 256n, 257, **9:**3, 287n, 292n, 354, 430–31,

433n, **12:**463, 467n; and election of 1908, **7:**310–11, 369, 370n, 374–75, 380, 384, 384n, 397, 398n, 410–11, 414–15, 415n, 421; *letters from,* **7:**300, 369; *letters to,* **7:**351–52, 414–15, **8:**255–56

Bryant, Louise, **12:**231, *232n*

Bryce, Joseph W., **8:**313, *314n*

Brydon Brothers Harness and Saddlery Co., **8:**148n

Buchanan, Frank J., **6:***,* 367, *369n,* 514, **8:***,* *184n,* **9:**153n, 292n; *letter to,* **8:**183–84

Buchanan, George, **5:**331n

Buchanan, John P., **3:**215n

Buchanan, Joseph R., **1:***,* 403, *404n,* **2:***,* 19, *23n,* 287, *288n,* **3:***,* *585n,* **4:**3, 249n, **8:***,* 416, *416n*

Buchanan and Lyall Tobacco Co., **1:**112, *115n,* **5:**117, 119n

Buchner, Charles, **3:**141, *143n*

Buck, L. W., **11:**113n

Buckler, William H., **10:***554n; letter from,* **10:**549–54

Buckley, James, **1:**17, *18n*

Buckley, John F., *5:111n; letter to,* **5:**110–11

Buck's Stove and Range Co., **8:**131n, 217; boycott, 1906–?, **7:**153–54, *154n,* 249n, 263, 287, 289, 295–96, 296n, 430, 434–35, **8:**271; settlement with, **8:**107–8, 108n, 161–63, 164n, 200; strike/lockout, 1906, **7:**153, *154–55n*

Buck's Stove and Range Co. cases: AFL and, **7:**426, 427n; AFL assessments for, **7:**267, 268n, 290, 426, 427n; AFL financial appeals for, **7:**290, 290n, 440–42, 448–49; *circular on,* **7:**440–42; contempt case, *7:249–50n,* 356–57, 387, 392, 394–95, 395n, 399, 426, 430–38, 438n, 439–41, 465, 478, 491, 492n, **8:**10–11, 11n, 12, 12n, 13–15, 16n, 17–18, 21, 23, 130, 133, 154, 161–64, 201, 204, 216–17, 217n, 240–41, 243n, 270–71, 292–93, 323n, 333, 335, 349, 358, 491, **9:**105, 106n, **10:**253, **11:**18n; injunction case, *7:247–49, 249–50n,* 253, 263, 266–67, 287, 289–90, 295–96, 296n, 426, 427n, 430–38, 440–41, 449, 453–54, 465,

8:108n, 154, 161–64, 164–65n, 204n, 269–70, **9:**106n, **10:**253; Mitchell and, **7:**249–50n, 356–57, 392, 426, 430–31, 434, 439–41, 478, 492n, **8:**10–12, 12n, 13–15, 16n, 17–18, 160–64, 217, 217n, 240–41, 266, 270, 292–93, 323n, 358, **9:**105, 106n, **11:**15, 18n; Morrison and, **7:**249–50n, 266, 356–57, 392, 426, 430–31, 434, 439–41, 478, 492n, **8:**10–11, 12n, 17–18, 160–64, 217, 217n, 240–41, 266, 270, 292–93, 323n, 333, 335, **9:**105, 106n, **11:**15, 18n; SG and, **7:**247–49, 249–50n, 253, 266, 289–90, 356–57, 387, 394–95, 395n, 399, 430–41, 453–54, 465–68, 476n, 478, 491, 492n, **8:**10–11, 12n, 17–18, 21, 23, 130, 133, 154, 161–64, 204, 216–17, 217n, 240–41, 243n, 269–71, 292–93, 323n, 333, 335, 349, 358, 491, **9:**105, 106n, **11:**15, 85, 85n

Buck's Stove and Range Co. v. American Federation of Labor et al., **7:**247–49, *249–50n,* 356–57. *See also* Buck's Stove and Range Co. cases: injunction case

Budd, Britton I., **9:**388, *390n*

Buffalo and Susquehanna Railroad, strike/lockout, 1909–10, **8:**33–35, *35n*

Buffalo (N.Y.) and Vicinity, Central Labor Council of, **12:**219–20, *221n*

Buffalo (N.Y.) Central Labor Council, **9:**406n

Buffalo (N.Y.) Copper and Brass Rolling Mill, strike/lockout, 1916, *9:406n*

Buffalo Creek Railroad, strike/lockout, 1892, **3:**185, 214n

Buffalo Union Furnace Co., **5:**382–83; strike/lockout, 1901, *5:383–84n*

Buffurton, George, *letter from,* **10:**459–60

Bugniazet, G. M., **12:**383n

Builders' Exchange (San Antonio), **6:**264

Builders of the U.S. of America, National Association of, **2:**170, *173n,* 175n

—convention: 1890 (St. Paul, Minn.), **2:**300, *301n*

Building Laborers' Union, Independent, **11:**325n

Building Material Drivers' Union (New York City), lockout by, 1903, *6:185–86n*

Building Material Handlers' Union (New York City), lockout by, 1903, *6:185–86n*

building trades, jurisdiction of, **11:**21–22, 22–23n, 60n

—conferences: Aug. 1903 (Indianapolis), **6:**173–74, *174–75n;* Oct. 1903 (Indianapolis), *6:175n;* 1907 (Indianapolis), **7:**182, 183n; 1914 (Boston), **9:**66, *68n,* 70, 73n

—convention: 1908 (Washington, D.C.), *7:276n*

—strikes/lockouts: 1892 (New York City), **3:**152, *153n;* 1903 (New York City), **6:**183–85, *185–86n;* 1906–7 (Lynn, Mass.), **7:**49–50, *50n;* 1910 (Gary, Ind.), **8:**159, *160n;* 1910 (Germany), **8:**198, *199n;* 1918 (Norfolk, Va.), **10:**409–10, *410n,* 411; 1919 (Winnipeg, Man.), **11:**75n; 1921–22 (Chicago), *11:496–97n,* **12:**57–58

Building Trades, United Board of (New York City), **6:**185–86n

Building Trades Alliance, Structural. *See* Structural Building Trades Alliance

Building Trades Council of America, National. *See* National Building Trades Council of America

building trades councils, **5:**350, 440, 518–19, **6:**492; in Boston, **9:**268n; in California, **6:**4, 5n, **7:**43n, **8:**122n, 221; in Chicago, **2:**175n, **3:**359n, **5:**214, 215–16n, **9:**261n, **10:**502n, **11:**27n, 496–97n, 530, **12:**55, 55n, 56–61, 356n; in Cincinnati, **12:**401n; in Dayton, Ohio, **12:**401n; in Denver, **6:**15, 17–18n; in Hartford, Conn., **7:**459–60, 461n; in Jacksonville, Fla., **7:**354–55; in Lawrence, Mass., **11:**351; in Milwaukee, Wis., **4:**182, 183n, **9:**354, **12:**122; in New Orleans, **3:**243n; in New York City, **3:**61–62n, **5:**447–48n, **6:**185–86n, **9:**292n, **11:**324, 324n, 352–53, 356–57, 378, 445, 467, 467–68n,

530, **12:**75; in Philadelphia, **2:**26n, **6:**44n, 414, 414n, **8:**52n; in San Francisco, **5:**338, 339n, 475, **6:**4, 5n, **9:**39n; in Seattle, **12:**274; in St. Paul, Minn., **10:**252, 253–54n; in Tacoma, Wash., **11:**50n; in Washington, D.C., **4:**175n; in Washington state and British Columbia, **3:**55n

Building Trades Employers' Association of New York, **6:**184–85, 186n

Building Trades Mechanics, United Board of (New York City), **6:**186n

Bulgaria, **10:**568n

Bullard, Arthur, **12:**286–87, *288n*, 291

Bullard, Robert L., **12:**546, 550, *552n*

Bullock, Jacob C., **2:***, 340, *343n*

bunching machines, **1:**417, 419, *421n*, 423, **2:**125

Bunker Hill and Sullivan Mining and Concentrating Co., **5:**93n, 97, 130–32

Burch, Frank, *12:350n; letter from,* **12:**349–50

Bureau of International Trade and Industrial Unions, **11:**488n

Burford, Robert E., **11:**83–84n, 314, 316–*17n*, 489–91, 491n

Burgess, William H., **6:**114, *115n*

Burgman, Charles F., **1:***, 227–28, *229n,* 242, **3:***, 47, *48n,* **9:**515n; and FOTLU Legislative Committee, **1:**231–34, 243

Burke, Edmund, **8:**482, *492n*

Burke, Frank, **11:**219, *220n*

Burke, James, **1:***, 103–6, *106n*

Burke, John P., **10:***, 259, *262n,* **12:***, 445, *446n*

Burke, Thomas, **3:**241n

Burkhard, Clemens D., *12:339n; wire from,* **12:**338–39

Burleson, Albert S., **8:**494, *495–96n,* **10:**482n, 514–15, 515n, **11:**93–94, 95n, 102–4

Burley Society, **8:**276n

Burlington, Charles G., **3:**460, *461n*

Burnett, John L., **8:**342, *346n,* 430, **9:**103n, 405n

Burnham, Daniel H., **3:**150–51, 153, *153n*

Burnquist, Joseph A. A., **10:**240, *241n*

Burns, John E., **2:***, 280, *281n,* 399, 407, 426, **3:***, 16, *18n,* 516, **4:***, 12,

15n, 18, 66, **9:**337; at AFL convention, **3:**517n, 589n, 596; *letters from,* **2:**352–53, **9:**326; *letter to,* **2:**350–51; mentioned in AFL Political Program debate, **3:**620, 622, 626, 634–35, 637–38, 640

Burns, Patrick J., **6:**398, *400n*

Burns, Simon, **7:***, 121, *122n*

Burns, William J., *8:214n,* 230, **9:**23, **11:**54n; and McNamara case, **8:**209n, 214, 248, 272–74, 293, 295n, 301, 305–6, 308–9; prosecution of, **8:**209n, 235–37, 238n, 254, 273–74, 350, 353

Burns Detective Agency, **12:**132n

Burress, James H., **12:**552, *554n*

Burt, Joseph H. (variously Burtt), **2:**74–75, *76n,* 79, **3:**131, *131–32n,* 135

Burt, Robert R., **11:***, 477, *478n*

Burt, Sidney, *11:189n; letter from,* **11:**188–89

Burt, Thomas, **3:***, 516, *517n*

Burton, Harry P., **9:**232–33, *233n*

Burton, Theodore E., **5:**326, *327n*

Busch, Adolphus, **5:**334n

Bush, Francis X., **7:**15

Bushe, J. F., *4:399n*

Bushway, Fred M., **4:**57

"Business Man and the Masses, The" (Bryan), *7:370n*

"Business Man's Vote, The" (Van Cleave), *7:370n*

Busse, Frederick A., **8:**149, *151n*

Bustillo Bros. and Diaz, strike/lock-out, 1902, *6:71n*

Busto, Serafín, **5:**182–83, 185, *188n,* 232

butchers, organization of, **4:**286–87

Butchers' Protective Union 1 (Denver), **5:**393, 396n

Butcher Workmen of America, Brotherhood of, **7:***, 343–45, 345–46n; jurisdiction of, **7:**343–45, 345–46n

Butler, Benjamin F., *1:269–70n,* **2:**382

Butler, Joseph, *letter from,* **10:**459–60

Butler, Michael T., **6:**166, *167n*

Butler, Mr. (Cook County, Ill., candidate for sheriff), **3:**646

Butler, Nicholas M., *8:24–25n; letter to,* **8:**23–24

Butler, Seymour, **11**:319n
Butler, Thomas S., **7**:80, *90n*
Butler, William K., **8**:498, *499n*
Butler, William M., **12**:296–97, *299n*
Butte (Mont.) Central Labor Council, **6**:284, *285n*, **12**:339, 340n
Butte (Mont.) miners' strike, 1917, **10**:126, *126–27n*
Butte (Mont.) Miners' Union. *See* Miners, Western Federation of: locals: local 1 (Butte, Mont.)
Butte (Mont.) Mine Workers' Union, *9:155n*, 181, 183n, 270–72
Butterworth, Frank, **11**:206n
Butterworth, Joshua, **10**:309n, 537, *538n*
Butts, Arthur C., **3**:299, *301n*
Byer, George, **4**:286, *287n*
Byoir, Carl, **10**:495–96, *496n*, 498
Byrne, Joseph F., **5**:*, 128, *129n;* attack on, **5**:454–55
Byrne, Michael J., **1**:218, *220n*, 242–43
Byrnes, Patrick S., **7**:108, *109n*
Bytal, A. L., **12**:541

Cabanas cigar factory, strike/lockout, 1907, **7**:220–21, *221n*
Cabet, Etienne, **1**:40, *44n*
Cabinet Makers' Employers' Association, strike/lockout, 1920–21, *11:358n*
Cable, James A., **5**:*, *84n,* 110n; *letter from,* **5**:219–20; *letters to,* **5**:82–84, 257–60
Cable, John L., **12**:185, *186n*
Cabrera, Luis, **9**:498–500, *500n*
Cabrini, Angiolo, **10**:552, *555n*
cabs, union, **9**:266–67, 267n
ca' canny, **4**:246–47, *249n*
Cachin, Marcel, **11**:39, *41n*
Caetani, Gelasio, **12**:415, *417n*
Caffery, Donelson, **5**:498, *501n*
Caffin, Charles H., **7**:442, *443n*
Cahan, Abraham, **3**:*, 85n, 298, *300n,* **10**:157n
Cahill, Martin, **11**:199, *199n*
Cahill, Thomas P., **4**:*, 431, *432n; letter from,* **4**:447–48
Cahill Iron Works, **4**:315, 317n
Cahillane, Patrick, **11**:86n
Caiger, Bill, **3**:516

Cain, George L., *7:115n; letter to,* **7**:114–15
Cain, James G., **5**:63n, 174–75, *176n*
Cain, John, **8**:230, *231n*
Cainey, Mr. (representative of U.S. Department of Justice), **10**:188
Caldara, Emilio, **10**:551, *555n*
Calder, William, *12:170n*
Calderhead, William A., **7**:80, *90n,* 94
Caldwell, Alonzo B., *4:331n; letter to,* **4**:330–31
Caldwell, Ben Franklin, **5**:189, *198n*
Caldwell, Henry C., **8**:491, *493n*
Caldwell, Howard H., **5**:340–41, *342n,* **6**:437–39, *439n*
California: Chinese workers in, **1**:48–49, 114, 115n, 125, **5**:45, 471, **6**:149, 340–41, **7**:111–12, 112n, 206, **9**:514; Democratic state convention in, 1908 (Stockton), **7**:383–84, *384n;* election of 1906, **7**:117; election of 1908, **7**:381–84, 384–85n, 413–14, 414n; Japanese students in, **7**:147, 148n, 195, **11**:89; Japanese workers in, **6**:149–50, 150–51n, 206, **9**:206n, 513–14, 515n; landholding by Asians in, **9**:206, 206n, **11**:89, *12:171n;* Mexican workers in, **6**:149–50, 150–51n, **7**:93n
California Farmers' Union, Inc., **8**:276n
California Industrial Welfare Commission, **8**:384n
California State Building Trades Council, **6**:4, *5n,* **7**:43n, **8**:122n, 221
California State Federation of Labor, **6**:243, *244n,* **7**:111, **8**:122n, **9**:206n, 513, 515
—conventions: 1914, **9**:206n; 1915, **9**:515n; 1916, **9**:515n
Call, Homer D., **5**:*, *18n,* 78, **6**:*, 16, *19n,* **7**:*, 344–45, *345n,* **9**:280n; at AFL conventions, **5**:164, 168n, 286, 287n; *letter to,* **5**:17–18
Call, Wilkinson, **1**:293–356 passim, *327n*
Callaghan, Edward F., **11**:510, *512n*
Callaghan, John M., **3**:172–73, *173n; letters to,* **3**:177–78, 241–43
Callahan, Patrick, **11**:86n
Calles, Plutarco Elías, **11**:404n,

12:120, *121n*, 392n, 525; inauguration of, 12:515, 515n, 535, 536n
Calumet and Hecla Mining Co., strike/lockout, 1913–14, 8:512, *512–13n*, 9:11–13, 13–14n, 25–28, 28n, 43–44, 44n, 46–47, 47–48n, 51–52, 52n, 64–67, 68n, 96n, 177, 181–83, 210, 211n, 301
Calumet (Mich.) *News*, 9:28n
Calvert, Alfred D., *6:479n*, 7:85, 91n; *letter to*, 6:478–79
Cambrai, 10:562
Cambrai, battle of, 10:293, *294n*
Cambria Steel Co., strike/lockout, 1919, 11:206, 206n
Camera del Lavoro (Chamber of Labor), 4:244n
Cameron, Andrew C., 1:22n
Camomile, David A., 9:343, *344n*
Campbell, Earl A., 10:505, *505n*
Campbell, George Douglas. *See* Argyle, duke of (George Douglas Campbell)
Campbell, Guy, 11:123n
Campbell, Henry C., 12:122, *123n*
Campbell, Humphrey B., 5:331, *332n*, 382n; *letter from*, 5:380–82
Campbell, James A., 3:250, *253n*
Campbell, John, 2:60, *63n*
Campbell, Philip P., 6:308n, 7:69, *69n*, 94
Campbell, Robert M., 3:250, *253n*, 377–78, 381, 383–84
Campbell, Thomas E. (government agent), 10:480, *481n*
Campbell, Thomas E. (governor), 10:150n, 338, *339n*
Campbell, Thomas M., 11:190, *191n*
Canada: AFL organizers in, 6:127, 128n (*see also* Brunet, G. R.; Flett, John A.; Varley, William); labor representatives of, meetings with AFL peace delegation, 11:55; One Big Union in, 11:75, 75–76n, 94, 281n, 380, 12:438, 442n; separatism in labor movement of, 6:21–22, 156–59, 7:236–37; unions in, expenditures for, 6:156–59, 160n, 11:280, 281n; unions in, income from, 6:160n, 11:280, 281n; unions in, membership of, 6:160n; unions in, religious,

9:14–15, 15n, 458–59, 460n, 12:438, 442n; workers from, 8:345, 11:341n
—strikes/lockouts: 1890–91 (miners), *3:56n;* 1909–10 (miners), 10:307, *308n;* 1910 (Grand Trunk Railway), 8:112–13, *114–15n;* 1918 (miners, threatened), 10:307–8, *308n;* 1919 (building trades workers), 11:75n; 1919 (general strike), 11:74–75, *75n,* 94, 380; 1919 (lathers), 11:72; 1919 (metal trades workers), 11:72–73, *74–75n;* 1919 (painters), 11:72–73, *74n;* 1923 (longshoremen), 12:442n
Canada, Trades and Labor Congress of, 4:471, *471n,* 8:120, 121n, 142, 142n, 11:380, 12:438, 442n; charters, issued by, 6:134–35, 8:142, 142n, 12:439–42; organizers, appointment of, 12:440–42; and per capita tax, 6:136n, 7:267, 268n, 8:421
—conventions: 1906 (Victoria, B.C.), 7:97, *98n;* 1913 (Montreal), 8:415, *416n;* 1914 (St. John, N.B.), *9:191n;* 1918, 11:75n; 1920 (Windsor, Ont.), 11:380, *381n*
Canada, Trades and Labor Congress of the Dominion of, 4:471, *471n*
Canadian and Catholic Confederation of Labor. *See* Confédération canadienne et catholique du travail
Canadian Electrical Trades Union, 11:381, *381n*
Canadian Federation of Labor, 8:120–21, *121n,* 9:15n, 11:380, 381n
Canadian Labor Congress (formed 1883), *4:471n*
Canadian Labor Congress (formed 1956), 11:76n
Canadian National Railroad, 12:413
Canadian Pacific Co., 5:327
Canal Zone, workers in, 9:496, 11:391–92, 392–93n, 433–34, 435n, 12:385–86, 410–11, 412n. *See also* "gold roll" employees, in Canal Zone; Panama Canal; "silver roll" employees, in Canal Zone
Canal Zone Central Labor Union. *See* Balboa (Canal Zone) Central Labor Union

Canal Zone Metal Trades Council,
11:393n
Cane, McCaffrey, and Co., 4:30, *30n*
Canfield, F. A., 10:369n
Cannon, Frank J., 4:507, *509n*
Cannon, James, *2:358n; letter to,*
2:357–58
Cannon, James, Jr., 5:94–95, 98n
Cannon, Joseph D., *8:286n,* 9:292n,
443n; at AFL conventions, 8:283–
84, 286n, 410, 9:25–26, 28n, 30,
346, 346n, 526n, 10:259, 262, 262n,
266n; *wire from,* 10:93
Cannon, Joseph G., 3:19, *20n,* 6:477n,
526, 527n, 529n, 7:6n, 43, 49,
80, 86–87, 91n, 288, 320n, 9:202,
10:434n; and election of 1906, 7:96,
101–2, 102n, 103, 106, 130, 140;
and election of 1908, 7:349, 350n,
357–60, 377, 387, 390, 398; election of, as Speaker of House, 7:334,
336n; *letters to,* 6:476–77, 7:3–6,
155–56; SG and, 7:92, 93n, 101–2,
334, 349, 350n
Cannon, William J., 2:267, *268n,* 269–
70, 391, 3:14n
Cannon, William P., *letter to,* 9:267–68
Canova, Leon Joseph, 9:443n
Cantonment Adjustment Commission, 10:114, 115n
Cantonment Construction Agreement, 10:114, 119, 119n, 128, 171,
176, 193n, 204, 229, 232–34, 314,
365, 526, 11:116, 117n; extension of,
10:115n, 171, 172n, 193n, 204, 229
cantonments, *10:115n*
Cantor, Jacob A., 1:446, *447n*
Čapek, Thomas, 1:46
Caperton, William, 9:311n
Capital and Labor (periodical), *1:354n*
capital punishment, 4:85, 9:278,
12:516, 516n
Cap Makers of North America, United
Cloth Hat and, 11:*, 135n
Cap Manufacturers' Association (New
York City), 7:207, *208n*
Caporetto, 10:343
Caporetto, battle of, 10:292, *294n*
Capper, Arthur, 11:338n
Capps, Washington L., 10:207n, 220,
221n

Carberry, C. B., 10:445n
car builders' union (Allegheny City),
2:89
Cárdenas, Julio de, 7:221n
Carders' Union (New Bedford,
Mass.), 4:428, *429n,* 477
Cardinale, Giuseppe, 8:342, *346n*
Carey, David A., 10:*, 265, *266n*
Carey, James, 3:238, *241n*
Carey, James F., 5:46, *48n,* 49–50, 53n,
6:199, 202, *204n*
Carey, Jeremiah T., 7:*, 202–4, *204n*
Carey, John D., 3:238, *241n*
Carey, P. W., 4:58, *58n*
Carey, W. M., 7:379
Carhartt, Hamilton, *5:417n*
Carl, Conrad, 12:393, *394n*
Carl, John H., 2:244
Carl, LeRoy, 3:439, *440n*
Carless, Harry, 4:103, *106n*
Carlin, Charles C., 9:91, *94n,* 97n
Carlisle, John G., 3:292, *292n,* 342,
343n, 404, 405n, 465–66, 613
Carlson, Harry G., *8:357n; letter to,*
8:355–56
Carlton, Albert A., 1:*, 403, *404n,* 2:19
Carlton, Newcomb, 10:486, *490n,* 515
Carlyle, Thomas, 3:451, 451n
Carmania (passenger liner), 11:37–38,
40n
Carmaux glassworkers' union. *See*
Chambre syndicale des verriers de
Carmaux
Carmody, Walter, *5:374n; letter to,*
5:373
Carnegie, Andrew, 2:35, *36n,* 3:210,
420, 481, 539, 542n, 582, 635,
637, 5:166, 169n, 6:235–36, 236n,
7:214n, 8:288–89
Carnegie Corporation, 12:185
Carnegie Endowment for Interna-
tional Peace, 9:274n
Carnegie Foundation for the Ad-
vancement of Teaching, 12:69, 73n
Carnegie Peace Association, 10:268
Carnegie Steel Co., 4:499n, 5:207n,
335n, 482n; boycott, 1892 (threatened), 3:232–34, 235n; and Homestead strike, 1892, 3:185, 188–89,
189n, 199, 207, 209, 217, 236–37,
239–40, 264, 4:492, 500n

Carney, Francis, **5:**89, *92n,* 307n
Carney, William A., **3:***, *75n,* 108, 189, 210, **4:***, 241, *242n;* at AFL conventions, **3:**255, 258, 258n, 260, 427
Carnova (Cuban newspaper editor), **7:**162–64
Carothers, Francis K., **9:***, 168, *169n*
Carpenter (trade union journal), **2:**133–34; *letter to,* **2:**180
Carpenter, Herbert L., **10:**310, *312–13n,* 512n
carpenters, mass meeting of, in New York City, *letter to,* **2:**295
Carpenters and Joiners, Amalgamated Society of (American union), **2:***, 296n, 305–6, 307n, 376, **3:**61n, 379, **6:***, 44n, 157; jurisdiction of, **6:**42–44, 44–45n, 51, 62–64, 66–67n, 175–76, 176n, 178–79, 210–11, 219–20, 326n
—local: local 683 (Washington, D.C.), **4:**285, 285n
Carpenters and Joiners, Amalgamated Society of (English union), **1:**71
Carpenters and Joiners, Progressive Association of, **2:**296n, 305, 342
Carpenters and Joiners, United Order of American, **1:**457, *458n,* **2:**99, *99–100n,* 136, 296n, 305–6
—local: local 22 (Newark, N.J.), **3:**70n
Carpenters and Joiners of America, Brotherhood of, **1:***, 275, 279–81, 385–86, 389, 390n, **2:***, 30n, 35, 67, 71n, 99, 99n, **3:***, **4:***, **5:***, **6:***, **7:***, **8:***, **9:***, **10:***, **11:***, **12:***
—locals: local 1 (Washington, D.C.), **2:**70, 71n, 129n (*see also* Carpenters' local 1 [Washington, D.C.; independent]); local 190 (Washington, D.C.), **2:**71, 71n
Carpenters and Joiners of America, United Brotherhood of, **1:***, **2:***, 99–100n, 118, 133–36, 165, 180, 235, 305, 376, **3:***, 61, 61–62n, 70n, 151–53, 267, 268n, 596, 649, **4:***, 95, 97n, 99, 341, 351, 450, 451n, **5:***, 18, 19n, **6:***, 8n, 173–74, **7:***, 56n, 282, 483, **8:***, 125n, 302n, 344, **9:***, 15n, 332, 333n, 342, 343n, 428, **10:***, 96n, 230, 233–35, 317–18, 318–19n, 359, **11:***, 325n, **12:***,

238, 241n, 469; and AFL Building Trades Department, **8:**149–50, 151n, 295, **9:**70, 73n, **11:**544–45, 545n, **12:**163n, 399–401, 401n; and AFL per capita tax, **6:**42–43; and black workers, **6:**114, 115n, **8:**278, 279n, **11:**84n, 366n; and Canadian labor movement, **6:**21–22, 156–57, **7:**268n, **9:**14–15, 458, 460n; and Chicago building trades arbitration case, **11:**496–97n; *circular of,* **6:**7, 8n; dues of, **2:**133–34, **7:**268n; and eight-hour movement, 1890, **2:**163–64, 290, 293–95, 296n, 298–301, 305–7, 314, 316–17, **3:**42, 54, 70n, 71–72, 268n, 623; executive board of, **2:**136, **5:**233, 398–99; executive board of, *letter to,* **2:**376; injunctions, **12:**400; injunctions against, **7:**50n, **10:**253, 254n; jurisdiction of, **3:**150, 153n, **5:**421–22, 422–23n, 484–85, **6:**42–44, 44–45n, 51, 52–53n, 62–66, 66–67n, 165–67, 167n, 175–76, 176n, 178–79, 181, 210–11, 211n, 219–20, 326n, 500, 503n, **7:**242–43, 243n, 272, **8:**151n, 295, **9:**70, 73n, 346–47, 347n, **10:**171, 171–72n, 405, 406n, **11:**60n, 545n, **12:**73, 163n, 399–401, 401n; label of, **6:**181; and McGuire, suspension of, **5:**398–99n, **6:**5–8, 8n, 38, 38n, 92, 130, **7:**54–56; organizing campaign in Bogalusa, La., **11:**366n; and painters' controversy, New York City, **5:**447–48n; and Structural Building Trades Alliance, **6:**414; withdrawal of, from AFL, **6:**317, 326n
—conventions: 1890 (Chicago), **2:**376, *376n;* 1892 (St. Louis), **3:**213; 1894, **6:**52n; 1896 (Cleveland), *4:263n;* 1898 (New York City), **5:**18, *19n;* 1902 (Atlanta), **5:**399n, **6:**7, *8n,* 22, 34, 38, 38n, 42–44, 44n, 326n; 1916 (Fort Worth, Tex.), **9:**347, *348n,* 496
—district councils: District Council 1, **3:**379; District Council, Newark, N.J., **3:**70n; District Council, New York City, **3:**150; District Council, San Francisco, **6:**5n; District Council, Washington, D.C., **10:**84n

—locals: local 8 (Philadelphia), **2:**133, **6:**546n, **7:**55; local 11 (Cleveland), **4:**451n, **9:**470; local 22 (San Francisco), **5:**339n; local 33 (Boston), **2:**133; local 39 (Cleveland), **4:**451n; local 55 (Denver), **7:**8, 9n; local 56 (Los Angeles), **2:**133; local 75 (Indianapolis), **12:**363; local 108 (Lynn, Mass.), **4:**187–88, 189n; local 119 (Newark, N.J.), **3:**70n; local 172 (Newark, N.J.), **3:**70n; local 190 (Washington, D.C.), **2:**71n, **4:**285, 285n; local 231 (Birmingham, Ala.), **2:**102; local 232 (Millburn, N.J.), **3:**70n; local 398 (Cleveland), **4:**451n; local 398 (Lewiston, Idaho), **10:**186n; local 449 (Cleveland), **4:**451n; local 468 (New York City), **3:**379, 382n; local 477 (Orange, N.J.), **3:**70n; local 492 (Reading, Pa.), **6:**263, 264n; local 513 (New York City), **2:**371n; local 524 (Nelson, B.C.), **6:**21; local 528 (Denver), **7:**8, 9n; local 533 (Montclair, N.J.), **3:**70n; local 563 (Scranton, Pa.), **4:**260, 262, 263n; local 595 (Lynn, Mass.), **7:**50n; local 652 (Elwood, Ind.), **3:**222n; local 717 (San Antonio), **6:**264–65, 265n; local 770 (Denver), **7:**8, 9n; local 913 (Balboa, Canal Zone), **9:**496, 497n; local 1039 (Cedar Rapids, Iowa), **10:**368, 369n; local 1131 (Waycross, Ga.), **8:**278, 279n; local 1313 (Demopolis, Ala.), **6:**106, 107n; local 1338 (Jonquière, Que.), **9:**15, 15n; local 1368 (Chicoutimi, Que.), **9:**15, 15n; local 1411 (Mobile, Ala.), **11:**486n; local 1456 (New York City), **9:**292n, 311n, **11:**324, 325n; local 1761 (Goldfield, Nev.), **7:**284, 286n; local 1782 (New Orleans), **6:**533–34; local 1793 (Trois-Rivières, Que.), **9:**14, 15n; local 1874 (Denver), **7:**8, 9n; local 2203 (Bogalusa, La.), **11:**366; locals in San Francisco, **5:**474–75
—strikes/lockouts: 1890 (Chicago), **2:**295, *296n,* 306; 1890 (Indianapolis), *2:299n;* 1891 (Newark, N.J.), **3:**70, *70n;* 1902 (Philadelphia), **6:**43–44, *44–45n;* 1903-? (Schenect-

ady, N.Y.), **6:**175–76, *176n,* 178–79; 1906–7 (Lynn, Mass.), **7:**49–50, *50n;* 1909 (New Britain, Conn.), **7:**460, *461n;* 1917 (threatened), **10:**171, 171–72n; 1918 (Baltimore), **10:**359–60, *362n;* 1918 (Beaumont and Orange, Tex.), **10:**317–18, *318n;* 1918 (Norfolk, Va.), **10:**409–10, *410n,* 411; 1918 (Staten Island, N.Y.), **10:**359–60, *362n;* 1920–21 (Mobile, Ala.), **11:**484–85, *486n*

Carpenters' Council of Chicago, United, **2:**296n

Carpenters' Council of St. Louis, **3:**344, 345n

Carpenters' local 1 (Washington, D.C.; independent), **2:**71n, 135–36, **4:**170, 171n

Carpenters of New York and Vicinity, United Order of. *See* Carpenters and Joiners, United Order of American

Carpenters' Union, International, **11:**544, 545n

Carpet Makers' Council (New York City), **3:**379

Carr, Alfred J., **2:**68, *69n*

Carr, Frederick J., *3:124n; letter to,* **3:**124

Carr, Maggie, **3:**140

Carr, Mrs., **3:**141

Carranza, Venustiano, *9:160n,* 438–39, **10:**499n, 545, **11:**300n, 303, 303n; **12:**121n; and Casa del Obrero Mundial, **9:**425, 426n, 498, 500n; declaration of martial law, **9:**498–500, 500–501n; land reforms of, **9:**439, 443n, 484n; and overthrow of Huerta, **9:**95–96n, 437; religious persecution under, **9:**440, 443n, 458; SG and, **9:**158–59, 427, 427n, 428, 458; and U.S. Punitive Expedition, **9:**426n, 431–33, 433–34n, 437; U.S. recognition of government of, **9:**306–7, 307n, 325–26, 326n, 327, 328n, 360–61, 437; and Villa, **9:**212n, 306, 437; *wire to,* **9:**434–35; and Zapata, **9:**306, 307n

Carriage and Wagon Workers' International Union of North America, **3:***, 509n, **5:***, 267–68n, **6:***, 312n, 384, **7:***, 245, 246n; affiliation of,

with AFL, **5:**265–68; jurisdiction of, **6:**311, 312n; *letter to,* **5:**265–67
—locals: local 5 (Denver), **5:**393, 396n; local 14 (New Orleans), **5:**377, 379n
Carriage Builders' National Association of the U.S. of America, **7:**245, 246n
Carrick, Michael P., **2:***, *315n,* **4:***, 346, *347n,* 359n, 372–73, 374–75n, 380, 416, **5:***, 408, *408n,* **6:***, *114n,* **9:***, 337, *341n; letters from,* **6:**113–14, 173–74; *letters to,* **2:**314–15, **5:**518–20
Carrizal, Mexico, battle at, *9:426n,* 431–32, 434–35n, 437, **10:**10
Carroll, Beryl F., **8:**297, *298n*
Carroll, Charles, *3:199n; letter from,* **3:**199
Carroll, Edward M., **4:***, 416, *417n*
Carroll, Michael J., **3:**464, *465n,* 534, 535n, 552, 589, **4:**144; *wire from,* **3:**532–33
Carry, Edward F., **10:**209n, 221, *221n*
Carson, James, **3:**141
Carson, John, **2:**332
Carter, Frederick S., **4:**306–7, *308n*
Carter, George R., **6:**473n
Carter, Thomas H., **5:**151n
Carter, William S., **4:***, *127n,* **8:***, *51n,* **9:***, 49, *50n,* 450n, 464n, **10:***, *251n,* 321n, **11:***, 460–61, *461n,* 462, 472n, 489, 491, 532n, **12:***, 499, *501n;* at AFL convention, **9:**521, 523n, 527; *letters from,* **4:**124–27, **10:**249–51; *letters to,* **8:**49–51, 249–53
Caruso, Enrico, **10:**45 ?, *452n*
Carvallo, Guillermo Z., **9:**429n, 467, *468n*
Car Workers, International Association of, **8:***, 296, 297n
Cary, Henry N., **9:**71, *74n*
Cary, William J., **7:**130, 139, *142n,* **8:**100–101; *letter to,* **7:**332–33
Casa del Obrero Mundial, *9:426n,* 427–28n, 433n, 436; agreement of, with Mexican government, **9:**425, 426n, 498, 500n; and general strike in Mexico City, 1916, **9:**426n, 501n; and IWW, **9:**427, 499; *letter to,* **9:**425–26
Case, Charles R., *7:109n; letter from,* **7:**107–9

Case, J. I., Threshing Machine Co., strike/lockout, 1905–6?, **7:**158n
Casey, Josephine, *9:99n,* *12:359n; letter from,* **9:**98–99
Cash, James G., **9:**351, *352n*
cash girls, **1:**304–5
Casserly, James A., **1:**457, *458n*
Castelli, Vincent, *10:180n; letter to,* **10:**180
Castle, Chauncey H., **5:**311, *311n*
Castle, Howard, **11:**454n
Castle Garden, **1:**361, *362n*
Casuss, R., **1:**432
Catholic Church: and trade unions, **3:**170; and trade unions in Canada, **9:**14–15, 15–16n, 458, 460n. *See also* trade unions: and religion
Catholic Labor Corporation of Three Rivers. *See* Corporation Ouvrière Catholique des Trois-Rivières
Catlin, Theron E., **8:**340, *346n*
Caton, Elijah F., *8:396n; letter to,* **8:**395–96
Catt, Carrie Chapman, *6:217n,* **11:**20n; *letter from,* **6:**216–17
Cattell, James M., *12:186n; letter to,* **12:**185–86
Cattermull, Alfred C., **6:**121, *122n,* 143
Cavanagh, Thomas, **10:**136n
Cavanaugh, George, **2:***, 376, *376n,* **3:***, 133, *134n*
Cavanaugh, Hugh, **1:***, 402, *404n,* **4:**123, *124n*
Cavanaugh, Peter, **8:**357n
Cavendish, Lord Frederick, **3:**241n
Cavis, Charles N., **10:**337–38, *339n*
censuses: 1880, **1:**331–34, **2:**239, 249; 1890, **2:**236–40, 248–49, 347–48
central bodies: affiliation of, with AFL, **2:**75, **3:**459; affiliation of locals in, **4:**189–91, 191n, 380–81, **5:**261, 440, **6:**273–75, **7:**353–55, **8:**141–42, 142n, **12:**88, 89n; and AFL organizers, **8:**355–56, 357n; black workers in, **5:**221–22, 261, 262n, 413–14, 430–31, 432n, 439n, 440, 460–62, **6:**19–20, 20n, 39, 91n, 108–9, 533–34, **8:**336–37, **9:**268, **10:**347; and boycotts, **5:**209–10, **8:**142–43, 144n; constitutions of, **9:**419–22; expulsion of locals from, **9:**203–5, 205n, 208–9, 209n; and

political conventions, **5:**210; political discussions in, **9:**164–66; powers of, **8:**174–75, 185–87; strike votes by, **11:**49, 50n, 94, 95n; and sympathy strikes, **8:**140–41, 141n

Centralia (Ill.) Central Trades and Labor Assembly, *6:266n*

Centralia, Wash., Armistice Day affair, **11:**216, *217n*

Central Loan and Trust Co. v. Campbell Commission Co., **8:**479, *492n*

Central New England Railroad, **9:**516

Central Pacific Railroad, **3:**551, 552n; strike/lockout, 1894, **3:**632, *659n*

Central Union Times (Jacksonville, Fla.), **7:**353–54

Central Vermont Railroad, strike/lockout, 1910, **8:**112–13, *114–15n*

Century Magazine (periodical), **8:**226–27n

Century Syndicate, **7:**256–57, 271

Cessna, William, **3:**258, *260n*

Chadbourne, Thomas L., Jr., **11:**168, *168n*

Chadwick, Mrs. T., **3:**141

Chafin, Dan, injunction against, **12:**265n

Chafin, Eugene W., **7:**397–98, *399n*

Chainmakers' National Union of the U.S. of America, jurisdiction of, **5:**516, 517n

Chair-Makers' Union (Tell City, Ind.), **7:**228

—strike/lockout: 1907, **7:**227–29, *229n*, 234–35

Challenge Accepted: Labor Will Not Be Outlawed or Enslaved, The (AFL), *11:426n*

Chalmers, Andrew, **4:**196, *197n,* **5:**452

Chalmers, Hugh, **6:**488, *489n,* **7:**168n; *letter from,* **7:**166–68

Chamberlain, George E., **10:**64n, 310, *312n*

Chamber of Labor. *See* Camera del Lavoro

Chambers, Jordan W., **11:**83–84n, 120n, 326n, 477, 478n; *wire from,* **11:**119

Chambre syndicale des verriers de Carmaux, **4:**77n

Chance, George, **4:***, *379n,* 383n,

388n, 452, **5:***, 126n, 175, *176n,* **6:***, 41, *42n,* **9:**336

Chandelier Workers' Benevolent and Protective Union (New York City), **3:**379, *382n*

Chandler, Charles F., **1:**152, *152n*

Chandler, D. L., **11:**475n

Chandler, Harry, indictment of, **9:**483, 484n

Chandler, Michael, **7:**205, *205n*

Chandler, William E., **3:**194, *194n, 487n; letter to,* **3:**487

Chapman, Pleasant T., **8:**132, *132n*

charitable organizations, **9:**50–51

Charleston (S.C.) and Vicinity, Central Labor Union of, **12:**207, *207n*

Charleston, S.C., earthquake, **6:**362, *364n*

Charter Oak Stove and Range Co., **8:**201

Chas. Wolff Packing Co. v. The Court of Industrial Relations of the State of Kansas, 11:280n

Chase, John, **9:**24n, 211, *211n*

Château-Thierry, battle of, **10:**565, *567n,* **11:**47, *49n,* 56, 118

Chattanooga (Tenn.) Central Labor Union, **4:**315, *317n*

check-off, **12:**354–55

Cheka, **11:**429–30, *432n*

Cherry, Edward H., *3:145n; letter to,* **3:**144–45

Cherry, Ill., mine disaster, 1909, **8:**6, *9n,* 32

Chesapeake and Ohio Railroad, **12:**413

Chevalier, F., Co., **6:**218

Cheyenne Street Railway Co., boycott, 1911–12, **8:**269, *277n*

Chicago, Amalgamated Building Trades Council of, **2:**175n

Chicago, Burlington and Quincy Railroad, strike/lockout, 1888–89, **2:**107, *108n*

Chicago: election of 1879, **2:**404, *409n;* election of 1886, **2:**404–5, *409n;* election of 1887, **2:**409n, **3:**646; election of 1894, **3:**646; election of 1915, **11:**263, 265n; election of 1919, **11:**263–64, 265n; factory inspection ordinance of, **2:**404,

409n; Labor Day in, **9:**453–54, 454n; police force of, violence against strikers by, **9:**354, 355n, 356–57, 386

Chicago, St. Paul, Minneapolis, and Omaha Railway Co.: injunction, **12:**373n; strike/lockout, 1922, **12:**373n

Chicago, Trade and Labor Assembly of, *1:166n*, 462n, **2:**63n, 128, 301, 304, **3:**103n, 286n, 358, 359n, 430, 538–39, **4:**80, 158, 159n, 176, *177n*, 269

Chicago Allied Printing Trades Council, **5:**342n

Chicago American, contempt case, **5:**415, *415n*

Chicago Associated Building Trades Council, **11:**497n

Chicago Association of Machinery Manufacturers, *5:216n*

Chicago Board of Education, injunction against, *9:419n*

Chicago Brass Manufacturers' Association, **6:**445n

Chicago Brick Exchange Insurance Department, **12:**353

Chicago Building Construction Employers' Association, **9:**261n, **11:**497n

Chicago Building Contractors' Council, **5:**214, *215*–16n

Chicago building trades arbitration case, **11:**496, *496–97n*, **12:**57–60, 61n

Chicago Building Trades Council, *3:359n*, **5:**214, 215–*16n*, **9:**260, 261n, **10:**502n, **11:**27n, 496–97n, 530, **12:**356n; SG, meeting with representatives of, **12:**55, 55n, 56–61

Chicago Central Labor Union, **1:**461, *462n*, **2:**60, *63n*, 202, 304

Chicago Chandelier Manufacturers' Association, **6:**445n

Chicago Civic Federation, **3:**521, 552, *553n*, 561, 589, 597, 605, **5:**215n, 217, 218n; industrial committee of, **3:**599, 606n

—conferences: 1894 (Chicago), **3:**552, *553n*, 561, 589–90, 599–606, **5:**218n; 1898 (New York City), **5:**218n; 1898 (Saratoga, N.Y.), **4:**505–6, *506n*, **5:**3–11, *11n*, 13–14,

15n, 217, 218n; 1899 (Chicago), **5:**217, *218n*

Chicago Commercial Association, **5:**29n

Chicago Daily News, boycott, 1898–1903, **5:**340, 341–*42n*

Chicago Defender, articles in, **10:**358–59, **11:**149, 149n

Chicago Drapers' and Tailors' Exchange, **5:**215, 216n

Chicago Elevated Railways, **9:**388, 390n

Chicago Employers' Association, **6:**453n

Chicagoer Arbeiter-Zeitung (labor journal), editor of, *letter to,* **4:**161–62

Chicago Federation of Labor, *1:166n*, 462n, *4:159n, 177n*, 269, 381, 382n, **5:**162n, 342n, 373, **6:**13n, 156n, 342, 407n, 453n, **8:**213n, 355n, **9:**203–4, 208, 261n, 371, **10:**5, 215–16, 218, 280n, 387, 502n, **11:**17n, 27n, 275–78, 368–73, 373n, 525n, 490; AFL financial support of, **12:**242–44, 244n; and election of 1905, **6:**468, 469n; and election of 1906, **7:**110n, 115; and election of 1908, **7:**363, 373, 386, 416–17, 417n; and industrial unionism, **11:**18n, **12:**54, 54–55n, 62–63, 67, 312–15; *letter from,* **11:**281–83; meeting of, 1898, **4:**469–70; Political Action Committee of, **7:**363; SG, *address before,* **8:**62–75, 75n; SG, meetings with representatives of, **12:**54, 54n, 55, 61–65

Chicago Industrial Workers' Club, **6:**447, 449n

Chicago Newspaper Publishers' Association, **9:**71, 74n

Chicago packinghouse workers, organization of, **10:**214–16, 218n

Chicago Peace Jubilee, 1898, **5:**20–29, *29n*

"Chicago Platform," **12:**21n

Chicago Platt Deutsche Gilde, **2:**60

Chicago Railway Co., strike/lockout, 1908, **7:**342, *342n*

Chicago Record, boycott, 1898–1903, **5:**340, 341–*42n*

Chicago Trade and Labor Congress, **4:**158, *159n*, 176, 177n

Chicago Trade and Labor Council,
1:166n
Chicago Typothetae: strike/lockout,
1905-?, **7:**11n; strike injunction,
7:11, 11–12n
Chicago-Virden Coal Co., strike/lock-
out, 1898, *5:30n*
Chicago Wholesale Clothiers' Association, **8:**277n
Chicherin, Georgi V., **11:**427, *432n,*
12:15n
Chihuahua, governor of, **9:**427n
Child, Richard, **12:**15n
child labor, **1:**268, 304–8, **2:**156, **4:**48,
167, **5:**475–77, 477n, **6:**214, **8:**331,
11:305, **12:**179; and black women's
clubs, **12:**83; and Child Labor Tax
Act, **10:**499n, **11:**15, 512–14, 514n;
in cigar industry, **1:**45, 50, 53–54,
66, 110–11, 172–210, 227, 291, 304;
and constitutional amendment
prohibiting, **12:**81, 82–83n, 91, 208,
276, 343, 346, 348n, 374, 453–54,
455n, 486–87, 510–11; and Keating-
Owen Act, **10:**85, 86n, 499n, **11:**15;
limitation of, **1:**37, 40, 270n, 361,
449, **2:**10n, 153, **3:**278–79, 550,
4:27, 28–29n, 232, 491, **5:**70, 70n,
312, 313n, 314–15, 316n, 341,
348–49, 349n, **6:**96, 108, 109–10n,
479, **7:**59, 59n, 106, 107n, 183–84,
185–86n, **8:**180, 182n, 345, **9:**214,
223–24n, **10:**57n, **11:**71n, 100, **12:**5;
prohibition of, **1:**225–27, 270n, 330,
2:3–4, 48, 83–84, 289, 289n, **3:**38,
43, 50, 192, 286, 395–96, 550, **4:**60,
100, 113, **5:**70n, **6:**108, 109–10n,
372, 478, **7:**59n, 185–86n, **8:**182n,
345, **9:**118, **10:**497, **11:**8n, 70–71n,
100, 159, 311, **12:**83–85, 91, 93, 161,
276, 343, 346, 348n, 374–75, 375n,
453–54; and wartime industrial production, **10:**85–86
Children's Dress Manufacturers' Association, **8:**442n
*Children's Hospital of D.C. v. Adkins et
al., 12:228n*
Children's Hospital of the District of
Columbia, **12:**228n
Childs, George W., **2:**35, *36n*
Childs-Drexel Home for Union Printers, **4:**369, *371n*

Chile, **10:**10–11, **12:**386n; and civil
war in Mexico, **9:**363n
Chillicothe (Ohio) Central Labor
Union, *10:129n*
Chillicothe (Ohio) Trades and Labor
Council, *10:129n*
Chilton, William E., *8:362n,* **9:**19, 22n;
letter to, **8:**361–62
China: revolution in, 1911–12, **8:**317,
320n; SG and, **4:**27, 36–37, 52,
5:297, 506; U.S. relations with,
10:37; workers in, **1:**345, **12:**285, 305
—workers from, **1:**218, 230, **4:**126,
409n, **5:**45, 280, 435–38, **6:**340–41,
521–22n, **7:**111–12, **11:**43, 149; in
California, **1:**48–49, 114, 115n, 125,
5:45, 471, **6:**149, 340–41, **7:**111–12,
112n, 206, **9:**514; and cigarmakers,
1:48–49, 114, 115–16n, 125, 126n,
7:308n; in Hawaii, **4:**488, **5:**xvi,
6:195, 471–72, **7:**332–33, **11:**483,
484n, 502–3, 503–4n, **12:**210–11,
415; membership of, in trade
unions, **12:**265; organization of,
6:149, 285–86, **8:**9, **9:**477, 478n;
and Panama Canal, **6:**512, 512n,
7:93, 93n, 119; in Philippines, **5:**62,
65; registration of, **3:**372n, **12:**345;
SG and, **1:**300–301, 373, **3:**53, 371,
488–89, **4:**342, 434, 484, **5:**466–67,
471–74, **6:**149, 150n, 195, 285–86,
338, 347, 471–72, **8:**46, 102, **9:**477,
12:210–11, 415; smuggling of,
5:326–27, **12:**32; on troopships,
5:13, 15n
—workers from, restriction of immigration of, **1:**242, 373, 387, **3:**135,
287, 343n, 371–72n, 488–89, **5:**426,
434–38, 456–58, 458–59n, **6:**261,
261–62n, 527n, **7:**206, 267, 268n,
9:100, 515n, **10:**37; SG and, **1:**300,
373, **3:**287, **4:**488, **5:**xvi, 7, 28, 406–
7, 407n, 431, 466–67, 470–74, 485–
86, 518, **6:**11–12, 12–13n, 150n,
286, 471–72, 472–73n, 512n, 513,
513n, 525, 527–29, **9:**514, **11:**342,
483, 484n, 502–3, **12:**415, 419. *See
also under* legislation, U.S.
—workers from, restriction of immigration of, conferences on: 1901
(San Francisco), **5:**457, *458n;* 1901
(Washington, D.C.), **5:**457, *458n*

Chindblom, Carl R., **11**:276, *278n,* 281
Chinese Question: Arguments against Exclusion Answered and Argument in Favor of Exclusion Presented, The (Morgan), **5**:406, *407n*
Chinese Summary Trial, **8**:479
Chipman, Miner, **9**:*229n*
Chism, Clarence A., **10**:19, *22n*
Chkheidze, Nikolai S., *10:45*–46n; *cable to,* **10**:45
Chlopek, Anthony J., **12**:*, *7n,* 49n, 390–91n, 441; *letter from,* **12**:7
Choate, Rufus, **12**:217n
Chopper, J. F., *letter to,* **3**:346–47
Christman, Elisabeth, **10**:*, *82n,* **11**:18, 532n, **12**:418n, 447n, 450–51; *letter from,* **11**:505–6, 507n; *wire from,* **10**:81–82
Christopher-Simpson Foundry Co., strike/lockout, 1904, **6**:244, *245n*
Christopherson, Elias S., **4**:208, *209n,* 269, 272n
Church, Thomas L., *10:278n*
Churchill, Horace W., **8**:81, *82n*
Churchill, Lord Randolph, **4**:100, *101n*
Churchill, Winston, **10**:537n
cigarmakers: Bohemian, **1**:46–47, 50–51, 53, 57, 66, 77, 96, 102–3, 107, 110; bunchmakers, **1**:45–46, 50, 53, 94, 417, 419, **2**:125 (*see also* Cigar Makers' International Union of America: and bunchmakers); and child labor, **1**:45, 50, 53–54, 66, 110–11, 172–210, 227, 291, 304; Chinese, **1**:48–49, 114, 115–16n, 125, 126n; and cigar mold or press, **1**:45–46, 49, **12**:304–5; Cuban, **1**:51, 457–58, 459n, **6**:70, 71n, **8**:25, 26n, 104; German, **1**:21, 46–47, 50–51, 66, 96, 102–3, 107, 110, 247, 259; Hillmann on, **1**:31, 42; in London, **1**:4, 74, 75n; packers, **1**:110, 374–75, 378–79, 381 (*see also* Cigar Makers' International Union of America: and packers); rollers, **1**:45, 49, 66, 94 (*see also* Cigar Makers' International Union of America: and rollers); Spanish, **1**:51; tobacco strippers, **1**:51, 94, 110, 304, **7**:306–8, 308–9n, **11**:412–19, 419–20n, 478n. *See also* bunching machines

Cigarmakers, Federation of Cuban, **1**:457–58, *459n*
Cigarmakers, United, *1:46*–49, 50n, 55–57, 60, 63–64, 66–67, 73–74; benefits of, **1**:47, 55, 58, 62; constitution of, **1**:47, 61–66; dues of, **1**:61–62; ethnic sections of, **1**:55–57, 65; officers of, **1**:63–64; strike provisions of, **1**:64
Cigar Makers' Association of the Pacific Coast, **1**:126n
Cigar Makers' International Union of America, **1**:*, 50n, 442, **2**:*, 13, 14n, 20, 25, 65, 67, 118, 165, 361, **3**:*, 15, 18n, 68, 76–77, 106, **4**:*, 10, 12, 15n, 72–74, 95, 132–33n, 149–51, 341, 474, **5**:*, 88, 88n, 234, 240, **6**:*, 31n, **7**:*, 221n, 483, 500, 501n, **8**:*, 20n, 344, **9**:*, 75n, 209, 209n, 537, **10**:*, 243n, 261, 264, 346, 350n, **11**:*, 10, 17n, **12**:*, 132n, 323, 446n, 517; AFL financial support of, **5**:xiv, 251–52, 253n, 255–56, 256n; and AFL per capita tax, **9**:478–79, 479n; and American Labor Union, **6**:203, 395; benefit system of, **1**:71–72, 80, 103–4, 127–29, 134–39, 146–48, 156–58, 158n, 338–39, 341–42, **2**:144–46, 146n, **5**:240–41, **7**:365, 365n, **8**:419, 421, 422n; and black workers, **1**:48, **6**:293, 293n, **11**:84n; board of appeals of, **1**:128–29, 132, 144–46; and bunchmakers, **1**:46, 417, 423, **2**:73, **5**:434–35, **12**:305, 308n (*see also* cigarmakers: bunchmakers); classes of membership in, **8**:419, 422n; constitution of, amendments to, **1**:127–29, 129n, 132–33, **6**:385–86, 386n, 433–34, 434–35n; dues of, **1**:72, 80, 91, 104, 134, 136, 145, 148–49, 258, **8**:419, 421, 422n; and eight-hour day, **9**:121, 223; and equalization of funds of, **1**:72, 135, 149, 338; and FOTLU, **1**:159, 165, 245n, 275; and industrial unionism, **8**:396–97, 419–20, 505; initiative and referendum in, **8**:284; injunctions against, **3**:26, 26n, 148, 148n, **5**:240–43, 243–44n; journal, official, of, **1**:74n; and KOL, **1**:248–49, 365–66, 380–401, 404n, 405–11, 415–20, 435–39, 464–65, **2**:20–21,

24, 35, 207–8, 208n, **4:**151; label of,
1:293, *327n,* 370, 374, 388, 392–94,
398, 400–401, 409–10, 413–14,
417, 449, **2:**124, **5:**434, **6:**203, 395,
7:462, **8:**422n, **10:**261, 264; labor
bureau of, **1:**105, 135, 138, 146; and
labor party, **3:**403, 403–4n; and La
Kurba Cigar Co. arbitration case,
12:132, 133n; members of, *letters
to,* **1:**238–45, 369–71, **2:**129–30,
144–46; members of, life expec-
tancy of, **9:**402, 403n; and National
Civic Federation, **8:**227n, 421, 422n;
New York District of, **1:**236–37, 269,
269n, 270–71, 271n, 272, 272n, 413,
419; officers of, election of, **3:**248,
249n, **4:**77, 77n, 107, 108n, 114–15,
8:172, 173n, 417, 420–21; officers
of, salaries of, **2:**235; organization
of, **5:**124, 127; organizing campaign
of, **1:**269–72, 359; and packers,
1:419, 420n, **2:**73, **3:**379, **7:**307 (*see
also* cigarmakers: packers); and
Progressive Cigarmakers, **1:**359–60,
365–66, 368–69, 375–79, 381, 383,
416–20, 422–24; and Puerto Rican
joint advisory board, **8:**19–20, 21n;
reform of, **1:**48–49, 71–72, 80–81,
103–6, 127–29, 134–51, 156–58;
representation of, at AFL conventions, **5:**397–98, 398n; and rollers,
1:66, 417, **2:**73, **7:**307, **12:**305, 308n
(*see also* cigarmakers: rollers); shop
delegates of, **1:**47, 109; shop stewards of, **1:**47, 63–64, 79–80; sinking
fund of, **1:**150; and strikebreakers,
1:389, 412; strike fund of, **1:**72,
109, 113, 118, 127–29, 132–33,
146–47, 337–39, 419, **6:**30, 31n,
294n; and tobacco strippers' locals,
2:73, **7:**306–8, 308–9n, **11:**412–19,
419–20n, 478n; and United Cigarmakers, **1:**46–49, 55, 60, 66–67; vice-
presidency of, SG and, **4:**77, 77n,
107, 108n, 114–15, **6:**224
—constitutions: 1879, **1:**127–29,
132–33, 140–51, 156–57, **7:**307,
308n; 1881, **1:**157n, 256–57; 1885,
1:369–71
—conventions: 1870, **1:**46; 1875 (Paterson, N.J.), **1:**46, 67, *67n;* 1877

(Rochester, N.Y.), **1:**71, 103–6,
106n, **8:**417, **12:**308, *309n;* 1879
(Buffalo, N.Y.), **1:**71, 134, *134n,*
135–40; 1880 (Chicago), **1:**72,
139n, 156, *157n,* 327n, **7:***308n,*
12:*308n;* 1881 (Cleveland), **1:**239,
245n, 257n, **4:**150, **12:**305, *308n;*
1885 (Cincinnati), **1:**368–69, *369n,*
2:130, *130n;* 1887 (Binghamton,
N.Y.), **2:**129–30, 130n, **5:**407, *407n;*
1889 (New York City), **2:**146n; 1891
(Indianapolis), **3:**248, *249n,* 403,
404n; 1893 (Milwaukee), **3:**402,
402n, 403, 403–4n, **4:**152–53; 1896
(Detroit), **4:**179, *180n,* 194, 219,
236–39, 248–49, **6:**434, **8:**417;
1912 (Baltimore), **8:**396–97, *397n,*
417–22, **9:**403n; 1920 (Cleveland),
8:422n, **11:**416, **12:**305, *308n;* 1923
(Chicago), **12:**298, *299n,* 303–8,
308n, 312
—locals: local 2 (Buffalo, N.Y.),
1:139n; local 5 (Syracuse, N.Y.),
1:139n; local 6 (Syracuse, N.Y.),
1:139n, **2:**13n, 340; local 8 (Hobo-
ken, N.J.), **1:**237, 237n; local 10
(New York City), **1:**373–74, 374n,
383, 419; local 10 (Progressive Cigar Makers; New York City), **3:**379;
local 13 (New York City), **1:**379,
380n, 419, **3:**379, 382n; local 14
(Chicago), **1:**134, 139n, 462n,
4:159n; local 15 (New York City),
1:5, 46, 50n; local 16 (Binghamton,
N.Y.), **3:**26n, 148, 148n; local 20
(New York City), **1:**96, 120n, 133,
134n; local 22 (Detroit), **4:**177n;
local 25 (Milwaukee), **1:**297–99,
327n, **6:**433–34, 435n; local 27
(Toronto), **1:**140n; local 28 (West-
field, Mass.), **6:**433, 435n; local 32
(Louisville, Ky.), **2:**308, 314n; local
42 (Hartford, Conn.), **2:**130n; local 43 (Williamsburg, N.Y.), **1:**116n;
local 44 (St. Louis), **4:**340n; local
55 (Hamilton, Ont.), **1:**134, 139n;
local 65 (Lynn, Mass.), **4:**187, 189n;
local 68 (Albany, N.Y.), **1:**262, 263n,
7:308n; local 78 (Hornellsville,
N.Y.), **3:**273; local 87 (Brooklyn,
N.Y.), **1:**50n, 111, 112n, 113–14,

419; local 90 (New York City), **1**:46, 50n, 55, 56n; local 90 (Progressive Cigar Makers; New York City), **2**:371n, **3**:76–77, 77n, 379, **4**:72, 74, 150–51; local 97 (Boston), **2**:208, 208n, **7**:308n; local 97 (Williamsburg, N.Y.), **1**:50n, 116n; local 100 (Philadelphia), **1**:359n, **3**:234, 235n, **4**:75n, 115; local 122 (Warren, Pa.), **1**:139n; local 126 (Ephrata, Pa.), **3**:561n; local 129 (Denver), **5**:393, 395, 395n, **6**:203, 385–86; local 131 (Jersey City, N.J.), **1**:237, 237n; local 132 (Brooklyn, N.Y.), **1**:237, 237n, 419; local 141 (New York City), **1**:379, 380n, 419, **3**:76–77, 77n, **4**:219, 219n; local 144 (New York City; *see separate subentry below*); local 149 (Brooklyn, N.Y.), **1**:413, 414n, 419; local 151 (Havana), **7**:220, 221n; local 165 (Philadelphia), **1**:359n, **4**:75n; local 213 (New York City), **1**:379, 380n, 419; local 218 (Binghamton, N.Y.), **3**:26n, 148, 148n; local 219 (Mobile, Ala.), **6**:293, 293n; local 220 (New Orleans), **6**:30–31, 31n; local 228 (San Francisco), **3**:551; local 237 (Morrisania, N.Y.), **1**:413, 414n; local 251 (New York City), **1**:419, 420n, **3**:379; local 281 (St. Louis), **4**:340n; local 284 (Barnesville, Ohio), **2**:75, 76n; local 284 (Detroit), **4**:177n; local 293 (Fort Smith, Ark.), **8**:227n; local 293 (Philadelphia), **4**:75n; local 316 (McSherrytown, Pa.), **5**:127–28, 128n; local 336 (Tampa, Fla.), **8**:26n, **11**:571n; local 433 (Mobile, Ala.), **6**:293, 293n; local 462 (Tampa, Fla.), **11**:571n; local 464 (Tampa, Fla.), **11**:571n; local 474 (Tampa, Fla.), **11**:571n; local 500 (Tampa, Fla.), **11**:571n; local 507 (Boston), **11**:420n; local 518 (Manchester, N.H.), **11**:420n; local 520 (Manchester, N.H.), **11**:420n; local 527 (Chicago), **12**:132
—local 144 (New York City), **1**:56n, 76, 103, 132–33, 236–37, 373–74, 419, **2**:146, 146n, **3**:111, 115n, 379, **4**:10,

12, 15n, 179, 194, 474, 476n, 502, **5**:236n, 324, 324n, 372n, **6**:397n, **8**:333–34, 397n, 417, 422n, **12**:517; benefit system of, **1**:71, 122; British influence on, **1**:71; charter of, 1875, **1**:68; constitution of, **1**:80–81; cooperative shop of, **1**:116–18, 121–24; corruption in, **1**:69, 93, 93n; factionalism in, **1**:97, 247–60, 264–66; and KOL, **1**:383; and mergers, **1**:96, 120–21, 133–34; organizing campaign of, **1**:73–74, 77–79, 98–100; and *Picket,* **1**:392; and politics, **1**:97, 171, 247–48; and Progressive Cigarmakers, **1**:272–74, 357; SG and, **1**:46–47, 73, 79–80, 91–92, 120, 250–55
—strikes/lockouts, **1**:336–38, **4**:72–74; 1870 (New York City), **1**:49, *50n;* 1873 (New York City), **1**:66; 1874 (New York City), **1**:56–57; 1877 (New York City), *1:95–96,* 106–14, 116–21, 123, 207; 1881 (Milwaukee), **1**:297–99, *327n;* 1883 (Chicago), **3**:640; 1883 (New York City), **1**:357–58; 1885–86 (Syracuse, N.Y.), *2:13n,* 340; 1886 (Buffalo, N.Y.), **1**:411–12, *412n;* 1886 (New York City), *1:365–66,* 375–79, 382–84, 407–8, 422–24, 465, **2**:340–41; 1888 (Boston), **2**:208, *208n;* 1890 (Binghamton, N.Y.), **3**:26, *26n,* 148, **5**:241, *244n;* 1894 (Philadelphia), **4**:72–73, *75n;* 1895–96 (Detroit), **4**:176, *177n;* 1896–97 (St. Louis), **4**:340, *340n;* 1898 (New York City), **4**:474, *476n;* 1899 (Ottumwa, Iowa), **5**:128, *129n;* 1900–1901 (New York City), **5**:234, *236n,* 240–43, 243–44n, 251–52, 253n, 255–56, 256n; 1902 (New Orleans), **6**:30–31, *31n;* 1903–4 (Mobile, Ala.), **6**:293, *293n;* 1918 (Benton Harbor, Mich.), **12**:133n; 1920–21 (Tampa, Fla.), **11**:567, *571n*
Cigar Makers' Mutual Association of London, **1**:74, *75n*
Cigar Makers' National Union of America, **1**:*, **2**:*, **3**:*, **4**:*, **5**:*, **6**:*, **7**:*, **8**:*, **9**:*, **10**:*, **11**:*, **12**:*
—locals: local 5 (Syracuse, N.Y.), **1**:139n; local 15 (New York City), **1**:5

Cigar Makers' Official Journal (trade union journal), *1:74n*, 115n, 149–50, 169, **3:**483; editor of, *letters to,* **1:**73–74, 79–81, 120, 132–33, 156–58, 252–54, **4:**72–77

Cigarmakers of New York, Central Organization of, *1:95*–96, 110, 112–13, 116–17, 121, 124

Cigarmakers of North America, United, **1:**247–48, *274n*

Cigarmakers' Progressive Union of America, *1:247–49*, 272–74, 356–58, *365–66*, 368, 369n, 375–79, 402n, 407–8, 412, 462n, **9:**209, 209n; and Cigar Makers' International Union, **1:**359–60, 365–66, 368–69, 369n, 375–79, 381, 412, 415–20, 422–24; and KOL, **1:**415–20

—convention: 1885 (Philadelphia), **1:**368, *369n*

—strike/lockout: 1883 (New York City), **1:**357–58

Cigarmakers' Society of England, **1:**4

Cigarmakers' State Union, New York, **1:**46

Cigar Manufacturers' Association, **5:**236n, 241, 251

Cigar Manufacturers' Association, American, **1:**358n, 418, *418n*, 422

Cigar Manufacturers' Association, National, **1:**116, *117n*

Cigar Manufacturers' Association, New York, **1:**358n, 375–79

Cigar Manufacturers' Association, United, **1:**357, *358n*, 365–66, 381, 409n, 417, 418n, 421–22, 424n

Cigar Manufacturers' Association of Tampa, Fla., **11:**571n

cigars, "Spanish," **12:**304, 308n

Cincinnati Agreement, **6:**90n, 134, *135n*, 208, 226, 326–27n

Cincinnati Arbeiter-Zeitung (labor journal), **4:**176

Cincinnati Brewing Co., **4:**399–400, 400n, 401–4; boycott, 1897, **4:**402–4; boycott, 1898, **4:**404n

Cincinnati Building Trades Council, **12:**401n

Cincinnati Central Labor Council, *1:212n*, **4:**176, **5:**503n

Cincinnati Central Labor Union, **1:**212n

Cincinnati Industrial Workers' Club, **6:**447, 449n

Cincinnati Trades and Labor Assembly, **1:**211, *212n*

Cintron (striker), **6:**425

Circle Check System, **4:**261–63, *263–64n*

citizens' alliances: in Beloit, Wis., **7:**157; in Birmingham, Ala., **6:**192, 193n; in Boston, **7:**50, 50n; in Calumet, Mich., **9:**43; in Colorado, **6:**279–80, 344n; in Cripple Creek, Colo., **6:**283n; in Denver, **6:**234, 282n; in Grand Rapids, Mich., **6:**230; in Illinois, **7:**346, 347n; in Los Angeles, **6:**213n; in Racine, Wis., **7:**157; in Ramsay and Dakota Counties, Minn., **12:**283–85; in San Francisco, **6:**234, 234n, 386; in Telluride, Colo., **6:**282n; in Waco, Tex., **6:**194. *See also* Citizens' Industrial Association of America

Citizens' Committee to Enforce the Landis Award, **11:**496–97n, **12:**58, 60

citizenship, **10:**265, 266n, 449–50, **11:**562–63

Citizens' Industrial Association of America, *6:193n*, 353, 354n, 362, **7:**48–49, 49n, 118n, 155n, 191–92, 245, 346, 347n; and IWW, **6:**384, 522

Citizens' Protective League (Colorado), **6:**282n

Citizens' Railroad Co., strike/lockout, 1892, *3:154n*

Citizens' Railway Co., strike/lockout, 1903, **6:**193–94, *194n*

City of Rio de Janeiro (steamship), sinking of, **7:**4, *7n*

City Record (periodical), **1:**201

Civil War, American, **1:**4, 32, **4:**59, **10:**52, 200–201, 559

Clabaugh, Harry M., **7:**248, 249–*50n*, **8:**161, 164n

Clabaugh, Hinton, **10:**69–70n, 242, 243n, 297

Claessens, August, **11:**262n

Claflin, Roy C., *9:466n; letter to,* **9**:465–
66
Claherty, Coleman, **11**:284, *286n*
Clancey, Daniel, **1**:361, *362n*
Clapp, Moses E., **9**:152, *153n*
Clark, Annie, **3**:141
Clark, C. Peter, **8**:34, *35n*
Clark, Edgar E., **4**:*, 273, *275n*,
5:464n, **11**:*, 348, *349n*
Clark, Ephraim W., **3**:117–18, *119n*,
280, **4**:322, **6**:206, 207n
Clark, Frank, *11:116n; letter from,*
11:114–15
Clark, George, **1**:*, 165, *166n*
Clark, George W., **2**:*, 407, *409n*
Clark, James B. "Champ," **8**:257, *258n*,
9:48n, 65, 98n, 111, 112n, **10**:13–14,
14n; *letter to,* **11**:384
Clark, Josephine, **3**:141
Clark, Theresa, **3**:141
Clarke, Albert, **5**:144–45, *146n*
Clarke, Edgar E., **6**:14n
Clarke, James P., **9**:111, *112n*
Clarke, John H., **10**:144, *147n*
Clarksburg (W.Va.) Fuel Co.: strike/
lockout, 1902, **6**:84n; strike injunction, **6**:80–81, 84n
Clark's O. N. T. Cotton Thread Co.:
boycott, 1891, **3**:53, *56n;* strike/
lockout, 1890–91, *3:56n*
class: divisions, Hillmann and, **1**:27,
29, 34, 38, 41; divisions, SG and,
3:75, 143, 237–38, 249, 281–82,
388–92, **4**:26, 35–36, 39–40, 44,
366–68, 422–23; struggle, **2**:419,
4:32, **12**:181
Clay, Arthur H., *11:565n; letter from,*
11:564–65
Clay, Henry, **12**:191, *192n*
Clay, Henry, and Bock Co., strike/
lockout, 1907, **7**:220–21, *221n*
Clay, John, **12**:91n
Clay, W. H., **5**:439, *439n*, 462
Clayton, Henry D., **8**:257, *258–59n*,
317, 373, 380–81n, 425n, 445–46,
9:10n, 90–92, 106n, 141n; *letter to,*
9:96–97
Clemenceau, Georges, **10**:563, *567n*
Clemmons, Ralph, **10**:430, *432n*
Clerks' International Protective Asso-

ciation, Retail, **2**:*, **3**:*, **4**:*, **5**:*, **6**:*,
176n, 192, **9**:*, 72n, **12**:*
—locals: local 7 (Denver), **5**:393, 395,
395n; local 262 (Washington, D.C.),
5:198–99, 199n; local 330 (Seattle),
6:19n; local 361 (Palestine, Tex.),
11:189, 191n
Clerks' National Protective Association of America, Retail, **2**:*, 355–56,
356n, **3**:*, 89, 90n, 244–45, 245n,
4:*, 174n, 502, **5**:*, 19, 20n, **6**:*, **9**:*,
12:*
—conventions: 1898, **5**:20n; 1899
(Kansas City, Mo.), **5**:19, *20n*
Cleveland, Grover, **2**:127, *127n*,
132–33, **3**:200, 292, 342, 613, **4**:14,
40, 69, 284n, **5**:464n, 511, **6**:302,
9:201, **10**:166n; and *Jefferson Borden*
mutineers, **3**:120n, 280, 281n; *letter
to,* **3**:598; and Pullman strike, 1894,
3:521, 523, 539, 559, 579n, **7**:24,
25n; *wires to,* **3**:532–33, 565
Cleveland, trade unionism in, **4**:450,
451n
"Cleveland Agreement," *12:48n*
Cleveland Board of Education, **9**:137,
137–38n
Cleveland Central Labor Union,
1:166n, **3**:402, *403n,* **4**:177, 354–55,
449–51, 451n; meeting of, 1900,
5:267n
Cleveland Chamber of Commerce,
12:177
Cleveland Citizen (labor journal),
4:449–51, 451n, **5**:72, 73n; proposed as AFL journal, **3**:402, 403n
Cleveland Electric Railway Co., **7**:342n
Cleveland Federation of Labor, *9:137–*
38n, **11**:319n
Cleveland Grade Teachers' Club,
9:137n
Cleveland Industrial Council, **1**:166n
Cleveland Street Railway Co.: strike/
lockout, 1918, **11**:19, *21n;* and
women workers, **11**:18–19, 20–21n
Cleveland Trades and Labor Assembly, **1**:165, *166n,* **3**:403n
Clew, John, **3**:118, *119n*
Clifford, Patrick H., **4**:*, 255–56, 266,
268n

Cline, Isaac, **1:***, 215–16, *217n,* 219, 228

Clinton, DeWitt, **1:**446, *446n*

Cloak and Suit Cutters' Association, United, **3:**379

—strike/lockout: 1890 (New York City), **2:**192, 348–49, *349n*

Cloakmakers, Italian branch of (New York City), **3:**379

Cloakmakers, Joint Board of (New York City), **7:**470n

Cloakmakers, United Brotherhood of, **3:**355n

Cloak Makers and Custom Tailors:

—local: local 38 (Montreal), **6:**447, 449n

Cloakmakers' and Operators' Union, *2:371n,* **3:**379

—strike/lockout: 1890 (New York City), **2:**192, 348–49, *349n*

cloakmakers, New York City:

—strike/lockout: 1910, **8:**109–13, *114n,* 218, 219n, 229, 269, 450; injunction against, **8:**114n

Cloakmakers' Union, Chicago:

—strike/lockout: 1898, **5:**101, *102n*

Cloak Makers' Union of America, International, **5:***, 103n; jurisdiction of, **5:**102, 102n

closed shop, **3:**324–25, 484, **5:**236n, 270, 384–85n, **6:**18n, 327–30, 337–38, 366, 401, 423n, 442n, 514, 516–17n, **7:**154, 222, 302, 377, **8:**40n, 74, 111–12, 114n, 119, 144n, 167–68, 201, 420, 440n, 442n, 471n, 489, **9:**248, **10:**61, 119, 119n, 128–29, 155n, 176, 229–30, 232–34, 235n, 254n, 287n, 318–19n, 376, 408n, **11:**162, 327, 343, **12:**3–4, 174–76, 182, 216, 217n

Clothiers' Exchange (Rochester, N.Y.), strike/lockout, 1891, *3:300n*

Clothing Contractors' Protective Association, **4:**206–7n

clothing cutters, New York City, **2:**385, 385n

—strike/lockout: 1893, **3:**295, 295n, 296, *296–97n,* 297–300, 300–301n, 302, 304–40, 340n, 341

Clothing Cutters' and Trimmers' Union (Boston), **4:**190

Clothing Cutters' Association, United, *2:338n,* **3:**457

Clothing Cutters' Progressive Union, **2:**367

Clothing Cutters' Union of New York, Independent, **2:**36, *37n*

Clothing Makers' Union of America, Custom, *6:50n*

Clothing Makers' Union of America, Special Order, *6:50n;* jurisdiction of, **6:**49–50, 50n

Clothing Manufacturers' Association (New York City), **1:**467n, **2:**348, 349n, **3:**295–97n, 297–300, 302, **6:**297n; injunction, **3:**293, 295–96n, 297–300, 302; and mediation of clothing cutters' strike, 1893, **3:**305–40

Clothing Workers of America, Amalgamated, **9:***, 205n, **10:***, 46–47, 48n, 138, 139n, 150, **11:**351–52n, **12:***, 350, 350n, 388, 389n; AFL 1914 convention and, **9:**205n, 227, 228n; injunction against, **11:**458n; organization of, **9:**74n, 203, 205n, 227n, 386, 391, 393; and Tailors' Industrial Union, **9:**236, 236n, 260, 261n

—strikes/lockouts: 1915 (Chicago), **9:**354, *355–56n,* 356–57, 370–71, 371n, 386–87, 391; 1917 (New York City), *10:336n;* 1918 (New York City), **10:**335, *336n*

Clough, Arthur H., *10:567n*

Cloutier, Emile, **9:**15n, 443n, 460n

Clover Leaf Railroad, **9:**516

Clowry, Robert C., **10:**515, *515n*

Cluett, Peabody, and Co.: boycott, 1905–6, **6:**484n; strike/lockout, 1905–6, *6:483–84n,* 492

Clyde Steamship Co. v. Walker, **10:**144, *147n*

Coach and Cab Drivers, Liberty Dawn Association of, *4:110n*

Coal Creek (Tenn.) mines, **3:**215n

Coal Wheelers' Union (New Orleans), indictment of members of, **8:**177, 182n, **9:**82

Coates, David C., **5:***, 90, *93n,* 115, **6:***, 18n, 191–92, *192n,* 467, **10:***, 388, *389–*90n; and IWW, found-

ing of, **6:**452, 455–65; *letter from,* **10:**418–19

Coates, Sarah Pearce, **10:**419n

Cochran, Negley Dakin, **8:**474, 474n

Cochrane, Aaron Van Schaick, **5:**327n, **8:**332n

Cochrane, Arthur D., **2:**212n

Cochren, Alexander, **7:**76, *90n*

Cockran, William Bourke, **9:**517, *518n*

Coefield, John, **12:***, 73, 73n, 225n, 550, *553n*

Coffey, Frank M., **9:***, *200n; letter to,* **9:**198–200

Coffin, Howard E., **10:**21n, *38n;* meeting with AFL Executive Council, **10:**23–31

Coffin, Josephine, *11:507n; letter from,* **11:**505–6

Coffin, L. S., **3:**553n

Cogan, William P., *3:199n, 5:99n; letter from,* **3:**199; *letter to,* **5:**99

Cohen, Fanny (Femmetje) Gompers, **1:***, 8, *8n,* 14, **3:***, 140, *142n,* **7:***, 499, 501n

Cohen, Henry L., **3:**656–57, *661n,* 662, *6:354n; letter from,* **6:**353–54

Cohen, J. H., **1:**10

Cohen, Jacob, **3:**140, *141n*

Cohen, Julius H., *8:440n; letter from,* **8:**439–40

Cohen, Simon, **3:**140, *142n*

Cohen, Simon A., **6:**277, *278n*

Cohen, William, **6:**374, *376n*

Cohn, Fannia M., *11:500n,* **12:**388, 389n; *letters from,* **11:**499–500, 533n, **12:**156–57, 360–61, 447–49

Cohnfeld's, wage reduction at, **2:**155, *155n*

Coit, Stanton, **3:**457, *458n*

Colbert, John, **12:**526, *526n,* 534

Colby, Bainbridge, **11:**300, *300n*

Colby, Josephine, **11:**395, *396n*

Cole, Harry, **2:**258

Cole, Martin, **8:**292n

Cole, Ralph D., **11:**375, *376n*

Cole, Raymond C., *11:376n*

Coleman, Griffin B., **5:**263, 263n

Coleman, John, **5:**286, 287n, **6:**169n

Coler, Bird S., **12:**550, *553n*

Coles, Richard T., *3:63n; letter to,* **3:**62–63

Collar and Shirt Manufacturers' Association (Troy, N.Y.): strike/lockout, 1886, **1:**466, 467n; strike/lockout, 1905–6, *6:483–84n*

Collar Starchers' Union:
—local: local 1 (Troy, N.Y.), **6:**483–84n, 492
—strike/lockout: 1905–6 (Troy, N.Y.), *6:483–84n,* 492

collective bargaining, **3:**303–4, **4:**472, **5:**505–10, **6:**82, 95–96, 125, 338–39, 417–23, 542–43, **7:**261, **8:**488, 490, **9:**55, 59, 85, 120, **10:**136, 184, 277, 408n, 461, 486, 490n, **11:**7n, 158, 167–82, 186, 230, 235, 242, 287–88, 327, 310, 386, 421–22, 424, 426n, 509, 536–39, **12:**3, 6, 173, 177, 216, 561. *See also* arbitration; conciliation; mediation of industrial disputes; strikes and lockouts

collective ownership of means of production and distribution. *See* government ownership: of means of production and distribution

College Settlement, **3:**160, *160n*

Colleran, Michael, **12:**81n

Collins, F. A., **10:**158n

Collins, J. J., **4:**20

Collins, James A., **8:**273, *277n,* 350

Collins, John M., **11:**264, *265n*

Collins, Patrick A., **5:**497n

Collins, Peter W., **7:***, 226, *227n,* 482n

Collins, S., **4:**57

Collins, William, **12:**339–40n

Colombia, and Pan-American Federation of Labor, **9:**466n

Colonel Sellers (Twain), *8:497n*

Colopovert, Joseph, **1:**111

Colorado, Industrial Commission of, **9:**456–57, 457n

Colorado: organizing in, **6:**15–17, 203; workday in, **6:**279, 281, 282–83n

Colorado Board of Arbitration, **5:**115n

Colorado Fuel and Iron Co., **9:**283n, 328–29, 329n; strike/lockout, 1913–14, **9:**23, *24n,* 210–11, 211n, 242, 301, 399, 400n. *See also* Ludlow, Colo., massacre

Colorado Industrial Plan, **9:**328–29, *329n*

Colorado miners' strike, 1913–14, **9:**23, *24n,* 210–11, 211n, 242, 301, 399, 400n (*see also* Ludlow, Colo., massacre); congressional investigation of, **9:**23, 24–25n, *48n,* 51–52, 52n, 96n, 97, 98n, 301, 302n

Colorado Springs (Colo.) Federated Trades Council, **6:**15, *17n*

Colorado State Federation of Labor, **5:**89, *92n,* 115n, **6:**18–19n, 87n

—conventions: 1899 (Denver), **5:**89, 91, *92n;* 1902 (Trinidad, Colo.), **6:**16–17, *19n*

Colored Helpers and Laborers, Executive Board of the Southeastern Railroads of, **10:**371–72, 372n

Colton, George R., **8:**88, *89n*

Columbian Exposition, World's, 1893 (Chicago), *2:233n,* 345, *346n,* **3:**86, 151–53, 356, 358, 359n, 365, 433, 495, 630; Board of Directors of (Directory), **3:**151–52, *153n,* 349, 358, 359n; Board of Lady Managers of, **3:**91; eight-hour workday at, **3:**151–53, 162; exhibition of women's and children's work at, **3:**91–92, 92n; French workers' delegation to, **3:**397–99, *399n,* 400–401; and nonunion labor, **3:**151–52; Sunday closing of, **3:**162, *163n*

Columbia River Fishermen's Protective Union, **6:**5n

Columbus, Hocking Valley, and Toledo Railroad, strike/lockout, 1894, **4:**4–5

Columbus (Ohio) Federation of Labor, *7:152n*

Columbus (Ohio) Trades and Labor Assembly, **1:**455n, **4:**5, 81, *82n,* **7:**152–53n

Comerford, Matthew, **7:***, 33, 35, *36n,* **9:**305n; *letter to,* **7:**218

Comintern. *See* Third (Communist) International (Comintern)

Commercial Acid Co., **10:**152n

commissary stores, **4:**27, 440–41

Commissioner of Corporations, **8:**361

Commission on International Labor Legislation, **11:**40, *41n; report of,* **11:**69, 70n, 99–102, 102n; SG and, **11:**40, 40–41n, 47–48, 53, 56–58

Commission Syndicale de Belgique, *11:57n*

Committee of Forty-Eight, *12:99n*

Committee of One Thousand on National Defense, **9:**358–59, 359n

Committee on Elimination of Waste in Industry. *See* Federated American Engineering Societies

Committee on Industrial Relations, **9:**420–21, *422n,* 464, 464n, **10:**106

Committee on Industrial Relations to Secure Appointment of Federal Commission on Industrial Relations, **8:**329, *331n,* 455–56, 456n. *See also* U.S. Commission on Industrial Relations

Committee on Public Information, *10:156n,* 403, 498; and American Alliance for Labor and Democracy, **10:**160–61n, 161–62, 313n, 382–83, 495–96, 496–97n, 499n

common carriers, government ownership of. *See* government ownership: of common carriers

Commons, John R., **3:***, *502n,* **6:***, 478, *480n,* **9:**172, 312n, **12:**17, 19; *letter to,* **3:**501–2

Commonweal of Christ, **3:**514–15, *515n*

Commonwealth Boot and Shoe Factory, strike/lockout, 1889, **2:**208, 209n

communications systems, public ownership of. *See* government ownership: of communications system; government ownership: of telegraph system; government ownership: of telephone system

communism: in Canadian labor movement, **12:**438; and trade unionists, **1:**110, 111, 209, 214, 262, 345–47; in United States, **12:**12, 172–73, 276, 366, 494n; in United States, accusations of, **12:**219–20, 224–27, 227n, 235, 253, 257–58, 263–64, 267, 271n, 272–73, 284, 294–95, 296n, 309–11, 327–29, 330n, 333, 337–38, 391, 403, 431–32, 438, 447, 452, 490–91 (*see also* "Bolshevism" in United States: accusations of)

Communist Manifesto (Marx and Engels), **1:**21, **12:**399

Communist Party of America, **11**:550n
—meeting at Bridgman, Mich., 1922, **12**:132, 132n, 338, 338n; raid on, **12**:131–32, *132n*
Communist Party of the U.S. of America, **11**:550n
Communist Youth League of the U.S. of America, **12**:277n
company benefits system, **6**:138, **8**:102–3, 103n, 157
company stores, **3**:56n, 521, 527, **4**:358, 376n, 440–41, **5**:263n, 273, **6**:151n, 247, **9**:87, 222, 307n, **11**:297n, **12**:280
company unions, **11**:173–74, 179, **12**:23n, 106n, 109, 115, 442n
Compton, Elias, **8**:257, *259n*
Compton, John L., **5**:394, *396n*, **6**:85, *87n*
Conant, Ernest L., **5**:186, *188n*
Conant, Luther, Jr., *11:334n; letter to,* **11**:333–34
Conard, Harry J., *10:365n; letter from,* **10**:365
Conboy, Sara A., **8**:*, 215, *216n*, **10**:*, *468n*, **11**:*, 97, *97n*, 128n, 240n, 275n, 460, 532n, **12**:*, 38n, 143, *146n;* at AFL conventions, **10**:467, 468n, **12**:97n; and AFL Women's Department, **12**:404, 406–7, 408n, 418n; *letter from,* **12**:417–18
Conboy, Thomas J., **11**:206, *206n; letter from,* **12**:125–26
conciliation, **3**:303–4, **4**:28, 38, 165–66, 472, **5**:295–99, 306, 310–11, 354, 505–8, 513, **6**:542, **9**:55, 457n, **12**:6. *See also* arbitration; mediation of industrial disputes
Concord Labor Club, **1**:140–41, 360, *361n*
Condition of the Working Class in England in 1844, The (Engels), **2**:149, *150n*, 156
Condition of Women Workers under the Present Industrial System, The (Van Etten), **2**:415–16, *417n*
Condon, Stephen J., *10:434n; letter to,* **10**:432–33
Confederación Regional Obrera Mexicana, **9**:305–7, 326–27, 436, 465, **10**:545, **11**:140n, **12**:319n,

392n, 533n, 536–37; SG, meeting with representatives of, **12**:356–58, 359–60n
—convention: 1924 (Ciudad Juárez), **12**:515, *515n*, 520n, 524, 534
Confédération canadienne et catholique du travail, **12**:438, *442n*
Confédération Générale du Travail, **7**:479, *479n*, **8**:186, **9**:238, 292n, **10**:540, 541n, 550–51, **11**:11, 440n; meetings with AFL peace delegation, **11**:39–40, 40–41n, 55, 57n, 140n
Confederation of Industrial Organizations:
—conference: 1892 (St. Louis), **3**:262, *263n*
Confederation of Swedish Labor Unions. *See* Svenska Landsorganisationen
Confederazione Generale del Lavoro, **10**:551, *555n*
Conference Board of Physicians in Industry:
—meeting: 1924 (New York City), **12**:419, 421n, 424, 424n
Conference for Progressive Political Action, **12**:433n, *467n;* and election of 1924, **12**:409, 409–10n, 432, 463–66, 467–68n, 469, 471, 472n, 473, 475n, 478, 480n, 481, 490; National Committee of, **12**:469, 474, 475n
—conventions: 1922 (Chicago), **12**:*467n;* 1924 (Cleveland), **12**:409–10n, 463–66, *467–68n*, 469; 1925, **12**:468n
Congregational Association of Ohio:
—meeting: 1894 (Cincinnati), **3**:506, *507n*
Congress of Negation, A (SG), **11**:336, *338n*
Congress on Industrial Conciliation and Arbitration, 1894 (Chicago), **3**:552, *553n*, 561, 589–90, 599–606
Conklin, Edward J., **2**:332, *337n*
Conklin, Mr. (of New York City), *letter to,* **2**:359
Conkling (labor inspector), **2**:343
Conlon, Peter J., **7**:355n, **8**:35n, 43, **12**:103–4, *106n*, 202–3; *letter from,* **8**:33–35

Conn, C. G., *4:286n*

Connecticut: election of 1906, **7:**112; and labor standards, maintenance of, **10:**76, 77n

Connecticut State Branch, AFL, **2:**25, *26n*, 140

Connellsville (Pa.) Central Trades and Labor Council, *7:181n*

Connelly, John F., **7:**185, *186n*

Conner, James P., **7:**28–30, *32n*

Connolly, Clarence P., *3:205n; letter to,* **3:**205

Connolly, James, **2:**288–89, *289n*, **3:**156, 156n

Connolly, John J., **12:**550, *553n*

Connolly, Patrick H., **6:**177, *177–78n*

Connolly, Thomas F., **4:***, 433, *435n*, 448, 449n

Connor, Washington E., **4:**351, *351n*

Connors, James B., **9:**212, *213n*

Connors, John, **11:**365n

Conrad, Jacob, **4:**401, *404n*

Conried, Heinrich, **6:**516–17, *517n*

Conroy, James B., **6:**367, *369n*, 502, 504n, **8:**413, *414n*

Conroy, James J., **11:**496, *497n*

Conry, Michael F., *8:85n; letter to,* **8:**82–85

conscription, **10:**62, 93, 93n; AFL and, **10:**30, 35–36, 42–43, 63, 265, 266n, **11:**292, 294, 301, **12:**454; provisions for, **10:**29–30, 64n; SG and, **10:**36–38, 272–73, **11:**292, 294, 294n; Sims and, **10:**216, 219n; and strikes, **10:**337–39, **11:**292; Wells and, **10:**397–98, 400n

conservation conferences: May 1908 (Washington, D.C.), **7:**322, *322n;* Dec. 1908 (Washington, D.C.), **7:**322n

Consolidated Coal Co., **5:**219n; injunction, **5:**219n

Consolidated Traction Co., **6:**13n

conspiracies: labor organizations as, **8:**65–66, 114n, 182n, 265, 462–63, 465–66, 481–83, 485, **9:**294–95; opposition to laws prohibiting, **1:**212–13, 218, 226, **2:**151, **3:**126, 130, **6:**353, 526n. *See also under* court cases; legislation, foreign; legislation, states and territories

Consten, Hermann, **9:**192, 194n

construction workers, Chicago, lockout, 1900–1901, **5:**214–15, *215–16n*, 233

consuls, U.S., and importation of labor, **1:**298–300

Consumers' League, National, **2:**155n

Continental Can Co., **10:**99

Continental Paper Bag Co., strike/lockout, 1906, **7:**104, *105n*

Continental Tobacco Co., **5:**117; boycott, 1899-?, *5:119n*

Continental Wall Paper Co., **8:**163

Continental Wall Paper Co. v. Louis Voight and Sons Co., **8:**163, *165n*

Contracting Carpenters' Association (Schenectady, N.Y.), **6:**176n, 179, 179n

contract labor, **1:**26, 218–19, 225–26, 287–88, **5:**29, 62, 326, **6:**478, **7:**91n, 93n, 155, 156n, 186n, 195–96, 197n, **8:**316, 316n, 429–30, 430n, **9:**101, **10:**165, 555n, **11:**338–41, 341n; in Hawaii, **4:**488, **5:**23–24, 29n, 44, **6:**195, **7:**332–33, **11:**483, 484n, 503

Contractors' and Material Men's Association (Denver), boycott, 1902, *6:18n*

Contractors' Union, New York City:
—strike/lockout: 1890, **2:**192, 348–49, *349n*

contributory negligence, **8:**32, 181, **9:**7, **12:**4

convict labor: Hillmann and, **1:**37, 40; opposition to, **1:**213, 215, 218, 225, 361, **9:**118, **11:**70n, 312, **12:**454; in Tennessee, **3:**185, 215n, 220, 252, **4:**40. *See also under* legislation, states and territories; legislation, U.S.

Conway, Frank, **6:**32–33, 33n

Conway, Henry J., **9:***, 69, *72n*

Conway, Mary, **11:**415, *420n*

Coogan, James J., **11:**10, *17n*

Cook, Henry W., **7:**339–40, *340n*

Cook, John H., **2:**374, *375n*

Cook, William, **5:**321, *322n*

Cook and Bernheimer, *4:218n*

Cooke, Morris, **12:**348n, 425, 426n

cooks, organization of, **6:**390–92

Coolidge, Calvin, **10:**243n, **11:**146, *146–47n*, 498n, **12:**299n, 372, 373n,

379, 380n, 416n; bust of, **12:**533n;
and election of 1924, **12:**463, 467n,
484–85, 492, 500, 508–10, 513n; SG,
meeting with, **12:**296–98, 298–99n
Coolidge, Louis, **10:**221n
Coombs, Frank, **5:**457, 458n
Cooney, Neil, **10:**489, *490n*
Cooney, William J. T., **2:**66, *68n*
Coonley, Howard, **10:**453n
Cooper, Ben, **3:**516, *517n*
Cooper, Edward, **2:**244, *245n*
Cooper, Henry A., *7:21n; letter to,*
7:20–21
Cooper, Jerry, **7:**444, 445n
Cooper, Peter, **1:**189, *192n,* **3:**380
Cooper, Wade, **9:**106n
Cooper Union, **1:**5, *192n*
Co-operative Clothing Co., *letter to,*
5:155
Cooperative Commonwealth, **4:**323,
324n, 341, *342n,* 360, **9:**245. *See also*
Social Democracy of America
Cooperative League, **7:**462n
Co-operative Packing Co., **4:**342
cooperatives, **1:**44n, 215–16, **11:**214n,
233, 238n, 335, 338n; and cigarmakers, **1:**116–18, 121–24; Hillmann
and, **1:**31, 35, 37, 42
Co-operative Union (of Great Britain), *7:490n,* **9:**238, *240n*
Coopers' International Union of
North America, **3:***, 470n, **4:***,
223n, **5:***, 84n, **11:***, 28n, 85n,
153n; jurisdiction of, **4:**329–30,
5:219–20, 221n, 257–60, 260n, 290,
292n, 503, 503–4n; and mechanization, **5:**83, 106–7, 107n, 108–9, 110n
—locals: local 7 (Albany, N.Y.), **4:**222–
23, 223n; local 30 (Milwaukee),
5:106–7, 107n; local 89 (Boston),
4:330, 330n; local 93 (Buffalo,
N.Y.), **5:**221n; local 94 (Chicago),
4:329–30, 330n
—strike/lockout: 1899 (Milwaukee),
5:106–7, *107n,* 151
Copeland, Royal, *12:170n*
Copeland, T. V., **6:**308n
Copely, DeWitt C., **6:**364, *365n*
Copperheads, **10:**160, *161n*
Cordell, William W., **9:**480, *480n*
Cordray, John F., **3:**55, *56n*

Coremakers' International Union of
America, **5:***, 285, 287n
Corey, William E., **4:**492, *500n,* **5:**387,
388n, 478–80
Corman, Alexander B., Sr., **5:**402–3,
404n
Cornelius, Richard, **6:**270, 271n
Corn Products Refining Co., antitrust
case against, **10:**322, 323n
*Corns v. Pattern Makers' Association of
Toledo,* **12:**302, *303n*
Cornwell, John J., **11:**295, *297n*
Coronado case, *10:323n,* **11:**174, 492,
494n, **12:**153, 227, 509. *See also
Coronado Coal Co. et al. v. United
Mine Workers of America et al.; Finley v.
United Mine Workers of America et al.;
United Mine Workers of America et al.
v. Coronado Coal Co. et al.*
Coronado Coal Co., **10:**323n
*Coronado Coal Co. et al. v. United Mine
Workers of America et al.,* *10:323n*
Coronado mine (Leadville, Colo.),
4:254
Corper, Joseph, **3:**141, *142n*
Corper, Sarah, **3:**141, 142n
Corporation Ouvrière Catholique des
Trois-Rivières, **9:**14, *15n*
Corporations Auxiliary Co., **7:**405–6,
406n
Corporation Tax Cases, **8:**484, *492n*
*Correspondence between Baker and Gom-
pers* (AFL), *12:183n*
Correspondenzblatt (German labor jour-
nal), *3:85n,* 86, 87n
Corrigan, W. J., **9:**267n
Cortelyou, George B., **5:**423, 425,
425n; letter to, **6:**195
Cosgrove, Joseph T., *4:314n; letter to,*
4:314
Costa Rica, **10:**11; and Pan-American
Federation of Labor, **9:**466n
Costello, John, **2:***, 332, *337n,* 343
Costello, P., **4:**118n
Costello, Patrick J., **5:**196, 198n
Costello, Thomas M., **7:**185, *186n*
Costello, Tony, **9:**62n; *letter to,* **9:**61
Costello, William F., **7:***, *158n; letter to,*
7:156–58
Coster, Benjamin, **3:**141, *142n*
Coster, Mrs. Benjamin, **3:**141

cost of living, **9:**525, 525–26n, 527, 529n, **10:**110–12, 117, 259, **11:**233, 388, 443, **12:**424
cost-plus system, **12:**424
Cotharin, William P., **12:**9, *10n*
Cotter, J. J., **11:**158, *160n*
Cotton Garment Manufacturers of New York, **8:**442n
Cotton Manufacturers Association, **10:**51
Cotton Yard Men's Benevolent Association, **5:**261, 262n
Coughlin, John E., **1:***, 165, *165n,* **3:***, 492–96, *497n*
Coughlin, John P., *9:63n,* **11:**457, 457n, **12:**504; *letter from,* **9:**62–63
Coughlin, William H., **1:**361, *363n*
Coulter, Clarence C., **12:***, 245, 247, *247n*
Counahan, Michael J., **4:***, 346, *347n,* 359n
Council of National Defense, **10:**18, *20–21n,* 87, 112, 115–17, 305, **11:**4–5; and AFL, **10:**464; and board of labor adjustment, **10:**74–75, 75n, 80; creation of, **9:**378, 435, 442n, **10:**20n, 96; and labor standards, **10:**54–56, 56–57n, 57–58, 58n, 59–60, 60n, 65–67, 76, 77n, 85, 91, 95, 98–102, 123, 174, 193n, 282–83, 285n, 458; *letter to,* **10:**121–22; and President's Mediation Commission, **10:**189n, 194, 205; SG appointment to Advisory Committee of, **9:**435, 511, 512n; and timber workers, **10:**184; and vocational training, **10:**277; and War Industries Board, **10:**412n; and war labor program, **10:**334n; and women workers, **10:**57n, 96–98
—Advisory Commission, *10:20–21n,* 31, 94–95, 112–13, 115–18, 121, 140, **11:**4, 348, **12:**412; and board of labor adjustment, **10:**75n; creation of, **10:**96; and labor standards, **10:**56n, 65, 76, 95; and President's Mediation Commission, **10:**194; SG appointment to, **10:**18, 96
—Committee on Labor, *10:21n,* 23n, 94–96, 407; Executive Committee of, **10:**52n, 54–56, 56n, 65, 97; fund-
raising efforts of, **10:**157–58, 159n; and labor standards, **10:**76, **11:**35; *letter to,* **11:**34–36; meeting with Wilson, **10:**101, 102n, 204, 282; organization of, **10:**50–52, 52n, 54, 73, 139–41; wartime accomplishments of, **11:**34–36; and women workers, **10:**57n, 81, 82n, 96–98, 98n, 108, 108–9n
—Committee on Women's Defense Work, **10:**97–98, 98n
—subcommittee on Cost of Living and Domestic Economy, **10:**94
—subcommittee on Welfare Work, **10:**158, **11:**35
—subcommittee on Women in Industry, **10:**82n, 96–98, 98n, 108, 108–9n, **11:**35–36
counsel, labor's right to, **3:**395, 602–3, **6:**96–97
court cases:
—*Adkins et al.* v. *Children's Hospital of D.C.,* **12:**227, *228n,* 230, 244, 246, 248–50, 370
—*Amalgamated Association of Street and Electric Railway Employes of America, Local Union No. 497* v. *Joplin and Pittsburg Railway Co.,* **11:**408, *409n*
—*American Lithographic Co.* v. *Castro,* **12:**302, *303n*
—*American Steel Foundries* v. *Tri-City Central Trades Council et al.,* **10:**252, *253n,* **12:**93n, 302
—*American Tobacco Co.* v. *U.S.,* **8:**153, *154n*
—*Arago* case. *See* court cases: *Robertson* v. *Baldwin*
—*A. R. Barnes and Co. et al.* v. *Chicago Typographical Union No. 16,* *7:12n*
—*Atchison, Topeka, and Santa Fe Railroad Co.,* v. *Matthews,* **8:**479, *492n*
—*Atchison, Topeka, and Santa Fé Railway Co.* v. *Gee et al.,* *11:458n*
—*Attorney General ex rel. Prendergast et al.* v. *Bedard et al.,* *8:502n*
—*Bailey* v. *Drexel Furniture Co.,* *10:499n, 11:514n,* **12:**82n, 84–85, 93n, 227, 230, 250
—*Bailey* v. *George,* *11:514n*
—*Baltic Mining Co. et al.* v. *Houghton Circuit Judge,* *9:13n*

—*Barbier* v. *Connolly*, **8:**479, *492n*

—*Bedford Cut Stone Co. et al.* v. *Journeymen Stone Cutters' Association of North America et al.*, **12:**398n

—*Berger et al.* v. *U.S.*, **11:**249n

—Buck's Stove and Range Co. cases. *See* Buck's Stove and Range Co. cases: contempt case; Buck's Stove and Range Co. cases: injunction case

—*Buck's Stove and Range Co.* v. *American Federation of Labor et al.*, **7:**247–49, *249–50n*, 356–57. *See also* Buck's Stove and Range Co. cases: injunction case

—*Central Loan and Trust Co.* v. *Campbell Commission Co.*, **8:**479, *492n*

—*Chas. Wolff Packing Co.* v. *The Court of Industrial Relations of the State of Kansas*, **11:**280n

—*Chicago American* contempt case, **5:**415, *415n*

—*Children's Hospital of D.C.* v. *Adkins et al.*, **12:**228n

—*Chinese Summary Trial*, **8:**479

—*Clyde Steamship Co.* v. *Walker*, **10:**144, *147n*

—*Continental Wall Paper Co.* v. *Louis Voight and Sons Co.*, **8:**163, *165n*

—*Corns* v. *Pattern Makers' Association of Toledo*, **12:**302, *303n*

—Coronado case, *10:323n*, **11:**174, 492, 494n, **12:**153, 227, 509. *See also* court cases: *Coronado Coal Co. et al.* v. *United Mine Workers of America et al.*, *Finley* v. *United Mine Workers of America et al.*, *United Mine Workers of America et al.* v. *Coronado Coal Co. et al.*

—*Coronado Coal Co. et al.* v. *United Mine Workers of America et al.*, *10:323n*

—*Corporation Tax Cases*, **8:**484, *492n*

—*Crane* v. *Campbell*, **10:**291n

—*C. W. Post* v. *American Federation of Labor et al.*, **8:**130, *131n*, 133, 149

—*C. W. Post* v. *Buck's Stove and Range Co. et al.*, **8:**130, *131n*, 133, 265

—Debs contempt case, **3:**524, 531–32n, 561n, *563n*

—*Debs* v. *U.S.*, *10:529n*

—*Dominick Connors* v. *Patrick Connolly et al.*, **8:**490, *493n*

—*Dorchy* v. *State of Kansas*, *11:280n*

—*Drake* v. *Perry*, **12:**302, *303n*

—*Dred Scott* v. *Sandford*, **6:**331–32, *340n*, **8:**74

—*Drexel Furniture Co.* v. *Bailey*, *11:514n*

—*Duplex Printing Press Co.* v. *Deering et al.*, **11:**406, *408n*, **12:**93n

—*Employers' Liability Cases*, **10:**145, *147n*

—*Erie Railroad Co.* v. *Winfield*, **10:**144, *147n*

—*Ex parte Sing Lee*, **8:**479, *492n*

—*Finley* v. *United Mine Workers of America et al.*, *10:323n*

—*Flint* v. *Stone Tracy and Co. See* court cases: *Corporation Tax Cases*

—*George J. Grant Construction Co.* v. *St. Paul Building Trades Council et al.*, **10:**252, *253–54n*

—*George* v. *Bailey*, **11:**512–14, *514n*

—*Gill Engraving Co.* v. *William Doerr et al.*, **9:**74–75n

—*Gompers* v. *U.S.*, **7:**250n. *See also* Buck's Stove and Range Co. cases: contempt case

—*Gray et al.* v. *Building Trades Council et al.*, **12:**303, *303n*

—*Greenfield* v. *Central Labor Council*, **12:**302, *303n*

—*Guaranty Trust and Safe Deposit Co.* v. *Mahon et al.*, **9:**208n

—*Gulf, Colorado, and Santa Fé Railway Co.* v. *Ellis*, **8:**479–80, *492n*

—*Hammer* v. *Dagenhart*, *10:499n*, **11:**15

—*Hammond Lumber Co.* v. *Sailors' Union of the Pacific et al.*, **7:**118n

—Hatters case. *See Loewe* v. *Lawlor*

—*Hawkins* v. *Bleakly*, **10:**143, *147n*

—Hitchman case. *See* court cases: *Hitchman Coal and Coke Co.* v. *Mitchell et al.*, *Mitchell et al.* v. *Hitchman Coal and Coke Co.*

—*Hitchman Coal and Coke Co.* v. *Mitchell et al.*, **10:**285–86, *287n*, 351–52, 372–73, **12:**23, 93n

—*Holden* v. *Hardy*, **4:**452, *453n*, 492, **5:**114, *115n*

—*Honomu Sugar Co.* v. *A. Sayewiz*, **5:**24, 29n

—*Honomu Sugar Co.* v. *Nikoleg Gzeluch*, **5:**24, 29n

—*Ice Delivery Company of Spokane* v. *Local No. 690 of Teamsters*, **12:**302, *303n*
—*Ingles et al.* v. *Morrison et al.*, **11:**280, *281n*
—*In re Frederick*, **9:***138n*
—*In re Morgan*, **5:**114, *115n*
—*In re Samuel Gompers, John Mitchell, and Frank Morrison*, **7:***250n*. See also Buck's Stove and Range Co. cases: contempt case
—*International Harvester Co. of America* v. *State of Missouri*, **9:**294, *296n*
—*Ives* v. *South Buffalo Railway Co.*, **8:***327n*, **9:**76n
—*Jaeckel et al.* v. *Kaufman et al.*, **12:**302, *303n*
—*James J. Reid et al.* v. *Frank J. McNulty et al.*, **9:**70, *73n*
—*J. M. H. Frederick* v. *John G. Owens*, **9:***138n*
—*John A. Kealey et al.* v. *A. L. Faulkner et al.*, **9:***83n*
—*John Bogni et al.* v. *Giovanni Perotti et al.*, **9:**454–55, *455n*, 520–21
—*John G. Owens* v. *Board of Education of Cleveland*, **9:***138n*
—*Kentucky Railroad Tax Cases*, **8:**479, *492n*
—*Kerbs et al.* v. *Rosenstein et al.*, **5:***244n*
—*Keuffel and Esser* v. *International Association of Machinists*, **12:**302, *303n*
—*Knickerbocker Ice Co.* v. *Stewart*, **11:**335, *338n*
—*Levy et al.* v. *Rosenstein et al.*, **5:***244n*
—*Lochner* v. *New York*, **6:***394n*, 420–21, **9:**243
—*Loewe* v. *Lawlor*, **6:**177, *177–78n*, 328, 440–42, **7:**304n, 310–11, 311–12n, 312–13, 319, 338, **8:**40, 42, 70, 74, 75n, 402–6, 406n, 463, 466, 488–90, **9:**150, *233n*, 294, 319; AFL assessment for appeal of decision, **8:**76n, 78, 86; AFL donation to Hatters, **9:**233n; appeal of decision, **8:**41, 76n, 77–78, 79n, 193–94, 194n, 203, 204n, 265, 402–6, 406n; and Sherman Antitrust Act, **6:**178n, **7:**320n, 323–25, 329–32, 346, 351, 372n, 389, 392, 409–10, 420, **8:**41, 42n, 62–68, **9:**248–50

—*Louis Bossert et al.* v. *Frederick Dhuy et al.*, **10:**253, *254n*
—*Louis Geib et al.* v. *The International Brotherhood of Electrical Workers et al.*, **9:**70, *73n*
—*Mack* v. *Wright et al.*, **8:**190–91, *191n*
—*Mahon et al.* v. *Guaranty Trust and Safe Deposit Co.*, **9:***208n*
—*McCray* v. *U.S.*, **11:**513, *514n*
—*Michaelson et al.* v. *U.S.*, **12:**373, *373–74n*
—*Milton Ochs Co.* v. *Amalgamated Clothing Workers of America*, **12:**302, *303n*
—*Minneapolis and St. Louis Railway Co.* v. *Beckwith*, **8:**479, *492n*
—*Mitchell et al.* v. *Hitchman Coal and Coke Co.*, **10:***287n*
—*Moore Drop Forging Co.* v. *McCarthy et al.*, **12:***10n*
—*Morrison et al.* v. *Ingles et al.*, **11:**280, *281n*
—*Mountain Timber Co.* v. *State of Washington*, **10:**143, *147n*
—*National League of Professional Baseball Clubs et al.* v. *Federal Baseball Club of Baltimore, Inc.*, **9:***238n*
—*New York Central Railroad Co.* v. *White*, **10:**143, *147n*
—*New York Central Railroad Co.* v. *Winfield*, **10:**144, *147n*
—*Nolde and Horst Co.* v. *Kruger et al.*, **9:***263n*
—*Norfolk and Western Railway Co.* v. *Earnest*, **10:**143, *147n*
—*Oregon* v. *Bock*, **7:***118n*
—*Pedersen* v. *Delaware, Lackawanna, and Western Railroad Co.*, **10:**143, *147n*
—*Pennsylvania Mining Co.* v. *United Mine Workers of America et al.*, **11:***494n*
—*Pennsylvania Railroad Co.* v. *U.S. Railroad Labor Board et al.*, **12:***30n*
—*People ex rel. Fursman* v. *City of Chicago et al.*, **9:***419n*
—*People* v. *Lochner*, **6:**392–93, *393–94n*
—*Perkins-Campbell Co.* v. *Albert Teeters et al.*, **7:**11, *11n*
—*P. M. Arthur et al.* v. *Thomas F. Oakes et al.*, **8:**491, *493n*

—*Pollock* v. *Farmers' Loan and Trust Co.*, **4**:*38n*, **6**:332, *340n*, **8**:264
—*Pre Catalan* v. *International Federation of Workers in the Hotel, Restaurant, Lunch Room, Club, and Catering Industry et al.*, **11**:455, *458n*
—*Railroad Cattle Damage Case. See* court cases: *Central Loan and Trust Co.* v. *Campbell Commission Co.*
—*Robertson* v. *Baldwin*, **4**:293, *294n*, **5**:8, 24, 62, 304–6, **6**:148, **7**:*7n*
—*Rogers et al.* v. *Evarts et al.*, **5**:*244n*
—*Ryan et al.* v. *U.S.*, **8**:*336n*
—*Sailors' Union of the Pacific et al.* v. *Hammond Lumber Co.*, **7**:*118n*
—*Samuel Gompers, Frank Morrison, and John Mitchell* v. *Buck's Stove and Range Co.*, **7**:*249–50n. See also* Buck's Stove and Range Co. cases: contempt case
—*Sarah Knisley* v. *Pascal P. Pratt et al.*, **9**:7, *9n*
—*Schwartz and Jaffee* v. *Hillman et al.*, **11**:455, *458n*
—*Second Employers' Liability Cases*, **10**:*147n*
—*Segenfeld and Kalin* v. *Friedman*, **12**:302, *303n*
—*Shanks* v. *Delaware, Lackawanna, and Western Railroad Co.*, **10**:143, *147n*
—*Southern Pacific Co.* v. *Jensen*, **10**:144–45, *147n*
—*Standard Oil Co. of New Jersey* v. *U.S.*, **8**:153, *155n*, 264, *276n*, **12**:*85n*
—*State of Nebraska* v. *Employers of Labor et al.*, **10**:252–53, *254n*
—*State* v. *Holden*, **5**:114, *115n*
—*Steers et al.* v. *U.S.*, **8**:*276–77n*
—*Stettler* v. *O'Hara et al.*, **9**:316, *317–18n*
—*Swift and Co.* v. *U.S.*, **12**:302–3, *303n*
—Taff Vale case, **6**:74, 78, 83, *83–84n*, **7**:24, 289n, 310, 326, 421, **8**:74
—*Third Avenue Railway Co.* v. *Patrick J. Shea et al.*, **12**:21–23, *24n*
—Toledo, Ann Arbor, and Northern Michigan Railroad case, *3*:*294n*, **7**:91–92n, **8**:487
—*Trade Press Publishing Co. et al.* v. *Milwaukee Typographical Union No. 23 et al.*, **12**:302, *303n*

—*Tri-City Central Trades Council et al.* v. *American Steel Foundries*, **10**:252, *253n*
—*Truax et al.* v. *Bisbee Local No. 380, Cooks' and Waiters' Union et al.*, **12**:*94n*
—*Truax et al.* v. *Corrigan et al.*, **12**:*93–94n*
—*United Mine Workers of America, Dist. No. 17, et al.* v. *Chafin et al.*, **12**:*265n*
—*United Mine Workers of America et al.* v. *Coronado Coal Co. et al.*, **10**:322, *323n*, **12**:93n
—*United Mine Workers of America et al.* v. *Pennsylvania Mining Co.*, **11**:492, *494n*
—*U.S. ex rel. Abern* v. *Wallis*, **12**:*278n*
—*U.S. Railroad Labor Board et al.* v. *Pennsylvania Railroad Co.*, **12**:*30n*
—*U.S.* v. *A. Haines et al.*, **9**:*83n*
—*U.S.* v. *American Tobacco Co.*, **8**:153, *154n*
—*U.S.* v. *Armstrong et al.*, **11**:*196n*
—*U.S.* v. *Bricklayers', Masons', and Plasterers' International Union*, **12**:*80n*
—*U.S.* v. *Cpl. John Washington et al.*, **10**:*326n*
—*U.S.* v. *Cpl. Robert Tillman et al.*, **10**:*326n*
—*U.S.* v. *E. J. Ray et al.*, **8**:*182n*, 265, 466
—*U.S.* v. *Frank J. Hayes et al.*, **11**:*196n*
—*U.S.* v. *Ollinger*, **4**:336, *337n*
—*U.S.* v. *Press Publishing Co.*, **8**:*204n*
—*U.S.* v. *Railway Employees' Department of American Federation of Labor et al.*, **12**:*87n*
—*U.S.* v. *Sgt. William Nesbit et al.*, **10**:*326n*
—*U.S.* v. *Steers et al.*, **8**:265, *276n*
—*U.S.* v. *Trans-Missouri Freight Association*, **4**:337, *338n*
—*U.S.* v. *Wells et al.*, **10**:397–400, *400n*
—*U.S.* v. *Wheeler et al.*, **10**:*324n*
—*Walsh* v. *New York, New Haven, and Hartford Railroad Co.*, **10**:143, *147n*
—*William D. Haywood et al.* v. *U.S.*, **10**:*243n*
—*Williams* v. *Great Southern Lumber Co.*, **11**:*366n*

—*Wilson* v. *New et al.*, **9:***450n*, **10:***17n*, **11:**251, *259n*, 331, **12:**497, 498n, 499

—*Wunch* v. *Shankland*, **6:**330, *339–40n*

Courtney, James E., **4:**425–26, *427n*

Court of Appeals of the District of Columbia, **7:**249–50n, 431, 440, 453–54, 465, 491, 492n, **8:**10, 11n, 17–18, 161, 163, 164–65n, 216, 217n, **12:**228n

courts, power of, **7:**264, **9:**125, **11:**8n, 232, 312, 422–23, **12:**68–72, 74, 91–93, 230. *See also* U.S. Supreme Court, amendment to curb veto power of

Covert, Clair, **10:***, *301n*, 417–18, 487, **11:***, 365, *366n; letter from,* **10:**299–301

Covington, J. Harry, **10:**320n

Cowen, Isaac, **3:***402n*, **5:**45, *48n*, 50; *letter to,* **3:**402

Cowen, Mr. (of Philadelphia), meeting with Tracy, **5:**357

Cowey, Edward, **4:***, 90, *91n*, 103, 106n

Cowper, John D., **7:**100, *101n*

Cox, Albert E., **3:**274n; *letter to,* **3:**273–74

Cox, Jacob A., **4:***481n; letter to,* **4:**480–81

Cox, James M., **11:**335–37, *337n*, 374–75, **12:**41, 122

Cox, Oscar, **5:**497n

Cox, P., Shoe Co.: strike/lockout, 1890–91, **2:**423, *427–28n*, **3:**20–21, 26; strike injunction, **3:**21, 26

Cox, Patrick, **3:**21, *23n*

Cox, Samuel S., **3:**449, *451n*

Coxen, E. R., **3:**222n

Coxey, Jacob S., **3:**365, *482n*, 514, 515n, 546, **6:**37n; *letter to,* **3:**482; march on Washington, D.C., led by, **3:**366, 482, *482n*, 514–15, 515n

Coyle, John E., **3:**21, *23n*

Coyne, Robert, **7:**15

Coyne Brothers Co., **7:**14–15, 15n; injunction, **7:**14, 15n

cracker bakers' union (proposed), **3:**455

Craftsman (trade union journal), *letter to,* **2:**39–41

"Craftsmen's Estate" (Handwerkerstand), *1:44n*

Craig, Thomas E., **7:**379, 381n

Craig, Walter A., **9:***256n; letter to,* **9:**256

Cramer, Robley D. "Bob," **9:***359n; letter to,* **9:**358–59

Cramp, Charles H., **4:**490–91, *499n*, 500, **5:**165, 169n, 205–6, 207n, 225–27, 230n

Cramp, Concemore T. T., **12:***, 526, *526n*, 534

Cramp, William, and Sons' Ship and Engine Building Co., **4:**490–91, **5:**165, 194, 198n, 207n, 230n; strike/lockout, 1891, **4:**491, *499n;* strike/lockout, 1899–1900, **5:**124, *126n*, 165, 205–6

Crampton, Herbert, **8:**8, *10n*

Crane v. *Campbell*, **10:***291n*

Cranston, Frederick P., **6:**459, *460n*

Cranwell, Thomas G., **10:***102n; letter to,* **10:**98–102

Crawford, George G., **10:**441, *444n*

Crawford, J. A., **3:**260, *261n*

Crawford, Mark L., **1:***, 161, 211, *212n*, 214, 216, 228, 230, 242–43

Crawford, Thomas J., **3:**206, 208, *210n; letter to,* **3:**217–18

Creamer, James J., **4:***, *79–80n*, **5:***, *287n*, **7:***, *281n;* at AFL conventions, **4:**79, 98–99, 99n, **5:**285, 287n, **7:**280, 281n

credit, **8:**26n, **9:**181, 307n, 351, 424n, **10:**6, 426, **11:**8n, 214n, 233, 235–36, 311, 422, 443n, 571n, **12:**114, 198

Creel, George E., **10:***156n*, 161–62, 382–83, 496–97n, 498, 512n; *letter from,* **10:**156; *letter to,* **10:**495–96

Creelman, James, **7:**372, *372n*

Cremer, William R., **2:***64n*, 79, **7:**211, *214n; letter to,* **2:**63–64

Cribben, William H., **8:**107, *108n*, 201

Crider (employing agent), **6:**122

crimping system, **7:**73

Crisp, Charles F., **8:**183, *184n*

Crispien, Artur, **12:**231, *232n*

Critchlow, Sylvester, **3:**265, *266n*

Critchlow, Walter G., **6:***, 398, *400n*, 403, 436

Critic (Baltimore, Md., labor journal), *letter to,* **2:**229

Crockett, George L., **6**:435, *439n*, **7**:102, 104n

Croft, G. W., **5**:312, 313n

Croker, Richard, **4**:64, *65n*

Croly, Herbert D., **10**:114n, **11**:470, *472n*

Cromer, George W., **7**:99, *99n*

Cromwell, Oliver, **12**:548, *552n*

Cronin, Frederick W., **6**:461, 463, *464n*

Cronin, John, *5:454n; letter to,* **5**:453–54

Crosby, Ernest H., **4**:349, *349n*, 351

Crosby, Thomas, **4**:410, *411n*, 414

Croskey, Richard E., *7:23n; letter from,* **7**:22

Crossfield, Sarah A., **5**:91, *93n*

Crothers, Austin L., **8**:245–46, *246n*

Crothers, Thomas, **9**:409n

Crough, Edward, **10**:518, *518n; letter from,* **10**:516–17

Crough, Katherine Dye, **10**:518n

Crouse, Alonzo B., **3**:260, 260n

Crow, James W., *5:264n; letter to,* **5**:264

Crowder, Enoch, **10**:451n, 540n

Crowe, Robert, **2**:184n, 194

Crowell, Henry P., **2**:38, *38n*

Crowley, Florence, *5:79n*

Crowley, Thomas F., **4**:57, *57n*

Crowley, Timothy M., **4**:*, 239, 241, *241n*

Crown Cork and Seal Co., **4**:319–20

Crumpacker, Edgar D., **7**:139, *143n*

Crumpacker, Maurice E., **10**:299, *301n*

Cruse, James, **9**:13n

Cuba: German intrigues in, **10**:37, 39n, 256, 257n; independence of, **4**:132, 132–33n, 273–74, 409–11, 464–65, 465–66n, 469, **5**:21–22, **10**:559, **11**:88, 92n; organizing in, **5**:280; revolt in, 1895–98, *4:465–66n;* revolt in, 1917, **10**:37, *39n;* SG trip to, 1900, **5**:xv–xvi, 156n, 179–87, *187*–88n, 199, 231–32; SG trip to, 1907, **7**:143–44, *144n*, 162–64, 220–21; suffrage in, **5**:139; workers from, **1**:51, 457–58, 459n, **6**:70, 71n, **8**:25, 26n, 104

—strikes/lockouts: 1899 (general strike), **5**:180, 185–86, *187n*, 232n; 1899 (masons), *5:187n;* 1900 (bakers), **5**:180; 1900 (cigarmakers),

5:180–84, *188n;* 1901 (dockworkers), **7**:162, *164n;* 1906 (general strike), **7**:162, *164n;* 1906 (street railway workers), **7**:162, *164n;* 1907 (cigarmakers), **7**:220–21, *221n;* 1907 (longshoremen), **7**:163, *165n;* 1916 (railroad workers), *9:534n;* 1916–17 (street railway workers), **9**:534, *534n;* 1917 (sugar mill workers), **10**:256, *257n*

Cuban Assembly Commission, **4**:133n

Cuban Railroad Co., strike/lockout, 1916, *9:534n*

Cuban Revolutionary Party, *4:132–33n; letter to officers and members of,* **4**:132

Cudahy meatpacking company, strike/lockout, 1921–22, *11:571n*

Culberson, Charles, **10**:434n

Cullen, Charles A., **7**:279, *280n*

Cullom, Shelby, **6**:232n

Culp, Mr. (Baltimore worker), **2**:35

Culross Brothers Bakery, strike/lockout, 1891, *3:105n*

Culver, E. O., **2**:332

Culver, Oscar D., **2**:332, *337n*

Cumberland Glass Co., strike/lockout, 1900, **5**:246

Cumberland Telephone and Telegraph Co., strike/lockout, 1902, **6**:32n

Cummin, Sherman, **1**:227–28, *229n*

Cumming, James M., *7:396n; letter to,* **7**:396

Cummings, Amos J., **3**:*, 137, *138n*, 245, 245n, 469, 539

Cummings, George, **5**:403, *404n*

Cummins, Albert B., **9**:207, *208n*, 319, 321n, 323, **11**:195n

Cunnane, William, **4**:477, *478n*

Cunnea, William, **10**:528, 529n

Cunningham, Cornelius, **4**:463–64, *465n*, 466–68

Cunningham, F. E., **7**:248, 357

Cuno, Theodore F., **4**:339, *339n*

Curley, James M., **8**:345, *346n*

Curran, Peter F., **7**:*, *476n*

Curran, Richard H., **12**:550, *554n*

Curran, Thomas J., **7**:104, *105n*

currency reform, **4**:326, 328. *See also* gold standard; silver question

Currier, Charles M., **3:**133, *134n*
Curtis, Charles, **7:**94, *95n*
Curtis, Edwin, **11:**146n, 319n
Curtis, T., **1:**125
Curtiss Corp., **10:**364
Cushing, Walter F., **3:**51, *55n*
Cushman, Francis W., **7:**108, *109n*
Cutters', Contractors', and Cloakmakers' Unions, Amalgamated Board of, **2:**349n
Cutters' Union, New England, **3:**269n
Cuyahoga County (Ohio), United Trades and Labor Council of, *7:282n, 9:137n*
Cuyler, Thomas D., **12:**114, *117n*
C. W. Post v. *American Federation of Labor et al.,* **8:**130, *131n*, 133, 149
C. W. Post v. *Buck's Stove and Range Co. et al.,* **8:**130, *131n*, 133, 265
"Czech Legion," *10:512n*
Czernin, Ottokar, **10:**344, *345n*
Czolgosz, Leon F., *5:390n*

Dacus, Solomon J., *11:366n; letter from,* **11:**365–66
Daggett, Floyd L., **7:**108, *109n*
Dahlstrom, George E., *6:189n; letter from,* **6:**186–89
Daily Mail, **9:**289–90n
Daily Mining Gazette (Houghton, Mich.), **9:**28n
Daily Mirror, **9:**289n
Daily Newspaper Association of Chicago, **5:**342n
Daily Worker, SG, *interview with,* **12:**427–28
Daisy, John, *letter to,* **3:**165
D'Alessandro, Domenico, **7:***, 444, *445n,* **8:***, 343, *346n,* **9:***, 71, *73n,* **10:***, 415, *416n,* **11:***, 324, *325n,* 353n; at AFL convention, **10:**468, 470n; *letter from,* **11:**378–79
Daley, Edward L., **1:***, 458, *460n,* 467, **2:***, 23n, *76n,* 228, **3:***, *131n,* 270; at AFL conventions, **2:**75, 267, **3:**130, 131n, 134, 137, 259, 260n, 662, 664n; *letter to,* **3:**224–25
Daley, James E., **5:**174, *176n*
Dallinger, Frederick, **12:**288n
Dally, Thomas, **9:**184n
Dalton, Hugh, **2:**373

Dalton, William, **1:**446, *447n*
Daly, Charles P., **1:**119, *120n*
Daly, Francis, **1:**360, 362n
Daly, James J., *2:408n,* **3:***, *253n;* at AFL conventions, **2:**392, 396, 398–99, 402, 408n, 410, 414, **3:**252, 253n, 260, 428, 436
Daly, Marcus, **3:**294, *295n*
Daly, Timothy M., **9:***, 222, *224n*
Dalzell, John, **7:**96, *98n,* 120, 123n
Damm, Peter, **5:**265, *267n*
Dampf, Henry, **3:**140, *141n*
Dampf, Isaac, **3:**140, *142n*
Dampf, Mamie (variously Mary), **3:**141, *142n*
Dampf, Meyer, **1:**255n, 260n, 438, *438n,* **3:**140, 298, 380, 382n, **4:**18, 18n, 54
Dampf, Rose, **3:**140, **4:**54
Dampf, Sophia, **1:**438n, **3:**140. *See also* Gompers, Sophia Dampf
Danbury Hat Manufacturers' Association, strike/lockout, 1893–94, **4:**105, *106n*
Danbury hatters, financial appeal for, **9:**344, *344n*
D'Andrea, Joseph, **8:**343, *346n*
Danger of Peace, The (Allen), **9:**365, *366n*
Daniel, F. Watt, **12:**197n
Daniel, John W., **7:**179–80, *181n*
Daniels, Josephus, **9:**98n, *10:54n,* 191, 220, 222, 274, 284n, **11:**191; and Cantonment Construction Agreement, **10:**115n, 172n, 204; and Labor Loyalty meeting, **10:**313n; and wages at Navy yards, **10:**53, 86–87, 87n
Danryid, Lemuel, **2:**163, 188n
Dant, Clements T., **2:**38, *39n*
Danville (Ill.) Trades and Labor Council, **7:**102n, 358, *360n;* Political Action Committee of, **7:**358
Danville (Va.) Central Labor Union, *5:439n,* **11:**66, 66n
Danville (Va.) Trades and Labor Council, **5:**370–71, *371n*
D'Aragona, Ludovico, **11:***, 372, *373n*
Dardis, James, **7:**427n
Darlington, Joseph J., **7:**250n, **8:**217, *217n,* **9:**106n

Darroch, William, **7:**139, *143n*
Darrow, Clarence S., **2:***, 301, 304, *304n*, **4:**45n, **5:***, 211, *211n*, 414–15, 415n, **6:***, 104, *104n*, 237, 238n, **7:**146n, **8:***, *238n*, 294, **9:**47n, 88n, **10:**237–38, **12:**516n; *letters from*, **8:**248–49, 299, 346–47; *letters to*, **6:**113, **8:**358–59; and McNamara trial, **8:**136n, 213–14n, 235, 237, 248–49, 249n, 299–300, 305, 305n, 346–47, 347n, 351, 358–59, 360n
d'Arschot-Schoonhoven, Guillaume, comte, **11:**56, *58n*
Das Kapital (Marx), **9:**5
Daugherty, Harry M., **11:**196n, 497, *498n*, **12:**87n, 133, 135–36, 137n, 152–54, 155n, 158; impeachment of, **12:**147, *147*–48n, 154–55, 166–67
Davenport, Daniel J., **6:**327–29, 333–38, *339n*, **7:**29, 250n, **8:**41, 198, 217, 217n, 319, **9:**221, 323, **11:**408n, **12:**398n
Davey, Martin, **11:**260n
Davidson, Herman, *1:271n*
Davies, Hywel, **9:**352, 352n, 489n, **10:**79n, **12:**212n
Davies, Joseph, **10:**72n
Davila, Felix Cordova, **11:**503n
Davis, Bernhard, **1:**457, *459n*, **3:**379–80, 382n
Davis, Charles R., **8:**79, *80n*
Davis, David, **3:**202, *204n*, 612, **11:**8
Davis, David J., **11:***, 98, *99n*, 124–25, 360; *wire from*, **11:**128–29
Davis, Edward H., **8:**273, *277n*
Davis, Jacob, **1:**17–18, *18n*, **9:**538
Davis, James J., **11:**410, *411n*, 451, 453n, **12:**32n, 212n, 260, 260n, 344–45, 348n; and election of 1924, **12:**463–64, 467–68n, 484–85, 492, 495–501, 508–9; *letter from*, **12:**344–45; *letters to*, **11:**494–95, **12:**31–32; SG, meeting with, **12:**210–12
Davis, John W., **8:**446, *448n*, **10:**323n
Davis, Jonathan M., *12:171n*
Davis, Mark, Sons and Co., strike/lockout, 1903–4, **7:**18, *19n*
Davis (water works employee), **5:**403–4
Davis, William J., **10:***, 522, *525n*

Davison, Emmett C., **10:***, 427, *431n*, **12:***, 391, *392n*
Davitt, Michael, **1:**285–86n
Dawes, Charles G., **12:**366, *367n*, 463, 467n, 486, 492
Dawes, Mr. (member of Congress?), SG interview with, **5:**248
Dawes Plan, *12:367n*
Dawkins, Clinton E., **2:**351
Dawley, William L., **4:***, 79, *79n*
Day, William R., **6:**421, 423n
daylight savings, **11:**79, 82n
Dayton, Alston G., **10:**285, *287n*
Dayton Manufacturing Co.: boycott, 1899–1900, **7:**194n; lawsuit against Metal Polishers' local 5, **7:**193, *194n*
Dayton (Ohio) Baseball Club, **6:**145n
Dayton (Ohio) Building Trades Council, **12:**401n
Dayton (Ohio) Central Labor Union, **6:**145n
Dayton (Ohio) Central Trades Council, **5:**379n, 460n
Dayton (Ohio) Employers' Association, **5:**365, *367n*, **6:**144, 145n
Dean, John J., **11:**510, *512n*
De Armay, Raymond, **1:**432
death benefits, **1:**39, 58, 72, 122, 156–57, 157n, 158, 158n, 341, **5:**112n, 240–41, **8:**421, **12:**6
De Bary and Co., strike/lockout, 1877, *1:95*
Debate between Samuel Gompers, President American Federation of Labor, and Henry J. Allen, Governor of Kansas . . ., *11:290n*
Deboos, George, **1:**7
Debs, Eugene V., **2:***, 219, *220n*, **3:***, *247n*, **4:***, 64, *65n*, 392–93, 453n, **5:***, *42n*, **6:***, 17n, *37n*, 397n, **7:***, *25n*, **8:***, 136n, 251, *253n*, 303, **9:***, *118n*, **10:***, 528–29, *529n*, **11:***, 259n, 318, 398n, **12:**132n; and Cooperative Commonwealth, **4:**323, 324n, 342n, 369, 377–78, 379n; and election of 1908, **7:**374–75, 375n, 401–5, 425, 427n, 486n; and IWW, **6:**37n, 384, 384n, 449, 452, 454, 457, 459–60, 464–65, 467, 468n, **7:**404, **9:**113–14, 116–17; and Leadville, Colo., strike, 1896–97, **4:**256,

385–86; *letters to,* **2:**361–62, **3:**246,
562–63; and miners' strike, 1897,
4:345n, 352–53, 357, 359–60n,
365, 372, 379n; and miners' strike,
1912–13, **8:**518, 519n; and Pullman
strike, 1894, **3:**186, 522–25, 526n,
531n, 534–35, 561n, 563n, 565–66,
579n, 639, **11:**250; SG and, **3:**586,
4:72, 178, 387–88, 392, **6:**36–37,
395, 432, 432n, **7:**24, 401–5, 425,
427n, **9:**113–17, **10:**533–34, **11:**397–
98, 398n, 532, 533n
Debs contempt case, **3:**524, 531–32n,
561n, *563n*
Debs v. *U.S.,* **10:***529n*
Decatur (Ill.) Federation of Labor,
3:362n
Deceit of the I.W.W., The (Zuckerman),
7:*19n,* 184
Declaration of Independence, **4:**25–
26, 35, 45, 301, **10:**325, 559, 566
De Costa, Moses, **3:**379, 381, *382n,*
383–84, 403
Dee, Richard P., **11:**314–16, *317n*
DeFalco, Vincenzo, **8:**343, *346n*
Defiance Assembly. *See* Knights of La-
bor (KOL): local assemblies (LAs):
LA 2458
DeForest, Robert E., *8:42n*
Defrem, Herman, **12:**87n, 97n
Degen, Robert, **3:**84, *86n*
Degetau Gonzalez, Federico, **6:**251,
257n
Dehan, Joseph, *10:329n,* 543, **11:**40n,
12:316n, 318–19; *letter from,* **12:**315–
16; *letter to,* **10:**328–29
Dehan, Lewis, **10:**328, *329n*
Dehan, Sophia, **10:**328, 329n
Delabar, August, **2:***, *202n,* 242, 417n,
421, **3:***, *27n,* 90n, 111–12; at AFL
conventions, **2:**385, 394–96, **3:**135,
138n; *letters from,* **3:**27, 65, 105; *letters
to,* **2:**201–2, **3:**65–66
Delahaye, Victor, **3:***, *91n,* 369, 379;
letter to, **3:**90–91
De la Vergne Refrigerating Co.,
5:332–33, 334n
DeLeon, Daniel, **2:**55n, **3:***, 397–99,
399n, 516, **4:***, 11, *15n,* 188–89n,
239, 305–7, 307n, 367, 437–38,
439n, 473, 476, **5:***, 72–73, *73n,*
74n, 147, 148n, 351–53, 429, 491,

6:*, 117, *118n,* 202, **8:***, 116, *117n,*
9:150n, **11:**570, 572n; and IWW,
founding of, **6:**444, 449, 455, 458–
59, 467, 468n; and Socialist Trade
and Labor Alliance, **4:**98n, 103,
106n, 135
Dellinger, Charles W., **8:**232, *234n*
Dĕlnické Listy, **1:***108n,* 191, *192n*
DeLong, Charles J., **4:**280, *281n*
Delves, Frank, **3:**636, *660n*
Democratic National Committee,
12:495, 501; AFL representatives,
meeting with, **12:**183–84
Democratic party, **6:**36, **8:**179, **10:**227,
12:41, 183–84; AFL demands of,
1908, **7:**309–10, 310n, 348, 348n,
349, 351–52, 369, 370n, 372, 372n;
AFL demands of, 1920, **11:**310–13,
313n, 330, **12:**269; AFL demands
of, 1924, **12:**453–55, 455n, 456–57,
457n, 458, 458n, 459–60, 461n;
and election of 1906, **7:**108; and
election of 1908, **7:**309–10, 310n,
311, 348, 348n, 349, 351–52, 353n,
361, 369, 370n, 372, 372n, 376–77,
377–78n, 380, 389, 410–11, 415n,
421, **8:**467, 477, **9:**4, 9; and election of 1912, **8:**386, 386n, 409, 467,
477, 494, **9:**4, 9, 77, 111; and election of 1920, **12:**122; and election
of 1922, **12:**169, 170n; and election
of 1924, **12:**453–55, 455n, 456–57,
457n, 458, 458n, 459–60, 461n,
462–64, 467–68n, 472, 472n, 473,
481, 484, 486–87, 491–92, 495–501,
505–6, 508–11, 513, 518–19; in
New York City, **1:**439n, 444, 448.
See also under elections in United
States, national
—conventions, national: 1868 (New
York City), **5:**159, *160n;* 1900, **5:**211,
211n; 1908 (Denver), **7:***310n,*
348–49, 351–52, 369, 389, **8:**257;
1916 (St. Louis), **9:**430n; 1920 (San
Francisco), **12:**269; 1924 (New York
City), **12:**456, 457n, 458, *458n,* 459,
461n, 462–63, 481, 484, 486–87,
501, 519
—conventions, state: **7:**348; 1906,
Washington, **7:**108, *109n;* 1908,
California, **7:**383–84, *384n;* 1908,
Nebraska, **7:***300n*

Demolition Contractors' Protective Association, **11**:353, *353n*

Demuth (friend of SG), **4**:136

Denby, Edwin, **6**:527n, **12**:200–201, *202n*

DeNedrey, Mrs. Samuel, **5**:452

DeNedrey, Samuel, **5**:328, *329n,* 371n, 420, 421n, 452, 453n, **7**:99–100, *100–101n,* 107n, **8**:*, *9n;* at AFL convention, **8**:7, 9n; *letter from,* **5**:369–71

Deneen, Charles S., **7**:363, *364n,* 416, 417n

Denison (Tex.) Labor Trades Council, **6**:19–20, *20n*

Dennis, Jere, *4:232n; letter to,* **4**:231–32

Denny, Albert G., **1**:*, 456, *458n,* 460

Denver: building contractors, boycott, 1902, *6:18n;* city council of, injunction against, **5**:97–98, 99n; divisions in labor movement in, **5**:394, 450, **6**:18–19n, 85–87, 87n; newspapers, boycott, 1903 (threatened), **6**:131, *131n,* 132, 132n; tramway controversy, 1899, **5**:97–98, *99n*

Denver Amalgamated Trades and Labor Assembly (independent), *6:18–19n,* 353

Denver Building Trades Council, **6**:15, 17–*18n*

Denver City Tramway Co., **5**:99n; injunction, **5**:97–98, 99n

Denver Federation of Labor, **6**:18n

Denver Incorporated Trades and Labor Assembly (AFL affiliate), *6:18– 19n,* 85–86, 87n, 353

Denver Times, editor of, *letter to,* **5**:94– 98

Denver Trades and Labor Assembly:
—AFL affiliate: **2**:287, *288n,* **5**:393–95, 396n, 450–52, **6**:16, 18–19n, 353; meetings of, **4**:195–96, 205
—independent: **6**:18, 85–86, 87n

Depew, Chauncey M., **2**:335, *338n,* **4**:64

depression of 1893, **3**:360, *363–66,* 544, 647, 660n, **4**:14, 46, 112–13, **11**:32; causes of, **3**:368–69, 377–78, 387, 418, 444–47; mass meetings and demonstrations during, **3**:364– 65, 367–69, 377–82, 382n, 383, 385, 457, 458n, 482, 482n, 514–15, 515n,

546; SG and, **3**:364–65, 367, 377–85, 607–8; and trade unions, **3**:360, 365, 376, 431–32, 504; unemployment during, **3**:363–65, 377–78, 383, 386, 394, 420, 445–46, 489, 555; unemployment relief during, **3**:363–65, 367, 377–85, 387, 396–97, 418, 433–34, 445–51, 458n, 600

Derflinger, William F., **4**:56, *57n*

Dernell, John C., **4**:452, *453n,* **5**:398n, 434, 435n, 438, 438n

Derossi, Karl, **2**:149, **4**:134, *137n,* 149–55

Desmerais, John S., **4**:57, *57n*

DeSpagna, Francis, **5**:280–81, 281n

detective agencies, **8**:49–51, 70, 225, 302, 311, 349–50, 353, **9**:279, **10**:391, **11**:422, 447n; Baldwin-Felts, **9**:24n, **11**:296n; Bergoff, **8**:50; Burns, **8**:214n, 248, 412, **12**:132n; Manufacturers', **5**:330–31, *331n;* National, **6**:432n; Pinkerton, **1**:454, *455n,* **3**:26, 52, 55n, 139, 140n, 185–86, 188, 189n, 190, 191n, 192–93, 207, 209, 214n, 237, 249, 254–56, 266n, 635, **4**:387, 388–89n, **5**:84, **6**:431; Thiel, **12**:132n; Waddell-Mahon, **8**:513n, **9**:11–12, 13n, 28n, 43, 182

Detlef, Conrad, **1**:125, *126n*

Detroit Cap Co., strike/lockout, 1905–6, **7**:18, *19n,* 184, 186n

Detroit Copper Mining Co., strike/ lockout, 1915–16, **9**:351–52, *352n,* 425

Detroit Council of Trades and Labor Unions, *10:108n*

Detroit Federation of Labor, *10:108n,* **11**:488n, **12**:326n, 339, 340n

Detroit Stove Works: boycott, 1896, **4**:227–29, *229n;* strike/lockout, 1896, **4**:227–28, *229n;* strike/lockout, 1918–19, **10**:447–49, *449n*

Detroit Street Railway Gazette (trade union journal), **3**:174, *175n*

Detroit Trade and Labor Council, **2**:67, *69n,* **3**:272, 272n, **5**:323

Deutelbaum, Julius, **11**:87n

Deutsch-Amerikanische Bäcker-Zeitung (trade union journal), **2**:241, 242n, *3:114n*

Deutsch-Amerikanische Buchdrucker-Zeitung (trade union journal), *2:213n*

DeValera, Eamon, **11:**86n
DeVeaux, Harry, **6:***, 517, *518n*
Devens, Henry F., **5:**275–77, *278n; letter to,* **5:**276
Devery, William S., **5:**33, *35n*
Devine, Edward T., *6:486n,* **8:**329, *332n,* 455, **10:**157–58
Devine, Michael, **5:**148, *151n*
Devitt, John, **1:**360, *362n*
Devlin, John, **2:***, 198, *198n,* 199, 332, 343
DeVore, Morris H., **3:**133, *134n*
Dewar, Ewen J., **4:**245, *246n*
Dewes, Jacob, *1:139n; letter from,* **1:**135–36
Dewey, Adelbert M., **2:***, *132n; letter from,* **2:**131–32; *letter to,* **2:**132–33
Dewey, George, **4:**466n, **5:**4, *11n,* 21
Dewey, John, *9:430n; letter to,* **9:**429
DeWitt, Samuel, **11:**262n
Diamond, Max, *11:378n; letter to,* **11:**376–77
"Diary of an Amateur Waitress, The" (Younger), **7:**239, *240n*
Diaz, Armando, **10:**550, *554n*
Díaz, Porfirio, **8:**193n, 317, *320n,* **9:**158, 212n, 324, 360, 432, 436
Dibble, Frederick W., **5:**31, 32n
Dick, John, **10:**541–42, 542n
Dickens, Charles, **6:**98, *100n*
Dickens, Frederick C., **5:**47, *48n*
Dickinson, Frances, *3:25n; letter to,* **3:**25
Dickinson, Frank G., *12:420n; letter to,* **12:**419–20
Dickinson, Jacob M., **8:**87–89, *89n*
Dickman, Franklin J., **12:**217n
Dickson, William, **11:**391n
Dicus, Thomas J., **4:**373–74, *375n*
Diefenbach, George, *10:69n; letter from,* **10:**67–69
Diego, José de, **8:**88, *89n*
Diehl, Fred. W., **2:**245
Dielman, Henry, **11:**20n
Dietrich, Charles E., **6:**411, *412n*
Diggs, James H., *letter from,* **9:**281
Dilke, Charles W., **6:**337, *340n*
Dilke, Lady Emilia, **4:**32, *33n*
Dill, Clarence C., *12:171n,* 187, 436
Dillard, James H., **10:**421–23, 430, *431n,* 462

Dillingham, William P., **9:**83n, 92, *94n*
Dillon, James C., **5:**460, *461n,* 462
Dillon, Thomas J., **10:**154, *154n*
Dillon, William J., **2:***, 167, 171–72, *172n,* 264, **3:***, *108n; letter to,* **3:**107–8
Dillworth, Daniel L., **6:**145n
Dingley, Nelson, **4:**329n
Dinkel, John A., **1:**113, *115n*
Dinkey, Alva C., **5:**478, *482n*
Disarmament: The American Federation of Labor: Its Declarations and Actions in Support of Disarmament and International Peace (AFL), **11:**548, *548n*
Disque, Brice P., **10:**245–46, *246n,* 295–96, 296n, 299–301, 486–90; *letter from,* **10:**375–76; *letter to,* **10:**416–18; *wire to,* **10:**503
distribution of wealth, **4:**71, 210, **5:**229
District Messenger Co., **1:**306
"Divide the Day" (Jones), **4:**394
Dix, John Adams, **1:**207, *210n*
Dix, John Alden, **8:**240n, 299; *letter to,* **8:**239–40
Dixon, Charles G., **2:**60, *63n*
Doak, William N., **11:**348, *349n,* 468, 470, **12:**345
Doane, Lester B., **11:**340, *342n*
Dobson, William, **7:***, *282n,* **10:***, 265, *266n,* **11:**23n, 529n, **12:***, 550, *553n; letter to,* **7:**281–82
Dock, Wharf, Riverside, and General Labourers' Union of Great Britain and Ireland, **5:**68, *69n*
Dock Builders' Union (New York City), **9:**292n, **11:**324, 325n
dock laborers (London): drinking habits of, **2:**350–52; organization of, **9:**337–38
Dodd, Alvin, *9:353n; wire from,* **9:**353
Dodge, Grace H., **4:**33, *33n*
Dodge Bros., **10:**365
Doggett, John W., **11:**73, *74n*
Doheny, Edward L., **12:**228n
Doherty, Jeremiah, **3:**125–26, 128, *128n,* 130, 135, 137, 208
Doherty, William, **12:**91n
Doherty and Co., strike/lockout, 1913, *8:503n*
Dohner, John H., **4:**460, 461n
Dolan, John, **3:**496, *498n*

Dolan, Patrick, **4:**346–47, *347n*, 359n, 365, **7:**121; *letters to,* **4:**363–64, **5:**408

Dolan, Thomas, *letter to,* **9:**470–72

Dold, Charles, **3:***, *128n*, **5:***, *56n*, **6:***, 469n, *497n,* **7:***, *141n;* at AFL conventions, **3:**125, 128n, 131, 137–38, 257, 258n, **5:**54, 56n, 57, **6:**495, 497n, **7:**128, 133, 136, 141n

Dold, Jacob, Packing Co., **5:**17

Dole, Sanford B., **5:**6, *11n*

Dolliver, Jonathan P., **8:**79, *79n,* 182

Dolphin, Michael M., **5:***, 124–25, *127n,* 307n

Domenech, Francisco, **10:**256, 257n

Dominick Connors v. *Patrick Connolly et al.,* **8:**490, *493n*

Dominion Coal Co.: strike/lockout, 1909–10, **10:**307, *308n;* strike/lockout, 1918 (threatened), **10:**307–8, *308n*

Dominion Trades and Labor Congress, *4:471n*

Domschke, C., **1:**195, *198n,* 199

Donath, August, *4:285n; letter from,* **4:**284–85

Donegan, Edward J., **3:**170, *171n*

Donegan, Mr. (acquaintance of Furuseth), SG conversation with, **6:**270

Doniger Brothers, strike/lockout, 1906, *7:18n,* 184

Donlin, John H., **10:***, 412n, 421, 427, *431n,* **11:***, *379n,* 401, 544, **12:***, 80, *80n,* 212n; and Canal Zone, workers in, **11:**392, 434; and Industrial Conference, 1919, **11:**128n; *letter from,* **12:**399–401; and New York City building trades situation, **11:**378, 445, 467, 467–68n; and Unemployment Conference, 1921, **11:**532n

Donnelly, James P., **1:**458, *460n*

Donnelly, John L., **10:***, *175n; wire to,* **10:**172–73

Donnelly, Michael J., **4:***, *287n,* **5:***, 164, *168n,* 453n, **6:***, 313, *315n,* 321, 326n, 468, 469n, **7:***, 363, *364n; letter from,* **4:**286–87

Donnelly, Patrick H., **2:***, *51n; letters to,* **2:**51, 101–2

Donnelly, Patrick J., **5:***, 106, *108n*

Donnelly, Samuel B., **5:***, 43–44, 46– 47, *48n,* 50, 174, 176n, 234; *letter to,* **5:**405–6

Donnelly, Thomas J., **4:**123, *124n,* 274, *275n*

Donoghue, Mortimer M., **9:***, 155n, 190, *191n*

Donohue, Patrick, **7:**90n

"Do Not Blame Me If I Sigh" (O'Donnell), **4:**391–92, *392n*

Donovan, Florence F., **1:**360, *361n,* **2:**7

Donovan, James A., **9:**454, 455n

Doody, Patrick H., **1:**434, *434n*

Doolittle, William H., **3:**477, *478n*

Dopheide, Henry, *3:533n; wire from,* **3:**532–33

Dorchy v. *State of Kansas,* *11:280n*

Döring, Sebastian, **1:**75, 76n

Dorn, Henry, **1:**461, *462n,* **2:**143

Dorsey, Hugh M., *11:76n; wire to,* **11:**76

Dougherty (delegate), **2:**367

Dougherty, John H., *1:448n; statement of,* **1:**446–47

Douglas, Charles A., **9:**327, *328n,* 430–33, 434n

Douglas, W. L., Shoe Co., **5:**112n, **7:**399, 400n

Douglas, William L., **6:**350n, **7:**378n

Douglass, C. C., **7:**121, *122n*

Dowell, Grant H., **10:**337, *339n*

Dower, George W., **4:***, 471, *471n*

Downer College, **9:**355n

Downey, Daniel, **6:**164, *164n*

Downey, John, **3:**152, 153n

Downey, Patrick J., **6:**53n, 166, *167n,* 211

Downing, William C., **6:**475, *476n*

Doyle, Charles W., **10:**399, *400n,* **12:**241, 271, 274–75, 322–24; *letter to,* **12:**324–26

Doyle, Edward L., *9:95*–96n, 97, 309, **10:**409n; *letter to,* **10:**408–9; *wire from,* **9:**95

Doyle, James G., **3:**381, *383n*

Doyle, John, **6:**475, *476n*

Doyle, John J., **2:**332, *338n; statement of,* **1:**446–47

Doyle, Martin F., **1:***, 83, *85n; letter from,* **1:**85

Doyle, Peter A., **12:**550, *553n*

Doyle, Peter F., **4:***, 410, *411n,* **5:***, 126, *127n*

draft. *See* conscription
Draft Bill for the Regulation of Public Utilities (National Civic Federation), **9:***164n*
Drage, Geoffrey, **3:**222–23, 224n
Drain, Parda D., *10:249n; letter to,* **10:**247–49
Drake, Barbara M., **12:**376, *377n*
Drake v. *Perry,* **12:**302, *303n*
Draper, Patrick M., **6:***, 134, *136n,* **9:***, *314n,* 409n, **12:***, 438–39, *442n;* letters to, **6:**156–58, **9:**312–14
Dreadnought (battleship), **8:**206, *208n*
Dred Scott v. *Sandford,* **6:**331–32, *340n,* **8:**74
Drees, Charles, **3:**404n
Dreier, Dorothea, **9:**302, 303n
Dreier, Mary E., **8:**301n
Dresler, Frederick E., **5:***, 140–41, *142n*
Dress and Waist Manufacturers' Association, and Protocol Agreement, **8:**439–40, 440n, 442n
Drew, Mr. (English worker?), **4:**508
Drew, Walter W., **8:**225, *227n,* 303, 309, **9:**221, 279, 280n, 284, 285n, 323, **10:**370, **11:**287
Drexel, Anthony J., **2:**35, *36n*
Drexel Furniture Co. v. *Bailey,* **11:***514n*
Dreyfus, Alfred, **4:**70n
Driazeloor, Joel, **1:**8
Driller, The (Niehaus), **7:**442
Drinkhouse, John A., **6:**341, *341n*
drinking: SG and, **2:**308–9, **3:**54, 183; by workers, **1:**215–16, 464, **2:**350–52. *See also* Gompers, Samuel: intemperance of, alleged; Prohibition; temperance movement
Driscoll, Dennis D., **5:***, 288, *292n,* **6:**11n, **7:**37n
Driscoll, John C., **7:**363–64, *364n,* 429
"Driscoll substitute," **6:**11n, 133, **7:**34, 37n, 216
Drucher, H., **3:**141
Drucher, Mrs. H., **3:**141
Drucker, Miss, **7:**492
Drummond, Charles L., **3:***, 532, *533n,* 534, *letter to,* **3:**548–49
Drummond Tobacco Co., **3:**304n; boycott, 1893, **3:**344, *345–46n*
Drury, Horace, **11:**391n

Dryer, Ferdinand, **2:**245
Dublin Trades Council, **4:**50n, 88–89, 91n
DuBois, W. E. B., *6:91n; letter to,* **6:**90–91
DuBose, G. P., **11:**39, *41n*
Dubue, Gustave, *letter from,* **7:**224–25
Ducey, Thomas J., **3:**386, *388n*
Duckworth, Robert F., **7:**59, *59n*
Dudek, Lawrence, **11:**142n
Duell, Holland, **11:**564n, **12:**39n
dues, union. *See* trade unions: dues of
Duffy, Frank, **5:***, *398n,* 399n, 423n, 448n, **6:***, *8n,* 290n, 473n, **7:***, *56n,* 243n, **8:***, 17n, *125n,* 138, **9:***, 145n, 148, *149n,* 207, **10:***, 360, *362n,* **11:***, *84n,* 345, 365, 366n, 544, 545n, **12:***, *117n;* at AFL conventions, **6:**64, 67n, 207, 207n, **8:**139n, **10:**469, 471n, **11:**83, 84n, 315–16, 317n, **11:**83, 84n, **12:**333, 334n; at AFL Executive Council meetings, **9:**436, 443n; and AFL mission to Europe, spring 1919, **11:**40n; and Canal Zone, workers in, **11:**365n, 435; election of, as AFL vice-president, **9:**38n, 226n, 348n, **10:**475, **11:**93n, 321, 321n, 482, **12:**97n, 338n; and election of SG's successor, **12:**555, 559–60; and Industrial Conference, 1919, **11:**128n; and jurisdiction questions, **6:**62–66, 176n; *letters from,* **5:**398, **7:**54–56, **8:**302, **9:**427–28, 496; *letters to,* **5:**421–22, 474–75, **6:**21–22, 42–44, 165–67, 178–79, 181, 264–65, 533–35, **7:**56–57, 242–43, **8:**123–25, **12:**352, 387–88, 470; and McGuire, **6:**6, 92–93, 546n
Duffy, Frank, Jr., **10:**471n
Duffy, George, **10:**471n
Duffy, Joseph, **10:**471n
Duffy, Patrick G., **1:**113, *115n*
Duffy, Peter E., *8:395n; letter to,* **8:**394
Duffy, Peter J., *11:66n; letter to,* **11:**65–66
Duffy, T. J., **7:**107n
Duffy, William, **10:**471n
Dugan, Bernard J., *3:122n; letter to,* **3:**122
Dugan, Martin, **3:**175, *175n*
Duggan, May, **1:**8

Duggan, Michael, **4:***, 432n, 433, *435n*
Duggan, Patrick W., **4:**190, *191n*
Dukes, Aaron N., **6:**140, 141n
Dullea, John D., **3:***, 461, *461n*
Dumas, P. E., **3:**70n
Duncan, Charles, **10:***, 309n, 537, *538n*
Duncan, James, **3:***, *260n,* **4:***, 4, 66n, *97n,* 288, 327–28, 338, **5:***, *56n,* 410n, 419–20n, 448n, 464n, **6:***, 4, *5n,* 116n, 217n, 232, 239, 259, 308n, 314, 316, **7:***, *7n,* 258n, 400n, 481, **8:***, *6n,* 80–81, 82n, 325, 450, **9:***, *14n,* 66, 68n, 107, 200n, 492n, 535, 539n, **10:***, *38n,* 44–45n, 313n, 544–45, 556–57, **11:***, *65n,* 93n, 221n, 345, 447, 544, 560n, **12:***, *98n;* and AFL Building Trades Department, **7:**276n, 277–78, **8:**149–50; at AFL conventions, **3:**260, 260n, 430, 434n, **4:**97n, 270–72, 272n, **5:**54, 56n, 158n, 163, 163n, 165, 288, 292n, **6:**54, 56, 57n, 64, 196, 197n, 200, 206, 212, 357–58, 360n, 362, 364–66, 370, 374–75, 492, 493n, 498–500, 502n, 512n, **7:**129, 142n, 423, **8:**3–4, 6n, 284–85, 286n, 290, 293, 402, 402n, 405–6, **9:**23–24, 25n, 34–36, 345–46, 346n, **10:**259, 263n, 266, 266n, **11:**315, 317n, 473, 475n, **12:**97; at AFL Executive Council meetings, **4:**239–41, 266–67, 321–23, **6:**133–34, **8:**503–4, **9:**366, 367n, 396, 397n, 436, 438–40, **10:**29–31, 35, 38, 39n, **11:**387–88; and AFL mission to Europe, spring 1919, **11:**40n, 48n; and Brewery Workmen, **7:**202n, 216; and Buck's Stove and Range Co. cases, **7:**248; *cable from,* **10:**120–21; and Canal Zone, workers in, **11:**365n; and election of 1906, **7:**111n; and election of 1908, **7:**310n, 415–16, 416n, **12:**459; and election of 1924, **12:**430, 432, 433n, 489, 491, 493; election of, as AFL vice-president, **4:**95, 278n, 414n, **5:**57n, 177n, 294n, 445, **6:**209, 376n, 509n, **7:**281n, 427n, **8:**18n, 295, **9:**38n, 226n, 348n, **10:**475, **11:**93n, 321, 321n, 482, **12:**97n,

338n; and election of SG's successor, **6:**171, **12:**555, 557–60; eulogy for SG, **12:**545, 549–50; illness of, **9:**363, *366n;* and Industrial Conference, 1919, **11:**128n; and industrial disputes, **4:**319–20, **6:**183–85, 217n; and International Labor Conference, 1919, **11:**110–11, 111n; and jurisdiction questions, **4:**148, **5:**78, 288, 438, 439n, 443–45; *letters from,* **3:**341–42, **5:**236–39, 418–19, **6:**146–47, 183–85, **8:**149–50, 259–60, **10:**373–74, 415–16, 528–29; *letters to,* **4:**481–83, 507–9, **5:**233–35, **7:**182, 205, 399–400, 415–16, **8:**218–19, 240–42, 500–501, **9:**69–72, 363–66, 396, **10:**191–93, 547–48, **11:**64–65, 110–11; and Root mission to Russia, **10:**72n, 120–21, 121n, 191–92, 311; and SG, death of, **12:**541; *testimony of,* **4:**452, 500; and "We Don't Patronize List" (AFL), **7:**312–13
Duncan, James A., **11:**81–82n, **12:**241, 271, 271n, 273, 273–74n, 275, 322–24, 436, 437n; at AFL conventions, **10:**474n, **11:**79–80, 81n, 87n, 94, 316, 317–18n, 321, **12:**334–35; *letters to,* **12:**223–25, 252–55
Duncan, Lillian Holman, **8:**242, 243n
Duncan, William, **3:**272n; *letter from,* **3:**272; *letter to,* **3:**274–75
Duncker, Franz, **1:**44n, **3:**639
Dundee (Scotland) and District Mill and Factory Operatives' Union:
—strikes/lockouts: 1893, *3:542n;* 1895, *3:542n*
Dunlap, Henry, **11:**454n
Dunlop, Robert, **11:**321n
Dunn, George F., **7:***, 90n, 233–34, *235n*
Dunn, John D., **2:**55
Dunn, William T., **4:**469, *470n*
Dunne, William F., **12:**96, *97–98n,* 326–27, 332n; at AFL 1923 convention, **12:**327–29, 330n, 338–39, 403, 404n
Dunsmuir, A., and Sons, strike/lockout, 1890–91, *3:56n*
Duplex case. See *Duplex Printing Press Co.* v. *Deering et al.*
Duplex Printing Press Co., **11:**408n

Duplex Printing Press Co. v. *Deering et al.,*
  11:406, *408n,* **12:**93n
Dupuy (French minister of interior),
  3:370n
Durr, Karl, **10:**90n
Duryea Starch Co., boycott, 1882,
  1:438n
Duse, Eleonora, **12:**340, *340n*
Dutton, E. P., and Co., **11:**522, 523n,
  12:378, 378n
Dwelle, E. C., **7:**186n
Dyche, James E., **11:**532, *533n*
Dyche, John A., **6:***, 276–77, 278n,
  518–19, 519n, **7:***, *165–*66n, 298n,
  470n, **8:***, 109–11, *114n,* 219n, **12:***,
  528, *532n; letter from,* **7:**297–98; *letters to,* **6:**473–74, **7:**165, 468–70
Dyer, David, **8:**131n
Dyer, Josiah B., **1:***, 385, *390n,* 426,
  464, **2:***, 207, *207n,* 281, **3:***, *79n,*
  405n; *letters from,* **1:**389–90, **3:**78–79;
  letters to, **2:**215–17, 293–94, **3:**79–80,
  404–5
Dyers' Helpers and Finishers of America, United, **6:**29n
Dykaar, Moses W., **12:**530, *533n,* 534

Earl, Charles, **7:**195, 197n
Easby-Smith, James S., **12:**155, *156n*
Easley, Crouch W., **10:**59, *60n; wire
  from,* **10:**59
Easley, Donna R., **9:**164, *164n*
Easley, Gertrude Beeks, **5:**218n. *See
  also* Beeks, Gertrude B.
Easley, Minerva Cheney, **9:**164, *164n*
Easley, Ralph M., **3:***, *590n,* **4:***, *506n,*
  5:*, 218n, *335n,* 355n, 464n, 483n,
  6:*, 105, 105n, 172, 236n, 237, 417,
  513, **7:***, 144n, *246–*47n, **8:***, 23,
  24n, 227n, 304n, **9:***, 132, *136n,*
  385n, **10:***, 52n, 73, *74n,* 141, 511,
  512n, **11:***, *530n,* **12:***, *47n,* 367n,
  550; *letters from,* **5:**334, 367–69,
  372, 387–90, 410–11, 482–83,
  489–90, **6:**235–36, 386–87, 489–90,
  7:244–46, **9:**138–39, **12:**43–47; *letters to,* **3:**589–90, **4:**505–6, **5:**477–78,
  494–96, **8:**202, 323–24, **9:**163–64,
  460–61, **10:**102–3, **11:**529–30,
  562–64; mediation of industrial disputes, **5:**361n, 366n, 367–69, 369n,

372, 387–90, 411n, 489–90, 497n;
  "Opposing Forces in the Industrial
  World," **7:**244, *246–*47n
Easley, Ronald M., **9:**164, *164n*
Eastern Counties' Labour Federation
  (Great Britain), **3:**146n
East India Matting Factory, **4:**139
East Liverpool (Ohio) *Evening Review,*
  article in, **7:**106
Eastman, Crystal, **8:**33n
Eastman Kodak Co., antitrust case
  against, **10:**322, 323n
Eastmans Co., **4:**229–30, 230–31n;
  boycott, 1896, **4:**231n; strike/lock-
  out, 1896, **4:**229–30, *230n*
East St. Louis (Ill.) race riots, 1917,
  10:129–33, *133–34n,* 135, 139n,
  142, 151–52, 152–53n, **11:**114
Eastty, George W., **11:**488, 491, *492n*
Eaton, Horace M., **4:***, *188n,* **5:***,
  112n, *492n; letters from,* **4:**185–88,
  5:490–92
Eatough, Henry, **11:**510, *512n,* **12:**252
Eberhardt, William F., **3:**182, *183n*
Ebert, Joseph W., **2:**32, *36n*
Eby, George M., **2:***, *356n; letters to,*
  2:355–56, 364–65
Echard, Charles E., **5:**440, *441n*
Echel, James, **6:**13n
Eckelmann, George J., **3:**495, 498n
Eckhardt, Heinrich von, **10:**34, 38n
Ecks, Henry, **1:**250, *251n*
*Economic and Social Importance of the
  Eight-Hour Movement, The* (Gunton),
  2:188n
Economic and Sociological Club,
  1:60n, *83,* 101n
economic readjustment, postwar. *See*
  reconstruction, postwar
Economics (Clay), **12:**191, *192n*
Edbrooke, Willoughby J., **3:**404, 405n
Eden Musee, **8:**230–31, 231–32n
Edge, Walter, *11:107n; letter to,* **11:**107
Edinburgh Trades Council, **10:**533
Edlar, Ottomar, **7:**495, *498n*
Edmonds, Charles N., **5:**92, *94n*
Edmonston, Gabriel, **1:***, 275–76,
  286n, 287, 361, *361n,* 371, 457,
  462n, **2:***, *28n,* 71n, **3:***, 119, *120n,*
  4:*, *288n,* **5:***, 232, *232n,* **6:***, 91–
  93, *93n;* at AFL convention, **2:**66,

71, 77; election of, as AFL treasurer, **1:**469–70, **2:**79; *letters to,* **2:**27–30, 38, 41, 123, 129, 159–60, 344, 356–57, **3:**211–12, **4:**288

Edmunds, George F., **8:**463, *468n*

Edmunds, George H., **10:**347, *350n*

education: compulsory, **1:**225, **11:**379; of immigrants, **12:**210, 212, 213n; public, **3:**286, 286–87n, **4:**101, 113, **6:**96, 100n, 479, **11:**8n; of women workers, **12:**449, 449n; and workingmen, **1:**105, **11:**499–500, 500n, **12:**382, 387–88, 389n

Edwards, Arthur, **3:**424, *425n*

Edwards, C. O., *wire from,* **10:**163

Edwards, Clarence R., **8:**87, *89n*

Edwards, Edward I., *12:171n*

Edwards, Enoch, **6:**62n

Edwards, James C., **4:**57, *57n*

Edwards, Thomas J., **6:***, *260n; letter from,* **6:**258–60

Edwoods, Prince L., *11:243n; letter from,* **11:**243

Eells, George, *8:156n; letter to,* **8:**155–56

efficiency. *See* scientific management; Taylor system

Egan, James P., **8:**408, *409n,* **12:**543, *544n*

Egan, John M., **3:**522, 524

Egan, John P., **1:**361, *362n*

Eggleston, William M., **1:**359, *359n*

Eggs, William L., **6:**15, *19n*

Egypt, workers in, **12:**305

Ehmann, John, **1:**390, *390n; letter to,* **2:**234–35

Eichelberger, Harry L., *8:47n,* 190n, **11:**489, 491, 525; *letter from,* **8:**47; *letters to,* **8:**188–89, 228–29

Eickoff, Anthony, **3:**18n

Eidlitz, Otto, **9:**200n

eight-hour campaigns:
—of 1872, **1:**66, *67n*
—of 1886, *1:276–77,* 363–64, 371, 387–88, 448–49, 454, 461, 467n, **2:**61–62, 149, 155–56, 170–71, 231, 260–61, 334, 344, **3:**567–68, **9:**241, **11:**9
—of 1890, *2:163–64,* 278, 294n, 298–99, 305–7, 334, **3:**42, 54, 71–72, 447, 567–68, 623, **9:**241; AFL 1888 con-

vention and, **2:**162–63, 165, 167–72, 276, 291, 307, 314; AFL 1889 convention and, **2:**163, 264–68, 276, 291, 307; AFL 1890 convention and, **2:**164; AFL Executive Council, *circular* in support of, **2:**299–301; assessment for, **2:**163, 266, 268, 291–92, 317; and Carpenters, **2:**163–64, 290, 293–95, 296n, 298–301, 305–7, 314, 316–17, **3:**42, 54, 70n, 71–72, 268n, 623; *circulars on,* **2:**278–80, 291–92, 295, 299–301; conferences on, **2:**223, 224n, 225; congressional resolution on, **2:**278, 278n, 280; correspondence with public figures to support, **2:**225, 226n, 231, 243, 253, 280, 314; financial appeal for, **2:**291–92, 299–301; and Furniture Workers, **3:**267, 268n; general strike to support, **2:**226–27, 334, 338n; International Labor Congresses, 1889, endorsement by, **2:**106; and KOL, **2:**163, 229–31, 242–43, 252–55, 255n, 267, 335–36, 342, 354; mass meetings in support of, **2:**163, 168, 183–84, 184n, 185–86, 189, 193–94, 223, 231–32, 243, 253, 279–80, 287–88, 295, 296n, 301–4, 307–16; *pamphlets* in support of, **2:**163, 168, 188, *188n,* 206, 253, 280; SG, *addresses by,* in support of, **2:**302–4, 308–14, 316; SG, *circular* in support of, **2:**291–92, 295; SG, *interview with,* in support of, **2:**298–99; SG, *letter to editor* in support of, **2:**284–86; strikes in support of, **2:**177–78, 244, 254; union to lead, choice of, **2:**266, 276–77, 283, 290–91, 293–94
—of 1891: assessment for, **2:**413–14; KOL and, **3:**72–74, 75n; Mine Workers and, **2:**163–64, 290, 318, 413–16, 430, **3:**23, 24n, 31, 32n, 33, 40, 42, 44, 54–55, 57, 60, 64, 64n, 69, 70n, 71, 71n, 72–74, 111, 168
—of 1892, **3:**162, 168–69

Eight-Hour League, **9:**220

Eight Hour Primer, The (McNeill), *2:188n,* 206n, 286

eight-hour workday, **1:**87, **3:**591, **11:**18n; AFL and, **3:**93, 547, **4:**92, 116, 323n, **5:**285–86, **7:**274–75,

275n, **9:**214–23, 223n, 240–41,
335, 349–50, 350–51n, 527, 529n,
532, **11:**14; hearings on, **5:**189–97,
201–7, 207n, 212–13, 222–30, 230n,
478–82, 482n, 497–500, **9:**224n; SG
and, **3:**49, 93–94, **4:**38, 111, 157–58,
5:186, **7:**483–84, **9:**240–44, 246,
335–40, 407, 494, 495n, **10:**83–84,
117, 443–44; Versailles Treaty and,
11:70–71n, 100; wartime suspension
of, **10:**13–14, 14n, 91–92, 230, 281,
365, 443–44, 458. *See also* eight-hour
campaigns; hours of labor
Eikhoff, Henry J., **3:***, *89–90n,* 662,
664n, **5:***, 239, *240n; letter to,* **3:**89
Eiland, J. H., **8:**247n
Einstein, Albert, **12:**277, *278n*
Einstein, Edwin, **3:**15, 18n, **4:**224,
225n
Eisendrath Glove Co., strike/lockout,
1920–21, *12:451n*
Eisenrath, William C., **6:**15, *19n*
Eisner, A. G., *letter to,* **6:**218–19
Ekern, Herman, **12:**494n
Elderkin, Thomas J., **3:***, *253n,* **4:***,
84n, **5:***, *38n;* at AFL conventions,
3:251, 253n, 437, 439, 610, 611n,
617, **4:**83, 84n, 405, 405n, **5:**37, 38n;
letters to, **3:**280–81, 358; *wire from,*
3:532–33
Eldorado (Ill.) Trades Council, **9:**240–
41, *244n*
elections in United States, national:
—1884, **9:**86–87
—1888, **2:**45
—1892, **3:**194n, 200–204, 224–25,
230–32
—1894, **3:**598, 598n, 612
—1896: AFL organizers and, **4:**239–
41, 268–72, 272n; McKinley and,
4:185n, 221n, 235, 247; SG and,
4:131, 178, 179n, 183–85, 195–96,
217, 217n, 221, 233–35, 240–41,
275–78
—1900, **5:**406n
—1902, **6:**285n
—1904, **6:**300–307, 307–8n
—1906: AFL and, **7:**126–41, 141–42n,
9:3; AFL Executive Council and,
7:60–64, 64n, 65–67, 126–41; AFL
financial report on, **8:**84, 85n, **9:**3,

8n; AFL organizers and, **7:**58–59,
96–97, 99–100, 102n, 104n, 105–7,
107n, 109n, 115, 121–22, 122n;
in California, **7:**117; Cannon and,
7:96, 101–2, 102n, 103, 106, 130,
140; Chicago Federation of Labor
and, **7:**110n, 115; in Connecticut,
7:112; Democratic party and, **7:**108;
Duncan and, **7:**111n; in Georgia,
7:58–59; Hamilton and, **7:**100,
104n, 107n; in Idaho, **7:**118–19; in
Illinois, **7:**96, 101–2, 102n, 109–10,
110n, 115, 140, 358, 360; Independence League and, **7:**110n; in
Indiana, **7:**99, 99n, 112–13, 139;
in Kansas, **7:**69, 94–95; Keefe and,
7:111n; Lennon and, **7:**96, 109,
110n; Littlefield and, **7:**58, 58n, 71,
89n, 99–101, 104n, 130; in Maine,
7:19–20, 57–58, 58n, 70–89, 96, 99–
100, 101n, 102–3, 107–8, 138–39,
143n, 183; in Maryland, **7:**119–20,
120n; Mitchell and, **7:**111; Morrison and, **7:**96–97, 110n, 122–23n;
in New Jersey, **7:**112; in New York,
7:96–97, 109–10, 110n; New York
City Central Federated Union and,
7:110n; O'Connell and, **7:**111n,
120; in Ohio, **7:**105–7, 107n; in
Pennsylvania, **7:**96, 112–13, 120–22,
122–23n, 132–33; Progressive Alliance and, **7:**110n; Republican party
and, **7:**89n, 99, 107n, 108; SG and,
7:19–20, 57–58, 58n, 68, 70–89, 96,
101n, 102–3, 107–8, 112–13, 138–
40, 143n, 183; Socialist party and,
7:110n; Taft and, **7:**103, 118–19;
United Labor party and, **7:**122n;
Walker and, **7:**101; in Washington
state, **7:**108, 109n; in Wisconsin,
7:64–67, 130–31, 139, 143n
—1908: AFL and, **7:**341–42, 342n,
373–74, 374n, 376–77, 377–78n,
381, 383, 384n, 389–93, 396–97,
413–14, 416n, 422–24, 424n, 425,
427n, **8:**90, **9:**3–4; AFL financial appeals for, **7:**342n, 390, 392, 393n;
AFL financial report on, **8:**84, 85n,
9:3, 8n; AFL organizers and, **7:**346,
347n, 350n, 358, 360, 373–74,
376–77, 377n, 380, 383–85, 387,

390, 394–95, 395n, 396–97, 398n, 416–17, 417n; Bryan and, **7:**310–11, 369, 370n, 374–75, 380, 384, 384n, 397, 398n, 410–11, 414–15, 415n, 421; in California, **7:**381–84, 384–85n, 413–14, 414n; Cannon and, **7:**349, 350n, 357–60, 377, 387, 390, 398; Chicago Federation of Labor and, **7:**363, 373, 386, 416–17, 417n; Debs and, **7:**374–75, 375n, 401–5, 425, 427n, 486n; Democratic party and, **7:**309–10, 310n, 311, 348, 348n, 349, 351–52, 353n, 361, 369, 370n, 372, 372n, 376–77, 377–78n, 380, 389, 410–11, 415n, 421, **8:**467, 477, **9:**4, 9; Duncan and, **7:**310n, 415–16, 416n, **12:**459; Furuseth and, **7:**382, 413–14, 414n; Hamilton and, **7:**346, 347n, 350n, 358, 360, 376, 377n, 387, 395n, 397, 398n, 416–17, 417n; in Illinois, **7:**346–47, 347n, 348–50, 350n, 357–62, 362n, 363–64, 377, 386–87, 390, 397–98, 416–17, 417n; Independence party and, **7:**369, 370n, 384; in Indiana, **7:**397–98; in Iowa, **7:**397; Keefe and, **7:**415–16, 416n, 422, 425, **12:**459; Lennon and, **7:**349–50, 350n, 363, 376, 377–78n, 396–98, 416–17, 417n; in Maine, **7:**377; Mine Workers, United, and, **7:**416–17, 417n; Mitchell and, **7:**415–16, 416n; Morrison and, **7:**350n, 377; in Nebraska, **7:**300, 300n, 353n; in New York, **7:**373, 374n; New York City Central Federated Union and, **7:**373, 374n; O'Connell and, **7:**377; in Ohio, **7:**397; in Oregon, **7:**414, 414n; in Pennsylvania, **7:**375; Perkins and, **7:**387; Prohibition party and, **7:**397–98, 399n; Republican party and, **7:**309, 310n, 328, 341, 348, 348n, 349, 351–52, 369, 370n, 371–72, 372n, 380–82, 389, 397–98, 398n, 410–11; Roosevelt and, **7:**397, 398n, 413–14, 414–15n; in San Francisco, **7:**381–82; SG and, **7:**333, 348–50, 350n, 351–52, 362n, 369, 370n, 371, 371n, 372–74, 374n, 376–77, 377n, 385–87, 391, 396, 396n, 397, 398n, 401–5, 408–11, 413–15, 415n,

416, 416n, 417–18, 421, 425, 427n, 486n, **8:**270; Socialist party and, **7:**374–75, 375n, 401–5, 425, 427n, 486n; St. Louis Central Trades and Labor Union and, **7:**373; Taft and, **7:**281, 281n, 362n, 369, 375, 385n, 397, 398n, 402, 410–11, 413, 414n, 415–16, 416n; in Texas, **7:**385–86; Typographical Union and, **7:**383–84, 384n; Union Labor party and, **7:**382, 382n, 383–84, 384n; Van Cleave and, **7:**369, 370n; Walker and, **7:**350n, 359, 416–17; in Washington state, **7:**414, 414n
—1910, **8:**91–92, 131–32, 134–35, 135n, 245–46; AFL and, **9:**3–4; AFL financial appeal for, **8:**76n, 86, 123–25, 125n; AFL financial report on, **9:**3, 8n; AFL organizers and, **8:**131–32; Wilson and, **8:**135
—1912, **8:**354, 355n, 385, 431, **12:**436–37; AFL and, **8:**386, 386–87n, 394, 409–11, **9:**4; AFL organizers and, **9:**4; Democratic party and, **8:**386, 386n, 409, 467, 477, 494, **9:**4, 9, 77, 111; Republican party and, **8:**386n, 409, **9:**4, 77, 111; SG and, **8:**386, 386–87n, 395–96; socialists and, **8:**409–11; Wilson and, **8:**386, 386n, **12:**511
—1916, **9:**462, 462n, 473, 487, 488n, 518, **12:**492
—1920, **11:**275–77, 283n, 330, 346–47, 374–77, 378n, 382, 384, 404–5, **12:**41, 269; AFL Executive Council and, **11:**239–40, 264; AFL organizers and, **11:**273; Democratic party and, **12:**122; Perkins and, **11:**283n; SG and, **12:**122
—1922, **12:**34–36, 40, 147, 464, 467n; AFL and, **12:**160–63, 169–70; AFL Executive Council and, **12:**162; AFL National Non-Partisan Political Campaign Committee and, **12:**162, 164n, 186–87, 189, 436; AFL organizers and, **12:**161–62; Democratic party and, **12:**169, 170n; La Follette and, **12:**121–23, 149–50, 170; SG and, **12:**121–23, 162, 169, 170–71n; Smith and, **12:**169, 170n
—1924: AFL and, **12:**409, 453–55,

455n, 456–57, 457n, 458, 458n, 459–60, 461n; AFL Executive Council and, **12:**453–57, 458n, 462, 465, 474, 475n, 480–81, 483n, 486–94, 494n, 498–99; AFL Legislative Committee and, **12:**433n, 461n, 462, 467n; AFL National Non-Partisan Political Campaign Committee and, **12:**433–34n, 456, 461n, 462, 465, 472n, 481, 486–94, 494n, 500–501; Berry and, **12:**468, 468n, 474; Bryan and, **12:**463–64, 467–68n, 492–93; Conference for Progressive Political Action and, **12:**409, 409–10n, 432, 463–66, 467–68n, 469, 471, 472n, 473, 475n, 478, 480n, 481, 490; Coolidge and, **12:**463, 467n, 484–85, 492, 500, 508–10, 513n; Davis and, **12:**463–64, 467–68n, 484–85, 492, 495–501, 508–9; Democratic party and, **12:**453–55, 455n, 456–57, 457n, 458, 458n, 459–60, 461n, 462–64, 467–68n, 472, 472n, 473, 481, 484, 486–87, 491–92, 495–501, 505–6, 508–11, 513, 518–19; Duncan and, **12:**430, 432, 433n, 489, 491, 493; Farmer-Labor party and, **12:**296n, 430, 432, 433n, 484, 490; Farmer-Labor Progressive party and, **12:**430–33, 433n, 490–91; Federated Farmer-Labor party and, **12:**296n, 409, 430–31; Foster and, **12:**432, 433n, 484–85, 485n, 490–91, 508; Frayne and, **12:**461n, 504; Green and, **12:**491, 493; Holder and, **12:**468, 474; Jewell and, **12:**474, 478–80, 481, 484n; Johnston and, **12:**431, 433n, 468–69, 470n, 474, 478–81, 490; La Follette and, **12:**389n, 409, 409–10n, 432, 433n, 463–67, 467n, 468–69, 470n, 471, 473–75, 475–76n, 478–84, 484n, 485, 487–89, 491–93, 494n, 497, 501, 504–7, 507n, 508, 510–13, 513n; Manly and, **12:**431–33, 433n, 474, 476n, 478; McGrady and, **12:**184n, 433, 433n, 456, 461n, 467n, 474, 483; Morrison and, **12:**184n, 433, 433n, 456, 459–60, 461n, 464, 466, 467n, 468, 468n,

470n, 472n, 474, 480–83, 483n, 489–92; Nelson and, **12:**430, 432, 433n, 481, 484n, 491; O'Connell and, **12:**184n, 433n, 456, 459–60, 461n, 481, 489–90; railroad unions and, **12:**479; Republican party and, **12:**453–55, 455n, 456–57, 457n, 458, 458n, 459–60, 462–63, 467n, 472, 472n, 473, 481, 484, 486–87, 491–92, 501, 505–6, 508–11, 513, 518–19; Roberts and, **12:**184n, 433n, 456, 460, 461n, 467n, 472n, 483n; SG and, **12:**227–28, 384, 409, 430–33, 433n, 456–57, 457–58n, 458–60, 461n, 462–69, 470n, 471–72, 472n, 473–75, 478–85, 485n, 486–501, 503–13, 518–20; Smith and, **12:**467n; Socialist party and, **12:**508; Tobin and, **12:**461n, 489, 491–93; Wallace and, **12:**432–33, 433n, 456, 461n, 467n, 468, 474, 483; Wheeler and, **12:**389n, 409n, 467–68n, 470n, 475–76n, 482, 484n, 487–89, 492–93, 505–6, 513; Wilson and, **12:**495–501; Woll and, **12:**456, 458n, 459, 461n, 465–66, 467n, 468–69, 470n, 471–72, 472n, 473, 473n, 474–75, 478–83, 483n, 489, 504–5, 507n; Workers' Party of America and, **12:**296n, 409, 431–32, 433n, 463, 484–85, 485n; Wright and, **12:**431, 433n, 461n, 467n, 468, 470n, 471, 474, 478–80, 502, 504

Electrical Workers, International Brotherhood of, **3:***, **4:***, **5:***, 277, 278n, 285, **6:***, 122n, **7:***, 90n, 461n, **8:***, 12n, **9:***, 38, 342, 343n, **10:***, 400n, 502n, **11:***, 28n, 85n, 99n, 281n, 344, 381, 381n, 475n, **12:***, 148n; and black workers, **5:**327, 327–28n, **12:**148, 343n; injunctions against, **8:**470, 471n, 490, **11:**189–90, 191n; jurisdiction of, **6:**297–99, 299n; and railroad shopmen's strike, 1919 (threatened), **11:**120n; secession movement in, **7:**480, *482n*, **8:**15–16, 16–17n, 137–39, 139n, 150, 159, 160n, 413–14, 414n, **9:**38, 38–39n, 40, 40n, 70, *73n*, 137n; and women workers,

organization of, **4:**323, 324n, **9:**99, 99n, **12:**371n
—conventions: 1903 (Milwaukee), **6:**139, *140n;* 1908 (St. Louis), **7:**482n
—locals: local 1A (Boston), **9:**270, 274n; local 4 (New Orleans), **6:**31, 31–32n; local 9 (Chicago), **8:**470, 471n, 490; local 100 (Jacksonville, Fla.), **5:**327, 327–28n (*see also* American Federation of Labor [AFL]: local unions [LUs], directly affiliated: LU 9001); local 134 (Chicago), **8:**470, 471n, 490; local 147A (Palestine, Tex.), **11:**189–90, 191n; local 189 (Quincy, Mass.), **7:**77; local 213 (Vancouver, B.C.), **11:**281n; local 353 (Toronto), **11:**381, 381n; local 355 (Wilkinsburg, Pa.), **6:**121–22, 122n; local 388 (Palestine, Tex.), **11:**189–90, 191n; local 397 (Balboa Heights, Canal Zone), **11:**391; local 405 (Cedar Rapids, Iowa), **10:**368, 369n; local 481 (Indianapolis), **12:**363; local 571 (Gary, Ind.), **8:**160n; local 572 (Regina, Sask.), **11:**381, 381n; local 810 (Mobile, Ala.), **11:**486n
—strikes/lockouts: 1902 (New Orleans), **6:**31, *31–32n;* 1914 (Toledo, Ohio), **9:**99, *99n;* 1919 (Palestine, Tex.), **11:**189–90, *191n;* 1919 (threatened), **11:**95n; 1920–21 (Mobile, Ala.), **11:**484–85, *486n*
electrical workers, wages of, **10:**86–87, 87n
Electrical Workers of America, National Brotherhood of, **3:***, 260, 442n, 533n, **4:***, 171n, **5:***, **6:***, **7:***, **8:***, **9:***, **10:***, **11:***, **12:***
—locals: local 2 (Milwaukee), **3:**494, 498n; local 26 (Washington, D.C.), **4:**170, 171n
Elevator Constructors, International Union of, and Chicago building trades arbitration case, **11:**496n
—local: local 50 (Toronto), **11:**380, 381n
Elgin Watch Co., **5:**31, 32n
Eliot, Charles W., **6:**356–59, *360n,* 417, 423n, **8:**135

Elizabeth (N.J.) Central Labor Union. *See* Union County (N.J.) Trades Council
Elizabeth (N.J.) *Daily Journal,* boycott, 1908, **7:**337–38, 338n
Elks, Benevolent and Protective Order of:
—lodges: Lodge 1 (New York City), **12:**517; Lodge 15 (Washington, D.C.), **12:**517
Elkus, Abram I., **8:***329n,* 389n, **9:**258, 259n; *letter to,* **8:**328–29
Elliott, Charles H., **5:***318n; letter from,* **5:**316–18
Elliott, Charles H., Co.: *letter to,* **5:**318–20; strike/lockout, 1900–1901, **5:***318n,* 320
Elliott, J. H., **11:**538, 539n
Elliott, James D., **10:**322, *323n,* **11:**174
Elliott, John T., **2:***, *76n,* **3:***, *61n,* 119, **4:***, 84n, 144, *145n,* 148, 454–55, 504; at AFL conventions, **2:**74, 275; *letters from,* **2:**417, **3:**61; *letters to,* **2:**120, 247–48, 283–84, 428–29, **3:**63–64, 157
Ellis, Mr. (National Cash Register official?), **4:**460
Ellis, William, **1:**10, *12n*
Ellis Island, **1:**362n
Ellison, Elias, **7:***118n; letters from,* **7:**116–17, 381–82
Elm, Johann Adolph von, **3:***, 639, 660n, **4:***, *137n,* 193, **6:***, *413n,* **11:***, 10–11, *17n; letters to,* **4:**133–37, 155–57, **6:**412–13
Elmira (N.Y.) Central Trades and Labor Assembly, **6:***152n*
El Salvador, and Pan-American Federation of Labor, **9:**466n
Elton, Charles, **6:**415, 417n
Ely, Frederick W., **9:***515n;* SG, *interview with,* **9:**512–15
Ely, Richard T., **2:***, 36, *36n,* 65, 78, 189, **3:***, 363, 656, *661n*
Ely, Smith, Jr., **1:**100, *102n*
Emancipation Proclamation, **12:**110
Emanuel, G. J., **1:**10
Emergency Federation of Peace Forces, **9:**274n
Emergency Fleet Corp., **10:**204,

207–*8n,* 209n, 220–21, 221n, 340n, **11:**52n, 63n

Emerson, Harrington, **12:**142, *146n*

Emerson, Nathaniel B., **1:**201–2, *203n,* 204

Emerson, Ralph Waldo, **12:**217n

Emery, James A., **8:**198, *199n,* **9:**85, 87, 88n

Emme, Julius F., **12:**326–27, *327n*

Emmendorf, M., **6:**276, *278n*

Emmet mine (Leadville, Colo.), **4:**255

Employers', Builders', and Building Material Men's Association of Gary (Ind.), **8:**160n

employers: interests of, **9:**131–32; liability of, **1:**231, 361, **3:**192, 278, 395, 454–55, **4:**113, **6:**479, **8:**32, 181–82, 190–91, 413, 443–47, 457–58, **10:**143–47, 147–48n, **12:**4 (*see also under* legislation, foreign; legislation, states and territories; legislation, U.S.); membership of, in AFL, **2:**375, 375n; membership of, in trade unions, **2:**33, **3:**247–48; political power of, **2:**83

Employers' Federation of Engineering Associations, **5:**68, *69n*

Employers' Liability Cases, **10:**145, *147n*

Employers' Parliamentary Council, *5:69n*

employment agencies, **11:**8n

employment bureaus, state, **9:**123

employment halls, **10:**476, 476n. *See also* "Fink Hall"

Empress of Ireland (passenger liner), sinking of, **9:**201, *203n*

Emrich, Henry, **1:***, 371, *372n,* 390, **2:***, 55, *55n,* 243, 358, **3:***, 176, *177n,* 298, **4:***, 152, *155n;* at AFL conventions, **1:**457, 471, **2:**77, 169, 171–72, 272, 387, 393, 395; at FOTLU convention, **1:**454, 462n

Endich, Judge, **9:**263n

Engel, Anton J., **6:***, 228–30, *231n*

Engel, George, **1:***, *462n,* **2:***, 53, *55n,* 56, 59

Engels, Friedrich, **1:**43n, **2:**149, 149–*50n,* 156, 159n, **3:**10n, 121, 121–22n, **4:**104, 339n, 474–75; *letter to,* **3:**7–10

Engineering Council, **11:**23n

Engineers, Amalgamated Society of, **6:***, 157, 158n, 447, 449n, **9:**385n

engineers, and labor, **11:**384–90, 391n, **12:**412–13

Engineers, Eccentric, Association of, local 3 (New York City), **2:**371n

Engineers, German, local 1 (New York City), **7:**217–19, 219n

Engineers, United, local 1 (New York City), **7:**217–19, 219n

Engineers' Committee on Waste in Industry. *See* Federated American Engineering Societies

Engineers of Great Britain and America, Amalgamated Society of, **1:**457

England. *See* Great Britain

English, Margaret, **3:**109, *109n,* 176

Ennis, Roscoe C., *11:486n; letter from,* **11:**484–85

Episcopal Eye, Ear, and Throat Hospital, **8:**468n

Eppenetter, Frank N., **1:**361, *362n*

Eppley, Francis, **7:**406n

equal rights amendment, *12:31n,* 37, 39n; AFL opposition to, **12:**31, 372

Erb, Charles M., *1:369n,* **2:**418; *report of,* **1:**368–69

Erdhaus, Henry B., **5:**502, 503n

Erdman, Constantine, **4:**142n, **5:**308n

Erfurt congress, 1872, **1:**26, 32, 42

Erie (Pa.), Central Labor Union of, *7:16n*

Erie Railroad, **9:**481; strike/lockout, 1892, **3:**185, 214n

Erie Railroad Co. v. *Winfield,* **10:**144, *147n*

Erlanger, Mitchell L., **11:**455, *458n*

Erwin, William W., **3:**265, *266n*

Erzberger, Matthias, **10:**344, *345n*

Esch, John, **11:**157n, 216n

Esdaile, James N., **7:**238, *238n*

Esper, Frank J., **11:**262–63, *265n*

Essex (N.J.) Trades Council, **10:**423, *431n*

Estenoz, Evaristo E., **5:**185, *188n*

Estes, Fred J., **4:**250–51, *251n*

Ethical Culture, New York Society for, Workingmen's School of the, **2:**94n

Ethical Culture, Young Men's Union for, **2:**94, *94n*

Ettor, Joseph J., **8:**325–26n, 501–2, *502–3n,* **9:**489n

Eunson, Andrew, **10:**533, 537n

Euphrat, Charles, **7:**198–99, *199n,* 230–31

Eureka (Calif.) Federated Trades Council, *7:112n;* and IWW, **7:**111

Evangelical Association, *2:319n*

Evans, Christopher, **1:***, 390, *391n,* 451, **2:***, 23n, *275n,* 283, 292, 301, 393, **3:***, *58n,* 107, 141, 217, 238, 302, 401, 411, 511, 667, **4:***, 353, *353n,* 366, 378, **6:**270, 271n; at AFL conventions, **1:**457, **2:**256n, 275, **3:**128, 261, 595, 597n, 610, 623, 626–27, 657; and clothing cutters' strike, 1893, **3:**298, 313, 338, 340n; and depression of 1893, **3:**367, 379, 382; and Homestead strike, 1892, **3:**199n, 206, 210, 218, 219n, 231; and KOL, **1:**386, 460, 464; *letters from,* **1:**395–96, 425–26, **3:**58; *letter to,* **3:**56–57; and organizing, **3:**105, 174, 607; and Pullman strike, 1894, **3:**532, 535, 563

Evans, E. Lewis, **4:***, *395n,* **5:***, *119n; letter from,* **5:**461–63; *letters to,* **5:**117–19, 460–61

Evans, Edward, **8:**131, *132n*

Evans, Edward J., **11:**98, *99n,* 124–25; *wire from,* **11:**128–29

Evans, Evan, **7:**359, *361n*

Evans, Evan A., **12:**154, *155n,* 219

Evans, Fred, *9:161n; letter from,* **9:**160–61

Evans, Joseph E., **8:***, 149, *151n*

Evans, Newton W., **5:***, 391, *391n*

Evans, P. F., *letter to,* **9:**251–52

Evening Copper Journal (Hancock, Mich.), **9:**28n

Everest, Wesley, **11:**217n

Everett (Wash.) Trades Council, **12:**237, *241n*

Evers, Charles, **7:**9n; *letter from,* **7:**8–9

excess profit tax, **10:**189–90, 190n, **11:**542, 543n, **12:**25, 424

Exler, John W., **1:**219, *220n*

expansionism, SG views on, **4:**482

Ex parte Sing Lee, **8:**479, *492n*

Exposition Universelle de 1900, **5:**91, *93n*

Faber, Leander B., **11:**455, *458n*

Fabrosky, Joseph, **1:**115n

Fahey, Charles P., **4:**407, *408n,* **6:**3, *4n*

Fahey, John, **4:**383n

Fairbanks, Charles W., **5:**470, *474n,* **7:**320n

Fairchild, Charles F., **4:**304n

Fairchild, G. W., *letter to,* **3:**247–48

Fairchild, Lewis W., **11:**42, *46n,* 394n; *letter from,* **11:**400; *letter to,* **11:**393–94

Fairgrieve, Alexander, **6:***, 455, *457n,* 462

Fairley, William R., *7:329n,* **9:**489n, **10:**79n, 376–77, *378n*

Fairview, Florence, **4:**15, *16n*

Fales, L. E., **7:**163, *164n*

Falkner, Roland P., **9:**139, *140n*

Fall, Albert B., **12:**228n

Falligant, Louis A., **4:**21–22, *22n*

Fallon, Michael, *3:497n; letter from,* **3:**490–97

Fallows, Samuel, **3:**424, *426n*

Fall River (Mass.) Textile Council, **6:**350n

Falú, Pedro, **6:**253, 258n

Fanz, Henry J., **4:**416, *417n*

Fargo (N.Dak.) Trades and Labor Assembly, *9:424n*

Farmer-Labor party, **11:**218n, 452, **12:**187, 236, 270; and election of 1924, **12:**296n, 430, 432, 433n, 484, 490

—convention: 1923 (Chicago), **12:**294, *296n,* 430–32, 490

Farmer-Labor Progressive party, and election of 1924, **12:**430–33, 433n, 490–91

—convention: 1924 (St. Paul, Minn.), **12:**430–33, *433n,* 490–91

Farmer-Labor Reconstruction League (Oklahoma), **12:**189n

farmers: AFL and, **7:**134, **8:**7–9, 9–10n, **9:**34, 36n, 422–24, **11:**132n, 187, 188n, **12:**188; black, **12:**425; label of, **5:**120, 121n; *letter from,* **11:**238–39, 239n; organization of, **3:**145–46, **5:**119–21, 177–78, **11:**213, 214n, 218n, 347n; SG and, **5:**119–21, **7:**301, 385, **8:**10n, 44–45, 45n, 72, **12:**285. *See also* farmers' alliances

Farmers' Alliance, National ("Northwestern Alliance"), **3:**24n
Farmers' Alliance and Co-operative Union of America, National ("Southern Alliance"), **3:**24n, 263n
Farmers' Alliance and Industrial Union of America, National, **3:**3, 24n, 105n, 263n, 442n, 511
farmers' alliances: and labor organizations, **3:**3–4, 6n, 24; SG and, **3:**3, 93, 99, 201, 262–63, 263n, 272–73. *See also specific alliances*; Knights of Labor (KOL): and farmers' alliances
—conferences: 1889 (St. Louis), **3:**3; 1890 (Ocala, Fla.), **3:**3, *6n;* 1891 (Indianapolis), **3:**104, *105n;* 1892 (St. Louis), **3:**262, *263n*
Farmers' and Laborers' Union of America, **3:**24n
Farmers' Educational and Cooperative Union of America, **7:***59n,* **8:**276n
—conventions: 1905 (Texarkana, Ark.), **7:***59n;* 1908 (Memphis, Tenn.), **7:**301, *302n;* 1908 (Fort Worth, Tex.), **7:**385, *387n;* 1910 (St. Louis), **8:**10n, *45n*
Farmers' Educational and Cooperative Union of Texas, **7:**301, 302n
Farmers' Mutual Benefit Association, **3:**105n, *263n*
Farmers' National Alliance and Cooperative Union, Colored, **3:***24n*
Farmers' National Congress, **8:***45n*
Farmers' Union, International, **5:**121n
farm laborer organizations, **1:**340, 353n, **3:**3, 93, 145–46, 146n, 201, 272–73
Farm Organizations, National Board of, and AFL Permanent Conference for Abolition of Child Labor, **12:**82n
Farnham, Milton G., **2:**98, *98n; letter to,* **3:**154
Farquhar, John M., **5:***, 142–46, *146n*
Farrel Foundry and Machine Co., **10:**281, 284n
Farrell, John H., **5:***123n; letter to,* **5:**123
Farrington, Frank, **9:***178n,* 272, **11:**481; *letters to,* **9:**176–78, **12:**294–95
Fascist movement, **12:**255–56, 366

Fauber, W. H., Co., boycott, 1898, **4:**500, *501n*
Faulkner, James E., **3:**138, *138n*
Faustus Labor Club, **1:**360, *362n*
Fay, Stephen, **6:**493n
F.B.Q. Clothing Co., strike/lockout, 1918, **10:**335, *336n*
Fear, Charles W., **4:***466n,* **7:***161n; article by,* **4:**463–65; *letters to,* **7:**158–61, 458–59
Featherstone, Daniel F., **10:**361, 363n
Feather Workers' Union:
—strike/lockout: 1889 (New York City), **2:***155n*
Fechner, Robert, **12:**202–3, *206n; letter to,* **12:**213–15
Federación de Sindicatos Obreros de la República Mexicana, **9:**305, *307n,* 363n, 427n, 429n, 467
Federación Libre de los Trabajadores de Puerto Rico, **5:**416n, 425n, **6:**252–54, *258n,* **9:**257, **11:**504n; injunction against, **6:**424–25, 428, 429n
—strike/lockout: 1905, **6:**424–25, 427–28, *429n*
Federación Obrera de la República de Panamá, **12:**411; SG, meeting with representatives of, **12:**385–86
—conventions: 1921 (Panama City, Panama), **12:**536, *538n;* 1924 (Panama City, Panama), **12:**536, *538n*
Federación Regional de los Trabajadores de Puerto Rico, **6:**252–54, *257–58n*
Federal Baseball League, **9:**237n
Federal Council of Churches of Christ in America, **9:**310n, **12:**415, 417n; and AFL Permanent Conference for Abolition of Child Labor, **12:**82n
Federal Employees, National Federation of, **11:***, 135n, 335, **12:**446n; and black workers, **11:**84n; and women workers, organization of, **12:**371n
Federal Party of Puerto Rico. *See* Partido Federal de Puerto Rico
Federal Reserve Board, **9:**300n, **12:**216
Federal Trade Commission, **9:**300n, 365, 449, 526n

Federated American Engineering Societies, **12:**142–43, 146n, 297, 413
Federated Farmer-Labor party, **12:**295, *296n,* 430, 490; and election of 1924, **12:**296n, 409, 430–31
Fédération du verre, **4:**77n
Fédération française des travailleurs du livre, *2:108n,* **4:**90, **10:**541n
Fédération Nationale des Coopératives de Consommation, **9:**238, *240n*
Federation of Organized Trades and Labor Unions of the U.S. and Canada (FOTLU), **1:**159–62, 243–44, 348, 354, 437, **2:**260; call of, for eight-hour day, **1:**212–13, 225, 281, 363–64; *circular of,* **1:**363–64; finances of, **1:**233–34, 239–40; and KOL, **1:**161–62, 275–76, 280, 282–83, 387–88, 440, 456, 460; merger of, with AFL, **1:**387, 461, 462n, 467–68, **9:**395; principles of, **1:**224–27, 241; and regionalism, **1:**238; SG and, **1:**163, 211, 214, 216–24, 227–35, 238–45, 277n, 286n, 371, 387, 440, 457, 462n; and socialism, **1:**213, 216; and strikes, **1:**280, 454; structure of, **1:**221–30, 239–40
—conventions: 1881 (Pittsburgh), **1:**161–62, 164–65, 238–44, **2:**155, *156n,* 260, **3:**202, 662, **9:**368, *370n,* 514, 515n, **12:**351, 375, 375n, 521–22; 1882 (Cleveland), **1:**231, *232n,* 275; 1883 (New York City), **1:**323, *328n;* 1884 (Chicago), **1:**276, 363, *364n,* **2:**61–62, *63n,* 155, 170, 260, **3:**106n, 567, *580n,* **9:**121, 136n, **12:**375, *376n;* 1885 (Washington, D.C.), **1:**276, 371, *371n,* 373n, **2:**155, *157n,* **3:**567, *580n,* **4:**141n; 1886 (Columbus, Ohio), **1:**387, 437, 451–52, **2:**261
—conventions, *accounts of:* 1881 (Pittsburgh), **1:**210–32; 1882 (Cleveland), **1:**282–85; 1886 (Columbus, Ohio), **1:**453–55, 457, 467
—Legislative Committee: **1:**223, 228, *229n,* 231, 239, 242–45, 276, 460; *circular of,* **1:**451–52; *letter to,* **1:**440; members, election of, **1:**231, 234n, 242–43, 286n; SG and, **1:**230–35, 239, 242–43, 277n, 286n, 371

—Legislative Committee, meetings, *minutes of:* Nov. 1881, **1:**232–36; Nov. 1882, **1:**286; Dec. 1885, **1:**371
Federation of the Organized Workers of the Republic of Mexico. *See* Federación de Sindicatos Obreros de la República Mexicana
Feehan, Francis, **7:**121, *122n*
Feeney, Edward, *3:340n,* **4:**57; and mediation of clothing cutters' strike, 1893, **3:**305–7, 313, 333–36, 338, 340
Fehrenbatch, John, **3:***, 469, *470n*
Feick, Frederick L., **10:**189n, 280n, 403, *404n*
Feinstone, Morris C., **12:**550, *553n*
Fell, Daniel A., Jr., **4:**442–44, *446n*
fellow-servant rule, **3:**192, 395, **6:**479, **8:**32, 181, **9:**7, **12:**4
Fellowship of Reconciliation, **12:**310, *311n*
Fels, Joseph, **10:**238n
Fels, Mary, **10:**236, *238n*
Feltman, William, **1:**185–86, 199
Felts, Albert, **11:**296n
Fenians, **3:**241n
Fenn, Albert P., **7:**227–28, *229n*
Fennessey, Thomas D., **7:**383–84, *384n*
Fenwick, Charles, **3:**223, *224n,* 516; *letter to,* **3:**348–49
Ferguson, Frank C., **5:**91, *93n*
Ferguson, William, *letter to,* **2:**371–74
Ferrell, Frank J., **2:***, 53, 55, *55n*
Ferrell, Wesley P., *5:485n; letter from,* **5:**484–85
Ferris, Howard, **7:**11, *11n*
Ferris, Woodbridge, **8:**513n, **9:**47n, 65, *68n,* 183
Ferry, Neal (variously Neil) J., **12:**550, *553n*
Fess, Simeon D., *12:171n*
Fessler, Arthur F., *11:267n; wire from,* **11:**265–66
Field, David D., **2:**289, *289n*
Fielden, Samuel, **1:***, *462n,* **2:***, 53, *55n,* 56, 59, **3:***, 350, *350n,* 358
Figolah, William, **7:***, 449, *451n*
Filene, Edward A., **7:**309n, 461–62, *462n,* **8:**110–12, **10:**310, **11:**523n
Findley, Alvin I., *letter to,* **6:**411
Fink, Reuben, *12:125n; letter to,* **12:**123–25

Finkelstone, Edward, **1:***, 457, *458n,*
  2:*, *98n; letter to,* **2:**98
"Fink Hall," **12:**390, *390n*
Finley, John H., **10:**310, *312n*
Finley v. *United Mine Workers of America*
  et al., **10:***323n*
Finn, Daniel E., **1:**446, *447n*
Finn, John J., **1:**360, *362n*
Finnell, Thomas C., **1:**206, *207n*
Finnie, Jennie, *letter to,* **4:**173–74
Finzer, John, and Bros., **4:**394, *395n*
Fire Fighters, International Association of, **11:***, 435n
Firemen, International Brotherhood
  of Stationary, **5:***, 162n, 396n, 446,
  6:*, 135n, **7:***, 36n, **8:***, 148n, 290n,
  10:502n, **11:***, **12:***; jurisdiction of,
  5:161, 162n, 169–71, 172n, 290,
  292n, 374–75, 375n, 433–34, 501–3,
  503–4n, 514–15, 515–16n, **6:**9–10,
  10–11n, 88–89, 89–90n, 101–2, 102–
  3n, 133–34, 135–36n, 208, 223–28,
  228n, 297–99, 299n, 317–26, 326–
  27n, 365–67, 368n, 452, 453n, 500–
  502, 502–3n, **7:**32–35, 36–37n, 152,
  152–53n, 199–201, 201–2n, 208–10,
  210–11n, 272–74, 274n, 317–18;
  withdrawal of, from AFL, **6:**317–18,
  323, 326n
—conventions: 1898 (Kansas City,
  Mo.), **6:**319, *326n;* 1904 (Washington, D.C.), **6:**317–26, *326n*
—locals: local 42 (Philadelphia),
  6:503n; local 49 (Cincinnati),
  5:374–75, 375n, 501–3, 503n, 514–
  15; local 56 (New York City), **7:**373,
  374n; local 75 (Belleville, Ill.),
  6:367, 369n; local 86 (San Francisco), **6:**101–2, 102–3n
—strikes/lockouts: 1901 (Cincinnati),
  5:374–75, *375n;* 1901 (Pennsylvania), **5:**381, *382n;* 1904–? (Belleville,
  Ill.), **6:**367, *369n*
Firemen and Engineers' Helpers'
  Union:
—local: local 158 (Denver), **5:**393–94,
  396n
Firemen and Oilers, International
  Brotherhood of, **6:***, **7:***, **8:***, **11:***,
  12:*

Firemen and Oilers, International
  Brotherhood of Stationary, **5:***, **6:***,
  7:*, **8:***, **11:***, 28n, 60n, 85n, 318–
  19n, 362, 480n, **12:***, 98n, 446n;
  and black workers, **11:**84n, **12:**299–
  300, 341–42, 342–43n; jurisdiction
  of, **11:**59–60, 60–61n, **12:**300, 341–
  42, 342–43n
—local: local 18 (Lawrence, Mass.),
  11:351, 352n
First American Conference for Democracy and Terms of Peace, 1917
  (New York City), **10:**93, *93n,* 94
First Conference for the Maintenance
  of Workers' Rights and Standards,
  1917 (New York City), **10:**127, *128n*
First International. *See* International
  Workingmen's Association
Fisch, Gustav, **12:**219n
Fischer, Adolph, **1:***, *462n,* **2:***, 53,
  55n, 56, 59
Fischer, Henry, **4:***, *395n,* **5:***, 430–31,
  432n, **6:***, *214n,* 400; *letters from,*
  4:394–95, **6:**214
Fischer, Jacob, **10:***, *475n,* **11:***, 128n,
  345, *345n,* **12:***, *117n,* 163n, 336,
  461n, 476; election of, as AFL
  vice-president, **10:**475, **11:**93n,
  321, 321n, 482, **12:**97n, 338n; and
  election of SG's successor, **12:**555,
  559–60
Fish, Nicholas, **2:**245, *247n*
Fisher, Frederick V., **10:***182n; letter to,*
  10:181–82
Fisher, James H., **10:**262, *263n*
Fisher, Robert, **4:***507n; letter to,*
  4:506–7
Fishermen of the Pacific, United, **6:**5n
Fishermen's Protective Union of the
  Pacific Coast and Alaska, **6:**5n
Fishler, Bennett, **9:**53, *54n*
Fitch, John A., **11:**154, *155n,* **12:**7, 8n
Fitchie, Thomas, **6:**111n
Fitzgerald, Anna, **7:**299n, **10:**218,
  11:240n, 275n, **12:**38n; *letter to,*
  7:298–99
Fitzgerald, Clarence A., **11:**149, 149n
FitzGerald, Edward H., **11:***, *502n,*
  12:*, *21n,* 86, 111, 112n; *letter from,*
  11:501–2; *wire to,* **12:**20

Fitzgerald, Frank A., **8:**355, *357n*
FitzGerald, James F., **7:***, *151n*, 203–4;
  letter from, **7:**150–51
Fitzgerald, John F., **5:**363n
Fitzgerald, John J. (boilermaker), **5:***,
  167, *169n*
Fitzgerald, John J. (congressman),
  8:468n, 492, *493n*, 496n
Fitzgerald, Theodore, **1:**135, *139n*
Fitzgerald, Thomas D., **4:**414, *416n*,
  8:327, *327n*, **9:**330, 332n, 491,
  10:329; *letter to*, **9:**400–403
Fitzgibbon, James H., **2:***, 137, *138n;*
  letter to, **2:**141–42
FitzPatrick, James, **12:**536n
Fitzpatrick, John, **4:**30, *30n*
Fitzpatrick, John E., **9:**80n
Fitzpatrick, John J., **6:**283, *285n*,
  7:350n, 361–62, 387, 387n, 417n,
  8:*, *75n*, **9:***, *205n*, 261n, 354, **10:***,
  5n, 215–17, 218n, 297, 327n, **11:***,
  18n, *85n*, 214, 263–64, **12:***, 38,
  40n, 42, 43n, 55, 190, 244n, 282–83,
  296n, 311–12, 315n, 490; at AFL
  conventions, **9:**348n, 349–50, 350n;
  circular of, **12:**312–15; *letters from,*
  7:302–4, **9:**203–5, **11:**141–42, 283–
  86; *letters to,* **9:**208–9, **10:**280–84,
  477–79, **11:**140–41, 496, **12:**242–44;
  and packinghouse workers, organization of, **10:**280n, 285n; and steelworkers' organizing campaign and
  strike, 1919, **11:**27n, 85, 99, 124–25,
  126n, 129n, 143–44, 148, 151–52,
  197n, 270n, 365n; *wires from,* **10:**5,
  279, **11:**128–29
Fitzpatrick, Patrick F., **1:***, 165, *166n*,
  451, **2:***, 21, *23n*, 25, **4:***, 123, *124n;*
  at AFL convention, **1:**457, 466, 470;
  and KOL, **1:**385–86, 460, 463–64;
  letters from, **1:**389–90, 395–96, 425–
  26; *letter to,* **2:**292–93
Fitzpatrick, Val, **4:**359n, **11:**250, *259n*
Flagler, John H., **5:**367–68, *368n*, 369
Flaherty, Martin D., **5:**331, *331*–32n,
  396n
Flaherty, Thomas F., **11:***, 476, *478n*
Flanigan, John, **1:**215, *217n*
Flannigan, Patrick M., **2:**22, 23n
Flaska, Mary, **7:**365, 365n

Flat Janitors:
—local: local 102 (Chicago), **6:**447,
  449n
Fleischmann, Charles, **2:**417n, **3:**270n
Fleischmann, Louis, **2:**417n, **3:**270n
Fleischmann and Co., boycott, 1889–
  93, **2:***417–18n*, **3:**270, *270n*
Fleming, Robert P., **4:**343, *344n*,
  5:254–55
Fleming, William H., **5:**326, *327n*
Fletcher, Albert H., **8:**143, *144n*
Fletcher, John, **2:**332
Flett, John A., **6:***, 21, *22n*, 134, 404,
  404n, **7:***, 236, *237n*, **9:***, *409n*,
  11:*, *381n; letter from,* **11:**380–81; *letter to,* **9:**408–9
Flint, Charles R., **5:**368, *368n*, **10:**89–
  90n
Flint and Pere Marquette Railroad,
  5:58–59, 59n, 60–61
Flint Glass Workers' Union, Ameri-
  can, **1:***, 458, 459n, **2:***, 134, 135n,
  3:*, 21, 23n, 505–6, **4:***, 472, 473n,
  5:*, 94n, **6:***, **7:***, **9:***, 34n; jurisdiction of, **6:**448, 450n, **7:**407, 408n;
  representation of, in central labor
  bodies, **7:**407, 408n
—conventions: 1898 (Zanesville,
  Ohio), **4:**503, *505n;* 1899 (Muncie, Ind.), **5:**92, *94n;* 1905 (Martins
  Ferry, Ohio), **6:**448–49, *450n*
—locals: local 6 (Marion, Ind.), **7:**407,
  408n; local 29 (Marion, Ind.),
  7:407, 408n; local 35 (Marion,
  Ind.), **7:**407, 408n
—strike/lockout: 1887–88, **2:**134, 197
Flint v. *Stone Tracy and Co.* See *Corporation Tax Cases*
Flood, Anna (daughter of Emmet
  Flood), **10:**304n
Flood, Anna (wife of Emmet Flood),
  7:233, *235n*, **10:**304
Flood, Emmet T., **6:**469, *469n*, **7:**100,
  104, 104n, 209, 229n, **8:***, *298n*, **9:***,
  46, 47n, 65, 354, *356n*, **10:***, *218n*,
  11:*, 450, *450n*, **12:***, 295, *296n; letters from,* **7:**227–29, 233–35, **8:**297,
  473–74, **10:**213–18, 302–4, **11:**451–
  53; *letter to,* **8:**298; *wire from,* **9:**438
Flood, Emmet T., Jr., **10:**304n

Flood, Evelyn, **10:**304n
Flood, Helen, **10:**304n
Flood, Henry, **10:**8n
Flood, Marie, **10:**304n
Flood, Raymond, **10:**304n
Flood, Rose, **10:**304n
Flore, Edward F., **10:***, *180n*
Flores, A. J., **12:**550
Florina, Nicola, **3:**513
Flour and Cereal Mill Employes, International Union of, **7:***, 304n; and Battle Creek Breakfast Food Co., Ltd., **7:**302–4, 304n; label of, **7:**303–4
Flower, Roswell P., *3:156n,* 365, 377, 385n, 387, 433; *letters to,* **3:**156, 385
Flynn, Edward, **6:**193
Flynn, Elizabeth Gurley, **8:**325, *326n,* 452–53n, 503n, **9:**489n
Flynn, John, **10:**361
Flynn, John J., **7:***, *44n; letter from,* **7:**44
Flynn, Patrick, **9:**38n
Flynn, Thomas H., **5:**392, *393n,* **6:**169n, 262–63, 268–69, 270n, **7:**48, 48n, 90n, 121–22, *122n,* 181, 190, **8:**189n, **10:**170, 517, 518n; *letters to,* **6:**167–70, **9:**150; *wire to,* **10:**170
Flynn, William J., **11:**54n, 219, *220n*
Foley, Cornelius F., **11:**316, *317n*
food: AFL and, **9:**525, 525–26n, 527; supply and prices, advisory committee on, **10:**74, 75n
Foraker, Joseph B., **4:**337, *338n,* 343n, **7:**87, 397, 398n
Foran, Martin A., **1:***, 283, *285n,* **2:***, 184, *184n,* **3:***, 469, *470n*
Forbes, Gerrit A., **5:**241–42, *244n*
Forbis (police chief), **10:**69–70n
Ford, C. M., *letter to,* **11:**221–23
Ford, Charles P., **9:***, 70, *73n*
Ford, Cornelius, **7:***, 469, 470–*71n,* **8:***, *358n,* **12:**66n; *letter to,* **8:**357–58
Ford, Henry, **9:**45, *45n,* **11:**449, 508n; *letter to,* **11:**507–8
Ford, Joseph E., **5:**91, *93n*
Ford, M. J., **5:**368, *369n,* 372
Ford, M. R., **11:**106n
Ford, Martha R., *12:66n; wire from,* **12:**66
Ford, Melbourne H., **2:**143n
Ford, Richard "Blackie," **9:**507n

Ford, Sheridan, **4:**118, *119n*
Ford, Thomas J., **1:***, 434, *434n,* **2:**257–58
Ford Investigating Committee. *See* U.S. House of Representatives: Select Committee on Importation of Contract Laborers, Convicts, Paupers, etc.
Ford Motor Co., **9:**45, 45–46n, **10:**365, **12:**10n
Fordney, Joseph, **12:**26n
Ford Plan, **9:**45, *45–46n*
foremen, eligibility of, for union membership, **5:**400–401
Fore River, Mass., shipyards, organization of, **8:**80–81, 81–82n
Fore River Ship Building Co., **10:**281, 284n
Foresters, Independent Order of, **4:**330–31, *331n;* court 1050 (Syracuse, N.Y.), **4:**330, *331n*
Forker, Max, **5:**429, *430n*
Forker, Reuben, *8:135n; letter from,* **8:**134–35
Forney, Frank, **8:**188, *190n*
Forrester, James J., **9:***, *517n,* **11:***, *84n,* **12:***, 112n, 344–46, *348n,* 433n; at AFL convention, **11:**83; at AFL Executive Council meeting, **11:**188n; and black workers, **11:**488, 502n, 551–52; *letter from,* **9:**516–17
Forrester, Rose Yates, *10:468n,* **12:**246–47, 247n. *See also* Yates, Rose A.
Forschner, August J., **1:***, *257n; letter from,* **1:**256–57
Forster, Rudolph, **10:**3, 4n
Fort, Franklin, **7:**456n
Fortschrittspartei, **1:**28, *44n*
Fortune, John, **1:***, 98, *101n,* 111, 259
Fort Wayne (Ind.) Federation of Labor, *8:9n*
Fort Worth (Tex.) Trades Assembly, **5:**221, *222n*
Forty Years of Action (AFL), **12:**188, *189n,* 437
Forward (New York City socialist journal), **11:**299, 299n
Forys, Frank, *letter from,* **8:**459–60
Fosdick, Eugene, **11:**450n
Fosdick, Sherman G., **6:**16, *19n*

Foss, Eugene N., **8:**325, *326n*
Foster, Addison, **5:**457, 458n
Foster, Charles, *3:195n; letter to,* **3:**195
Foster, David, **6:**527n
Foster, Frank K., **1:***, 282, *283n,* 287, **2:***, *173n,* **3:***, *14n,* 356, 419, 441, 480, 503, 517, 517n, 655, **4:***, 9, *9n,* **6:***, *364n,* **7:***, *68n,* 238, 481; at AFL conventions, **2:**171–72, 259, 269, 275, 390–91, 398–99, 410–11, 413–14, **3:**12–13, 126, 128n, 137, 251–52, 253n, 256, 259, 430, 434n, 436, 438–39, **6:***, 362–63, 364n, 375–76, 504–5, 508, 508n, **7:**130, 134–35, 141–42n; *letters to,* **3:**606–7, **7:**67–68
Foster, Israel, **12:**83n
Foster, John, **11:**460n
Foster, John T., **12:**438–39, *442n*
Foster, John W., *6:378n; letter to,* **6:**377–78
Foster, Martin D., **9:**96n, 97, *98n*
Foster, Murphy J., **3:**243n
Foster, Volney W., *6:232n*
Foster, William H., **1:***, 211, *212n,* 287, 458, **2:***, 62, *63n;* and FOTLU Legislative Committee, **1:**230–36, 242–44, 286, 286n, 371; and KOL, **1:**382, 383n, 385, 440; *letter from,* **1:**389–90
Foster, William Z., **8:**260, *260–61n,* **9:***, *454n,* **10:***, *218n,* **11:***, *27n,* **12:***, *47n,* 48, 434n; at AFL conventions, **10:**468, **12:**96–97; arrest of, **12:**125, 126n, 132n; and Chicago Federation of Labor, **12:**311, 431; and election of 1924, **12:**432, 433n, 484–85, 485n, 490–91, 508; and Illinois State Federation of Labor, **12:**334n; and industrial unionism, **12:**43–47, 48n, 55n, 62–65, 67–68, 126, 220, 403, 403n; and IWW, **8:**260, **10:**215, **12:**64; *letters from,* **10:**477–79, **11:**26–27, 153–55, 561, **12:**67–68; *letters to,* **9:**453–54, 461–62; and packinghouse workers, **10:**214–15, 280n, 302; raid on office of, **12:**131, 132n; and steelworkers' organizing campaign, 1918, **10:**477–79, 479–80n, 500–502; and steelworkers' organizing campaign and strike, 1919, **11:**28n, 99,

124–25, 126n, 129n, 141–42, 144n, 148, 152, 155n, 206n, 228–29, 360, **12:**279, 281n; and Trade Union Educational League, **11:**561n; western tour of, **12:**125–26, 126–27n; *wires from,* **10:**279, **11:**126, 128–29, 206, **12:**484–85
Foster and Hilson, **1:**192, *193n,* 199, 423
Fostoria (Ohio) Trades Assembly, **7:**408n
FOTLU. *See* Federation of Organized Trades and Labor Unions of the U.S. and Canada (FOTLU)
Foulger, Sydney, **7:**489, *490n*
Foundry Employes, International Brotherhood of, **7:***, 54n, **8:***, 200, 202n, **11:**28n, 85n
—local: local 5 (Troy, N.Y.), **7:**53–54, 54n
—strike/lockout: 1906 (Troy, N.Y.), **7:**53–54, *54n*
Fourier, François Marie Charles, **1:**40, *44n*
Fourteen Points, **10:**309, *310n,* 353, 464–65, 473n, 530–32, 544n, 551, 553, 567n, **12:**156
"Fourth Estate" (Workingmen's Estate), **1:**28–29, *44n*
Fowler, Chester A., **7:**158n
Fowler, Henry H., **3:**541, 542n
Fox, Charles, **11:***, 262–63, *265n*
Fox, Harry W., **12:**87–88n, *191n; letter to,* **12:**191
Fox, Martin, **3:***, *434n,* 535n, **4:***, 79, *80n,* 123, 315, 317n, 472, **5:***, *216n,* 311, *311n,* 368, 464n; at AFL conventions, **3:**430, 434n, 436, 439, 662, 664n; *letter from,* **4:**324–25; *letter to,* **4:**334; memorial to, **8:**389, 389n
Fox, William W., **12:**503, 504n
Fraeber (delegate), **2:**367
France, **4:**41, **10:**559; "Bolshevism" in, **11:**28; conditions in, **10:**112, 292, 342–43, 445–46, 465–66, 551–52; industrial courts in, **5:**300–301; labor representatives of, at Leeds (England) conference, 1916, **9:**470n; mission of, to United States, **10:**71, 72n; and outbreak of World War I, **9:**163n, **10:**559; socialists in, **4:**63,

68–69, **7:**479, **10:**343, 356n, 446, 465, 522–23, 550–52, 554–55n, 561, **11:**11; trade unions in, **1:**164, 281, 345, **3:**640, **4:**62–63, 68, 90, **7:**479, **11:**11; wartime industrial production in, **10:**25–26
—strikes/lockouts: 1895 (glassworkers), **4:**76, *77n;* 1920 (general strike), **11:**438, *440n*
France, Hugh, *5:98n*
France, Joseph I., **12:**13, *15n*
Francis, Charles S., **2:**341, *343n*
Francis, David, **10:**45–46n, 90n
Francis, Earl N., **10:**167, *169n; wire to,* **10:**167–68
Franck, Charles H., *11:51–52n; wire from,* **11:**51, 52n
franc-tireur, **9:**477n
Frank, Anton, **1:***, *425n; letter from,* **1:**424
Frank, H. C., *letter to,* **10:**340–41
Frank, Leo M., **9:**278, *278–79n,* **12:**210n
Frank, Solomon, *11:380n; letter to,* **11:**379–80
Frankel, Joseph, **6:**277, *278n*
Frankel, Lee, **10:**52n
Frankfurter, Felix, **10:**56n, *75n,* 195n, 337, 546n; *letter from,* **10:**74–75
Franklin, Joseph A., **8:***, 322, *323n,* **9:***, 49, *50n,* **10:***, 19, *21n,* 223n, 334n, 340n, 503, **12:***, 128n, 341–42, *343n; wire to,* **10:**340
Franklin, Stella Miles, **9:**234, *235n,* 302
Franklin-Bouillon, Henry, **10:**191, *193n*
Franklin Brewing Co.: boycott, 1907, **7:**209–10; strike/lockout, 1907, **7:**209–10, *210n*
Franks, Bernard J., **8:**440, *440n*
Franks, Robert, **12:**516n
Franz, G. A., **9:**351, *352n*
Franz Ferdinand, Archduke, **9:**160n
Frayne, Hugh, **7:**96, *98n,* **8:***, 36, *38n,* 231n, 456, **9:***, 107–8, *110n,* 161n, 168, 169n, 311n, **10:***, 61, *62n,* 103n, 156–57n, 313n, **11:***, *111n,* 140n, 243n, 324–25n, 354, 357, 454, 533n, **12:***, 50, *51–52n,* 242, 368, 550; and election of 1924,

12:461n, 504; and International Labor Conference, 1919, **11:**110–11, 111n; *letters from,* **8:**230–31, 439–40, **10:**330–31, **11:**323–24, 549; *letters to,* **8:**397–98, **9:**490–92
Frazier, Arthur H., **10:**540, *541n*
Frazier, Lynn J., **12:**170, *171n*
Frazier, William H., **5:***, 164, *168n,* **7:***, *101n*
Frederick, J. M. H., **9:**138n
Fredericks, John D., **8:**248, *249n,* 291
Freedman, John J., *5:243n;* injunction against picketing, **5:**240–43, 243–44n
Free Federation of the Workers of Puerto Rico. *See* Federación Libre de los Trabajadores de Puerto Rico
Freeman, William E., **11:***, *280n; letter to,* **11:**279–80
Free Trade (Marx), **2:**148, *149n*
freight handlers, **1:**296–97; union of (New Orleans), **5:**261
—black, **11:**182–83, 183n, 326, 349–50, 501–2, 502n; at AFL conventions, **11:**83n, 313–16, 316n; meeting of, **11:**488–91, 491–92n; Worthey and, **11:**550–51, 551n, 552–54, 558–59
Freight Handlers' and Warehousemen's International Union, Interior, **7:***, 44n; and IWW, **7:**44; and Socialist Labor party, **7:**44
—local: local 4 (Chicago), **7:**44
Freisinger, Victor, **8:**496, *497n*
Frelinghuysen, Joseph S., **12:**169, *171n*
French (Cigar Makers' organizer), **6:**31n
French, George W., **5:**311, *311n*
French, Thomas A., **9:***, *468n,* **10:***, *150n; letter to,* **9:**466–68; *wires from,* **10:**149
Fresno (Calif.) Farmers' Union, **8:**263, *276n*
Freund, John C., **6:**396, *397n*
Frey, John P., **6:***, 147, *147n,* **7:***, *122n,* 489, **8:***, 17n, *293n,* **9:***, *25n,* 90–91, 94n, 188–89n, **10:***, 44n, *333n,* 357n, **11:***, *61n,* 240n, 404n, 473, 475n, 560n, **12:***, 38n, *54n,* 388, 550; at AFL conventions, **8:**293, 293n, **9:**23, 25n, 32, 37,

214, 216–17, 223n, 529n, **10:**464, 467n, **11:**79–80, 81n, **12:**91n; and AFL mission to Europe, fall 1918, **10:**470n, 529, 549–50, 553, 567n; *cable to,* **10:**546n; *letter from,* **7:**120–22; *letters to,* **9:**454–55, **10:**332, 372–73, **11:**63–64, 225–27, **12:**53–54, 167–68, 226–27; and Sadie Gompers, death of, **10:**546n, 547; and SG, death of, **12:**541

Frey, Michael, *5:209n; letter to,* **5:**207–9

Frey Brothers, **1:**194, *198n*, 199

Frick, H. C., Coke Co., **3:**58n

Frick, Henry C., **3:**67, *68n*, 217, 237, 420, 481, **4:**492, **5:**84, 85n, **8:**288–89; attempted murder of, **3:**209, 211n, 238

Friedenwald, Joseph, **4:**319–20

Friedman, Julius, *3:486n; letter to,* **3:**486

"Friendly Inn," **3:**364

Friends of Russian Freedom, **10:**129, *134n*

Frinke, John W., *3:116n*

Fritz, Adolph J., **11:***, 262, *264n*

Froats, Arthur S., *letter from,* **10:**363–64

Frohlichstein Cigar Manufacturing Co., strike/lockout, 1903–4, **6:**293, *293n*

Frohnhoefer, Henry, **1:**68, *69n*

Fromme Brothers, **3:**453

From Politics to Industry (SG), **12:**420, *421n*

Frost, Henry E., *7:89n*

Fryatt, Charles A., **9:**475, *477n*

Frye, William P., **4:**323n, **5:**168n, *7:6n,* 89n, **9:**202; *letter to,* **7:**3–6

fuel, **9:**525–26n; wartime restriction of, **10:**316–17, 317n

Fuhrman, Alfred, **2:***, *203n,* **3:***, 30n, 47, *48n,* 82, 87; *letter to,* **2:**202–3

Fuller, Hugh R., **6:**544, *545n,* **7:**457

Fuller, Warren, and Co.: boycott, 1884–86, 1886-?, *1:402n,* **2:**8; strike/lockout, 1884, **1:**399, *402n*

Fulton, Harry W., *9:317n; letter to,* **9:**314–17

Fulton Bag and Cotton Mill Co.: strike/lockout, 1897–98, **4:**425–27, *427n,* 428; strike/lockout, 1914, **9:**170–71, *171n,* 191n

Funk, August J., **10:**188, *189n*

Funk, Isaac K., **3:**217, *218n*

Furlong, Thomas, **2:**224, *224n*

Furniture Manufacturers' Association (Grand Rapids, Mich.), **6:**229–30, 231n

Furniture Manufacturers' Association (New York City), **3:**268n

Furniture Workers' Union of America, International, **1:***, 362n, 390, 391n, **2:***, 173n, **3:***, 268n, **4:***, 8n, 155n; AFL financial support of, **3:**266–67, 268n; and eight-hour movement, **3:**267, 268n; and KOL, **3:**268n

—convention: 1890, **3:**268n

—locals: local 7 (New York City), **2:**384, **3:**152, 153n, 267, 268n; local 39, **2:**371n

—strike/lockout: 1892 (New York City), **3:**267, *268n*

Furuseth, Andrew, **3:**535n, **4:***, *93n,* 462, **5:***, *14*–15n, 69n, **6:***, 11, *12n,* **7:***, *16n,* 81–82, **8:***, *139n,* 491, **9:***, 91, *94n,* 305n, 359n, 454, **10:***, 44n, 253, *254n,* **11:***, *92n,* 152, **12:***, 345–46, *348n,* 433, 501; at AFL conventions, **4:**91–92, 93n, 283, **5:**45, 48n, 168n, 171, 437, 438n, 470n, **6:**212, 212n, 374–75, 376n, 501, 503n, 507, 509n, **7:**134, 142n, 419, 423, **8:**138, 291, 292n, 293, 400–401, 404, 407–11, **9:**212, 214n, 225–26, 226n, 345, 346n, 520–21, 521n, 524, **11:**88–90, 92n, 473–74; and Chinese exclusion, **5:**406–7, 437; and Cuba, **4:**274, 275n, 410; and eight-hour legislation, **5:**481; and election of 1908, **7:**382, 413–14, 414n; and Hawaii, annexation of, **4:**405, 406n, **5:**45; and injunctions, **7:**92–93, 117; *letters from,* **4:**172, **5:**338–39, **6:**261, **7:**42–43, 92–93, 310–11, 413–14; *letters to,* **4:**141–43, 382–83, 389–91, **5:**13–14, 455–56, **6:**170–71, 270–71, **7:**16, 253–54; lobbying by, **4:**113n, 142n, 452; and seamen's legislation, **5:**67, 74–76; and ship subsidy legislation, **5:**164, 166–67

Fur Workers, and black workers, **11:**84n

Gage, Lyman J., **3**:*, 151–52, *153n,*
4:419n, **5**:426, 426n; *letter from,*
4:417–19; *letters to,* **3**:215–16, **4**:421–
25
Gahan, D. F., *3:348n; letter to,* **3**:347–48
Gainor, Edward J., **11**:*, 474, *476n*
Gale, Zona, **12**:427n
Gallagher, Agnes, **11**:414–15, 417–19,
420n
Gallagher, Andrew J., **7**:384, *385n;*
at AFL conventions, **7**:419, **8**:138,
139n, 141, 143, 145–46, 410–11,
412n, 413, **9**:218–19, 221, 224n;
letters from, **8**:174–75, 301; *letters to,*
8:185–88, 302
Gallagher, Daniel J., **2**:27, *28n,* 29,
4:379n
Gallagher, John, **6**:546n
Gallagher, John J., **8**:139n, 291, *292n*
Gallagher, Peter W., **4**:373, *375n*
Gallagher, Thomas (Boston teamster),
5:410n
Gallagher, Thomas (Illinois congress-
man), **11**:276, *278n*
Galley, Alford A., **6**:398, *400n*
Gallinger, Jacob H., **3**:469, *469n,* **7**:7n,
8:132n
Galloway, Earl, **11**:93n
Gallup, N. Mex., deportations from,
10:167–68, 169n
Gallup-American Fuel Co., strike/
lockout, 1917, **10**:167, *169n*
Galveston, Tex., flood, **6**:362, *364n,*
11:31
Galveston (Tex.) Labor Council,
4:38n
Galveston Cotton Mills, strike/lock-
out, 1895, **4**:38, *38n*
Gambrinus brewery, **7**:208
Gannon, Lawrence J., **3**:47, *48n*
Gansser, August H., *5:330n; letter to,*
5:329–30
Ganter, Francis X., **5**:107, *108n,*
269–71, 271n; boycott, 1899–1900,
5:107, *108n,* 271n
Gantt, Thompson F., **1**:455, *456n,* 460
Garaty, Amelia, **1**:14
Gardner, Frederic W., **8**:107–8, *108n,*
162; *letter from,* **8**:200–201
Gardner, John J., **4**:329, *329n,* 453n,
5:189, 197–*98n,* 201, 206–7, 212,

222, 411n, 455–56, 478–79, 482n,
498, **6**:526, 527n, 529n, **7**:26–27,
311n, **8**:134, 135n, 183, 344
Gardner, Jonathan E., **5**:473, *474n*
Gardner, Mrs. Frederic, **8**:201
Garfield, Alex H., *7:227n; letter to,*
7:225–26
Garfield, Harry A., **10**:287–88, *288n,*
317n, **11**:307
Garfield, James A., **12**:511, *513n*
Garland, Charles, **12**:227n
Garland, Mahlon M., **3**:*, 206, *210–*
11n, 233–34, 234n, 253n, 535, 535n,
553n, **4**:*, 97n, **6**:*, 235, *236n,* **10**:*,
16n; at AFL conventions, **4**:95, 97n,
281, 281n, 413, 414n; at AFL Executive Council meetings, **4**:240–41,
266–67, 321–23; election of, as AFL
vice-president, **4**:95, 278n, 414n; *letters to,* **3**:265–66, **10**:15–16; and miners' strike, 1897, **4**:345, 359n; *wire*
from, **3**:532–33
Garland Fund, **12**:226, *227n,* 257, 264
Garlington, Ernest A., **10**:114, *115n,*
204
Garman, John M., **4**:444, *446n*
Garment Makers' Trades Council
(New York City), **3**:379
Garment Worker (trade union journal),
editor of, *letter to,* **4**:29–30
Garment Workers' Association,
United, **2**:349n
Garment Workers of America, United,
3:*, 107, 108n, 299, 355n, 379,
382n, 589n, **4**:*, 20, 21n, 99, 135–
36, 137n, 148–49, **5**:*, 102, 102–3n,
6:*, 3, 4n, 116, 116n, **7**:*, 98n, 178,
8:277n, 344, **9**:*, 71, 73–74n, 203,
261n, **10**:*, 92n, 150, 335, 336n,
12:*, 444, 446n; AFL financial support of, **3**:453–54, 454n, **4**:147–48,
148–49n, **6**:294, 297n, 355n, 405,
409–10, 410n; and clothing cutters' strike, 1893, *3:296–97n,* 302,
305–40, 453–54, **4**:148, 149n; injunctions against, **3**:293, 295–96n,
297–300, 302, **6**:406–7n; jurisdiction of, **5**:102, 102n, **6**:49–50, 50n,
189–90, 191n, **9**:74n; and KOL,
3:107–8, 108n, 295–96, 296n, 299,
300–301n, 318, 320–24, **4**:20; seces-

sion movement in, **9:**203, 205n, 227, 228n, 386, 391, 393; SG organizing trip for, 1895, **4:**19–20, *20–21n,* 21–49; wages of, **10:**61–62, 62n; and women workers, organization of, **12:**371n
—conventions: 1891 (New York City), **3:**107, *108n;* 1904, **6:**297n; 1914 (Nashville, Tenn.), *9:205n,* 227, 393
—locals: local 1 (Boston), **3:**179, 180n; local 2 (New York City), **9:**227, 228n; local 4 (New York City), **3:**111, 115n, 296n, 297, 297n, 298–300; local 20 (New York City), **10:**61, 62n; local 110 (Philadelphia), **6:**297n; local 127 (Indianapolis), **12:**363; local 136 (Rochester, N.Y.), **6:**297n; local 139 (Denver), **5:**395, 396n
—strikes/lockouts: 1892 (Boston), *3:180n;* 1893 (New York City), **3:**295–96, *296–97n,* 297–300, 300–301n, 302, 304–41 (*see also* Knights of Labor [KOL]: and clothing cutters' strike, 1893); 1894 (New York City and Newark, N.J.), **3:**587–88, *589n,* **4:**20; 1896 (New York City), **4:**206, *206n,* 207, *207n;* 1902 (Chicago), **6:**50n; 1903–8 (Rochester, N.Y.), *6:297n;* 1904 (New York City), **6:**294–96, *297n,* 313; 1904 (Philadelphia), *6:297n;* 1904–5 (Chicago), **6:**405–6, *406–7n,* 409–10, 410n; 1910–11 (Chicago), **8:**269, *277n;* 1913 (New York City), **8:**452, 453n
Garner, John Nance, **12:**184, *184n*
Garretson, Austin B., **8:***, 332n, 455, *456n,* **9:***, 49, *50n,* 136, 312n, 322, 422n, **10:***, *252n; letter to,* **10:**319–20
Garrett, Finis J., **9:**5, *9n,* **12:**184
Garrett, John, **6:**70, 71n
Garrison, Lindley, **11:**358n
Garrison, William Lloyd, **4:**406, *408n,* **6:**333, **12:**135
Garrison School (Kansas City, Mo.), *3:63n*
Garrod, Heathcote W., **10:**72n
Garside, Thomas H., **4:**367, *368n*
Gary, Elbert H., **5:**384n, **8:**225, *227n,* **10:**441, **11:**27n, 125, 126n, 151,

169–70, 172, 390, **12:**121, 123, 185, 212, 260, 279–81; *letter to,* **11:**98–99; *wire from,* **10:**386; *wire to,* **10:**385–86
Gary, Ind., building trades strike, 1910, **8:**159, *160n*
Gary Plan, **9:**429, *430n*
Gassner, Jacob, **3:**47, *48n*
Gas Workers and General Labourers of Great Britain and Ireland, National Union of, **3:**33, *33n*
Gates, Philetus W., **5:**214, *216n*
Gatewood, David, **10:**372n
Gatica, Manuel, **5:**180, 184, *188n,* 232
Gaul, Joseph, **6:**15, *19n*
Gaumer, Clarence, *8:255n; letter to,* **8:**254–55
Gauthier, Victor S., *12:403n; letter to,* **12:**403
Gavegan, Edward J., **7:**457, 458n
Gaver, Lavina A., **5:**392, *393n*
Gawanus Building Material Co., **11:**323, 324n
Gaylord, Winfield R., **10:**261, *263n*
Geissenhainer, Jacob A., **3:**513, *514n*
Gelotte, Dominick, **11:**206n
Gelson, James, **4:***, 6–7, 96, *97n*
General Commission of German Trade Unions. *See* Generalkommission der Gewerkschaften Deutschlands
General Confederation of Labor (French). *See* Confédération Générale du Travail
General Confederation of Labor (Italian). *See* Confederazione Generale del Lavoro
General Electric Co.: strike/lockout, 1906, *7:41n;* strike/lockout, 1914, **9:**99, *99n;* strike/lockout, 1919 (threatened), **11:**186–87; wage reduction by, **11:**411
General Federation of Trade Unions of Great Britain and Ireland, **5:**68, *69n,* 210–11, **8:**4, 6n, **9:**238, 470n, 474, **10:**522, **11:**11, 17n, 569, *572n*
—conventions: 1899 (Manchester), *5:69n;* 1900 (Nottingham), **5:**211; 1909 (Blackpool), **7:**473n, 474–76, *476n*
General Federation of Women's Clubs, and AFL Permanent Confer-

ence for Abolition of Child Labor, **12**:82n

General German Workingmen's Association. *See* Allgemeiner Deutscher Arbeiterverein

Generalkommission der Gewerkschaften Deutschlands, **3**:660n, **4**:134, *137n,* **7**:484, **8**:186

General League of Cuban Workers. *See* Liga General de Trabajadores Cubanos

General Managers' Association, *3:580n;* and Pullman strike, 1894, **3**:522–24, 526n, 566, 571, 579n

General Munitions Board, **10**:74, *75n*

General Slocum (steamship), burning of, **7**:4, *7n*

general strikes, **2**:226–27, 334, 338n; **3**:568, **8**:508–9

—specific strikes: 1892 (New Orleans), **3**:185–86, 241–42, *243n,* 252, 295n, **5**:344, 346n; 1894 (threatened), **3**:523–25, 526n, 534–38, 565–69, 579n, 625, 659n, **11**:250–51; 1899 (Cuba), **5**:180, 185–86, *187n,* 232n; 1900 (Puerto Rico), **5**:415n, 423–24, 425n; 1902 (Denver), *6:18n;* 1906 (Havana), **7**:162, *164n;* 1909 (Sweden), **7**:484, *486n;* 1914 (miners, threatened), **9**:97, *98n;* 1915 (New York City, threatened), **9**:269; 1916 (Mexico City), **9**:426n, 499–500, 500–*501n;* 1916 (New York City, threatened), **9**:490–91, *492n;* 1917 (agricultural workers, threatened), **10**:176n; 1917 (metal miners, threatened), **10**:176n; 1918 (Germany, antiwar), **10**:342, *344–45n,* 353; 1918 (Mooney, on behalf of, threatened), **10**:387, 396, 420, 420n; 1919 (Boston, threatened), **11**:146n; 1919 (Mooney, on behalf of, threatened), **11**:6, 7n, 86, 87n, 94; 1919 (Seattle), **11**:61, *62–63n,* 94; 1919 (Tacoma, Wash.), **11**:49–50, *50n;* 1919 (threatened), **11**:207, 215; 1919 (Winnipeg, Man.), **11**:74–75, 75n, 94, 380; 1920 (Europe, threatened), **11**:437–38, *439–40n;* 1920 (France), **11**:438, *440n;* 1920

(threatened), **11**:368–69, 372, 373n; 1922 (Rand Revolt, South Africa), **12**:43, *47n;* 1922 (threatened), **12**:133–34, 136–37, 137n, 147

General Railway Co., **6**:13n

Genesee Brewing Co., **4**:332

Genoa conference, 1922, **12**:12–14, *15n*

Gentlemen's Agreement (with Japan), *7:148n,* **9**:514, **10**:37

George, Annie Fox, **4**:393n; *letter to,* **4**:393

George, Henry, **1**:*, 288, 431, *431n,* 454, **2**:*, 45, 47, *48n,* 51, 369, **3**:*, *10n,* **4**:49n, 392, *392n,* 393, **8**:133–34, **12**:33, 33–34n; debate with Shevitch, **2**:398, *408n,* **3**:10; *letter from,* **1**:432; mayoral campaign of, *1:429*–34, 438n, 439, 441–49, **8**:133–34, **11**:9, **12**:33, 34n

George, Henry, Jr., *5:361n;* SG, *interview with,* **5**:357–61

George, Herbert, **6**:234, *234n*

George, James Z., **1**:291–356 passim, *327n,* **8**:463, *468n*

George, John E., *4:473n; letter to,* **4**:472–73

George V, **10**:563, *567n*

"George Grey Barnard: A Virile American Sculptor" (Knaufft), **7**:442, *443n*

George J. Grant Construction Co., injunction, **10**:252, *253–54n*

George J. Grant Construction Co. v. St. Paul Building Trades Council et al., **10**:252, *253–54n*

George v. Bailey, **11**:512–14, *514n*

George Washington (passenger liner), **11**:111n, 460n

George Washington Club, **2**:211, 212n

Georgia, election of 1906, **7**:58–59

Georgia Federation of Labor, *7:59n*

—convention: 1906 (Augusta), **7**:59, *59n*

Georgia Immigration Association, **7**:196, *197n*

Geraldine, Dion, **3**:151–52, *153n*

Gerard, James W., **10**:274, *278n*

Gerber, William E., *12:260n; letter to,* **12**:259–60

Gerling, Asmus, **12**:399, *399n*

German-American Independent Citizens' Association of the Tenth District of New York City, **1:**260n
German Central Labor Union of Baltimore, **2:**388, *408n*
German Exchange Bank, **2:**36
German Federation of Trade Unions. *See* Allgemeiner Deutscher Gewerkschaftsbund
German Society of New York, **1:**362n
German Trades, United (Brooklyn, N.Y.), **3:**85n
German Trades of the City of New York, United, **1:**457, *459n*
German Trades Unions, Congress of, 1886 (Berlin), **4:**136, *137n*, 193
German Workers' Educational Association, **11:**549n
German Workingmen's Associations, Federation of. *See* Verband der deutschen Gewerkvereine
Germany, **10:**558–60, 564, 568n, **11:**47–48; atrocities of, **9:**192, 193–94n, 195; Belgium, invasion of, **9:**163n, 193n, 295, 296n, 364, **10:**559; communists in, **11:**28, 150, **12:**369; conditions in, **4:**41, **9:**173–74, 175n, 264, **10:**381, **12:**368–69, 435, 435n; Cuba, intrigues in, **10:**37, 39n, 256, 257n; Economic Congress of, **12:**144–45; Great Britain, air raids on, **9:**289, 290n, 474; Imperial Commission of, on U.S. cigar and tobacco production, **1:**125, *126n;* indemnities imposed by, **10:**88; industrial conference boards in, **11:**164, 167n; and International Labor Conference, 1919, **11:**136–37, 137–38n; Japan, intrigues in, **10:**35, 37; Mexico, intrigues in, **10:**34–35, 38n; militarism of, **5:**11, 23, **10:**30, 35, 88–89, 129, 132, 202, 268–71, 309, 352, 508, 558–59, 564, 566, **11:**118; peace proposals of, **10:**543, 543–44n, 553; and Polish boundary dispute, **11:**48, *49n;* Reichstag of, **12:**144; and reparations, **12:**13–14, 367n; and Russian treaty, **10:**344–45n, 353, 355n, 564; socialists in, **3:**639–42, **4:**41, 68, 306, **9:**379, **10:**89, 90n, 269–70, 275–76, 278n, 342–44, 344–45n, 508–9, **11:**11; and spring offensive, 1918, **10:**413, 414n; and submarine warfare, **9:**253, 254n, 263–64, 287n, 474–75, 477n, **10:**4n, 35, 38n, 49, 49n, 93n, 200, 326n; trade unions in, **1:**345, **3:**639–42, **4:**62, 68, 90, **6:**412–23, **7:**485, **11:**10–11; trade unions in, AFL financial support of, **12:**367–69, 369n, 377; trade unions in, and war, **10:**3, 4n, 35–36, 49, 276, 342, 344–45n, 353, 536, 566; transatlantic cables, cutting of, **9:**173, 175n; United States, intrigues in, **10:**157n, 435; United States, outbreak of war with, **10:**3, 4n, 12, 17, 49, 49n, 200, 202–3; United States, possible invasion of, **10:**28–29, 34, 37; workers from, **1:**4, 21, 47, 50–51, 66, 95–96, 98, 102–3, 110, 247–48, 259, **7:**217–19, 219n (*see also specific unions*); working class in, **1:**23, 32; and World War I, outbreak of, **9:**160n, 163n; and World War I, responsibility for, **11:**47, 48–49n, 55
—strikes/lockouts: 1910 (building trades workers), **8:**198, *199n;* 1918 (antiwar), **10:**342, *344–45n,* 353
Germany and the Next War (Bernhardi), *9:193n*
Germer, Adolph F., **8:***, 518, *519n,* **9:***, *224n,* 364, **10:***, 510–11, *512n;* at AFL conventions, **9:**217–18, 221–22, 344–45, 346n, 348n
Gernon, James, *7:368n;* letter to, **7:**365–68
Gerry, John, **2:**332
Gessner, Frank M., **1:***, 390, *390n*
Gewerkverein, Der (German labor journal), *1:44n*
Ghent, William J., **9:**378, *383n,* **10:**160, 181, 228n
Ghent unemployment relief program, **9:**174, *175n*
"Giant Power." *See* power network
Gibbs, George, **10:**310, *312n*
Gibson, David H., **9:**418n; *letter from,* **9:**416–18
Gibson, David R., **1:***, 402, *404n*
Gibson, George W., **8:***, 296, 297n

Gibson, J. S., **10**:137–38n
Gibson, Lewis H., **11**:342–43, 343n
Gideon, David, **1**:262, 263n
Gifford, Orrin P., **3**:424, *425n*
Gifford, Walter S., **10**:73, *73–74n*, 140, 303
Gilbert, Newton, **7**:91n
Gilbert, Simeon, **3**:424, *425n*
Gilded Age, The (Twain), *8:497n*
Gilded Age, The: A Tale of To-Day (Twain and Warner), *8:497n*
Giles, John E., **10**:469, *471n*, **12**:541, *541n*, 543
Gill, Alfred H., **8**:*, 116, *117n*
Gill, Charles M., *6:102n; letter from,* **6**:101–2
Gill, Frank H., *4:480n; letter to,* **4**:479–80
Gill, Patrick F., **10**:403, *404n*
Gill Engraving Co., injunction, *9:74–75n*
Gill Engraving Co. v. William Doerr et al., *9:74*–75n
Gillett, James N., **7**:118n
Gillmore, Frank P., **12**:*, 550, *553n*
Gilmore, Solon T., **7**:158, *161n*
Gilmour, J. H., **10**:424, *431n*
Gilroy, Thomas F., **3**:365, 377, 380–81, *382n*, 383–85, 387, 445–46, 600
Gilthorpe, William J., **5**:*, 164–65, *168n*, **6**:473n, **7**:*, 176, *177–78n; letter to,* **5**:488–89
Giolitti, Giovanni, *10:556n*
Giolittism, **10**:552, *556n*
Giovannitti, Arturo, **8**:326n, 511n, **9**:489n
girls, education of, **12**:52–53. *See also* women workers
Gitlow, Benjamin, **12**:485, *485n*
Gitterman, Alice Sterne, **6**:267, 268n
Glackin, Everett, **2**:55, *55n*
Gladden, Washington, **4**:45n
Gladstone, William E., **3**:429n, 565, *580n*, **6**:335, **12**:217
Glass, Carter, **10**:8n
Glass Bottle Blowers' Association of the U.S. and Canada, **3**:*, **4**:*, 505n, **6**:*, 62n, **7**:*, 408n, **8**:*, 256, 258n, 475, **10**:*, 540n, **11**:84n, **12**:446n; jurisdiction of, **6**:448, 450n, **7**:407, 408n; and Miners, Western Federation of, **6**:505, 509n

—conference: 1901 (with manufacturers), **5**:341, *342n*
—conventions: 1898 (Muncie, Ind.), **4**:503, *505n;* 1901 (Milwaukee), **5**:341, *342n;* 1904, **6**:509n
—locals: local 8 (Bridgeton, N.J.), **5**:286n; local 19 (Bridgeton, N.J.), **5**:286n
—strike/lockout: 1899 (Bridgeton, N.J.), **5**:283, *286n*
Glasso, Charles, **2**:340, 343n
Glassworkers, Federation of. *See* Fédération du verre
Glass Workers' Association of the U.S. and Canada, United Green, **3**:*, 442n, 511, 512n, **4**:*, **6**:*, **7**:*, **8**:*, **10**:*
Glass Workers' International Association of America, Amalgamated, **7**:*, 451n; and AFL Building Trades Department, **7**:449–50, 451n; jurisdiction of, **7**:449–50, 451n
—local: local 1 (Chicago), **6**:448, 450n
Gleaves, Albert E., *12:554n*
Gleaves, Elsie M., **11**:460, *460n*, **12**:16
Gleaves, Walter, **12**:551
Gleaves, William H., *12:554n*
Gleaves, William T., **11**:460n, *12:554n*
Gledhill, Edwin, **7**:184, *186n*
Glenn, Frank J., *9:155n; wire from,* **9**:154
Glenn, John M., **11**:287, *289n*
Glenn, S. B., **4**:407, *409n*
Glenning, Mrs. William, *letter from,* **10**:219
Glennon, James H., **10**:191–92, *193n*
"Glenwood Plan," **12**:382, *383n*, 412–13
Glidden, Benjamin F., **3**:362, *362n*
Globe (Ariz.) Miners' Union, Ladies' Auxiliary, **10**:301
Glove Workers' Union of America, International, **7**:*, 275n, **10**:*, 82n, **12**:*, 446n, 450–51, 451n; AFL financial support of, **9**:191n
—locals: local 4 (Chicago), **12**:451n; local 18 (Chicago), **12**:451n
—strikes/lockouts: 1914 (New York City), **9**:191n; 1920–21 (Chicago), **12**:451, *451n*
Glyn, Henry, *3:182n; letter to,* **3**:181–82

Gobel, E. F., **3:**466n
Godchaux, Leon, **4:**30
Godfrey, Hollis, **10:**21n
Godfrey, Samuel W., *3:497n; letter from,* **3:**490–97
Goethals, George W., **7:**244, *246n*
Goettache, Edward, **2:**60
Goff, John W., **3:**297, *298n*
Golden, Clinton S., **12:**350, *350n*
Golden, John, **6:**:*, 113–14, *115n,* **7:**:*, *185n,* **8:**:*, 49n, *117n,* 324n, 360–61, **9:**:*, *171n,* **10:**:*, *294n,* **11:**:*, *351n;* at AFL convention, **6:**355, 355n; *letters from,* **7:**183–85, 236–37, **8:**215–16, 324–25, **9:**170–71; *letters to,* **8:**115–16, **9:**261–62, **11:**350–51
Goldensmith, W. R., **5:**151n
Goldfield (Nev.) Businessmen's and Mine Owners' Association, **7:**286n
Goldfield (Nev.) Federated Trades Council, **7:**283, *286n*
Goldfogle, Henry M., **8:**342, *346n*
Goldman, Emma, **3:**:*, *383n,* **11:**:*, *432n;* and depression of 1893, **3:**364, 382, 382n; and Russia, **11:**427, 432n
Goldowsky, Bernard M., *6:432n; letter from,* **6:**430–32
"gold roll" employees, in Canal Zone, **11:**392–93n, 433–34, 435n, **12:**386, 386n
Goldsmith, Isaac, **1:**8
Goldsmith, Marcus K., **1:**:*, 103–6, *106n*
gold standard, **4:**417–19, 421–25
Goldstein, David, **6:**118n
Goldstein, I., **4:**219n
Goldstone, Jacob, **9:**31, *34n*
Goldwater, Samuel, **2:**:*, *69n,* **3:**:*, *128n,* **4:**:*, *479n;* at AFL conventions, **2:**66, **3:**125, 128, 128n, 131, 134, 136, 251, 253n, 260; *letters to,* **2:**96–97, **3:**225–29, 415–16, **4:**478–79
Goldzwig, Emanuel, **6:**489, *489n*
Gomez, José Miguel, **10:**39n
Gomez, Natalie, **12:**276, *278n*
Gompers, Abraham, **1:**:*, 153, *154n*
Gompers, Abraham J., **1:**:*, 153, *154n,* **3:**:*, 140, *142n,* **4:**:*, 198–99, *199n,* 296, 297n, **5:**:*, *407n,* **6:**:*, *35n,* 108n; death of, **5:**xvi, **6:**35n, 107, 117, 130,

232n; illness of, **5:**xvi, 407, 407n, 420, **6:**34, 35n, 41, 130; *letter to,* **4:**199–200
Gompers, Alexander, **1:**:*, 14, *14n,* 16, **3:**:*, 140, *141n,* **4:**:*, *502n,* **5:**:*, 324, *324n,* **7:**:*, 499, *501n,* **8:**:*, 77, *77n,* **9:**:*, 537, 539n, **11:**:*, *54n,* 367, 368n; *letter to,* **4:**501–2
Gompers, Alexander J., **1:**:*, 96, 153, *154n,* **3:**:*, 140, *142n,* **4:**:*, 199, *200n,* **5:**:*, 256, *257n,* **6:**:*, 34, *35n,* 238, 238n, **7:**:*, 492, 492n, **9:**:*, 537, 539n, **11:**:*, 53–54, *54n,* **12:**:*, 517, 517n, 551
Gompers, Catherine, **1:**:*, 8, *8n,* 14, 153, **5:**324n, **7:**:*, 499, 501n
Gompers, Clara. *See* Le Bosse, Clara Gompers
Gompers, Elizabeth Tate, **1:**:*, 153, *154n*
Gompers, Ella Applebaum, **11:**54, *54n,* 298, 299n
Gompers, Emanuel, **1:**:*, 153, *153n,* **4:**50n, **5:**:*, 324, 324n
Gompers, Esther, **11:**54, 54n
Gompers, Ethel, **7:**492, *492n*
Gompers, Fannie (SG's cousin), **1:**:*, 153, *154n*
Gompers, Fanny (Femmetje; SG's aunt). *See* Cohen, Fanny (Femmetje) Gompers
Gompers, Florence (SG's granddaughter), *4:175n,* 197, **7:**492, 501, **8:**267, 277n, 347, **9:**537, **11:**53, *54n,* 57, 487n; *letter from,* **10:**383–84; *letter to,* **4:**174–75. *See also* MacKay, Florence Gompers
Gompers, Florence (Mrs. Louis Gompers, wife of SG's French cousin), **11:**39, 41n, 52–53, 54n
Gompers, George, *9:156n; letter to,* **9:**155–56
Gompers, Gertrude Annersly Gleaves, **11:**:*, 459–60, *460n,* 543, **12:**:*, *16n,* 517, 546, 550–52, 554n; *letters to,* **12:**15–16, 340
Gompers, Harriett, **1:**:*, 14, *14n,* 16, **11:**:*, 367, 368n
Gompers, Harry Boyd. *See* Gompers, Samuel Harry
Gompers, Henrietta (SG's grandmother), **1:**:*, 8, *8n,* 14, 14n

Gompers, Henrietta (SG's sister), **1**:*, 153, *153n. See also* Isaacs, Henrietta Gompers

Gompers, Henry, **1**:*, 14, *14n,* 16, **3**:*, 140, *141n,* **7**:*, 499, *501n,* **9**:*, 537, 539n, **11**:*, *54n,* 367, 368n

Gompers, Henry J., **1**:*, 153, *154n,* **2**:26n, **3**:*, 140, *142n,* 341–42, **9**:*, 156, *156n,* 367, 367n, 537–38, 539n, **10**:491n, **12**:*, 517, 517n, 551; *letter to,* **9**:308

Gompers, Isabella, **1**:*, 153, *153n. See also* Isaacs, Isabella (Bella) Gompers

Gompers, Jacob, **1**:*, 16, *16n,* 153, **3**:*, 140, *141n,* **9**:311n, **11**:*, 367, 368n

Gompers, Leah Lopez, **3**:140, 141n

Gompers, Louis (SG's brother), **1**:*, 14, *14n,* 16, 153, **3**:*, 140, *141n,* **4**:*, 502, *502n,* **5**:*, *257n,* 325n, **7**:*, *492n,* 498–99, **8**:*, 77, *77n,* **9**:*, 537, 539n, **11**:*, *54n,* 367, 368n; death of, **11**:291, *291n; letters to,* **5**:256–57, 324–25, **7**:491–92

Gompers, Louis (SG's cousin), **1**:153, **11**:39, *41n,* 52–53, 54n

Gompers, Louis (son of Henry J.), **9**:156, *156n*

Gompers, May, **11**:54, 54n

Gompers, Minnie, **1**:153

Gompers, Rachel Bickstein, **3**:140, 141n

Gompers, Rose, **1**:*, 153, *153n. See also* Mitchell, Rose Gompers

Gompers, Sadie J., **4**:*, 56, 57n, 199, 502, **5**:*, 256, *257n,* **6**:*, 12, *14n,* 33, 41, **7**:*, *101n,* 471, 481, **8**:*, 185n, 241–42, *243n,* **9**:*, 156, *156n,* 354, 537, 539n, **10**:*, *491n,* **11**:*, *18n,* 562, **12**:*, 323, 324n; death of, **10**:544–45, 546n, 547, 564–65, **11**:16, 18n, 23, 291; *letter from,* **8**:416

Gompers, Samuel: ancestry of, **1**:3, **5**:41; autobiography of (*Seventy Years of Life and Labor*), **11**:68, 68n, 117, 119n, 522–23, **12**:316, 318–19, 321, *322n,* 365, 365n, 378, 384, 533–35, 535n; as automobile driver, **9**:327; birth of, **1**:3; *birth certificate of,* **1**:7; birthday of, **9**:61, 62n, 535–39, **11**:40, 246, **12**:16–17; black eye of, **1**:449; bust of, **12**:530, 532, 533n,

534; childhood of, **1**:3–4, **9**:287; cigarmakers' locals, membership in, **1**:5, 46–47, 71, 289, 327n; citizenship of, **8**:340; *citizenship application of,* **1**:18–19; death of, **12**:536n, 541–44, 560; and death threat, **7**:393, 393n; description of, **2**:214, 297, **3**:42, 48–49, 59, 386, 458, 543, **4**:25, 70, 110, **5**:39–41, **6**:160, **11**:297–99; education of, **1**:3–5, 13; elections of, as AFL president, **2**:72, 79, 165, 226, **3**:117, 127–28, 133, 135, 429, 437–38, 464, 609–11, 661–65, **4**:6–7, 9, 78–79, 82, 94–99, 134, 278n, 389–91, 414n, **5**:57n, 177n, 294n, 445, **6**:208, 210n, 376n, 509n, **7**:280, 427n, **8**:17–18, 18n, 144, 295, 414–15, **9**:37, 38n, 225, 226n, 348, 348n, **10**:266, 475, **11**:93n, 321, 321n, 480–82, **12**:90, 95, 97n, 337, 549; employment of, early, **1**:3–6, 289, **12**:304, 393, 394n, 399; eyesight of, **11**:486, 487n; family life of, **1**:3, 5–8, 14, 16–18, 96, 153–55, 327n, **4**:296, **6**:12, 128–29, **11**:297–98; finances of, personal, **1**:96, **4**:138, 198–99, 202–3, 203n, 226–27, **12**:323, 514; and flag incident, **8**:280–81, 281n, 282; and fraternal societies, membership in, **1**:5, **4**:56, 57n, 138, 330–31, **12**:517, 550; funeral of, **12**:545–52, 554; and grand jury, appearance before, **9**:366n; idealism of, **12**:222; immigration of, to United States, **1**:4, 16; intemperance of, alleged, **1**:410, 465–66; Jewish heritage of, **1**:3–4, **3**:476, **11**:298, **12**:548; KOL, membership in, **1**:289, 327n; *Labor in Europe and America, 7:474n;* leadership, views of, **5**:40–41, **6**:321–22, **9**:526–29, **11**:64, 498–99, **12**:16–17; *marriage certificate of,* **1**:17–18; nominations of, for public office, **2**:45, 244–47, 249–51, 359, 369, **3**:17, 110, **4**:152–53, 155n, **5**:488–89, 489n, **7**:411, 414–15, 415n; and pacifism, **4**:108–9, 147, 301–3, 465, **6**:377–78, **7**:211–14, **8**:205–8, **9**:346, 364, 366n, 372–73, **10**:36, 198–99, 201, 260, 267–70, 272–73, **12**:179; poem inscribed to, **4**:295, *296n;* protection

of, **10**:480–81, **12**:123; recording of, **9**:44–45, 45n; relatives of, employment of, **2**:26n, **7**:492; residence of, in New Jersey, **1**:5–6, 289, 327n; signing authority for, **10**:73; successor, election of, **12**:554–60; temperament of, **4**:247; tributes to, **12**:526–30, 544–45; wedding of, 1867, **1**:5; wedding of, 1921, **11**:459–60; work schedule of, **2**:28, **4**:xiv–xv, 177, 179, 247, **5**:xvi, 67–68, 158n, 231, **6**:126, 128–29, **7**:394–95, 395n

—accidents: 1899, **5**:155–56, *156n,* 157, 163, 179, **7**:170; 1901, **5**:377–78, *378–79n,* 380, **6**:257n; 1919, **11**:67, *67n,* 69–70, 91, 93n

—*addresses by,* **2**:3–10, 32–35, 57–58, 81–88, 100–101, 169–70, 184–86, 257, 259–63, 302–4, 308–16, 321–23, 325, 348–49, 392–402, 405–8, **3**:35–40, 52–54, 75–76, 95–102, 208–10, 236–38, 295–96, 299–300, 377–78, 388–96, 425, 430–34, 438, 458, 599–606, 611–13, 662–63, **4**:21–22, 24–28, 30–42, 45–49, 59–60, 108–10, 301–4, 432–39, 469–70, **5**:3–11, 20–29, 129–38, 294–307, 475–77, 505–10, **6**:93–100, 245–57, 317–39, 345–50, 417–23, **7**:70–89, 211–14, 214n, 258–65, 474–78, 483–85, **8**:31–33, 62–75, 128–30, 175–82, 261–76, **9**:57–60, 367–70, 372–82, 443–48, 508–10, 535–39, **10**:50–52, 196–207, 267–78, 507–12, 532–37, 556–67, **11**:8–16, 157–58, 161–66, 170–82, 192–94, 249–58, **12**:17–20, 303–8, 520–23, 524n, 525, 530–32, 536–38

—addresses by, mentioned, **4**:76, 106n, 149n, 161–62, 162n, 176–77, 465n, **5**:13, 67, 85–86, 89–90, 94n, 126n, 150, 182–84, 199, 243n, 245, 245n, 257n, 263n, 336n, 357n, 512–13, 514n, **6**:31n, 35n, 158n, 191n, 314n, 378n, 389, 486n, **7**:71, 96, 120n, 169n, 336n, 385–87, 387n, 395n, 399, **8**:75n, 133, 134n, 222–23, 227n, 258n, 276n, **9**:52–53n, 62–63n, 64–67, 68n, 69–70, 72n, 138n, 153n, 167, 167n, 178n, 208n, 256, 256n, 276n, 292n, 303n, 309,

310n, 354, 355n, 364, 366n, 373, 492n, 522, 523n, **10**:102, 103n, 178, 179n, 192, 194n, 219n, 241n, 313n, 363n, 388, 389n, 520–22, 523–24n, 525–27, 551–53, 555n, **11**:14, 17–18n, 23–25, 25n, 37, 40n, 220, 221n, 320n, 458–59n, 524n, 532, 532–33n, **12**:10n, 11, 39n, 53, 54–55n, 142, 146n, 159n, 162, 164n, 170–71n, 278n, 285, 286n, 299n, 319n, 419, 421n, 424, 424–25n, 534

—*articles by,* **1**:172–210, **2**:378–82, **3**:44–46, 200–204, 287–91, 445–51, 527–31, **4**:439–45, **5**:179–87, **6**:426–28, 480–82, **7**:291–94, **8**:417–22, **9**:412–16, **12**:289, 303–8, 507–13

—articles by, mentioned, **5**:363, 363n, **6**:484n, **7**:370n, **8**:166, 169n, 198, 199n, 202, 203n, 224, 226, 227n, 309, 334, 335n, **9**:55, 57n, 151–52, 252, 253n, 295, 296n, 310n, 316, 317n, 407, 408n, 465, 466n, 532, 533n, **10**:16, 17n, 152–53n, 248, 253, 254n, **11**:277, 278n, 299n, 336, 338n, 391n, 447, 447–48n, **12**:33, 34n, 162, 365, 376, 377n, 381–83

—*circulars of,* **1**:445–46, **4**:119–21, 183–85, 340, **5**:70, 335–36, 349–51, 485–86, 501–3, 517, **6**:24–25, 158–59, 192–93, 405–6, 433–34, **7**:12–13, 48–49, 408–12, **8**:27–30, 389–91, **9**:51–52, 141–42, 153–54, 194, 246–51, 510–11, **10**:96–98, 110–12, 239, 413–14, **11**:108–9, 224–25, 280–81, 349–50, 391–92, 483, 554–56, **12**:370–71, 371n

—circulars of, mentioned, **5**:91, 93n, **6**:136n, 218, **7**:17n, 180n, 195, 206, 206n, 268n, 311n, 341, 398n, 407, 408n, 412, 412n, 413–14, 414–15n, **8**:85, 108, 108n, 370, 391n, 453, **9**:65, 68n, 145n, 154–55n, 157n, 190, 191n, 227, 227n, 236n, 251n, 262, 262n, 469n, 488n, **10**:20, 22n, 453, 454n, **11**:207, 207n, 215, 226, 227n, 393n, 509, 509n, **12**:127, 128–29n, 147, 147n, 229, 229n, 346, 348n, 369n, 371n, 377, 377n, 491, 494n

—debates: with Allen, **11**:289–90, 290n, 298–99, 304–8, 320n; with

Brandeis, **6:**71–83; with Roosevelt, **10:**129–33, 138, 139n, 142
—*editorials by,* **2:**58–59, 80, **3:**514–15, 539–42, 580–82, 669–71, **4:**128–29, 145–47, 360–62, 366–68, 473–76, **5:**342–46, 486–88, **6:**25–29, 123–25, 394–96, **7:**329–32, 401–5, **8:**102, 243–44, 506–11, 513–17, **11:**515–16, **12:**26–30
—editorials by, mentioned, **5:**39n, 112n, 486, 488n, 497n, 517, 517n, **6:**11, 12–13n, 451, 453n, **7:**216, 217n, 232, 232n, 251, 252n, 295–96, 296n, 349, 350n, 356, 357n, 372, 399, **8:**23, 24n, 41, 42n, 50, 52n, 139n, 154, 155n, 332n, **9:**56, 57n, 150–52, 152n, 229, 230n, 238n, 244, 252, 253n, 284, 285n, 302, 303n, 310n, 316, 317n, 399, 407, 408n, 455, 456n, 465, 466n, 502, 507n, 532, 533n, **10:**16, 17n, 247, 252–53, 254n, 281–82, 285n, **11:**372, 373n, 536, 539n, **12:**12, 15n, 259, 260n, 379, 380n
—illnesses of: 1895, **4:**39, 42–43, 49, 54; 1896, **4:**xiv, xxin, 116, 118–19, 128, 132–33, 138, 141, 144, 160; 1899, **5:**94n; 1901, **5:**372n; 1903, **6:**190; 1904, **6:**381, 381n, 382; 1906, **7:**143, 162; 1912, **8:**416, *416n,* 428; 1913, **8:**461, *468n,* 469–71, 477, 493n, 495–501, **9:**44, 79; 1915, **9:**363; 1919, **11:**57; 1923, **12:**218, *219n,* 221–22, 222n, 243; Feb.–Apr. 1924, **12:**424, *424n;* May–Oct. 1924, **12:**447n, 455–56, *457–58n,* 461, 462n, 470, 481, 489, 500, 502–3, 503n, 504, 504n, 505, 514, 519, 534, 536n; final, **12:**536n, 538–43
—*interviews with,* **1:**117–18, 404–5, **2:**46–48, 64–66, 124–26, 160–62, 276–77, 298–99, 338–43, 423–27, **3:**42–44, 49–50, 59–60, 189–90, 231–32, 386–87, 396–97, 444–45, 543–47, 608–9, **4:**22–23, 61–68, 70–72, 99–101, 110–13, 157–58, 464–65, **5:**12, 39–42, 357–61, **8:**128–30, 299–301, 347–55, **9:**512–15, **11:**536–39, **12:**222, 427–28
—*memoranda by,* **9:**88–93, 167–68, 353–55, 498–500, **10:**73, 297–98,

304–6, 310–12, 387, **11:**37–40, 46–48, 55–57, 497–98, **12:**296–98
—*statements of,* **1:**446–47, **4:**344–45, **6:**276–78, 278n, **7:**417–18, **8:**90–91, 120–21, 221–22, 306–12, 370–80, **9:**88–93, 166–67, 167n, 184–87, 187n, 286–87, 328–29, 383, 498–500, 508–10, **10:**63, 64n, 189–90, 285–87, 316–17, 346–49, 402–3, 413–14, 420, 451, **11:**150, 512–14, **12:**84–85, 426–27, 499–501, 518–23, 524n
—statements of, mentioned, **7:**83, 257n, **8:**137, 139n, 145, 227n, 281n, 386–87n, **9:**321n, 354, 355n, 356, 357n, 490–91, 492n, 513, 515n, **10:**67, 67n, **11:**66n, 198n, 220, 221n, 247n, 384n, 445, 446n, 447, 447n, 527, 528n, 548, 548n, **12:**12, 15n, 105, 106–7n, 118, 118n, 162, 195, 197n, 213, 226–27, 227n, 351, 352n, 484, 485n
—*testimony of,* **1:**287, 289–356, **3:**563–79, **4:**489–99, **5:**142–46, 146n, 189–97, 201–7, 212–13, 222–30, 230n, 466–67, 470–74, 478–82, 482n, 497–500, **6:**537–45, **7:**26–32, **8:**94–99, 209–12, 317–20, 339–45, 430–37, 442–47, **9:**3–8, 83–88, 112–36, **10:**441–44, **11:**31–34, **12:**68–80
—testimony of, mentioned, **8:**40, 42n, 258, 259n, 457, **9:**40, 90, 137–38, 138n, 139, 139n, 224n, 279–80, 280n, 284, 285n, 300, 323, 324n, **10:**15–16, 17n, **11:**81n, 85n, 146n, 153n, 156, 157n, 246, 247n, 260n, 319n, 502, 503n, **12:**82–83n, 148n, 208
—trips: Dec. 1887 (Northeast), **2:**65–66; Jan.–Feb. 1888 (Northeast, Midwest, and West), **2:**81–88, 90, 92–93, 97, 157; June 1888 (New England), **2:**123, *123n;* Feb.–Apr. 1891 (West), **3:**27, *27n,* 30–33, 42–43, 59, 72; May 1893 (Midwest), **3:**343–45; Apr.–July 1895 (South), **4:**19–20, *20–21n,* 21–49, 52, 167; Aug.–Sept. 1895 (Europe), **4:**50, *50n,* 52–53, 55–63, 66, 85–91, 193, **11:**10–11; Apr. 1896 (Northeast), *4:142n,* 143–44, 148, 155, 157–58, 160, 169; May 1896

(Illinois), **4:**168; June 1896 (Midwest), **4:**176–77, *177n;* July 1896 (Illinois), **4:**198; July 1896 (Michigan), **4:**193–94; Aug. 1896 (Northeast), **4:**206–7; Jan.–Feb. 1897 (Midwest), **4:**296, *297n;* May 1897 (New York), **4:**331–33; Aug. 1897 (mining region), **4:**365, *366n;* Oct. 1897 (Northeast), **4:**386, *388n;* Apr. 1898 (Northeast and Midwest), **4:**460, *461n,* 463–65, 465n, 466–70; May–June 1898 (Midwest), **4:**503, *505n;* Sept. 1898 (West), *5:16n;* Apr.–May 1899 (West), **5:**48n, 85–86, *87n;* May–June 1899 (West), **5:**48n, *87n,* 88–92, 124–26, 130, 149–50; Oct. 1899 (Pennsylvania), **5:**124, *126n,* 127; Nov. 1899 (Midwest), *5:148n;* Dec. 1899 (New York City), **5:**157; Jan. 1900 (Chicago), **5:**156n; Jan.–Feb. 1900 (Cuba), **5:**xv–xvi, 156n, 179–87, *187*–88n, 199, 231–32; Aug. 1900 (New Jersey), *5:257n;* Sept. 1900 (Pennsylvania), **5:**262, 263n; Oct.–Nov. 1900 (Chicago), *5:271n;* Nov. 1900 (New York City), *5:271n;* Jan. 1901 (New York City), **5:**324, *324n;* Apr. 1901 (Northeast), **5:**339, *341n,* 346; May 1901 (Midwest), **5:**357, *361n;* May 1901 (New York City and Connecticut), **5:**356, *357n;* May 1901 (Philadelphia), **5:**357, 357n; June 1901 (New York City), *5:372n;* Oct. 1901 (Scranton, Pa.), *5:400n;* Nov. 1901 (New York City), **5:**411, *411n;* Mar.–Apr. 1902 (Midwest), **5:**501, *511n;* July–Aug. 1902 (West), *6:23n;* Aug.–Sept. 1902 (New Orleans), **6:**30, *31n;* Sept. 1902 (New York City and Pennsylvania), **6:**38, *40n;* Jan. 1903 (Philadelphia), **6:**92; Apr.–May 1903 (Canada and New England), **6:**109, *110n,* 140, 159n; July 1903 (Kentucky), **6:**158, *158n;* July–Aug. 1903 (Midwest), *6:170n;* Oct. 1903 (Chicago), **6:**189–90, *191n;* Oct. 1903 (New York City), **6:**183–84, *186n;* Dec. 1903 (New York City), *6:217n;* Feb.–Mar. 1904 (Puerto Rico), **6:**217n, 228, *228n,* 231–32, 232n,

235, 237–39, 245–57, 426–27, 470, 7:232, **8:**20, **9:**79; Mar. 1905 (Ohio), **6:**409; May–June 1905 (Midwest), **6:**430, *430n;* Sept. 1905 (Pennsylvania and New York City), **6:**478, *479n;* Dec. 1905 (New York City), **6:**512–13; June 1906 (Maine), **7:**70, *89n;* Aug.–Sept. 1906 (Northeast), **7:**58, *58n,* 70, *101n,* 103, 448, 449n; Sept.–Oct. 1906 (New York City and Chicago), **7:**109, *110n;* Dec. 1906– Jan. 1907 (Cuba), **7:**143–44, *144n,* 162–64, 220–21; Feb. 1907 (Midwest), **7:**182, *183n;* Apr. 1907 (New York and Midwest), *7:210n;* Aug. 1907 (Midwest), **7:**244, *246n;* Sept. 1907 (New York City), **7:**250, 283, *286n;* Feb. 1908 (New York City), **7:**315, 316n; Apr.–May 1908 (Midwest), **7:**334, *336n;* July 1908 (Chicago and Denver), **7:**350n; Sept. 1908 (Indiana), *7:395n,* 399n; Sept. 1908 (Ohio), *7:395n,* 399; Sept. 1908 (St. Louis, Texas, and Illinois), **7:**370n, 385–87, 387n, 394; Oct. 1908 (Pennsylvania, New York, and Midwest), *7:395n;* Nov. 1908 (New Jersey and New York City), *7:395n;* Apr. 1909 (New York City), *7:462n;* June–Oct. 1909 (Europe), **7:**472, *473–74n,* 474–81, 483–85, 487–91, 492n, **8:**21, 22n, 241, **10:**563; Dec. 1909 (New York City, Cincinnati, and Pittsburgh), **8:**22, *22n;* June 1910 (New York City), **8:**109, 114n; July 1910 (Midwest), **8:**107, *108n;* mid-July 1910 (New York City), **8:**110, *114n;* late July 1910 (New York City), **8:**110, *114n;* Sept.– Oct. 1910 (Midwest), **8:**133, *134n;* Apr.–May 1911 (Midwest), **8:**213, *213–14n,* 220; May 1911 (New York City), **8:**218–19, 219n; June–July 1911 (Midwest), **8:**242; July–Aug. 1911 (Midwest and New York City), **8:**257–58, *259n;* Aug. 1911 (New York City), **8:**258, *259n;* Aug.–Sept. 1911 (Pacific Coast), **8:**256, *258n,* 261–76, 280–81, 281n, 282, 300, 339, 352; mid-Jan. 1912 (New York City), **8:**322, *323n;* late Jan. 1912

(New York City), **8:**333, *334n;* July 1912 (Trenton, N.J.), **8:**386; July 1912 (Utica, N.Y., and Cincinnati), **8:**386, *386n;* Aug.–Sept. 1912 (Ohio), **8:**394, *395n;* mid-Dec. 1912 (New York City), *8:427n;* late Dec. 1912 (New York City), **8:**428, *429n;* later Dec. 1912 (New York City), **8:**428, *429n;* Jan. 1913 (Albany, N.Y., and New York City), *8:439n,* 448–49; Jan. 1913 (New York City), **8:**451, *452n;* Feb. 1913 (Indianapolis), **8:**470, *471n;* Nov.–Dec. 1913 (San Francisco and New York City), *9:39n,* 40; Jan. 1914 (New York City), *9:51n;* Jan.–Feb. 1914 (Indianapolis and New York City), **9:**64, *68n;* Feb.–Mar. 1914 (Chicago), **9:**72, *74n;* Mar.–Apr. 1914 (Puerto Rico), **9:**78–80, *80n;* Apr. 1914 (New York City and New Haven, Conn.), *9:93n;* May 1914 (Cleveland), **9:**137, *138n;* May 1914 (New York City), **9:**137, *138n;* June 1914 (Buffalo, N.Y., and New York City), **9:**155–56, *156n;* July 1914 (New York City), **9:**164, *164n;* Aug. 1914 (Atlantic City, N.J., and Schenectady, N.Y.), **9:**176, 178, *178n;* Feb. 1915 (Chicago, Cleveland, Buffalo, N.Y., and New York City), **9:**234, *235n;* Mar. 1915 (Chicago), **9:**258, *258n,* 260–61, 263, 266, 266n, 267, 267n; May 1915 (New England and New York City), **9:**276, *276n;* June 1915 (New York City), **9:**290, 292n; July–Aug. 1915 (New York City, Midwest, and Philadelphia), *9:310n;* Aug. 1915 (New York City), **9:**310, *311n;* Oct.–Dec. 1915 (West Coast and Midwest), **9:**353–55, *355n,* 363; Dec. 1915 (New York City), **9:**363, *366n;* Jan. 1916 (New York City), **9:**363, 363n; Mar. 1916 (New York City and Albany, N.Y.), **9:**406, *408n;* May–June 1916 (Midwest), **9:**429, *430n*; Sept. 1916 (New England and New York City), **9:**490, *492n;* Oct. 1916 (New York City and Atlantic City, N.J.), **9:**498; Feb. 1917 (New York City), *10:15n;* May 1917 (New York City and Pittsburgh), **10:**102–3, *103n;* June–July 1917 (New York City), **10:**127, *127–28n;* Aug. 1917 (New York City), *10:163n;* Aug.–Sept. 1917 (New York, Pennsylvania, and Midwest), **10:**192, *194n,* 195; Sept.–Oct. 1917 (New York City and Buffalo, N.Y.), **10:**225, *228n;* Jan. 1918 (Newark, N.J., New York City, and Indianapolis), **10:**320, *320–21n,* 328; Jan.–Feb. 1918 (New York City), **10:**329, *330n;* Feb.–Mar. 1918 (New York and Chicago), *10:363n;* Apr.–May 1918 (Canada, Boston, and New York City), **10:**432, *434n;* Aug.–Nov. 1918 (Europe), **10:**468, *470n,* 492–93, 503–4, 504n, 506, 519–23, 525–27, 529–37, 540, 541n, 543, 546n, 549–54, 554–55n, 557–58, 560–65, **11:**6n; Nov. 1918 (Chicago), **10:**544–45, *546n,* 547, 556–67; Nov.–Dec. 1918 (New York City), *11:18n;* Dec. 1918 (New York City), *11:17n;* Jan.–Apr. 1919 (Europe), **11:**25, 25n, 37–40, *40n,* 46–48, 52–59, 62n, 63–64; Apr. 1919 (New York City), **11:**66–*67n;* July 1919 (New York City), *11:113n;* July–Aug. 1919 (Europe), **11:**110, *111n,* 113n, 118, 119n, 460n; Sept. 1919 (New York City), *11:138n,* 140n; Nov. 1919 (New York City), *11:199n;* June–July 1920 (San Francisco), **11:**328; Dec. 1920 (New York City), **11:**469, *472n;* Jan. 1921 (Mexico), **11:**402, *404n,* 407; Mar. 1921 (Boston), **11:**417–18, *420n;* Oct. 1921 (New York City), **11:**532, *533n;* Jan. 1922 (New York City and Springfield, Mass.), **12:**8, *10n,* 15–16; Feb.–Mar. 1922 (New York City and Albany, N.Y.), **12:**36, *39n;* Mar. 1922 (Northeast), **12:**53, *54n;* Apr. 1922 (Chicago and Northeast), **12:**53–55, *55n;* Oct. 1922 (Indianapolis), **12:**160, *163n;* Oct. 1922 (New Orleans), **12:**158, *159n,* 162; Nov. 1922 (New Jersey, New York City, and New Haven, Conn.), **12:**162, *164n;* Feb. 1923 (New York City), **12:**208, *209n;* Mar. 1923 (New York

City), *12:219n*, 243; June 1923 (Chicago and New York City), *12:277–78n;* Aug.–Sept. 1923 (Midwest, New York City, and Philadelphia), **12:**298, *299n*, 312; Sept.–Nov. 1923 (West), **12:**319, *319n*, 321, 356, 365; Dec. 1923–Jan. 1924 (Panama), **12:**383, *383–84n*, 385, 536, 538n; Apr. 1924 (New York City, Pennsylvania, and Chicago), **12:**418, *418n*, 422, 424, 425n; May 1924 (New York City), **12:**456, *457n*; Nov.–Dec. 1924 (Texas and Mexico), **12:**518, *520n*, 534–35, *536n*
—*will of,* **12:**516–17
Gompers, Samuel (SG's cousin), **1:***, 153, *154n*
Gompers, Samuel Harry, **10:**203, *207n*, 276, 491n, 540, **11:**53, 54n, 57; *letter from,* **10:**519; *letter to,* **10:**491
Gompers, Samuel J., **1:***, 6, 153, *153n*, 438n, **2:***, 344, *344n*, 356–57, **3:***, 119, *120n*, 140, 211–12, **4:***, *175n*, 197, **6:***, *35n*, **7:***, 492, 492n, 501, **8:***, 267, 277n, **9:***, 537–38, 539n, **12:***, 457n, 517, 517n, 543, 551; *letters to,* **4:**174–75, 197–98
Gompers, Samuel Moses, **1:***, 3, 7, *7n*, 14, **8:***, 347, 355n, **9:***, 536, 539n, **12:***, 323, 324n
Gompers, Sarah (SG's aunt). *See* Levy, Sarah Gompers
Gompers, Sarah (SG's cousin), **1:**153
Gompers, Sarah Rood, **1:***, 3, 7, *7n*, 8, 14, 16–17, 153, **5:***, xvi, 14, *16n*, 41, **7:***, 500, *501n*, **9:***, 537, 539n, **11:***, 367, 368n; death of, **5:**14, 16n; *marriage certificate of,* **1:**7
Gompers, Sarah Wennick, **3:**140, 141n
Gompers, Simon (SG's brother), **1:***, 153, *153n*, **3:***, 140, *141n*, **7:***, 499, *501n*, **9:***, 537, 539n, **11:***, *54n*
Gompers, Simon (SG's uncle), **1:***, 8, *8n*, 14, 153, 154n, **2:***, 367, 370, *371n*, **3:***, 111, *115n;* death of, **5:**16n
Gompers, Solomon (SG's cousin), **1:**153
Gompers, Solomon (SG's father), **1:***, 3–4, 7, *7n*, 14, 14n, 16–17, 153, **3:**516, **5:***, 41, *42n*, **7:***, 498–500, 501n, **8:***, 76–77, 77n, 267, 347, **9:***,

367n, 537–38, **10:***, 444–45, 445n, **11:***, 54, 54n, 367, 368n; death of, **11:**129n, 138, 138n, 141, 144, 291; *marriage certificate of,* **1:**7; *wire to,* **9:**367
Gompers, Sophia (daughter of Alexander J. Gompers), **11:**54, 54n
Gompers, Sophia Bickstein, **3:**140, 141n, **7:**492n
Gompers, Sophia Dampf, **1:**438n, **3:***, 140, 141n, 212, **4:***, 174, *175n*, 198, **9:**538, 539n; *letter to,* **4:**174–75
Gompers, Sophia Julian, **1:***, 5, 17, *18n*, 153, **3:***, 140, *141n*, **4:***, 56, 57n, 144, 160, 169, 194, 199, 432, 502, **5:***, 154n, *421n*, **6:***, 34, *35n*, 41, 117, **7:***, 126, *126n*, 471, 481, **8:***, 184n, 241–42, 243n, **9:***, 156, *156n*, 354, 537–38, **10:***, 419n, 546n, **11:***, 23, 24n, 67, 562, **12:***, 323, 324n; *cable to,* **10:**549; death of, **11:**291, *291n;* illness of, 1890, **2:**430; illness of, 1911, **8:**184, *184–85n*, 194, 201, 204, 258, 259n; illness of, 1919, **11:**63; *letters to,* **8:**416, **11:**52–54; *marriage certificate of,* **1:**17–18
Gompers, Sophia Spero, **3:**140, 141n, **9:**311n
Gompers, Sylvain, **11:**39, 41n
Gompers, William, **9:**310, *311n*, **10:**276
Gompers family: entries for, in 1851 *census returns,* **1:**8; entries for, in 1861 *census returns,* **1:**14–15; entries for, in 1880 *census returns,* **1:**153–55; entries for, in *passenger list* of ship *London,* **1:**16; reunion of, **7:**498–501
Gompers v. U.S., **7:**250n. *See also* Buck's Stove and Range Co. cases: contempt case
Gomperz, Rosa, **7:**500, *501n*, **8:**241
González García, Salvador, **9:**426–27n, 436, 443n
Goodacre, James J., **2:**129–30, *130n*
Goode, Armistead, **10:**177n, 424, 426, 430, *431n*
Goodnow, Frank J., **10:**310, *312*–13n, 512n
Goodrell, Harry B., **7:**447n; *letter to,* **7:**446–47

Goodwin, Francis, **1:**205, *207n*
Gordon, F. G. R., **6:**117, *118n,* **9:**139
Gordon, H. F., *letter to,* **12:**206
Gordon, Kate M., **6:**532, *532n*
Gordon, Sadie, *letter to,* **9:**530–33
Gordy, Eva, *wire from,* **10:**301
Gore, Thomas P., **9:**194, *195n*
Gorey, John W., **12:**56, *61n*
Gorman, James, **7:**315n
Gorman, Owen D., **11:**315, *317n*
Gorozave, Eusebio, **12:**101n
Goschen, George J., **2:**325, *326n,* 349–52; *letter from,* **2:**351; *letter to,* **2:**350
Gosling, Harry, **9:**487, 488n, **10:***, 522, *524n*
Gotha congress, 1875, **1:**43n, **2:**159n
Gould, Ashley M., **7:**249n, 287, *287n,* 289, 296, 430, 453, 465, **8:**161, 269
Gould, E. R. L., **3:**602, *606n*
Gould, Jay, **1:**99, *101n,* 343, 402n, 432, 433n, **2:**33, 341, **3:**637, **9:**218
Gourley, James, **3:**341
government contracts, wartime: clothing, **10:**61–62, 62n, 91, 138, 139n, 150, 151n, 204; construction, **10:**136, 137n, 452–53 (*see also* Cantonment Construction Agreement); and eight-hour day, **10:**91–92, 365, 366n; harnesses and saddlery, **10:**281–82, 284–85n, 365; naval engines, **10:**281, 284n
government employees, **1:**320–27; Blanton and, **10:**453–54, 456–59; hours of, **3:**93, **4:**111, 326, **5:**189–97, 201–7, 207n, 212–13, 222–30, 230n, 350, 478–82, 482n, 497–500, **6:**478, **7:**3, 6–7n, 327, 335, **8:**341, **9:**215, 219, 224n, 532, **10:**401, 453–54, 454–55n, 456–59, 459n; KOL and, **7:**314; organization of, **7:**114–15, 313–14, 314–15n; pensions of, **9:**525, 526n; rights of, **7:**5, **8:**377, **11:**311; wages of, **9:**19, 22n, 532, **10:**41, **12:**249. *See also under* legislation, states and territories; legislation, U.S.
government ownership: of common carriers, **9:**254–55, 255n; of communications system, **3:**574 (*see also* American Federation of Labor [AFL]: Political Program); of means

of production and distribution, **5:**282, 284, 286n, **6:**196, 197n, 199, 205n; of mines, **12:**173–74; of railroads, **1:**227, 288, **3:**258–59, 260n, 401, 475, 551, 574, 635, **9:**254–55, 255n, 494, **10:**340–41, **11:**130–31, 131n, 214n, 319–20, 320n, 329, 472–75, 475n; of telegraph system, **1:**227, 288, **3:**258–59, 260n, 401, 635, **9:**494, **10:**341, 515; of telephone system, **3:**258–60, 260n, 401, **10:**341, 515; of transportation system, **3:**258–59, 260n, 401, 574 (*see also* American Federation of Labor [AFL]: Political Program); of utilities, **5:**361, **10:**340–41, **11:**8n, 18n
governors, conference of, 1911 (Spring Lake, N.J.), **8:**269, *277n*
Grace, Lawrence A., *6:172n; letter to,* **6:**172
Grace, William R., **1:**172, *173n,* **2:**244
Gracy, George W., **6:**243, *244n*
Grade Teachers' Union, *10:439n*
Grady, Michael R., **4:**157, *159n,* **5:**215, *216n*
Grady, Thomas F., **1:**260, *263n,* **8:**239, *240n*
Graham, George, **11:**260n
Graham, Wade B., *11:191n; letter from,* **11:**189–90
Graham, William H., **5:**190, *198n*
Graham, William T., **5:**387, *388n*
Grambarth, Charles, **3:**47, *48n*
Gran Círculo de Obreros Libres, **9:**307n
Grand Army of the Republic, **3:**212, 212n, 652, *660n*
Grand Circle of Free Workers. *See* Gran Círculo de Obreros Libres
Grand Trunk Railroad, strike/lockout, 1910, **8:**112–13, *114–15n*
Grange, **6:**303, *308n,* **8:**45
Granget, John P., **1:**205, *206–7n*
Granis, Capt., **10:**229, 232
granite cutters, **2:**116
Granite Cutters' International Association of America, **1:***, **2:***, **3:***, **5:***, **6:***, **7:***, 142n, **9:***, 136n, **10:***, 374n, **11:***, 65n, 544, **12:***, 129n, 223; and eight-hour day, **9:**120; jurisdiction of, **8:**188n

—strike/lockout: 1921-?, **12:**127, *129n*
Granite Cutters' National Union of
the U.S. of America, **1:***, 165, 166n,
275, 339, 385, **2:***, 116–17, 117n,
217n, 235, **3:***, 79n, 165–66n, **5:***,
79n, **6:***, 147n, **7:***, **9:***, **10:***, **11:***,
12:*; AFL financial support of, **3:**79,
5:xiv, 233–35, 235n, 236–39; and
black workers, **6:**115–16, 116n, 146–
47, 147n; jurisdiction of, **4:**481–82,
483n; National Union Committee
of, **2:**293–94
—local: Lithonia, Ga., branch, **6:**120,
121n
—strikes/lockouts: 1892, **3:**165, *165–*
66n; 1900, *5:235n,* 237
Granite Manufacturers' Association
(Barre, Vt.), **2:**294, *294n*
Granite Manufacturers' Association of
New England, **3:**165, 165–66n
Grant, Hugh J., *2:377n; letters to,*
2:377, **3:**161–62
Grant, James, **2:**271, 272n, **3:**166n
Grant, Luke, *6:445n,* 450n; *letters from,*
6:465–66, 468–69; *reports on IWW*
founding convention, **6:**442–64, 465n,
467n, 469n
Grant, Ulysses S., **1:**320, 323, *328n,*
3:119n, **10:**201, 207n, **12:**519
Grassmann, Peter O., **12:***, 526, *526n,*
534, 537, 538n
Graves, Frank N., **6:**387–88, *388n*
Grawer's Brewery, **3:**112
Gray, George, **6:**14n
Gray, Horace, **6:**340n
Gray, James A., **6:**241, *244n*
Gray et al. v. Building Trades Council et
al., **12:**303, *303n*
Grayson, Cary, **11:**41n
Great Britain: anti-German feeling in,
9:192–93, 194n, 195–97, 288–89,
289–90n, 474–76; Blue Book of,
9:192, *193n;* Board of Trade of,
5:87–88, *88n;* "Bolshevism" in,
11:28–29; child labor in, **5:**314;
conditions in, **4:**41–42, **6:**418,
10:342–43, 465–66; diplomatic relations with United States, **2:**63, 64n,
4:301, 303, 304n, **5:**21; election of
1906, **7:**63, 421; election of 1918,
11:28–29, 30n; German air raids on,

9:289, 290n, 474; Germany, blockade of, **9:**263–64; industrial councils
in, **11:**164, 166–67n, 244; and International Labor Conference, 1919,
11:136, 137n; labor mission of, to
United States, 1917, **10:**71, *72n,*
102, 103n, 113; labor mission of, to
United States, 1918, **10:**309, *309n,*
332; mission of, to United States,
1917 (Balfour mission), **10:**71,
72n; and outbreak of World War
I, **9:**163n, **10:**559; trade unions in,
1:281, 345, **4:**10–11, 61–64, 67–68,
85–89, 100, **5:**34, **6:**78, 80, 157, 418,
7:68, 401n, 474–76, 478, 489–91,
9:337–38, **10:**66, **11:**11–12 (*see also*
specific unions); wartime industrial
production in, **9:**376, 384, **10:**24–26,
74, 99, 113, 116–18; women workers
in, **5:**314, **10:**27, 81; working class
in, **1:**23–24, 32, 41, 340–41
—strikes/lockouts: 1877–78 (stonemasons), **3:**639, *660n;* 1889 (dockworkers), **2:**279–80, *281n,* 325,
3:78n, 504; 1893 (jute mill workers), *3:542n;* 1893 (miners), **3:**426,
429n, 432, 565, 575; 1895 (jute mill
workers), *3:542n;* 1900 (railroad
workers), **6:**74, 78, *83n;* 1919 (railroad workers), **11:**164, *167n;* wartime, **10:**60n
Great Eastern Telephone Co., **7:**406n
Greathouse, Charles, **10:**49n
Great Northern Railroad, strike/lock-
out, 1894, **3:**521, *547n*
Great Southern Lumber Co., organization of, **11:**365, 366n
Greece, workers from, **5:**152, **8:**115,
155, **9:**170
Greeley, Horace, **1:**446, *446n,* **4:**68
Green, Frank, *letter to,* **2:**196–97
Green, M. F., **9:**479n
Green, Samuel S., **1:***, 371, *372n*
Green, William, **9:***, 39, *40n,* 52n,
98n, 283n, 309, 490n, **10:***, 168,
169n, 372, **11:***, 25n, *92n,* 313n,
335, 345, 390, 430, 560n, **12:***,
82–83n, 120n, 150, 544n; at AFL
conventions, **9:**529n, **10:**266n,
11:89–90, 321–23, **12:**327–29,
330n, 520, 524n; at AFL Executive

Council meetings, **9:**271–74, 436, 440; and AFL mission to Europe, spring 1919, **11:**40n; and election of 1924, **12:**491, 493; election of, as AFL president, **12:**555, 557–60; election of, as AFL vice-president, **9:**42n, 226n, 348n, **10:**475, **11:**93n, 321, 321n, 482, **12:**97n, 338n; and Industrial Conference, 1919, **11:**128n; and International Labor Conference, 1919, **11:**111n; *letters to,* **9:**282–83, **12:**81; *wire from,* **9:**63–64

Greenawalt, Elmer E., **3:***, 279, *279n,* **4:**108n, **7:***, 122, *122n,* **8:***, *191n;* *letter to,* **8:**190–91

Greenbaum, Leon, **6:**203, *204n*

Greenberger, Jesse, *6:474n*

Greene, Ellen, **5:**274n

Greene, Michael F., **12:***, 550, *553n*

Greene, Prince W., **4:***, 335, *335–36n,* 426, 428, **5:***, *274n,* 336, 336n, 370, 418–19, 420n; *letter from,* **5:**271–73

Greene, William, **12:**228n

Greene, Willie, **5:**273, *274n*

Greenfield v. *Central Labor Council,* **12:**302, *303n*

Greenhalgh, Charles, **3:**632–33, 659n

Greenhall, Abraham, **1:**75, 76n

Greenman, Leon, **4:**236, *238n*

Greenstein, Abraham, **12:***, *221n*

Greenville brewery, **3:**112

Greenwood, Ernest H., **11:**401, *404n,* 405

Gregg, Laura A., **6:**532, *533n*

Gregor, Edward C., lynching of, **12:**192–93, *196n*

Gregory, Thomas W., **10:**92, *92–93n,* **11:**210, 220, 221n, 336; and Bisbee deportations, **10:**321–22, 323–24n, 336–39; and IWW, **10:**243n, 297–98, 298n; *letter to,* **10:**321–22

Grenell, Judson, **1:***, 282, *283n*

Gresham, Walter Q., **3:**342, *343n,* 488

Grey, Edgar, **9:**160

Grice, Benjamin F., **8:**48, *49n*

Grieb Rubber Co., strike/lockout, 1904, **6:**260n

Griffith, Arthur, **11:**86n

Griggs, Everett G., **10:**489, *490n*

Griggs, John W., **5:**326, *327n*

Grimes, James F., **3:**213, *214n, 6:93n,* 237, 264–65, 265n, **7:**16n, 82; *letter to,* **6:**91–93

Grimké, Archibald H., **10:**345, *350n,* 421, 462

Grimshaw, Frank, **10:***, *449n; letter from,* **10:**447–49

Griscom, William S., *4:316n,* 324, 334; *letter from,* **4:**314–16; *letter to,* **4:**317–18

Grocery Employes' Union:
—local: local 167 (Denver), **5:**393, 396n

Gronland, Laurence, **2:**288n, **6:**395, *397n*

Gronna, Asle, **11:**338n

Grosscup, Peter S., **3:**523, 527, 530, *531–32n,* 559, 576–77, 587, 592; *letter to,* **3:**554–61

Grosse, Edward, **1:***, 258–59, *260n*

Grossi, Col., **10:**553

Grossman, Herman, **6:***, 276–77, *278n,* **7:**166n

Grosvenor, Charles H., **6:**232n, **7:**84, 90n, *91n*

Grout, Adelbert (variously Albert) B., **6:***, 443, *446n,* **7:**427n

Grove, Ernest J., **4:**25, *28n*

Grow, Cyrus F., **11:**94, *95n*

Gruber, Charles W., **8:**232–34, 234n

Gruber, Henry C., **2:**332, *337n*

Gruelle, Thomas M., **3:***, 175, *175n,* 227; *letter to,* **3:**511–12

Grundy, Thomas, **4:**374, 375n

Guaranty Trust and Safe Deposit Co. v. *Mahon et al.,* **9:**208n

Guard, R. Lee, **5:***, 91, *93n,* 155, 413n, **6:***, 150n, 154n, 161, *163n,* 512n, **7:***, *126n,* 481, **8:***, 258, *259n,* 427–28, 429n, 451, 472n, 493n, **9:***, 78n, 93, 490n, 498, *500n,* **10:***, *74n,* 140, 192, 327n, 547–48, **11:***, *31n,* 53, 64, 68n, 93n, **12:***, 131n, 156, *157n,* 428n, 433n, 483n; *letters from,* **5:**399–400, **6:**169–70, 237–38, **7:**126, 182, 205, 394–95, **8:**499–500, **10:**102–3, 543, **11:**67, 117–19, **12:**365, 470, 533–35, 538–39; *letters to,* **5:**105, 380–82; *memoranda by,* **11:**300, **12:**502, 543–44; and SG, death of, **12:**543–44; and SG, illness of, 1923, **12:**218; and SG, illness of, May–Oct.

1924, **12:**458n, 461, 462n, 470, 502, 503n; and SG, illness of, Dec. 1924, **12:**538–39; and SG, memoirs of, **12:**365, 378n, 385n, 533–34; and SG, security of, **10:**480; and SG, signing authority for, **10:**73; *wires from,* **12:**218, 539
Guatemala, **10:**11; and civil war in Mexico, **9:**363n; and Pan-American Federation of Labor, **9:**466n
Gubbins, George P., **6:***, 173, *175n*
Guerin, Theobold M., **10:**172n, 318–19n, 360, *362n*
Guest, William J., **12:**36, *38–39n*
Guggenheim, Daniel, *10:158–*59n; *letter to,* **10:**157–58
Gulf, Colorado, and Santa Fé Railway Co. v. *Ellis,* **8:**479–80, *492n*
Gulick, Sidney L., **9:**513, *515n,* **12:**417n
Gullett, Francis M., **7:**378, *381n*
Gunter, R. L., **5:**312, 313n
Gunther, Charles F., **7:**361, *362n*
Gunther, William, **12:**57–58, *61n*
Gunton, George, **2:**163, 188n, **3:***, 588, *589n,* **5:**483, 483n
Gurko, Vasily I., **10:**292, *294n*
Gutenberg Bund, **2:**26n
Gutstadt, Herman, **1:***, 237, *237n,* **5:***, 407, *407n,* **6:***, *12n,* **8:***, *134n; letters to,* **6:**11–12, **8:**133–34
Gutstadt, Richard, **8:**133, *134n*
Guyer Hat Co., **7:**455
Gzeluch, Nikoleg, **5:**29n

Haag, Harry O., **5:**328, *329n*
Haas (cigarmaker), **2:**125–26
Haas, Louis, **1:**260, 262, *263n*
Haase, Hugo, **10:**344, *345n*
Haberman, Roberto, **12:**359n
Hacker (brewer), *letter to,* **3:**261–62
Hackett, Carhart, and Co.: boycott, 1894–95, **4:**20, *21n;* SG campaign against, **4:**19–20, *20–21n,* 21–49, 57n
Haddock, William S., **11:**122, *123n,* 153n
Haeselbarth, A. C., **6:**426–28
Hagan, Edward P., **1:**446, *447n*
Hagerty, Thomas J., *6:445n;* and IWW, founding of, **6:**443, 448, 450, 452, 454–55, 457–60, 462, 465, 467

Haggerty, Charles, **8:**214n
Haggerty, John, *1:133n; letter from,* **1:**132–33
Haggerty, Thomas T., **12:**495, *498n*
Haggott, Warren, **6:**282n
Hague, Ethel V., **11:**476–77, *478n*
Hague, The: Permanent Court of Arbitration (*see* arbitration: international); Permanent Court of International Justice (*see* World Court)
Hague conferences: 1899, *5:15n;* 1907, **5:**15n, **7:**180, *180–81n,* 206n, 214n
Hahn, Charles F., **4:**181, *182n*
Hahn, William, **5:**198
Hahn, William, and Co., **5:**198, 199n
Haig, Douglas, **10:**273, *278n,* 550, 554n
Hainer, Eugene, **3:**471n
Haines, Elijah H., **2:**62n
Haiti, U.S. intervention in, **9:**311n
Hale, Marshall, **6:**386, *387n*
Hale, Matthew, **10:**160, *161n*
Hale, Prentis C., **6:**386, *387n*
Hale, Reuben B., **6:**386, *387n*
Hale, William W., **10:**516–17, *518n*
Hale Brothers, Inc., **6:**386–87, 387n
Haley, Margaret A., *10:83n; wire from,* **10:**81–82
Hall, E. G., **12:**333n
Hall, Frank, **11:**206n
Hall, George C., **10:**215, 359, *360n*
Hall, Goldsmith P., **1:**455, *455n,* 460, 466
Hall, Harry L., **12:**337, 337n, 550, *552n*
Hall, Horatio J., *5:400n; letter to,* **5:**399–400
Hall, J. E. A., **3:**70n
Hall, John M., *8:393n; letter to,* **8:**392–93
Hall, John S., **9:**23–24, *25n,* 27, 28n, 35, 36n
Hall, William L., **6:**408, *409n*
Hallahan, H. F., **1:**255n, **3:**141, *143n*
Haller, Frederick, **1:***, 366, *374n,* 397, 399, 419–20, 432, **2:***, 55, *55n;* at AFL convention, **2:**166, 171; *letter of agreement,* **1:**373–74; *letter to,* **2:**120–21
Hamburger, I., and Sons, **2:**189, 189n

Hamburger Echo, editor of, *letter to,*
4:149–55
Hamburg (Germany) Trades Council,
4:50n
Hamerand, John, 2:332, *337n*
Hamill, James A., 8:460, *468n,* 469,
494
Hamilton, Albert H., 12:320, *321n*
Hamilton, M. Grant, 6:18n, 191, *192n,*
262, 262n, 284, 285n, 7:340n, 495,
8:*, 110–11, *114n,* 257, 375, 9:*,
44n, 46, 47n, 65, 82n, 90–92, *94n,*
98n, 10:*, 64n, 78, *79n,* 296n; and
election of 1906, 7:100, 104n, 107n;
and election of 1908, 7:346, 347n,
350n, 358, 360, 376, 377n, 387,
395n, 397, 398n, 416–17, 417n; *let-
ter from,* 7:343–45; *letters to,* 7:105–7,
394–95, 9:326–28, 456–57, 493–95
Hamilton, Marie, 9:328, *328n*
Hamilton, Robert R., 1:447, *448n*
Hamilton, Thomas H., 7:162, *164n*
Hamilton (Ohio) Trades and Labor
Council, *4:400n,* 402
Hamilton (Ont.) Trades and Labor
Council, 9:409n
Hamlin, Charles A., 11:*, *347n; letter
to,* 11:346–47
Hamlin, Frank D., *2:252n; letter to,*
2:251–52
Hammer (trade union journal), 2:112
Hammerling, Louis N., 8:342, 344,
346n
Hammerstein, Oscar, 1:418, *418n*
Hammer v. *Dagenhart, 10:499n,* 11:15
Hammet, Allen K., *11:529n; letter from,*
11:528–29
Hammond, John H., 8:323, *324n*
Hammond Lumber Co.: strike/lock-
out, 1906, 7:117, 118n; strike in-
junction, 7:117, 118n
Hammond Lumber Co. v. *Sailors' Union
of the Pacific et al., 7:118n*
Hampton, George P., 11:187, *187–
88n,* 468, 471
Hamrick, William P., *10:86n; letter to,*
10:85–86
Hamrock, Patrick, 12:127n
Hancock, Charles, 11:67, *67n*
Hancock, James T., 4:436–37, 439,
439n

Hancock, John, 6:332–33, 349, 7:88
Hand-in-Hand Benevolent Society,
4:56, *57n,* 138
Handley, John J., 9:*, *47n; letter to,*
9:46–47
Hanecy, Elbridge, 5:415, 415n
Haney, Mary E., *10:83n; wire from,*
10:81–82
Hanford, Benjamin, 7:375, *375n*
Hanger, G. Wallace, 6:237, *238n,*
11:538, 539n
Hanlon, John F., 1:457, *459n,* 460
Hanly, David, *12:31n; letter to,* 12:30–
31
Hanly, Martin A., 2:*, 53, 55, *55n*
Hanna, Daniel R., *5:383n; letter from,*
5:382–83
Hanna, M. A., and Co., 5:383n
Hanna, Marcus A., 4:221, *221–22n,*
240, 5:165, 215n, 248, 335n, 382–
83, 406n, 426, 508, 6:17n, 122,
138, 167–70, 170n, 212, 379, 9:132;
death of, 6:235, 236n, 379–80n; *let-
ter to,* 6:40; and National Civic Fed-
eration, 5:463–64, 464n, 482, 497n,
511
Hannahan, James, 9:282n, 497n
Hannahan, John J., 6:*, 235, *236n*
Hannon, William, 11:98, *99n,* 124–25,
129n; *wire from,* 11:128–29
Hanscom, Charles W., 7:77, 8:81, *82n;
letter from,* 7:77
Hansen, Ernest, 10:185–86, *186n*
Hansen, Julius, *10:186n; letter from,*
10:185–86
Hanson, Morris, 4:294n
Hanson, Ole, 11:63n
Hanson, William S., 12:540, *540n,*
541–42
Hapsburgs, 10:89
Harada, J., *letter to,* 9:17–18
Hardie, J. Keir, 3:*, 505, *505n,* 516,
640, 7:*, 130, *142n,* 477, 489
Harding, Chester, 11:393n
Harding, Florence M. K., 12:296, *299n*
Harding, John C., 3:*, *128n,* 7:387n;
at AFL convention, 3:125–26, 128n,
131, 135, 137–38
Harding, Warren, 10:243n, 11:374,
376n, 404–6, 410, 524n, 532n, 539n,
548n, 12:13, 26n, 39n, 48n, 260,

281n, 310; bust of, **12:**533n; death of, **12:**299n; and railroad shopmen's strike, 1922-?, **12:**86–87n, 103, 105, 106n, 116, 135, 137n, 203; SG, meetings with, **11:**449, 450n, 484n, 497–98, 498n; and World Court, **12:**209, 210

Hardman, George S., **6:**146, *147n*

Hardwick, Thomas W., **7:**58, *59n*

Harlan, John Marshall, **4:**293, *294n*, **5:**8, 305–6, **6:**421, 423n, **8:**491

Harlan and Hollingsworth Co., **4:**499n

Harlin, Robert H., **11:**481, *482n*

Harmon, Gilbert, **12:**22, *24n*

Harmony Mills: strike/lockout, 1880, *1:268n;* strike/lockout, 1882, **1:**264, *265n,* 267–68, 293–96, **3:**318, 340n

Harney, Michael J., *5:363n; letter to,* **5:**362–63

Harper, Robert L., **7:**354, *356n*

Harper, Samuel N., **10:**310, *312n*

Harper, Thomas W., **4:**293, *294n*

Harrah, Charles J., Jr., **5:**189–97, *198n*

Harriman, Charles A., **6:**398, *399–* 400n, 403–4, 405n, 435–39, 439n, **7:**86, 91n; *letter from,* **7:**86

Harriman, E. H., **3:**552n

Harriman, Florence Jaffray, **9:**312n, **10:**97, *98n*

Harriman, Job, **8:**136, *136n,* 291

Harriman, Mrs. Borden. *See* Harriman, Florence Jaffray

Harriman System Federation, **8:**322–23n, 367

Harris, Daniel, **1:***, 107, *108n,* 111, **2:***, 184, *186n,* 393, **3:***, 176, *177n,* 188, 298–99, 367, 452, 472, **4:***, 15, *16n,* 57, 222, **5:***, 429, *429n,* **8:***, *327n,* 427n, 449, **9:**80n, **12:***, 393, *394n; letter from,* **8:**326–27; *letters to,* **4:**219, **8:**426–27

Harris, G. B. "Barney," *9:342n; letter from,* **9:**341–42

Harris, George, **1:***, 390, *391n,* 457, 469–70, **2:***, 27, *28n*

Harris, George W. (Chicago newspaper editor), *4:391n*

Harris, George W. (New York newspaper editor), **10:**330–31, *331n,* 347, 350n

Harris, George W. (Tennessee newspaper owner), **6:**119, *119n*

Harris, Isaac, **8:**297n

Harris, Joel Chandler, **11:**68n

Harris, R. F., *letter from,* **7:**21–22

Harris, William V., **6:**15, *19n*

Harrisburg (Ill.) Trades and Labor Assembly, *8:132n*

Harrison, Ark., strike, 1921–23, **12:**192–95, *196–97n*

Harrison, Benjamin, **2:**233n, 277, *278n,* 346n, **3:**200, 214n, 283; and *Jefferson Borden* mutineers, **3:**117–19, 120n, 157, 158n, 280

Harrison, Byron P., *12:380n; letter to,* **12:**378–80

Harrison, Cabel, **12:**132, *132n*

Harrison, Carter, **2:**57, *58n,* 409n, **3:**364–65

Harrison, J. E., *letter from,* **10:**459–60

Harrison, Thomas H., **5:**255n, **6:**498–99, *499n,* **9:**479n

Harry, George Y., **6:**237, *238n,* **10:**209n; *letters to,* **6:**532, 536–37

Hart, Charles, **3:**51, *55n*

Hart, George H., **3:**297, *298n*

Hart, I., **1:**10

Hart, John F., **10:***, 303, *304n*

Hart, Lee M., **3:***, *520n,* 539, **4:***, *122n,* **5:***, *176n,* **6:***, *496n;* at AFL conventions, **5:**175, 176n, 284, 286n, **6:**494, 496n; *letters to,* **4:**121–22, **5:**450–51

Hart, Matthew, **4:**449n

Hart, Schaffner, and Marx, **8:**277n, 410

Hartford (Conn.) Building Trades Council, **7:**459–60, 461n

Hartford (Conn.) Central Labor Union, **7:**459, *461n*

Hartmann, Louis, **2:***, *128n; letter to,* **2:**128

Hartwig, Otto R., **10:***, 487, *490n,* **11:***, *51n,* **12:**212n; *wire from,* **11:**51, 52n

Hartzell, Charles, **6:**424–25, *429n*

Harvey, James F., **4:**416, *417n*

Harvey, William H., **4:**371n

Harzbecker, Frank H., **5:**453n, **6:***, 10n, *393n; letter to,* **6:**392–93

Haskell, Burnette G., **2:***, 287, *288n,* **5:**504

Haskell, Henry, **9:**274n
Haskell, William E., *6:299n; letter from,* **6:**297–99
Haskins, William H., **6:**67–68, *70n*
Haslam, James, **5:***, 154, *154n*
Hassenpflue, Peter, *9:137n; letter to,* **9:**136–37
Hasson, Samuel B., **2:***, 65, *68n*
Hastings, Charles E., *12:17n; letter to,* **12:**16–17
Hat and Cap Makers of North America, United Cloth, **6:***, 407n, **7:***, 18n, **9:***, 110n, **11:***; AFL financial support of, **6:**355n, 405, 407n, 409–10, 410n; agreement of, with Cap Manufacturers' Association, **7:**207–8, 208n; and IWW, **7:**18, 18–19n, 207; jurisdiction of, **9:**107–10, 110n
—convention: 1906 (New York City), **7:**17, *18n*
—locals: local 5 (Chicago), **9:**107, 110n; local 24 (New York City), **9:**108, 110n
—strikes/lockouts: 1903–4 (New York City and New Jersey), **7:**18, *19n;* 1904–5 (New York City and New Jersey), **6:**405–6, *407n,* 409–10, 410n; **7:**207; 1905–6 (Detroit), **7:**18, *19n,* 184, 186n; 1905–6 (New York City), **7:**18, *18n,* 184
Hatch, Leonard W., *10:456n; letter to,* **10:**455–56
Hatfield, George, **3:**236, *240n*
Hatfield, Henry, **8:**519n
Hatfield, Sidney, **11:**296n
Hat Finishers' Association, Brooklyn, N.Y., **1:**361, *362n*
Hat Finishers of the U.S. of America, National Trade Association of, **1:***, 390, 390n
Hatters case. See *Loewe v. Lawlor*
Hatters of North America, United, **4:***, 140–41, 141n, 389n, **5:***, 73n, **6:***, 177–78n, **7:***, 313n, **8:***, 42n, **9:***, 110n, **12:**446n; AFL financial support of, **7:**454–55, 455–56n; jurisdiction of, **9:**107–10, 110n; label of, **7:**455–56n, **8:**74. See also *Loewe v. Lawlor*
—strikes/lockouts: 1902 (Danbury, Conn.), *6:177n;* 1909 (Connecticut,

New York, and New Jersey), **7:**454–55, *455–56n,* **8:**77
Hatton (priest), **3:**424
Haugen, Gilbert N., *11:338n*
Hausler, Mary, **1:***, 108, *109n,* 110, 119
Havana Central Railroad Co., strike/lockout, 1916–17, **9:**534, *534n*
Havana Electric Railway Co., strike/lockout, 1906, **7:**162, *164n*
Havana Herald, **5:**184, 186, 188n
Havana Journal, **5:**184
Havana Tobacco Co., strike/lockout, 1907, **7:**220–21, *221n*
Havens, Munson A., *10:245n; wire from,* **10:**244; *wire to,* **10:**244
Hawaii: annexation of, **4:**405, 405n, 487–88, *488–89n,* **5:**xv, 4–6, 22–24, 44–45; Asian labor in, **6:**471–72, 472–73n; Chinese workers in, **4:**488, **5:**xvi, **6:**195, 471–72, **7:**332–33, **11:**483, 484n, 502–3, 503–4n, **12:**210–11, 415; contract labor in, **4:**488, **5:**23–24, 29n, 44, **6:**195, **7:**332–33, **11:**483, 484n, 503; Filipino labor union in, **12:**211, 212n; Japanese workers in, **6:**151n, 195, **7:**332–33, **12:**415; Korean workers in, **6:**195, 195n; workers from, **7:**93n; working conditions in, **5:**xv–xvi, 5–6, 8, 22–24, 44, 139, **6:**372, **12:**211, 212n
Hawkins, John T., **8:**210, *212n*
Hawkins, William M., *4:480n*
Hawkins v. Bleakly, **10:**143, *147n*
Hawley, Frank T., **7:***, 423, *424n,* 457
Hawley, Joseph R., **5:**248, *249n*
Hay, Arthur A., **6:**415, 416–*17n; letter from,* **7:**383–84; *letter to,* **7:**305–6
Hay, John, **4:**133n, **6:**378n
Hayden, James H., *5:207n,* 225–26, 230n, **7:**28–29
Hayes, Denis A., **5:***, *172n,* 341–42n, **6:***, *67n,* 450n, **7:***, *7n,* 111n, 123n, 202n, 251, 453n, **8:***, *125n,* 256, 258n, 501, 503–4, **9:***, *14n,* 436; at AFL conventions, **5:**170, 172n, 283–84, 286n, **6:**63, 67n, 199, 204n, 361, 364n, **8:**18n, 288, 295, 408; election of, as AFL vice-president, **5:**294n, 445, **6:**209, 376n, 509n, **7:**281n,

427n, **9:**38n, 226n, 348n; *letter to,*
 5:339–41
Hayes, Dora Schneider, **8:**22n
Hayes, Everis A., **7:**382n, 384, *385n*
Hayes, Frank, **8:***, 407, *409n,* 413, **9:***,
 40n, 98n, 210, *211n,* 443n, **10:***,
 181, *182n,* 308n, 334n, 372, 407
Hayes, Isaac I., **1:**152, *152n*
Hayes, John, **5:**491, *492n*
Hayes, John W., **1:***, *401n,* 426, 466,
 467n, **2:***, 24n, 131–32, *132n,* 181,
 212, 219, 230, 243, 332, 342–43,
 3:*, 414, *415n,* **5:***, 153, *154n,* **7:***,
 256, *257n,* **8:***, 72, *76n; letter from,*
 1:409–11; *letter to,* **3:**441–42; *report of,*
 1:399–401
Hayes, Max S., **4:***, 450, *451n,* **5:***,
 48n, 72, **6:***, *62n,* **7:***, *422n,* **8:***, *6n,*
 9:*, *36n,* 139, 139–40n, **10:***, *262n,*
 11:*, 262–63, *265n,* **12:***, *89n;* at
 AFL conventions, **5:**44–45, 48n, 50,
 162n, 166, 169n, 281–82, 284, 286n,
 437, 438n, 440, **6:**59, 62n, 63–64,
 67n, 69, 196, 197n, 200, 202, 204n,
 501, 503n, **7:**419, 422n, 423, **8:**4,
 6n, 11, 285, 289, 290n, 405, 406n,
 409, 415, 416n, **9:**35, 524, 525n,
 10:259, 262n, **11:**474, **12:**88, 94–96,
 332–33; *letters to,* **6:**485–86, **8:**21–22,
 9:333–34
Hayes, Rutherford B., *2:225n; letter to,*
 2:225
Haymarket: and Amnesty Association,
 2:60, 63n; bombing, *1:277,* **3:**568,
 9:241, **11:**9; defendants, **1:**461,
 462n, 467, **2:**53–55, 55n, 56–58,
 58n, 59–62, **3:**350, 358, 359n
Haynes, George E., **8:**504, *504n,*
 9:169n, **10:**327n, 367n, 421, 428,
 463
Hays, Arthur G., **12:**265n
Hays, John W., **8:***, 30, *31n,* 53, **9:***,
 168, *168n,* **11:***, 94, *95n,* **12:***, 126,
 127n
Hays, William H., *12:263n; letter to,*
 12:261–63
Hayward, Stuart A., **9:**406, *406n*
Hayward, William, **12:**80n
Haywood, William D., **6:***, *283n,* **7:***,
 146n, **8:***, *104n,* 415, 416n, **10:***,
 176n, *529n,* **11:***, *113n;* and AFL

affiliation, **7:**284, 286n; arrest and
 extradition of, **7:**144–46, 146n; and
 Colorado miners' strike, 1903–4,
 6:281, 282n, 344n, 504–6, 509n;
 conviction of, **10:**528, 529n, 533–34,
 11:113, 113n; and IWW, **6:**37n,
 406n, 442, 450–52, 456–57, 459,
 461–63, **7:**245, 247n, **8:**103, 104n,
 326n, 501, 503n, **9:**489n; *letter to,*
 6:343–44
Head, Franklin, **5:**218n
Healey, Martin, **4:**57, *57n*
health insurance: AFL Executive
 Council and, **9:**400–401; in Great
 Britain, **9:**193n; SG and, **9:**400–403,
 407; state, **10:**329, 329–30n
Healy, John P., **4:**416, *417n*
Healy, Timothy, **6:***, *57n,* **7:***, 33, *36n,*
 210, **8:***, 30, *31n,* **11:***, *60n,* **12:***,
 98n, 299–300, 342–43n, 467n; at
 AFL conventions, **6:**56, 57n, 501,
 503n, **8:**289, **11:**82n, **12:**96–97; *letters
 from,* **11:**59–60, **12:**341–42
Heaphy, Richard A., *11:262n; letter to,*
 11:260–61
Hearst, William, **10:**278n
Hearst, William Randolph, *5:63–64n,*
 415n, **6:**213, 213n, 521, 521–22n,
 7:90n, 104n, 110n, 311, 311n, 369,
 397, 398n; *editorial by,* **5:**64–66
Hearst newspapers, attacks on SG,
 11:366–68, 368n, 447, 447–48n
Heathcote, Thomas, **3:**521
Heberling, Samuel E., **9:***, 30, *34n,*
 11:*, 249, *259n,* 461
Hebrew Labor Federation of the U.S.
 and Canada, **3:**355n
Hebrew Mutual Benefit Society,
 2:117n
Hebrew Trades, United. *See* United
 Hebrew Trades
Hebrew Trades of Greater New York,
 Federated, **3:**355n
Hecker, A., **2:**367, 371n
Hedley, Frank, **6:**475, *476n,* **9:**492, *493n*
Hedrick, George, **8:**151n, **12:**383n
Heenan, Frank C., **5:***, 427, *428n*
Hefferman, Etta M., **7:**286n
Heffernan, John, **2:**271, 272n
Heim, Ferdinand, Brewing Co.,
 strike/lockout, 1900, **5:**260n

Heimerdinger, David S., **4:**10–12, 15, *15n*, 236

Heine, C., **1:**183–84, *184n*, 199

Heine, Heinrich, **6:**419, *423n*, **10:**50

Heinze, Frederick A., *6:285n*

Heitfeld, Henry, **5:**151n, 457, 458n

Helgesen, Henry T., **8:**345, *346n*

Heller, Charles, **6:**222, 223n

Heller, Jacob J., **11:**90, *92n*

Hell Gate Power Station, **12:**68, 72, *73n*

Helm, John L., *7:105n; letter from,* **7:**104–5

Heltmann, William, **1:**199

Hemleben, Ernst, *letter from,* **3:**455

Hempstead, H. K., **12:**184n

Henderson, Arthur, **10:***, *294n*, 522, 549, 551, 554n, **11:***, 12, *17n*, 28–29, 30n; and AFL mission to Europe, spring 1918, **10:**445–46; and Labour party, constitution of, **10:**293, 294n; and proposed mission to United States, **10:**388, 390n; and "Stockholm" movement, **10:**343, 356n

Henderson, David B., **7:**80, *90n,* **8:**183

Henderson, George, **12:**195, 197n

Henderson, James "Pitchfork," **10:**187–88, *189n*

Henderson, W. M., *letter from,* **10:**494

Henderson Shipbuilding Co., strike/lockout, 1920–21, **11:**484–85, *486n*

Henley, John J., *8:199n; letter to,* **8:**195–99

Henneberry, Thomas T., **1:***, 243, *245n*

Henning, Edward J., **12:**546, 550, *552n*

Henry, Alice, **9:**302, *303n*

Henry, Patrick, **8:**74

Henry, Robert L., **8:**374–75, *381n*

Henry VIII, **5:**303, 309n

Henry Steers Co., **10:**171–72n

Hensel, Otto, *12:457n*, 503, 504n

Henson, James, **9:**477n, 487

Hepburn, William P., **5:**363n, **7:**322n, 333n, 336n, **8:**361, *363n*

Heraldo Habanero. See *Havana Herald*

Herbert, Hilary A., **4:**181, *182n*, **5:**201–3, *207n*, 228, 231n, 481

Herbrand, Louis, **2:***, *42n*, 113; *letter to,* **2:**42

Hereford, Fred, *wire from,* **11:**51, 52n

Hering, Frank E., *12:218n; letter to,* **12:**217–18

Hermalin, David, **10:**163n

Hermann, Mrs. Paul, **3:**141

Hermann, Paul, **3:**141, *142n*

Hernsheim factory, strike/lockout, 1902, **6:**31n

Herrick, Myron T., **10:**158, *159n*

Herrin (Ill.) massacre, **12:**99, *99n*, 195, 197n, 329, 330n; Lewis and, **12:**99n; SG and, **12:**99–100n

Herwegh, Georg, *6:423n*

Herzberg, George, **3:**484, *485–86n*

Herzl, Theodor, **9:**405n

Hesketh, Robert B., **12:***, 258, *259n*

Hess, Rosa, **3:**141, *142n*

Hessler, John, *11:267n*, 481; *wire from,* **11:**265–66

Heurtaux, Alfred, **1:**204, *206n*

Hewer, The (Barnard), **7:**442

Hewitt, Abram S., **1:***, 126, *127n*, 207, 429, 431n, 441, 443–44, **5:**411, **8:**330, **11:**9

Hewitt, Fred, **11:**401, *403n*, 474

Hexagon Labor Club, **4:**57n

Hexter, H., **1:**108, *109n*

Heywood, Charles, *4:396n*

Hibbert, Albert, **5:***, 418, *419n,* **6:***, *119n*, 358; *letter to,* **6:**118–19

Hibernians, Ancient Order of, **4:**261, *264n*

Hickey, John H., *12:300n; letter to,* **12:**299–300

Hickey, Thomas, **5:**429, *430n*

Hickory Steel-Grip Glove Co., strike/lockout, 1920–21, *12:451n*

Hicks, Henry A., **2:**332, *338n*

Higgins, John M., **3:**474, *477n*

Higgins, Samuel, **11:**538, 539n

Higginson, Thomas H., **6:**356

High, James L., **8:**491, *493n*

High School Teachers' Union (Washington, D.C.), *9:466n*

Hilfers, Henry F., **9:***, *54n*, 167, **12:***, 305, *308n; letter to,* **9:**53–54

Hilkene, Jacob, *3:69n; letter to,* **3:**68–69

Hill, Albert, **5:**279n

Hill, Andrew, **9:**518n

Hill, David B., **2:***, 6–7, 9, *11n,* 110n, 320n, 359, **3:***, *28n*, 508, **4:**113n,

143, *143n*, 153, 323n; *letters to,* **2:**108–10, 320, 363–64, **3:**28
Hill, James J., **3:**547n
Hill, Joe, **9:**343, *343*–44n
Hillman, Sidney, **9:***, 227, *228n*, 354, 357, **10:***, 138, *139n*, 150
Hillmann, Carl, **1:***, 22, *43n;* on carpenters, **1:**39; on cigarmakers, **1:**31, 42; on class divisions, **1:**27, 29, 34, 38, 41; on cooperatives, **1:**31, 35, 37, 42; on fraternal organizations, **1:**39; on goldsmiths, **1:**31, 42; on guilds, **1:**24, 30, 34, 38–39; on hatmakers, **1:**31, 38, 42; on journeymen's associations, **1:**39, 41; *Praktische Emanzipationswinke* (pamphlet by), **1:**23–43; on printers, **1:**31, 38, 42; on silversmiths, **1:**31; on suffrage, universal, **1:**26, 32; on trade unions, **1:**27–28, 30–31, 34–42; on typesetters, **1:**39
Hillquit, Morris, **9:***, *117n*, 378, **10:***, 90n, *94n*, 138, 261, 263n, **12:***, 208, *209n;* interrogation of, by SG, **9:**112–17; interrogation of SG by, **9:**118–35, 138–39; socialist program, summary of, **9:**139, 139n; *wire from,* **10:**93
Hillstrom, Joseph. *See* Hill, Joe
Hillyer, Granby, *9:283n*, 309, 310n
Himmelsbach, Henry, *2:252n; letter to,* **2:**251–52
Hinchcliffe, John, **6:**29n
Hindenburg, Paul von, **11:**49n
Hinder, Herman, **7:***, 207, *208n*
Hines, Walker D., **11:**128n, 238–39, *239n*, 249, 254, 259n; and railroad shopmen's strike, 1919 (threatened), **11:**120n
Hinkle, Charles C., *11:229n; letter from,* **11:**228–29
Hints to Unions, Organizers, and Others (AFL), **5:**399, *400n*, **7:**126n
Hirsch, David, **1:**21, 75, *76n*, 96, **12:**393, 394n, 399
Hirsch, Edward, **4:**319, *320n*, *7:120n; letter from,* **7:**119–20
Hirsch, Henry, **1:**449, *449n*
Hirsch, Louis, *11:444n; letter to,* **11:**443–44
Hirsch, Max, **1:**33–34, *44n*, **3:**639

Hirsch-Duncker Workingmen's Associations. *See* Verband der deutschen Gewerkvereine
Hirschhorn and Bendheim, **1:**187, *188n*, 199, 262
Hirschhorn, L., and Co., **1:**112, *115n*
Hirth, Frank, **1:***, 71, 103–6, *106n*
Hiscock, Frank, **2:**123, *123n*
History and Philosophy of the Eight-Hour Movement (Danryid), *2:188n*
History of Germany in the Nineteenth Century, The (Treitschke), *9:194n*
History of Trade Unionism, The (Webb and Webb), *8:304n*
Hitchcock, Frank H., **8:**495, *496n*
Hitchcock, Samuel M., **7:**388n
Hitchcock, Thomas, **2:**286n. *See also* Marshall, Matthew
Hitchman case. See *Hitchman Coal and Coke Co. v. Mitchell et al.*; *Mitchell et al. v. Hitchman Coal and Coke Co.*
Hitchman Coal and Coke Co., injunction, **10:**285–86, 287n, 322, 323n
Hitchman Coal and Coke Co. v. Mitchell et al., **10:**285–86, *287n*, 322, 323n, 351–52, 372–73, **12:**23, 93n
Hitt, Robert R., **6:**232n, 261–62n, **7:**80, *91n*
Hixson, C. E., **5:**120, 121n
Hoar, George F., **8:**463, *468n*
Hoard, Otto E., **10:**19, *21n*
Hobbs, Algernon G., *11:247n; wire to,* **11:**247
Hobby, William, **11:**426n
Hobson, Richard P., **5:**4, *11n*, 21; *letter to,* **9:**178–79
Hochstader, Albert F., *3:340n;* and mediation of clothing cutters' strike, 1893, **3:**305–12, 314–16, 318–35, 337–38
hod carriers, **5:**440; and black workers, **3:**80, 409; jurisdiction of, **2:**131, 131n
Hod Carriers', Building and Common Laborers' Union of America, International, **6:***, **7:***, **8:***, **9:***, 71, 73n, 251, **10:***, 415–16, 416n, **11:***, 72, 74n, 85n, **12:***, 238, 241n; and black workers, **9:**480, 480n, **10:**135, **11:**84n; jurisdiction of, **10:**405, 406n

—locals: local 95 (New York City), **11:**323–24, 324–25n, 352–53, 378; local 120 (Indianapolis), **12:**363, 364n; local 224 (Cedar Rapids, Iowa), **9:**464; local 228 (Lawrence, Mass.), **11:**351, 352n

Hod Carriers' and Building Laborers' Union of America, International, **2:***, **6:***, 173–74, 175n, **7:***, 282, 282n, **8:***, 346n, **9:***, **10:***, **11:***, **12:***; reorganization of, **7:**443–44, 445–46n

—local: local 4 (Chicago), **7:**445n

Hodge, John, **7:***, 288, *289n*

Hodges Boiler Works, strike/lockout, 1920–21, **11:**484–85, *486n*

hod hoisting engineers' union (New York City), **2:**295

Hoehn, Gottlieb A., **2:***, 388, *408n*, **4:**339n, **6:**196, *197n; letter to,* **4:**338–39

Hoffman, Clara C., **3:**598, *599n*

Hoffman, Edward, *letter to,* **4:**165–66

Hoffman, Fred W., **8:**297, *298n*

Hoffmeyer, Volmer A. H., **3:**47, *48n*

Hoffstot, Frank N., **10:**77, *79n*

Hofher, Philip A., **3:**628, *659n*

Hogan, C. H., *letter to,* **8:**46

Hogan, Thomas J., **8:**107, *108n*, 201

Hogg, Charles E., **10:**372, *373n*

Hohenzollerns, **10:**88

Holcomb, Walter L., **5:**489, *489n*

Holden, Henrietta, **12:**222, *222n*

Holden v. Hardy, **4:**452, *453n*, 492, **5:**114, *115n*

Holder, Arthur E., **5:***, *455n*, **7:***, 169, *177n*, 288, 347n, 458n, **8:***, 101, *101n*, 158, 257, **9:***, 54, *56n*, 90–92, 97–98n, 371, **10:***, 19, *22n*, 49n, 64n, 181, **11:***, 466, *467n*, **12:***, *470n;* and election of 1924, **12:**468, 474; *letter to,* **5:**454–55

Holdom, Jesse, **7:**11, *11n*, **12:**366, *367n*

Holland, James J., **2:***, 332, *337n*, 343

Holland, James P., **7:***, 279, *280n*, **10:***, 127, *128n*, 196, 236, 238n, **11:**⁽ⁿ⁾, 354–55, *358n*, **12:***, 550, *553n*

Holland, Thomas, **2:**75, *76n*, 79

Hollis, Henry, **11:**31, *34n*

Hollis, Lawrence P., **9:**170, *171n*

Hollister, Frank C., **3:**465n; *letter to,* **3:**463–64

Hollister, William C., *3:464n; letter to,* **3:**463–64

Holm, Walter E., *10:150n; wire from,* **10:**148

Holmes, David, **3:***, 517n, 589n, 596, *597n,* **4:***, 66, *70n*

Holmes, Oliver Wendell, **6:**421, 423n, **10:**144, *147n*

Holmes, Shipley R., *2:375n; letter to,* **2:**374–75

Holmqvist, Mr. (San Francisco worker lost in earthquake), **7:**42

Holston Manufacturing Co., injunction, **9:**262–63n

Holt, Edwin M., family of, **5:**272–73, *274n*

Holt, Thomas M., **5:**273, *274n*

Holzmann and Deutschberger, **1:**112, *115n*, 197, *198n*, 199

Home Club, **1:**402–3, *404n*, 420, **2:**14, *14–15n*, 21, 23n

Homestead strike, 1892, **1:**455n, *3:189n*, 213, 214n, 420, **4:**492, 500n, **5:**84, **6:**235; advisory committee of Iron and Steel Workers and, **3:**189n, 210–11n, 233, 233n, 234, 235n, 253n; AFL Executive Council and, **3:**188, 191, 206–8, 210n, 231–34, 236–40, 250, 266, 266n; AFL financial support of, **3:**206–8, 218–19, 219n, 250–52, 265, 266n; arrests and legal proceedings during, **3:**186, 210–11n, 217, 232, 233n, 237–38, 240–41n, 264–65, 266n, 299; and Carnegie Steel Co. boycott (threatened), **3:**232–34, 235n; *circular on,* **3:**206–8, 217; congressional investigation of, **4:**387, **9:**51, *52n;* "Homestead Day," **3:**250, *253n,* 265; and KOL, **3:**190, 217–18, 218n; mass meetings to support, **3:**206, 208–10, 231, 234, 236–40; SG and, **3:**188–91, 193, 195, 206–10, 213, 217–19, 219n, 231–34, 236–38, 265–66; strikebreakers in, **3:**186, 188, 189n, 190, 195, 199, 199n, 208, 239; suppression of, **3:**185–86, 189n, 191, 191n, 208, 255–56, **4:**105; and sympathy strikes, *3:234n,* 238,

250–51; violence in, **3:**185, 188–89, 189n, 190, 193, 209–10, 237–38
home work, **8:**393–94, **11:**71n
Home Work Congress, International, 1912 (Zurich), **8:**393, *394n*
Honolulu Trades and Labor Council, **6:**151n
Honomu Sugar Co., **5:**24
Honomu Sugar Co. v. A. Sayewiz, **5:**24, 29n
Honomu Sugar Co. v. Nikoleg Gzeluch, **5:**24, 29n
Hood, Thomas, **2:**80, *80n,* 83
Hooker, Mr. (English worker), as correspondent of SG, **3:**588
Hooper, Ben Wade, **11:**538, 539n
hoops, driving (tightening) of, **4:**330, *330n,* **5:**221n
Hoover, Herbert C., **10:**75n, 303, *304n,* 315n, **11:**210, 384–88, 390, 391n, 515n, 532n, **12:**30n, 142, 146n, 191, 192n, 413; SG, meetings with, **12:**12–15, 381, 382n
Hopkins, J. A. H., **10:**160, *161n,* **12:**99n; *wire from,* **12:**99
Hopkins, John J., **1:**361, *362n*
Hopkins, John P., **3:**521, 523–24
Horn, George L., **3:***, *471n; letter to,* **3:**470–71; *wire from,* **3:**532–33
Hornthal, Lewis M., *3:340n;* and mediation of clothing cutters' strike, 1893, **3:**305, 307, 313, 316, 326, 335–36, 338–39
horse car drivers, **1:**301–3
horse car railroad employees, **2:**150
Horseshoers of the U.S. and Canada, International Union of Journeymen, **4:***, 99, 99n, **5:***, 162n, **9:***, 209, 209n; jurisdiction of, **5:**161, 162n
—locals: local 11 (Milwaukee), **3:**497, 498n; local 29 (Denver), **5:**393, 396n
Hosick, James, **8:**209n, 272–73, *277n;* prosecution of, **8:**209n, 235–37, 238n, 254, 273–74, 350, 353
Hotel and Restaurant Employees' International Alliance and Bartenders' International League of America, **3:***, **4:***, **5:***, 140–41, 142n, 161, 162n, 396n, **6:***, 286n, 390–92,

7:*, 22, 23n, **8:***, 44n, 451, 452n, 475, **9:***, 245, 246n, **10:***, 82n, **11:***, 46n, **12:***, 259n; and black workers, **10:**180, **11:**42–46, 84n; and Chinese workers, **11:**43; injunction against, **12:**94n; and Japanese workers, **11:**43; jurisdiction of, **11:**42–46, 46n
—convention: 1899 (Chicago), **5:**142n
—locals: local 14 (Denver), **5:**395, 396n, **6:**15; local 18 (Denver), **5:**393, 396n, **7:**22; local 33 (Seattle), **12:**259n; local 362 (Albany, N.Y.), **8:**449, 452n; local 380 (Bisbee, Ariz.), **12:**93n; local 520 (Tell City, Ind.), **7:**235, 236n; local 767 (Washington, D.C.), **6:**390
—strike/lockout: 1913 (Albany, N.Y.), **8:**448–49, *452n*
Hotel and Restaurant Employees' National Alliance, **3:***, 401n, 417, 484–85, 485–86n, **4:***, 270–71, 272n, 381, **5:***, **6:***, **7:***, **8:***, **9:***, **10:***, **11:***, **12:***
—convention: 1894, **3:**486n
—local: local 40 (Chicago), **4:**381, 382n
—strike/lockout: 1893 (Brooklyn, N.Y.), *3:485–86n*
Hotel Workers' Union, International: —strikes/lockouts: 1913 (Albany, N.Y.), **8:**448–49, *452n;* 1913 (New York City), **8:**449, *452–53n*
Hough, D. J., **9:**74n
hours of labor, **1:**83, 98, 219; AFL and, **3:**547, **4:**100, **11:**8n, 79, 82n, 504, 504n; Gary and, **12:**279–80, 281n; hearings on, **1:**315–26, 328–30 (*see also* eight-hour workday: hearings on; government employees: hours of); overtime, **5:**16–17, **6:**32n, **10:**84, 99–101, 281, 285n, 444, **11:**159; SG and, **1:**78, 372–73, **2:**85–86, 153–54, 325, **3:**44–46, 53–54, 229–30, 393–94, 450, 605, 609, **4:**27, 36–37, 173–74, 392–94, 433–34, **5:**137–38, 198, 349–51, **6:**418–22, **7:**490, **8:**345, **9:**119–22, 341n, 408n, **12:**304–5. *See also under* government employees; legislation, states and territories; legislation, U.S.; strikes and lockouts; women workers

House, Edward M., **10**:71n, **11**:41n, 48, *49n*, 58n
House of the World Worker. *See* Casa del Obrero Mundial
House Wreckers' Union (New York City), **11**:323, *324*–25n. *See also* American Federation of Labor (AFL): federal labor unions(FLUs): FLU 14,949; Hod Carriers', Building and Common Laborers' Union of America, International: locals: local 95 (New York City) —strike/lockout: 1920 (New York City), **11**:353
housing plans, wartime, **11**:35. *See also* Cantonment Construction Agreement; cantonments
Houston, Clinton C., **6**:107n, **9**:*, 457, *457n*
Houston, David F., **10**:274, *278n*
Houston, race riot in, 1917, **10**:326, *326n*
Houston Ice and Brewing Co., boycott, 1907, **7**:222
Howard, Charles P., **11**:*, 474, *476n*
Howard, George, **3**:579n
Howard, John, **1**:449, *449n*
Howard, Robert, **1**:*, 217–18, *220n*, 228, 286n, 329, 390, **2**:*, 17, *259n*, **4**:*, *204n*, **12**:376n; at AFL convention, **2**:259, 271–72; *letter to*, **4**:250–51
Howard, W. Schley, **10**:366–67, *368n*
Howat, Alexander, **11**:321n, 481, *481–82n*
Howe, Frederic, **9**:422n
Howe, Louis M., *10:223n; letter from*, **10**:222–23
Howe, Walter, **1**:93, *93n*
Howes, John W., **1**:387, 455, *456n*, 460, **2**:33, 35
Howey, James W., *10:385n; letter from*, **10**:384–85
Howland, Henry E., **4**:304n
Howlin, William H., **12**:543, *544n*
Hoxie, Robert F., *9:189n*, 505; *letter to*, **9**:187–89
Hoyt, Henry W., **5**:311, *311n*
Hüber, Anton, **7**:487–88, *488n*
Huber, Henry, **12**:215n
Huber, Jacob, **3**:112, *115n*, **6**:90n

Huber, William D., **5**:*, 398, *398*–99n, 474, **6**:*, 6–7, *8n*, 44, 45n, 92–93, 546n, **7**:*, *7n*, 55–56, 111n, 243, 312–13, 453n, **8**:*, 106n, *125n*, **9**:*, *14n;* at AFL Executive Council meetings, **8**:379, 501, 503–4; election of, as AFL vice-president, **6**:509n, **7**:281n, 427n, **8**:18n, 295
Huberwald, Florence F., **4**:31, *33n*
Huck, Louis, **1**:*, 85, *86n*
Huddell, Arthur M., **12**:*, 550, *553n*
Huddleston, George, **10**:378, *378n*, **11**:468
Hudson, Manley O., **12**:210n
Hudson, Oliver, **6**:308n
Hudson, W. G., *letter to*, **10**:449–50
Hudson County (N.J.), Central Labor Federation, **3**:83–84, *85n*, 112–13
Hudson County (N.J.), Central Labor Union, **3**:85n
Huebner, Adam, **6**:*, 487, *488n*, **8**:*, 91, *92n*
Huerta, Adolfo de la, **9**:467, *468n*, **11**:340–41, 404n, **12**:391–92, 392n
Huerta, Victoriano, *9:160n*, 325, 432; and Madero, **9**:158–59, 436; overthrow of, **9**:96n, 159n, 306, 361, 437; Villa and, **9**:212n; Zapata and, **9**:307n
Huggs, John A., *11:96n; letter from*, **11**:96
Hughes, Andrew C., **11**:*, 151, *153n*
Hughes, C. N., **5**:438, *439n*, 443–45
Hughes, Charles Evans, **8**:120n, 258, *259n*, **11**:261, 262n, 443n, 524n, **12**:12–13, 210n, 211, 294n, 417n, 492; bust of, **12**:533n; labor record of, **9**:488n; *letter from*, **12**:290–94, *letters to*, **11**:440–42, **12**:100, 255–56, 286–88
Hughes, Harley, **9**:223n
Hughes, James F. (bricklayer), **11**:350, *351*–52n
Hughes, James F. (sheet metal worker), **4**:*, 346, *347n*
Hughes, Samuel T., *letters to*, **9**:287–88, 397–98
Hughes, Thomas, **9**:267n
Hughes, William, **8**:100, *101n*, 492, 494, **9**:92, **12**:496; and eight-hour bill (H.R. 9061), **8**:259n; and indus-

trial relations commission bill (H.R. 21,094), **8:**381n; and sundry civil appropriation bill (H.R. 25,552), **8:**132n, 460, 469

Hughes, William M., **10:**492–93, *493n,* 521, **11:**409

Hugo, Victor, **9:**537

Huhta, John, **9:**184n

Hulbert, George M., **12:**546, 550, *552n*

Hull, Cordell, **12:**184, *184n*

Hull, Harry, **12:**348n

Hullehan, Mr. (New York City worker), **7:**373

Hull-House, **5:**316n

Hulse, E. J., **10:**521, *524n*

Hulse, H., **10:**521, 524n

Humphrey, Charles F., **5:**184, *188n,* 231

Humphrey, H. Ben, *letter to,* **12:**515–16

Humphrey, J. Otis, **10:**252, *253n*

Humphrey, William E., **7:**108, *109n*

Hungary, workers from, **12:**415

Hunger, Jacob, **3:**492–95, *497n*

Hunt, George W. P., **9:**351, *352n,* 467, **10:**338, *339n*

Hunt, John T., **7:**183n

Hunt, Russell R., **7:**47–48, *48n*

Hunt, William H., **5:**416n, 423–25, **6:**254–55

Hunter, Robert, *8:335n,* **10:**181

Hunter, Samuel N., **12:**99n

Hunter, W. A., **11:**73, *74n*

Huntington, Henry, **12:**265n

Huntington, Henry E., **6:**415–16, *417n, 8:136n*

Huntington (W.Va.) Central Labor Union, *6:62n*

Huntley, Frederick, **2:**332, *337n*

Hupp Motor Co., **10:**365

Hurley, Edward N., **10:**207n, 220, *221n,* 360, 362n, 546, **11:**41n, 523n; *letter to,* **10:**452–53

Hurley, John D., **8:**285, *286n*

Hurst, George, **1:***, *66n,* 68; *letters to,* **1:**75–78

Hushing, William C., **12:**246, *247n,* 383n

Husted, Joel E., **3:**227, *229n*

Hutcheson, William L., **10:***, *171*–72n, 318–19n, 334n, 360–61, 362–63n,

407, **11:***, 23n, 434, *435n,* 477, 529n, **12:***, 550, *553n; letter from,* **10:**232–35; *letters to,* **10:**228–31, **11:**544–45; *wires from,* **10:**176, 317–18, 410–11; *wires to,* **10:**171, 409–10

Hutchinson, Lee C., *2:175n; letter to,* **2:**175

Huysmans, Camille, **7:**488, *489n,* **11:**28, *30n*

Hylan, John F., **9:**430n, **10:**236, *238n,* **12:**546, 550

Hyman, Celia, **3:**140

Hyman, Miss Mary, **3:**141

Hyman, Mrs. Mary, **3:**141, *142n*

Hynes, John J., **10:***, *410n,* **11:**23n, 111n; *wire to,* **10:**409–10

Hynes, William F., **4:**292, *294n*

Hysell, Nial R., **2:***, 256n, 271, *272n,* **3:***, 648, 654, *660n*

Hyde, John S., **7:**77, *90n*

Iams, William L., **3:**238, *240–41n*

Ice Delivery Company of Spokane v. *Local No. 690 of Teamsters,* **12:**302, *303n*

Idaho, election of 1906, **7:**118–19

Idaho State Federation of Labor, *10:186n*

Idaho State Tribune (trade union journal), **5:**97, *98n*

Idar, Clemente N., **11:**338–40, *341n,* **12:**358–59, 525, 541; *letter from,* **12:**120–21

Ide and Co., George P., strike/lock-out, 1886, *1:467n*

Iden, George, *3:193n,* 255, 258n; *letter to,* **3:**192–93

Iffland, Charles, **9:***, *244n; letter from,* **9:**242–43

If I Were an Employer (Crowther), **12:**419, *421n*

Iglesias Pantín, Santiago, **5:***, xvi, 281n, *415n,* **6:***, 232n, 248, 252–54, *257n,* 424–27, 429n, **7:***, *52n,* **8:***, 19, *20n,* 87–88, 470, **9:***, *80n,* 410, 443n, 533–34, **10:***, 9, *13n,* 436, 438n, 499, **11:***, *503*–4n, **12:***, *201*–2n, 356, 358, 391; arrest of, **5:**415–16n, 423–25, 425n; *letters from,* **5:**415, **10:**313–15; *letters to,* **6:**382–83, 470, **7:**51–52, 231–32, **9:**78–80, **11:**502–3; SG, meeting

with, **12**:197–201; and U.S. Commission on Industrial Relations, **9**:257–58, 258n, 280, 311–12
Illinois: election of 1906, **7**:96, 101–2, 102n, 109–10, 110n, 115, 140, 358, 360; election of 1908, **7**:346–47, 347n, 348–50, 350n, 357–62, 362n, 363–64, 377, 386–87, 390, 397–98, 416–17, 417n
Illinois Central Federation of Shop Employees, **8**:322–23n, 367
Illinois Central Railroad, strike/lockout, 1911–15, **8**:321–22, *322–23n*
Illinois Conference for Progressive Political Action, **12**:409, 410n
Illinois Malleable Iron Co., strike/lockout, 1916, **9**:438, *443n*, 452
Illinois Manufacturers' Association, **11**:287, *289n*
Illinois Mine Managers, **5**:494n. *See also* Mine Managers' and Assistants' Mutual Aid Association, National
Illinois State Board of Arbitration, **5**:215–16n, 509, *510n*, **6**:314n
Illinois State Council of Defense, Labor Committee of the, **10**:151, 152n
Illinois State Federation of Labor, **2**:202, *202n*, **3**:562n, **4**:268, 271, **7**:102n, 363, *364n*, **9**:204, 511, **10**:48, **11**:452; and industrial unionism, **11**:17–18n, **12**:295, 296n, 314; SG, meeting with representatives of, **12**:54
—conventions: 1922 (Rockford), **12**:295, *296n*, 314; 1923 (Decatur), **12**:295, *296n*, 334n
Illinois State Miners' Political Committee, **7**:359
Illinois Women's Alliance, *2:176n*
Iloilo, Philippines, **5**:63, 64n
Imerson, Thomas H., **4**:10, 12, 15, *15n*
immigrants: "Americanization" or education of, **4**:128, **8**:97, 517, **11**:312, **12**:51n, 210, 212, 213n, 297, 348n, 378; intelligence tests for, **12**:185, 186n; and IWW, **10**:265; literacy tests for, **7**:91n, 155–56, **8**:330, **9**:80–81, 82–83n, 102, 103n, 403–4, 405n, 413–16, **10**:164–65, 166n, **12**:164; and padrone system, **3**:508, 508n, 512–13, **12**:210; registration of, **12**:50–51, 211–12, 213n, 344–45,

348n, 379, 380n; surveillance of, **12**:50–51. *See also specific nationalities*
immigration, restriction of, **3**:115–16, 162, 287–91, 346, 513, **4**:242–44, 244n, 283–84, 284n, 326, 412–13, 413–14n, **5**:152, **7**:155–56, 196, 260, 486n, **8**:339–44, **9**:412–16, **10**:164–66, 166n, **11**:8n, 160, 312, 387, 422, **12**:124–25, 164–66, 166n, 259–60, 260n, 297, 344, 348n, 378, 414–16, 416–17n. *See also specific nationalities*
income tax, **12**:454. *See also under* legislation, U.S.
Independence League, and election of 1906 (Illinois), **7**:110n
Independence party, and election of 1908, **7**:369, 370n, 384
Independent Labor League (Maine), **7**:86, 91n
Independent Labor party (New York), **7**:110n
Independent Trade Union Educational League, **8**:261n
India, **5**:506, **12**:223, 234–35
Indiana: election of 1906, **7**:99, 99n, 112–13, 139; election of 1908, **7**:397–98; organizing in, **6**:141; SG, *address before* legislature of, **8**:175–82
Indiana, State Federation of Trades and Labor Unions of the State of, *6:141n*
Indiana Federation of Labor, *6:141n*
Indiana Federation of Trade and Labor Unions, *3:229n*
Indiana Labor Commission and Arbitration Board, **5**:300, 308n
Indianapolis Central Labor Union, **1**:165, *166n*, **3**:512, *512n*, **8**:213n, 355n, **12**:362–64, 364n
"Indianapolis Plan," **3**:364
Indianapolis Traction and Terminal Co., **9**:208n
Indianapolis Trades Assembly, **1**:165, *166n*
Indiana State Federation of Labor, *3:229n*, *6:141n*, **8**:213n, 303n, 355n, **9**:511, **11**:268
industrial commissions. *See under* legislation, states and territories
Industrial Conference, First, 1919 (Washington, D.C.), **11**:127, *128n*, 145, 153, 160n, 230, 287, 386,

390, 538; black representation at, **11**:142–43, 143n; and collective bargaining, **11**:158, 167–82; *proceedings of,* **11**:157–82; and steel strike, 1919–20, **11**:126n, 144n, 147

Industrial Conference, Second, 1919–20 (Washington, D.C.), **11**:246, *247n*

industrial conference boards, **11**:159–60; in Germany, **11**:164, 167n

Industrial Congress, **3**:204n

industrial councils, in Great Britain, **11**:164, 166–67n, 244

industrial courts, **11**:424; in France, **5**:300–301. *See also* Kansas Court of Industrial Relations

Industrial Education (AFL), *7:427n*

industrial education, **9**:353, 353n; in wartime, **11**:35. *See also under* legislation, U.S.; vocational education

industrial hygiene, **12**:419

industrial mobilization, wartime, **12**:422–23, 424n

"industrial peace," SG and, **11**:77

industrial service, by workers in wartime, **10**:42–43

industrial unionism: AFL and, **5**:171, 290, 381, 433–34, 438, 439n, 443–44, 444n, 445–46, **6**:501, **8**:296, 363, 402, 406–8, 411–12, 412n, 505, **9**:115–17, 212, 213n, **12**:86–87, 87n, 88–89, 101–2, 102n, 307, 330–31, 332n; AFL Executive Council and, **8**:296–97n, **9**:71, 73n, 104, 104n, 116, 245, 246n, **12**:55n; AFL Railway Employes' Department and, **12**:66, 66n; Bakery Workers and, **9**:148–49; Brewery Workmen and, **5**:433–34, **8**:406, **9**:148–49, 502, **12**:62; Chicago Federation of Labor and, **11**:18n, **12**:54, 54–55n, 62–63, 67, 312–15; Cigar Makers and, **8**:396–97, 419–20, 505; Foster and, **12**:43–47, 48n, 55n, 62–65, 67–68, 126, 220, 403, 403n; Illinois State Federation of Labor and, **11**:17–18n, **12**:295, 296n, 314; industrial workers' clubs and, **6**:449n; Iron, Steel, and Tin Workers and, **12**:62; IWW and, **6**:455–57, **8**:363, 406–7, 505; Ladies' Garment Workers and, **6**:518; Laundry Workers

and, **9**:148–49; Longshoremen and, **9**:104n; Machinists and, **5**:291, **9**:62, **12**:62–63; Mine Workers, United, and, **5**:381, 433–34, **6**:501, **8**:406–7, 411, **9**:52n, 502, **12**:62; Minnesota State Federation of Labor and, **12**:126, 127n; Quarry Workers and, **12**:395–98; railroad workers and, **12**:66, 66n; SG and, **3**:573, **5**:xiv, 99, **8**:366, **9**:71, 103–4, 143, 245, 502–3; socialists and, **6**:264, **8**:412; Tailors and, **9**:71, 74n; Teamsters and, **9**:149; Timber Workers and, **12**:62; Typographical Union and, **5**:291, **9**:502, **12**:62, 66n. *See also* One Big Union

Industrial Unionism (Debs), **9**:115, *118n*

Industrial Unionism in Its Relation to Trade Unionism (AFL), **9**:71, *73n,* 245, 246n

industrial workers' clubs, **6**:449n

Industrial Workers of the World (IWW): American Labor Union and, **4**:453n, **6**:443–44, 447, 461–63, 468; Barnes and, **10**:264; Bolsheviks and, **11**:163, 165, 184, 194; Brewery Workmen and, **6**:487, **7**:8, 34, **9**:30; in Butte, Mont., **9**:154, 180, 270–72; in California, **7**:111; Casa del Obrero Mundial and, **9**:427, 499; in Centralia, Wash., **11**:216, 217n; Chicago faction of, **9**:150, 150n, 230, 504–5, **10**:247; Cigar Makers and, **8**:103; and Citizens' Industrial Association of America, **6**:384, 522; Coates and, **6**:452, 455–65; constitution of, **6**:454–62; Debs and, **6**:37n, 384, 384n, 449, 452, 454, 457, 459–60, 464–65, 467, 468n, **7**:404, **9**:113–14, 116–17; DeLeon and, **6**:444, 449, 455, 458–59, 467, 468n; Detroit faction of, **9**:150n, 230, 504–5, **10**:247; Easley and, **7**:245, 247n; Foster and, **8**:260, **10**:215, **12**:64; free speech campaigns of, **8**:502, 503n; Freight Handlers and, **7**:44; Germer and, **9**:218; Grant and, **6**:442–64, 465n, 467n, 469n; Gregory and, **10**:243n, 297–98, 298n; Hagerty and, **6**:443, 448, 450, 452, 454–55, 457–60, 462, 465, 467;

Hat and Cap Makers and, **7:**18, 18–19n, 207; Haywood and, **6:**37n, 406n, 442, 450–52, 456–57, 459, 461–63, **7:**245, 247n, **8:**103, 104n, 326n, 501, 503n, **9:**489n; Hillstrom and, **9:**343, 343n; Hotel Workers and, **7:**22; and immigrants, **10:**265; Industrial Conference, 1919, and, **11:**175; Industrial Council of Metal and Machinery Workers of, **7:**41n; and industrial unionism, **6:**455–57, **8:**363, 406–7, 505; Jones and, **6:**443, 453; journal, official, of, **9:**245; label of, **6:**451, 457; Ladies' Garment Workers and, **6:**518; Laundry Workers and, **7:**111; Little and, **10:**163, 163n; Longshoremen and, **7:**111, **12:**48, 389–90; Machinists and, **7:**41n; membership of, **9:**230; Miners, Western Federation of, and, **6:**405, 406n, 447, 451, 457, 461–62, 506–7, 508n, **7:**247n; Mooney and, **10:**420n, **11:**6; National Women's Trade Union League and, **8:**398; Perkins and, **8:**103–4, 505, **10:**242–43, 297; Plumbers and, **7:**47–48; prosecution of, during World War I, **10:**185, 188, 223, 242, 243n, 248, 297–98, 435, 484, 528, **11:**218–19; in Schenectady, N.Y., **7:**40, 41n, 47; Seattle Central Labor Council and, **12:**253–54, 257, 266–67, 272; SG and, **6:**451, 467, 522, **7:**34, 40, 42n, 191, **8:**195, 229, 507–11, **9:**31, 230, 503–5, **10:**149, 168, 173–74, 182–84, 193n, 205, 247–49, 260, 297–98, 298n, 534; Sherman and, **6:**443–44, 452, 455, 457, 459, 461, 463–67; Shingle Weavers and, **7:**111; socialists and, **6:**444, 455, 458–60, 466–68; Socialist Trade and Labor Alliance and, **4:**98n, **6:**447, 449, 468; Spargo and, **10:**389n; Textile Workers and, **7:**184–85, **8:**115–16, 117n, **9:**170, **11:**350; Timber Workers and, **12:**234; Trautmann and, **6:**384, 385n, 449, 452, 459–61, 463, 466, 468; Walker and, **10:**296; in Washington state, **7:**108, 111, **11:**225; Woodsmen and Sawmill Workers and, **7:**111; in Youngstown, Ohio, **7:**40, 41–42n, 48

—conventions: 1905 (Chicago), **6:**384, 384–85n, 408, 442–68; 1906, *6:461n*

—locals: local 20 (textile workers, Lawrence, Mass.), **8:**324, 326n; local 77 (miners, Goldfield, Nev.), **7:**286n; local 152 (textile workers, Paterson, N.J.), **8:**503n; local 300 (lumbermen, Eureka, Calif.), **7:**111, 112n; local 310 (tinners and slaters, Youngstown, Ohio), **7:**41n; local 374 (barbers, Brooklyn, N.Y.), **8:**503n; local 397 (mill workers, Skowhegan, Maine), **7:**184–85, 186n; local 500 (lumber workers, Pacific Northwest), **10:**155n; Metal Mine Workers' Industrial Union (Bisbee, Ariz.), **10:**125, 126n; Metal Mine Workers' Industrial Union (Butte, Mont.), **10:**125–26, *126*–27n; Metal Mine Workers' Industrial Union (Mesabi Range), **9:**489n

—strikes/lockouts: 1906 (metal and machinery workers, Schenectady, N.Y.), *7:41n;* 1906 (tinners and slaters, Youngstown, Ohio), *7:41–42n;* 1907 (mill workers, Skowhegan, Maine), **7:**184–85, *186n;* 1912 (textile workers, Lawrence, Mass.), **8:**324–25, *325–26n*, 360, 406, 450, 501–2, 502n, 517, 518n, **9:**229, 230n, 489n, 504, **10:**247; 1913 (barbers, Brooklyn, N.Y., and New York City), **8:**501–2, *503n;* 1913 (cooks and waiters, Albany, N.Y.), **8:**448–49, *452n;* 1913 (cooks and waiters, New York City), **8:**449, *452–53n*, **9:**489n; 1913 (textile workers, Paterson, N.J.), **8:**502, *503n*, 517, **9:**489n, 504–5, **10:**247–48; 1913, 1914 (hop field workers, California), **9:**504, *507n*, **10:**247; 1916 (iron ore miners, Mesabi Range), **9:**488, *489–90n*, 504–5, **10:**247; 1916 (laborers, Buffalo, N.Y.), **9:**406, *406n;* 1916 (steelworkers, Pittsburgh), **9:**504, *507n*, **10:**247; 1917 (copper miners, Arizona), **10:**125, *126n*, 148–49, 167–68, 259, 262, 301, 321, 323–24n, 336–39; 1917 (metal miners, Butte, Mont.), **10:**126, *126–27n;* 1917 (tim-

ber workers, Pacific Northwest),
10:154, *155n*, 182
Industry's Manifest Duty (AFL Executive Council), 12:420, *421n*
influenza pandemic, 1918, 10:543–44, *544n*, 546n, 547, 552
Ingersoll, Raymond V., 10:310, *312n*
Ingersoll, Robert G., 2:184, *184n*, 289, 4:498, *500n*
Ingles, Ernest, 11:281n
Ingles et al. v. *Morrison et al.*, 11:280, *281n*
Ingraham, George L., 3:295n, 453
Ingram, John K., 6:335
inheritance tax, 12:454
initiative, 4:235, 6:302–6, 308n, 8:282–85, 382, 384n, 397, 413, 417, 420, 9:124, 11:422
Injunction Reform League, 7:387n
injunctions in labor disputes, 3:420, 4:112–13, 5:326, 414–15, 6:331, 344, 353, 537–45, 7:83–84, 160, 245, 263, 335, 350n, 408–11, 423–24, 430–34, 438–39, 465, 8:177, 266, 317, 349, 434, 10:299, 11:226, 254, 257, 12:495–96; AFL and, 3:125–27, 129–31, 295–96n, 297, 4:100, 7:324, 372n, 389, 391–92, 422–24, 8:53, 293, 385, 491, 9:520–21, 521n, 528, 11:231, 421–24, 454–57, 458–59n, 515–16, 12:317–18, 318n, 453; Cannon and, 7:93n; Democratic platform and, 7:351, 370n, 12:486; Furuseth and, 7:92–93, 117; model state law on, 9:262, 262n, 320, 423; Post and, 8:131n; Progressive (Bull Moose) platform and, 8:478; Progressive (La Follette) platform and, 12:487, 510; Republican platform and, 7:351, 12:486; Roosevelt and, 6:510, 511n, 513, 7:415n; Taft and, 3:293, 294n, 295, 299, 302, 559, 576, 7:87, 91–92n, 118–19, 251, 252n, 281, 379, 398n, 410, 8:152–54, 478, 487
—in specific labor disputes: and AFL City Policemen's Union 16,718, 11:146n; and AFL Railway Employes' Department, 12:87; and American Railway Union, 3:523–25, 526n, 530, 531n, 537, 547n, 559, 561n, 563n, 576, 632–33; and American Steel Foundries, 10:252, 253n; and Auburn (Maine) Shoe Manufacturers' Assn., 3:412n; and Bedford Cut Stone Co., 12:398n; and Best, 5:123; and Binghamton Cigar Manufacturers' Assn., 3:26, 26n, 148n; and Blacksmiths, 12:9n, 267; and Boot and Shoe Workers, 3:21, 26, 26n, 412n; and Bossert and Son, 10:253, 254n; and Brewery Workmen, 6:90n, 226, 228n, 442n; and Brine Transportation Co., 5:497n; and Carpenters, 7:50n, 10:253, 254n, 12:400; and Chafin, 12:265n; and Chicago Board of Education, 9:419n; and Chicago, St. Paul, Minneapolis, and Omaha Railway Co., 12:373n; and Chicago Typothetae, 7:11, 11–12n; and Cigar Makers, 3:26, 26n, 148, 148n, 5:240–43, 243–44n; and Cincinnati Brewers' Exchange, 5:516n; and Clarksburg (W.Va.) Fuel Co., 6:80–81, 84n; and cloakmakers, 8:114n, 11:571n; and Clothing Manufacturers' Assn. (New York City), 3:293, 295–96n, 297–300, 302; and Clothing Workers, 11:458n; and Consolidated Coal Co., 5:219n; and Cox Shoe Co., 3:21, 26; and Coyne Brothers, 7:14, 15n; and Denver City Council, 5:97–98, 99n; and Denver City Tramway Co., 5:97–98, 99n; and Debs, 4:360n, 7:405 (*see also* injunctions in labor disputes: in specific labor disputes: and American Railway Union); and Electrical Workers, 8:470, 471n, 490, 11:189–90, 191n; and Federación Libre de los Trabajadores de Puerto Rico, 6:424–25, 428, 429n; and Garment Workers, 3:293, 295–96n, 297–300, 302, 6:406–7n; and Gill Engraving Co., 9:74–75n; and Grant Construction Co., 10:252, 253–54n; and Hammond Lumber Co., 7:117, 118n; and Hitchman Coal and Coke Co., 10:285–86, 287n, 322, 323n; and Holston Manufacturing Co., 9:262–63n; and Hotel and Restaurant Employees, 12:94n; and hotel workers, 11:458n; and Ladies'

Garment Workers, **11:**448–49, 456, **12:**428, 428n; and Lasters, **3:**412n; and Leather Workers, **11:**571n; and Levy and Co., **5:**241, 243–44n; and Locomotive Engineers, **3:**294n, 295–96, 559, 576; and Loewe Co., **6:**440–41; and Logan Coal Operators' Assn., **12:**265n; and Los Angeles metal trades unions, **8:**121, 122n; and Machinery Manufacturers' Assn., **7:**51n; and Machinists, **7:**50, 50–51n; and Marine Cooks and Stewards, **7:**117, 118n; and Marine Firemen, **7:**117, 118n; and Master Builders' Assn., **7:**50n; and Merchants' and Manufacturers' Association of Los Angeles, **8:**121, 122n; and Mine Owners' Protective Assn. of Coeur d'Alene, Idaho, **3:**214n; and Miners, Western Federation of, **6:**344n, **9:**12, 13n; in miners' strike, 1897, **4:**353, 358–59, 360n, 362–63, 363n, 364–65; and Miners' Union of Coeur d'Alene, Idaho, **3:**214n; and Mine Workers, United, **5:**219n, 322n, **6:**80–81, 84n, **10:**285–86, 287n, 323n, **11:**192n, 195, 196n, 197–201, 203–4, 206, 208–12, 213n, 220, 252–53, 336, **12:**265n; and *Montgomery County* (Ohio) *Reporter,* **5:**459, 460n; and Moore Drop Forging Co., **12:**9–10n; and Murdock, Kerr, and Co., **3:**125–27, 128n, 129–31, 139, 263–64; and National War Labor Board, **11:**21n; and New Orleans Workingmen's Amalgamated Council, **3:**243n; and New York City Board of Walking Delegates, **3:**61, 63; and New York City Cloak, Suit, and Skirt Manufacturers' Protective Assn., **8:**114n, **11:**571n; and Northern Pacific Railroad workers, **3:**559, 561n; and Northwestern Brewers' Assn., **6:**440, 442n; and Painters, **3:**61, 63; and Palestine (Tex.) Telephone Co., **11:**191n; and Pennsylvania Railroad, **12:**27, 30n, 109, 115; and Perkins-Campbell Co., **7:**11, 11n; and Photo-Engravers, **9:**74–75n; and Plumbers, **7:**14, 15n; and Print-

ing Pressmen, **3:**125–27, 128n, 129–31, 139, 263–64; and Pullman strike, 1894, **3:**186, 523–25, 526n, 530, 531n, 538, 559–60, 561n, 563n, 639; and Railroad Labor Board, **12:**27, 30n, 109, 115; in railroad shopmen's strike, 1911, **8:**322n; in railroad shopmen's strike, 1922-?, **12:**87, 133–36, 137n, 147, 147n, 152–55, 158–59, 161, 167, 248, 486; and Railway Servants, **6:**74, 78, 83, 83–84n, **8:**74; and Sailors, **7:**117, 118n; and San Francisco Labor Council, **6:**440–41, 442n; and San Francisco Steam Ship Assn., **7:**93n; and Seattle Brewing and Malting Co., **6:**442n; and Springfield, Mass., Central Labor Union, **12:**10n; and Steam Engineers, **5:**516n; and St. Paul Building Trades Council, **10:**252, 253–54n; and Stove Mounters, **10:**449n; and Street Railway Employes, **6:**194, **7:**342n, **9:**206–7, 208n, 220, **12:**21–23, 24n; and Taff Vale Railway Co., **6:**74, 78, 83, 83–84n, **8:**74; and Team Drivers, **5:**497n; and Teamsters, **7:**98n, **10:**252–53, 254n, **11:**455, 458n; in Tell City, Ind., **7:**234; and Textile Workers, **9:**262–63n; and Theis, **5:**459, 460n; and Third Avenue Railway Co., **12:**21–23, 24n; in Toledo, Ann Arbor, and Northern Michigan Railroad case, **3:**294n, 295–96, 559, 576, **8:**487; and Tri-City (Ill.) Central Trades Council, **10:**252, 253n; and Typographical Union, **3:**125–27, 128n, 129–31, 139, 263–64, **7:**11–12n; and Upholsterers, **6:**229–30; and Van Owners' Association of Greater New York, **11:**458n; and Waddell-Mahon detectives, **9:**12, 13n; and Woodsmen and Sawmill Workers, **7:**378–79. *See also* Buck's Stove and Range Co. cases: injunction case

Inland Steel Co., strike/lockout, 1913, **8:**391n

Innis, George A., **5:***, 391, *391n*, 410n; *letter from,* **5:**409–10

In re Frederick, **9:***138n*

In re Morgan, **5:**114, *115n*
In re Samuel Gompers, John Mitchell, and Frank Morrison, **7:***250n. See also* Buck's Stove and Range Co. cases: contempt case
Inskip, William, **5:***, 39n, 68, *69n*
inspection of workplaces: AFL and, **4:**100, **9:**118; in Chicago, **2:**404, 409n; FOTLU and, **1:**231; in Massachusetts, **3:**278; of mines, **1:**231, **4:**506–7; in New York, **3:**278–79, 279n; in Ohio, **3:**279; in Pennsylvania, **3:**278–79, 279n; SG and, **3:**192, 277–79, **4:**506–7, **12:**4; and women inspectors, **2:**176, 288–89, 289–90n. *See also under* legislation, states and territories
Institute for Crippled Soldiers and Sailors, **10:**158
insurance, health. *See* health insurance
insurance, unemployment. *See* unemployment insurance
insurance companies, **5:**416–17, **6:**492, 493n
intelligence tests, **12:**167–68, 168n; and immigration, restriction of, **12:**185, 186n
"intelligencia" and labor movement, **11:**470, **12:**26, 42–43. *See also* trade unions: and "outsiders"
Inter-Allied Labour and Socialist Conference, Feb. 1918 (London), **10:**355, *355–56n,* 530
Inter-Allied Labour and Socialist Conference, Sept. 1918 (London), **10:**493, 493n, 503–4, *504n,* 522, 529–37, 551–52, 561, 567n, **11:**11–14, 16, 30n, 37, 48n; declaration of war aims by, **10:**529–32, 532n
Inter-American Peace Conference, **9:**434n
Interborough Rapid Transit Co., **6:**475, **7:**69–70, 70n; strike/lockout, 1905, **6:**407, *408n,* 452, 521n; strike/lockout, 1916, **9:**490–92, *492n,* **12:**23n
Inter Mountain Publishing Co., **6:**284
Intermountain Worker (Salt Lake City, Utah, labor journal), editor of, *letter to,* **9:**80–82

International Committee of Women for Permanent Peace, **9:**274n
International Conference on Limitation of Armaments, 1921–22 (Washington, D.C.), **11:**523–24, *524n,* 533, 543, 547, 548n, **12:**13, 180, 310, *311n;* and advisory committee to American delegation, **11:**547, 548n
International Conference on Safety of Life at Sea, 1913–14 (London), *9:112n*
International Conference on Workers' Education, 1922 (Uccle, Belgium), **12:**156–57, *157n*
International Congress of Women, 1915 (The Hague), **9:**270, *274n*
International Congress of Working Women, 1919 (Washington, D.C.), **11:**132–34, *135n*
International Congress of Working Women, 1921 (Geneva), *11:525n*
International Congress on Social Insurance, **9:**68n
International Convention on the Safety of Life at Sea, **9:**111, *112n*
International Federation of Trade Unions, *8:394n,* **9:**265, **11:**38–39, 135–37; AFL and, **9:**174, 175n, **11:**223–24, 224n, 436–39, 479, 480n, **12:**137–39, 139–40n, 357–58, 360n; headquarters of, **9:**238–39, 240n, 289n, 470n; and Russo-Polish War, **11:**437–38
—meetings: 1915 (Amsterdam), **9:**288, *289n;* 1915 (San Francisco), **9:**106, *107n,* 174, 175n; 1917 (Stockholm), *10:90n,* 104–5, 271; 1919 (Berne, Switzerland), **11:**28, *30n,* 55; 1919 (Amsterdam), *11:111n,* 118, 135, 460n; 1920 (London), **11:**438, *440n;* Apr. 1922 (Rome), **12:**138–39, *139n;* Dec. 1922 (The Hague), **12:**140n
International Harvester Co., antitrust case against, **10:**322, 323n
International Harvester Co. of America v. State of Missouri, **9:**294, *296n*
International Joint Conference Council of Commercial and Periodical Branches of the Printing Industry, **11:**570n

International Labor Conference, 1919
(Washington, D.C.), **11**:70, *71–72n*,
110, 118, 135–37, 137–38n, 194,
195n
International Laborers' Union, **6**:403–
4, 435–39; label of, **6**:436
—local: local 196 (Rockland, Maine),
6:399n, 436–39, 439n
—strike/lockout: 1905 (Rockland,
Maine), **6**:436–39, *439n*
International Labor News Service,
12:277
International Labor Organization,
11:41n, 101, 135, 137, 405, **12**:190;
publications of, **12**:231–32, 232n
International Labor Union, **1**:84
International Labour and Socialist
Conference, 1919 (Berne, Switzerland), **11**:28–29, *30n*, 38–39, 41n,
47, 48–49n, 55
International Paper Co., strike/lock-
out, 1907, **7**:202–4, *204n*
International Peace Society, **10**:199,
268
International Secretariat of the National Centers of Trade Unions,
7:473–74n, 486n, 487–89, **8**:115,
394n
—meetings: 1907 (Christiania, Norway), **7**:399, *401n;* 1909 (Paris),
7:399–400, 401n, 485, *486n,*
487–89, **8**:205, **9**:213, 364, *366n,*
10:198, *207n,* 268; 1911 (Budapest),
8:219n, 260, *260n,* 393; 1913 (Zurich), *8:506n,* **9**:254n
International Socialist Bureau, **10**:90n
international trades secretaries, conference of, 1913 (Zurich), *8:506n*
International Workers' Defense
League, **11**:7n, 86, 87n, 94
International Workers' Defense
League of San Francisco, **9**:517n
International Workingmen's Association, **1**:21, *22n,* 24, 26, 36, 83, 84n,
8:151n; General Council of, **1**:25–
26, *43–44n;* and trade union movement, **1**:25–26, 31
—conferences: 1866 (Geneva), **1**:25,
43n; 1869 (Basel, Switzerland),
1:22n, 25, *43n;* 1871 (London),
1:25, *44n;* 1872 (The Hague), **1**:25,
44n

International Working People's Association, **1**:462n
Interstate Commerce Commission,
3:301n, **5**:363, 363n, **8**:361, **9**:365,
11:195n, 216n, 238, 274n, **12**:115
Interstate Council on Immigrant Edu-
cation, **12**:50
Invincibles, *3*:241n
Iowa, election of 1908, **7**:397
Iowa State Federation of Labor,
5:455n, **8**:16
Ireland, **1**:164, 218–20, 223, **2**:79; in-
dependence of, **11**:85–86, 86n, 87,
89–90, 92n, 108; recognition of,
11:319, 320n, 473, 476n; workers
from, **1**:51, 248
Ireland, American Committee for the
Relief of Famine in, **2**:377, *377n*
Ireland, Arthur E., **7**:121, *122n*, 241,
8:251, 253n
Irish, Ernest O., **11**:53, *54n*
Irish Immigrant Society, **1**:362n
Irish National Land League, *1:285–*
86n
Irish World, **12**:33, 34n
Iron, Steel, and Tin Workers, Amalgamated Association of, **1**:*, **2**:*,
3:*, **4**:*, **5**:*, **6**:*, 57n, **7**:*, 464n,
473n, **8**:*, 9n, 189, 453, **10**:*, 79n,
101, 502n, **11**:*, 28n, 85n, 99n,
269–70, 270n, 360, 365n, **12**:*,
66n, 281n, 333n; and black workers, **10**:135, **11**:285; and immigrant
workers, **10**:77–78; and industrial
unionism, **12**:62; jurisdiction of,
12:221n; organizers, **10**:67–69,
69–70n
—conventions: 1902 (Wheeling,
W.Va.), **6**:55, *57n,* 103, 104n; 1917
(Granite City, Ill.), *10:69n*
—local: local 81 (Yorkville, Ohio),
10:79n
—strikes/lockouts: 1909–10, **7**:472,
473n, 480, **8**:7, 9n, 12, 12n, 27–30,
54–55; 1917 (Yorkville, Ohio),
10:79, *79n*
Iron Age (periodical), **12**:164, 166n
Iron and Steel Workers, National
Committee for Organizing: and
black workers, **11**:283–86, 286n;
creation of, **10**:501–2, **11**:99n;
and Iron, Steel, and Tin Workers,

11:269–70, 270n; organizing campaign of, 11:26–27, 27–28n, 85, 124–25, 125n, 128–29, 129n; reorganization of, 11:359–60, 365n; and steel strike, 1919–20 (*see* steel strike, 1919–20); *wire from*, 11:128–29
iron and steel workers (unorganized), foreign-born workers among, 8:345
—strikes/lockouts: 1910 (So. Bethlehem, Pa.), 8:43, *44n;* 1913 (Rankin and Braddock, Pa.), 8:391n, 453, *455n*
Iron and Steel Workers of the U.S., Amalgamated Association of, 1:*, 159, 165, 166n, 167, 211, 272n, 339–40, 353n, 385–86, 2:*, 134, 135n, 235, 3:*, 21, 23n, 68, 420, 535, 575, 4:*, 95, 97n, 99, 472, 490–91, 499n, 5:*, 386n, 482, 6:*, 7:*, 8:*, 10:*, 11:*, 12:*; advisory board of, 5:386; and Homestead strike, 1892, 3:185, 188–89, 189n, 190, 219, 231, 233n, 236, 238–39, 250, 265
—convention: 1901, 5:384n
—lodge: lodge 15 (Brilliant, Ohio), 2:340, 343n
—strikes/lockouts: 1882 (Pittsburgh), 1:272, *272n*, 339–40, *353n;* 1887 (Mingo Junction, Ohio), 2:24, *24n,* 40, 339–40; 1887–88 (Brilliant, Ohio), 2:340, *343n;* 1888, 2:134, *135n*, 197; 1892 (Beaver Falls, Pa.), 3:*234n,* 238; 1892–93 (Union Mills, Pittsburgh), 3:*234n,* 238; 1901, 5:384, *384n*, 385, *385n,* 386–88, 388n, 389–90, 411, 411n, 479, 6:104n. *See also* Homestead strike, 1892
Iron and Steel Workers of the U.S., Finishers' Union of, 3:232, *233n,* 238–40
Iron City Trades Council of Pittsburgh, 8:454
"iron law of wages," 1:27, 31, *44n,* 87
Iron League Erectors' Association, 11:399n
Iron League of New York City, 7:12
Iron Molders, National Union of, 1:*, 217n, 2:*, 4:*, 5:*, 7:*, 8:*, 9:*, 11:*
iron molders' union (New York City), 2:332
Iron Molders' Union of North America, 1:*, 159, 165, 166n, 167, 216, 385, 2:*, 16n, 165, 235, 4:*, 79, 80n, 99, 228–29, 325n, 341, 472, 5:*, 175, 176n, 277, 285, 7:*, 32, 36n, 8:*, 9:*, 11:*; and black workers, 4:314–17, 317n, 318, 324, 334, 11:84n, 284
—locals: local 2 (Troy, N.Y.), 7:53–54, 54n; local 10 (St. Louis), 7:153, 155n; local 14 (Pittsburgh), 1:217n; local 31 (Detroit), 4:228, 229n; local 45 (Dayton, Ohio), 6:144, 145n; local 53 (Chattanooga, Tenn.), 4:317n; local 72 (Springfield, Ohio), 1:165, 166n; local 103 (Lynn, Mass.), 4:187, 189n; local 181 (Dayton, Ohio), 1:165, 166n; local 286 (Sheboygan, Wis.), 4:325n; local 306 (Auburn and Lewiston, Maine), 7:58n
—strikes/lockouts: 1896 (Chattanooga, Tenn.), 4:315, *317n,* 318; 1897 (Sheboygan, Wis.), 4:325, *325n;* 1906 (St. Louis), 7:153, *155n;* 1906 (Troy, N.Y.), 7:53–54, *54n*
Iron Trades Council, 5:432–33n
Irwin, John T., 8:131, *132n*
Isaacs, Henrietta Gompers, 7:*, 499, *501n,* 9:*, 537, *539n,* 11:*, 54, *54n. See also* Gompers, Henrietta (SG's sister)
Isaacs, Isabella (Bella) Gompers, 7:*, 499, *501n,* 9:*, 537, *539n,* 11:*, 54, *54n. See also* Gompers, Isabella
Isaacs, Rosa, 7:499
Isaacs, Sophia, 7:499
Ishii, Kikujirō, 10:191, 193n
Italy: "Bolshevism" in, 11:28; conditions in, 10:112, 342–43, 551–52; emigration from, 10:552, 555–56n, 12:415; labor representatives of, at Leeds (England) conference, 1916, 9:470n; mission of, to United States, 10:72n; socialists in, 10:356n, 550–53, 555–56n, 561–62; workers from, 3:379, 508, 508n, 512–13, 4:242, 5:386–87, 387n, 6:290, 290–91n, 7:45, 218, 8:34, 115, 155, 345, 9:171, 12:210, 282–83, 415; workers in, 1:281, 4:242, 244
itinerant workers. *See* migrant workers
Itō, Hirobumi, 9:17, *18n*
Ittner, Anthony, 9:54n

Ives, Eben C., **2:**170, 172, *173n,* 268
Ives, Harry M., **2:***, 267–68, *268n,* **3:***,
  236n; letters to, **3:**235–36, 276–77,
  281–82
Ives v. *South Buffalo Railway Co.,*
  8:*327n,* **9:**76n
IWW. *See* Industrial Workers of the
  World (IWW)

Jablinowski, Ludwig, **1:***, 432, *433n,*
  2:*, 367, *371n,* **4:**236, *237n,* 239
Jackson, Giles B., **10:**327, *327n,* 367n,
  11:286n; *letter from,* **10:**366–67
Jackson, H. R., **4:**359n
Jackson, John J., Jr., **4:**360n, 365, **6:**80–
  81, *84n,* **12:**495, *498n*
Jackson, Joseph G., **5:***, 418, *419n*
Jackson, Lee L., **7:**112, *113n*
Jackson, Richard H., **10:**540, *541n,*
  549
Jackson (Miss.) Trades and Labor
  Council, **6:**182, *182n*
Jacksonville, Fla.: longshoremen's
  case, **9:**82, *83n;* newspapers, boy-
  cott, 1886, **2:***343n;* newspapers,
  strike/lockout, 1886, **2:**340–41,
  343n
Jacksonville (Fla.) Central Trades and
  Labor Council, **7:**353–55, 355–*56n;*
  Building Trades Section of, **7:**354–
  55
Jacobson, Hugo W., **11:**391, *393n*
Jacoby, M., and Co., **1:**196–97, *198n,*
  199
Jaeckel et al. v. *Kaufman et al.,* **12:**302,
  303n
Jaehne, Henry, **1:**444, *444n*
Jahelka, John, **3:**15, 18n, **4:**224, 225n
Jahns, Louis O., **5:**47, *48n*
Jallonen, Hjalmer, **9:**182, 184n, 190–
  91, 191n
James, Charles E., **8:**3, *6n*
James, Newton A., **10:***, 421, *431n,*
  12:*, 247, *247n*
James J. Reid et al. v. *Frank J. McNulty et
  al.,* **9:**70, *73n*
James Ormond Wilson Normal
  School, **10:**439n
Jamestown Street Railway Co., strike/
  lockout, 1901–2, **5:**378, *379n*
Jameton, Marie S., **12:**541, *542n*
Jamieson, William D., **8:**100, *101n*

Jane, Arthur, **9:**184n
Jane, Henry, **9:**184n
Japan: German intrigues with, **10:**35,
  37; mission of, to United States,
  10:72n, 191, 193n; National Civic
  Federation commission to (proposed), **7:**245–46; and outbreak of
  World War I, **9:**173, 175n; peace
  delegation of, **11:**38, 41n; students
  from, in San Francisco, **7:**147, 148n,
  195, **11:**89; U.S. relations with,
  7:148n, **9:**17–18, 514, **10:**37, 193n
—workers from: in Hawaii, **6:**151n,
  195, **7:**332–33, **12:**415; landholding
  by, in California, **9:**206, 206n, **11:**89,
  12:171n; organization of, **4:**53,
  6:149–50, 150–51n, **7:**93n, **8:**9, 46,
  9:513–15, 515n, **11:**43, 149, **12:**336;
  and railroad shopmen's strike,
  1922–?, **12:**119; restriction of immigration of, **5:**435–38, **6:**150n, **7:**147,
  148n, 195, 206, 267, 268n, **8:**102,
  10:37, **11:**69, **12:**415, 416–17n;
  smuggling of, into United States,
  12:32, 211
Japanese and Korean Exclusion
  League. *See* Asiatic Exclusion
  League
Japanese-Mexican Protective Association:
—strike/lockout: 1903 (Oxnard, Calif.), **6:**150, *151n,*
Jaquith, Leon, **2:**198–99n
Jarrett, John, **1:***, *212n;* at FOTLU
  convention, **1:**212, 214, 216, 218–
  19, 223–24, 227–28, 230, 238
Jaurès, Jean, **4:**69, *70n*
Jay Street Terminal Co., **10:**381
Jefferson, Thomas, **1:**446, **3:**476,
  6:333, **8:**74, 85, **11:**232, **12:**135, 291,
  294n
Jefferson Borden (cargo ship), mutiny
  on, **3:**117–19, *119–20n,* 157, 158n,
  280, 343n, **4:**322
Jeffries, James J., **7:**23, *25n*
Jenkins, Helen P., **5:**159, 160n
Jenkins, James G., **3:**559, *561n*
Jenkins, John H., **4:**59, *60n*
Jenks, Jeremiah W., **5:**388–*89n; letters
  from,* **5:**387–88
Jenney, Charles A., **2:***348n; letter to,*
  2:347–48

Jennings, James F., **3:**252, *253n*
Jennings, Patrick H., **10:**469, *470–71n*
Jensen, Sofus, *4:342n,* 363; *letter to,* 4:342
Jesse, Paul C., **1:**73, *74n*
Jewell, Bert M., **10:***, 176, *177n,* 358n, **11:***, *131*–32n, 190, 227, 348, 460–62, 469, 472n, 474, **12:***, *11n;* and election of 1924, **12:**474, 478–81, 484n; and Industrial Conference, 1919, **11:**128n; *letter from,* **12:**148; *letters to,* **11:**130–31, **12:**10–11, 146–47, 158–59, 382–83; and railroad shopmen's strike, 1922-?, **12:**86, 87n, 105, 106–7n, 118, 127–28, 128–29n, 131n, 204, 206n; *wire from,* **11:**271; *wires to,* **12:**106–7n, 153, 248, 373
Jewelry Workers' Union, International, **12:***, *221n*
Jewish Congress Organization Committee, **9:**405n
—conference: 1916 (Philadelphia), **9:**405n
Jewish Daily Forward (New York City socialist journal), **10:**157n, *12:321n*
Jewish Socialist Federation, **11:**549n
Jewish workers: AFL and, **5:**102, **9:**404, 405–6n; and Americanization movement, **10:**156, 157n; immigration of, **12:**415–16; organization of, **4:**98n, **5:**102n, **7:**281–82, 282n, 297–98, **11:**449, **12:**527; pogroms against, in Russia, **6:**491, 491n, **10:**132; SG and, **6:**518–19, 519n, **8:**363, **9:**57–60, 403–5, 405n, **10:**521, **11:**298–99, **12:**124, 415–16, 435
Jews' Free School, **1:**3, 9–12, *12n,* 13, 17, **11:**117
"Jim Crow," **10:**359
jingoism, SG and, **4:**108, 145–47, 302, 482
J. M. H. Frederick v. John G. Owens, 9:138n
Joffre, Joseph, **10:**72n, 563, *567n*
Johannsen, Anton, **8:**291, *292n*
John A. Kealey et al. v. A. L. Faulkner et al., 9:83n
John Bogni et al. v. Giovanni Perotti et al., **9:**454–55, *455n,* 520–21
John G. Owens v. Board of Education of Cleveland, 9:138n

Johnson, A. G., Jr., **2:**55, *55n*
Johnson, Agnes, *10:83n; wire from,* **10:**81–82
Johnson, Albert, **11:**483, *484n,* 503, 504n, **12:**39n, 52n, 165, 166n, 211, 213n, 416–17n
Johnson, Alexander, **2:**171, *173n*
Johnson, C. R., **6:**243
Johnson, Claude M., *5:232n;* SG and charges against, **5:**231, 232n
Johnson, Edwin, **1:**208, 210n
Johnson, Edwin L., *12:426n; letter to,* **12:**425–26
Johnson, Frederick E., *12:375n; letter to,* **12:**374–75
Johnson, Granville T., *9:497n; letter from,* **9:**497
Johnson, Hiram, **8:**273, *277n,* **10:**147n, **11:**337n, **12:**170
Johnson, Hugh S., **10:**450, *451n*
Johnson, Jacob E., **6:**443–44, *446n*
Johnson, James S., *3:279n; letter to,* **3:**277–79
Johnson, Jesse, **4:***, 357, 359–*60n,* 408n
Johnson, Magnus, **12:**432–33, 433–*34n,* 491, 494n
Johnson (mayor of Gary, Ind.), **10:**70n
Johnson, Robert C., *6:194n; letter from,* **6:**193–94
Johnson, Robert U., **8:**220, *226n*
Johnson, Samuel, **9:**183n
Johnson, Theodore, *letter to,* **10:**105–7
Johnson, William L. A., **3:***, 282, *282n*
Johnston, Robert, **1:**267, *268n*
Johnston, William H., **8:***, 322, *323n,* **9:***, 49, *50n,* 71, **10:***, 19, *21n,* 181, 333n, 412n, **11:***, *125n,* 128n, 143, 144n, **12:***, 341–42, *342*–43n, 383n, 467n, 550; at AFL conventions, **8:**415, 416n, **10:**475; at AFL Executive Council meetings, **11:**124, 151, 365n, 468–70; and election of 1924, **12:**431, 433n, 468–69, 470n, 474, 478–81, 490; *letter from,* **10:**187–89; *letter to,* **12:**349–50; and National War Labor Board, **10:**408n; and War Labor Conference Board, **10:**334n, 407
Johnstone, John W., **10:**215, *218n*
Johnstown, Pa., flood, **2:**213, *213n,* **6:**362, *364n,* **11:**31

John Swinton's Paper (New York City labor journal), *1:203n,* **2:**39n; editor of, *letter to,* **1:**364
Jolin, Mazaire, *12:301n; letter to,* **12:**300–301
Jonas, Alexander, **3:***, 298, *300n*
Jonas, Morris, **1:**108, *109n*
Jones, A. W. "Puggy," **6:**59, *62n*
Jones, Addison P., **1:**261, *263n*
Jones, Andrieus A., **12:**170, *172n*
Jones, Arthur R., and Co., **2:**208
Jones, Benjamin, **10:**445, *447n*
Jones, Christopher C., **3:**482n
Jones, David R., **1:***, 221, *229n*
Jones, Edward, **4:**442, *446n*
Jones, Eugene K., *9:169n,* **10:**345, 421, 423, 462–63; *letters from,* **9:**168–69, **10:**461–63, **11:**142–43
Jones, George C., **4:**481, *481n*
Jones, J. R., *letter from,* **7:**21–22
Jones, James E., **10:**177, *177n,* 424, 431n
Jones, James K., **4:**276–77, *278n*
Jones, James L., **3:**173, *174n*
Jones, Jerome, **3:***, *285n,* **5:***, *287n,* 378, **6:***, *38n,* **7:***, *190n,* **8:***, 373–74, *381n,* **10:***, 481, *482n,* **11:***, 526, *527n,* **12:***, *112n,* 159n; at AFL conventions, **3:**135, 430, 434n, **5:**285–86, 287n, **7:**271, 272n; *letter from,* **7:**187–89; *letters to,* **3:**284–85, **6:**37–38, 180, **12:**111–12, 148
Jones, John P., **3:**132, *134n*
Jones, Luther C., **4:**406–7, *408–9n,* **5:**70, *70n*
Jones, Mary Harris "Mother," **6:***, 84n, 262, *262n,* 270, **8:**519n, **9:***, *211n,* 443n, **12:***, 495, *498n;* at AFL conventions, **9:**210–11, 520; at IWW founding convention, **6:**443, 453
Jones, Samuel I., **4:**25, *28n*
Jones, Samuel M. "Golden Rule," *4:394n; letter to,* **4:**393–94
Jones, Theodore S., **4:***, 416, *417n*
Jones, Thomas J., **10:**345, 349, *350n,* 421, 462
Jones, Wesley L., **7:**108, *109n,* **12:**228n
Jones, William, **9:**372n
Jones, William T., **10:**346, *350n*
Jones and Laughlin Steel Works, **12:**212

Jones rail mill, **3:**481
Joplin (Mo.) Central Labor Union, *5:151n*
Jordan, David S., **9:**433n
Jordan, Edward L., **6:**110, *111n,* 492, 493n
Josephs, Samuel, and Co., **1:**189–90, *192n,* 199, 209, 262
Jouhaux, Léon, **9:***, *239n,* 289n, 385n, 469, **10:**72n, **11:***, 39, *41n,* 223, **12:**369n; *letters from,* **9:**238–39, 488–89
Journal of the Knights of Labor (KOL journal), **1:**391n, **3:**69, 70n
Journal of United Labor (KOL journal), **2:**132, 132n
Joyce, John J., **10:***, 460, *460n*
Joyce, Joseph J., *10:481n; report of,* **10:**480–81
Joyce, Martin T., **9:***, 454, *456n,* **10:***, 469, 470–*71n*
Joyner, Austin F., *10:482n; letter from,* **10:**481
Joyner, James Y., *8:79*–80n; *letter to,* **8:**79
Juárez, Benito Pablo, **9:**498, *501n*
Juárez decree, **9:**498, *500–501n*
Judge, Michael T., **4:**25, *28n*
judges, **5:**62, 123, 301–3, 308n, **6:**75, 80–83, 322, **7:**24, 310, 323–24, 391, 432, 467–68, 478, **8:**67, 263–64, 462, 482–83, 485, **9:**125, 248, 322, 353, 455, 521, **10:**323–24n, **11:**232, 335, 383, 512–14, 563, 568, **12:**4, 39n, 52, 210n; election of, **7:**359, **11:**232, 312, 422, **12:**487, 511; and injunctions, **5:**266, 326, 414, **6:**301, 331, 539–40, **7:**60, 83, 87, 92, 263–64, 408–11, 422–23, **8:**269, 385, **9:**521, **11:**231, 257, 305, 424, 449, 455, **12:**495–96; recall of, **8:**404, 413. *See also specific cases and specific judges*
Judson, Frederick N., **7:**245, *246n*
Judson, Henry P., **8:**258, *259n*
Julian, Catherine, **1:**17
Julian, David H., **1:***, 17, *18n*
Julian, J., **3:**140
Julian, Mrs. J., **3:**140
Julian, Sophia. *See* Gompers, Sophia Julian
Julien, Mortimer, **7:**470n

Julier, H. S., *6:289n; letter from,* 6:287–89

Jumel, Eliza B., 4:175, *175n;* estate of, 4:174–75, *175–76n*

Junio, John J., 1:*, 68, *69n,* 2:*, 12, *13n,* 340, 4:*, 12, 15, *15n,* 249n

Junius, 8:482, *492n,* 507, 511n, 9:455

Junta Organizadora del Partido Liberal Mexicano, 8:193n, 12:392n

Juranovich, Philip S., *10:152n; letter to,* 10:151–52

jurisdictional disputes (*see also specific unions*):
—AFL Carriage and Wagon Laborers' Union 5635 v. Painters, 3:149
—AFL Federal Labor Union 7204 v. Carpenters, 5:484–85
—AFL Federal Labor Union 8276 v. Mine Workers, United, 5:336–37, 338n
—AFL Gas Workers' Union 9840 v. Stationary Firemen, 6:101–2, 102–3n
—AFL Ladies' Straw and Felt Hat Workers' Union 12,675 v. Hat and Cap Makers, 9:107, 110n
—AFL Ladies' Straw and Felt Hat Operators' Union 14,440 v. Hat and Cap Makers, 9:110n
—AFL Railroad Helpers' and Laborers' Union 15,920 v. Machinists, 10:505, 505n
—AFL Riggers' Union 10,315 v. Bridge and Structural Iron Workers, 6:210, 211n
—AFL Sash, Door, and Blind Workers' Union 5150 v. Carpenters, 3:150, 153n
—AFL Shingle Weavers' Union 9891 v. Carpenters, 6:44, 45n
—AFL Stationary Engineers' Union 5658 v. Machinists, 3:462, 463n
—AFL Water Department Workers' Union 6356 v. Machinists, 5:76–78
—Bakers v. Teamsters, 9:143, 145n, 147–49
—Blacksmiths: v. Chainmakers, 5:516, 517n; v. Horseshoers, 5:161, 162n; v. tool and hardware makers, 5:516, 517n; v. Tunnel and Subway Constructors, 9:347, 347–48n
—Boot and Shoe Workers v. Leather Workers, 5:491, 492n
—Boston Central Labor Union v. Machinists, 4:144, 144–45n, 148, 169
—Brewery Workmen: v. Coopers, 4:329–30, 5:219–20, 221n, 257–60, 260n, 290, 292n, 503, 503–4n; v. Machinists, 7:221–22, 222n; v. Painters, 5:292n; v. Stationary Firemen, 5:161, 162n, 169–71, 172n, 290, 292n, 374–75, 375n, 433–34, 501–3, 503–4n, 514–15, 515–16n, 6:9–10, 10–11n, 88–89, 89–90n, 133–34, 135–36n, 208, 223–28, 228n, 317–26, 326–27n, 365–67, 368n, 452, 453n, 500–502, 502–3n, 7:32–35, 36–37n, 152, 152–53n, 199–201, 201–2n, 208–10, 210–11n, 272–74, 274n, 317–18; v. Steam Engineers, 5:161, 162n, 170–71, 172n, 290, 292n, 433–34, 503, 503–4n, 514–15, 515–16n, 6:9–10, 10–11n, 88–89, 89–90n, 133–34, 135–36n, 208, 223–28, 228n, 365–67, 368n, 452, 453n, 500–502, 502–3n, 7:32–35, 36–37n, 152, 152–53n, 199–201, 201–2n, 208–10, 210–11n, 272–74, 274n, 317–18, 451–52; v. Teamsters, 5:292n, 501–3, 503–4n, 514–15, 6:365–67, 367–68n, 452, 500–502, 7:36n, 199–201, 201–2n, 272–74, 274n, 317–18, 493–97, 9:143–45, 146n, 148
—Bricklayers: v. hod carriers and masons, 2:131, 131n; v. Stone Cutters, 9:73n
—Bridge and Structural Iron Workers: v. AFL Riggers' Union 10,315, 6:210, 211n; v. Carpenters, 10:171, 171–72n; v. Longshoremen, 10:405, 406n
—building trades unions v. Maintenance of Way Employes, 11:60n. *See also* National Board for Jurisdictional Awards in the Building Industry
—Butcher Workmen of America, Brotherhood of, v. Meat Cutters and Butcher Workmen, 7:343–45, 345–46n
—Carpenters: v. AFL Federal Labor

Union 7204, **5:**484–85; v. AFL Sash, Door, and Blind Workers' Union 5150, **3:**150, 153n; v. AFL Shingle Weavers' Union 9891, **6:**44, 45n; v. Amalgamated Carpenters, **6:**42–44, 44–45n, 51, 62–64, 66–67n, 175–76, 176n, 178–79, 210–11, 219–20, 326n; v. Bridge and Structural Iron Workers, **10:**171, 171–72n; v. Longshoremen, **10:**405, 406n; v. Machinists, **9:**346–47, 347n; v. Maintenance of Way Employes, **11:**60n; v. Sheet Metal Workers, **8:**151n, 295, **9:**70, 73n, **11:**545n, **12:**73, 163n, 400, 401n; v. Shipwrights, **7:**242–43, 243n; v. Wood-Workers, **5:**421–22, 422–23n, **6:**51, 52–53n, 64–66, 66–67n, 165–67, 167n, 181, 211, 211n, 500, 503n, **7:**272

—Carpenters, Amalgamated, v. Carpenters, **6:**42–44, 44–45n, 51, 62–64, 66–67n, 175–76, 176n, 178–79, 210–11, 219–20, 326n

—Carriage and Wagon Workers v. Metal Polishers, **6:**311, 312n

—Chainmakers v. Blacksmiths, **5:**516, 517n

—Cloak Makers v. Garment Workers, **5:**102, 102n

—Coopers v. Brewery Workmen, **4:**329–30, **5:**219–20, 221n, 257–60, 260n, 290, 292n, 503, 503–4n

—Firemen and Oilers: v. Maintenance of Way Employes, **11:**59–60, 60–61n; and railroad shop craft workers, **12:**300, 341–42, 342–43n

—Flint Glass Workers v. Glass Bottle Blowers, **6:**448, 450n, **7:**407, 408n

—Garment Workers: v. Cloak Makers, **5:**102, 102n; v. Special Order Clothing Makers, **6:**49–50, 50n; v. Tailors, **6:**189–90, 191n, **9:**74n

—Glass Bottle Blowers v. Flint Glass Workers, **6:**448, 450n, **7:**407, 408n

—Glass Workers v. Painters, **7:**449–50, 451n

—Granite Cutters: v. marble and freestone cutters, **4:**481–82, 483n; v. Paving Cutters, **8:**188n

—Hat and Cap Makers: v. AFL Ladies' Straw and Felt Hat Workers' Union 12,675, **9:**107, 110n; v. AFL Ladies' Straw and Felt Hat Operators' Union 14,440, **9:**110n; v. Hatters, **9:**107–10, 110n

—Hatters v. Hat and Cap Makers, **9:**107–10, 110n

—hod carriers and masons v. Bricklayers, **2:**131, 131n

—Hod Carriers v. Longshoremen, **10:**405, 406n

—Horseshoers v. Blacksmiths, **5:**161, 162n

—Hotel and Restaurant Employees: v. Railroad Trainmen, **11:**42–46, 46n; v. Seamen, **11:**42, 46n

—Laundry Workers v. Teamsters, **9:**143, 145n, 148–49

—Leather Workers v. Boot and Shoe Workers, **5:**491, 492n

—Locomotive Engineers: v. Locomotive Firemen and Enginemen, **10:**250–51; v. Street Railway Employes, **11:**78, 78n, 308–9, 309n, 328–29

—Locomotive Firemen and Enginemen v. Locomotive Engineers, **10:**250–51

—Longshoremen: v. Bridge and Structural Iron Workers, **10:**405, 406n; v. Carpenters, **10:**405, 406n; v. Hod Carriers, **10:**405, 406n; v. marine sack sewers and cargo repairers, **7:**224–25, 225n; v. Seamen, **6:**51, 52n, 53–55, 373–76, 377n, 497–99, 499n, 502, **7:**270

—Machinists: v. AFL Railroad Helpers' and Laborers' Union 15,920, **10:**505, 505n; v. AFL Stationary Engineers' Union 5658, **3:**462, 463n; v. AFL Water Department Workers' Union 6356, **5:**76–78; v. Boston Central Labor Union, **4:**144, 144–45n, 148, 169; v. Brewery Workmen, **7:**221–22, 222n; v. Carpenters, **9:**346–47, 347n; v. Metal Mechanics, **5:**331, 332n; v. Miners, Western Federation of, **8:**105, 106n, 144–45, 170; v. Typographical Union, **3:**457, **5:**103–4, 104–5n, 112–13, 113n, 172–76, 288–92, 292n, 445, **6:**339n

—Maintenance of Way Employes: v. building trades, **11:**60n; v. Carpen-

ters, **11**:60n; v. Firemen and Oilers, **11**:59–60, 60–61n
—marble and freestone cutters v. Granite Cutters, **4**:481–82, 483n
—marine sack sewers and cargo repairers v. Longshoremen, **7**:224–25, 225n
—Meat Cutters and Butcher Workmen v. Butcher Workmen of America, Brotherhood of, **7**:343–45, 345–46n
—Metal Mechanics v. Machinists, **5**:331, 332n
—Metal Polishers v. Carriage and Wagon Workers, **6**:311, 312n
—metal trades unions v. Street Railway Employes, **9**:388–90, 390n
—Miners, Western Federation of: v. Machinists, **8**:105, 106n, 144–45, 170; v. Steam Engineers, **6**:352n
—Mine Workers, United: v. AFL Federal Labor Union 8276, **5**:336–37, 338n; v. Stationary Firemen, **5**:433–34; v. Steam Engineers, **5**:433–34
—musicians v. Theatrical Stage Employes, **4**:121–22, 122–23n
—Painters: v. AFL Carriage and Wagon Laborers' Union 5635, **3**:149; v. Amalgamated Association of Painters, **5**:446–47, 447–48n, 449; v. Brewery Workmen, **5**:290, 292n; v. Glass Workers, **7**:449–50, 451n; v. Paper Hangers, **5**:161, 162–63n; v. Sign Writers, **5**:427–28, 428–29n, 518
—Painters, Amalgamated Association of, v. Painters, **5**:446–47, 447–48n, 449
—Paper Hangers v. Painters, **5**:161, 162–63n
—Paper Makers v. Pulp, Sulphite, and Paper Mill Workers, **7**:150–51, 151–52n, 202–4, 204n
—Paving Cutters v. Granite Cutters, **8**:188n
—Piano and Organ Workers v. Wood-Workers, **6**:66n
—Plumbers v. Steam, Hot Water, and Power Pipe Fitters, **6**:342, 343n, **7**:272, **8**:151n, 296, 399–402, 402n, 413, 414n, **12**:68–69, 72–73, 73n
—Pulp, Sulphite, and Paper Mill

Workers v. Paper Makers, **7**:150–51, 151–52n, 202–4, 204n
—Quarry Workers v. Steam Engineers, **12**:394–98, 398n
—Railroad Trainmen: v. Hotel and Restaurant Employees, **11**:42–46, 46n; v. Switchmen, **8**:251–52, 253n, **10**:250
—railroad yardmen, **9**:341–42, 342–43n
—Railway Conductors v. Street Railway Employes, **11**:78, 78n
—Seamen: v. Hotel and Restaurant Employees, **11**:42, 46n; v. Longshoremen, **6**:51, 52n, 53–55, 373–76, 377n, 497–99, 499n, 502, **7**:270
—Sheet Metal Workers v. Carpenters, **8**:151n, 295, **9**:70, 73n, **11**:545n, **12**:73, 163n, 400, 401n
—Shipwrights v. Carpenters, **7**:242–43, 243n
—Sign Writers v. Painters, **5**:427–28, 428–29n, 518
—Special Order Clothing Makers v. Garment Workers, **6**:49–50, 50n
—Stationary Firemen: v. AFL Gas Workers' Union 9840, **6**:101–2, 102–3n; v. Brewery Workmen, **5**:161, 162n, 169–71, 172n, 290, 292n, 374–75, 375n, 433–34, 501–3, 503–4n, 514–15, 515–16n, **6**:9–10, 10–11n, 88–89, 89–90n, 133–34, 135–36n, 208, 223–28, 228n, 317–26, 326–27n, 365–67, 368n, 452, 453n, 500–502, 502–3n, **7**:32–35, 36–37n, 152, 152–53n, 199–201, 201–2n, 208–10, 210–11n, 272–74, 274n, 317–18; v. Mine Workers, United, **5**:433–34
—Steam, Hot Water, and Power Pipe Fitters v. Plumbers, **6**:342, 343n, **7**:272, **8**:151n, 296, 399–402, 402n, 413, 414n, **12**:68–69, 72–73, 73n
—Steam Engineers: v. Brewery Workmen, **5**:161, 162n, 170–71, 172n, 290, 292n, 433–34, 503, 503–4n, 514–15, 515–16n, **6**:9–10, 10–11n, 88–89, 89–90n, 133–34, 135–36n, 208, 223–28, 228n, 365–67, 368n, 452, 453n, 500–502, 502–3n, **7**:32–35, 36–37n, 152, 152–53n, 199–201, 201–2n, 208–10, 210–11n, 272–74,

274n, 317–18, 451–52; v. Miners, Western Federation of, **6:**352n; v. Mine Workers, United, **5:**433–34; v. Quarry Workers, **12:**394–98, 398n
—Stone Cutters v. Bricklayers, **9:**73n
—Street Railway Employes: v. Locomotive Engineers, **11:**78, 78n, 308–9, 309n, 328–29; v. metal trades unions, **9:**388–90, 390n; v. Railway Conductors, **11:**78, 78n
—Switchmen v. Railroad Trainmen, **8:**251–52, 253n, **10:**250
—Tailors v. Garment Workers, **6:**189–90, 191n, **9:**74n
—Teamsters: v. Bakers, **9:**143, 145n, 147–49; v. Brewery Workmen, **5:**290, 292n, 501–3, 503–4n, **6:**365–67, 367–68n, 500–502, **7:**36n, 199–201, 201–2n, 272–74, 274n, 317–18, 493–97, **9:**143–45, 146n, 148; v. Laundry Workers, **9:**143, 145n, 148–49
—textile workers, **4:**431, 432n, 447–49, 449n
—Theatrical Stage Employes v. musicians, **4:**121–22, 122–23n
—tool and hardware makers v. Blacksmiths, **5:**516, 517n
—Tunnel and Subway Constructors v. Blacksmiths, **9:**347, 347–48n
—Typographical Union v. Machinists, **3:**457, **5:**103–4, 104–5n, 112–13, 113n, 172–76, 288–92, 292n, 445, **6:**339n
—Wood Carvers v. Wood-Workers, **5:**161, 162n
—Wood-Workers: v. Carpenters, **5:**421–22, 422–23n, **6:**51, 52–53n, 64–66, 66–67n, 165–67, 167n, 181, 211, 211n, 500, 503n, **7:**272; v. Piano and Organ Workers, **6:**66n; v. Wood Carvers, **5:**161, 162n
Jusserand, Jean-Jules, **10:**191, *194n*
Justi, Herman, **5:**311, *311n,* 353, 367–68, **6:**123–24, 126n
Justice (trade union journal), **11:**499
Justice and the Poor (Smith), **12:**69, *73–74n*
jute industry: in India, **3:**540–42; in Scotland, **3:**539–42
Juul, Niels, **11:**276, *278n,* 281
Juuntunen, John, **9:**182, 184n, 190–91, 191n

Kaefer, Jacob H., **5:***, *277n; letter to,* **5:**275–77
Kahn, Julius, **5:**459n, **7:**117, *118n,* 382n, **10:**64n, **11:**294n
Kaiserhof Hotel (Chicago), fire at, **9:**263, 266n
Kalamazoo (Mich.) Trades and Labor Council, *9:28n*
Kalan, John, **9:**26, 28n
Kalanianaole, Jonah K., **11:**484n, 502, *503n*
Kaminski, George, *8:455n*
Kane, John, **1:**457, *459n*
Kaneko, Kentarō, *9:18n*
Kansas, election of 1906, **7:**69, 94–95
Kansas City (Mo.) Industrial Council, **4:**287, *287n,* **5:**125–26, 127n
Kansas City (Mo.) Railways Co.: strike/lockout, 1918–19, **11:**20, *21n;* and women workers, **11:**19–20, 21n
Kansas City (Mo.) Typothetae, **5:**236n
Kansas Court of Industrial Relations, **11:**320, 320–21n, 409, 409n, 481n. *See also* Allen, Henry J.; legislation, states and territories: Kansas
Kansas State Federation of Labor, **3:**276, *277n,* **11:**346–47, 347n, 557–58
Karston, Carl E., **12:**335, *337n*
Kassel, Charles, **2:**275, *275n*
Kasten, Frank M., **12:***, *355n; letter from,* **12:**353–55
Katō, Tomosaburō, **12:**12, *15n*
Katz, Rudolph, **4:**10, 12, 15, *15n*
Katzenmayer, Richard, **2:**113–14, *115n*
Kaufman, Mr. (New York City worker), **3:**378
Kaufmann, Berthold W., **1:***, 83, *90n; letter from,* **1:**89–90
Kaufmann Brothers, **1:**197, 199
Kaufmann Brothers and Bondy, **1:**186–87, *188n,* 199
Kautsky, Karl J., **8:**241, *242–43n*
Kavanaugh, William, **11:**86n, 96n
Kean, Edward J., **1:***, 360, *361n,* 449, **2:***, 363–64, *364n,* **3:***, 28, *28n*
Kean, John, *6:341n; letter from,* **6:**340–41; *letter to,* **9:**103–4
Keating, Edward, **9:**25n, 48n, **10:**124, *125n,* **11:**131n, 154, 470, **12:**432, 433n, 474, *475n,* 479
Kee, Walter D., **5:**392, *392n*

Keefe, Daniel J., **5:***, *249*–50n, 368, 464n, 474–75, **6:***, *57n*, 235, 259, 470, 513, **7:***, *7n*, 187–89, 310n, **8:***, *316n*, **12:***, 459, *461n;* at AFL conventions, **6:**53–55, 375–76, 376n, 498–99, 499n, **7:**424n; and election of 1906, **7:**111n; and election of 1908, **7:**415–16, 416n, 422, 425, **12:**508; election of, as AFL vice-president, **6:**209, 376n, 509n, **7:**281n; *letter from,* **8:**316; *letters to,* **5:**248–49, **7:**162–64

Keegan, John J., **6:**121, *122n,* 140n, **7:**376, *378n,* **12:**493, *494n; letter from,* **6:**139

Keene, Rufus, **6:**182, *182n*

Keep, Arthur, *9:482n,* **12:**96; *letter to,* **9:**481–82

Kehoe, William F., **11:**454–55, 457, *458n,* 467n

Keightly, Fred, **12:**212n

Kelby, Walter, **1:**134, *139n; report of,* **1:**140–51

Kelleher, Mary J., **12:**252, *252n,* 406, 408n

Kelleher, William, **12:**551

Keller, Oscar E., **12:**147–48n, 433, *433–34n*

Kelley, Florence, **2:***, *149*–50n, **10:***, 151n, 335, *336n,* **12:***, 81, *82n; letters to,* **2:**148–49, 155–56

Kellington, Alfred E., **7:***, 302–3, *304n*

Kellogg, Frank B., **12:**169, *171n,* 210n, 431, 434n

Kellogg, Paul U., **10:**388–89, *389n,* 415

Kells, David, **1:**360, *361n*

Kelly, Cornelius F., **9:**180–81, 184n, 270–71, *275n*

Kelly, James T., **3:***, 420, 614, *616n,* **4:***, *171n,* 324n; *letter to,* **4:**170–71

Kelly, John, **1:**100, *102n,* 169

Kelly, John A., **8:**282, *282n*

Kelly, John J., **5:**30–31, *32n*

Kelly, Josephine T., **9:**410, *410n*

Kelly, José W., **12:**356, 358–59, *359n,* 524–25

Kelly, Michael J., **2:**55, *56n*

Kelly, Patrick J., **3:**430, *434n*

Kelly, W., **10:**127

Kelly, William J., **9:**32, *34n*

Kelly Drydocks, strike/lockout, 1920–21, **11:**484–85, *486n*

Kelso, Charles, **8:**188–89, 190n

Kemper, Louis, **6:***, 9, *10n,* 449, 487, **7:***, 32–33, *36n,* 202n, **8:***, 91, *92n;* at AFL conventions, **6:**210, 210n, 366, 368n, 500–502, 503n, **7:**274, **8:**415; *letter from,* **8:**423; *letters to,* **6:**88–89, 223–28

Kendall, Maude, *letter from,* **7:**197–99

Kendrick, John B., **11:**338n, **12:**170, *171n*

Kendrick, Samuel J., *7:355n; letter from,* **7:**353–55

Kenefick, John J., **3:**148, *148n*

Kenehan, Roady, **4:***, 195, *197n,* 267, **6:***, *508n;* at AFL conventions, **4:**280, 281n, 282, 407, 409n, 413, **6:**504, 508n

Kenna, Edward D., **5:**294–96, *307n,* 311

Kennaday, Paul, **6:**485, *486n*

Kennedy, Adolphus, *6:116n; letter from,* **6:**115–16

Kennedy, Frederick E., *5:121n; letter to,* **5:**119–21

Kennedy, James, **7:**105–6, *107n*

Kennedy, John (Canadian fraternal delegate), **6:**62n

Kennedy, John (priest), *7:456n*

Kennedy, John J., **7:**58, 58n, 343

Kennedy, John L. (of Nebraska), **7:**107n

Kennedy, John L. (of Washington, D.C.), **3:**119, *120n,* **4:**197, *198n,* **5:**266–67, 268n

Kennedy, Thomas, **12:***, 550, *552n*

Kennedy, William E., *6:122n,* 139, 493n; *letter from,* **6:**121–22

Kenney, Horace, **3:**342, *343n*

Kenney, John, **8:**233, 234n

Kenney, Mary E., *3:160n,* 162, 180, 251, 253n, 428; *letters to,* **3:**159–60, 219–20. *See also* O'Sullivan, Mary Kenney

Kenny, John F., **1:**446, *447n*

Kenny, Patrick F., **12:**68, *73n*

Kent, A. W., **5:**181, *188n,* 231

Kent, Alexander, **5:**181, *188n,* 231

Kent, Sidney J., **5:***, 48n, 165–66, *169n,* 171

Kentucky farmers' case, **8:**265, 276–77n

Kentucky Railroad Tax Cases, **8:**479, *492n*

Kenworthy, Robert J., **12:**551–52, *554n*
Kenyon, William S., *8:424n,* **11:**31, 33, 297n, 336, 338n; *letter to,* **11:**294–96
Keogh, Mae, **6:**492, *493n*
Keough, Michael J., **12:***, 550, *553n*
Kerbs, Wertheim, and Schiffer, strike/lockout, 1900–1901, *5:236n,* 241, 244n, 251–52
Kerbs and Spiess, *1:58n,* 110, *112n, 198n,* 365, 373–74, 378, 407, 423; strike/lockout, 1873, **1:**66; strike/lockout, 1874, **1:**56–57; strike/lockout, 1877, **1:**113; and tenement production, **1:**194–95, 198n, 199, 210, 260, 262
Kerbs et al. v. Rosenstein et al., 5:244n
Kerby, Frederick M., **9:**397, 398n
Kerensky, Aleksandr, **10:**279n
Kern, Charles W., *11:267n,* **12:**363; *wire from,* **11:**265–66
Kern, Frederick, **5:**458n
Kern, Howard L., **10:**313, *315n*
Kern, John W., **8:**519n, **9:**194, *194n*
Kernon, John D., **3:**579n
Kerr, Archie R., **12:**551, *554n*
Kerr, Charles H., **9:**115, 118n
Kerr, Nathaniel B., **4:**434–35, *435n*
Kerr, Robert B., **5:**435n, **6:***, 188, *189n*
Kerwin, Hugh, **10:**307n, **11:**123n
Kessler (foreman), **4:**485
Ketcham, John H., *3:19n; letter to,* **3:**19
Ketterer, William, **6:**291–92, *292n*
Keufer, Auguste, **2:***, 18, 105, *108n,* **3:***, *91n,* **10:**72n; *letters to,* **2:**107–8, 133–35, 173–74, 317–18, **3:**368–70
Keuffel and Esser v. International Association of Machinists, **12:**302, *303n*
Keuping, Henry G., **7:**192, *194n*
Keyes, John, **6:**201, *204n*
Keys, Ida B., *3:161n; letter to,* **3:**161
Keystone Carmen, **8:**51, 52n, 70
Kidd, Edward C., *11:267n; wire from,* **11:**265–66
Kidd, Frank A., **3:**136, *138n*
Kidd, Thomas I., **3:***, *138n,* **4:***, *272n,* **5:***, *56n,* 271n, 372n, **6:***, *17n,* 134, 165, 408n, 432n, 468–69, **7:***, 463, *464n;* at AFL conventions, **3:**138, 138n, **4:**270, 410, 411n, **5:**53–54, 56n, 169–70, 171n, 175, 284, 286n, **6:**63, 65–66, 67n, 198, 204n, 508, 509n; election of, as AFL vice-presi-

dent, **5:**57n, 177n, 294n, 445, **6:**209, 210n, 376n; and jurisdiction questions, **5:**162n, 169–70, 172n, 175; *letters from,* **4:**379–81, **5:**401–4, 414–15, **6:**15–17, 316; *letters to,* **5:**269–71, 364–66, **6:**191–92, 432; mediation of industrial disputes, **5:**340, 342n, 366n; resignation of, **6:**316, 317n; *wire from,* **3:**532–33
Kiernan, James G., **1:**206, *207n*
Kiev, capture of, **10:**342, 345n
Kilgallan, John C., **3:***, 234, *234n*
Killoran, John, **2:**332, *337n*
Kilmainham Treaty, *1:286n*
Kimble, Andrew, **5:**107, *108n;* boycott, 1899–?, **5:**107, *108n*
Kimbrough, Eugene R. E., **7:**358–59, *361n*
King, A. E., **8:**244–45n, **9:**450n, 464n
King, Alexander C., **11:**195, *196n*
King, Andrew J., **2:**68, *69n*
King, Burnice W., *10:378n; letters from,* **10:**376–78, 517–18
King, Edward, **1:**288, **2:***, 53, 55, *55n,* 62, 184, **3:***, 472, *472n*
King, George G., **1:***, 371, *372n*
King, J. S., **3:**505
King, John W., **11:**528, *529n*
King, Joseph H., **11:**489, 491, *492n*
King, Laura G., **11:**413, *420n*
King, Mr. (supervisor of machine shops at Midvale Steel Co.), **5:**196
King, Sidney S., **11:**382, *383n*
King, Stanley, **10:**412n
King, William H., **12:**170, *171n*
King, William L. Mackenzie, **8:**114n, **9:**85–86, *88n,* 329n
King County (Wash.) Triple Alliance, **11:**218n
Kingman (boiler maker), **8:**81
Kinkead, Eugene F., **10:**436n, 528, *529n*
Kinnear, John, **1:**165, *166n*
Kinsella, John T., **8:***, *160n,* 402
Kinsella, William L., **4:**448, *449n*
Kipling, Rudyard, **5:**472, 474n
Kirby, James, **7:***, 443, *445n,* 460, 461n, **8:***, 150, *151n,* **9:***, *15n;* letters from, **9:**14–15, 69–70
Kirby, John, **3:**301, *302n,* **5:**35–36, 38n, 44, 57
Kirby, John, Jr., *5:367n,* **6:**98–99, *100–*

101n, **7:**193, 194n, **8:**70, 90, 198, 307, 494, 506–7, 511; and McNamara case, **8:**223, 225, 301n
Kirchner, Emil, **4:**102, *106n,* 118
Kirchner, G. F., **2:**106
Kirchner, John S., **1:***, *369n,* 387, 437, 440, 454, 457, 462n, **2:***, *71n,* 156, 187, 361n, **3:***, 31, *32n,* 234, 235n, **4:***, 119, *119n,* **7:***, *375n;* at AFL conventions, **2:**70, 72–74, 77, 79, 166–67, 171, 263, 272; and KOL, **1:**366, 398–99, 409; *letter from,* **7:**374–75; *letters to,* **2:**179, 187, 360–61, **3:**105–6; *report of,* **1:**368–69
Kirchner, Maggie B., *3:107n*
Kirkby, William, **3:**294n
Kirkpatrick, Charles G., **6:***, 443, *445n,* 461, 487–88n
Kirstein, Louis E., **10:**151n, 335, *336n*
Kirwan, Daniel M., *4:300n; letter to,* **4:**300
Kissinger, William B., **5:**321, *321*–22n; *letter from,* **5:**321
Kitchin, Claude, **10:**190n, **12:**496, *498n*
Klapetzky, William E., **4:***, *82n,* **5:***, *169n,* **6:***, 16, *19n;* at AFL conventions, **4:**80, 95, 407, **5:**167, 169n
Klarsfeld, Jerome R., *9:311n; letter from,* **9:**310
Kleffner, George J., **5:**282, *286n*
Kleiber, Victor, **11:***, *249n*
Klein, John, **2:**116–17
Klein, Samuel, **5:**89, *92n*
Kline, James W., **8:***, 322, *323n,* **9:***, 49, *50n,* **11:***, *27*–28n, 151, **12:***, *113n,* 128n, 237; *letters from,* **11:**504, **12:**112; *letters to,* **11:**26–27, **12:**118
Klinger, Louis F., *letter to,* **3:**80
Kliver, William H., **2:***, 171, *173n,* **3:***, 150, *153n*
Knaufft, Ernest, **7:**443n
Kneeland, Frederick J., **5:***, 284, *287n,* **6:***, 205, *206n*
Kneeshaw, J. W., **10:**532–35, *537n*
Knickerbocker Ice Co. v. Stewart, **11:**335, *338n*
Knife Grinders' and Finishers' National Union of America, Pen and Pocket, **3:***, 196
—strike/lockout, 1892, **3:**197, 197n
Knife Makers' National Protective

Union of America, Spring, **3:***, 196, 197n
Knight, Andrew E., *9:367n*
Knight, Charles E., **9:**367, 367n, 538, 539n
Knight, John C., **3:**345, *346n*
Knight, Sophia Gompers, **9:**367, *367n,* 538, 539n
Knights of Industry, **1:**160
Knights of Labor (KOL): and AFL, **1:**387–88, 460–64, 466–69, **2:**17–19, 39–40, 69–71, 71n, 73–74, 78–79, 208–9, 217–18, 273–75, 332–36, 339–43, 353–55, **3:**182, 622, 654, **4:**3, 123–24, 170, 332–33, 333n, 356, **5:**77, **8:**5, 72, 505, **9:**257, 391, 394–95; and American Protective Association, **3:**660n; and Bakers, **3:**105, 105n, 270, 270n; and Barbers, **2:**35; and Boot and Shoe Workers, **2:**208–9, 209n, 212, **4:**187–88, **7:**39; boycotts, **1:**365, 467n; and Brewery Workmen, **4:**83, 144, 145n, 222–23, 331–32, **5:**244–45, 245n; and Bricklayers, **1:**385–86; and Carpenters, **1:**385–86, **2:**35; and Cigar Makers, **1:**248–49, 365–66, 380–401, 404n, 405–11, 415–20, 435–39, 464–65, **2:**20–21, 24, 35, 207–8, 208n, **4:**151; and Clerks, **3:**244–45, 245n; and clothing cutters' strike, 1893, **3:**295–96, 296n, 299, 300–301n, 318, 320–24; education fund of, **2:**101–2, 102n; and eight-hour movement, **1:**276–77, 388, **2:**163, 170, 229–31, 242–43, 252–55, 255n, 267, 335–36, 342, 354, **3:**72–74, 75n, 93; factions in, **2:**19, 174 (*see also* Knights of Labor, Founders' Order of the; Knights of Labor, Improved Order of the); and farmers' alliances, **3:**3, 6n, 24; and FOTLU, **1:**161–62, 275–76, 280, 282–83, 387–88, 440, 456, 460; and Furniture Workers, **3:**268n; and Garment Workers, **3:**107–8, 108n, 295–96, 296n, 299, 300–301n, 318, 320–24, **4:**20; General Executive Board of, **1:**399–401, *401n,* 402–3, **2:**20–21, **3:**58; and George mayoral campaign, **1:**429–30; and government employees, **7:**314; and Granite Cut-

ters, **1:**385; and granite cutters' strike, 1892, **3:**166n; and Hatters, **4:**140–41; Home Club of, **1:**402–3, *404n,* 420, **2:**14, *14–15n,* 21, 23n; and Homestead strike, 1892, **3:**190, 217–18, 218n; and industrial organization, **5:**381, **8:**505; and Iron and Steel Workers, **1:**385–86, **2:**24, 24n; and Iron Molders, **1:**385; label of, **1:**366, 380, *380n,* 381–82, 384, 393–94, *394n,* 395, 397, 400, 405n, 408, 410–11, 420, 435; and labor congress, international, 1891 (Brussels), **3:**84–85; and Lasters, **3:**268–69, 269n, 270; membership statistics, **2:**19, 134; and Miners and Mine Laborers, **2:**30–32, 32n, 35; and miners' strike, 1891 (Pennsylvania), **3:**67–68; and miners' strike, 1891 (Tennessee), **3:**215n; and Mine Workers, United, **3:**173; and New Orleans general strike, 1892, **3:**243n; and New York State Workingmen's Assembly, **2:**11–12, 13n, 14; officers of, election of, **2:**227; and Painters, **3:**61; and People's party, **3:**3–4, 442n; principles of, **1:**160, **4:**104–5; and Pullman strike, 1894, **3:**526n; SG and, **1:**283, 386, 388, 397–99, 405, 420–21, 438–40, 463–66, **2:**17–18, 33–35, 39–40, 102, 194–95, 204, 207–10, 292–93, **3:**67–68, 244–45, 270, 296, 344–45, **4:**19–20, **5:**289, 331n, 449, **8:**151n, **9:**506, **11:**415; and Street Railway Employes, **3:**226, 228; and strikebreakers, **1:**395, 397–98, 406–7, 409–11, **2:**234n; structure of, **1:**159–60, 385; and Theatrical Stage Employes, **4:**123n; and trade unions, **1:**159–63, 385–89, 395–98, 401–3, 404n, 406–9, 425–27, 436–40, 453–55, 460–62, 466–69, **2:**17–22, 22n, 24, 30–31, 33–35, 39–40, 49, 102, 194–95, 195n, 198, 204, 207–9, 212, 292–93, **3:**416, 516; and Typographical Union, **1:**385–86, 389, 438; and women workers, **3:**133

—AFL conferences with: Feb. 1889 (Philadelphia), **2:**178–79, 181, 194, 198–201, 204–5, 210n, 212, 215, 217–20; Aug. 1889 (Philadelphia),

2:229–32, 234; Oct. 1889 (Philadelphia), **2:**232n, 242–44, 274; Apr. 1894 (Philadelphia), *3:442n;* June 1894 (St. Louis), **3:**441–42, *442n,* 511, 517, 606

—district assemblies (DAs): DA 1 (Philadelphia), **2:**38–39n; DA 3 (Pittsburgh), **1:**167, *167n;* DA 5 (Scranton, Pa.), *3:174n;* DA 9 (West Elizabeth, Pa.), **1:**167, *168n;* DA 16 (Scranton, Pa.), **3:**173, *174n;* DA 17 (St. Louis), **1:**160; DA 25 (Maryland), **1:**286n; DA 30 (Massachusetts), **2:**24n, **3:**269, *269n,* 270; DA 36 (Rochester, N.Y.), **4:**187, 189n; DA 45 (telegraphers), **1:***, 353n, **2:***, 335, 338n, 339; DA 49 (New York City), **1:**248, 366, 382, *383n,* 384, 387, 397, 399, 404n, 405, 407–8, 411, 415, 419–20, 435–36, 438n, 439, 467n, **2:**14–15n, 20, 23n, 55n, 58n, 142, **3:**14n, 65, 166n, 218n, **4:**11, 15n, 97n, 105, 106n, **5:**245; DA 57 (Chicago), **2:**296n; DA 66 (Washington, D.C.), **2:**71, *71n;* DA 68 (Troy, N.Y.), **1:**402n; DA 75 (Brooklyn, N.Y.), **2:**197n, **4:**94n; DA 89 (Denver), **2:**21, *23n;* DA 126 (carpet workers, New York City), **1:**420, *421n;* DA 148 (lake seamen, Milwaukee), **3:**496, 498n; DA 197 (Jersey City, N.J.), *2:337n,* **3:**218n; DA 198 (machinists, New York City), **3:**14n; DA 220 (Brooklyn, N.Y.), *2:338n,* **3:**270n; DA 246, **2:**382n; DA 253 (building trades, New York City), *2:337n,* **3:**218n, 268n

—general assemblies: 1878, **1:**159; 1880, **1:**160; 1884, **3:**106n; 1885 (Hamilton, Ont.), *1:380n;* 1886 (Cleveland), **1:**386, 391, *392n,* 395, 399–403, 403n, 405–6, 425; 1886 (Richmond, Va.), **1:**386, 425–26, *426n,* 427, 435, 437, 439, **2:**20–21, *23n,* 342, **5:**289; 1887 (Minneapolis), **1:**435n, **2:**50n, 78; 1889 (Atlanta), **2:**227, *228n,* 230–31, 243, 252–55, 255–56n; 1890 (Denver), **3:**72, *75n;* 1892 (St. Louis), **3:**245n; 1893 (Philadelphia), **3:**414, *415n,* 441, 442n; 1896 (Rochester, N.Y.), *4:286n*

—local assemblies (LAs): LA 80 (Boston), **2:**208, 208n; LA 92 (Allegheny County, Pa.), **4:**145n; LA 300 (window glass workers), **1:***, 215, 217n, 388; LA 767 (Queen City Clerks' Assembly, East St. Louis, Ill.), **3:**244, 245n; LA 952 (Chicago), **4:**381, 382n; LA 1562 (Spread the Light Club, Brooklyn, N.Y.), **1:**237n, 276, 438n, **12:**33, 34n; LA 1630 (Pittsburgh), **1:**217, 220n; LA 1644 (Washington, D.C.), **4:**285, 286n; LA 1748 (Washington, D.C.), **2:**71n, **4:**285, 285n; LA 1809 (Syracuse, N.Y.), **2:**13n; LA 2025 (Fort Bragg, Calif.), **6:**242, 244n; LA 2327 (Denver), **2:**20, 22n; LA 2410 (New York City), **2:**99n; LA 2412 (New York City), **2:**337n; LA 2458 (Defiance Assembly, New York City), **1:**248, 327n, 383–84, 399–401, 408, 438; LA 2531 (New York City), **2:**99n; LA 2588 (New York City), **2:**99n; LA 2814 (Progressive Labor Club, New York City), **1:**248, 399, 402n; LA 2853 (New York City), **2:**338n, 349n; LA 2888 (New York City), **2:**337n; LA 2914 (New York City), **2:**337n; LA 3275 (Clinton, N.Y.), **1:**402n; LA 3662 (Lynn, Mass.), **4:**188, 189n; LA 3973 (New York City), **2:**337n; LA 4333 (Albany, N.Y.), **4:**223, 223n; LA 5214 (New York City), **2:**338n; LA 5371 (New York City), **1:**462n; LA 5938 (St. Louis), **4:**123n; LA 6085 (Syracuse, N.Y.), **2:**13n; LA 7086 (Philadelphia), **2:**39n; LA 7087 (Philadelphia), **2:**39n; LA 7148 (New York City), **2:**337n; LA 7482 (Pittsburgh), **2:**315n; LA 7643 (New York City), **2:**337n; LA 7789 (New York City), **4:**57n; LA 8390 (New York City), **2:**337n, **5:**244–45, 245n; LA 8546 (Albany, N.Y.), **4:**222, 223n; LA 9426 (Albany, N.Y.), **4:**222–23; Harlem Assembly (New York City), **3:**14n; James Watt Assembly (New York City), **3:**14n; Joan of Arc Assembly (Troy, N.Y.), **1:**467n; in Pittsburgh, **2:**234, 234n
—national trade assemblies (NTAs):

NTA 35 (brewery workers), **4:**83, 84n; NTA 126 (carpet weavers), **2:**74, *76n;* NTA 135 (miners), **1:**391n, **2:***, 30–31, 32n, 51, 256, **3:***, 58n, 70, 71n; NTA 210 (painters and paperhangers), *2:337n,* **3:**62n; NTA 216 (shoe workers), **2:**18, 212, 213n, **3:**269n; NTA 226 (railroad workers), **2:**150, *150n,* 197n, 286, 286n, 337n; NTA 231 (clothing cutters), **2:**349n, **3:**107, *108n,* 296n, 300n
—state assembly: Alabama, *2:355n*
—strikes/lockouts: 1882 (miners, western Maryland), **1:**284, *286n;* 1883 (telegraphers), **1:**101n, 343, *353n;* 1884 (stove mounters, Troy, N.Y.), **1:**399, *402n,* **2:**8; 1885 (railroad workers), **1:**399–400, *402n,* 409–10; 1886 (clothing cutters, New York City), **1:**466, *467n;* 1886 (collar and cuff workers, Troy, N.Y.), **1:**466, *467n;* 1886 (packinghouse workers, Chicago), **1:**466, *467n,* **2:**22, 23n, 341, 343n; 1886 (railroad workers), **1:**101n, *402n,* **2:**341; 1886 (tanners and curriers, Salem, Peabody, and Stoneham, Mass.), *1:471n;* 1887–88 (railroad workers, Pennsylvania), **2:**92n, 108n; 1889 (street railway workers, New York City and Brooklyn, N.Y.), **2:**197, *197–98n,* 286; 1890 (railroad workers, New York), **2:**378–79, *382n,* 399, **11:**330; 1891 (clothing cutters, Rochester, N.Y.), **3:**299, *300n;* 1894 (coat makers, Brooklyn, N.Y., New York City, and Newark, N.J.), **3:**587–88, *589n,* **4:**20; 1895 (street railway workers, Brooklyn, N.Y.), **4:**92, *94n,* 105
Knights of Labor, Founders' Order of the, **2:**19, 174, *174n*
Knights of Labor, Improved Order of the, **2:**19
Knights of St. Crispin, **2:**411, *413n,* **5:**55
Knollin, James C., *12:285n; letter to,* **12:**283–85
Knotts, Thomas E., **8:**473, *474n*
Know-Nothing party, **12:**352
Knox, Philander, **6:**14n, **7:**415n
Knoxville Iron Co., **3:**215n

Knoxville Woolen Mills: boycott,
1900–1903, **6:**118–19, *119n;* strike/
lockout, 1900–1903, **6:**118–19, *119n*
Koenen, Bernard, **3:***, *268n; letter from,*
3:266–67
Koeser, Ignatz, **3:**141, *142n*
Koeser, Mrs. Ignatz, **3:**141
Kohler, Haysen, and Stehn Manufac-
turing Co., strike/lockout, 1897,
4:325, *325n*
Kohn, Joseph, **1:**113, *115n*
Kohout, Frank, *3:153n*
KOL. *See* Knights of Labor (KOL)
Kolb, Robert, **6:**147, *147n*
Kollontai, Aleksandra M., **12:**231,
232n
Konenkamp, Sylvester J., **10:***, 482n,
485, *490n,* 515n, **11:***, 103, *104n*
König, Ludwig, **8:**241, *243n*
Koopman, John, *8:334n*
Koralek, Frank, **7:**8, *9n*
Korea, workers from, **6:**195, 195n,
471, **7:**268n
Korn, Moses, **3:**51, *55n*
Kostial, T., **1:**204, 206n
Koveleski, Emanuel, **8:***, 449, *452n,*
12:*, 550, *553n*
Krasin, Leonid B., **12:**14, *15n*
Krause, L., **12:**145, 146n
Krausse, John, **5:**279n
Krchov, Anton, **4:**219n
Kreeft, Harry, *3:197n; letter to,* **3:**196–
97
Kreft, Ernst, **4:**410, *411n,* 415, **6:**208,
210n
Kretlow, Henry, **3:**47, *48n*
Kreusi, Walter, **10:**151n, 335, 336n
Kreyling, David J., **4:**148n, **5:***, 250,
251n, **7:***, 153, *155n,* **8:***, 128, *131n,*
10:*, *352n,* 431n; *letter to,* **10:**351–52
Kronburg, David, **1:***, 83, 84n, 85, *86n*
Krowizek, Stephen, **11:**142n
Kruger, Charles O., **8:**69, *76n*
Krumbein, Charles, **12:**275, *278n*
Kruttschnitt, Julius, **8:**321, *323n*
Kuenstler, Rudolph, **1:**237, *237n*
Kugler, Albert J., **8:**407, *408n,* **9:**32
Kugler (delegate), **3:**397, *399n*
Kuhn, Conrad, **12:**304, *308n*
Kuhn, Henry, **3:**199n, **5:**429, *430n*
Kuhn, I. B., **7:**427n

Ku Klux Klan: AFL and, **12:**89–90,
90n, 352, 352n, 421–22; and In-
dianapolis Central Labor Union,
12:362–64, 364n; murders by, in
Louisiana, **12:**194, *197n;* SG and,
11:527, 528n, **12:**352, 366
Kumler, Alvin W., **7:**193, *194n*
Kunart, William, **1:**111, *112n*
Kuntz (delegate), **3:**380
Kunzler, J., **4:**359n
Kuppenheimer, B., and Co., **7:**179n;
boycott, 1907-?, **7:**178–79, *179n;* let-
ter to, **7:**178–79
Kurkowski, Frank, **11:**206n
Kurtzer, F., *3:533n; wire from,* **3:**532–33
Kurzenknabe, Ernst, **2:***, 203, *203n,*
384–85, 397, **3:***, *88n,* 112–13, 344,
4:*, *223n; letters to,* **3:**87–88, **4:**222–
23, 264–66; *wire from,* **3:**532–33
Kutscher, William, and Co., **1:**187–88,
199
Kvale, O. J., **12:**433n
Kyle, Hugh G., **9:**262, 263n
Kyle, James H., **4:**489, 492, *499n,* 507–
8, **5:**498, 501n

Labadie, Joseph A., **2:***, *272n,* **3:***,
585n, **4:***, *180n,* **6:***, *108n;* at AFL
convention, **2:**269, 272; *letters to,*
3:584–85, **4:**179–80, **6:**107
labor, as creator of wealth, **2:**82–83
*Labor, Its Grievances, Protests, and De-
mands* (AFL), **11:**132n, 188n, 229–
37, 238n, 256, 260n
Labor and Antitrust Legislation (SG),
9:89, *93n*
Labor at Rest (Barnard), **7:**442
Labor Conference for the Relief of
the Unemployed (New York City),
3:364, 384–85, **4:**152–53
labor conferences: Sept. 1881 (Terre
Haute, Ind.), **1:**160–61, 164–65,
212; Sept. 1888 (Troy, N.Y.), **2:**151,
152n; Mar. 1891 (Oakesdale,
Wash.), **3:**51, *55n;* July 1892 (Pittsburgh), **3:**197, *199n;* Aug. 10, 1893
(New York City), **3:**364, 367n;
Aug. 20, 1893 (New York City),
3:364, 367, 377–83, 385; Aug.–Sept.
1893 (Chicago), **2:**345, *346n,* 383,
3:365, 369, 379, 388–96; Apr. 1894

(New York City), **4:**11–12, *15n;* Apr. 1894 (Philadelphia), *3:442n;* June 1894 (St. Louis), **3:**4, *442n,* 511, 517, 606; July 8, 1894 (Chicago), **3:**564, *579n;* July 12, 1894 (Chicago), **3:**523–24, 532–38, 548, 564– 69, 579n; July 1894 (Springfield, Ill.), **3:**4, 561, *562n;* July 1897 (Pittsburgh), **4:**344–45, *345n,* 346–57, 362–66, 372–73, 375, 389; July 1897 (Wheeling, W.Va.), **4:**353–59, *359n,* 363n, 364–65, 366n, **5:**386, **9:**337; Aug. 1897 (St. Louis), **4:**369–71, *371n,* 372–74, 374n, 379n, 382–83, 390–91, 391n; Sept. 1897 (Chicago), **4:**256, 370, *371n,* 374, 376, 383–86, 390–91; Mar. 1906 (Washington, D.C.), *7:6n,* **9:**89–90; Mar. 1908 (Washington, D.C.), **7:**319–20, *320n,* 323–29, 341, 342n, 346, 389–90, **9:**89–90, 165, 166n; Dec. 1909 (Pittsburgh), *7:473n,* **8:**7, 12n, 22–23; Dec. 1913 (Lansing, Mich.), **9:**46, *47n,* 65, 68n; Mar. 1917 (Washington, D.C.), **10:**20, *22n,* 39, **11:**225, 227n, 420, 426n, 521n; Jan. 1919 (Chicago), **11:**7n; Jan. 1919 (Pittsburgh), **11:**27, 28n; Nov. 1919 (Chicago), **11:**213, *214n;* Dec. 13, 1919 (Washington, D.C.), **11:**132n, 187, *188n,* 188, 197–98, 225–27, 228n, 229–37, 238n, 256, 271, 329, 332n; Dec. 29, 1919 (Washington, D.C.), **11:**241, *241n;* Feb. 1920 (Washington, D.C.), **11:**249–58, *258–59n;* Mar. 1920 (Emporia, Kans.), *11:347n;* Dec. 1920 (Washington, D.C.), **11:**401–2; Feb. 1921 (Washington, D.C.), **11:**401–2, 404n, 420–26, *426n,* 470; Apr. 1921 (Washington, D.C.), **11:**460–61, *461n,* 462; July 1921 (Washington, D.C.), **11:**488–91, *491–92n;* Oct. 1922 (Washington, D.C.), **12:**152– 55, *155n,* 159
—AFL conferences with KOL: Feb. 1889 (Philadelphia), **2:**178–79, 181, 194, 198–201, 204–5, 210n, 212, 215, 217–20; Aug. 1889 (Philadelphia), **2:**229–32, 234; Oct. 1889 (Philadelphia), **2:**232n, 242–44,

274; Apr. 1894 (Philadelphia), *3:442n;* June 1894 (St. Louis), **3:**441–42, *442n,* 511, 517, 606
labor conferences, international, **10:**89, 90n, 104–5, 271, 278n
—specific conferences: 1866 (Geneva), **1:**25, *43n;* 1866 (Sheffield, England), **1:**24, 43n; 1869 (Basel, Switzerland), **1:**22n, 25, *43n;* 1871 (London), **1:**25, *44n;* 1872 (Erfurt, Germany), **1:**26, 32, 42; 1872 (The Hague), **1:**25, 44n; 1875 (Gotha, Germany), **1:**43n; 1888 (London), **2:**105, 134, *135n,* 158–59, 165, 166n, 174, *letter to,* **2:**152–54, 156; 1889 (Paris), **2:**105–6, 159n, 166n, 174, 279, 318, **3:**84, *86n,* 197, *letter to,* **3:**369–70, 370n; 1889 (Zurich), **2:**158, *159n,* 174; 1891 (Brussels), **2:**383, *383n,* **3:**10n, 84–85, *85n,* 86, 90, 197, 199n; 1893 (Zurich), **3:**197, *199n,* 223, 349; 1896 (London), **4:**93, *94n,* 96, 130, 474; 1915 (London), **9:**238, *239–40n,* **10:**530; 1916 (El Paso, Tex.), **9:**425, 427–28, 428n, 437; 1916 (Leeds, England), **9:**469, *470n,* 474, 485; June 1917 (Stockholm), *10:90n,* 104–5, 271; Aug. 1917 (Stockholm), *10:90n,* 105, 271; Oct. 1917 (Berne, Switzerland), *10:90n,* 271; Dec. 1917 (Westminster, England), **10:**309, *309–*10n, 353, 356n; Feb. 1918 (London), **10:**355, *355–56n,* 530; Sept. 1918 (London), **10:**493, 493n, 503–4, *504n,* 522, 529–32, 532n, 533–537, 551–52, 561, 567n, **11:**11–14, 16, 30n, 37, 48n; 1919 (Berne, Switzerland), **11:**28– 29, *30n,* 38–39, 41n, 47, 48–49n, 55; Oct.–Nov. 1919 (Washington, D.C.), **11:**70, *71–*72n, 110, 118, 135–37, 137–38n, 194, 195n
labor conferences, proposed: 1893 (Chicago), *2:346n,* **3:**50, 85–86, 194n, 198, 215–16, 223, 224n, 348– 49; 1893 (London), **3:**223, *224n,* 348–49; 1899 (Chicago), **5:**100– 101, *101n,* 114; 1914 (Houghton, Mich.), **9:**46, *47n;* 1919 (Washington, D.C.), **11:**77, 77n; 1920 (railroad), **11:**347–49, 349n

—postwar: AFL proposal for, **9:**226, 226n, 469–70n, 488n, **10:**104, 535–36, 538n; Appleton and, **9:**468, 469n; and Confédération Générale du Travail, **9:**291, 292n; and Leeds (England) conference, 1916, **9:**469, 470n, 474, 485; Legien and, **9:**265, 485; in Paris, **11:**28, 30n, 40n, 48n; SG and, **9:**226, 226n, 468–69, 469n, 484–87, 488n; Wilson, J. H., and, **9:**473–76

Labor Day, **3:**106, *106–7n,* 219, 355–56, 358, 359n, **6:**197n, 202–3, **8:**237, **9:**201, 453–54, 454n, **11:**86, 87n, **12:**289

labor disputes, conciliation or mediation of. *See* conciliation; mediation of industrial disputes

laborers, proposed organization of, **5:**440

Laborers' Friendly Society. *See* Yūaikai

Laborers' International Protective Union of America, Building, **4:***, 117–18, 118n

—convention: 1896 (Holyoke, Mass.), **4:**117, 118n

Laborers' Union, International, **6:***, 397–98, 399n

Labor Forward Movement, **8:**391, 474, *474n,* **9:**62, 63n, 310n

Labor Herald (Trade Union Educational League journal), **11:**561, *561n,* **12:**44, 63, 66n

Labor in Europe and America (SG), *7:474n*

Laboring Men's Council, **10:**528, 529n

Labor Injunction (Frey), **12:**166

"Labor Is Not a Commodity" (SG), **12:**249, 250n

labor journals, mailing, as second-class matter, **5:**412, 413n

Labor Loyalty Week, **10:**311, *312–13n,* 324, 330n

labor party, **1:**387, **3:**23–24, **4:**415, **5:**51, 412, **7:**142n, 319, **10:**419, **11:**262–69, 282, 452, **12:**94; AFL and, **5:**444n, **7:**128–30, 133–35, 269, 269n, 418–22, **8:**283–84, 410–11, **9:**34–36, 36n, **12:**296n, 332–33, 333n, 410n, 468n; SG and, **3:**6, 78n, 202, 403, 421, 479–81, 504, 608, 612, **8:**404–5,

11:8–16, 17n, 24–25, 226, 265–67, 275–77, **12:**187–89, 430, 436–37. *See also* Farmer-Labor party; Farmer-Labor Progressive party; Federated Farmer-Labor party; Labor Party of Illinois; Labor Party of Indiana; Labor Party of New York, American; National Labor party; Progressive Labor party (New York); Social Democratic Workingmen's Party of North America; Socialist Labor party (SLP); United Labor party; Workingmen's Party of the U.S.

Labor Party of Illinois, **11:**17n

Labor Party of Indiana, **11:**265n

—convention: 1920 (Indianapolis), **11:**262–65, *265n,* 268

Labor Party of New York, American, **11:**17n

Labor Party of the U.S. *See* National Labor party

Labor Press of America, Associated, **4:**389–90, *391n*

"labor problem," SG and, **11:**77

"Labor's Bill of Grievances" (AFL), **6:**535, 535n, **7:**3–6, *6n,* 20, 61, 94, 106, 107n, 127, 135, 409, **8:**71, **9:**165, 166n, 202; reaction to, **7:**21–25

"Labor's Fourteen Points," **11:**13, *17–18n*

Labor's National Peace Council, **9:**366n

"Labor's 1912 Political Programme" (AFL), *8:386–87n*

Labor's Political Banner Unfurled (SG), **11:**277, *278n*

"Labor's Political Demands" (AFL), **12:**453–55, 455n, 456, 458n

"Labor's Political Duty" (AFL), **7:**391, *393n*

Labor's Position in the 1924 Campaign (AFL National Non-Partisan Political Campaign Committee), **12:**486–89, 501, *502n,* 510–11, 513n

Labor's Protest against Rampant Tragedy (SG), **11:**336, *338n*

"Labor's Protest to Congress" (AFL), *7:320n,* 323–29, 342n, 410, **8:**71, **9:**165, 166n

Labor Standard (New York City labor

journal), *1:83, 203n,* **2:**29; editor of, *letters to,* **1:**85–90

Labor World (Columbus, Ohio, socialist journal), **7:**215, *217n*

Labour, Its Wrongful Claims and Rightful Dues, Its Actual Present and Possible Future (Thornton), *3:102n*

Labour Department of the Board of Trade (Great Britain), **3:**94n

Labour party (of Great Britain), **7:**419, 421, 475, 477–78, **10:**293, 294n, **11:**11–12, 30n, 38, **12:**505; constitution of, **10:**293, 294n; executive committee of, **11:**11; postwar reconstruction program of, **10:**356, 357n, 388, 389–90n

Lacey, John, **11:**84n

Lacey, Thomas, **4:**118, *119n*

Lachman, Tillie, **7:**198–99, 199n

Lackner coal cutting machine, **3:**481

Ladd, Edwin F., *12:6n; letter to,* **12:**3–6

Ladies' and Panama Hat Blockers, **9:**108

ladies' garment workers, organizing of, **7:**165, 166n

Ladies' Garment Workers' Union, International, **3:**355n, **6:***, 156n, 276–78, **7:***, 165, 166n, **8:***, 114n, **9:***, 99n, **10:***, 62n, 379, **11:***, 92–93n, 318–19n, 531, **12:***, 91n, 156, 157n, 371n, 389n, 414–15, 444, 446n, 527–32, 532n; and black workers, **11:**84n; Educational Department of, **11:**499–500, 500n; and industrial unionism, **6:**518; injunctions against, **11:**448–49, 456, **12:**428, 428n; joint board of sanitary control of, **9:**402, 403n; journal, official, of, **7:**297, 298n; label of, **6:**276, **12:**529; and Protocol Agreement, **8:**439–40, 440n, 442n

—conventions: 1904 (Boston), **6:**276–77, *278n;* 1907, **7:**470n; 1910 (Boston), **8:**109, *114n;* 1914 (Cleveland), **9:**137, *138n;* 1924 (Boston), **12:**447, *449n*

—locals: local 1 (New York City), **6:**276, 278n, **8:**114n; local 6 (New York City), **6:**278n, 473–74, 474–75n; local 7 (Philadelphia), **6:**278n; local 9 (New York City), **6:**276,

278n, **8:**114n; local 10 (Cleveland), **6:**278n; local 10 (New York City), **6:**475n, **7:**468–70, 470–71n, **8:**114n, 442, 442n; local 11 (New York City), **8:**114n; local 12 (New York City), **6:**278n; local 14 (Cleveland), **6:**278n; local 15 (New York City), **6:**278n, 473, 475n; local 15 (Philadelphia), **8:**56n; local 17 (New York City), **8:**114n; local 20 (Philadelphia), **6:**278n; local 23 (New York City), **6:**276, 278n, **8:**114n; local 25 (New York City), **8:**40n, 442n; local 26 (Boston), **6:**278n; local 35 (New York City), **6:**276, 278n, **8:**114n; local 38 (Montreal), **6:**279n; local 41 (New York City), **8:**442n; local 50 (New York City), **8:**442n; local 53 (New York City), **7:**470n; local 62 (New York City), **8:**442n; local 63 (Philadelphia), **6:**278n; local 64 (New York City), **8:**114n; local 68 (New York City), **8:**114n; local 100 (Chicago), **12:**428n

—strikes/lockouts: 1903 (Chicago), **6:**155, *156n;* 1909–10 (New York City), **8:**39, *40n;* 1909–10 (Philadelphia), *8:56n,* 269; 1910 (New York City), **8:**109–13, *114n,* 218, 219n, 229, 269, 450, **12:**528–29, 531; 1913 (New York City), *8:442n,* 450, **9:**98; 1917 (New York City), **10:**61, *62n;* 1921 (Chicago), **11:**567, *571n;* 1921 (Philadelphia), **11:**567, *571n;* 1921–22 (New York City), **11:**567, *571n;* 1924 (Chicago), **12:**427–28, *428n*

La Du, Dwight, **12:**382n

Lafferty, Abraham W., **9:**19, *22n*

La Follette, Robert M., **7:**90n, **9:**10n, **11:**407n, 468–70, *471n;* and election of 1922, **12:**121–23, 149–50, 170; and election of 1924, **12:**389n, 409, 409–10n, 432, 433n, 463–67, 467n, 468–69, 470n, 471, 473–75, 475–76n, 478–84, 484n, 485, 487–89, 491–93, 494n, 497, 501, 504–7, 507n, 508, 510–13, 513n; SG, meetings with, **12:**471, 472n, 504–7

La France Fire Engine Co., **6:**152

Laidler, Harry W., **12:**387–88, *389n*

Laird, J. George, **10:**368, *369n*

Lake, Emmett J., **2**:*, *150n; letter to,*
  2:150
Lake, Obadaiah R., **2**:*, 172, *173n,* 213
Lakey, George H., **11**:434, *435n*
La Kurba Cigar Co.: arbitration
  case, **12**:132, 133n; boycott, 1917,
  12:133n; strike/lockout, 1918,
  12:133n
Lamar, Joseph R., **8**:152–53, *154n*
Lamb, Charles, **7**:382, *382n*
Lamb, Harry, *letter to,* **5**:200–201
Lambert, Frederick J., **3**:139, *140n,*
  264, **6**:6–7, *8n*
Lamoreux, Forrest P., **8**:261, *276n*
Lampert, Florian, **12**:346, *349n*
Land, Horace, *letter to,* **5**:400–401
land, ownership of: **1**:218–20, **3**:627,
  629, 631; and wages, **1**:282
Landauer, Strauss, and Co., **1**:188,
  188n, 199
Landers, Samuel L., **7**:97, *98n,* 236; *let-
  ter to,* **9**:285–86
Landis, Kenesaw M., **9**:237n, **11**:496,
  496–97n, **12**:30n, 57–59, 61n, 80,
  159n
Lane, Dennis, **10**:*, 213–15, *218n,*
  280n, 302, 404n, **11**:*, 381, *381n,*
  451; *wires from,* **10**:279, 403–4
Lane, Franklin K., **9**:466, *466n,* 484n,
  498, **10**:320n, **11**:160n, 182n, 191,
  259n, **12**:499; *letter to,* **9**:482–84
Lane, Harry, **9**:371, *372n*
Lane, Horatio H., **1**:458, *459n*
Lang (detective), **3**:381
Lang, Harry, *11:299n; letter from,*
  11:297–99; *letters to,* **11**:358–59n,
  530–32; SG, meeting with, **12**:320
Langdon, William H., **7**:117, *118n*
Langer, Louis E., **12**:530, *533n,* 550
Lanphere, Emma, **6**:386–87, *387n*
Lansbury, George, **12**:231, *232–33n*
Lansing, Robert, **9**:431–32, *434n,*
  443n, **10**:71n, 191, 274, 326n, 567n,
  11:40, 41n, 48, 58n, 93n; *letter from,*
  10:256; *letter to,* **10**:70–71; and
  Mooney-Billings case, **10**:93n
Lansing, Theodore F., **6**:195, *195n*
Lansing-Ishii Agreement, *10:193n*
Lappard, John, **3**:*, 257, *258n*
Laredo (Tex.) Trades Council, **8**:47,
  47n
lares, **12**:151, *152n*

Larger, Bernard A., **6**:*, 406, *407n,*
  7:*, 489, *490n,* **9**:*, 227, *228n,* **10**:*,
  150, *151n,* **11**:*, 460, *460n; letter
  from,* **10**:335; *letter to,* **10**:401–2
Larkin, Michael, **1**:283, 285n
Larkin, Walter, *10:69n,* 78, 79n; *letter
  from,* **10**:69; *letter to,* **10**:67–69
Larraga, Manuel, **12**:101n
Lassalle, Ferdinand, **1**:26–28, 43–*44n,*
  259, **3**:639
"Lassalleans," **1**:84n
Lasters' Protective Union, New England, **1**:*, 458, 460n, **2**:*, 235, **3**:*
—strike/lockout: 1887 (Worcester
  County, Mass.), **2**:24, *24n*
Lasters' Protective Union of America,
  1:*, **2**:*, **3**:*, 140n, 268, 269n; injunction against, **3**:412n; and KOL,
  3:268–69, 269n, 270
—strikes/lockouts: 1891–95 (Brockton, Mass.), *3:269n;* 1893–94 (Auburn, Maine), **3**:411, *412n,* 460–61
Latin America, commercial union
  with, **9**:527, 529n
Latrobe, Ferdinand C., **2**:66–69, *68n*
Lattimer massacre, **4**:376, *376–77n,*
  380, 381–82n, 383, 387, 388n, 439–
  45, 464, **5**:26, **8**:303; trial, **4**:377n,
  387, 388n, 439–40, 442–45, 446n
Latz, Alla Herschfield, *11:291n; letter
  to,* **11**:291
Latz, Mack, death of, **11**:291, *291n*
Lauck, W. Jett, **11**:401, *404n,* 471n
Lauer, Martin, *2:319n; letter to,* **2**:318–
  19
Laughlin, Gail, **6**:532, *533n*
Laughlin, Irwin, *10:554n; letter to,*
  10:549–54
Laughlin and Junction Steel Co.,
  2:24n
Laughran, P. Frank, **4**:387, *388n*
Laughton, Charles E., **3**:51–52, *55n*
laundry workers: and black workers,
  5:264, **8**:47; organization of, **8**:47,
  47n
Laundry Workers' International
  Union, **6**:*, **9**:*, 145n, **11**:*, 478n;
  and black workers, **11**:84n; and in-
  dustrial unionism, **9**:148–49; jurisdiction of, **9**:143, 145n, 148–49
Laundry Workers' International
  Union, Shirt, Waist, **6**:*, 493n,

7:111, **9:***, **11:***; AFL financial support of, **6:**484n, 492
—locals: local 2 (Troy, N.Y.), **6:**484n, 492; local 165 (Denver), **5:**393, 396n; local in Bellingham, Wash., **7:**111
—strike/lockout: 1905–6 (Troy, N.Y.), *6:484n,* 492
Laurell, Carl Malcolm Ferdinand, **1:***, 21, 22n, 46, 71, 83, 84n, **5:***, *514n,* **9:***, *408n,* **12:***, 315–16, *316n,* 318–19, 393, 399; *letters to,* **5:**512–14, **9:**406–7
Laurell, Clara, *12:316n*
Laurell, Emma, *12:316n*
Laurell, Louisa, **12:**315, 318, *319n*
Laurell, Margaret, *12:316n*
Laurell, Sophia, *12:316n*
Lavery, John T., *2:355n,* **6:**367, 368–69n; *letter to,* **2:**353–55
Lavery amendment, **6:**367, 368n, 502, 504n, **7:**36n, 201n
Lavin, Charles, **6:**197, *204n,* **7:**128, 141n, **8:**293, 293n
La Vine, John W., **2:**169, 172, *172n,* 301
Law, William J., **3:***, 227–28, *229n,* 359
Lawlor, Martin, **9:***, 107–8, *110n,* **12:***, 550, *553n*
Lawrence, Abraham R., **3:**293, 295n, 296
Lawrence, Groce, **8:**290n
Lawrence, Joseph M., **6:***, 536n; *letter to,* **6:**535
Lawrence (Mass.) Building Trades Council, **11:**351
Lawrence (Mass.) Central Labor Union, *11:351n*
Lawrence, Mass., textile workers' strike, 1912. *See* textile workers: strikes/lockouts: 1912 (Lawrence, Mass.)
Lawrence, Sidney B., **5:**395, 396n
Lawson, John R., **9:**282, *283n,* **10:**409n; *letter to,* **9:**308–9; protest meetings on behalf of, **9:**309, 310n
Lawson, Victor, **5:**342n
Lawyer, Charles E., **8:***, 30, *31n,* 53
Layet, Alexandre, **1:**204, *206n*
Layton, Harry B., **2:**430, *430n*
Layton, Robert D., **1:***, 161–62, *167n,* 228, 287; *letter from,* **1:**167

Lazarus, H. E., and Co., strike/lockout, 1917, *10:62n*
Leadbetter, Frederick W., **10:**245, *246n,* 296n, 417, 503
Leader (Henry George journal), **1:**429–30, 438n, *459n,* **2:**48n
Leadville, Colo., strike, 1896–97, **4:**245–46, 246n, *253–56, 257n,* 323, 385; AFL and, **4:**255, 257–58n, 259, 259n, 266–67, 268n, 279, 297–98, 304, 309
Leadville (Colo.) Trades and Labor Assembly, **5:**89–90, 92n
League for Industrial Democracy, **12:**387, 389n
League for Industrial Rights. *See* American Anti-Boycott Association
League of Nations, **10:**179n, **11:**40, 41n, 100–101, 136–37, 212, 404–6; AFL and, **9:**527, 529n, **11:**87–91, 91n, 102n, 321–23, 367, **12:**455; SG and, **11:**87, 91, 321–22, **12:**10, 209
League of Nations Covenant, **11:**58–59, *59n,* 101–2, 108–9, 137, 166, **12:**210n
League of Nations Union, **11:**58, *59n*
League to Enforce Peace, **8:**208n, **10:**178–79, *179n,* **11:**212, 212n
—conferences: 1915 (Philadelphia), **10:**179n; 1916 (Washington, D.C.), *10:179n*
Leahy, Jeremiah J., **2:***, 181, *182n*
Leak, Walter R., *6:402n*
Leake, Harry P., **6:**424, 428, *429n*
Leary, John J., Jr., **11:**297n, *12:210n,* 506–7; *wire to,* **12:**209
Leather Workers, Amalgamated, jurisdiction of, **5:**491, 492n
—locals: local 20 (Lynn, Mass.), **5:**492n; local 21 (Lynn, Mass.), **5:**492n
Leather Workers' International Union, United, **7:***, **10:***, **11:***, 319n, 558n, **12:**446n; and black workers, **11:**84n; injunction against, **11:**571n
—strikes/lockouts: 1919–20 (Indianapolis), **11:**569, *571n;* 1920 (Boston), **11:**569, *571n;* 1920 (St. Louis), **11:**569, *571n;* 1920–22 (Chicago), **11:**569, *571n;* 1921 (Peabody, Mass.), **11:**569, *571n*

Leather Workers on Horse Goods, United Brotherhood of, **7:***, 11n, **9:**205n, **10:***, 284n, **11:***; eight-hour case, **10:**281–82, *284–85n*, 365
—locals: local 17 (Chicago), **9:**203, 205n; local 49 (Cincinnati), **7:**11n
—strikes/lockouts: 1905-? (Cincinnati), **7:**11n; 1910, *8:148n;* 1910–12 (Los Angeles), **8:**147, *148n*
Le Bosse, Clara Gompers, **1:***, 8, *8n*, 14
Le Bosse, Louis, **10:**521, *524n*
Lederman, Michael C., **1:**414, *414n*
Ledyard, H. C., *11:534n; letter to*, **11:**533–34
Lee, Algernon, **10:**90n
Lee, Elisha, **10:**52n, 55, *56n*
Lee, Ernest, **9:**477
Lee, Fitzhugh, **5:**21, *29n*
Lee, Frank W., **4:**196, *197n*
Lee, Ivy L., **9:**399, *400n*
Lee, John F., **8:**130
Lee (labor inspector), **2:**343
Lee, Robert E. (attorney), **8:**234, *234n*
Lee, Robert E. (general), **10:**201, 358
Lee, Robert E. (machinist), **6:**31, *31n*
Lee, Uriah M., **5:**221, *222n*
Lee, William G., **9:***, 49, *50n*, **10:***, *252n*, **11:***, 42–43, *46n*, 249–50, 393–94, 400n, 460–62, 470, 472n; at AFL convention, **9:**521, 523n, 527
Lee, William S., **2:**82, *88n*
Leffingwell, Samuel L., **1:***, 165, *166n*, 211, 230, 242–43, **6:***, 523, *525n*
Lefkowitz, Abraham, *10:395n*, **11:**326n; *letter from*, **10:**393; *letter to*, **10:**394–95
Legassie, James, **12:**89–90n
Legien, Carl, **3:***, 85n, *87n*, 660n, **4:***, 136–37, *137n*, **7:***, 399–400, *400n*, 486n, 488, **8:***, 116, *117n*, 241, 252, 409, 412n, 518, **9:***, *107n*, 239, 240n, 289n, 385n, 485, **10:***, *4n*, 535–36, 538n, **11:***, 10–11, *17n*, 39; *cables to*, **9:**160, **10:**3, 49; *letters from*, **9:**173–74, 263–65; *letters to*, **3:**86–87, **8:**393–94, **9:**106–7
legislation, foreign:
—Australia: Commonwealth Conciliation and Arbitration Act (1904), **9:**212, *213n*, 217; eight-hour law (1870), **1:**318–19, *327n*

—Canada: Immigration Act, **11:**75n; Industrial Disputes Investigation Act (Lemieux Act, 1907), **8:**115n, **9:**86, *88n*, 212, 213n, 312–13, 314n, 408–9, 409n, 529n; labor agitation bill (1903), **6:**158–59, *159–60n*
—England: "poor laws" (1597, 1601), **5:**303, *309n;* Statute of Labourers (1351), **5:**303, *308–9n*
—Germany: Workmen's Compensation Act (1911), **9:**199, *200n;* Zuchthausvorlage (penitentiary bill, 1899), **5:**301–2, *308n*
—Great Britain: act regarding combinations and trade societies (1824), **8:**466–67, *468n;* Conciliation Act (1896), **3:**94n, **9:**54, *57n;* Conspiracy and Protection of Property Act (1875), **2:**151, *152n;* Corn Laws (1815), *1:44n;* Employers' Liability Act (1880), **8:**457, *459n;* Factory Act (1867), **2:**109, *110n;* Insurance Act (1911), **9:**192, *193n;* Land Act (1881), **1:**285–86n; Masters and Servants Act (1823), **5:**304, *309n;* Military Service Act (1916), **9:**382n; Munitions of War Act (1915), **9:**384, *385n*, **10:**114n, 171, *171n;* Munitions of War (Amendment) Act (1916), **9:**384, *385n*, **10:**114n, 171, *171n;* Trade Disputes Act (1906), **7:**288, *289n*, 326, 415n, 457, **8:**74, 467, 490, 494; Treasury Agreement (1915), **9:**384, *385n;* Workingmen's Compensation Act (1906), **7:**288, *289n*, **8:**457, **9:**199
—Hungary: legislation regarding strikes, **5:**301–2
—New Zealand: Industrial Conciliation and Arbitration Act (1894), **5:**300, 302–3, *307–8n*, **9:**212, 213n, 217
—Sweden: legislation regarding strikes, **5:**301
legislation, states and territories:
—Alabama: antiboycott law (1903), **6:**108, *110n*, 192, 193n, 293, 293–94n, 388; child labor bill (1898–99), **5:**70, *70n;* child labor bill (1900–1901), *5:70n*, 315, *316n*, 341; child labor law (1903), **6:**108, *109–10n;* compulsory education bill (1900–

1901), **5:**315, *316n;* eight-hour law for women and children (1887), **4:**27, *28–29n,* 232; ten-hour bill (1898–99), **5:**70

—Arizona: eight-hour law (1903), **7:**24, 25n

—California: Alien Land Act (1913), *9:206n,* **11:**89; antiboycott bill (1891), **3:**53, *56n;* child labor legislation, **12:**5; cigar box stamp bill (1878), **1:**125, *126n;* industrial commission law (1913), *8:384n,* **9:**19, *21n*

—Colorado: compulsory investigation law, **12:**5; eight-hour law (1899), **5:**114, *115n,* **6:**279, 281, *283n,* **9:**242; industrial commission law (1915), **9:**456–57, *457n;* minimum wage commission law (1913), **9:**19, *21n*

—Connecticut: labor standards suspension law (1917), **10:**76, *77n*

—Florida: child labor legislation, **12:**5

—Georgia: child labor law (1906), **7:**59, *59n;* child labor legislation, **12:**5

—Hawaii: Masters and Servants Act, **5:**24, 29n

—Idaho: minimum wage law for women, **9:**314

—Illinois: arbitration law (1895), **3:**553n, **5:**300, 302–3, *308n;* constabulary bill (1921), **11:**452–53, *453–54n;* employer liability laws (1891, 1895), **4:**231, *233n*

—Indiana: arbitration law (1897), **5:**300–303, *308n;* child labor law (1911), **8:**180, *182n;* eight-hour law (1889), **3:**221–22, *222n*

—Iowa: workmen's compensation law (1913), **10:**143, *147n*

—Kansas: court of industrial relations law (1920), **11:**279–80, *280n,* 289–90, 290n, 304–6, 308, 346, 347n, 408, 563, **12:**3, 5, 36

—Louisiana: suffrage restriction (1898), **5:**239, 240n

—Maine: child labor law (1907), **7:**183, *185–86n;* child labor legislation, **12:**5; woman and child labor bill (1907), **7:**183, *185n*

—Maryland: compulsory labor law

(1917), **10:**174, *175n;* political campaign law (1908), **8:**246

—Massachusetts: anti-injunction law (1914), **9:**262, *262–63n,* 321–22, 454–55, 455n, 520–21; Commonwealth Defense Act (1917), **10:**76, *77n;* election law (1889), **4:**231–32, *233n;* eleven-hour bill (1850), **3:**282, *282–83n;* employer liability law (1894), **4:**231, *232n;* fifty-eight-hour law (1892), **3:**282, *283n,* **4:**435, **8:**180, 182n; fifty-four-hour bills (1897, 1898, 1899), **5:**315, *316n;* fifty-four-hour law (1911), **8:**324, *325n;* minimum wage commission law (1912), **9:**19, *21n;* ten-hour bill (1853), **3:**282, *282–83n;* ten-hour law (1874), **1:**290, *327n,* 329–30; twelve-hour law, **3:**282; woman and child labor law (1890), **7:**184, *186n;* woman and child labor law (1902), **7:**184, *186n;* woman and child labor law (1907), **7:**183–84, *186n;* workmen's compensation law (1911), **9:**75, *76n*

—Michigan: child labor legislation, **12:**5; mine accident reporting law (1913), **9:**27, *28n;* workmen's compensation law (1912), **9:**75, *76n*

—Minnesota: minimum wage commission law (1913), **9:**19, *21n*

—Mississippi: antisedition law (1920), **11:**247, *247–48n;* child labor legislation, **12:**5

—Missouri: antiboycott law (1907), **7:**158–61, *161n;* antitrust law (1899), **9:**296n; antitrust law (1907), **7:**158–61, *161n;* antitrust law (1909) **9:**296n; employees, bill regulating discharge of (1909), **7:**458–59; miners' eight-hour law (1899), **9:**242, *244n;* minimum wage commission bill (1913), **9:**19, *22n;* Oliver law (1911), *8:493n;* Orr law (1913), *8:493n*

—Montana: child labor legislation, **12:**5

—Nebraska: eight-hour law (1891), **3:**93, *94n,* 147; minimum wage commission law (1913), **9:**19, *21n;* workmen's compensation law (1913), **9:**198–200, *200n*

—New Jersey: apprenticeship bill (1913, 1914), **9**:53, *54n;* child labor bill (1882), **1**:269, *270n;* workmen's compensation law (1911), **9**:75, *76n*

—New Mexico: personal injury law, **8**:132n

—New York: antistrike bill (1921), **11**:447, *447n;* anti-tenement bills (1880, 1881, 1882), **1**:151, *152n,* 208–9, 261–62, 269, 270n, 292–93; anti-tenement law (1883), **1**:169–70, 358, *358n;* arbitration laws (1886, 1887), **2**:5, *10n;* bakers' ten-hour law (1895, 1896, 1897), **6**:393, 393–*94n,* 420–21, **9**:242–43; bureau of labor statistics bill (1880), **1**:151; bureau of labor statistics laws (1883, 1886), **2**:5, *10n;* child labor law (1886), **2**:3–4, *10n;* conspiracy law (1881), **3**:299, *301n;* conspiracy laws (general), **2**:6, 151, 152n; contract convict labor bill (1880), **1**:151; contract convict labor bill (1882), **1**:169; contract convict labor laws (1884, 1888), **2**:4–5, *10n,* 320, 320n, 363; contract convict labor law (1894), **4**:231, *233n;* detective agency investigation bill (1921), *11:447n;* Duell-Miller Industrial Relations bill (1922), **12**:36, *39n;* eight-hour bill (1880), **1**:151; election law (1891), **4**:231–32, *233n;* employer liability bill (1885), **1**:361; employer liability law (proposed), **4**:231, 233n; employment offices, bill to establish free public (1894), **3**:452, *452n;* factory inspection law (1887), **2**:7, *11n,* 288–89, 289–90n; factory inspection law (1893), **3**:278–79, *279n;* fire hazard law (1913), **8**:471–72, *472n;* health insurance bill (1916), **9**:400, *403n,* 407; health insurance bill (1918), **10**:329, *329–30n;* industrial relations court bill (1922), **11**:563, *564n;* injunctions, bill to limit (1891), **3**:25–26, *26n;* Labor Day law (1887), **2**:6, *11n;* labor standards suspension bill (1917), **10**:76, *77n,* 99–100; lien bill (1880), **1**:151, 226, 258, 361; lien law (1885, 1887), **2**:5, *10–11n;* lien

law (1895), **4**:231, *233n,* **6**:372, 479; New York Charter, Greater (1897), *3:472n;* open air meetings in New York City, bill to allow (1892), **3**:158, *159n;* penal code, **8**:239–40, *240n,* **9**:321–22, *323–24n;* picketing, provision regarding, **9**:321–22, *323–24n;* prison labor bill (1880), **1**:151; private police, act to regulate (1892), **3**:26, *26n;* railroad employees, twelve-hour law for (1886), **2**:4, *10n;* Saturday Holiday Act (1887), **2**:108–10, *110n;* Spring bill (1915), **9**:277, *277–78n;* state printing office bill (1885), **1**:361; state printing office bill (1887), **2**:7, *11n;* tenement law (1901), *5:254n;* ten-hour law, **3**:185, 214n; trade union incorporation bill (1885), **1**:361; trade union incorporation laws (1871, 1895), **2**:6, *11n;* tramp law (1880), **1**:258, *260n;* Wilson-Fullagar bill (1916), **9**:406, *408n;* woman suffrage bill (1892), **3**:159, *159n;* women and children, legislation limiting hours of labor of (1891, 1892, 1894, 1895, 1896), **3**:29, *29n,* 452; workmen's compensation law (1910, mandatory), *8:327n,* *9:76n;* workmen's compensation law (1910, voluntary), **9**:75, *76n;* workmen's compensation law (1913), **8**:327, 327–28n, **9**:75, *76n,* 200, **10**:143–44, 147n; workmen's compensation law (1914), *9:76n,* **10**:143–44

—Ohio: child labor bill (1906), **7**:106, *107n;* child labor legislation, **12**:5; employer liability laws (1888, 1890), **4**:231, *233n;* run-of-mine payment laws (1914, 1915), **9**:282, *283n;* workmen's compensation law (1911), **9**:75, *76n*

—Oklahoma: "Coach Law" (1907), **8**:46, *46n*

—Oregon: industrial commission law (1913), **9**:19, *21n;* minimum wage law for women, **9**:316

—Pennsylvania: building construction safety law (1893), **8**:190, *191n;* compulsory arbitration bill (1901), **5**:328, *329n;* conspiracy

law, **3:**126; employer liability law (1915), **8:***191n;* factory inspection law (1889), **3:**278, *279n;* full crew law (1911), **10:**124, *125n,* 204; semimonthly payment law (1887, 1891), **3:**147, *147–48n;* workmen's compensation law (1915), **8:***191n*
—Puerto Rico: eight-hour law (1904), **6:**254–55, *258n;* homestead law (1917, 1921), **12:**198, *201n;* land grant law, **12:**199
—Rhode Island: antistrike bill (1922), **12:**36, *38n;* trade union incorporation bill (1922), **12:**36, *38n*
—South Carolina: child labor bill (1901), **5:**312–13, *313n;* child labor legislation, **12:**5
—South Dakota: child labor legislation, **12:**5
—Tennessee: child labor law (1893, 1901), **5:**348, *349n*
—Texas: AFL financial support of lobbying in, **6:**387–88, 389n; antitrust bill (1903), **7:**160–61, *161n;* child labor legislation, **12:**5; garnishment of wages law (1905), **6:**388, *388n;* Open Port Law (1920), **11:**422, *426n;* poll tax law, **6:**388, 388n; railroad safety laws (1905), **6:**388, *388n*
—Utah: eight-hour law (1896), **4:**452, *453n,* 491–92, **5:**114, 115n; minimum wage law for women (1913), **9:**19, *21n*
—Washington: anti-Pinkerton bill (1891, 1893), **3:**52, *55n;* eight-hour day initiative (1914), **9:**214–16, 220–22, *224n;* industrial commission law (1913), **9:**19, *21n;* timecheck bill (1891), **3:**52, *55–56n;* workmen's compensation law (1911), **9:**75, *75n,* **10:**143, 147n; workmen's compensation law (1913), **9:**75, *75n,* **10:**143, 147n
—West Virginia: compulsory labor law (1917), **10:**174, *175n*
—Wisconsin: minimum wage law for women and minors (1913), **9:**19, *22n;* unemployment compensation bills (1921, 1923), **12:**214, *215n;* workmen's compensation law (1911), **9:**6, 75, *75–76n*

legislation, U.S.: (The date in parentheses after an act is the year the law was passed; the date in parentheses after a bill number is the year the legislation was introduced in Congress.)
—Adamson Act (1916), **9:***450n,* 493–95, 495n, 522, 523n, 527, **10:**15–16, 17n, **11:**251, 259n, 331, **12:**497, 498n, 499; H.R. 17,700 (1916), **9:***450n*
—agricultural extension law (1914), **9:***10n;* H.R. 7951 (1913), **9:**9, *10n*
—alien contract labor law (1885), **3:**195, *195–96n,* 271, 287, 290, 292, 292n, 360–61, 487, **5:**15n, 326, **7:**185, 186n, 195–97, 197n, 332–33, **8:**316, **9:**101; amendment of (1891), **2:**366, *366n*
—aliens, resident, bill to federalize state-level suits against, S. 1943 (1921), **12:**169, *171n*
—anarchism, bills to repress (1901), **5:**404, 405n
—antisedition bills: H.R. 10,650 (1919, Davey-Palmer bill), **11:**253, *260n,* 301; S. 3317 (1919–20, Sterling bill), **11:**245n, 253, *260n,* 301; H.R. 11,430 (1920, Graham bill), **11:**245n, 253, *260n,* 301
—arbitration bill, S. 3259 (1904), **6:**231, *232n*
—Army Appropriations Act for 1917 (1916), **9:**435, *442n,* **10:**20n, 96
—Army Reorganization Act (1920), *11:***294n;* H.R. 12,775 (1920), **11:**292–94, *294n,* 300
—Baer bill, H.R. 13,526 (1920), **11:**336, *338n*
—barge towing, bill for regulation of, H.R. 471 (1905), **7:**78–79, *90n,* 170–71
—bonus bill, H.R. 10,874 (1922), **12:**25–26, *26n*
—Borland amendment regarding federal employee workday (1918), **10:**454, *455n,* 456–59
—Bureau of Labor, law to establish (1884), **8:**95, *100n*
—campaign contribution law (1910), **8:***85n;* H.R. 2250 (1909), **8:**82–85, *85n*

—Capper-Volstead Act (1922), *11:338n;* H.R. 2373 (1921), *11:338n*

—census laws: 1879, **2:**236, *240n,* 249; 1889, **2:**236–40, *240n,* 249

—child labor, law to regulate in the District of Columbia (1908), *8:132n;* S. 4812 (1908), **8:**132, *132n*

—child labor amendment: H.J. Res. 407 (1922), *12:82–83n,* 208; S.J. Res. 232 (1922), *12:82–83n,* 208; H.J. Res. 184 (1924), *12:83n,* 453–54, *455n*

—Child Labor Tax Act (1919), *10:499n,* **11:**15, 512–14, 514n, **12:**82n, 84

—Chinese exclusion bills: H.R. 6525 (1901), **5:**456, *458n;* S. 1450 (1901), **5:**457, *458–59n;* H.R. 9330 (1902), **5:**457–58, *458–59n,* **6:**48, 48n; H.R. 13,031 (1902), *5:459n,* **6:**11, 12–13n, 48, 48n; S. 2960 (1902), **5:**457–58, *458–59n,* 466–67, 467n, 470–74, 485–86, **6:**48, 48n; H.R. 15,167 (1904), **6:**261, *261n;* H.R. 12,973 (1906), **6:**525, 527, *527n,* 529; H.R. 18,022 (1906), **6:**525, *527n*

—Chinese exclusion laws: 1882, **1:**454, *455n,* **3:**371n, 490n, **5:**15n; 1902, *5:458–59n,* **6:**286n, 471; 1904, **6:**286, *286–87n,* 372, 472n, **7:**268n

—Chinese workers, bills to admit, into Hawaii: H.J. Res. 158 (1921), **11:**483, *484n,* **12:**37; H.J. Res. 171 (1921), **11:**483, *484n,* 502–3, 503–4n, **12:**37, 210–11, 212n

—Clayton Act (1914), *9:94n,* 207, 220, 233, 237, 423, **10:**123–25, 286, 351, 373, 526, **11:**14–15, 226, 310, 335–36, 406, 408n, 424, **12:**71, 134, 373–74n, 496–97, 499; amendment of, **12:**91, 93; Golden and, **9:**261–62, 262n; SG defense of, **9:**246–51, 262, 279, 280n, 292–95, 318–21, 321n, 322–23, 324n, 446–47; Spelling and, **9:**279, 280n, 323; Wickersham and, **9:**250, 292–95, 295n, 319, 323. *See also under* legislation, U.S.: Sherman Antitrust Act (1890), bills to amend

—coast defense bill, S. 1159 (1896), **4:**145–46, *147n*

—Coinage Acts: 1837, **3:**613, *616n;* 1873, **3:**613, *616n*

—common carriers' liability laws: 1906, **10:**145, *147n;* 1908, **8:**458, *459n,* **10:**143–44, 146, 147n

—contempt bills: S. 2984 (1896), **4:**112, *113n, 323–24n;* H.R. 2471 (1897), **4:**321, *323–24n;* H.R. 22,591 (1912), **8:**424, *425n*

—contract labor law. *See* legislation, U.S.: Foran Act (1885)

—convict labor bills: H.R. 5450 (1900), **5:**325, *327n,* **8:**330, *332n;* H.R. 9958 (1902), **5:**456, *456n;* H.R. 10,006 (1904), **6:**231, *232n;* H.R. 12,318 (1906), **7:**182, *183n;* H.R. 5601 (1911), **8:**330, *332n*

—Cummins bills: first, S. 2906 (1919), **11:**195n; second, S. 3288 (1919), **11:**194, *195n,* 207, 215, 232, 238, 241, 253, 271, 274n, 301, 330

—deficiency bill, H.R. 12,320 (1906), **6:**525–26, *526n,* 527–28, **7:**3, 94, 105, **8:**132, 132n, 341, 371

—Department of Commerce and Labor, law to create (1903), *8:100n*

—Department of Industry and Commerce, bill to create, S. 624 (1897), **5:**13, *15n*

—Department of Labor: appropriations (1913, 1914), **9:**9, *10–11n;* cabinet status, H.R. 4514 (1893), **3:**477, *478n*

—Department of Labor, bills to create: H.R. 3646 (1909), **8:**94–99, *100n,* 331, 332–33n; H.R. 13 (1911), **8:**331, *333n;* H.R. 22,913 (1912), *8:333n,* 376, 395, 424–25, 425n, 470

—Department of Public Welfare, bills to create (1921), **12:**37, 39n

—diplomatic and consular service appropriation act of 1915, *9:300n,* **10:**6

—diplomatic and consular service appropriation act of 1917, *10:8n;* H.R. 19,300 (1916), **10:**5, *8n*

—District of Columbia Appropriation Act (1918), *10:439n;* H.R. 11,692 (1918), **10:**438, *439–40n*

—eight-hour bills: H.R. 6449 (1890), **3:**19, *19n;* S. 2705 (1896), **4:**143, *143n;* H.R. 7939 (1896), **4:**143, *143n,* 172, **5:**497–98, 501n; H.R. 7389 (1898), **4:**452, *453n,* 489–99,

499n, 500–501, 503–4, 505n, 507–8, **5:**14, 66–67, 165, 498, 501n; H.R. 6882 (1900), **5:**189–97, *197–98n*, 201–7, 207n, 212–13, 222–30, 230n, 248–49, 249–50n, 325, 327n, 498–99, 501n, **6:**48, 48n, **7:**26; H.R. 3076 (1901), **5:**410–11, *411n*, 456, 478–82, *482n*, 497–500, **7:**26; H.R. 4064 (1903), **6:**231, *232n*, 302–6, 308n, 477, 525, **7:**26; H.R. 8134 (1903), **6:**308n; S. 489 (1903), **6:**231, *232n*, **7:**26; H.R. 11,651 (1906), **6:**527, *529n*, **7:**26–32, 32n, 43, 43n, 48–49, 101; H.R. 15,651 (1908), **7:**310, *311n*, 327, 335, 346

—eight-hour law of 1868, **1:**67n, 151, 212, 225, *229n*, 281, 287–88, 320–26, 351, **2:**165–66, 166n, 264, **9:**242

—eight-hour law of 1888 (letter carriers' eight-hour law), **5:**362, *363n*

—eight-hour law of 1892 (public works' construction laborers' eight-hour act), **3:**343n, 404, *405n*, 449, 465–66, **4:**336, **8:**371, **10:**13; and Panama Canal workers, **6:**525–28

—eight-hour law of 1912, *8:259n;* H.R. 9061 (1911), **8:**257, *259n*, 370–72, 379, 380n, 395, 459–60, **10:**281, 284n, 458

—eight-hour law of 1912 (letter carriers' eight-hour law), *8:495n;* H.R. 21,279, **8:**494, *495–96n*

—employer-employee relations, bill to improve, S.J. Res. 44 (1919), **11:**107, *107–8n*

—employer liability bill: H.R. 16,734 (1908), **7:**327, *329n*, 335, 346; AFL bill (1909), **7:**452–53, 453n

—employer (railroad) liability law (1908), *8:459n;* H.R. 20,310 (1908), **8:**458, *459n*, **10:**143–44, 146, 147n

—Erdman Act (1898), **4:**142, *142n*, 273, 275n, 283, 292–93, 295, 296n, **5:**308n, **11:**330

—Esch bills: first, H.R. 4378 (1919), **11:**156, *157n*, 216n; second, H.R. 10,453 (1919), **11:**157n, 215, *216n*, 241, 253, 271, 274n, 301, 330, 332n

—Esch-Cummins Law. *See* legislation, U.S.: Transportation Act of 1920

—Espionage Act (1917), *10:64n;* H.R. 291 (1917), **10:**62–63, *64n*, **11:**80, 91, 93n, 248n, 319n

—extradition bill, S. 657 (1921), **12:**37, *39n*

—farmer cooperative legislation: H.R. 13,931 (1920), *11:338n;* S. 4344 (1920), *11:338n;* H.R. 2373 (1921), *11:338n. See also* legislation, U.S.: Capper-Volstead Act (1922)

—Federal Farm Loan Act (1920), **11:**311, *313n*

—Food Control and District of Columbia Rents Act (1919), *11:338n;* H.R. 8624 (1919), **11:**336, *338n*

—food survey law (1917), **9:**526n, 529n

—Foraker Act (1900), **8:**88, *89n;* bill to amend, H.R. 19,718 (1910), **8:**88–89, *89–90n*

—Foran Act (1885), **3:**195, *195–96n*, 271, 287, 290, 292, 292n, 360–61, 487, **5:**15n, 326, **7:**185, 186n, 195–97, 197n, 332–33, **8:**316; amendment of (1891), **2:**366, *366n;* H.R. 7897 (1894), **3:**513, *514n*

—free lecture appropriation for Washington, D.C. (1904), **6:**267, *268n*

—Gage financial bill, H.R. 5181 (1897), **4:**417–19, *419n*, 421–25

—Geary Act (1892), **3:**343n, *371–72n*, 488–89, 490n, **5:**7, 33, 326–27, 406, 407n, 431, 435, 456–57, 458n, **6:**261, 262n

—Hawaii, bills to admit Chinese workers into: H.J. Res. 158 (1921), **11:**483, *484n*, **12:**37; H.J. Res. 171 (1921), **11:**483, *484n*, 502–3, 503–4n, **12:**37, 210–11, 212n

—Hawaii, bill to admit immigrant workers into, H.R. 10,568 (1907), **7:**332, *333n*

—immigrant intelligence screening bill, H.Res. 476 (1922), **12:**185, *186n*

—immigrant literacy test bills: S. 3175 (1911), **9:**80–81, 82–*83n;* H.R. 6060 (1913), **9:**102, *103n*

—immigrant naturalization bill, H.R. 10,860 (1922), **12:**50, *52n*

—immigration bills: H.R. 14,273 (1923), **12:**211, *213n;* S. 2365 (1924), *12:348n*

—immigration law of 1903, **7:**197n;
bill to amend, S. 4403 (1906), **7:**87,
91n, 195
—immigration law of 1917, *9:405n;*
H.R. 10,384 (1916), **9:**403–4, *405n,*
414–15, 470, **10:**37, 164–66, 166n
—immigration law of 1921, **12:**39n,
416n
—immigration law of 1922, H.J. Res.
268 (1922), **12:**37, *39n*
—immigration law of 1924, *12:416n;*
H.R. 101 (1923), **12:**415, *416–17n;*
S. 35 (1923), **12:**415, *417n;* H.R.
6540 (1924), *12:417n;* H.R. 7995
(1924), **12:**414–16, *416n*
—income tax law of 1894, **3:**546,
548n, **4:**36, 38n, **6:**332, 340n, **8:**264
—income tax law of 1913, **9:**90
—industrial education bill, S. 3
(1913), **9:**9, *10n*
—Industrial Relations Commission,
law to create (1912), *8:381n;* H.R.
21,094 (1912), **8:**376, *381n*
—injunctions, bills to limit: S. 2984
(1896), **4:**112, *113n;* H.R. 8917, S.
4233 (1900), **5:**211, 211n, 242, *244n,*
325–26; H.R. 11,060 (1902, Grosvenor bill), **7:**84, *91n;* H.R. 89 (1903),
6:231, *232n,* 301–6, 308n; H.R. 4445
(1905), **6:**525, *526n,* 527, 537–45;
H.R. 9328 (1905, Gilbert bill), **7:**81,
91n; H.R. 18,752 (1906, Pearre bill),
6:525, *526–27n,* **7:**83, 91n, 101, 288,
8:373, 380n; H.R. 94 (1907, Pearre
bill), **7:**310–11, *311n,* 327, 335, 346,
415n, 457, **8:**373, 380n; H.R. 3058
(1909, Wilson bill), **7:**457–58, *458n;*
H.R. 21,334 (1910, Moon bill),
8:100, *101n,* 152, 158, 159n; H.R.
25,188 (1910, Wilson bill), **8:**100,
101n, 158, 159n, 373, 380n; H.R.
11,032 (1911, Wilson bill), **8:**257,
258–59n, 354, 355n, 373, 380, 380n;
H.R. 23,635 (1912, Clayton bill),
8:259n, 373–75, 380–81n, 424–25,
438n, 445, 448n, **9:**91, 94n
—internal revenue bill, H.R. 4414
(1878), **1:**126–27, *127n,* 131, 207–8
—Interstate Commerce Act (1887),
3:301n, **4:**26, 35, 338n; bill to

amend, S. 1479 (1897), **4:**337, *338n,*
343, 343n; use of, against strikes,
3:293, 295n, 299–300, 523, 530,
531n, 559–60, 576, 632
—interstate commerce court bill, S.
7051 (1905), **6:**353–54, *354n*
—Interstate Railroad Act (1917),
10:125n; S. 2356 (1917), **10:**123–25,
125n
—intoxicating liquors, law prohibiting
transportation of (1913), *8:424n;* S.
4043 (1911), **8:**423, *424n*
—Jones Act (1917), *9:371–72n;* H.R.
9533 (1916), **9:**371, *371–72n*
—judiciary law (1911), *8:159n;* H.R.
23,377 (1910), **8:**158, *159n;* S. 7031
(1910), **8:**158, *159n*
—Keating-Owen Act (1916), **10:**85,
86n, 499n, **11:**15
—labor dispute investigation bill,
H.R. 15,447 (1908), **8:**132, *132n*
—land, public, loan bill, H.R. 10
(1877), **3:**448, *451n*
—letter carriers' forty-eight-hour bill,
H.R. 11,075 (1900), **5:**362, *363n*
—Lever Food and Fuel Control Act
(1917), **9:**526n, 529n, *10:112n;*
H.R. 4961 (1917), **10:**111–12, *112n,*
124–25, 289, **11:**79–80, 81n, 196n,
210–11, 211n, 220, 221n, 336
—lobbying bill, H.R. 22,912 (1912),
8:377–79, *381n*
—Lodge-Corliss bill, H.R. 7864
(1896), **4:**283, *284n,* 412
—longshoremen's compensation law
(1917), *11:337n;* S. 2916 (1917),
11:335, *337n*
—Maguire Act (1895), **4:**294n, **7:**4,
7n, 72–73
—mail, bills prohibiting obstruction
of (1894), **3:**413, *414n*
—mail service law of 1891, **7:**175,
177n
—mail train bill, S. 1214 (1893),
5:301, *308n*
—meatpacking industry legislation:
S. 2199 (1919), **11:**336, *338n;* S.
2202 (1919), **11:**336, *338n;* S. 3944
(1920), **11:**336, *338n;* H.R. 6320
(1921), *11:338n. See also* legislation,

U.S.: Packers and Stockyards Act
(1921)
—merchant marine law of 1884,
7:174, *177n*
—Militia Act (1903), **6:**201, *204n*
—minimum wage bills: for government employees, H.R. 4901 (1913),
9:19, *22n;* for women, S. 579
(1913), **9:**19, *22n*
—minimum wage commission bills:
H.R. 1803 (1913), **9:**19, *22n;* S.
1925 (1913), **9:**19, *22n*
—minimum wage law for women in
the District of Columbia (1918),
12:228n
—munitions, manufacture of, bills regarding: H.R. 2702 (1923), **12:**346,
348–49n; S. 742 (1923), *12:348–49n*
—National Defense Act (1916),
9:525n, **11:**294n
—Naval Appropriation Act (1917),
10:14n; H.R. 20,632 (1917), *10:14n,*
54n, 87, 87n, 91–92, 281, 284n,
366n, 443–44, 458
—naval holiday bill, H.Res. 298
(1913), **10:**535, *538n*
—Newlands Mediation, Conciliation,
and Arbitration Act (1913), **9:**55,
57n, 212, 450n; bill to amend, H.R.
19,730 (1917), **10:**15–16, *17n;* bill
to amend, H.R. 20,752 (1917),
10:15–16, *16n;* bill to amend, S.
8201 (1917), **10:**16, *17n*
—New Mexico personal injury resolution (1908), S.R. 37 (1908), **8:**132,
132n
—Oates bill, H.R. 12 (1892), **3:**162, *163n*
—oleomargarine law (1886, 1902),
11:513, *514n*
—Olney arbitration bill, H.R. 8556
(1895), **5:**301, *308n*
—Overman bill, S. 3771 (1918),
10:412, *412n*
—Packers and Stockyards Act (1921),
11:338n; H.R. 6320 (1921), *11:338n*
—pension bill, H.R. 14,494 (1909),
12:217, *218n*
—periodicals, bill to classify as second-class matter, H.R. 4897 (1893),
3:470, *471n*

—phosphorus matches, law banning
(1912), **11:**513, *514n*
—pilotage bill, H.R. 5281 (1905),
7:75–76, 86, *90n,* 101
—Poindexter bill: S. 4204 (1920),
11:406–7, *407n,* 469, **12:**436; S. 16
(1921), **11:**407n
—political coercion of employees, bill
to prohibit, H.R. 11,177 (1911),
8:245–46, *246n*
—Pomerene bill, S. 1256 (1919),
11:157n
—Post Office Appropriation Acts:
1894, *5:413n;* 1912, *8:495n;* H.R.
21,279 (1912), **8:**494, *495n*
—Post Office resolution (1913), H.J.
Res. 80 (1913), **8:**495, *496n*
—public land pasturage bill, H.R.
4805 (1880), **1:**230, *232n*
—railroad accident reporting law
(1901), *5:363n;* H.R. 10,302 (1901),
5:362–63, *363n*
—railroads, bill to limit hours of labor
on, S. 5133 (1906), **7:**79, *90n*
—refugee immigration bill, S.J. Res.
252 (1922), **12:**211, *213n*
—Revenue Acts: of 1918, *11:543n;* of
1921, *11:543n*
—Sabotage Act (1918), *10:434n;* S. 383
(1917), **10:**433, *434n,* 447–49, 449n
—Safety Appliance Act (1893), **3:**283,
284n, **5:**362, **6:**372, **8:**181, **11:**330
—sales tax bills: H.R. 14,956 (1920),
12:38, *39–40n;* H.R. 2,226 (1921),
12:38, *39–40n;* S. 202 (1921), **12:**38,
39–40n
—Scott Exclusion Act (1888), **3:**488–
89, *490n*
—seamen's accommodation bill, H.R.
7061 (1883), **1:**352, *354n*
—seamen's bills: H.R. 6399 (1896),
4:321, *323n;* H.R. 9685 (1902),
7:72, *89n;* H.R. 23,673 (1912),
9:111, *112n*
—seamen's law of 1790, **7:**174, *177n*
—seamen's law of 1898 (White Act),
5:15n; S. 95 (1897), **5:**14, *15n,* 67,
69n, 74–76, **6:**371, **7:**4, 7n, 73, 89n;
amendment of, S. 7337 (1903),
7:73, *89n*

—seamen's law of 1915, *9:10n*, 201–3,
446–47, **11:**14–16, 88, 311, **12:**501;
S. 4 (1913), **9:**9, *10n*, **10:**204, 526; S.
136 (1913), **9:**9, *10n*, 111
—Selective Service Acts: of 1917,
10:62, *64n*, 514n; of 1918, **10:**513–
14, *514n*
—Sherman Antitrust Act (1890),
4:26, *28n*, 35, 324n, 337–38, 338n,
6:178n, **7:**80, 473n, **8:**131n, 154–
55n, 165n, 362, 410, **9:**237, 237–
38n, **10:**123–24, 322, 323n, **11:**196n,
492–93, 494n, **12:**85n; AFL and,
7:323–25, 389, 392, 410; amendment of, **7:**310–11, 320n, 325, 372n,
8:153, 355n, 402–6, 413; and labor
organizations, **8:**41, 53, 62–63, 65–
68, 264–66, 318–19, 385, 463, 465–
66, 469–70, 477, 479–81, 483, 487–
88, 490, **9:**39, 40n, 72, 74–75n, 77,
82, 83n, 89, 247–50, 295, **12:**80n; re-
peal of (proposed), **12:**91–93, 453;
SG and, **7:**320n, 329–31, 335, 351,
420, **9:**76–78; use of, against strikes,
3:186, 243n
—Sherman Antitrust Act (1890), bills
to amend: H.R. 2808 (1897), **4:**343,
343n; H.R. 10,539 (1900, Littlefield
bill), **7:**80–81, *90n;* H.R. 19,745
(1908, Hepburn bill), **7:**320–21,
321–22n, **8:**361–62, 363n; H.R.
20,584 (1908, Wilson bill), *7:322n,*
325–26, 329n, 335, 346, 457, 458n;
S. 6440 (1908, Warner bill), **8:**362,
363n; H.R. 23,189 (1912, Bartlett
bill), **8:**374–75, 380, *381n,* **9:**93n;
H.R. 23,635 (1912, Clayton bill),
8:259n, 373–75, 380–81n, 424–25,
438n, 445, 448n, **9:**91, 94n; S. 6266
(1912, Bacon bill), **8:**374–75, 380,
381n, **9:**93n; Chilton bill (1912),
8:361–62; H.R. 1873 (1913, Bartlett
bill), **9:**9, *10n*, 40, 40n, 72, 89–90,
93n; H.R. 4659 (1913, Clayton bill),
9:91, *94n;* H.R. 5484 (1913, Clayton
bill), **9:**91, *94n;* S. 927 (1913, Bacon
bill), **9:**9, *10n*, 40, 40n, 72, 89–90,
93n; H.R. 15,657 (1914, Clayton
bill), **9:**10n, 88–93, *94n,* 96–97, 97n,
105, 140–41, 141n, 146, 146n, 152–
53, 153n, 154, 154n, 167–68, 168n,

175–76, 194, 197–98, 200–201,
208n, 446. *See also under* legislation,
U.S.: Clayton Act (1914)
—Sherman Silver Purchase Act
(1890), **3:**373, *375n*, 387, 554, 615,
4:14
—ship subsidy bills: H.R. 64, S. 727
(1899), **5:**164–68, *168n;* S. 529
(1905), **7:**4, *7n*, 73–75, 89–90n,
169–76, 177n; H.R. 10,644 (1922),
12:228, *228n;* H.R. 12,021 (1922),
12:228, *228n;* H.R. 12,817 (1922),
12:228, *228n;* S. 3217 (1922),
12:228, *228n*
—Sims bill, H.R. 8157 (1919), **11:**130–
31, *131n*
—Smith-Hughes Act (1917), **10:**47, *49n*
—Soviet Union, request for information regarding, H.Res. 635 (1921),
12:286–87, *288n*, 291
—sundry civil appropriation act for
1911, *8:132n;* H.R. 25,552 (1910),
8:132, *132n*, 460, 469, 492; H.R.
25,552, Hughes amendment of,
8:132, *132n*, 158, 460, 469, 492
—sundry civil appropriation act for
1914, *8:468n;* H.R. 2441 (1913),
8:468n, 469, 491–92, 494, 495n
—sundry civil appropriation bill for
1914, H.R. 28,775 (1913), **8:**460–61,
468n, 469, 478–79, 484, **9:**81–82,
82n, 353; H.R. 28,775, Hamill
amendment of, **8:**460–61, *468n*,
469, 478–79, 484, **9:**81–82, 82n, 353
—tariff act of 1890 (McKinley Tariff),
3:224–25, *225n*, 554n
—tariff act of 1894 (Wilson-Gorman
Tariff), **3:**548n, 553–54, *554n*, **4:**36,
38n, **6:**340n, **8:**264
—tariff act of 1897 (Dingley Tariff),
4:329, *329n*
—tariff act of 1909, *8:492n;* H.R. 1438
(1909), **8:**484, *492n*, **9:**89
—tariff act of 1913 (Underwood
Tariff), *8:493n;* **9:**89–90; H.R. 10
(1913), **8:**484–85, *493n;* H.R. 3321
(1913), *8:493n*
—trade union incorporation bill, S.
2474 (1883), *1:354n*
—trade union incorporation law
(1886), *1:354n*

—Transportation Act of 1920, **11**:216n, *274n*, 281, 312, 329–30, 469, 536, **12**:3, 103, 108–9, 113, 135, 300, 454

—uniform car coupler law (1893). *See* legislation, U.S.: Safety Appliance Act (1893)

—universal military training bills: H.R. 92 (1917), **10**:62, *64n*; S. 1 (1917), **10**:62, *64n*

—vessels in domestic commerce, bill to regulate, S. 3216 (1888), **2**:123, *123n*

—vocational education bills: H.R. 20,374 (1910), **8**:79, *80n*; S. 4675 (1910), **8**:79, *80n*, 182, 182n; S. 3 (1911), **8**:376, *381n*, 398–99, 399n

—vocational education resolution (1914), S.J. Res. 5 (1913), **9**:9, *10n*

—Volstead Act (1919), **12**:206, 429, 454

—War Expenditures Revenue Act (1898), *5:84n*

—War Revenue Act (1917), *11:543n;* H.R. 4280 (1917), *10:190n*

—War Risk Insurance Act (1917), *10:213n*, **11**:35; H.R. 5723 (1917), **10**:212, *213n*

—Webster amendment (to Esch railroad bill, 1919), **11**:332n

—woman suffrage amendment (proposed), **3**:25n, **10**:401, 402n; H.J. Res. 200 (1917), *10:471n. See also* U.S. Constitution: Nineteenth Amendment

—workmen's compensation bills: AFL bill (1909), **7**:452–53, 453n; S. 5382 (1912), **8**:442–47, *448n*, 457

—workmen's compensation law of 1908, *9:200n;* H.R. 21,844 (1908), **9**:199, *200n*, **11**:337n

—workmen's compensation law of 1916, *11:337n;* H.R. 15,316 (1916), **11**:335, *337n*

—workmen's compensation suit law (1917), *10:147–48n;* S. 2916 (1917), **10**:146, *147–48n*

Legislative Achievements of the American Federation of Labor (AFL), **9**:470–71, *472n*

legislative records of political candidates, AFL reports on, **6**:47–48, 492–93, 493n, **7**:16, 16n, 19, 58, 69, 72–84, 94–95, 99, 105–6, 333, 346–47, 347n, 391, 416, **8**:131–32, 387n, 395–96, **9**:165, **12**:34–35, 160–61, 169, 187, 436–37, 487–88

Lehigh Valley Railroad: strike/lockout, 1892, **3**:185, 214n; strike/lockout, 1893, **3**:432, *434n*

Lehmann, Frederick W., **8**:130

Leib, Francis, **1**:251, *251n*

Leipart, Theodor, **12**:369n

Leitch, Andrew S., **3**:205, *206n; letters to,* **3**:244–45, 248–49

Lelyfeld, Louis, **1**:414, *414n*

Lelyveld, Bessie, **3**:141, *142n*

Lelyveld, Hariet, **3**:141, *142n*

Lelyveld, Rosa, **3**:141, *142n*

Lelyvelt, Sadie, **3**:141

Lemieux, Rodolphe, **9**:314n

Lemke, James, **11**:*, *520n*, 547n; *wire to,* **11**:519–20

Lemmler, Mr. (New York City worker), **3**:378

Lenahan, John T., **4**:440, 444, *446n*

Leng, John, **3**:541, 542n

Lenin, Vladimir I., **10**:279n, 342, *344n,* 508–10, 512n, **11**:112, 371–72, 427, **12**:14, 64–65, 96, 98, 288n, 293, 294n

Lennon, John A., **4**:377, *379n*

Lennon, John B., **2**:*, 243, *244n*, 258, **3**:*, 14n, 58, *58–59n*, 107, 141, 397, 401, 411, 420, 430, 441, **4**:*, 4, 7n, *82n*, 106n, 127n, 357, 359n, 377, **5**:*, 20n, *38n*, 211, 365, 391n, 410, **6**:*, 19n, *57n*, 128n, 163n, 239, **7**:*, 7n, 453n, 455–56n, **8**:*, *6n*, 332n, **9**:*, *10n*, 71, 74n, 208n, **10**:*, *258n*, 306, 544, **11**:*, *22n;* at AFL conventions, **2**:263, 270, 391, 410, **3**:128, 128n, 135–36, 253n, 255, 427, 438, 613–14, 616n, 622, 647–48, **4**:82, 97, 270, 272n, 281, **5**:37, 38n, 40, 49, 52, 160n, 171, 172n, 173–74, 432, 432n, 437–38, **6**:54, 59–60, 207, 207n, 369, 373n, 492, 493n, 501, **7**:133–34, 142n, 269n, 277, 280n, 419, 422n, 423, **8**:6, 6n, 8–9, 16, 18n, 146n, 283, 286n, 295, 407, 409n, 411, **9**:23, 25n, **10**:257, 258n, 265–67, **11**:79–

81, 81n; at AFL Executive Council meetings, **4:**240–41, 266–67, 321–23, **6:**133–34, **8:**371, 501, 503–4, **9:**271–72, 436, 438; and cloakmakers' strike, 1910, **8:**110–12; and clothing cutters' strike, 1893, **3:**297–98; and Committee on Industrial Relations, **9:**422n; and election of 1906, **7:**96, 109, 110n; and election of 1908, **7:**349–50, 350n, 363, 376, 377–78n, 396–98, 416–17, 417n; election of, as AFL treasurer, **3:**661, **4:**95, 278n, 414n, **5:**57n, 177n, 294n, 445, **6:**209, 376n, 509n, **7:**281n, 427n, **9:**38n, 226n, 348n; and Granite Cutters' assessment, **5:**234, 237; and Homestead strike, 1892, **3:**206, 210, 218, 231, 238–39, 250; and jurisdiction questions, **5:**171, 173–74, 446–47, **11:**21–22, 22n; *letters from,* **3:**178–79, **5:**390–91, 446–47, **6:**464–65, 509–11, **7:**361–62, 396–98, 454–57; *letters to,* **4:**171–72, 207–9, **5:**385–86, 406–7, 448–50, **6:**126–27, 189–90, 312–14, 467–68, 512–13, **7:**215–17, **8:**35–38, 92–94, 171–73, 386, **9:**256–58, **11:**21–22; and Mc-Namara case, **8:**235, 238n; mediation of industrial disputes, **5:**106–7, 107–8n, 109, 340, 342n; and Northern Michigan copper miners' strike, 1913–14, **9:**12, 14n, 47n, 65; and printers' strike, 1891–92, **3:**125, 127, 130, 264; and Pullman strike, 1894, **3:**532; and temperance, **8:**38n, 92–94, 94n; and U.S. Commission on Industrial Relations, **8:**455–56, **9:**9, 138, 171–72, 311, 312n, 322

Lennon, Juna J. Allen, **3:**141, 142n, **7:**361; *letter to,* **6:**523–25

Lennon, Thomas, **4:**57

Lenox Hill Hospital, **12:**219n, 221, 222n, 456, 457n, 461, 462n

Lens: battle of, **11:**57, *58n;* capture of, **10:**522

Lentz, John J., **5:**326, *327n*

Lenz, Charles, **1:**346, *354n*

Leonard, Edwin F., **12:**9, *10n*

Leonard, James, **3:**241, *243–44n,* **4:**343, **6:**182–83, 183n, **7:***45n,* 225n, 498n; *letter from,* **7:**45; *letters to,* **5:**254–55, **6:**182–83

Leonard, William, **4:**123

Leopold, Nathan, Jr., **12:**516, 516n

Lesem, Samuel, **3:**386, *388n*

Lesley, A. F., **7:**286n

Leslie, Charles, **10:**252, *254n*

Lester, John A., *4:431n; letter to,* **4:**430–31

Lester, William, **4:**57, *57n*

Letter Carriers' Association, National Rural, **10:***,* 230, 231n

Letter Carriers of the U.S. of America, National Association of, **5:***,* 363n, **7:***,* 114, 115n, **10:***,* 230, 231n, **11:***,* 476n; and black workers, **11:**84n

—local: local 39 (Indianapolis), **12:**363

Letts, Frank C., **5:**17, *18n*

Leveling, C. J., **4:**416, *417n*

Leventritt, Edgar M., **8:**387, 389, *389n*

Lever, Asbury F., **9:**10n, *10:86n*

Levi, Abraham G., **8:**230, 231n

Levi, Isaac M., *8:244n,* 246–47; *letter from,* **8:**244

Levi and Co., **8:**230, 231n

Levin, Abraham, **4:**136, *137n*

Levin, Max, **11:**499–500, *500n*

Levy, M., **1:**237

Levy, Marcus, **1:***,* 18–19, *20n*

Levy, Myles J. K., **4:**262, 264n

Levy, Nathan E., **2:**244

Levy, Samuel, **8:**127

Levy, Sarah Gompers, **1:***,* 8, *8n,* 14, **3:***,* 141, *142n*

Levy, Sigismond, and Co.: injunction, **5:**241, 243–44n; lockout, 1900, **5:**241, 243n

Levy and Ullmann, **1:**113, *115n*

Levy Brothers, **1:**193–94, *198n,* 199, 408, 409n, 417–18; strike/lockout, 1886, **1:**374–77, 379, 381–82, 392

Levy et al. v. Rosenstein et al., **5:***244n*

Lewelling, Lorenzo D., **3:**276, *277n*

Lewis, Ansel M., **1:**237, *237n*

Lewis, Charles H., *10:108n; letter to,* **10:**107–8

Lewis, David J., **9:**90–92, *94n,* 98n

Lewis, J. C., **12:**550

Lewis, J. Harry, **4:**468, *468n*

Lewis, James H., **7:**361–62, *362n,* **9:**19, *22n,* 194

Lewis, Jesse L., *letter from,* **9:**464

Lewis, John L., **8**:*, 279–80, *280n*, **9**:46, 47n, 65, **11**:*, 128n, *138n*, 199, 212, 213n, 322, 473–74, 532n, **12**:*, 29–*30n*, 105, 297, 329, 469, 550; AFL presidential candidacy of, **11**:480–82, **12**:90; and Brackenridge, Pa., murders, **11**:123n; and Herrin, Ill., massacre, **12**:99n; *letters from,* **8**:475–76, **11**:492–93, **12**:150–51; *letter to,* **12**:377; and miners' strike, 1922, **12**:146; and permission to circularize Mine Workers, United, **12**:377, 377n; SG, *telephone conversations with,* **11**:200–205; *wire from,* **11**:198–99; *wires to,* **11**:138, 191–92, 195–96, 205–6, **12**:312, 315n

Lewis, Joseph, *letter to,* **11**:327–28

Lewis, Matt, *11:183n*, 315, 317n; *letter to,* **11**:182–83

Lewis, Reuben A., Jr., *12:403n; letter to,* **12**:401–3

Lewis, Thomas L., **4**:359n, **5**:*, *57n*, **6**:*, *70n*, **7**:*, *424n*, **8**:*, *9n*, 30, 93, 94n, 106n, 170; at AFL conventions, **5**:56, 57n, **6**:67, 70n, 366, 368n, 508, 509n, **7**:423, 424n, **8**:7, 137, 139n, 288, 290n

Lewiston (Idaho) Central Labor Union, *10:186n*

Lewiston (Maine) *Evening Journal,* **7**:87, 92n

Lewyn and Martin, **1**:419

Lian, Ole O., **9**:*, *507n; letter to,* **9**:501–7

Libby (company), strike/lockout, 1904, **6**:313–14, 314–15n

Liberal party (in United States), **12**:99n

Liberator (American Communist party journal), **11**:561n

Liberty League of Bisbee, Ariz., **10**:321

Liberty Loan drive, **10**:543

Lichtenstein, Benjamin, **1**:260, *263n*

Lichtenstein Brothers and Co., **1**:58, *59n*, 181–84, *184n*, 199, 418; *letter from,* **1**:392–94

Licking River Lumber Co., strike/lockout, 1908, **7**:378–80

Liebig, Albert F., **6**:*, 291, *292n*

Liebknecht, Karl, **10**:270, *278n*, 344, 344n

Liebknecht, Wilhelm, **1**:43n, *2:159n*, **3**:639, **4**:68; *letter to,* **2**:158–59

Liebold, E. G., **11**:508n

Lies, George P., **2**:125, *126n*

Life of John Marshall (Beveridge), **12**:171n

Liga General de Trabajadores Cubanos, **5**:182, *188n*

Liggett and Meyers Tobacco Co., **3**:304n, 343–44, 345n, 462, **5**:118

Light and Power Council of California, strike/lockout, 1913–14, **9**:38, 38–*39n*

Lighthall, George, **6**:*, 60, *62n*

Lightner, Hamilton W., **8**:232–34, 234n

Liley, Henry F., **11**:124, *125n*

Lilien, Herman, **7**:445n

Lilly, James H., **9**:480, *480n*

Linck, A. J., **10**:470n

Lincoln, Abraham, **1**:332, **3**:633, **4**:434, **5**:6, 506, **6**:333, 335, **8**:85, **9**:291, 293, 383, **10**:132, 206, 526, 566, **12**:92, 110, 135, 269, 511, 548, 562

Lincoln Motor Co., **10**:365

Linderman, Robert P., **4**:490–91, *499n*

Lindner, Henry, **3**:379, *382n*

Lindsay, Martha M., **12**:81, *82n*

Lindsay, Samuel M., **8**:455–56, *456n*, **12**:82n

Lindstrom, Ellen, **6**:483, *484n*

Linehan, James J., **3**:85, *86n*, 151, **4**:51, 157, 217n; at AFL conventions, **3**:252, 253n, 259–60, 613, 616n, 620, 646, **4**:93, 94n, 99, 99n; *letters to,* **3**:538–39, **4**:225–26

Lingg, Louis, **1**:*, *462n*, **2**:*, 53, *55n*, 56, 59

Linihan, J. E., **7**:302–4, *304n*

Linn, A. R., **11**:365n

Lipe, Morris, **2**:417, *418n*

Lipke, Edward, **10**:447, 449n

Lipman, Miss, **1**:11

Lippmann, L., and Sons, boycott, 1891–92, **3**:107, *108n*

Lippmann, Walter, **10**:115n, 138, *139n*, 204

Listman, George P., **11**:217, 217–*18n*

Litchman, Charles H., **2**:*, *50n*, 323; *letter to,* **2**:48–50

literacy test, for immigrants, **7**:91n,

155–56, **8:**330, **9:**80–81, 82–83n, 102, 103n, 403–4, 405n, 413–16, **10:**164–65, 166n, **12:**164; and right to vote, **11:**379–80, 380n

Lithographers, National Association of Employing, **7:**244, *246n*

Lithuania, workers from, **8:**345

Little, Frank H., **10:**126n, 163, *163n,* 173

Little, John, **6:**526n

Little, John E., **7:**48, *48n*

Littlefield, Charles E., **5:**326, *327n,* **6:**537, 539–43, **7:**90n; and election of 1906, **7:**58, 58n, 71, 89n, 99–101, 104n, 130; legislative record of, **7:**19, 72–84; SG campaign against, **7:**19–20, 58, 58n, 70–89, 96, 101n, 102–3, 107–8, 138–39, 143n, 183

Littleton, Martin W., **10:**132, *134n*

Littlewood, Herbert, **4:***, 250, *251n*

Livernash, Edward J., **5:**474n, **6:**261, *261–62n,* 270–71, **7:**139–40, 143n, 311, **8:**491

Liverpool Trades Council, **4:**88, 91n

living wage, **3:**395, 575, 604, **4:**446–47n, 489–90, **5:**319, **6:**148, **9:**20, 259n, **10:**408n, **11:**7–8n, 71n, 77n, 100, 159, 165, 233, 443, **12:**248. *See also* minimum wage; wages

Lizarraras, J. M., **6:**150n

Llewellyn Iron Works, bombing of, **8:**131n, 209n, 299n

Lloyd, George K., **3:**106n, 298, *300n,* **4:**109

Lloyd, Henry, **3:***, *129n,* 517n, 588, **4:***, 50, *50n,* 249n, 370, 432n, **5:***, *48n,* **7:***, 377, *378n;* at AFL conventions, **3:**126, 129n, 134, 614–15, 616n, 644–45, 651, 656–57, **4:**271, 272n, 283, 406–7, 408n, 412, 417n, **5:**44, 48n, 55; *letter to,* **3:**515–17

Lloyd, Henry D., **2:***, 301, *304n,* **3:***, 4, 463, *465n; letter from,* **3:**561–62; *letter to,* **3:**552–53

Lloyd George, David, **10:**71, *72n,* 74, 520, 565, **11:**30n, 357; statement of war aims, **10:**309, 310n

Loar, James A., **3:**67, *68n*

lobbying, **5:**153, **9:**3–8, 229, 230n

Lobster Fishermen's International

Protective Association, **7:***, 447–48, 449n

Lochner, Joseph, *6:393*–94n

Lochner, Louis P., **9:**274n, *10:93n; wire from,* **10:**93; *wire to,* **10:**94

Lochner v. New York, 6:394n, 420–21, **9:**243

Lockhart, R. H. Bruce, **10:**509–10, *512n*

Lockman, Frank, **6:**32n

Lockwood, Charles, **11:**399n

Lockwood Committee, **9:**292n, **11:**324n, 399, *399n,* **12:**80n; SG, *testimony before,* **12:**68–73, 73n, 74–80

Locomotive Engineers, Brotherhood of, **1:***, 339, 343, 353n, **2:***, 108n, 335, 339, **3:***, 94n, 331, 413, 442n, 511, 547n, **4:***, 273, 275n, **7:**91n, **8:***, 251, 253n, 313, **9:***, 450n, **10:***, 251n, **11:***, 78, 78n, 131n, 539n; affiliation of, with AFL, **2:**146–48, **3:**93, 466–68, **11:**78, 78n, 308–9, 309n, 328–32, 345; injunctions against, **3:**294n, 295–96, 559, 576; jurisdiction of, **10:**250–51, **11:**78, 78n, 308–9, 309n, 328–29

—conventions: 1888 (Richmond, Va.), **2:**146, 148, *148n;* 1912 (Harrisburg, Pa.), **9:**522, *523n;* 1921 (Cleveland), **11:**309, *309n*

—local: local 105 (New York City), **6:**408n

—strikes/lockouts: 1882 (Southwest, threatened), **1:**343, *353–54n;* 1888–89 (Chicago, Burlington, and Quincy Railroad), **2:**107, *108n,* 341, **11:**330; 1893 (Toledo, Ann Arbor, and Northern Michigan Railroad), *3:294n,* 329–31, **11:**330; 1905 (New York City), **6:**407, *408n,* 452, 521n

Locomotive Engineers and Firemen, Amalgamated Society of:

—strike/lockout: 1919 (Great Britain), **11:**164, *167n*

Locomotive Firemen, Brotherhood of, **1:***, 390, 391n, **2:***, 108n, 182n, 218, 335, **3:***, 94n, 215n, 246, 442n, 511, 547n, **4:***, 127n, 273, **6:***, 37n, 7ı*, 8ı*, 51n, 302n, **9:***, **10:***, **12:***; affiliation of, with AFL, **3:**93, 572, **4:**124–27, 211–16, **6:**36, **7:**402–3, **8:**249–53; and black workers,

4:125–26, 213, **8:**250, 253n, **10:**249; members of, *letter to,* **4:**211–16; and Southern Railway Co., **8:**253n

—conventions: 1890 (San Francisco), **2:**361, *362n,* 1892 (Cincinnati), **7:**403, *405n;* 1894 (Harrisburg, Pa.), **4:**125, *127n;* 1896 (Galveston, Tex.), **4:**125, *127n,* **10:**249

—local: local 149 (New York City), **6:**408n

—strike/lockout: 1905 (New York City), **6:**407, *408n,* 452, 521n

Locomotive Firemen and Enginemen, Brotherhood of, **1:***, **2:***, **3:***, **4:***, **6:***, **7:***, 400n, **8:***, **9:***, 50n, **10:***, 251n, **11:**131n, 539n, **12:***; affiliation of, with AFL, **10:**249–51; and black workers, **8:**253n, **10:**249; jurisdiction of, **10:**250–51

—conventions: 1908 (Columbus, Ohio), **7:**399, *400n;* 1910 (St. Paul, Minn.), *8:52n;* 1915 (Cincinnati), **9:**310n

Locomotive Firemen's Magazine (trade union journal), **3:**246

Lodge, Henry Cabot, **4:**145, *147n,* **5:**457, 459n, **6:**212, **7:**103, **8:**430, **12:**299n, 417n

Loeb, Daniel. *See* DeLeon, Daniel

Loeb, Richard, **12:**516, 516n

Loeb, William, Jr., **7:**229n, 388n

Loebenberg, Abraham B., **3:***, *132n,* 175, 227, 244, **4:**208, *209n;* at AFL convention, **3:**131, 132n

Loefler, E., **3:**430, 434n

Loewe, Dietrich E., **7:**409, **9:**233, 233n; boycott, 1902, *6:177–78n,* 440–42; injunction, **6:**440–41; strike/lockout, 1902, *6:177n.* See also *Loewe* v. *Lawlor*

Loewe v. *Lawlor,* **6:**177, *177–78n,* 328, 440–42, **7:**304n, 310–11, 311–12n, 312–13, 319, 338, **8:**40, 42, 70, 74, 75n, 402–6, 406n, 463, 466, 488–90, **9:**150, *233n,* 294, 319; AFL assessment for appeal of decision, **8:**76n, 78, 86; AFL donation to Hatters, **9:**233n; appeal of decision, **8:**41, 76n, 77–78, 79n, 193–94, 194n, 203, 204n, 265, 402–6, 406n; and Sherman Antitrust Act, **6:**178n, **7:**320n,

323–25, 329–32, 346, 351, 372n, 389, 392, 409–10, 420, **8:**41, 42n, 62–68, **9:**248–50

Logan Coal Operators' Association, injunction against, **12:**265n

Logansport (Ind.) Trades and Labor Assembly, **3:**583, *584n*

Lomax, Essex L., **3:**119, *120n*

London, Meyer, **8:**110–11, *114n,* 127, 127n, **9:**274n, 292n, **12:**39n, 208, 209n

London (packet ship), *1:16n; passenger list of,* entries for Gompers family in, **1:**16

London and Counties Labour League (Great Britain), **3:**146n

Londoner, Wolfe, **3:**34–35, *41n*

London Trades Council, **2:**399

Long, Breckinridge, **10:**120, *121n*

Long, Chester I., **7:**80, *91n*

Long, John D., **4:**395–96, *396n,* 490

Long, Norman, **7:**387

Longfellow, Henry Wadsworth, **6:**81, 84n, **8:**511n

Long Island Protective Association, *2:338n*

Longshoremen, Marine, and Transport Workers' Association, International, **4:***, **5:***, **6:***, 52n, 126, 127n, **7:***, 164n, **9:***, **10:***, **12:***; and black workers, **7:**187–89, 190n, 224–25, 225n, 460n; and IWW, **7:**111; jurisdiction of, **5:**445, **6:**51, 52n, 53–55, 373–76, 377n, 497–99, 499n, 502, **7:**270

—locals: local 251 (New Orleans), **7:**224–25, 225n; local 634 (Brunswick, Ga.), **7:**190n; local 681 (Havana), **7:**163, 164n; local in Tacoma, Wash., **7:**111

—strike/lockout: 1907 (Brunswick, Ga.), **7:**187–89, *190n*

Longshoremen's Association, International, **4:***, 99, 99n, **5:***, 249n, **6:***, **7:***, **9:***, 103, **10:***, 138n, 208n, 460, **12:***, 7n, 238, 241n, 268, 389–90, 440–41, 442n; and black workers, **9:**83n, **10:**459–60, **11:**84n; German intrigues with, **9:**304, 305n; indictment of members of, **9:**82, 83n; and industrial unionism, **9:**104n; and

IWW, **12:**48, 389–90; jurisdiction of, **10:**405–6, 406n; Pacific Coast District of, **9:**103, 104n, **10:**405–6, 406n; wage scale of, **12:**7
—convention: 1901, **5:**379n
—locals: local 38-A2 (Seattle), **12:**237–38, 241n, 267–68; local 38–18 (San Pedro, Calif.), **12:**48, 49n; local 231 (New Orleans), **5:**377, 379n; local 237 (New Orleans), **5:**377, 379n; local 251 (New Orleans), **5:**377, 379n; local 348 (Jacksonville, Fla.), **9:**83n; local 652 (Jacksonville, Fla.), **9:**82, 83n; local 797 (Jacksonville, Fla.), **9:**83n; local 847, ser. 2 (New York City), **10:**432; local 979 (New Orleans), **10:**459
—strikes/lockouts: 1917 (Seattle, threatened), **10:**137, 137–38n; 1918 (New York harbor, threatened), **10:**380–81, *381–82n,* 432–33, 434n; 1920 (Galveston, Tex.), **11:**426n; 1923 (Vancouver, B.C.), **12:**442n
Longshoremen's Protective Union and Benevolent Association (New Orleans), **5:**261, 262n
Longshoremen's Union, American, *4:249n*
Longuet, Frédéric J. L., **10:**551, *554–55n,* **11:**13–14
Longworth, Nicholas, **12:**346, *349n*
Looking Backward (Bellamy), **4:**305, *307n*
Loom Fixers' Association (New Bedford, Mass.), **4:**428, 429n
Lord, Alice M., **12:**241, *242n,* 271, 273
Lord, Frank B., *11:97n; wire to,* **11:**97
Lord, J. Walter, **9:**200n
Lord, James, **9:***, 271, *275n,* 352n, **10:***, 52n, 181, *182n,* 499n, **11:***, 139, *140n,* 391–92, 401, **12:***, 150–51, *152n; letter from,* **9:**351–52
Loree, Leonor F., **12:**103, *106n,* 114
Los Angeles, **6:**414–16, 416n, **7:**305–6, **8:**121–22, 122n
Los Angeles, Merchants' and Manufacturers' Association of, **8:**121, 122–23n, 146–47, *148n,* 248, 272; injunctions, **8:**121, 122n
Los Angeles breweries, boycott, 1910-?, **8:**148n

Los Angeles Central Labor Council, **8:**148n
Los Angeles County Council of Labor, *4:480n,* **6:**151n
Los Angeles Examiner, **6:**213, *213n*
Los Angeles Founders' and Employers' Association, **8:**122–23n
Los Angeles Metal Trades Council, *8:122n*
Los Angeles metal trades unions, injunctions against, **8:**121, 122n
Los Angeles Railway Co., strike/lockout, 1903, **6:**415, *416n*
Los Angeles Saddlery and Finding Co., **8:**148n
Los Angeles Times, **6:**415, **8:**349, **10:**390; boycott, 1893-?, **6:**212–13, *213n,* 417n; and Los Angeles brewery workers' strike, 1910–11, **8:**148n; and Los Angeles metal workers' strike, 1910–12, **8:**123n; and McNamaras, **8:**131n, 209n, 299n; SG, photo of, **8:**280, 281n, 282; strike/lockout, 1890–92, 1893-?, **6:**212–13, *213n,* **8:**129, 146
Los Angeles Times building, bombing of, 1910, **8:**128–30, *130–31n,* 136, 306–7, 349–50; SG, condemnation of, **8:**129, 220–24, 271–72, 349
Losky, Woyt, **3:***, *417n; letter to,* **3:**416–17
Lossie, William A., **5:**36–37, *38n*
Loucks, Henry L., **3:**262, *263n*
Loud, Eugene, **5:**457, 458n
Lougheed, James, **6:**159n
Loughran, Edward, **3:**139, *140n*
Louis Bossert et al. v. Frederick Dhuy et al., **10:**253, *254n*
Louis Geib et al. v. The International Brotherhood of Electrical Workers et al., **9:**70, *73n*
Louisiana Purchase Exposition, 1904 (St. Louis), **6:**121, *123n,* 237, 238n
Louisiana State Federation of Labor, *9:400n*
Louisville (Ky.) Federation of Labor, **7:**234, *236n,* 380
Louvain, destruction of, **9:**192, 193n, 195
Love, John W., **1:**408, 409n
Loveira y Chirino, Carlos, **9:**426–27n,

430, 432, *433*–34n, 436, 443n, 534,
10:9–11
Lovejoy, Elijah, **3:**633, *659n*
Lovejoy, Francis T. F., **3:**209, *211n*
Lovejoy, Owen, **3:**633, *659n*
Lovely, Collis P., **6:***, 15, *17n*, 233,
11:*, *288n; letter to,* **11:**287–88
Lovering, William C., **4:**500n
Lovestone, Jay, **12:**485n
Lovett, Robert S., **8:**321, *323n*
Low, A. Maurice, **9:**54, *57n*
Low, Seth, **4:**304n, **7:***321n*, **8:**118,
227n, 304n, 323, 324n, **9:**163; *letters
to,* **7:**320–21, **8:**220–26, 321–22
Lowden, Frank, **10:**263n
Lowe, Archibald B., **9:***, *49n; letter
from,* **9:**48–49
Lowe, Walter, *letter from,* **11:**148–49
Lowell, Abbott L., **8:**258, *259n*
Lowell (Mass.) Central Labor Union,
4:435n
Lowell (Mass.) Trades and Labor
Council, *4:435n*
Lowenthal, Daniel, **3:**140, *141n*
Lowman, John H., **6:**485, *486n*
Loyal Legion of Loggers and Lum-
bermen, *10:246n*, 299–300, 375,
417–18, 418n, 486–87, 489, 503,
12:234, 241n
—convention: 1918 (Spokane,
Wash.), **10:**487–88, *490n*
loyalty leagues, **10:**167, 183, 224, 338
Lozier, Henry, **1:**414
Lubin, David, *3:477n; letter to,* **3:**474–77
Lubitz, Yetta, **8:**243
Lucas, Edward, **7:**154, *155n*
Luce, Cyrus G., **2:**384, *385n*, 419
Luchtenburg, William H., *letter to,*
3:167–68
Ludlow, Colo., massacre, **9:**24n, 95,
95–96n, 97, 98n, 210, 221, 301, 329
Ludlow, William, **5:**180, 185–86, *187*–
88n, 231, 232n
Ludlow Valve Co.: boycott, 1906
(threatened), **7:**53–54, 54n; strike/
lockout, 1906, **7:**53–54, *54n*
Luke, Charles, **2:**35, *36n*
Lumbermen's Protective Association,
10:155n
Lumber Workers' Industrial Union,
12:442n

Lumber Workers' Union of Canada,
12:439–42, *442n*
Lunn, George, **10:**434n
Lusitania (passenger liner), sinking
of, *9:287n*, 288, 289–90n, 332n,
474–75, **10:**274, 560
Lusk Committee, **8:**398n
Lustig, Adolph, **1:**432, *433n*
Luther, Archie E., **11:**435, *435n*
Luther, Martin, **1:**29
Lux, Mrs., **3:**141
Luxburg, Karl-Ludwig von, **10:**326n
Luxemburg, Rosa, **10:**278n, 344n
Lynch, Charles D., **1:**231, *232n*
Lynch, David, **3:**207, *211n*, 240
Lynch, Edward J., **4:***, *229n,* **5:***, 157,
158n, 275, 366n, 377n, 435n, **6:***,
112, *112n*, 312n, 443; *letters from,*
4:227–29, **5:**276, **6:**311
Lynch, James, **1:***, 221, 228, *229n*, 259
Lynch, James E., *3:594n; letter to,*
3:593–94
Lynch, James M., **5:***, *293n*, 311, 464n,
6:*, 132n, *213n,* **7:***, 166, *169n*,
195n, **8:***, *6n*, 439n, **9:**280n, **12:***,
550, *553n;* at AFL conventions,
5:290–91, 293n, **7:**279, 280n, 423,
8:4–5, 6n, 13, 138, 142–43, 290; *letter
from,* **8:**302; *letters to,* **6:**212–13, **7:**301
Lynch, John J., **4:**157, *159n,* **5:**324,
324n
Lynch, Joseph L., **12:**541, *542n*
Lynch, M. W., *12:32n*
lynching, AFL condemnation of,
11:96, 96n, 114–15. *See also under
specific individuals*
Lynn (Mass.) Central Labor Union,
4:187–88, *189n*, 307n, **5:**491
Lynn (Mass.) Metal Trades Council,
11:186
Lyons, Joseph H., *11:50n; wire from,*
11:49; *wire to,* **11:**50–51

MacArthur, Walter, **3:***, *659n,* **4:***,
453n, *463n*, 486, **5:***, 406–7, *407n*,
464n, 474, **6:***, *206n,* **7:***, 42, *43n,*
8:*, 133, *134n;* at AFL conventions,
3:618, 620–21, 659n, **6:**205, 206n,
207–8, 375–76, 376n, 498, 499n; *letter to,* **4:**462–63
Macaulay, Mary J., **8:**404, *406n*

Macaulay, Thomas B. (Lord Macaulay), **11**:563, *564n*
MacDonald, Alexander, **1**:*, 219, *220n*, 235, 336
Macdonald, J., **4**:85, *91n*
MacDonald, James Ramsay, **3**:635, 637, *660n*, **10**:445, *446–47n*, 522, **11**:28, 373n
MacDonald, William, **9**:48n
Macfadyen, Alfred N., **5**:316n, *349n; letter to*, **5**:347–49
Macfarland, Charles S., **7**:*443n; letter to*, **7**:442–43
machinery. *See* mechanization
Machinery Manufacturers' Association: strike/lockout, 1906–7, **7**:50, *50–51n;* strike injunction, **7**:51n
Machinists, International Association of, **2**:*, **3**:*, **4**:*, 98–99, 99n, 270, 319–20, 500, 501n, **5**:*, 104n, **6**:*, 152n, 240n, 384, **7**:*, 115n, **8**:*, 35n, 56–61, 148n, 302n, **9**:*, 63n, 191n, **10**:*, 21n, 502n, **11**:*, 37n, 87n, 120n, 131n, 149, 319n, 344, 475–76n, 480n, **12**:*, 66n, 91n, 96, 337n, 349–50; AFL financial support of, **5**:xiv, 432, 432n; and black workers, **2**:297n, **3**:124, 135, 166–67, 167n, 343, 405–7, **4**:4, 7n, 130, 213, **11**:36–37, 37n, 148–49, 149n, 285, **12**:148, 341, 342–43n; disaffiliation of, from AFL, threatened, **9**:71, 73n; and Duplex case, **11**:406, 408n; and industrial unionism, **5**:291, **9**:62, **12**:62–63; injunction against, **7**:50, 50–51n; and IWW, **7**:41n; jurisdiction of, **3**:457, **4**:144, 144–45n, 148, 169, **5**:76–78, 103–4, 104–5n, 112–13, 113n, 172–76, 288–92, 292n, 331, 332n, 445, **6**:339n, **7**:221–22, 222n, **8**:105, 106n, 144–45, 170, **9**:346–47, 347n, **10**:505, 505n; and legislation for shorter workday, **9**:214–16, 220–22, 224n, 350–51n, **11**:82n; *letters to,* **3**:166–67, **5**:103–4; and Murray Hill Agreement, **5**:216n, 275, 278n, 332, 333–34n, 367, 432n; and National Cash Register Co., **6**:489; nine-hour campaign of, **5**:233, 332, *333–34n*, 340–41, 341n, 350, 356, 357n, 366n, 367–69, 369n, 372, 381; organizers,

8:189n, **10**:187–88, 189n; and steelworkers' organizing campaign and strike, 1919, **11**:28n, 85n, 362
—conventions: 1891 (Pittsburgh), **3**:124, *124n*, 166, 407; 1892 (Chicago), *3:167n;* 1893 (Indianapolis), **3**:343, *345n*, 405; 1901 (Toronto), **5**:367, *368n*
—locals: local 21 (Galeton, Pa.), **8**:35n; local 47 (Denver), **5**:394, 396n, **6**:15, 18n; local 159 (Philadelphia), **5**:126n; local 168 (Livingston, Mont.), **7**:25n; local 186 (Baltimore), **4**:319–20, 320n; local 204 (Schenectady, N.Y.), **7**:41n; local 217 (Philadelphia), **5**:126n; local 230 (Scranton, Pa.), **5**:331, 332n; local 252 (Vallejo, Calif.), **11**:149, 149n; local 257 (Jacksonville, Fla.), **7**:353–54, 355n; local 261 (Mobile, Ala.), **11**:486n; local 264 (Boston), **4**:145n, **5**:76, 78, 79n; local 303 (Philadelphia), **5**:126n; local 334 (Lynn, Mass.), **4**:187, 189n; local 348 (Philadelphia), **5**:126n; local 365 (Troy, N.Y.), **7**:53–54, 54n; local 368 (So. Bethlehem, Pa.), **8**:43, 44n; local 388 (Rock Island and Moline, Ill., and Davenport, Iowa), **6**:215n; local 421 (Elmira, N.Y.), **6**:152n; local 466 (Bath, Maine), **7**:77, 90n; local 471 (Lynn, Mass.), **7**:50, 50–51n, 115n; local 634 (Charlestown, Mass.), **7**:115n
—strikes/lockouts: 1896 (Cleveland), **4**:177, *178n;* 1899 (Rock Island and Moline, Ill., and Davenport, Iowa), **6**:215, *215–16n,* 1899–1900 (Philadelphia), **5**:124, *126n,* 205–6; 1900 (Chicago), **5**:214, *216n;* 1900 (Cleveland, Detroit, Philadelphia, and Paterson, N.J.), *5:216n,* 233; 1901–2, *5:333–34n,* 367–69, 369n, 372; 1901–2 (Denver), **6**:15, *18n;* 1903–5 (Elmira, N.Y.), **6**:152, *152n,* 1906 (Troy, N.Y.), **7**:53–54, *54n;* 1906–7 (Lynn, Mass.), **7**:50, *50–51n;* 1907 (Houston), **7**:222, *222n;* 1909–10 (Galeton, Pa.), *8:35n;* 1915 (Bridgeport, Conn.), **9**:304, *305n;* 1917 (Michigan Central Railroad, threatened), **10**:187–88, *189n;*

1920–21 (Mobile, Ala.), **11**:484–85, *486n*

Machinists, National Association of, **2**:*, 297n, 409, **3**:*, 63n, **4**:*, **5**:*, **6**:*, **7**:*, **8**:*, **9**:*, **10**:*, **11**:*, **12**:*; and black workers, **2**:296–97, 297n, 409–11, **3**:62

Machinists' Union of America, International, **2**:*, 297n, **3**:*, 62, 63n, 407, 407n, 649–50, **4**:*, 144n; jurisdiction of, **3**:457, 462, 463n, **4**:144, 144–45n, 148, 169

—convention: 1891 (New York City), *2:413n*, **3**:77–78

—locals: local 2 (New York City), **3**:457; local 28 (Boston), **4**:145n; local in St. Louis, **3**:462

MacIntyre, Frank, **12**:200, *202n*

Mack, Norman, *7:377n*, 387; *letter to,* **7**:376–77

MacKay, Florence Gompers, **11**:486, 487n, **12**:457n. *See also* Gompers, Florence (SG's granddaughter)

MacKay, Shirley, *11:487n; letter to,* **11**:486–87

MacKay, William H., **11**:486, *487n,* **12**:457n

Mackenzie, Kenneth, **1**:214, *216n,* 231, 260, 262, 263n

Mackey, Thomas J., **3**:297, *298n*

Mackie Fuel Co., George K., strike/lockout, 1921, **11**:481n

Mack v. *Wright et al.,* **8**:190–91, *191n*

MacNair, William, **2**:332, *337n*

MacNaughton, James, **9**:183, *184n*

Macrae, John, **11**:522, *523n,* **12**:322n, 378; *letters to,* **12**:321, 365, 384–85, 533–35

MacStay, Arnold B., *8:77n; letter to,* **8**:76–77

MacSwiney, Terence, **11**:357, *358n*

MacVeagh, Franklin, **5**:294, *307n,* 310, 311n, 464n, **6**:13n

Macy, R. H., and Co., strike/lockout, 1904-?, **6**:380, *381n*

Macy, V. Everit, **10**:52n, 220–21, *221n,* 318n, 361, 363n

Madden, Henry, **8**:233, 234n

Madden, Martin B. (congressman), **12**:346, *349n*

Madden, Martin B. "Skinny" (steamfitter), **6**:469n, **7**:364, *364n,* 429, **8**:149

Madden, Michael, **3**:103n

Madden, Stephen, **3**:*, 207, *211n,* **4**:*, 345–46, *347n*

Mader, Fred, **12**:56, *61n*

Madera, Adolph, **3**:345, *346n*

Madero, Francisco, *9:160n,* 360, 425, 432; overthrow of, **9**:96n, 158, 436–37; and overthrow of Díaz, **8**:193n, 320n, **9**:158, 212n, 324; reforms of, **9**:325, 327, 436, 443n; Zapata and, **9**:307n

Madison, Edmond H., **8**:479, *492n*

Madras (India) Labor Union, **12**:241n

Madsen, John A., *10:137n,* 476, **12**:389–90, *390–*91n; *wire from,* **10**:137

Magna Carta, **9**:290

Magnes, Judah L., *10:94n; wire from,* **10**:93

Magnolia Brewery, strike/lockout, 1907, **7**:222, *222n*

Magón, Ricardo Flores, *8:193n; letter to,* **8**:192–93

Magoon, Charles E., **7**:163, *164–*65n, 221

Maguire, James, **7**:413, 414n

Mahan, James B., **11**:40n, 57, *58n*

Mahany, Rowland, **10**:62n

Maher, Edward, **2**:301, 304

Maher, James J., **5**:*, 91, *93n,* 149–50

Maher, James P., **8**:41, *42n,* 77

Mahon, William D., **3**:*, *660–*61n, **4**:*, *93–*94n, 182, 191n, **5**:*, *39n,* 250, **6**:*, *57n,* 234n, 270, 271n, 531n, **7**:*, *70n,* 342n, **8**:*, 30, *31n,* 173n, **9**:*, *34n,* 65, 208n, 255, 337, **10**:*, 33–35, *38n,* **11**:*, 19, *21n,* 345, 404n, 488n, 532, **12**:*, *23n,* 295; and AFL affiliation of railroad brotherhoods, **11**:78n, 308–9; at AFL conventions, **3**:653–54, 661n, **4**:92, 94n, 275–76, 278, 278n, 280, 407, 409n, **5**:37, 39n, 42–43, 49–50, 52, 57, 167, 169n, 171, **6**:53–54, 56, 504, 509n, **8**:139, 293, 293n, **9**:31–32, **12**:87n; election of, as AFL vice-president, **10**:475, **11**:93n, 321, 321n, 482, **12**:97n; as fraternal delegate to TUC, **9**:162, 469, 485; and Industrial Conference, 1919, **11**:128n, 167; and industrial disputes, **6**:13n, 142, 194n, 408n, 414–16, 416n,

9:47n; *letters from,* **4:**118–19, **5:**346–47, 377–78, **6:**529–31, **7:**69–70, 240–42, 341–42, **8:**304–5, **9:**206–7, 388–90, **11:**197–98, **12:**21–23; *letters to,* **4:**115, **5:**262–63, **6:**407–8, **9:**533–34, **11:**446–47; and miners' strike, 1897, **4:**346, 348, 350, 357, 359n, 366; and SG, death of, **12:**541; *wire to,* **11:**78

Mahon et al. v. *Guaranty Trust and Safe Deposit Co.,* **9:**208n

Mahoney, Charles E., **7:***285–86n,* **9:**65; indictment of, **9:**182–83, 184n; *letter to,* **7:**283–85

Mahoney, Jeremiah F., **1:**457, *459n*

Mahoney, Nellie, **6:**484n

Mahoney, Timothy S., **6:**463, *464n*

Mahoney, William, **12:**431, *433–34n*

Mailly, William, **7:**144–45, *146n*

Maine (battleship), **4:**464, 466n, 469–70

Maine: election of 1906, **7:**19–20, 57–58, 58n, 70–89, 96, 99–100, 101n, 102–3, 107–8, 138–39, 143n, 183; election of 1908, **7:**377; organizing in, **6:**397–99, 402–4, 435–39

Maine State Federation of Labor, **6:***439n*

—conventions: 1905 (Bangor), **6:**438, *439n;* 1906 (Lewiston), **7:**71, *89n*

Maintenance of Way Employes, International Brotherhood of, **4:***, **5:***, **9:***, 50n, 342, **11:***

Maintenance of Way Employes and Railway Shop Laborers, United Brotherhood of, **4:***, **5:***, **9:***, **10:**431n, **11:***, 60n; and black workers, **11:**46n, 84n; jurisdiction of, **11:**59–60, 60–61n, 105

—strike/lockout: 1920 (threatened), **11:**249–58, *258–59n*

Maisel, Robert, **10:**128n, *162–63n,* 236, 241n; and creation of American Alliance for Labor and Democracy, **10:**156–57n, 160n; *letters to,* **10:**161–62, 225–28, 382–83

Majestic Manufacturing Co., **8:**200

Malby, George R., **3:***456n; letter to,* **3:**456

Male Nurses' Association of Massachusetts, **9:**416–18

Malines, German defeat at, **9:**193n

Malley, James, **2:**8, *11n*

Mallinson, John, **4:**248, *249n*

Mallory, William J., **7:***22n; letter from,* **7:**21–22

Malloy, John, **4:**123

Maloney, Elizabeth, **10:***82n; wire from,* **10:**81–82

Maloney, Robert S., **6:**355–57, 360n

Maloy, James, **1:**218, *220n*

Mammoth Vein Coal Co., **10:**323n

Mance, Alfred W., **6:**466, *467n*

Manchester (England) Trades Council, **4:**88, 91n

"Manchester Martyrs," *1:285n*

Manee, James T., **7:***461n; letter from,* **7:**459–61

Mangan, John, **6:**496, *497n,* **8:**402, *402n*

Manhattan Single Tax Club, **4:**15n

Manion, Edward J., **11:***, 460–61, *461n,* **12:**467n

Manley, Joseph, **12:**431–32, *434n*

Manly, Basil M., **9:**312n, **11:**18n, 468, 470–71, *471n,* **12:**167; and election of 1924, **12:**431–33, 433n, 474, 476n, 478

Manly, Thomas I., *11:547n; letter from,* **11:**546

Mann, A. J., **5:**336–37

Mann, Horace, **6:**100n

Mann, James R., **9:**24, *25n,* **11:**276, *278n,* 281

Mann, Thomas, **2:***, 352, *353n,* 399, 407, **3:***, 16, *18n,* 94n, 516, **4:***, 249, *249n,* **9:**337; *letters to,* **3:**92–94, 222–24, 504–5, 587–89

Manning, Henry Edward Cardinal, **6:**335, *340n,* **11:**32–33, 34n

Manning, James F., **9:***166n; letter to,* **9:**164–66

Manning, John J., **11:***, 401, *403n,* **12:***, 126, *127n,* 301, 443–45, 445n, 450, 461n; and SG, death of, **12:**543

Mannison, Edward, **11:**122, *123n*

Man Nobody Knows, The (Barton), **9:**17n

Manrique, Aurelio, **12:**392n

Mansfield, Frederick W., **9:**454, 455n

Mansion, Joseph R., **2:**12, *13n,* **4:**222–23, *223n*

Mantle, Lee, **4:**490, 492, 496–98, *499n*

Manual of Common Procedure (AFL), **2:**142, *142n,* 202–3, **5:**400, *400n*

Manuel, Joseph C., **3:***, 228, *229n*
Manuel II, *8:320n*
Manufacturers' Information Bureau, **5:**330–31, *331n*, **8:**50
Manufacturers' Union (Havana), **7:**221n
Manvury (manager, Porto Rico Sugar Co.), **6:**424
marble and freestone cutters (Baltimore), **4:**481–82, 483n
Marble Cutters, Reliance Labor Club of, **2:**337n
Marble Polishers, Whitestone Association of, **2:**337n
Marburg, Theodore, **5:**483, *483–84n*
Marbury, Elisabeth, **8:**39, *40n*
Marden, William H., **1:***, 458, *460n*, **2:***, 23, *24n*, **3:***, 256, *258n*, 532; *letter from*, **3:**268–69; *letter to*, **3:**269–70
Mares, Baudilio, **5:**185, 188n
Marine Band, U.S., SG and, **4:**180–81
Marine Cooks' and Stewards' Union of the Pacific, injunction against, **7:**117, 118n
—strike/lockout: 1906 (San Francisco), **7:**93, *93n*, 118n
Marine Engineers' Beneficial Association of the U.S. of America, National, **11:***, 435n
Marine Firemen's Union, Pacific Coast, injunction against, **7:**117, 118n
—strike/lockout: 1906 (San Francisco), **7:**93, *93n*, 118n
marine sack sewers and cargo repairers (New Orleans), **7:**224–25, 225n
Marine Trades Council of the Port of New York and Vicinity, **7:**170, 177n
Marion (Ind.) Central Trades Council, **7:**407, *408n*
Maritime Association (Brunswick, Ga.), strike/lockout, 1907, **7:**187–89, *190n*
Mark Cowen and Co., strike/lockout, 1917, *10:336n*
Markel, Herman, **11:**355
Markel, Lester, *12:228n; letter to*, **12:**227–28
Marks, Marcus M., **6:**236, *236n*, **8:**40n; *letter to*, **8:**166–69
Marot, Helen, **9:**422n
Marron, Thomas, **2:**332

Marsh, Albert, **2:**149, *150n*, 156
Marsh, Benjamin, **12:**433n
Marsh, Ernest P., **10:***, 154, *154–55n*, 195, 195n, 262
Marshall, Isaac D., **3:**482, *482n*
Marshall, John, **12:**250
Marshall, Leon C., **10:**304–6, *306n*
Marshall, Matthew, **2:**284–86, *286n*
Marshall, Richard C., Jr., **11:**116, *117n*
Marshall, Thomas R., **8:**273, *277n*, 386n
Marston Worsted Mills, strike/lockout, 1907, **7:**184–85, *186n*
Martel, Arthur, **9:**458, 460n
Martí, Jose, **4:**132n
Martin, Abraham, **1:**8
Martin, Franklin, **10:**21n, 103n
Martin, J. Henry, **4:**40, *42n*
Martin, James (blacksmith), **12:**8, *10n*
Martin, James (sheriff), **4:**376–77n, 380, *381n*, 383, 387, 439–40, 442, 445, 464
Martin, John A., **8:**89, *90n*, 100
Martin, Thomas R., **4:**444, *446n*
Martin, Thomas S., **8:**492, *493n*, 495, **10:**366–67
Martin, William, **2:***, *79–80n*, 243, 283, **3:***, 59, *61n*, **7:***, 463, *464n;* at AFL conventions, **2:**76, 79, 269; *letters to*, **2:**81, 429–30
Martine, James, **9:**195n
Martínez, Edmundo E., *9:307n*, 326–27, 426–27n, 436–38, 443n, 465; *letter from*, **9:**305–7; *letter to*, **9:**360–62
Martinez, Joseph N., *6:31n; letter from*, **6:**30–31
Martinez, Vincente, **10:**256, 257n
Martinez and Co., *1:109n;* strike/lockout, 1877, **1:**108
Martyr to His Cause, A (McNamara Ways and Means Committee), *8:249n*
Marx (clothing manufacturer), *3:340n;* and mediation of clothing cutters' strike, 1893, **3:**314, 316–17, 319
Marx, Karl, **1:**21, 22n, 23, 34, *43n*, 432, **2:**159n, 426, **3:**10, 640–41, **4:**104, 154, 338–39, **5:**511, **9:**5
Maryland, election of 1906, **7:**119–20, 120n
Mary of Teck, **10:**563, *567n*

Mason, Arthur, **12:**426n
Mason, John W., **4:**360n, 363n, 365
Mason, T. H., **11:**84n
Mason, William, *letter to,* **6:**220–22
Mason Forwarding Co., **9:**83n
Masons, Ancient Free and Accepted:
—lodges: Dawson Lodge 16 (Washington, D.C.), **12:**517; St. Cecile Lodge 568 (New York City), **12:**550
Massachusetts: constitutional convention, 1917–19, *10:161n;* and labor standards, maintenance of, **10:**76, 77n
Massachusetts Bureau of Statistics of Labor, **1:**290, *327n,* 329
Massachusetts State Board of Arbitration, **2:**24n
Massachusetts State Board of Conciliation and Arbitration: and Boot and Shoe Workers, **7:**37, 39n; and Douglas, W. L., Shoe Co., **7:**400n; and Team Drivers, **5:**496–97n
Massachusetts State Federation of Labor, **2:**269, *272n,* **7:**313, *314n,* **11:**146n
Master Builders' Association: strike/lockout, 1906–7, **7:**49–50, *50n;* strike injunction, **7:**50n
Master Painters', Paper Hangers', and Decorators' Association (Dayton, Ohio), **6:**144, 145n
Master Teamsters of Boston, **5:**496n
Masters, Edgar Lee, **6:**237, *238n*
Matewan (W.Va.) incident, **11:**294–96, *296*–97n
Mathews, James W., *9:422n; letter to,* **9:**419–22
Matteson, Harry T., *7:25n*
Matthews, May, **11:**89
Mattill, Henry, *2:319n; letter to,* **2:**318–19
Mattyeser, Isaac, **3:**141, *142n*
Maurer, James H., **10:***, *241n,* **11:***, 263, *265n,* **12:***, 388, *389n; letter from,* **10:**240–41
Mauretania (passenger liner), **11:**111n, 460n
Mawdsley, James, **4:***, 90, *91n,* 100, 101n, 103, 106n
Maximalists, **10:**275
Maximon, Selma C., *12:321n;* SG, meeting with, **12:**320

Maxwell Motor Co., **10:**365
May, Mathilde H., *12:462n,* 503, 504n, 541–42
May, Moses, **3:**141, *142n*
May, Mrs. Moses, **3:**141
May Day, **3:**370; in Seattle, **12:**254, 266–67, 272
Mayer, Julius M., **6:**392–93, *394n*
Mayo, P. H., and Bro., **4:**394, *395n*
mayors, conference of, 1914 (Philadelphia), **9:**206–7, *208n*
Mayor's Committee on National Defense, **9:**358–59, 359n
Mazur, Paul M., *9:229n; letter to,* **9:**228–29
McAdoo, William G., **5:**363n, *9:299*–300n, 358, 437, **10:**546n, **12:**409, 467n; as Director General of Railroads, **10:**320n, 366, 382n, 494, 505n, **11:**238; General Order No. 27 of, **10:**320n, 505n; *letters to,* **9:**296–99, **10:**5–8; and Pan-American financial conferences, **9:**299–300n, **10:**9n
McAnarney, Henry A., **11:**274, *275n*
McAnnich, Elisha H., **3:**196n
McArdle, Peter J., **7:***, *329n,* 472, 473n, 480, **8:***, *9n,* 30, 31n, 53–55; at AFL convention, **8:**7, 12n
McArdle, Thomas E., **9:**276n; *letter to,* **9:**275–76
McAteer, L. H., *letter to,* **4:**167–68
McAuliffe, Patrick F., **1:***, 371, *371n*
McBride, C. F., **3:**69, *70n*
McBride, John, **1:***, *458n,* **2:***, *32n,* 127, **3:***, 31, *32n,* 272, 356, 430, 480, 481n, **4:***, *53n,* 106n; at AFL conventions, **1:**457, 460, 470, **2:**72–75, 78, 411–14, **3:**126, 128, 128n, 137, 252, 253n, 256, 259, 434n, **4:**80, 92, 96, 273, 275n; and AFL presidency, **4:**3–7, 7n, 53, 55, 66, 124–25; charges against, **4:**4–5, 7–8n, 80–81; illness of, **4:**4; *letters from,* **2:**30–32, **4:**55, 66; *letters to,* **3:**173–74, 220–21, 301–2, 663, 667–68; and Pullman strike, 1894, **3:**579n
—AFL presidential candidacy: 1893, **3:**437–38, 441; 1894, **3:**610, 662–63, 665, 669; 1895, **4:**78–79, 82, 93–96, 98–99
McBryde, Patrick, **2:***, 221, *222n,* **3:***,

69, *70n,* 535, 586, **4:***, *82n,* **9:***, 336, *341n;* at AFL conventions, **3:**644–45, 655–56, 660n, **4:**82; *letter to,* **2:**255–56; *wire from,* **3:**532–33
McCabe, Felix, **6:**291, *292n*
McCabe, Frank M., **6:**408, *409n,* 461
McCabe, Robert C., *wire to,* **10:**477
McCabe, William, **1:***, *446n; circular of,* **1:**445–46
McCabe, William P., *6:442n; letter to,* **6:**440–42
McCall, Samuel W., **7:**87, *92n,* **8:**82
McCallin, Andrew, **3:**661, *664n*
McCallister, H. G., **7:**234, 236n
McCallum, Alfred, **4:**94–95n, 236, *237n*
McCammon, Joseph K., **5:**203, 205–6, *207n,* 225, 230n, 478–81
McCann, John A., **11:**526, *526–27n*
McCarthy, Daniel J., **12:**56, *61n*
McCarthy, Dennis, **1:**261, *263n*
McCarthy, Frank H., *3:253n,* **5:**286n, **6:**287–88, *289n,* **8:***, *81–82n,* **9:**418n, 492n, **10:***, *542n,* **11:***, *146n,* **12:***, 53, *54n;* at AFL conventions, **3:**251, 253n, 257, 259, **5:**284, 286n, 290; *letter from,* **10:**541–42; *letter to,* **8:**80–81; *wire to,* **11:**145–46
McCarthy, James S., *11:376n; letter to,* **11:**374–76
McCarthy, Jeremiah G., **3:**599, *606n*
McCarthy, Patrick F., **6:***, 439, *439n*
McCarthy, Patrick H., **5:**338, *339n,* 518, **7:**383–84, **8:**282, **11:**89–90, 92n, 313n
McCartney, George, *3:41n*
McCauley, James, **6:**276–77, *278n*
McChord, Charles, **10:**320n
McCleary, James T., **4:**172, *172n,* **5:**497, 499
McCleary, William H., **3:**190–91, *191n*
McClellan, Heard S., **11:**219, *220n*
McClelland, John, **1:**288
McClelland, W. W., **1:**390
McClennan, A. G., **3:**23
McClintic, George W., **12:**169, *171n*
McClory, Joseph E., **9:**311n, **10:***, 265, *266n,* 370
McClure's Magazine (periodical), **7:**240n
McClurg, Harry O., **9:**487, *488n*
McCollum, J. Brewster, **8:**191, *191n*

McComas, Louis E., **6:**232n, **7:**85, *91n*
McConegly, William F., **3:**208, *211n,* 218
McConville, Matthew A., **7:**148, *150n*
McCord, William H., **2:**332, *337n*
McCormack, George B., **10:**288, *288n*
McCormick (AFL representative), **7:**198
McCormick, F. A., **6:**287
McCormick, Joseph M., **11:**453, *454n,* **12:**82n
McCounder, John, **2:**332
McCoy, Edwin T., **10:**321, *323n; letter from,* **10:**336–39
McCoy, Frank, and Co., strike/lockout, 1886, **1:**379, 381–82, 392
McCoy, Robert T., **11:**284, *286n*
McCrackan, George B., **5:**279n, *313n; letter from,* **5:**312–13
McCracken, Eugene, **11:**551n, 553
McCraith, Augustine, **3:***, *611n,* 667, **4:***, 5, 66n, 78, 295, 392, 392n, 394, **8:***, 120, *121n;* at AFL conventions, **3:**609, 611n, 627–30, 657–58, 662, **4:**97n; and AFL organizers, **4:**239–41, 269; charges against, **4:**278n; charges against SG, **4:**275–78; election of, as AFL secretary, **3:**667, **4:**95; *letter to,* **4:**192; SG and, **4:**xxin, 279n
McCray v. U.S., **11:**513, *514n*
McCreash, Timothy A., **10:**213–14, *218n*
McCullen, Edward J., **6:**494–95, *496–97n*
McCulley, W. J., *7:119n; letter to,* **7:**118–19
McCullough, Ezra S., **8:**53, *54n,* 146, 146n, 289, 290n
McCullough, John (police officer), **2:**331, *336n*
McCullough, John (shipwright), **7:**243n
McCullough, John H., **1:**110, *112n,* **2:**331, *336n*
McCullough, Theodore W., *7:422n;* at AFL conventions, **7:**419, 422n, 423, **9:**212, 213n, 345, 346n, **11:**83, 84n
McCurdy, Robert, **10:**359
McDermott (delegate), **4:**109
McDermott, James, **1:**457, *459n*
McDermott, James T., **7:**457, *458n,* **8:**100

McDermott, John A., **10**:329, 330n

McDonald, Daniel, **5**:*, 469, *470n*, **6**:*, 408, *408n*, 448, 459, 462–63

McDonald, Duncan, **8**:*, *290n*, **9**:*, *52n*, **11**:17n, **12**:433n; at AFL conventions, **8**:286–88, 404; at Mine Workers', United, convention, **9**:52, 52n, 62–63, 63n, 66–67, 68n, 69–70, 72n

McDonald, George, **6**:153, *154n*

McDonnell, Joseph P., **1**:*, *85n*, 108, **2**:*, *29n*, 156, 184, 214, 241, **4**:*, *295–96n*, **5**:*, 16n, 286, *287n;* and Amalgamated Trades and Labor Union, **1**:98–100, 152; and *Labor Standard,* **1**:203n, 264; *letters to,* **2**:28–29, 137, **4**:294–95; and *New York Unionist,* **1**:268n; and Workingmen's Party of the U.S., American Section, **1**:83, 84n, 85

McDowell, Claude K., **12**:99n

McDowell, Mary Eliza, **6**:483, *484n*

McDowell, William, **12**:82n

McEnerney, Mary, *10:83n; wire from,* **10**:81–82

McFeely, James M., **1**:455, *456n*, 460

McGahren, John, **4**:444, *446n*

McGann, Lawrence, **5**:308n

McGeory, William J., **11**:316, *317n*

McGhee, Richard, **9**:477n, 487

McGill, James, **3**:*, 133, *134n*

McGill, Patrick, **7**:493, *498n*

McGillicuddy, Daniel J., **7**:138–39, *143n,* **11**:337n

McGinley, John P., **8**:43, *44n*, 449

McGivern, Edward, **12**:225n

McGlynn, Edward, **2**:*, 369, *371n,* **3**:*, 217, *218n*, 428

McGlynn, Michael M., **3**:430, *434n*

McGoorty, John P., **7**:361, *362n*, 363

McGovern, Francis E., **9**:353, *355n*

McGrady, Edward F., *10:77n*, 266n, **11**:476n, **12**:347, 452n, 550; as AFL Legislative Committee member, **11**:401, 465–66, 525, **12**:147n, 212n, 423, 424n; and election of 1924, **12**:184n, 433, 433n, 456, 461n, 467n, 474, 483; *letter to,* **10**:76 77

McGrath, John J., **3**:429–30, *434n,* **4**:157, *158n*

McGrath, William J., **12**:551, *554n*

McGregor, Hugh, **1**:*, *60n*, 83, **2**:*, 66, *69n*, 99, 106, 276, **3**:*, 369, *370n,* **4**:*, 387–88, *388n*, **5**:*, 91–92, *93n,* 116–17, 149, 151n, 356–57, 357n, **6**:*, 34, *35n; letters from,* **1**:59–60, **5**:155–56

McGuigan, Bernard, *5:17n; letter to,* **5**:16–17

McGuire, Christine, *6:546n,* **7**:55–57; *letter from,* **6**:546

McGuire, James, **10**:434n

McGuire, James G., **7**:254, *254n*

McGuire, John J., **3**:400

McGuire, Kate, **6**:546n

McGuire, Lillian, **6**:546n

McGuire, Myrtle, **6**:546n

McGuire, Patrick C., **2**:332, 338n

McGuire, Peter, **6**:546n

McGuire, Peter J., **1**:*, *166n*, 287, 335, 353n, 387, **2**:*, 23n, *24n,* 103, 111, 156, 206n, 316, 423–24, **3**:*, *32n,* 58, 106, 211, 246, 264, 267, 430, 512n, **4**:*, *50n,* 82n, 115, 119, 282, 288, 327–28, 338, 383n, 385, 388–89n, 500, **5**:*, *19n,* 126n, 157, 158n, 356, 357n, **6**:*, *8n,* 34, **7**:*, *56n,* **9**:*, 336–37, *341n;* and AFL conventions, **1**:457, 469–70, **2**:26n, 70–72, 75, 77–79, 165–66, 170, 259, 272, 411–13, **3**:127–28, 129n, 133, 135–36, 250–51, 253n, 258–59, 434n, 438, 626, 628, 644, 648–51, 654–55, 659n, 664, **4**:79, 99, 270–72, 272n, 279, 415, **5**:18, 50–51, 53n, 161, 162n; at AFL Executive Council meetings, **4**:240–41, 266–67, 323; and AFL per capita tax, **2**:133; and Amalgamated Carpenters, **2**:376; and arbitration, **1**:349–50; and black workers, **4**:407, 408–9n, 430; charges against, **6**:5–8, 8n, 38, 38n, 92, 130, **7**:56n; and charges against McBride, **4**:5, 81; and Chicago Civic Federation, **3**:553n; circular of, mentioned, **6**:7, 8n; death of, **6**:546; as delegate to TUC, **4**:50, 50n, 55, 58–60, 66, 85–91, 508; election of, as AFL vice-president, **3**:661–63, **4**:95, 278n, 414, **5**:57n, 177n; and Granite Cutters' assessment, **5**:233, 238; Harrison, meeting with, **3**:157;

and Haymarket defendants, **2:**55n; and Homestead strike, 1892, **3:**206, 210; and immigration restriction, **4:**283–84; *interviews with,* **4:**61–64, 66–68; and KOL, **1:**275–76, 385–86, 455, 460, 463–64, **2:**181, 219, 230, 232, 243, **3:**182, 441, 517, 517n, 606; *letters from,* **1:**279–81, 389–90, 395–96, 425–26, 436–37, 450–51, **2:**27–30, 38, 129, 178–79, 199, 218, 228, **3:**69–70, **6:**308–9; *letters to,* **2:**23–25, 99, 183–84, 186–88, 194–95, 198–201, 204–5, 209–10, 212–13, 290–91, **3:**31–32, 64, 83–85, 138–40, 147, 150–53, 221–22, 233–34, 245, 595–97, **4:**147–48, 369–71, 376–79, 383, 386–88, 431–32, 503–4, **5:**116–17, **6:**129–30; money for family of, **6:**546n, **7:**55–57; and non-partisan political action, **3:**130–31, 256–57; and Pittsburgh congress, 1881, **1:**161, 165; and Powderly, **2:**215, 217; and Pullman strike, 1894, **3:**532, 534, 535n, 562; as secretary of AFL, **2:**180, 186–87; SG, criticisms of, **2:**27, 29–30, 38; and Social Democratic Workingmen's Party, **1:**84n; suspension of, from office, **5:**398, 398–99n; and Terre Haute, Ind., congress, 1881, **1:**160; and textile workers' strike, 1898, **4:**430–31, 477

McGuire, Thomas B., **1:***, 420, *421n,* 436, 439, **2:***, 18, 331–32, *336n,* 341–42, **4:***, 249n, 332–33, *333n*

McHenry, Michael J., **2:**66, 68, *68n,* 75

McHugh, Edward, **4:***, 247–48, *249n*

McHugh, James F., **4:***, 285, *286n*

McHugh, John, **6:**277, *278n*

McHugh, Larkin C., **1:**460, *462n*

McIntosh, Edward S., **1:***, 390, *390n*

McIntyre, David, **1:**282, *283n*

McIntyre, Frank, **9:**72, *74n,* **10:**438n

McIntyre, Peter J., **3:**257, *258n*

McKaughan, Benjamin F., *5:414n; letter to,* **5:**413–14

McKay, Charles, **6:**443, *445n*

McKay Starching Machine, **3:**109n

McKee, Robert, **5:**453n, **6:***, 502, *504n,* **7:***, 33, *36n*

McKee, Sidney S., **5:**416n, 424, *425n*

McKees Rocks, Pa., steel plants, **10:**170, 170n

McKenna, Charles F., **6:**424–25, 428, 429n

McKiernan, Michael F., **2:**14, *15n*

McKillop, Daniel P., **10:**468, *470n,* 472n

McKim, James, **3:**156, *156n,* **4:**57

McKimmie, Oscar A. M., **8:**498, *499n*

McKinley, Alexander B., **3:**34, *41n*

McKinley, Ida Saxton, *5:390n; letter to,* **5:**390

McKinley, William, Jr., **3:**19, *19n,* **4:**45, 221n, 405n, 464, 466n, 489n, 506n, **5:**15n, 64n, 67–68, 69n, 148, 151n, **12:**511; AFL Executive Council, meeting with, **4:**321–22; assassination of, **5:**390, *390n,* 404, 405n, **6:**437; and Boer War, **5:**122n; and election of 1896, **4:**185n, 221n, 235, 247; *letter to,* **4:**419–20; SG, meetings with, **4:**343, 503–4, **5:**67

McKinley National Memorial Association, **5:**426, 426n

McKinney, Joseph W., **3:***, *533n,* **4:***, 83, *83–84n,* 359n, 454; *wire from,* **3:**532–33

McKinney, William H., *2:139n; letter to,* 138–39

McKinnon, Charles H., **6:**454

McKinstry, Delia, **4:**108, 108n

McKinstry, William H., *4:108n; letters to,* **4:**106–8, 114–15

McLaren, James, **3:**280, *281n*

McLaughlin, Daniel, **1:***, *459n,* **2:***, *69n,* 243; at AFL conventions, **1:**457, 460, **2:**66–67, 79

McLaughlin, John P., **10:**165, *166n*

McLean, H. C., **3:**404, *405n*

McLean, James H., **1:**352, *354n*

McLean, Robert E., **5:**453, 453n, 454, *454n*

McLean County (Ill.) Coal Co., **7:**417n

McLeod, Duncan, **10:**228n, 273

McLuckie, John, **3:**207, *211n*

McMackin, John, **1:***, 360, *362n,* **2:***, 369, *371n,* **5:**361n

McMahon, James, **6:***, 168, *169n*

McMahon, Martin T., *3:29n; letter to,* **3:**28–29

McMahon, Mr. (National Cash Register informant), **7:**193
McMahon, Thomas F., **12:***, 53, *54n,* 97n, 550; and AFL women's department, considered, **12:**406, 408n, 445, 450, 451n
McManigal, Ortie, **8:**306, 309, *312n*
McManus, John, **1:**263n
McMenimen, Walter L., **11:**348, *349n,* 538, 539–40n
McMillan, James, **5:**308n
McMorrow, Edward, **9:**388, *390n*
McMurphy, George L., *3:478n; letter to,* **3:**477–78
McMurtry, George G., **5:**387, *388n*
McNab, Gavin, **10:**209n
McNally, Gertrude M., **11:***, 466, *467n,* **12:***, 245–47, *247n,* 347
McNally, John, **1:***, 85, *85n,* 108
McNamara, James B., **8:***, 214, *214n,* 274–75, 300, 305n, 352; arrest of, **8:**131n, 213, 273–74, 294, 307, 350; confession of, **8:**299, 299n, 300–302, 306, 311, 352, 359; trial of, **8:**131n
McNamara, John J., **6:***, *515*–16n, **7:***, *13n,* **8:***, *209n,* 274–75, 300, 352; arrest of, **8:**131n, 209, 209n, 213n, 230–31, 231n, 235, 238n, 249n, 273–74, 294, 307–8, 310, 350; confession of, **8:**299, 299n, 300–302, 306, 311, 352, 359; *letter from,* **6:**514–15; *wire to,* **8:**214
McNamara, Patrick J., **11:**348, *349n*
McNamara case, *8:131n,* **9:**280n; AFL Executive Council and, **8:**213, 213–14n, 234–38, 238n; AFL organizers and, **8:**231n, 237; Burns and, **8:**209n, 214, 272–74, 293, 295n, 301, 305–6, 308–9, 350, 353; Darrow and, **8:**136n, 213–14n, 235, 237, 248–49, 249n, 294, 299–300, 305, 305n, 346–47, 347n, 351, 358–59, 360n; and financial appeals, **8:**213, 213–14n, 234–38, 238n, 249n, 254, 274–76, 290–91, 350–51, 359; movie on McNamara, kidnapping of, **8:**249n; SG and, **8:**209, 213, 213n, 214, 214n, 224–26, 235–37, 249n, 273–76, 299–305, 308–10, 313–15, 347, 350–52, 360n, 428, **9:**279, 300; trial, **8:**335, *336n,* 358–59, 412–14,

414n, 431–37. *See also* McNamara, James B.; McNamara, John J.
—conferences: Apr. 1911 (Indianapolis), *8:213n,* 350; Apr.–May 1911 (Indianapolis), **8:**213, *213–14n,* 310, 312n, 350–51, 355n; June 1911 (Indianapolis), **8:**236, *238n,* 241, 254, 255n, 310; Dec. 1911 (Indianapolis), **8:**302, *302–3n*
McNamara Defense Fund, **8:**238–39n, 249n, 291, 294, 300, 311, 351, 359, 413, **9:**279
McNamara Legal Defense Committee, **8:**236, 413
McNamara Ways and Means Committee, **8:**237, 249n, 254, 257; *circular of,* **8:**306–12
McNeil, John A., **7:***, 75, *89n*
McNeil (member of National Civic Federation), **5:**483
McNeill, Adeline J. Trefethen, **4:**50, 50n
McNeill, George E., **1:***, 83, 259, *260n,* 437, **2:***, *184n,* 381, 382n, **3:***, 12, *14n,* 480, 640, 655, **4:***, 9, *9n,* 50n, 249n, 432n, **5:***, *39n,* **6:***, 34, *35n;* at AFL conventions, **2:**264, 267, 270–71, 413–14, 416, **3:**126, 128, 128n, 129–30, 136–37, **4:**271, 272n, 273–74, 278, 405, 406n, **5:**37–38, 39n, 46, 55; and depression of 1893, **3:**377–82; and eight-hour campaign, **2:**163, 184, 188, 188n, 264, 267, 288, 413–14; *letters to,* **2:**248–49, **4:**49–50, 203–4
McNulty, Frank J., **7:***, *279n,* 482n, **8:***, 16, *17n,* 138, 139n, 149, 151n, **9:***, *38n,* **11:***, *92n;* at AFL conventions, **6:**493n, **7:**276–79, 279n, **8:**17n, **9:**38n, **11:**88–89, 92n
McPadden, Myles, **1:***, 162, 167, *167n*
McPherson, John, **2:**332, *337n*
McPherson, Robert, **4:**330n
McPherson, Smith, **8:**131n
McQuade, Thomas J., **12:**541, *541–42n*
McReynolds, J. C., **9:**106n
McSorlcy, William J., **8:***, 115, *116n*
McSweeney, Edward F., **3:***, 360–61, *361n,* 487, **4:**56, **5:**326; *letters to,* **3:**507–8, 668–69

McTaggart, James, **5**:365, 366n
McVey, David A., **12**:332–33, *333–34n*
McVey, George H., **2**:*, 55, *55n*, 370, **3**:*, 298, *300n*
McVicker, Louis E., **7**:337, *338n*
McWade, Robert M., **10**:189n, 371, *372n*, **11**:512n
McWhinney, Thomas A., **12**:69, *74n*
McWilliams, J., *letter to*, **2**:89–90
Meade, Claude, **11**:36, *37n*
Meador, C. H., **9**:494, 495n
Meadows, Spurgeon P., *12:364n; letter from*, **12**:362–64
Meat Cutters and Butcher Workmen of North America, Amalgamated, **4**:*, 286, 287n, **5**:*, 18n, **6**:*, 315n, **7**:*, 343–45, 345–46n, **10**:*, 218n, 280n, 403–4, **11**:*, 381, 381n, 453n; and black workers, **11**:84n; jurisdiction of, **7**:343–45, 345–46n; label of, **5**:78, 79n; and women workers, **5**:17
—locals: local 34 (Buffalo, N.Y.), **5**:17; local 127 (Stockton, Calif.), **6**:39, 40n; local 188 (Toronto), **11**:381, 381n; local 634 (Denver), **10**:214, 218n
—strikes/lockouts: 1904, **6**:313–14, *314–15n*, **7**:345, **11**:567, 571n; 1917–18 (Chicago, threatened), **10**:279, *280n*, 285n, 302–3, 442, **11**:453n; 1921 (Chicago, threatened), *11:453n;* 1921–22, *11:453n*, 567, *571n*
Meatie, W. R., **5**:39n
meatpacking arbitration, 1918–21, *10:280n*, 363n, **11**:84, 451, *453n*
Meat vs. Rice. See Some Reasons for Chinese Exclusion. Meat vs. Rice (Gutstadt)
Mecartney, Harry S., **7**:395n
mechanization, **1**:90, 282, 315–17, **2**:91, **3**:109n, 556, **5**:33, 45–46, 50–51, 138, 159, 183, 190, 195, 203–4, 213, 225, 229, **6**:418–19, 480, 543, **7**:258, 261, 264, 294, **8**:33, 263, 319, 514, **9**:53, 118, 139n, 502, 531, **10**:117, **12**:182, 521; in brewing industry, **5**:106–7, 107n, 108–9, 110n; and Chicago Building Trades Council, **5**:215n; in cigar industry, **1**:45–46, 49–50, 53, 90, 94, 417, 419, *421n*, 423, **2**:73, 124–25, **5**:434–35, **12**:303–8, 308n; and coopers, **5**:83, 106–7, 107n, 108–9, 110n; in garment industry, **12**:306; in glass bottle industry, **12**:305; labor-saving, **1**:94, 105, 282, 316–17, 328–30, 363, 366, 419, 423; in mining industry, **9**:273, **12**:306; in printing industry, **4**:392, **5**:83, 291, **12**:305–6; SG and, **1**:328, **2**:153, **4**:243, **5**:82–83, 106–9, 110n, 152, **6**:418, **12**:304–8; in shoe industry, **7**:39n, **12**:306; in textile industry, **1**:328–30, **12**:304
mediation of industrial disputes, **3**:303–4, **5**:115n, 218n, 307–8n, 379n, 384n, 411, 411n, 489–90, 490n, 496–97n, **6**:13–14n, 29n, 46n, 104n, 245n, 314n, 453n, 484n, **7**:164n, 187–89, 190n, 340n, 378–80, 400n, 456n, 473n, **8**:40n, 114n, 205, 253n, **9**:57n, 307n, 450n, 457n, 507n, **10**:57n, 242, 280n, 288n, 306n, 408n, 539, **11**:140, 164, 453n, **12**:6, 315n; SG and, **3**:283, 303–4, 304n, 305–40, 343–44, 601–2, 605, **4**:167n, 176–77, 229–30, 230–31n, 319–20, 332, 340, 394, 395n, 399–400, 400n, 401–4, 404n, 456–60, 460–61n, 483–85, 500, 501n, **5**:236n, 247n, **6**:40, 45–46, 103–5, 241, 484n, **7**:309n, 399, **8**:110–12, 114n, 452n, **9**:54–56, 85. *See also* arbitration; conciliation
Medina Dam, **8**:316, *316n*
Mee, John, **3**:*, 400, *401n*
Meeker, Royal, **8**:455, *456n*
Meiklejohn, George D., *5:100n; letter from*, **5**:100
Melhorn, Sallie F., **8**:493n, 495–96, *497n*, 498
Mellen, James H., **2**:48, *50n*
Mellor, Thomas, *7:151–52n*
Melms, Edmund T., **7**:130, *142n*
Melnotte, Claude, **6**:79
Melon, José R., **7**:163, 165n, 220, *221n*
Melville, Albert L., *12:390n; letter from*, **12**:389–90
Mems (British labor leader), **2**:352
Menche, Adam, **2**:*, *288n*, 410, **3**:*, 34, *41n; letter to*, **2**:287–88
Mendel Brothers, **1**:195, *198n*, 199

Mendelsohn, George, *9:236n; letter from,* **9:**235–36
Mendelsohn, Herman S., *3:340n;* and mediation of clothing cutters' strike, 1893, **3:**309, 319, 334–35
Menge, Edward, **9:**213n
Menke (business agent, Ladies' Garment Workers), **6:**155
Menocal y Deop, Mario G., **10:**71, *72n,* 256, 257n
Mercer County (N.J.) Central Labor Union, **8:**134–35, *135n*
Merchant Marine League, **7:**169
Merchants', Manufacturers', and Employers' Patriotic League of America, **10:**183
Merchant Tailors' Association of the U.S., **6:**191n
Mergenthaler typesetting machine, **12:**306
Merlino, F. Saverio, *4:244n; letter to,* **4:**242–44
Merriam, Charles E., Jr., **8:**483, *492n*
Merriam, Henry C., **5:**93n, 95–96, *98n,* 114–15, 133–34, 149, 151n
Merrick, William M., **7:***, *15n,* 48; *letter from,* **7:**14–15
Merrill, Albert G., **7:**77, 90n
Merrill, Oscar C., **12:**347, 348–*49n*
Merriman, Henry S., **7:**23, *25n*
Merriss, L. W., **6:**140; *letter from,* **6:**140–41
Merritt, Charles H., **9:**284, *285n*
Merritt, Charles L., *2:22n,* **4:**196; *letter from,* **2:**20–22
Merritt, Harry D., **5:**468, *470n*
Merritt, James S., *6:292n; letter from,* **6:**291–92
Merritt, Walter G., **9:**284, *285n,* **11:**408n, **12:**398n
Merritt Expanded Metal Fireproofing Co.: boycott, 1903–6, *6:292n;* strike/lockout, 1904–6, **6:**292, *292n*
Mertens, Corneille, **11:***, 223, *224n,* **12:**369n
Mesabi Range strike, 1916, **9:**488, *489–90n,* 504–5
Mesker Brothers, and Tin, Sheet Iron, and Cornice Workers, **4:**36, 147, *148n*
Messemer, Michael J. B., **1:**206, *207n*

messenger boys, **1:**306–7
Metal Mechanics, International Association of Allied, **4:***, **5:***, 275–77, 278n, 285, 330–31, 332n, 460n, **6:***, 240n; dues of, **5:**323; jurisdiction of, **5:**322–23, 331, 332n; label of, **6:**239, 240n
—local: local 29 (Dayton, Ohio), **5:**460n
—strike/lockout: 1901–2 (Dayton, Ohio), *5:366n*
Metal Pattern Makers, Filers, and Fitters, **5:**323
Metal Polishers', Buffers', and Platers' International Union of North America, **3:**356n, **4:***, **5:***, **6:***, **7:***, **8:***, **9:***, **11:***
—convention: 1891 (Toledo, Ohio), **3:**89–90n
—strike/lockout: 1893 (Chicago), **3:**356n
Metal Polishers', Buffers', Platers', and Brass and Silver Workers' Union of North America, **5:***, **6:***, **7:***, **8:***, **9:***, 224n, **11:***
Metal Polishers', Buffers', Platers', and Brass Workers' Union of North America, **4:***, 227–28, 229n, **5:***, 275–77, 278n, 285, 376, 377n, **6:***, **7:***, **8:***, **9:***, **11:***
—locals: local 1 (Detroit), **4:**227–28, 229n; local 5 (Dayton, Ohio), **5:**366n; local 133 (Dayton, Ohio), **5:**366n
—strike/lockout: 1896 (Detroit), **4:**227–28, *229n*
Metal Polishers', Buffers', Platers', Brass Molders', and Brass and Silver Workers' International Union of North America, **5:***, **6:***, 311n, **7:***, 155n, **8:***, **9:***, **11:***; jurisdiction of, **6:**311, 312n
—locals: local 5 (Dayton, Ohio), **7:**193, 194n; local 6 (Chicago), **6:**443, 445n, 446, 446n, 448; local 13 (St. Louis), **7:**154n; local 83 (Chicago), **6:**445–46n; local 127 (Chicago), **6:**445–46n; local 143 (Chicago), **6:**445–46n; local 212 (Chicago), **6:**445–46n
—strikes/lockouts: 1904 (Chicago),

6:443, *445–46n;* 1906 (St. Louis), **7:**153, *154n*

Metal Polishers', Buffers', Platers', Brass Molders', and Brass and Silver Workers' Union of North America, **5:***, **6:***, **7:***, **8:***, 200, 201n, **9:***, **11:***

Metal Polishers', Buffers', Platers', Brass Molders', and Brass Workers' Union of North America, **5:***, **6:***, **7:***, **8:***, **9:***, **11:***
—strike/lockout: 1901–2 (Dayton, Ohio), **5:**364–65, *366–67n,* 460n, 489–90

Metal Polishers' International Union, **5:***, **6:***, **7:***, **8:***, **9:***, **11:***, 85, 262n; and black workers, **11:**84n
—local: local 21 (Toronto), **11:**381, 381n

Metal Trades, Federated, **4:**126, *127n,* 347n

Metal Trades Association of the Pacific Coast, **5:**432–33n

Metal Trades Council of St. Louis and Vicinity, **5:**278n, 287n, **7:**154n

metal trades councils, **5:**380–81, 382n, 519, **6:**492; in Birmingham, Ala., **10:**376–77, 378n, 385–86, 440–41; in Canal Zone, **11:**393n; in Los Angeles, **8:**122n; in Lynn, Mass., **11:**186; in Norfolk, Va., **10:**222–23; on Pacific Coast, **5:**432–33n; in Portland, Ore., **10:**208–9, 209n; in Schenectady, N.Y., **11:**411; in Seattle, **11:**62, 63n, **12:**266, 272; in St. Louis, **5:**278n, 287n, **7:**154n

Metal Trades Federation of North America, **5:**287n, 382n, **6:**112, 174, 175n; officers of, **5:**435, 435n

metal trades unions, **2:**110–12, 115–16; jurisdiction of, **9:**388–90, 390n
—conferences: 1900 (Louisville, Ky.), **5:**284–85, 287n; 1900 (Washington, D.C.), **5:**275, *278n;* 1901 (St. Louis), **5:**285, *287n,* 381–82, 382n
—national alliance of, **5:**284–85, 287n, 381–82, 382n; AFL and, **5:**284–85, 287n; and Machinists, **5:**275–77, 278n, 285; SG and, **5:**275–77, 287n. *See also* Metal Trades Federation of North America
—strikes/lockouts: 1901–2 (San Fran-cisco), **5:**432, *432–33n;* 1910–12 (Los Angeles), **8:**121–22, *122–23n,* 136, 147, 221; 1919 (Toronto), **11:**72–73, *74n;* 1919 (Winnipeg, Man.), **11:**75n

Metal Workers' International Union of America, United, **5:***, 277, 278n, **6:***, 443, 445n, 447, 452, 457, 462–63, 468

Metal Workers' National Union of North America, **1:***, 390, 391n, **2:***, 110–12, 111n, 115–16, 235

Metcalf, Henry B., **2:**325, *326n*

Metcalf, Richard H., **3:***, 624, *659n*

Metcalf, Victor H., **5:**457, 458n, **6:**477, *477n,* 527n, **7:**147

Metropolitan Opera Co., strike/lock-out, 1906, **6:**516–17, *517–18n*

Metropolitan Street Railway Co., **5:**81, 82n

Mettee, Charles H., **2:**66, *69n*

Metz, Herman, *letter to,* **4:**127–28

Metzger, Martin, **5:**357, 357n

Mexican-American War, **9:**434n

Mexican Confederation of Labor. *See* Confederación Regional Obrera Mexicana

Mexico: AFL and, **9:**158–59, 324, 326, 326n, 360–61, 436, 458, 462; agrarian reforms in, **9:**307n, 439, 443n, **12:**391, 392n; German intrigues in, **10:**34–35, 38n; religious persecution in, **9:**440, 443n, 458; schools in, **9:**465; uprising in, 1911, **8:**317, *320n;* uprising in, 1923–24, **12:**391–92, *392n;* wages in, **9:**439; workers in, **9:**427–28, 429n, 439, 467, **12:**391, 392n (*see also specific unions*)
—strikes/lockouts: 1907 (textile work-ers), **9:**306, *307n;* 1916 (general strike), **9:**426n, 499–500, 500–*501n*
—and United States, relations with: American exploitation of, **11:**312–13; American prisoners in, **9:**426n, 434–35, 435n, 437; anti-American feeling in, **9:**439; Tampico incident, **9:**95, *95–96n;* under Taft, **8:**192, 193n; U.S. intervention in, possible, 1915, **9:**306, 307n, 326–27, 361, 363n, 437; U.S. Punitive Expedi-tion in, 1916–17, **9:**212n, *426n,* 437;

U.S. recognition of government of, **12:**100, 100–101n; U.S. war with, threatened, 1916, **9:**428, 430–33, 433n, 434, 434n, 435, 435n, 438–39, **10:**10
—workers from, **6:**149–50, 150–51n, **9:**352n, 425, 443n, **11:**285, **12:**32, 282–83; importation of, **8:**316, 316n, 429–30, 430n, **10:**164–66, 166n, **11:**338–41, 341–42n, 494–95, 495–96n; organization of, **8:**46–47, **9:**43, 443n, 456, 466–68, **10:**265, 266n; and railroad shopmen's strike, 1922-?, **12:**120; as strike-breakers, **7:**93n, **9:**438–39, **11:**285, 495

Meyer, Aaron N., **7:**230–31, 231n
Meyer, Henry, **4:**400, 400n, 401–3
Meyers, H. B., *3:465n*
Meyers, John C., **3:***, 455, *455n*
Meyers, Mr. (bricklayer?), **3:**145
Meyling, Herman, **9:**173
Michaels, Joseph R., **5:***, 141, *142n*
Michaelson, Joseph, **6:**277, *278n*
Michaelson et al. v. *U.S.,* **12:**373, *373–74n*
Michels, James L., **1:**219, *220n*, 228
Michigan Central Railroad, strike/lockout, 1917 (threatened), **10:**187–88, *189n*
Michigan State Court of Mediation and Arbitration, **5:**59n
Michigan State Federation of Labor, **6:**230, *231n*
Michigan Stove Co., strike/lockout, 1918–19, **10:**447–49, *449n*
Micou, Benjamin, **5:**228, *231n*
Middleton, George W., **3:**381, 383n
Midvale Steel Co., **5:**189–90, 192–97
migrant workers, **8:**9, 339, **9:**142, 143n, 507n
Mikel, George E., **12:**88, *88n*
Mikol, Maurice, **7:***, 18, *19n*
Milburn, William H., **3:**34, *41n*
Milchrist, Thomas E., **3:**522–23
Miles, Charles A., **8:**49n, 116, *117n*
Miles, Herbert E., **10:**483, *484n*
Miles, Nelson A., **3:**521, **5:**21, *29n*
Milholland, Chief Inspector, **2:**343
Milian, Francisco, **6:**71n
militarism: AFL and, **9:**524, 524–25n,

529, **10:**43; German, **5:**11, 23, **10:**30, 35, 88–89, 129, 132, 202, 268–71, 309, 352, 508, 558–59, 564, 566, **11:**118; and imperialism, **5:**10, 23, 135–36; and workers, **4:**108, 145–47, 301–2, **5:**10–11, 23, **8:**206–7, **9:**380–81, **10:**35
military training, **9:**332n; AFL and, **9:**345–46, 379, 524, 524–25n, 526; SG and, **9:**329–30, 374–75, 380, 382, **10:**37–38
Military Training Camps Association of the U.S., **9:**332n
militia, **6:**361–63, **8:**326, 357, 512, **9:**379, 382
Milke, Frederick K., **1:***, 390, *391n*
Mill and Factory Operatives' Union, Dundee (Scotland) and District, **3:**540, *542n*
—strikes/lockouts: 1893, *3:542n;* 1895, *3:542n*
Miller, Abraham, *9:227n; letter from,* **9:**227
Miller, Alfred E., **11:**62, *63n*
Miller, Amasa S., **3:**51, *55n*
Miller, Bert, *letter to,* **12:**101–2
Miller, Charles, **11:**564n, **12:**39n
Miller, Charles L., **2:**332, *338n*
Miller, Charles S., *letter to,* **3:**178–80
Miller, Cyrus, *letter from,* **10:**324–26
Miller (delegate), **3:**132
Miller, Frank C., **1:**397, *398n*
Miller, Fred, **11:**391n
Miller, George, **3:**117–18, *119n*, 280
Miller, Guy E., **6:**459, *460n*, **9:**179, *183n*
Miller, Hall, and Hartwell Co.: boycott, 1891–92, *3:109n,* 164, *164–65n,* 176; strike/lockout, 1891–92, **3:**109, *109n*
Miller, Henry, **3:***, 260, *260n*, 436–37, 437n
Miller, Hugo A., **1:***, 371, *372n*, 457, 462n, **2:***, 25, *25n,* **5:***, *511n; letter from,* **5:**510–11
Miller, Isaac B., **2:**74–75, *76n*
Miller, James M., **7:**94, *95n*
Miller, John A., *11:207n; letter from,* **11:**207; *letter to,* **11:**215–16
Miller, Joseph D., *12:33–34n; letter to,* **12:**32–33

Miller, Louis E., **10:**156, *157n,* 162
Miller, Max, **6:**277, *279n*
Miller, Owen, **3:***, 135, 137, *138n,* **4:***, 410, *411n,* **5:**453n, **8:**12n; *letter to,* **3:**498–99; *wire from,* **3:**532–33
Miller, Spencer, Jr., **12:**191, *192n,* 227
Miller, Thomas, **8:**80n
Miller, William H. H., **3:**404, *405n*
Miller, William J. (cigarmaker), **1:***, 68, *69n*
Miller, William J. (typographer), **3:**436, *437n*
Miller Brothers, strike/lockout, 1892, **3:**197, 197n
Millet, Jean-François, **7:**442, *443n*
Mills, Ernest, **9:***, *44n; wire from,* **9:**43–44
Mills, Henry S., **4:***, 335, *335n,* 429–30, 431, 432n, **5:***, 43, *48n,* 52; *letters to,* **4:**425–27, 447–49
Mills, Ogden, **9:**403n
Mills, Walter T., **3:**223, *224n*
Milton Ochs Co. v. Amalgamated Clothing Workers of America, **12:**302, *303n*
Milwaukee, Industrial Council of, **3:**459, 490, 497
Milwaukee Brewers' Association, **5:**107n, **6:**453n
Milwaukee Building Trades Council, **4:**182, *183n,* **9:**354, **12:**122
Milwaukee Central Labor Union, *1:217n. See also* Milwaukee, Industrial Council of
Milwaukee-Downer College, **9:**354, *355n*
Milwaukee Federated Trades Council, **2:**65, *68n,* **3:**459, *460n,* 490–97, **4:**6, 119, 119n, 183n, *6:25n; circular of,* **6:**24–25, 25n; *letter from,* **7:**64–67
Milwaukee Female College, **9:**355n
Milwaukee Journal, **12:**122–23
Milwaukee Leader (socialist journal), **12:**122
Milwaukee Sentinel, **3:**495
Milwaukee Street Railway Co., strike/lockout, 1896, **4:**166, *166–67n,* 182–83
Milwaukee Trades Assembly, **1:**216, *217n*
Milwaukee Vessel Owners' Association, **3:**496

Milwaukee Volkszeitung (socialist journal), **3:**493, 497n
Mine, Mill, and Smelter Workers, International Union of, **4:***, **5:***, **6:***, **7:***, **8:***, **9:***, **10:***, 126n, 169n, 430, 502n, **11:***, 28n, 85n, 219, 220n; and black workers, **11:**84n; jurisdiction of, **12:**396
—strike/lockout: 1917 (copper miners, Ariz.), **10:**125, *126n,* 148–49, 167–68, 259, 262, 301, 321, 323–24n, 336–39
Mine Managers' and Assistants' Mutual Aid Association, National, **5:***, 492–94, 494n
—convention: 1902, **5:**492, 494n
Mine Operators' Association (Colorado), **6:**282–83n, 344n
Mine Owners' Protective Association (Coeur d'Alene, Idaho), **3:**214n; injunction, **3:**214n
miners, **2:**30–31, 91, 92n, 220–21, **9:**222; and mechanization, **12:**306; run-of-mine method of paying, **9:**282, 283n
Miners, Western Federation of, **4:***, 192n, **5:***, 92n, **6:***, 15–16, 19n, **7:***, 244, 246, **8:***, 104n, 411, **9:***, 28n, 115, 118n, **10:***, 169n, **11:***; and AFL, **4:**192, 253, 255–56, 257–58n, 266–67, 268n, 297–99, 304–5, 308–13, 323, 324n, 385, **5:**90–91, 114–15, 149–50, 431, **6:**17n, 270, 271n, **7:**283–85, 286n, 404, **8:**104–6, 106n, 144–45, 169–70; AFL financial support of, **6:**279–81, 282n, 343–44, 405–6, 407n, 504–8, 508–9n, **9:**11–13, 14n, 27–28, 28n, 48n, 65–66, 181–83, 190–91, 191n; amalgamation of, with Mine Workers, United, **9:**176–78, 178n, 271–74; and American Labor Union, **6:**37; in Butte, Mont., **9:**154, 155n, 179–82, 190; and eight-hour day, **9:**121; injunctions, **6:**344n, **9:**12, 13n; and IWW, **6:**405, 406n, 447, 451, 457, 461–62, 506–7, 508n, **7:**247n; jurisdiction of, **6:**352n, **8:**105, 106n, 144–45, 170; and Mexico, **9:**443n; officers of, indictment of, **9:**182–83, 184n; and Western Labor Union, **4:**452–53n, 486

—conventions: 1896 (Denver), **4:**192, *192n;* 1897 (Salt Lake City), **4:**258n, *299n,* **5:**90–91, 150; 1898 (Salt Lake City), **4:**486; 1899 (Salt Lake City), **5:**91, *93n,* 97, 114; 1901, **6:**352n; 1902 (Denver), **6:**17n; 1904 (Denver), **6:**270, *271n;* 1905 (Salt Lake City), **6:**504–7, *508–*9n; 1910 (Denver), **8:**105–6, *106n;* 1914, **9:**178n
—locals: local 1 (Butte, Mont.), **9:**155n, 180, 182, 270–72; local 18 (Wardner, Idaho), **5:**93n, 95–97, 131–32, 134, 138n; local 74 (Butte, Mont.), **6:**447, 449n; local 83 (Butte, Mont.), **6:**352n; local 93 (Denver), **6:**282n; local 125 (Colorado City, Colo.), **6:**282n; local 220 (Goldfield, Nev.), **7:**286n
—strikes/lockouts: 1896–97 (Leadville, Colo.; *see* Leadville, Colo., strike, 1896–97); 1899 (Denver and Pueblo, Colo.), **5:**114, *115n;* 1899 (Wardner, Idaho), **5:**90, *92–93n,* 95–97, 101n, 114, 129–36, 148–50, 151n, 231, 232n, **7:**24, 25n; 1903–4 (Colorado), **6:**279–81, *282–83n,* 343–44, 344n, 361–62, 452, 504–6, 509n, **7:**24, 25n; 1907 (Goldfield, Nev.), **7:**283, *286n;* 1913 (Mineville, N.Y.), **9:**177, *178n;* 1913–14 (Northern Michigan), **8:**512, *512–13n,* **9:**11–13, 13–14n, 25–28, 28n, 43–44, 44n, 46–47, 47–48n, 51–52, 52n, 64–67, 68n, 96n, 177, 181–83, 210, 211n, 301; 1915–16 (Arizona), **9:**351–52, *352n,* 425
Miners' Amalgamated Association, Ohio, *2:72n*
Miners' Amalgamated Association of Pennsylvania, *1:229n,* 390, *391n*
Miners and Drivers, Amalgamated Association of Pittsburgh, **1:**211, 221, *229n*
Miners and Mine Laborers, National Federation of, **1:***, 390, 391n, **2:***, 30–32, 32n, 35, 51, 67, **4:**473n
—convention: 1887 (Indianapolis), **2:**51, *51n*
Miners and Mine Laborers, National Progressive Union of, **1:***, 391n, **2:***, 221, 222n, 235, 256

Miners' and Mine Laborers' Amalgamated Association of Pennsylvania, *1:391n,* **2:**32n, 92n
—strike/lockout: 1887–88, **2:**91, *92n,* 107
Miners' and Mine Labourers' Protective Association of Vancouver Island, B.C., **3:**56n
—strike/lockout: 1890–91, *3:56n*
miners and mine operators, conferences of, **4:**473n, **5:**297–98; 1886, **4:**473n; 1891 (Pittsburgh), **3:**32n, 40, *41n,* 72–73; 1894 (Cleveland), *3:547n;* 1898 (Chicago), **4:**472, *473n;* 1900 (Indianapolis), **5:**322n; 1901 (Columbus, Ohio), **5:**321, *322n;* 1901 (Hazelton, Pa.), **5:**328, 329n, 334; 1914, 1915 (Ohio), **9:**282, 283n; 1919, **11:**192n; 1920, **11:**192n; 1923, **12:**297
Miners' Benevolent and Protective Association of Illinois, Coal, **2:**51
Miners' Federation of Great Britain, **3:**429n, **6:***, 157, 158n
—strike/lockout: 1893, **3:**426, *429n,* 432, 565, 575
Miners' Magazine (trade union journal), *5:464n;* excerpt of *article in,* **5:**463–64
Miners of the U.S., Amalgamated Association of, **1:**391n
miners' strike, 1892 (Tennessee), **3:**185–86, 213, *215n,* 220–21, 251–53, 420, **4:**40
miners' strike, 1897, *4:345n,* **5:**297, 386, 486, 488n, **7:**417n, 472, 483–84, **8:**229, 269, **9:**33, 86–88, 337, **11:**567; boycott of West Virginia coal, **4:**345n, 503, *505n;* Chicago conference, **4:**256, 370, 371n, 374, 376, 383–86, 390–91; Columbus, Ohio, conference, **4:**375–76, 376n, 378; financial support of, **4:**347–49, 350n, 351, 354–55, 357, 369–70, 371n, 372–73, 384; and food assistance, **4:**363–64; injunctions against, **4:**353, 358–59, 360n, 362–63, 363n, 364–65; organizers and, **4:**347–48, 350–53, 353n, 357, 359, 365–66, 366n, 375, 384; Pittsburgh conference, **4:**345, 345n, 346–47;

settlement of, **4:**345, 375–76, 376n, 378, 384; SG and, **4:**344–53, 353n, 354, 354n, 355–57, 359n, 362–63, 363n, 364–66, 366n, 372–73, 375, 389; St. Louis conference, **4:**369–71, 371n, 372–74, 374n, 379n, 382–83, 390–91, 391n; sympathetic strikes and, **4:**357; Wheeling, W.Va., conference, **4:**353–59, 359n, 363n, 364–65, 366n, **5:**386, **9:**337. *See also* Lattimer massacre

miners' strike, 1902 (anthracite), **6:**12, *13–14n,* 22–23, 26–27, 34, 35n, 40, 40n, 45–46, 46n, 97–98, 100n, 103–4, 104n, 162, 197, **7:**484, **8:**5, 229, 269, **9:**13, 86–88, 337, **11:**567, 571n, **12:**179

miners' strike, 1919, *11:192n,* 194, 233, 386, 566; AFL Executive Council, *statement on,* **11:**208–11; injunction against, **11:**192n, 195, 196n, 197–201, 203–4, 206, 208–12, 213n, 220, 252–53, 336; SG negotiations during, **11:**191–92, 195–96, 198–205, 205n, 206

miners' strike, 1922, **12:**44, *47–48n,* 86, 87n, 99n, 103, 127–28, 134, 140, 146, 179, 195, 285, 309, 311n, 328, 330n

Miners' Union of Coeur d'Alene, Idaho, **3:**214n
—strike/lockout: 1892, **3:**185–86, 213, *214n,* 251–52, 255, 293–94, 420, **5:**93n, **6:**452; injunction against, **3:**214n

mines: government ownership of (*see* government ownership: of mines); inspection of, **1:**231, **4:**506–7; and safety legislation, **3:**559, **6:**96, 372, 479, **8:**181–82, 318

Mine Workers of Alabama, United:
—strike/lockout: 1894, *4:28n*

Mine Workers of America, Independent Union of, **10:**408–9, *409n*

Mine Workers of America, Reorganized United, **11:**482n

Mine Workers of America, United, **2:***, **3:***, 173–74, 535, **4:***, 82n, 98–99, 473n, **5:***, 218n, 493, 494n, **6:***, 22n, 501, **7:***, 69n, **8:***, 9n, **9:***, 24n, 66, 115, 118n, 121, **10:***, 22, 23n, 430, 435, **11:***, 28n, 85n, 174, 296n, **12:***, 30n, 96, 119, 150–51, 264, 377, 440, 469, 495, 558–59; AFL financial support of, **6:**22–23, **11:**492–93, 493–94n; and black workers, **10:**347, **11:**84n; and Coronado case, **10:**322, 323n; and eight-hour movement, **2:**163–64, 290, 318, 413–16, 430, **3:**23, 24n, 31, 32n, 33, 40, 42, 44, 54–55, 57, 60, 64, 64n, 69, 70n, 71, 71n, 72–74, 111, 168; and election of 1908, **7:**416–17, 417n; exposé on communists in labor movement, **12:**310–11n, 329, 330n; and Hitchman case, **10:**285–86, 287n, 322, 323n, 351, 372; and industrial unionism, **5:**381, 433–34, **6:**501, **8:**406–7, 411, **9:**52n, 502, **12:**62; injunction, **12:**265n; injunctions against, **5:**219n, 322n, **6:**80–81, 84n, **10:**285–86, 287n, 323n, **11:**192n, 195, 196n, 197–201, 203–4, 206, 208–12, 213n, 220, 252–53, 336; jurisdiction of, **5:**336–37, 338n, 381, 382n, 433–34, 445, **8:**104–6, 145, 170, **10:**408–9, 409n, **12:**396; and Mexico, **9:**436, 443n; and Miners, Western Federation of, **6:**506–7, **9:**176–78, 178n, 271–74; and Mine Workers of America, Independent, **10:**408–9, 409n; officers of, indictment of, **9:**39, 40n, 89; organization of, **3:**301–2, **9:**336–37, **10:**78, **12:**280; and women workers, **4:**60
—conventions: 1891 (Columbus, Ohio), **3:**31, *32n,* 72; 1893 (Columbus, Ohio), **3:**302, *302n;* 1894 (Columbus, Ohio), **3:**545, *547n;* 1901 (Indianapolis), **5:**321, *322n;* May 1902 (Shamokin, Pa.), *6:13n,* 98, 100n; July 1902 (Indianapolis), **6:**14n, 22, *22n,* 26–27; Oct. 1902 (Wilkes-Barre, Pa.), **6:**14n, 45–46, *46n;* 1911 (Columbus, Ohio), **8:**170, *170n,* 287, 289, 290n; 1912 (Indianapolis), **8:**287, *290n;* 1914 (Indianapolis), **9:**40, *40n,* 52, 52–53n, 63n, 64–67, 68n, 69, 176, 178n; 1918 (Indianapolis), **10:**347, *350n;* 1919–20 (Cleveland and Columbus,

Ohio), **11:**138, *138n,* 192, 192n, 208–9, 268, 269n, **12:**236, 241n
—districts: District 4 (western Pennsylvania), **3:**58n; District 5 (western Pennsylvania), **3:**70, *70*–71n, **5:**408, **11:**121–23, 123n; District 11 (Indiana), convention, 1919 (Terre Haute), **11:**268, *269n;* District 12 (Illinois), **6:**447–48, 450n, **9:**181; District 14 (Kansas), **11:**557; District 15 (Colorado), **10:**409n; District 18, **11:**75n; District 20 (Alabama), **2:**414n, **10:**288n; District 21 (Arkansas), **10:**323n; District 22 (Wyoming), **11:**199, 199n; District 23 (Kentucky and Tennessee), *5:322n;* District 26 (Nova Scotia), **10:**308n
—locals: local 128 (Scranton, Pa.), **3:**174; local 746 (DeSoto, Ill.), **5:**336–37, 337–38n; local 1771 (Red Lodge, Mont.), **6:**447, 449n, 462; locals in Pittsburg, Kans., **6:**447, 449n
—strikes/lockouts: 1890–91 (Alabama), **2:**414, *414n;* 1891 (Connellsville, Pa.), **3:**56–58, *58*–59n, 64n, 66, 66n, 67–68, 68n, 73–74; 1891 (Iowa), **3:**69, *70n;* 1894, **3:**542–44, *547n;* 1897 (*see* miners' strike, 1897); 1898 (Illinois), **5:**26, *30n,* 43–44; 1900 (Maryland), **5:**217–18, *218–19n;* 1900 (Pennsylvania), **5:**262, *263n,* **7:**484, **8:**229, 269, **9:**337, **11:**567, 571n; 1900–1903? (Kentucky), **5:**321, *322n;* 1901 (Pennsylvania), **5:**382n; 1902 (anthracite; *see* miners' strike, 1902 [anthracite]); 1902 (Clarksburg, W.Va.), **6:**81, 84n; 1909–10 (Cape Breton, Canada), **10:**307, *308n;* 1913–14 (Colorado), **9:**23, *24n,* 210–11, 211n, 242, 301, 399, 400n (*see also* Ludlow, Colo., massacre); 1914 (threatened), **9:**97, 98n; 1915 (Arkansas), *11:494n;* 1917 (Alabama, threatened), **10:**287–88, *288n;* 1917 (copper miners, New Mexico), **10:**167, *169n;* 1918 (Cape Breton, Canada, threatened), **10:**307–8, *308n;* 1919 (*see* miners' strike, 1919); 1921 (Kansas), **11:**481–82n, 558; 1922

(*see* miners' strike, 1922); 1923, *12:315n*
Mine Workers of Nova Scotia, Amalgamated, **10:**308n
Mine Workers' Progressive Union, Northern Mineral, **4:***
—strike/lockout: 1896–97 (Norway, Mich.), *4:165n*
minimum wage, **3:**316–18, 575, 604, **4:**446–47n, 489–90, **6:**338, **7:**293, **8:**168, 382–84, 384n, **9:**20, 22n, 119, 122, 126, 215, 258–59, 259n, 314–17, 460–61, 461n, 530–32, **10:**459, **11:**18n, 159, **12:**5, 392; for teachers, **10:**438–39, 439–40n; in wage contracts, **4:**472, **5:**216n, 338n, **6:**17–18n, 148, 176n, 401, **7:**52n, 53, 154, **8:**503n, **9:**11n, 26, 46n, 305n, 352n, 416, **10:**53, 364, 487, **11:**21n, 167n, 387, 571n, **12:**77, 354–55; for women, **6:**83n, **7:**52n, **8:**382, 384n, **9:**19–21, 21–22n, 258–59, 259n, 314–17, 317–18n, **12:**227, 228n, 230, 244–47, 247n, 248–50, 370, 372. *See also under* legislation, states and territories; legislation, U.S.; living wage; wages
Minimum Wage Law, The (Brown), **9:**316, *318n*
Minneapolis and St. Louis Railway Co. v. *Beckwith,* **8:**479, *492n*
Minneapolis Central Labor Union, *12:337n*
Minneapolis Civic and Commerce Association, **10:**240, 241n
Minneapolis Trades and Labor Assembly, *12:337n;* and industrial unionism, **12:**126, 127n
Minnesota State Federation of Labor, **7:**225–26, *227n*
—convention: 1922 (Crookston), **12:**126, *127n*
Minute Men of the Constitution, **12:**366, *367n*
Missanabie (passenger liner), **10:**470n, 520, 523n
Mississippi State Federation of Labor, **11:**51, *52n*
Missouri and North Arkansas Railroad, strike/lockout, 1921–23, **12:**192–95, *196*–97n

Missouri Socialist (socialist journal), 5:491

Missouri State Federation of Labor, *7:161n*

"Mistakes of Gompers," 2:97

Mitch, William A., *11:267n; letter from,* 11:267–69; *letter to,* 11:265–67; *wire from,* 11:265–66

Mitchel, John P., 9:358–59, *359n,* 430n, 492, 10:129–30, 132–33

Mitchell, Aronette, 11:23, *24n; letter from,* 11:543; *letter to,* 11:547–48

Mitchell, Ethel, 5:153, 154n, *11:24n,* 562, 12:517; *letter to,* 11:23–24

Mitchell, Henrietta, *3:79n,* 4:43, 161, 5:153, 154n, 12:517; *letters to,* 11:23–24, 562

Mitchell, Isaac H., 5:*, 210–11, *211n*

Mitchell, James, 6:430, 430n

Mitchell, John (AFL vice-president), 5:*, *218n,* 322n, 492, 6:*, *22n,* 162, 270, 410n, 450n, 513, 7:*, *64n,* 309, 309n, 322n, 400n, 8:*, *6n,* 40n, 173n, 337n, 342, 456, 9:*, *13n,* 200n, 280n, 359, 359n, 10:*, *147n,* 286, 11:*, *18n,* 12:558; at AFL conventions, 5:281, 6:197–98, 204n, 356, 358, 492, 494, 496n, 507, 7:424, 424n, 8:5–6, 6n, 18n, 287, 289, 295, 407–8, 411, 9:38n; at AFL Executive Council meeting, 8:501, 503–4; and anthracite mining region, labor disputes in, 5:329n, 334, 335n, 411, 411n; and anthracite strike, 1902, 6:13–14n, 35n, 40, 40n, 45–46, 98; and boycotts, 8:14–15; and Buck's Stove and Range Co. cases, 7:249–50n, 356–57, 392, 426, 430–31, 434, 439–41, 478, 492n, 8:10–12, 12n, 13–15, 16n, 17–18, 160–64, 217, 217n, 240–41, 266, 270, 292–93, 323n, 358, 9:105, 106n, 11:15, 18n; death of, 11:138n; death threat against, 7:393; and election of 1906, 7:111; and election of 1908, 7:415–16, 416n; election of, as AFL vice-president, 5:57n, 177n, 294n, 445, 6:209, 376n, 509n, 7:281n, 427n; and Granite Cutters' assessment, 5:237; and jurisdiction questions,

5:288, 338n, 438, 443–45; and labor legislation, 8:371–72, 375, 377–80; *letters from,* 5:387–90, 426, 6:22, 8:117–20, 160–64, 170–71; *letters to,* 5:217–18, 321, 328–29, 336–37, 504–5, 6:45–46, 103–4, 262, 409–10, 430, 7:112–13, 461–62, 10:143–47; and McNamara case, 8:227n, 235, 306; and Miners, Western Federation of, 8:106n; and National Civic Federation, 5:217, 311, 351–52, 387–88, 388n, 389–90, 464n, 482–83, 6:235, 8:170–71, 171n; as New York commissioner of labor, 8:439n; and Northern Michigan copper miners' strike, 1913–14, 9:12, 14n, 28n, 44n, 47n, 65; retirement of, 9:37–38, 41; Shaffer's charges against, 6:104n; and temperance, 8:93, 94n

Mitchell, John (of Connellsville, Pa.), *7:181n; letter from,* 7:181; *letter to,* 7:190–92

Mitchell, John (senator), 5:457, 458–59

Mitchell, Katherine, 6:430, 430n

Mitchell, Margaret Katherine, 6:430, 430n

Mitchell, Mark J., 3:103n

Mitchell, Marie, 6:430, *430n*

Mitchell, Mildred, 11:23, *24n*

Mitchell, Pauline Wiener, 11:23, *24n*

Mitchell, Richard, 6:430, 430n

Mitchell, Robert, 6:430, 430n

Mitchell, Rose Gompers, 3:79n, 4:*, 43, *43n,* 56, 57n, 432, 5:*, xvi, *87n,* 154n, 11:24n; *letter to,* 4:161; SG, and death of, 5:85–86. *See also* Gompers, Rose

Mitchell, Samuel, 3:*, 79n, 140, *142n,* 4:*, *43n,* 5:*, 153, *154n,* 11:*, 23, *24n; letters to,* 4:42–43, 161, 205–6

Mitchell, William P., 2:244, *245n*

Mitchell et al. v. *Hitchman Coal and Coke Co., 10:287n*

Mobile (Ala.) Central Labor Union, 6:293n

Mobile (Ala.) Central Trades Council, *4:28n,* 6:293n

Modest, Rudolph, 3:298, *300n*

Modie, Frank E., 6:287, *289n*

Moffett, Edward A., **7:**244, *246n; letter from,* **8:**303
Moffitt, John A., **5:***, 72, *73n,* **6:***, 67–69, *70n,* 178n, **7:**395n, **8:***, *42n,* 77, 513n, **12:***, *303n; letters to,* **6:**177, **8:**40–42, **12:**301–3
Mohns and Mohns, **6:**218
Molders' Union of North America, International, **1:***, **2:***, **4:***, **5:***, **7:***, **8:***, **9:***, 34n, **10:**502n, **11:***, 28n, 85n, 153n, 362, **12:**446n; and black workers, **11:**84n, 284; and women workers, **8:**387–89, 389n
Moley, Daniel M., **9:**99, *99n*
Molle, Jessie M., **11:**427–28, *432n*
Molloy, Annie E., **9:**270, *274n*
Monaghan, Frank B., **6:***, 366, *368n,* 373
Monahan, Joseph E., **5:**393, 395, *396n*
Monck, Richard S., **5:**386, *387n*
Monckton, James H., **1:***, 85, *86n*
Mondell, Franklin W., **6:**512n, **12:**211, *213n*
Monness, Harry M., **12:**460, *461n,* 543, 550
Monnett, Francis S., *7:439n,* **8:**53; *letter to,* **7:**438–39
Monon Railroad, **9:**516
monopolies, **1:**212–13, 285, **5:**281–82, 358–61
Monroe, James, **4:**44, *45n*
Monroe (steamship), sinking of, **9:**201, *203n*
Montana Federation of Labor, *9:155n*
Montana State Federation of Labor, *9:155n*
Montana Trades and Labor Council, *9:155n*
Monte Grappa, **10:**562, 564, 567n
Montgomery, William H., **3:**34–35, 40, *41n,* **4:**246n, 258n, 267, **5:**393, 395, **6:**15, *18n,* 191; *letter to,* **4:**245–46
Montgomery County (Ohio) *Reporter,* **5:**460n; injunction against, **5:**459, 460n
Montgomery Ward and Co., strike/lockout, 1905, **6:**452, *453n,* 469, 502
Montreal Wage Earners' Union, **6:**447, 449n
Montsec, **11:**47, *49n*
Montz, James O., **6:**222–23
Moon, John, **8:**495n

Moon, Reuben O., *8:101n,* 159n
Moonelis, Adolph, **1:**189, *192n,* 199, 260
Mooney, Rena, **9:**517–18n, *11:535n; letter to,* **11:**541
Mooney, Thomas J., **9:***, 343, *344n,* 517–18n, **10:***, 92, *93n,* 533, **11:***, *7n,* 113, 541, **12:**90, 91n; general strike on behalf of, 1918 (threatened), **10:**387, 396, 420, 420n; general strike on behalf of, 1919 (threatened), **11:**6, 7n, 86, 87n, 94; *letter from,* **11:**534–35
Mooney-Billings case, **9:**517, *517–18n,* **10:**92, *92–93n,* 215, 387, 387–88n, 395–97, 397n, 420, 468–69, 470n, 497, 506, 507n, 533–34, **11:**7, 7n, 86, 87n, 534–35, 541, **12:**90, 91n
Moore, Charles, **11:**321n
Moore, Charles A., **5:**464n, 482, *483n,* **6:**235, *236n*
Moore, Edward S., **4:**410, *411n,* 413
Moore, Frederick R., **10:**345, *350n,* 421, 426, 429, 462; *letter from,* **10:**461–63
Moore, John, **10:**358n
Moore, John B., **12:**210n
Moore, Mark W., *1:167n; letter from,* **1:**164–65
Moore, Tom, **12:***, 20, *21n,* 438–40
Moore, William B., **1:**16, *16n*
Moore, William H., **7:**108, *109n*
Moore Drop Forging Co.: injunctions, **12:**9–10n; strike/lockout, 1920–21, *12:9n;* yellow-dog contracts at, **11:**507–8, **12:**8–9
Moore Drop Forging Co. v. *McCarthy et al.,* *12:10n*
Morales, Nieves G., *letter to,* **9:**43
Moral Overstrain (Alger), *8:493n,* **12:**69, 74n
Moranete, John, **1:**108
"more," **1:**317, **2:**151, 302–3, 313, **3:**36–37, 54, 396, 447, 561, **4:**48, 60, 162, 174, 493, **5:**226–27, **8:**268, 384, **9:**127–30, **10:**197–98, **11:**14, 233, **12:**222
Morgan, Anne, **8:**39, *40n*
Morgan, Elizabeth C., **2:***, *176n,* **3:***, *103n,* 663, 664n; *letters to,* **2:**175–76, **3:**102–3, 154–55
Morgan, J. Edward, **9:**517, *517–18n*

Morgan, J. Pierpont, **5:**334, *335n,*
384n, 385, 483, **6:**14n, **12:**121, 123
Morgan, John T. (laborer), **5:**406,
407n, 436–37, 438n
Morgan, John T. (senator), **3:**560,
561n, 576, **6:**212
Morgan, Thomas J., **2:***, *408n,* 420,
422, 426, 429, **3:***, *14n,* 420, 463n,
4:*, 44, *45n;* at AFL conventions,
2:398, 400, 402–6, 410–12, 415–16,
3:256–60, 365, 426–27, 429n, 435–
36, 613–14, 616n, 619–20, 623–25,
634–43, 646, 649–51, 653, 664; and
Homestead strike, 1892, **3:**250–51,
253n; *letter from,* **3:**457; *letter to,*
3:286; and Pullman strike, 1894,
3:525, 538–39, 625; and Socialist Labor party, **3:**12, 16, 83
Morgan, William Y., **12:**169, *171n*
Morgan continuous billet mill, **3:**481
Morgen Journal, arbitration case,
2:371–74
Moriarty, James, **9:**479n
Morones Negrete, Luis N., **9:***, 426–
27n, 436, *443n,* **11:***, *140n,* 300,
302–3, 303n, **12:***, 360n, 525, *526n;*
letter to, **11:**139–40
Morrin, Paul J., **11:***, 151, *152n*
Morris, Esther, **7:**471, *471n*
Morris, Gouverneur, **12:**294n
Morris, James, **12:**195, 197n
Morris, Julia G., **5:**199n, *7:471n; letter
to,* **7:**471
Morris, Max, **4:***, 502, *502n,* **5:***, *20n,*
89–90, 92n, 342n, 407n, 421n, 452,
6:*, *17n,* 85–86, 87n, 133–34, 164n,
239, 270, 271n, 386–87, 430, **7:***,
7n, 9n, 111n, 453n; and AFL conventions, **5:**160n, **6:**210n, 212; death
of, **7:**471, 482n; election of, as AFL
vice-president, **5:**57n, 177n, 294n,
445, **6:**209, 376n, 509n, **7:**281n,
427n; *letter from,* **6:**15–17; *letters to,*
5:19–20, 198–99
Morris, Melvin, **7:**471, *471n*
Morris meatpacking company,
10:152n; strike/lockout, 1921–22,
11:571n
Morrison, Alice Boswell, **7:**482n,
8:258, **11:**460, **12:**251
Morrison, Cameron A., **11:**510–11,
512n

Morrison, Erwin, **7:**479–80, *482n*
Morrison, Frank, **4:***, *272n,* 338, 356,
359n, 465, 503–4, **5:***, *92n,* 112,
113n, 257, 322, 329, 346, 400, 451,
455, 470n, 510–11, **6:***, *17n,* 108,
161, 227, 232, 238, 309–10, 382,
403, 409, 440, 452, **7:***, *7n,* 27, 145,
309n, 455, 455n, 457, **8:***, *10n,*
101, 120, 124, 158, 370–72, 375,
428, 453–54, 456, **9:***, *14n,* 48n, 64,
157n, 359n, 464n, 488n, 508, **10:***,
15n, 19, 156–57n, 241n, 305, 412n,
11:*, *18n,* 140n, 345, 407, 410,
459–60, 565–66, **12:***, *21n,* 190,
212n, 221n, 344–45, 347, 373; address by, mentioned, **12:**236, 241n,
252, 252n; at AFL conventions,
4:268–70, 272n, 273, 278, **5:**49n,
173, 176n, 432, 432n, **6:**54–55,
57n, 210n, 375, 376n, 496, 497n,
501, 503n, **8:**8, 10n, 18n, 141–42,
142n, 145, 295, **9:**29, 33, 34n, 214n,
11:473, 475, 476n; at AFL Executive Council meetings, **4:**321–23,
6:133–34, 151n, 531n, 546n, **8:**503–
4, **9:**271–74, 436, **10:**26, 28, 32–33,
11:430, **12:**554–55, 559–60; and
AFL headquarters, **7:**446–47; and
AFL Labor Representation Committee, **7:**63; and AFL National
Non-Partisan Political Campaign,
11:272, 274; and AFL organizers,
7:104n, 181, 190, 231, 233, 428,
8:36–37, **11:**502n, 517, 554; and
American Alliance for Labor and
Democracy, **10:**160n; and black
workers, **9:**282n, **10:**371, 372n, 421,
423–24, 427–28, 430–31, **12:**341–
42, 342–43n; and Boston building
trades conference, 1914, **9:**68n, 70,
73n; and Brackenridge, Pa., murders, **11:**123n; and Buck's Stove
and Range Co. cases, **7:**249–50n,
266, 356–57, 392, 426, 430–31, 434,
439–41, 478, 492n, **8:**10–11, 12n,
17–18, 160–64, 217, 217n, 240–41,
266, 270, 292–93, 323n, 333, 335,
9:105, 106n, **11:**15, 18n; *cable to,*
11:52n; and carpenters' strike,
1918, **10:**361; and Central Trades
and Labor Council of Greater New
York and Vicinity meeting, **11:**354;

and Cincinnati Agreement, **6:**135n; and Clayton bill, **9:**90–91, 97–98n, 153; and cloakmakers' strike, 1910, **8:**109; and coal strike, 1919, **11:**195, 198, 198n, 200–203, 211n, 213n; and Committee on Labor, Council of National Defense, **10:**52n; and communist sympathizers in labor movement, **12:**295; and conservation conference, 1908, **7:**322n; Coolidge, meeting with, **12:**296, 298, 298–99n; and Denver trade unions, **6:**19n; and election of 1906, **7:**96–97, 110n, 122–23n; and election of 1908, **7:**350n, 377; and election of 1924, **12:**184n, 433, 433n, 456, 459–60, 461n, 464, 466, 467n, 468, 468n, 470n, 472n, 474, 480–83, 483n, 489–92; election of, as AFL secretary, **4:**272n, 278, 278n, 414n, **5:**57n, 177n, 294n, 445, **6:**209, 376n, 509n, **7:**281n, 427n, **9:**38n, 226n, 348n, **10:**475, **11:**93n, 321, 321n, 482, **12:**97n, 338n; and election of SG's successor, **12:**555, 559–60; and Granite Cutters' assessment, **5:**233, 237–38; and Hearst papers, attack by, **11:**366–67; Hoover, meeting with, **11:**387–88; and Iglesias, **5:**424, **12:**197, 201; and Industrial Conference, 1919, **11:**128n; and International Federation of Trade Unions, **9:**174, 175n, **11:**224n; and International Labor Conference, 1919, **11:**110–11, 111n; and jurisdiction questions, **5:**173–75, 375n, 448n, **7:**151n, 152, 152–53n, 204n, 208–10, 210n, **9:**107–8, **12:**398n; and Lawson protest, **9:**309; *letters from,* **4:**383, **6:**15–17, 478–79, **7:**96–97, 152, 208–10, 225–26, **8:**160–64, 323–24, 500–501, 512, **11:**112–13, 113n, 119–20; *letters to,* **4:**289–90, 379–81, 453–56, **5:**88–92, 156–58, 377–78, 384, 467–70, **6:**149–50, 397–99, 529–31, 546, **7:**49–50, 102–4, 209, 250–52, 413–14, 472–73, 479–81, **8:**33–35, 91–92, 256–58, 396–97, 473–76, 494–95, 501, **9:**39–40, 227, 260–61, 281, 464, **10:**119, 176–77, 405–6, 415–16, 434–36, 447–49,

491–92, 528–29, 538–42, **11:**42–46, 59–60, 72–74, 105–6, 323–24, 460–61, 484–85, 510–12, 556–58, 558n, **12:**219–21, 251–52, 394–98, 544–45; and McNamara case, **8:**235–37, 238n, 335, 351, 358; and meatpackers' strike, 1917 (threatened), **10:**280n, 303; and military intelligence, collection of, **10:**434–36, 436n; and Miners, Western Federation of, **7:**404; and National Civic Federation, **6:**235, **8:**323–24, 324n; and National War Labor Board hearing, **10:**433; and National Women's Trade Union League, **11:**132, 135n; and One Big Union, **11:**113n; and open shop campaign, **11:**401; and People's Legislative Service, **11:**468–71; and Plumb Plan, **11:**130, 131n; and political prisoners, **11:**449–50n; and railroad brotherhoods, **11:**187, 241n, 447, 462; and railroad shopmen's strike, 1922–?, **12:**106n, 155n; and Russia, conditions in, **10:**512n; and Sabotage Act, **10:**449n; and Sadie Gompers, death of, **10:**544–45, 546n; salary of, **9:**213, 214n; and *San Francisco Call* boycott, **8:**144n; and SG, death of, **12:**541, 543; and SG, illness of, 1923, **12:**218, 219n, 221; and SG, illness of, 1924, **12:**503, 503n, 504, 514, 539; and southern textile organizing campaign, **11:**525–26; *statement of,* **12:**540–41; and steelworkers' organizing campaign, 1918, **10:**478–79; and steelworkers' organizing campaign and strike, 1919, **11:**148, 360–64, 365n; and "Stockholm" movement, **10:**104; and timber industry, **10:**295, 296n; and Trades and Labor Congress of Canada, **12:**20; and trade union movement in Canada, **9:**15–16n; tribute to SG, **12:**554–55; trip to Northwest, 1922, **12:**236, 241n, 252, 252n; and "We Don't Patronize List" (AFL), **7:**312–13; Wilson, meetings with, **8:**386, 424; *wires from,* **9:**146, **10:**245, **11:**50–51, 78; *wires to,* **9:**371, **10:**137, **11:**49, 112–13, **12:**338–39; and women

workers, **11**:18–19, **12**:238, 246–47, 247n; and Zaranko, **11**:325n
Morrison, Harry, **9**:145n
Morrison, John (grocer), **9**:343, 343–44n
Morrison, John (organ maker), **2**:66
Morrison, John (SG friend), **1**:*, 420, *421n,* **2**:23n, **5**:*, 274n, 418, *419n,* **6**:*, *8n,* **7**:*, *257n,* 377n, 396, **8**:231n, **10**:549, **11**:*, 459, *460n; letters from,* **6**:5–8, **7**:256–57; *letters to,* **10**:244, 484
Morrison et al. v. Ingles et al., **11**:280, *281n*
Morrissey, Patrick H., **3**:*, *533n,* 579n, **4**:*, 357, 359n, *360n; wire from,* **3**:532–33
Morrow, Dennis J., **4**:433, *435n*
Morrow, Hugh, **5**:316n
Morrow, Jay J., **12**:383n, 410–11, *411*–12n
Morse, Sidney, *12:51n; letter to,* **12**:49–51
Morton, Joseph W., **8**:*, 410, *412n*
Morton, Levi P., **4**:14, *16n*
Morton, Lew, **6**:*, 517, *518n,* **7**:*, *41n; letter to,* **7**:40–41
Moscow, Harry, *letter to,* **8**:333–34
Mosely, Edward A., **11**:330, *332n*
Mosher, Aaron A. R., **12**:*, 20, *21n*
Moskowitz, Henry, **12**:529, *533n*
Mosses, William, **10**:309n
Most, Johann, **2**:*, 384, *385n,* **4**:368n
motion picture industry, and trade unions, **12**:261–62
Moton, Robert R., **10**:331, *331n,* 345, 358–59, 421, 428, 462
Mott, John R., **10**:310, *312n*
Mott, Luther, **12**:39n
Mountain Timber Co. v. State of Washington, **10**:143, *147n*
Moxley, James F., **2**:409, *410n*
Moyer, Charles H., **6**:*, *352n,* 406n, 457, 459, 461–62, 504–6, 509n, **7**:*, 144–46, *146n,* **8**:*, *106n,* 144, 170, **9**:*, *44n,* 65, 154, 155n, 274, **10**:*, *126n,* **11**:*, *220n,* 365n; attack on, **8**:513n, **9**:43–44; criticism of AFL, **6**:506, **9**:52n, 67, 68n; indictment of, **9**:182–83, 184n; *letters from,* **8**:104–6, **9**:179–83, **10**:516–18, **11**:218–19; *letters to,* **6**:351–52,

9:189–91, **10**:167–69, 516–18; *wires from,* **10**:125–26, 167; *wire to,* **10**:167
"Mr. Gompers and His Two Million Men" (Creelman), *7:372n*
Mudd, Sydney E., **7**:119, *120n*
Mudge, William, **4**:*, 221, *222n*
Mulback, John, **10**:186n
Muldoon, Frank M., **3**:51, *55n*
Mulhall, Martin M., **7**:85, *91n*
Mulhall investigation, **7**:91n, **8**:500
Mulholland, Frank, **8**:79n, 130, *131n,* 194n, 213, 213n, 234n, 350, 404, **12**:152, 154–55, 155n, 196n; *letter from,* **8**:232–34; *letters to,* **8**:160–64, 193–94
Mulholland, John F., **4**:*, 359n, 458, 460, *461n,* **5**:*, 157, *158n,* 275, 332n, 438, 443–45, **6**:*, *240n; letters from,* **5**:276, 330–31, **6**:238–40
Mullen, William H., **1**:*, 402, *404n,* **5**:*, 462, *463n*
Mulligan, P. J., **6**:311, *312n*
Mullin, William, **8**:*, 116, *117n*
Mulliner, Gabrielle, **8**:39, *40n*
Mulraney, Edward, **1**:457, *459n,* 461
Mulready, Edwin, **10**:366n
Mulvey, Joseph, **2**:245
Municipal Traction Co., strike/lockout, 1908, **7**:342, *342n*
Munroe, James, **10**:49n
Munson steamship line, strike/lockout, 1901, **7**:162, *164n*
Murch, Thomas H., **3**:*, 469, *470n*
Murdock, Kerr, and Co., **3**:128n, 263; injunction, **3**:125–27, 128n, 129–31, 139, 263–64
Murdock, Victor, **7**:94, *95n,* **9**:98n
Murillo, Gerardo, **9**:433n
Murphy, Arthur P., **8**:100, *101n*
Murphy, Franklin, **6**:29n
Murphy, James J., **3**:367, *367n*
Murphy, James W., **7**:482n, *8:160n*
Murphy, John, **8**:52n
Murphy, Joseph F., **12**:220, *221n*
Murphy, Lawrence E., *5:79n*
Murphy, Patrick, **4**:3, **5**:430n
Murphy, Thomas J., **4**:411, *412n,* 432n
Murray, Arthur C., **10**:332, *333n*
Murray (cigarmaker), **2**:331
Murray, Edward W., **3**:257, *258n*
Murray, George E., **2**:332, *336n*
Murray, George F., **1**:403, *404n*

Murray, James, **12:**196n
Murray, John, **9:**430–31, *433*–34n, 436, 438, 443n, **10:**9, 181, 499n, *11:31n*
Murray, Philip, **11:***, *123n*, **12:***, 327–28, *330n*, 550; *wire from,* **11:**121–23
Murray Hill Agreement, *5:216n*, 275, 277–78n, 332, 333–34n, 367, 368n, 432n
Murtha, Thomas, **7:**90n
Musée Social (Paris), *3:370n*
Mushet, William, **9:**213n
Musical Mutual Protective Union (New York City), **2:**37, 37n, **4:**397–98, 399n, **9:**168–69, 169n
Musical Protective Union, Manhattan, **4:**56, 57n, 397–98, 399n
Musical Society, Chicago, **4:**381, 382n
Musical Union of Baltimore, **2:**228n, **3:**283, 284n
Musicians, American Federation of, **3:***, **4:***, 289–90, 291n, 295, 381, 398, **8:***, 12n, 344, **9:***, 169n, **11:**319n, 520, 520n; and black workers, **9:**168–69, 169–70n, **11:**84n
—locals: local 6 (San Francisco), **6:**233; local 10 (Chicago), **4:**381, 382n; local 41 (Washington, D.C.), **4:**396n; local 130 (New York City), **6:**518n; local 209 (Goldfield, Nev.), **7:**284, 286n; local 310 (New York City), **9:**168–69, 169n
Musicians, Chicago Federation of, **4:**382n
Musicians' Mutual Protective Union (Butte, Mont.), **4:**289–90, 291n
Musicians' Mutual Protective Union (San Francisco). *See* Musicians, American Federation of, locals: local 6
Musicians of the U.S., National League of, **2:**37n, 235, **3:***, 283, 284n, 496, 498–99, 499n, **4:***, 122, 123n, 144, 181, 289–90, 398
—conventions: 1894 (Baltimore), **3:**498–99, *499n;* 1896 (Washington, D.C.), **4:**122, *123n*, 144
—locals: local 1 (New York City), **4:**399n; local 17 (Baltimore), **3:**283, 284n; local 39 (Butte, Mont.), **4:**289–90, 291n
Musicians' Protective Association, Columbia (Washington, D.C.), **4:**396n

Musicians' Union, American (Chicago), **4:**381, 382n
Musicians' Union, Pacific Coast (San Francisco). *See* American Labor Union, locals: local 435
musicians' union (Pittsburgh), **2:**341
Muskegon (Mich.) Employers' Association, **10:**187
Mussey, Henry R., **11:**468, *472n*
Mussolini, Benito, **9:**489n, **10:**555n, **12:**255, *256n*, 415
Mutual Beneficial Association of Pennsylvania Railroad Employes, **9:**48, *50n*
Myers, Bert, *letter to,* **8:**422–23
Myers, Charles H., **4:**412, *414n*
Myers, Joseph S., **9:**352, 352n
Myers, Morris H., **1:**11, *12n*
Myrup, Andrew A., **9:**145n, **12:***, 406, *408n*
Mystic Tie Association of Sash, Door, and Blindmakers, *2:337n*

Nagel, Charles, *8:430n; letter to,* **8:**429–30
Napoleon I, **5:**6
Napoleon III (Louis Napoleon), **5:**10, *11n*
Nashville (Tenn.) Trades and Labor Council, **4:**180, *182n*, **5:**279n
Nasmyth, George, **10:**317, *317n*
Nathan, Abel L., **3:**257, *258n*
Nation (periodical), **12:**41–43
National Adjustment Commission, **10:**476, 476n
National American Council, **12:**49–51, *51n*
National Arbitration and Peace Congress, 1907 (New York City), **7:**206n, 211–14, *214n*
National Association for Universal Military Training, *9:451n*
National Association of Builders, *5:355n*
National Association of Burlesque Theatre Owners, **11:**520n
National Association of Clothiers, **6:**297n
National Association of Colored Women, **12:**83, *84n*
National Association of Manufacturers, **5:**13, *15n*, **7:**48–49, 49n, 192,

245, **8**:309, 311, **9**:78, 82, 135; and
attempted bribery of SG, **7**:256–57,
257–58n, 269–70, 270n, 271–72,
280, **8**:49, 52n, **11**:287; hearings on,
9:229, 230n, **10**:390–91; hostility
of, toward unions, **6**:105, 431, **7**:12,
232, 232n, 267, 339, **8**:49–50, 70,
121, 146–47, 198, 237, 272, 348–50,
354, 434, **9**:3, 221, 230, **10**:51
—conventions: 1905 (Atlanta), **7**:85,
91n; 1907, **7**:246n; 1910 (New York
City), **8**:90, *91n;* 1911 (New York
City), **8**:225, *227n;* 1913 (Detroit),
8:506, *511n;* 1917 (New York City),
10:101, *102n*
*National Association of Manufacturers
Exposed* (AFL), **9**:229, 230n
National Association of Master Builders, **8**:199n
National Association of Stove Manufacturers, **5**:367, *368n*
National Board for Jurisdictional
Awards in the Building Industry,
11:21–22, *22–23n*, 387, 544–45,
545n
National Boot and Shoe Manufactur-
ers' Association, **11**:288, *289n*
National Brotherhood Workers of
America, **11**:188–89, *189n*
National Building Trades Council,
2:175, *175n*
National Building Trades Council of
America, **4**:183n, *416–17n*, **6**:17–
18n, **7**:276, 278; AFL and, **4**:416,
417n, **5**:277; and painters' controversy, **5**:448n
—conventions: 1897 (St. Louis),
4:416, *417n;* 1898 (Kansas City,
Mo.), **4**:416, *417n*
National Business League, **5**:29n
National Cash Register Co., **6**:144,
239–40; boycott, 1901–2, *5:366n,*
460n, **6**:240n; boycott, 1907 (threatened), **7**:167–68, 168n, 193, 194–
95n; convention, 1898, **4**:461n; and
open shop, **6**:488–89, **7**:166–67,
169n, 192; strike/lockout, 1898,
4:457–60, *460n;* strike/lockout,
1901–2, **5**:364–65, *366–67n*, 460n,
489–90; strike/lockout, 1906–?,
7:166, 168–*69n*, 193; workday at,
7:166–68, 168–69n, 192

National Catholic Welfare Council, and AFL Permanent Conference for Abolition of Child Labor,
12:82n
National Child Labor Committee, and
AFL Permanent Conference for Abolition of Child Labor, **12**:82n
National Citizens' Alliance, **3**:6n
National Civic Federation, **1**:438n,
5:218n, **6**:17n, 452, **7**:70, 371n,
8:303, 304n, **9**:138–39, 140n; criticisms of, **5**:463–64, 491, 511, **6**:492,
521, **8**:170, 195–99, 227n, 286–90,
290n, 421, 422n; mediation of industrial disputes, **5**:433n, **6**:13n,
186n, 408n, **7**:473n; and minimum
wage laws, **9**:460–61, 461n; Mitchell
and, **5**:217, 311, 351–52, 387–88,
388n, 389–90, 464n, 482–83, **6**:235,
8:170–71, 171n; model bill on public utilities, **9**:163–64, 164n; organization of, **5**:217, 218n; presidency
of, **6**:235–36, 236n; SG and, **5**:xv,
217, 218n, 509, 511, **6**:172, 314n,
380, 380n, 381, 394–96, 396–97n,
417–23, 475, **8**:226, **9**:132–36,
10:389n; and unemployment insurance, **12**:17–20; and workmen's
compensation laws, **9**:199, 200n
—advisory committee, **5**:217, *218n*
—annual meetings: 1903 (New York
City), **6**:379, *379n;* 1904 (New York
City), **6**:350n, 378–79, *379n*, 394–
96, 396–97n, 417, 423n; 1907 (New
York City), *7:286n;* 1916 (Washington, D.C.), **9**:372–82, *382n;* 1921
(New York City), **11**:419n; 1922
(New York City), **11**:562, **12**:17–20,
20n
—Committee on Conciliation and
Arbitration, **5**:310–11, **6**:235; and
labor disputes, **5**:354–55, 387–88,
388n, 389–90, 479; meeting, 1901
(New York City), *5:335n*, 351–53,
355n; *report of,* **5**:353–55, 355n; SG
and, **5**:334, 335n, 352–53, 355n,
357n, 367–68, 368n, 369, 372, 385n,
411n; subcommittee of, *letters from,*
5:387–90
—Committee on the Plan and Scope
of the Department on Pure Food
and Drugs, **8**:323, 324n

—Conciliation Department, **8:**118
—conferences: 1900 (on industrial arbitration, Chicago), **5:**294–307, *307n,* 309–11, 353; 1901 (on industrial conciliation, New York City), **5:**463, *464n,* 477, 478n, 486, 488n, 491, 492n, 512–14; 1903 (Chicago), **6:**191n, 312, *314n;* 1905 (on immigration, New York City), **6:**472, *473n,* 490, *490n,* 513, 513n, 521–22n; 1907 (on trusts and combinations, Chicago), **7:**245, *246n,* 256, 258–65, 321n; 1910 (on uniform legislation, Washington, D.C.), **8:**31–33, *33n*
—Department on Regulation of Interstate and Municipal Utilities, **9:**163, 164n
—executive committee, *5:218n;* meeting, 1908, **7:**316n, *321n*
—executive council, *5:218n;* meeting, 1914, **9:**51n; meeting, 1917, **10:**15n
—finance committee, **5:**483
—Industrial Committee meeting, 1921 (New York City), **11:**529, 530n
—Industrial Department, *5:218n,* 463–64, *464n,* 477–78, 483n, 497n; local branches of, **6:**105, 105n; SG and, **5:**463–64, 464n, 477–78, 482–83, 486–90, 490n, 491, 492n, 507, 513–14, **6:**104–5
—Industrial Economics, Department of, meeting, 1905 (New York City), **6:**417–23
—Minimum Wage Commission, **9:**461n
—organizing committee, *5:218n*
—Trade Agreement Department, **8:**117–19
—Welfare Department, **7:**244
National Civil Liberties Bureau, **10:**484, *485n*
National Committee for Constructive Immigration Legislation, **12:**415, 417n
National Committee for Organizing Iron and Steel Workers. *See* Iron and Steel Workers, National Committee for Organizing
National Committee on American-Japanese Relations, **12:**415, 417n

National Conference on U.S. Foreign Policy, 1898 (Saratoga, N.Y.), **4:**505–6, *506n,* **5:**3–11, *11n,* 13–14, 15n, 217
National Congress of Mothers' and Parent-Teachers' Associations, and AFL Permanent Conference for Abolition of Child Labor, **12:**82n
National Conservation Commission, **7:**322n
National Constitutional Prohibition Committee on Cooperation, **9:**179
National Consumers' League, **6:**180, *180n,* **8:**487, *493n*
National Convention for the Extension of the Foreign Commerce of the U.S., 1907 (Washington, D.C.), **7:**166, *168n*
National Council for Industrial Defense, **6:**101n, **7:**155n, *246n*
National Council for Limitation of Armaments, **12:**310, *311n*
National Council for Prevention of War, **12:**310, *311n*
National Council of Catholic Women, and AFL Permanent Conference for Abolition of Child Labor, **12:**82n
National Council of Jewish Women, and AFL Permanent Conference for Abolition of Child Labor, **12:**82n
National Council of Women, and AFL Permanent Conference for Abolition of Child Labor, **12:**82n
National Detective Agency, **6:**432n
National Educational and Economic League, **4:**49, *50n*
National Emergency Peace Conference, 1915 (Chicago), **9:**269, *274n*
National Erectors' Association, **6:**515n, **7:**12, *8:227n,* 237, 272, 309, 311, 350, 434, **9:**221, **10:**390, **11:**287, 399n
National Federation of Afro-American Women, **12:**84n
National Federation of Consumers' Cooperatives. *See* Fédération Nationale des Coopératives de Consommation
National Founders' Association, **5:**367, *368n,* **12:**261–62

—convention: 1916 (New York City), **9**:523, *523n*

National Fur Felt Hat Manufacturers' Association, **7**:455–56n

National Glass Budget (trade union journal), **3**:420, 478

National Guard, **8**:513n

National Guard Association of New Jersey, **8**:358n

National Industrial Conference Board, **9**:523, *523n*, **10**:334, 334n, 391, 407, **11**:127, 287–88

National Industrial Council, **6**:101n. *See also* National Council for Industrial Defense

Nationalist movement, **3**:355n, *4:307n*

National Labor Bureau of Clothing Manufacturers, *6:297n*

National Labor Defense Council, **10**:106–7, *107n*

National Labor party, **11**:17n, 262–66

—convention: 1919 (Chicago), **11**:214, *214n*

National Labor Publicity Organization, **10**:127, *128n*, 156–57n, 226

National Labor Reform party, **3**:204n

National Labor Tribune (labor journal), **3**:186

National Labor Union, **1**:22n, **3**:202, *204n*, 612, **4**:184, **9**:241, **11**:8, **12**:521

—conventions: 1866 (Baltimore), **3**:204n; 1868 (New York City), **5**:159, *160n;* 1872 (Columbus, Ohio), **3**:202, *204n*

National League (baseball), **9**:237n

National League of Colored Women, **12**:84n

National League of Professional Baseball Clubs et al. v. Federal Baseball Club of Baltimore, Inc., **9**:*238n*

National League of Women Voters, **6**:217n

National League on Urban Conditions among Negroes, **8**:504, *504n*

National Metal Trades Association, **5**:275–77, *277–78n,* **7**:50, 50–51n; Administrative Council, meeting, 1901 (Chicago), **5**:369, *369n;* Committee on Finance and Strikes of, **5**:369n, *372n;* and Machinists' nine-

hour campaign, **5**:332, 333–34n, 367–69, 369n, 372; and Murray Hill Agreement, **5**:216n, 432n

National Metal Trades Council. *See* metal trades unions: national alliance of

National Organization for Public Health Nursing, and AFL Permanent Conference for Abolition of Child Labor, **12**:82n

National Packing Co., strike/lockout, 1904, **6**:313–14, 314–15n

National party, **10**:225–27, *228n*, 235–38, 357, 388, 418–19

—conference: 1917 (Chicago), **10**:225, 228, *228n*, 236–37

National Race Congress, **11**:143n

National Service party, **11**:277–78

National Society for the Promotion of Industrial Education, **9**:353, *353n*

National Society for Vocational Education, *9:353n*

National Trades and Labor Congress (of Canada), *8:121n*

National Trades and Workers Association, **8**:313–14, *314n*

National Urban League, *8:504n*

National War Labor Board, *10:408n,* **11**:20, 103, **12**:450; and Birmingham, Ala., steelworkers' strike, 1918, **10**:378n, 440–44; creation of, **10**:334n, 408n, 490n; injunction against, **11**:21n; and New York harbor workers' strike, 1918 (threatened), **10**:382n, 432–33; and Springfield, Ill., street railway workers' strike, 1917–18, **10**:263n; and telegraphers' strike, 1918 (threatened), **10**:481, 482n, 486, 490n, 515n

National Watch Co., **5**:30–31, 32n

National Wheat Conference, 1923 (Chicago), **12**:285, 286n

National Wholesale Tailors' Association, **6**:50n, 406n

National Woman's party, **12**:31n, 372, 373n

National Woman's Union, **11**:506

National Women's Relief Society, and AFL Permanent Conference for Abolition of Child Labor, **12**:82n

National Women's Trade Union League, *6:483n,* **7:**237, **8:**40n, 397, **9:**108, 286, 332, 333n, 371, **10:**401, **11:**21n, 132–34, 135n, 505–6, 523–24, 525n, **12:**245, 247n, 404, 406, 417–18, 418n, 449–51; AFL financial support of, **8:**398, 398n; **9:**234, 235n; and AFL Permanent Conference for Abolition of Child Labor, **12:**82n; Chicago branch of, **9:**302–3, 371, 452; and Clayton Act, **9:**318–21, 321n; New York branch of, **9:**110n. *See also* Woman's Trade Union League
—conference: 1923 (Washington, D.C.), **12:**244, *247n*
—conventions: 1913 (St. Louis), **8:**513, *517n;* 1915 (New York City), **9:**302, *303n,* 318, 321n
"Naval Holiday," **10:**535, 537–38n
Navarro, Pedro A., **5:**182, *188n*
Neal, Elbridge H., **8:**326, 327n
Neary, Anna, **11:**240n, 275n, 525–26, *526n,* **12:**38n
Neary, Timothy F., *9:267n,* 453; *letter to,* **9:**266–67
Nebraska: Democratic state convention, 1908, *7:300n;* election of 1908, **7:**300, 300n, 353n
Nebraska State Federation of Labor, **7:**481, *482n*
—convention: 1909 (Lincoln), **7:**481, *482n*
Nee, William C., *10:177n; letter from,* **10:**176–77
Neebe, Oscar W., **1:***, *462n,* **2:***, 53, *55n,* **3:***, 350, *350n,* 358
Neely, Matthew M., *12:171n*
Neff, William B., **9:**138n
Negro Artisan, The (DuBois, ed.), *6:91n*
Neighborhood Guild (New York City), **3:**458n
Neihaus, Herman, **6:**389, *390n*
Neill, Charles P., **7:**285, *286n*
Nejedly, Joseph E., **1:**432, *433n*
Nelson, Charles B., **7:**340, 340n
Nelson, Henry J., **5:**280, *281n,* 283
Nelson, John M., **12:**346, *349n;* and election of 1924, **12:**430, 432, 433n, 481, 484n, 491
Nelson, Knute, **8:**132n, 362, *363n,* **9:**10n, 92, **12:**39n

Nelson, Oscar F., **10:***, 242, *243n,* 297, **12:***, 67, *68n,* 490
Nelson, Robert, **2:**301, *304n,* 409n
Nelson Morris (company), strike/lockout, 1904, **6:**313–14, 314–15n
Nesbit, Robert B., *7:25n; letter from,* **7:**23–25
Nesmith, Charles C., **6:**293, *294n*
Nestor, Agnes, **7:***, *275n,* **8:**456n, **9:**422n, **10:***, *82n,* 97, 333n, **12:***, 418n, 451, *451n;* at AFL conventions, **7:**275, 275n, **10:**467, 468n; *wire from,* **10:**81–82
Netherlandisch Isralitiche Sickefund, *letter to,* **2:**116–17
Nettleton, A. E., Co., **8:**157, 157n; boycott, 1907, **7:**186n; shop association of, **7:**339–40; strike/lockout, 1906–7, **7:**185, *186n,* 339
Nettleton, Albert E., **7:**339–40, *340n*
Neuroth, William B., **4:***, 77, *77n,* 107
neutrality, American, **9:**254n, **10:**199–200
Nevin, A. Parker, **10:**52n
Newark (N.J.) Central Labor Federation, **4:**97n, 105, *106n*
New Bedford, Mass., textile workers' strike, 1898. *See* textile workers: strikes/lockouts: 1898 (New Bedford, Mass.)
New Haven, Central Labor Council of, **1:**459n
New Haven Trade Council, **1:**458, *459n*
New Jersey: election of 1906, **7:**112; and labor standards, maintenance of, **10:**99; state police of, **8:**357–58, 358n
New Jersey, Federation of Trades and Labor Unions of. *See* New Jersey State Federation of Labor
New Jersey Board of Arbitration, **3:**434n
New Jersey Bureau of Statistics of Labor and Industries, **1:**328, 340, *353n*
New Jersey State Federation of Labor, *8:135n*
—conventions: 1910 (Newark), **8:**135, *135n;* 1914 (Newark), **9:**168, *168n*
Newlands, Francis G., **4:**488n, **5:**457, 458n, **9:**55, *57n,* 92, **10:**17n
New Majority (Chicago labor journal), **12:**311

Newman, Jennie, *10:369n; letter from,*
  10:368–69
Newman, M. H., **4:**254–55, 257n
Newmark, Bernhard, **1:**384, *384n*
New Mexico: AFL organizers in,
  8:279–80, 280n; copper miners'
  strike in, 1917, **10:**167, *169n,* 248
New Orleans Board of Trade, **3:**186,
  243n
New Orleans Building Laborers'
  Council, **3:**243n
New Orleans Central Labor Union,
  5:261, *262n,* **6:**534, **10:**460
New Orleans Central Trades and Labor Council, *3:244n,* **5:**240n, 262n,
  6:533–34, **7:**493–97, 498n, **8:**355–56,
  357n
New Orleans Dock and Cotton Council, indictment of members of,
  8:182n, **9:**82
New Orleans general strike, 1892,
  3:185–86, 241–42, *243n,* 252, 295n,
  5:344, 346n
New Orleans longshoremen's case,
  8:177, *182n,* 265, 466, **9:**82
New Orleans United Labor Council,
  7:494, *498n*
New Orleans Workingmen's Amalgamated Council, **3:**186, 243n; injunction against leaders of, **3:**243n
Newport News Ship Building and Dry
  Dock Co., **4:**499n, **10:**410n
New Republic (periodical), **10:**356,
  357n
newsboys, **1:**307–8, **5:**475–77, 477n
*New Slavery, The: Investigation into the
  Sweating System as Applied to the Man-
  ufacturing of Wearing Apparel* (Morgan), *3:103n*
Newspaper Enterprise Association,
  9:397
"New Trade Unionism," **3:**77, *78n,*
  113–14, 181, 403, 420, 503, **4:**10,
  16–18, 89, 98n, 102
New York, New Haven, and Hartford
  Railroad Co., **5:**497n, **9:**516
New York, Workingmen's Federation
  of the State of, *1:361n,* **2:**96n
New York and Porto Rico Steamship
  Co., strike/lockout, 1905, **6:**470,
  470–71n
New York and Vicinity, Central Federated Union of Greater, *1:379n,*
  8:208n, **9:**167, 269, 274n, 278n,
  291n, **11:**17n, 357–58n
New York and Vicinity, Central Trades
  and Labor Council of Greater,
  11:357–58n, 445–46, 449, 449n,
  458–59n, 467, 467n, 533n, **12:**170n;
  executive board, meeting, *minutes
  of,* **11:**454–57; organizational meeting of, **11:**354–57, 358–59n
New York Association of Housedress
  and Kimono Manufacturers, **8:**442n
New York Call (socialist journal),
  10:394
New York Central and Hudson River
  Railroad: strike/lockout, 1890,
  2:378–79, *382n,* 399, **11:**330; strike/
  lockout, 1892, **3:**215n
New York Central Railroad Co.,
  strike/lockout, 1900, **5:**247, *247n*
New York Central Railroad Co. v. White,
  10:143, *147n*
*New York Central Railroad Co. v. Win-
  field,* **10:**144, *147n*
New York Charter, Greater, **3:**471–72,
  472n
New York City: above-ground cables
  in, **1:**432, 433n; breadline raid
  in, **5:**33–34, *35n;* building trades
  unions of, *letter to,* **6:**183–85; election of 1886, *1:429–34,* 438n, 439,
  441–49, **2:**45; election of 1887, **2:**45;
  free lectures in, **6:**267, 268n; Gary
  Plan for education in, **9:**429, 430n;
  and George mayoral campaign,
  1:429–34, 438n, 439, 441–49, **8:**133–
  34, **11:**9, **12:**33, 34n; Grand Central
  Station explosion in, **8:**307, *312n;*
  rapid transit system in, **5:**81–82,
  82n; trade unions in, *letter to,* **3:**367
New York City Allied Printing Trades
  Council, **9:**153n; investigation of,
  9:72, *74n,* 89
New York City and County, Board of
  Aldermen of, *letter to,* **3:**410–11
New York City and Vicinity, Central
  Federated Union of, **10:**392–95;
  and People's Council of America
  for Democracy and Peace, **10:**127,
  127n, 156, 157n, 206, 226
New York City Board of Business
  Agents, **11:**445

New York City Board of Civil Justices, **3:**377

New York City Board of Estimate and Apportionment, **3:**385, 385n

New York City Board of Health, **1:**47, 50, *54n,* 56, 56n, 58, 67, 79, 103, 111, *112n,* 130, 200, 208

New York City Board of Trade and Transportation, **7:**168n, **11:**564n

New York City Board of Walking Delegates, **2:**120n, 305, **3:**61, *61–62n,* 63, 190, 268n; injunction against, **3:**61, 63

New York City breweries: boycott, 1888–1902, **2:**100–101, *101n,* 107, 341, **6:**89n; boycott, 1902, **6:**89, 90n

New York City Building Trades Council, **3:**61–62n, **5:**447–48n, **9:**292n, **11:**324, 324n, 352–53, 356–57, 378, 445, 467, 467–68n, 530, **12:**75

New York City Cap Manufacturers' Association, **6:**407n

New York City Central Federated Union, *1:379n,* **5:**446, 448n, **6:**10n, 518n, **7:**15, 346n, 470n; and election of 1906, **7:**110n; and election of 1908, **7:**373, 374n; formation of, **1:**379n, **2:**192; Miners' Relief Committee of, **6:**35n; and National Civic Federation, **6:**394, 396, 396–97n

New York City Central Labor Federation, *1:379n,* **2:**426, **3:**62n, 85n, 353, 378, 397–98, **4:**11, 15n, 16–18; *circulars of,* **3:**110–14, 132; meetings, *news accounts of,* **2:**249–51, 367–70, 382–83, **3:**11–14; *reports to,* **4:**65–70, 70n; and Socialist Labor party, membership in, **3:**8–9, 11, 65–66; and Socialist Trade and Labor Alliance, founding of, **4:**97n, 105, 135

—1889: chartering of, by AFL, **2:**191, 195, 206–7, 213, 387, 392, **3:**8; conflict of, with Central Labor Union, **2:**193, 195, 206–7; formation of, **1:**379n, **2:**191, 386, 392, **3:**8; merger of, with Central Labor Union, **2:**191, 358, 387, 392–93, **3:**8; and SG nomination for senator, **2:**245, 247n, 249–51, **3:**110, **4:**152

—1890: AFL 1890 convention and, **2:**192, 378, 383, 386–408, 417–18,

421–24, **3:**9, 12–13, 17, 110, 655, **4:**368, 368n; application for new AFL charter, **2:**192, 362–63, 367–70, 377–78, 387, 391, 394–95, **3:**8; application for old AFL charter, **2:**192, 358–59, 387, 391, 393–94, **3:**8; reorganization of, **1:**379n, **2:**191–92, 387, 393, **3:**8

—1899: merger of, with Central Labor Union, **2:**192

New York City Central Labor Union, *1:379n,* **2:**114, **3:**62n, 65, 378, **4:**15n, 18, 56, 230, 248, 348, 399n, **5:**64n; and Amalgamated Trades and Labor Union, **1:**101n; Building Trades Section of, **2:**120, 120n; and Central Labor Federation, **2:**192–93, 195, 206–7, 392–93, **3:**8; and Cigar Makers, **1:**376–79, 407; corruption in, **2:**191, 207, 392; and eight-hour movement, **2:**183, 184n; factions in, **2:**191, 392–93; formation of, **1:**248, 379n; and Haymarket clemency campaign, **2:**55n, 58n, 61; and KOL, **1:**191, **2:**292–93; and Labor Day, **3:**106n; *letter to,* **1:**411–12; and party politics, **1:**248, 379n, 429–30, 433n, **2:**45, 161, **3:**115n; re-formation of, **3:**115n; and SG nomination for senator, **2:**245, **4:**152

New York City Cloak, Suit, and Skirt Manufacturers' Protective Association, **8:**111, **11:**571; injunction, **8:**114n; injunction against, **11:**571n

New York City Committee of One Hundred, **3:**161–62

New York City Department of Docks, ·**3:**384, 385n

New York (City) Federation of Labor, **3:**111, 113–14, *115n,* 133

New York City Rapid Transit Commission, **5:**82n

New York City United Board of Building Trades, *3:62n*

New York commissioner of labor, **8:**427, 438–39, 439n

New Yorker Staats-Zeitung, **1:**310, **2:**124, 126n; boycott, 1892, *3:486n;* strike/lockout, 1892, **3:**484, *486n*

New Yorker Volkszeitung (socialist journal), **1:**97, 169, 207, 252–54, 263n,

359, 429, 459n, **2:**191, 400, **3:**17, **5:**72–73, 74n; editor of, *letters to,* **2:**211–12, **4:**65, 75–76; and Garment Workers, **4:**135–36, 137n; and SG, **4:**65, 65n, 75–77, 77n, 134, 137n, 154, 155n, **5:**512–13, 514n; and Tailors, **4:**137n

New York Evening Journal, **5:**63n, **6:**521, 521–22n; editor of, *letter to,* **5:**61–63

New York Evening Post, and sympathy strikes, **6:**25–27, 29n

New York Harbor Wage Adjustment Board of Arbitration, **10:**381–82n; wage awards of, **10:**380–81, 381–82n, 434n

New York Joint Board of Cloakmakers' Unions, **11:**571n

New York Life Insurance Co., **6:**493n

New York Maritime Exchange, *7:177n*

New York News Dealers' and Stationers' Protective Association:
—strike/lockout: 1918 (New York City), **10:**335, *336n*

New York Office of Factory Inspection, **3:**456, *456n*

New York Peace Society, **7:**214n, **8:**205, *208n;* mass meeting, 1911, *8:208n*

New York Press, letter to, **2:**349–53

New York Public Service Commission, **10:**15n

New York Railroad Commission, **2:**4, *10n*

New York Railways Co., strike/lockout, 1916, **9:**490–92, *492n,* **12:**23n

New York State: election of 1906, **7:**96–97, 109–10, 110n; election of 1908, **7:**373, 374n; election of 1922, **12:**169; jury duty in, **2:**8; and labor standards, maintenance of, **10:**76, 77n, 99–100; literacy test and right to vote in, **11:**379–80, 380n; New Capitol Commission of, **4:**16n
—constitutional conventions: 1887, proposed, **2:**6, *11n;* 1894, **3:**273–74, *274n,* 410–11, 411n, 549–50, 550n, 593–94, 594n, **4:**152–53; 1915, **9:**279–80, *280n,* **10:**311

New York State Board of Arbitration, **2:**5, 7, *10n,* **4:**153

New York State Board of Mediation and Arbitration, **2:**5, *10n,* 101n, 197n, 427, **3:**109n, 297n, 303, 428, 434n, 456, 456n, **4:**230, 230–31n, **5:**236n, 247n, 379n, 384n, **6:**484n, **8:**114n; and mediation of clothing cutters' strike, 1893, **3:**305–40

New York State Board of Trade and Transportation, **12:**39n

New York State Branch, AFL, **1:**361n, *2:81n, 96n,* 121
—convention: 1888 (Albany), **2:**81, *81n*

New York State Bureau of Employment, **11:**243, 243n

New York State Bureau of Labor Statistics, **1:**151, 258, *364n,* **2:**5, *10n,* **3:**303, 456, 456n

New York State Department of Labor, **3:**456n, **9:**277, 277n

New York State Factory Investigating Commission, **8:**219n, 299, *301n,* 323n, 389n, 429n, 438, 471–72, **9:**137, 138n, 156, 258–59, 259n, 316; *report of,* 1912, **8:**328–29, 329n

New York State Federation of Labor, *1:361n, 2:96n,* **8:**326–27, **9:**62, 278n, 280, 280n, 408n, **10:**329–30n, **11:**458n
—conventions: 1914 (Schenectady), **9:**178n; 1917 (Jamestown), **10:**192, *194n,* 196–207

New York state industrial board, **9:**277n

New York State Industrial Commission, **9:**277n, **10:**76, 143, 146, 455

New York State Printing Office, **2:**7, *11n*

New York State Tenement House Commission, **5:**253–54, *254n*

New York State Workingmen's Assembly, **1:**360–61, *361n,* 402n, **2:**96n, **3:**303
—conventions: 1886, **2:**9; 1887 (Albany), **2:**3–10, *10n,* 11–13, 13n, 14; 1895 (Albany), **4:**10–15, *15n;* 1903 (Schenectady), **6:**179, *179n*

New York State Workingmen's Assembly, Political Branch of the, *1:447n,* **2:**8–9; *circular of,* **1:**446–47
—convention: 1886 (Syracuse), **2:**8–9, *11n*

New York state workmen's compensation commission, **9:**277, 277n

New York Sun, **1**:169; boycott, 1899–
1902, *5:236n,* 477, 477n; editor of,
letters to, **1**:123–24, **2**:284–86, **8**:337–
38; strike/lockout, 1899–1902,
5:234, *236n,* 405, 406n
New York Supreme Court, **2**:427n,
3:148
New York Unionist (labor journal),
1:268n
New York Working Women's Society,
2:154, *155n,* 289n, **3**:29n
New York World: editor of, *letters to,*
3:553–54, **5**:309, **9**:45; editor of, *wire
to,* **11**:246; libel case, **8**:203, *204n*
Nicaragua, **10**:11, **12**:389n
Nicholas II, **5**:14, *15n,* **6**:491n, **10**:45n,
310
Nicholls, Thomas D., **7**:96, *98n,* 113,
130, 142n, 457, **8**:89, 100–101
Nichols, Alvah E., **12**:552, *554n*
Nichols, William B., **10**:404, *404n*
Nickel Plate Railroad, strike/lockout,
1892, **3**:215n
Nickelsberg, Kaufman, **1**:68, *69n,* 74,
93
Niederstein, John, **1**:384, *384n*
Niehaus, Charles H., **7**:442, *443n*
Nielsen, Dagmar J., *8:62n; letters to,*
8:56–61, 125–26
Nietzsche, Friedrich W., **11**:298, *299n*
Niglutsch, John C., **1**:260, *263n*
Nimmo, John, **9**:283n
Nineteenth Century Club, **4**:446, *446n*
Nishimura, Yoshio, *12:120n; letter from,*
12:119–20
"Noble Movement and a Valiant
Leader, A" (Walsh), *4:296n*
Nockels, Edward N., *6:342n,* 469n,
7:347, 347n, 350n, 387, 417n,
9:91, 205n, 354, **10**:215–17, 302–3,
11:18n, **12**:55, 55n, 311–12, 315n;
circular of, **12**:312–15; *letters from,*
7:357–60, 362–64, **11**:281–83; *letters
to,* **6**:342, **11**:275–78, 368–73; *wire
from,* **10**:5
Noe, Ralph W., *12:217n; letter to,*
12:215–17
Nolan, Edward, **9**:517–18n
Nolan, J. C., *3:468n; letter to,* **3**:466–68
Nolan, John I., **11**:152, *153n*
Nolan, Mr. (New York City worker?),
4:296

Nolda, Henry, **9**:214n
Nolde and Horst Co., **9**:263n
Nolde and Horst Co. v. Kruger et al.,
9:263n
Nolte, Ed, *letter to,* **9**:166–67
Non-Partisan League, **11**:227, *228n,*
347n
non-partisan political campaign com-
mittees, local, **12**:40, 160–61, 170
Non-Partisan Successes (AFL National
Non-Partisan Political Campaign
Committee), **12**:170, *172n,* 186–87,
437, *438n*
Noonan, James P., **11**:191n, 365n,
12:*, 104–5, *107n,* 280, 349n, 433n,
550
Noonan, John J., **12**:551, *554n*
Noonan, Martin J., *4:431n,* **5**:46–47,
48–49n, **6**:3, *4n*
Norfolk and Norwich Amalgamated
Labourers' Union (Great Britain),
3:146n
*Norfolk and Western Railway Co. v. Ear-
nest,* **10**:143, *147n*
Norfolk (Va.) Central Labor Union
(Colored), *10:177n*
Norfolk (Va.) Metal Trades Council,
10:222–23
Norfolk (Va.) Navy Yard, strike at,
1917, **10**:222–23, *223n*
Noriega, R. F., **12**:412n; *letter to,*
12:410–11
Norland, John M., **11**:*, 365, *366n*
Norman, Carl A., *12:414n; letter to,*
12:412–14
Norris, George W., **7**:27, 31, *32n,*
8:446
North Carolina: and alien contract la-
bor law, **7**:185, 186n; organizing in,
6:400–402
North Carolina State Federation of
Labor, *6:48n,* **11**:511
Northcliffe, Charles W. H., *9:289n*
Northcliffe press, **9**:288, 289–90n
North Dakota Non-Partisan League,
9:422, *424n*
Northern Coal Co., **5**:94–95
Northern Michigan copper miners'
strike, 1913–14, **8**:512, *512–13n,*
9:11–13, 13–14n, 25–28, 43–44,
44n, 46–47, 64–67, 177, 181–83,
210, 301; congressional investiga-

tion of, **9:**28n, 46, 47–*48n,* 51–52,
52n, 65–66, 68n, 96n
Northern Pacific Railroad: injunction,
3:559, 561n; strike/lockout, 1894,
3:561n
"Northwestern Alliance." *See* Farmers'
Alliance, National ("Northwestern
Alliance")
Northwestern Brewers' Association:
boycott, 1905, **6:***442n;* strike/lock-
out, 1905, **6:***442n;* strike injunction,
6:440, 442n
Northwestern Federation of Colored
Women's Clubs, **12:**83, *83–84n*
North Yakima (Wash.) Trades and La-
bor Council, *10:185n*
Norton, George L., **3:***, 162–63, *163n,*
177–78; *letters to,* **3:**170–73, 275–76,
350–51
Norton, Miner G., *12:26n; letter to,*
12:25–26
Norton, Sleeper, and Co., **2:**208;
strike/lockout, 1888, *2:208n*
Notton, Frank M., *3:409n; letter to,*
3:408
Novel Proposition, A (Lubin), **3:**474, *477n*
Noyes, Crosby S., **5:**243n
nurses, male, **9:**416–18
Nye, Frank M., **8:**444, 446, *448n*

Oakes, Elmer, **5:**279n
Oakes, John, *11:106n; letter from,*
11:106
Oates, William C., **3:**163, **4:**232, *233n*
Oberlin Summer School of Christian
Sociology, **4:**44, *45n*
Oberwager, Charles, **6:**396, 397n
Obregón Salido, Alvaro, **9:**160n, 306,
307n, 427n, **11:**300, 300n, 303n,
340–41, 404n, **12:**121n, 392n, 525;
letters to, **11:**302–3, **12:**391–92; and
U.S. recognition of government of,
12:100, 100–101n
O'Brien, John, **3:***, *82n,* 255, 257,
258n, 259, 371–72n; *letters to,* **3:**81–
82, 213–14, 370–71
O'Brien, John R., **6:***, 176, *176n*
O'Brien, Michael, **1:**283, 285n
O'Brien, Michael F., **7:***, *314n; letter
from,* **7:**313–14
O'Brien, Patrick, **9:**13n
O'Brien, Patrick L., **2:**129, *129n,* 135–36

O'Brien, William J., **5:**153, *154n,*
6:516n
Observer (British newspaper), **9:**289n
O'Callaghan, John, **1:***, 134, *139n; report of,* **1:**140–51
Ochart, Bolivar, **10:**313
O'Connell, James, **3:***, *407n,* **4:***, *80n,*
106n, 157, 177, 222n, 370, 371n,
5:*, *31–32n,* 126n, 157, 158n, 365,
6:*, 19n, *67n,* 112, 135n, 190, 216n,
232, 259, 488–89, **7:***, *7n,* 145, 209,
244, 446, **8:***, *31n,* 62, 144n, 173n,
454, 494, 495–96n, **9:***, *10n,* 71,
157n, 488n, 508, **10:***, 52n, 305,
307n, 544, **11:***, 272, 274, *275n,*
12:*, 246, *247n;* at AFL conventions, **4:**97n, 99n, 270, 272n, 407,
408n, **5:**37, 38n, 172–75, 176n,
435–38, 438n, **6:**62, 67n, 210n, 370,
500, 503n, **7:**135–36, 142n, 271,
272n, **8:**18n, 289, 290n, 295–96,
415, 416n, **9:**224–25, 225n; at
AFL Executive Council meetings,
4:240–41, 266–67, 321–23, **8:**503–4,
9:272, 436; and AFL Labor Representation Committee, **7:**63, **8:**124;
and AFL per capita tax, **5:**57, 58n;
and black workers, **4:**4, 407, **10:**421,
424–27; and Clayton Act, **9:**91; and
Committee on Industrial Relations,
9:422n; and conservation conference, 1908, **7:**322n; and election of
1906, **7:**111n, 120; and election of
1908, **7:**377; and election of 1924,
12:184n, 433n, 456, 459–60, 461n,
481, 489–90; election of, as AFL
vice-president, **4:**95, 98–99, 278n,
414, **5:**57n, 177n, 294n, 445, **6:**209,
376n, 509n, **7:**281n, 427n, **9:**38n,
226n, 348n; and Granite Cutters'
assessment, **5:**233, 238; and jurisdiction questions, **5:**78, 103–4,
104–5n, 113n, 172, 172n, 173–75,
257, 290–91, 292n, 448n, **7:**148–49,
150n, 204n, **9:**388, 390n; *letters from,*
5:30–31, 103–4, 276, **6:**151–52,
9:171–72; *letters to,* **3:**405–7, **4:**221,
500–501, **5:**112–13; and Machinists'
nine-hour campaign, **5:**333, 340,
357n, 367–69; and McNamara case,
8:237, 257; mediation of industrial
disputes, **4:**178n, 319–20, 501n; and

metal trades unions, national alliance of, **5:**275; and Miners, Western Federation of, **8:**105, 106n, 144–45, 170; and Murray Hill Agreement, **5:**214; and National Civic Federation, **5:**464n, **8:**324n; and organizing, **5:**43, 47; retirement of, from AFL vice-presidency, **10:**475; and SG 1895 presidential candidacy, **4:**79; and steelworkers' strike, 1909–10, **8:**30, 53; and steelworkers' strike, 1918 (Birmingham, Ala.), **10:**440–41; and U.S. Commission on Industrial Relations, **8:**332n, 455–56, 456n, **9:**9, 138, 171–72, 311, 312n, 322; and "We Don't Patronize List" (AFL), **7:**312–13

O'Connell, John, **9:**518n
O'Connell, John A., *10:92n; wire to,* **10:**92
O'Connell, John H., **3:**190, *190n*
O'Connell, John J., **2:**332, **5:**244–45, *245n*
O'Connor, Julia, **11:**20n
O'Connor, Thomas V., **9:**83n, 104n, **10:***, 381n, 433, *434n,* 460, **11:**532n
O'Dea, Thomas, **1:***, 390, *390n,* 458, **2:***, *131n,* **3:***, 145, *145n; letter to,* **2:**131
Odell, Benjamin, **5:**361n
Odessa, capture of, **10:**342, 345n
O'Donnell, Edward, **4:**190, *191n,* 270, 272n, **5:**78, *79n; letter to,* **4:**391–92
O'Donnell, Hugh, **3:**207, 210–*11n,* 217–18, 218n
O'Donnell, John R., **3:**472, *472n*
O'Donnell, Thomas, **4:***, 477, *478n,* **5:***, 418, *419n*
Oederlin, Frederick, **10:**543n
O'Fallon, Daniel W., *4:140n; letter to,* **4:**138–40
Ogden, Harry M., **2:**70, *71n,* 73, **4:**123
Ogden, John W., **10:***, 522, *524n*
Ogg, Robert Y., **2:**213, *213n,* 268, 275, **3:**136–37, **4:**179, *180n*
Oglesby, Richard J., **2:**53, *59n,* 60–62, 62n; *letter to,* **2:**59
O'Gorman, James A., **9:**194, *194n*
O'Hagan, M., **5:**90, *93n*
O'Hanlon, John M., **11:**447, *448n*
O'Hara, John J., *9:233n; letter from,* **9:**232–33

Ohio: election of 1906, **7:**105–7, 107n; election of 1908, **7:**397
Ohio Federation of Labor, *1:455n, 8:17n*
Ohio Railroad Commission, **3:**294n
Ohio State Bureau of Labor Statistics, **1:**336, *353n,* **2:**143
Ohio State Federation of Labor, **8:**16, *17n,* **9:**511
Ohio State Trades and Labor Assembly, **1:**453, *455n,* **8:***17n*
Ohio Valley Trades and Labor Assembly, **1:**390, *390n,* **2:**75, *76n,* **11:**270
Olander, Victor A., **9:***, 91, *94n,* **10:***, 46–47, *48n,* 131, 134n, 215, **11:***, 452–53, *454n,* **12:***, 38, *40n,* 295, 311–12, 315n, 333, 334n; *letter to,* **12:**366–67; and War Labor Conference Board, **10:**334n, 407
O'Leary, John, **5:**435n
Oliver, Lucien S., **2:**60, *63n*
Ollinger, William, **4:**337n
Olmsted, Marlin, **8:**89n
Olney, Richard, **3:**343n, 404, *405n,* 522–23, 647, **4:**304n, **5:**308n, **7:**250n; *letter to,* **7:**247–49
Olsen, P. H., **4:**294n
Olsen, S. A., *letter to,* **9:**422–24
Omaha (Nebr.) Central Labor Union, **5:**160n
O'Mahoney, Thomas F., **3:**34, *41n*
O'Malley, Timothy T., **2:***, 256, *256n*
O'Meara, Patrick, **11:**321n
Omholt, Andrew, **12:**49n
One Big Union, **9:**103, 245, **11:**112–13, 149, 218, 412, 415, 550n, **12:**63, 87–88, 101–2, 219–20, 234, 307; in Canada, **11:**75, 75–76n, 94, 281n, 380, **12:**438, 442n
—Lumber, Camp, and Agricultural Workers' Department, *12:442n*
O'Neil, Edward J., **6:**15, *19n*
O'Neil (labor spy), **5:**331
O'Neil, Michael J., **5:**38, *39n*
O'Neill, John, **7:**387, *387n*
O'Neill, John J., **2:**123, *123n*
O'Neill, John M., **6:**452, *453n,* 454
O'Neill, Joseph F., **7:**44, *44–45n*
Open Letter to Ministers of the Gospel, An (AFL), *8:442n*
open shop, **6:**401, **11:**216, **12:**207, 284, 486; AFL response to, **11:**401–2,

420–21, 423, 426n; Drew and,
8:227n; efforts by employers to im-
pose, **5:**367n, **6:**406, 407n, 442n,
445–46n, 488–89, 515n, **7:**11n,
12, 19n, 49–50, 50n, 69–70, 70n,
158n, 166–67, 169n, 183n, 192,
235, 302–4, 304n, 434, 456n, 461n,
472, 473n, 480, 496, **8:**148n, 160n,
10:254n, 287n, **11:**339, 342–43,
519–20, 520n, **12:**58, 169, 216, 262,
408n, 451n; Gary and, **11:**169; and
government contracts, **10:**229–30,
232–34; and labor turnover, **11:**333,
555; and Rochester (N.Y.) Central
Trades and Labor Council, **11:**456,
459n; SG and, **6:**327–30, 334, 337,
339n, **8:**168, **11:**342–43, 383, 444,
519–20, **12:**174–76, 179, 181, 183n
Oppeit, E. J., **1:**210n
Oppenheim, Joseph, **1:**408, *409n,* 418
Oppenheim, Simeon, **1:**7, *7n*
Oppenheimer, Moses, *5:76n; letter to,*
5:74–76
Oppermann, Charles, **3:**397, *399n*
"Opposing Forces in the Industrial
World" (Easley), **7:**244, *246–47n*
Orange Free State, **5:**122n
Orchi, John A., **4:**39, *42n*
Order and the Cigar-Makers, The (KOL),
1:401n, 411n, 464, **2:**21, 23n, 142–43
Oregon: election of 1908, **7:**414,
414n; and senators of the United
States, direct election of, **6:**536–37,
537n; and woman suffrage, **6:**532,
533n
Oregon Industrial Welfare Commis-
sion, **9:**317n
Oregon State Federation of Labor,
10:490n, **11:**51
Oregon v. Bock, 7:118n
O'Reilly, Leonora, **11:**134, *135n*
O'Reilly, Thomas, **1:**:*, 390, *391n,* **2:**:*,
55, *55n*
O'Reilly, Thomas J., **2:**332, *338n*
Orenburg, capture of, **10:**342, 345n
organize, right to, **1:**354–55, **4:**483,
5:83, **6:**213, 340n, **7:**11, 252n, **8:**228,
519n, **9:**24, 183, 262n, 293, 301,
316, 418, 492n, 506, **10:**45, 167,
187, 198, 252, 284, 408n, 486, 489,
490n, 514, **11:**11, 18n, 94n, 146n,
242, 304, 433, **12:**174–76, 306, 486,

487n; AFL and, **10:**346, **11:**7n, 186,
230–33, 235, 310, 327, 422, **12:**91;
and Industrial Conference, 1919,
11:158–59, 168, 173, 177–82
Organizing Committee of the Mexi-
can Liberal Party. *See* Junta Orga-
nizadora del Partido Liberal Mexi-
cano
Organ Makers, United Association of,
2:69n
Orgler, Solomon, **1:**75, 76n
O'Rielly, Thomas F., *letter to,* **3:**469
O'Rourke (delegate), **2:**245
O'Rourke, Eugene F., **5:**50, *53n,* 175,
176n
O'Rourke, Matthew J., *3:373n; letter to,*
3:372–73
Orr, Samuel, **11:**262n, 447n
Osborne, George W., **1:**165, *166n*
Osborne, Loyal A., **6:**136, 139, 139n
O'Shea, John E., **2:**315, *315n*
O'Shell, Thomas J., **4:**374, *375n*
O'Sullivan, John F., **2:**:*, *409n,* **3:**:*,
119, *120n,* 607, 607n, **4:**:*, *93n,*
118n, 169, 432n, **5:**:*, *38n,* **6:**:*, *35n;*
news accounts of AFL 1901 convention,
5:430–32, 432n, 433–35, 438–40,
444–45; at AFL conventions, **2:**407,
3:647, 655–56, 660n, **4:**91–92,
93n, 271, 272n, 283, **5:**36, 38, 38n;
death of, **6:**33–35, 35n, 38, 40–41,
117; *letter from,* **4:**189–91; *letters to,*
3:414–15, 586–87, **4:**144, 340–41,
5:124–26, 153–54
O'Sullivan, Kenney, **4:**191, *191n*
O'Sullivan, Mary Kenney, **4:**:*, 144,
144n, 191, **5:**:*, *154n,* **6:**:*, *41–42n,*
483, 484n, **7:**:*, 237–38, *238n;* at
AFL convention, **6:**355, 355n; *letters
to,* **6:**40–41, 117–18. *See also* Kenney,
Mary E.
O'Sullivan, Michael, **7:**41–42n, **8:**:*,
149, *151n,* 322
Otis, Harrison G., **6:**213, *213n,*
415–16, **7:**383, **8:**280, 309, 435–36,
9:484n; and *Los Angeles Times* building, bombing of, **8:**128–30, 131n,
221, 223, 307, 349
Ott, Godfrey (variously Gottfried) A.,
10:92n; letter to, **10:**91–92
Ottawa (Ont.) Trades and Labor
Council, **6:**156, *158n*

Ottendorfer, Oswald, **3**:484, *486n*
Oudegeest, Jan, **9**:*, 240n, 265, *266n*,
289n, **10**:*, 90n, *105n*, **11**:*, 223,
224n, 440n, **12**:*, *139*–40n, 369n;
cable from, **10**:104; *cable to,* **10**:104–5;
letters to, **11**:436–39, **12**:137–39
Oulmann, Peter, **5**:*, 418, *419n*
Ouray Building, **7**:446–47
Our Toiling Children (Kelley), **2**:156,
157n
out-of-work benefits, **1**:47, 62, 71,
103–4, 122, 134, 136–38, 139n, **2**:86,
144–46, 146n, 153, **5**:240–41
output, restriction of, **2**:153, **10**:116,
340, 340n
"outsiders" and labor movement. *See*
trade unions: and "outsiders"
Overcoat and Suit Makers' local 30
(New York City), **3**:379
Overman, Lee S., *10:412n*
overproduction, SG and, **4**:25, 37
overtime work, **5**:189, 216n, 250n,
7:42, **8**:43, 44n, 61, 440n, **9**:215–16,
10:119, 232, **11**:159; AFL and, **5**:16,
8:58–59, **10**:83–84, 84n, **11**:504n;
pay for, **5**:107n, 278n, 496n, **6**:13n,
18n, 32n, **7**:52n, **8**:59, 61, 114n,
122n, 277n, 322n, 325–26n, 440n,
442n, 452n, 503n, **9**:305n, **10**:14n,
83–84, 92, 234, 245, 246n, 280n,
281, 284n, 318n, 376, 404n, 454,
459n, 489, **11**:27n, 61n, 120, 126n,
159, 352n, 408, 453n, 539–40n,
12:9; on railroads, **10**:21n, **11**:408,
539–40n, **12**:27–28, 86n, 107n, 203;
SG and, **5**:16–17, 350, **10**:83–84,
99–100, 245, 281, 443–44, 454n,
456–59, **11**:408–9
Owen, Fred L., **12**:38n
Owen, Robert, **1**:217n
Owen, Robert D., **1**:217n
Owen, Robert L., **10**:310, *312n*
Owen, William C., *3:355n; letter to,*
3:353–54
Owen, William L., **7**:111, *112n*
Owens, Charles E., **2**:*, 305–6, *307n*
Oxman, Frank, **10**:92–93n
Oyler, Charles P., **2**:*, 65, *68n; letter to,*
2:224
Oyster, Edward W., **2**:70, *71n*, 79
Oyster, Guy H., **10**:470n, 522–23,
524n, **11**:67, 91, 459, 543, 547,

12:12, 155n; and AFL mission to
Europe, spring 1919, **11**:40n, 57;
and AFL mission to Europe, summer 1919, **11**:111n, 117–18, 460n;
and AFL mission to Mexico, 1921,
11:404n
oystermen, **2**:67–68

Pabst, Gustav G., **5**:106, *108n*, **9**:354,
355n
Pabst Brewing Co.: boycott, 1899,
5:106–7, *107n*, 108–9, 110n; *letter
from,* **5**:108–9; *letter to,* **5**:109; strike/
lockout, 1899, **5**:106–7, *107n*
Pacelli, Tito, *6:290n*, **7**:*, *150n; letter
from,* **7**:148–49; *letter to,* **6**:290
Pacific Coast, Representative Assembly of Trades and Labor Unions of
the, **1**:231, *232n*
Pacific Coast, Representative Council
of the Federated Trades and Labor Organizations of the, **1**:*, 458,
460n, **2**:*, 122, 123n, **3**:*, 27, 27n,
30, 31n, 477n
—convention: 1893 (Seattle), **3**:214,
215n
Pacific Gas and Electric Co., strike/
lockout, 1913–14, **9**:38–*39n*
Pacific Mills, strike/lockout, 1882,
1:296, *327n*, 355–56
pacifists: SG and, **10**:201, 260, 270;
and war effort, **9**:378, **10**:93, 93n,
193n, 258–59
Packard Motor Co., **10**:365
Packer, Launcelot, **7**:452, *453n*
packinghouse workers, organization
of, **10**:213–16, 218n, 403–4
Padgett, Frank H., **3**:119, *120n*
padrone system. *See* immigrants: and
padrone system
Page, Alice Wilson, **10**:521, *524n*
Page, Carroll S., *8:381n*, **9**:10n
Page, George, **12**:30n
Page, Walter H., **10**:521, *524n*
Pages, Baltasar, **9**:426–27n, 430, 432,
433–34n, 436, **10**:10–11
Paine, Robert T., **5**:13–14, *15n*
Paine, Thomas, **4**:235, *235–36n*, **8**:96,
100n, **11**:367
Painter (trade union journal), **2**:248,
248n
Painters, Decorators, and Paperhang-

ers of America, Brotherhood of, **2**:*, **3**:*, **4**:*, **5**:*, 79n, **6**:*, 115n, 173–74, **7**:*, 451n, **8**:*, 22n, **9**:*, 34n, 62, 191n, **10**:*, 449, 450n; and black workers, **6**:113–14, 115n, **8**:278–79, 279n, **11**:84n; divisions in, **5**:160n; jurisdiction of, **5**:161, 162–63n, 290, 292n, 427–28, 428–29n, 446–47, 447–48n, 449, 518, **7**:449–50, 451n; unification of, **5**:160n, 260, 260n
—conference: 1900 (Washington, D.C.), **4**:456n, **5**:160n, 260, *260n*
—convention: 1909 (Cincinnati), **8**:22, *22n*
—locals: local 25 (Augusta, Ga.), **6**:114, 115n; local 26 (Augusta, Ga.), **6**:114, 115n; local 47 (Indianapolis), **12**:363; local 151 (Toronto), **11**:74n; local 194 (Chicago), **6**:448, 450n; local 275 (Chicago), **6**:448, 450n; local 398 (Danville, Ill.), **7**:358, 360n; local 584 (Chicago), **6**:447–48, 450n; local 596 (Tucson, Ariz.), **10**:338, 339n; local 602 (Waycross, Ga.), **8**:278, 279n; local 631 (Waycross, Ga.), **8**:278, 279n; local 847 (Selma, Ala.), **6**:106, 107n; local 983 (Bisbee, Ariz.), **10**:337, 339n; local 1099 (Toronto), **11**:74n; local 1133 (Toronto), **11**:74n; local in Tell City, Ind., **7**:235
—strikes/lockouts: 1900 (Augusta, Ga.), **6**:115n; 1919 (Toronto), **11**:72–73, *74n;* 1920–21 (New York City), **11**:356, *358n*
Painters, Decorators, and Paperhangers of America, National Amalgamated Association of, **5**:446–47, *447*–48n, 449
Painters, National Alliance of, *5:448n*
Painters, New York Mutual Benevolent and Protective Society of Operative, **1**:361, *362n*
Painters and Decorators of America, Brotherhood of, **2**:*, 76n, 118, 120, 120n, 235, **3**:*, 61, 61–62n, 63–64, **4**:*, 83, 84n, 144, 453–56, 456n, 504, **5**:*, **6**:*, **7**:*, **8**:*, **9**:*, **10**:*; dues of, **2**:284; executive board of, **2**:417, *417n;* injunction against, **3**:61, 63; jurisdiction of, **3**:149

—conventions: 1894 (Buffalo, N.Y.), **4**:454, *456n;* 1897 (eastern and western factions, Cleveland), **4**:454, *456n;* 1898 (eastern faction, Buffalo, N.Y.), **4**:453, 455–56, *456n*
—local: local 182 (paperhangers, New York City), **3**:62n, 63–64, 111, 115n
Painters' Union 1, Progressive, **2**:332, 337n
painters' unions (New York City), **2**:120, 120n
Palda, Lev J., **1**:*, 107, *108n,* 119, 130
Palestine, **9**:403–5, 405n
Palestine (Tex.) Telephone Co.: injunction, **11**:191n; strike/lockout, 1919, **11**:189–90, *191n*
Palmer, A. Mitchell, **11**:191n, 195–96, *196n,* 220–21n; *letters to,* **11**:216–17, 220–21; SG, meetings with, **11**:197, 198n, 200–203, 203n, 204–5, 319n; SG, *telephone conversations with,* **11**:205, 205n, 206
Palmer, Bertha Honoré, *3:92n; letter to,* **3**:91–92
Palmer, Charles E., *3:455n; letter to,* **3**:454–55
Palmer, Courtland, **2**:57, *58n*
Palmer, Henry W., **4**:440, *446n*
Palmers Manufacturing Co.: boycott, 1903–5, *6:223n;* strike/lockout, 1903–4, **6**:222, *223n*
Pana Coal Co., strike/lockout, 1898–99, *5:30n*
Panama Canal, **6**:382–83, 383n, **9**:328n, **12**:385–86; and Chinese workers, **6**:512, 512n, **7**:93, 93n, 119; hours of labor, **6**:525–28, **7**:3, 94, 105, **8**:132, 132n, 341, 370–72, 380n; and immigration, **8**:340; and Puerto Rican workers, **6**:382–83, 383n; working conditions at, **7**:244. *See also* Canal Zone, workers in; "gold roll" employees, in Canal Zone; "silver roll" employees, in Canal Zone
Panama Canal Commission, **11**:392, 393n
Panama Federation of Labor. *See* Federación Obrera de la República de Panamá
Panama-Pacific International Exposition, 1915, **9**:326, *328n*

Pan-American Federation of Labor, **9:**443n, 465, 500, 534, **10:**8, 9n, 10, 12, 499n, **11:**139–40, 140n, 392, 393n, **12:**319n, 356, 359n, 561
—conventions: 1918 (Laredo, Tex.), *9:466n,* **10:**545, *546n,* 547, **11:**139; 1919 (New York City), **11:**113n, 139, *140n;* 1921 (Mexico City), **11:**404n; 1924 (Mexico City), **12:**536, 536n, 537–38, *538n*
Pan-American Federation of Labor Conference Committee, **9:**443n, **10:**8, 9n; *circular of,* **10:**9–12
Pan-American Financial Conference, First, 1915 (Washington, D.C.), **9:**296–99, 299–*300n,* 327, 358, 437, **10:**5; commission of, **9:**298, 299–300n, 358
Pan-American Financial Conference, Second, 1920 (Washington, D.C.), **10:**5, *8n*
Pan-American Labor Press: El Obrero Panamericano (bilingual newspaper), *10:499n*
Pani, Alberto J., **9:**498–500, *500n*
panics: of 1857, **3:**614; of 1873, **1:**321, 328n, **3:**373, 448, 614–15; of 1878, **1:**340; of 1893, **3:**363, 544 (*see also* depression of 1893); of 1907, **7:**291, *294n,* 484
Pape, Ernest G., **7:***, *112n,* 378; *letters from,* **7:**111–12, 206
Pape, George, **1:**414, *414n,* **3:**141
paper, print, **9:**525, 526n
Paper Box, Bag, and Novelty Workers' International Union, **7:***, 105n
—locals: local 10 (Rumford Falls, Maine), **7:**105, 105n; local 12 (Rumford Falls, Maine), **7:**105
—strike/lockout: 1906 (Rumford Falls, Maine), **7:**104–5, *105n*
Paper Hangers' Protective and Beneficial Association of America, National, **5:***, 162n; jurisdiction of, **5:**161, 162–63n
Paper Makers, Pulp, Sulphite, and Paper Mill Workers, International Brotherhood of, **6:***, 205n, **7:***, 151n, **10:***; and American Labor Union, **6:**203, 395; jurisdiction of, **7:**150–51, 151–52n, 202–4, 204n; label of, **6:**131–32, 203, 395

—convention: 1907 (Northampton, Mass.), **7:**151–52n, 204n
—locals: local 9 (Rumford Falls, Maine), **7:**104, 105n; local 28 (Fort Edward, N.Y.), **7:**204, 204n; local 34 (Denver), **6:**131n; local 91 (Denver), **6:**131n
—strike/lockout: 1907 (Fort Edward, N.Y.), **7:**202–4, *204n*
Paquette (Canadian organizer), **7:**236–37
Paris Exposition of 1900. *See* Exposition Universelle de 1900
Paris Labor Exchange. *See* Bourse du travail (Paris)
Park, Noel R., **1:**113, *115n*
Parker, Alton B., **6:**394n, **7:**295–96, *296n,* 441, 458n, 462n, **8:**31, 257, 429n, **9:**97n, 141, 153, 536, **10:**253, 372, **12:**550; and Buck's Stove and Range Co. cases, **8:**11, 240, 323n; *letters to,* **7:**465–68, **8:**23, 160–64, 203–4, 427–29, 499–500; and *Loewe v. Lawlor,* **8:**79n, 194, 194n
Parker, C. M., **3:**67, *68n*
Parker, E. W., **6:**14n
Parker, Gilman M., *12:173n; wire to,* **12:**172–73
Parker, Harry C., **7:**375, *375n,* **8:**172
Parker, Henry P., **10:**103, *103n,* 546n, 547
Parker, John, **12:**197n
Parker, Lewis W., **9:**171n
Parker, Mary Louise Schoonmaker, **8:**429n
Parker, Willard, **1:**204, *206n*
Parker, William C., **2:**120–21, *121n*
Parker, William N., **5:**128, *129n*
Parks, George A., **10:**185, *186n*
Parks, Samuel J., **6:**186n, *339n,* **12:**75
parliamentary procedure, SG and, **6:**523–25
Parnell, Charles S., **1:**286n, *4:91n*
Parral, Mexico, battle at, **9:**426n
Parry, David M., **6:**124–25, *126n,* 328–29, 333, 335–38, 510, 522, **7:**49n, 138, 153, 245, 401–2, 405, **8:**273, **11:**382, 383n
Parry, J. S., **7:**384n
Parsons, Albert R., **1:***, *462n,* **2:***, 53, *55n,* 56, 59
Parsons, John N., **5:***, 153, *154n*

Parsons, Lucy Eldine Gonzalez, **6:**453, *453n*
Parsons, Solomon, **2:**324, *326n*
Parsons, Thomas C., **7:***329n*
Partido Federal de Puerto Rico, **6:**258n
Partido Obrero Socialista de Puerto Rico, **6:**258n
Partido Republicano de Puerto Rico, **6:**258n
Pascoe, David M., **1:***, 426, *427n*, 464
Pass, Joseph, **10:**400n, **11:**113
Pass, Morris, **10:**400n, **11:**113
Paterson, N.J., silk weavers, **1:**98
Paterson, N.J., textile workers' strike, 1913. *See* textile workers: strikes/lockouts: 1913 (Paterson, N.J.)
Paterson (N.J.) Trades Council, **6:**29n
Patriots of America, **4:**369, *371n*
Patrons of Husbandry. *See* Grange
Patten, Simon N., **6:**482n
Pattern Makers' Association of New York and Vicinity, **8:**77n
Pattern Makers' League of North America, **4:***, **5:***, 214, 216n, 275–77, 285, **8:***, 123n, **9:***, 34n, **10:***, 54n, **11:**28n, 85n
—strike/lockout: 1917 (Brooklyn, N.Y., threatened), **10:**52–53, 54n
Pattern Makers' National League of North America, **4:***, 127n, 347n, **5:***, **8:***, **9:***, **10:***
Patterson, Corydon T., **3:**117–18, *119n*
Patterson, David F., **3:**139, *140n*, 263–64
Patterson (Illinois Democratic politician), **7:**361
Patterson, J. H. (paving cutter), **6:**116n; *letter from*, **6:**120–21
Patterson, John H. (National Cash Register president), **4:**461n, **5:**364, 366n, **6:**144, 488, **7:**166; *letters from*, **4:**457–59, **7:**192–94
Patterson, Thomas M., *6:131*–32n, 286–87n, 354, 354n; *letter from*, **6:**131–32; *letters to*, **6:**131–32
Patterson, William M., **3:**117–19, *119n*
Pattison, Robert E., **3:**185, 189n, 191, *191n*, **6:**212, 212n
Paulding, James K., **5:**74–76, *76n*
Pauncefote, Julian, **4:**304n
Pavelk, Max, **1:**432

Pavers and Rammermen, **11:**319n
Paving Cutters' Union of the U.S. and Canada, **3:***, 165, **6:***, **12:***
—strike/lockout: 1892, **3:**165, *165–66n*
Paving Cutters' Union of the U.S. of America, **3:***, **6:***, **12:***; and black workers, **6:**115–16, 116n, 120–21, 146, 147n
Paving Cutters' Union of the U.S. of America and Canada, International, **3:***, **6:***, **12:***, 223, 223n; jurisdiction of, **8:**188n
—local: local 71 (San Francisco), **8:**188n
Paxson, Edward M., **3:**233n, 299, **4:**419–20, *420n*
Payne, George W., **3:**257, *258n*
Payne, Sereno E., **4:**323n, **5:**168n, **8:**492n
Payne Engine Co., strike/lockout, 1903–5, **6:**152, *152n*
Payson, Louis E., **4:**490, *499n*, **7:**28–31
Peabody, James H., **6:**279–80, 282–*83n*, 344, 344n, 362, **7:**25n
peace movement, **9:**254, 366n, 430, 433n, **10:**88–89, 90n, 93, 93n, 94; AFL Executive Council and, **9:**231. *See also* American Peace Society; Carnegie Endowment for International Peace; Carnegie Peace Association; Emergency Federation of Peace Forces; International Committee of Women for Permanent Peace; International Peace Society; Labor's National Peace Council; League to Enforce Peace; New York Peace Society; pacifists; People's Council of America for Democracy and Peace; Socialist Party of America; socialists: in United States, antiwar; Woman's Peace party; Women's International League for Peace and Freedom; World War I
—meetings: Apr. 1907 (New York City), **7:**206n, 211–14, *214n;* Jan. 1915 (Washington, D.C.), **9:**231, *232n;* Feb. 1915 (Chicago), **9:**269, *274n;* Apr. 1915 (New York City), **9:**269, *274n;* Apr.–May 1915 (The Hague), **9:**270, *274n;* May 1915 (Cleveland), **9:**269, *274n;* June

1915 (NewYork City), **9:**290, *291–92n;* June 1915 (Philadelphia), **10:**179n; May 1916 (Washington, D.C.), *10:179n;* May 1917 (New York City), **10:**93, *93n,* 94; June–July 1917 (NewYork City), **10:**127, *128n;* autumn 1917 (Chicago), **10:**161n
"peace reigns in Warsaw," **3:**37, **4:**490, *499n*
Pearce, Grafton, **1:**453, *455n*
Pearce, William C., **4:***, 350n, *353n,* 359n, 365, **5:***, 211, *211n,* **9:***, 336, *341n; letter to,* **4:**352–53
Pearl, Emma, **10:**185, 186n
Pearl, Jack, **12:**80n
Pearl, Philip J., **10:**185, *186n,* **12:**322–24, *324n*
Pearre, George A., **6:**527n, **7:**83, *91n,* 289n, 311n; *letter to,* **7:**287–88
Peasants' Revolt, **1:**29
Peavey, Hubert, **12:**433n
Peck, Charles F., **2:**29, *29n,* **3:**28
Peckham, George, **7:**413, 414n
Peckham, T. A., **6:**151n
Pedersen v. *Delaware, Lackawanna, and Western Railroad Co.,* **10:**143, *147n*
Peeke, Erastus C. B., *4:218n; letter from,* **4:**218
Peetz, Charles, **7:**380, *381n*
Peltier, Eugene, **4:**261–63
penates, **12:**151, *152n*
Pender, Edward J., **2:**66, *69n*
Peninsular Stove Co., strike/lockout, 1918–19, **10:**447–49, *449n*
Penna, Philip H., **3:***, *253n,* **4:***, *82n;* at AFL conventions, **3:**250, 252, 253n, 259, 438, 440n, 630–31, 654–55, 659n, 662, **4:**82, 93, 272, 272n, 277
Penning, George C., **6:**186, 189n
Pennsylvania: American Civil Liberties Union activities in, **12:**309, 311n; election of 1906, **7:**96, 112–13, 120–22, 122–23n, 132–33; election of 1908, **7:**375; and labor standards, maintenance of, **10:**99; state police of, **8:**44n, 52n, 357–58, 358n
Pennsylvania, United Labor League of Western, **4:**145n, *374n,* **5:**174, 176n; meeting, 1897, **4:**371–74

Pennsylvania, University of, SG address banned by, **9:**256, 256n
Pennsylvania Board of Pardons, **5:**84–85, 85n
Pennsylvania Giant Power Survey, **12:**348n
Pennsylvania Mining Co., strike/lockout, 1915, *11:494n*
Pennsylvania Mining Co. v. *United Mine Workers of America et al.,* *11:494n*
Pennsylvania Railroad, **9:**481, 511, 516, **11:**504, **12:**299–300; injunction, **12:**27, 30n, 109, 115; organization of, **8:**188–89, 189–90n, **9:**48–49, 49–50n; strike/lockout, 1910, *8:190n;* strike/lockout, 1914, *9:50n*
Pennsylvania Railroad Co. v. *U.S. Railroad Labor Board et al.,* *12:30n*
Pennsylvania State Branch, AFL, *10:241n*
Pennsylvania State Federation of Labor, *3:279n,* **8:**52n, 189, 191, 191n, *10:241n*
—convention: 1911 (Harrisburg), **8:**189, *190n*
Pennsylvania state labor convention, **2:**156
Pennsylvania Supreme Court, **3:**148
Penrose, Boies, *5:85n,* 466, 467n, 471, 473, 474n, 485–86; *letter to,* **5:**84–85
pensions, **6:**58–60, 363–64, 492, **8:**413, **9:**122–23, 525–26; for government employees, **9:**525, 526n; and international unions, **12:**223; legislation on, **12:**217–18, 218n; and U.S. Steel Corp., **11:**333; and Western Union Telegraph Co., **11:**334
People ex rel. Fursman v. *City of Chicago et al.,* *9:419n*
People (New York City socialist journal), *3:14n,* 626, **4:**10–18, 18n, 66–70, 77n, 135, **5:**72–73, 73–74n, **11:**572n; *letter to,* **3:**671
People's Council of America for Democracy and Peace, **10:**93n, 127–28n, 159–60, 161n, 241n, 258, 260–62
—conferences: 1917 (Chicago), **10:**161n; 1917 (NewYork City), **10:**127, *128n*

People's Legislative Service, **11:**468–71, *471n*, **12:**433n, 472n

People's party, **3:**3–4, 6, 201–2, 277, 281–82, 366, 442n, 491, 562, 562n, **4:**11, 15n, 178, 390

—conventions: 1891 (Cincinnati), **3:**3–4, 6, *6n;* 1892 (Omaha, Nebr.), **3:**4, 263n

People's Street Railway Co.: boycott, 1901–4, *5:379n*, **6:**142–44, *145n;* strike/lockout, 1901–4, **5:**378, *379n*, **6:**142–44, *145n*

People v. *Lochner*, **6:**392–93, *393–94n*

Peregrine, Philip A., **6:***, 15, *19n*

Pergler, Charles, **10:**160, *161n*

Perham, Henry B., **7:***, 457, *458n*, 481, 482n, **8:***, *10n*, **9:***, 9, *10n*, 343n, 495n, **10:***, 475, *475n;* at AFL conventions, **8:**9, 10n, **10:**475n; at AFL Executive Council meetings, **8:**501, 503–4, **9:**436; election of, as AFL vice-president, **8:**18n, 295, **9:**38n, 226n, 348n

Perina, Anton, **1:**125, *126n*

Perkins, Chester O., **7:***126n; letter to,* **7:**123–25

Perkins, Edgar A., **6:***, *141n,* **7:***, 199n, 376, *378n,* **9:***, 64, *68n,* 69; *letter to,* **6:**140–41

Perkins, Frances, *8:472n; letter to,* **8:**471–72

Perkins, George C., **4:**492–93, 498, *500n*

Perkins, George W. (of Cigar Makers), **2:**13n, **3:***, *77n,* **4:***, 51, *52n,* 72, 127n, 157, 176, **5:***, *73n,* **6:***, 30, *31n,* **7:***, *221n,* 464n, **8:***, *20n,* 30, 53, 172, 173n, 227n, **9:***, *75n,* 80n, 254n, 260, 354, 403n, **10:***, *243n,* **11:***, *67n,* 401, **12:***, *66n,* 133n, 190, 312, 315n, 471n, 550; at AFL conventions, **10:**264n, 472, 473n, **11:**479; and AFL financial support of Cigar Makers, **5:**251–52, 253n; and AFL postwar reconstruction program, **10:**358n; and AFL Women's Department, considered, **12:**406–7, 408n, 443–45; and Cigar Makers' 1896 convention, **4:**236, 238, 249; and Cigar Makers' 1912 convention, **8:**422n; and Cigar Makers' 1923 convention, **12:**305; and Dampf embezzlement, **4:**54; and election of 1908, **7:**387; and election of 1920, **11:**283n; and IWW, **8:**103–4, 505, **10:**242–43, 297; and Kirchner, **4:**119; *letters from,* **5:**214–15, 251–52, **6:**519–20, **8:**25–26, 103–4, 505–6, **9:**253–54, **10:**242–43, **12:**131–32, 544–45; *letters to,* **3:**76–77, 148, 483, **4:**77–79, 116–17, 216–17, **5:**71–73, 126–27, 397–98, **6:**104–5, 283–84, 385–86, **7:**220–21, 306–8, 308n, 463–64, **8:**19–20, 54–55, 517–18, **9:**75, 237, 478–79, **11:**67, **12:**226–27; and miners' strike, 1897, **4:**357, 359n; near-drowning of, **4:**217n, 225–26; and tobacco strippers' locals, **7:**306–8, 308–9n, **11:**412–13, 418–19, 419n; and Trade Union Educational League, **11:**561n; *wires from,* **3:**532–33, **12:**66; and Workers' Education Bureau, **12:**226–27, 388; and Workers' Party of America, **11:**549

Perkins, George W. (of U.S. Steel), **5:**483, *484n*

Perkins-Campbell Co., strike/lockout, 1905–?, **7:**11n; strike injunction, **7:**11, 11n

Perkins-Campbell Co. v. *Albert Teeters et al.*, **7:**11, *11n*

Permanent Court of International Justice (World Court), **12:**209, *210n*, 455

Perry, Edwin, **8:***, *170n; letter to,* **8:**169–70

Perry, F. J., *10:150n; wire from,* **10:**148

Perry, George A. P., **2:**8, *11n*

Perry, H. Francis, *4:202n; letter to,* **4:**200–202

Perry, H. H., **8:**380–81

Perry, Isaac G., **4:**16n

Perry, James H., **2:**169, 171–72, *172–73n; letter to,* **2:**177–78

Perry, John B., *12:49n; letter from,* **12:**48–49

Perry, Theodore, *4:182n,* 359n; *letter to,* **4:**180–81

Pershing, John J., **9:**212n, 426n, **10:**564, *567n,* **12:**13; attack on SG by, **11:**520–21, 521n; bust of, **12:**533n

Persion, Achille, **9**:*, *480n; letter from,* **9**:480
personnel administration, **12**:419–20
Persons, Charles E., **11**:560, *560n*
Peru, **10**:11
Peru (Ind.) Central Labor Union, **6**:140, *141n*
Peru (Ind.) Contractors' Association, **6**:140
Pestaña Nuñez, Angel, **11**:372, *373n*
Peteet, J. Walton, **6**:264–65, *265n*
Peters, Andrew J., **10**:154, *155n*, **11**:146n; *wire to,* **11**:145–46
Petkewicz, Joseph, **12**:195, 197n
Petrograd Council of Workers' and Soldiers' Deputies, Executive Committee of the, *cable to,* **10**:88–89, 89–90n
Petrograd Council of Workers' Deputies, Provisional Executive Committee of the, **10**:45n
Petry, Charles W., **7**:17, *17n*
Pettibone, George A., **7**:144–46, *146n*, **8**:274
Pettigrew, Richard F., **5**:248, *249n*, **8**:358–59, *359n*
Pettingill, Millard F., *7:20n; letter to,* **7**:19–20
Pettingill, Noah B. K., **6**:428, 429n
Pettipiece, R. Parmenter, *9:478n; letter to,* **9**:477–78
Pfahler, William H., **5**:367–68, *368n*, 369, 464n, **6**:236
Pfeiffer, John J., **7**:*, *11n*, 141n; *letter from,* **7**:11
Pfrommer, Julius, **1**:250, *251n*
Phagan, Mary, **9**:279n
Phaire, Frank, **11**:326n
Phelan, Frank W., **7**:92n
Phelps Dodge Copper and Coal Mining Corp., **10**:167, 169n, 337–39, 339n
Philadelphia: building trades dispute in, 1902, **6**:43–44, 44–45n; conference of trade and labor unions of, 1889, **2**:179, *179n*, 187
Philadelphia, United Labor League of, *2:179n*, 232, 4:144, **5**:340
Philadelphia and Reading Railroad, **3**:434n; strike/lockout, 1887–88, **2**:92n, 108n

Philadelphia Building Trades Council, **2**:26n
Philadelphia Central Labor Union, **2**:26n, 179, *179n*, **6**:503n, **8**:52n; Building Trades Section of, **6**:414, 414n; and Poth boycott, 1902–3, **6**:44–45n
Philadelphia Central Short-Hour League, **2**:179n
Philadelphia Council of Allied Building Trades, *6:44n,* **8**:52n
—strike/lockout: 1902, **6**:43–44, *44–45n*
Philadelphia Manufacturers' Association, **8**:56n
Philadelphia Rapid Transit Co., strike/lockout, 1910, *8:52n,* 69–70
Philadelphia Tageblatt, **3**:643–44; arbitration case, **2**:25, *26n*, 37; boycott, 1886–87, *2:25–26n*
Philadelphia Typothetae, strike/lockout, 1905–8, **7**:85, *91n*
Philipp, Emanuel L., **9**:353, *355n*
Philippines: annexation of, **5**:xv–xvi, 4, 6–11, 23, 25–26, 28, 32–33, 44–46, 62–64, 64n, 136; Chinese workers in, **5**:62, 65; suffrage in, **5**:139
Phillips, Agnes, **8**:473–74, 474n
Phillips, Albert, **11**:538, 539n
Phillips, Anthony, **8**:473–74, *474n*
Phillips, Cyrus, **9**:200n
Phillips, George, **9**:83n
Phillips, Hannah B. L., **1**:11, *12n*
Phillips, Hyman, **1**:103–6, *106n*
Phillips, James E., **12**:241, *242n*, 271, 274–75
Phillips, John, **1**:*, 361, *363n*, 390, **4**:*, *141n*, 271, 272n; *letter from,* **4**:140–41
Phillips, John R., **10**:499n
Phillips, Mrs., **3**:141
Phillips, Samuel, **3**:15, 18n
Phillips, Thomas W., **4**:143, *143n*, 172, 321, **8**:183
Phillips, Wendell, **2**:379, *382n*, **3**:633, 660n, **4**:406, 434–35, **6**:333, 335, **12**:135
Phillips, William, **12**:101n, 256n
Phoenix Park murders (Dublin), *3:241n*
Phoenix Preferred Accident Insurance Co., **8**:103, 103n

Photo-Engravers' Union of North America, International, **7:***, 422n, **9:***, 94n, **10:***, 48n, **11:***, 337n, **12:***, 127n; injunction against, *9:74–75n*
—conventions: 1914 (Indianapolis), **9:**163, *163n*, 168; 1923 (Milwaukee), **12:**299n
—local: local 1 (New York City), **9:**74–75n
Piano, Organ, and Musical Instrument Workers' International Union of America, **7:***, 133, 142n, **12:**446n
Piano and Organ Workers' International Union of America, **7:***; jurisdiction of, **6:**66n
Piano Makers' Union, **2:**235
Pichon, Stéphen-Jean-Marie, **10:**541n
Picket (trade union journal), *1:366,* 383, 392, 394, 406, 412, 421, **2:**15, 16n, 344, **8:**133
picketing, **1:**119, 373n, **3:**128n, **5:**240–43, 243–44n, **6:**81, 83–84n, 124–25, 242, 282n, **7:**11, 11n, 19n, 50n, 289n, 370n, **8:**34, 40n, 114n, 121, 122n, 297, 298n, 313, 513n, **9:**12, 13n, 94n, 183, 249, 263n, 430n, **10:**215, 253, 253n, 377, 449n, 538, **11:**126n, 448, 456, 458n, 511, 571n, **12:**9n, 94n, 154, 301–3, 303n, 428n. *See also* strikes and lockouts
Pierce, Abby G., *5:247n; letters to,* **5:**246–47, 420–21
Pierce, George P., **1:**167, *167n*
Pierce, Jefferson D., **4:**432n, **5:***, *246n,* 247, 247n, 338–39, 339n, 396n, 420, 421n, **6:***, 4, *5n,* 15–16, 87n, 128n, 260n, **7:***, 96–97, *98n,* 152–53n, 346, 347n, **8:***, 53, *54n,* 134, 135n, 157n, 189–90n; financial affairs of, **6:**163–64, 164n; *letters from,* **6:**85–87, **7:**152, 209, **8:**188–89; *letters to,* **5:**246, 451–52, **6:**163–64, **7:**115, 428
Pierce, John F., **6:**473, *474n*
Pierce, Walter L., **5:**367, *368n,* 369, 372
Pierce, Willis H., **9:**48, *49–50n*
Piez, Charles, **10:**360–61, *362–63n*
Pillsbury, Charles, **3:**547n
Pilots' Association, Sandy Hook, **2:**332
Pimpin, Edward F., **6:**153–54, 154n
Pinard, William O., **4:**42, *42n*

Pinches, John, Co., **7:**461n
Pinchot, Amos, **9:**422n, 433n
Pinchot, Gifford, **7:**322n, **9:**309, *310n,* **12:**206n, 315n
Pinckney, Walter S., *1:115n*
Pingree, Hazen S., **2:**384, *385n*
"Pingree Potato Scheme," **3:**364
Pinkerton, Allan, **1:**455n
Pinkerton, Robert A., **4:**387, *388–89n*
Pinkerton Detective Agency, **1:**454, *455n,* **3:**139, 140n, 192–93, 214n, 249, 254–56, 635, **5:**84, **6:**431; and Homestead strike, 1892, **3:**185–86, 188, 189n, 190, 191n, 207, 209, 237, 266n, **4:**387, 388–89n; legislation on, **3:**26, 52, 55n
Pinkofsky, Louis, **12:**530, *533n*
Pinner, Reuben E., **1:***, 237, *237n,* **3:***, 141, *142n*
Pintado, José González, **5:**185, 188n
Pintó, Domingo G., **5:**185, *188n*
Pioneer Hat Works, **7:**230–31
Pitney, Mahlon, **10:**144, *147n*
Pittman, Key, **12:**170, *171n*
Pittsburgh Central Trades Council, **5:**408, *408n*
Pittsburgh Commercial Gazette, editor of, *letter to,* **3:**116–17
"Pittsburgh Experiment," **12:**382, *383n,* 412–13
Pittsburgh Meter Co., **6:**137
Planten, G. H., **9:**48, *49n*
plasterers: and black workers, **11:**84n; and Chicago building trades arbitration case, 1921, **11:**496n; in Milwaukee, **3:**494
Plasterers' Association, Employing (New York City), **2:**292
Plasterers' International Association of the U.S. and Canada, Operative:
—local: local 96 (Washington, D.C.), **4:**285, 286n
Plasterers' Society of the City and County of New York, Operative, **4:**110n
Plasterers' Union, Operative (New York City), **2:**292, 295
Plate, Augustus F., *1:139n; letter from,* **1:**136–37
Plate, Martin D., **1:***, *54n*
Plate Printers' Union of North Amer-

ica, International Steel and Copper, **10:***, 229, 231n
—locals: local 1 (Philadelphia), **5:**318n, 320; local 8 (Brooklyn, N.Y.), **6:**380, 381n
—strikes/lockouts: 1900–1902 (Philadelphia), *5:318n*, 320; 1904-? (Brooklyn, N.Y.), **6:**380, *381n*
Platt, James P., **6:**178n, **8:**42n, 68
Platt, Orville H., **4:**507–8, *509n*, **6:**48n, 212
Platt, Thomas C., **4:**196, *197n*, 205
Platt, William A., *6:71n; letter from,* **6:**70–71
Plattsburgh (N.Y.) Business Men's Camp, **9:**330–31, *332n*
Plevna, siege of, **1:**121, *121n*
"pluck-me" stores, **4:**27, 358, **6:**247, **9:**87, 222
Plumb, Glenn E., **11:**131n
Plumb, Preston B., **3:**137, *138n*
Plumb, William F., **4:**99, 99n
Plumbers, Gas Fitters, Steam Fitters, and Steam Fitters' Helpers of the U.S. and Canada, United Association of Journeymen, **4:***, 347n, **6:***, 145n, 173–74, **7:***, **8:***, 159–60, 160n, 344, **10:**502n, **12:***; and AFL Building Trades Department, **8:**151n, 296; injunction, **7:**14, 15n; and IWW, **7:**47–48; jurisdiction of, **6:**342, 343n, **7:**272, **8:**151n, 296, 399–402, 402n, 413, 414n
—convention: 1900 (Newark, N.J.), **5:**257n
—local: local 75 (Milwaukee), **3:**494, 497, 498n
Plumbers, National League of Journeymen, **7:**15n
Plumbers, Steam Fitters, and Gas Fitters, International Association of Journeymen, **1:***, 458, 460n
Plumbers and Steam Fitters of the U.S. and Canada, United Association of Journeymen, **4:***, **6:***, **7:***, **8:***, **11:**28n, 85n, **12:***, 76; jurisdiction of, **12:**68–69, 72–73, 73n
—local: local 463 (New York City), **12:**76, 80n
Plumb Plan, **11:**130–31, 131n, 320n, 329

Plumb Plan League, **11:**188n
Plummer, Charles H., **8:**122, *123n*
Plummer, Edward C., **7:**76, *90n*
Plummer, Mr. (Denver worker), **3:**34
Plummer, William P., **6:**243, *244n*
Plunket, Thomas J., **1:**449, *449n*
Plunkett, Charles P., **12:**546, 550, *552n*
Plunkett, George, **11:**86n
Plunkett, John E., **2:**282n; *letter to,* **2:**281–82
Plymouth Rock Pants Co.: boycott, 1892, **3:**179, *180n;* strike/lockout, 1892, *3:180n*
P. M. Arthur et al. v. Thomas F. Oakes et al., **8:**491, *493n*
Pocatello (Idaho) Trades and Labor Council, **6:**284, *285n*
Poincaré, Henriette Benucci, **10:**564–65, *567n*
Poincaré, Raymond, **10:**550, *554n*, 563–65
Poindexter, Miles, **10:**420, *420n*, *11:407n*, **12:**169, 171n, 187, 436, 437n
Polakoff, Sol, **6:**276, *278n*
Poland: crisis with Germany, 1918–19, **11:**48, *49n;* crisis with Russia, 1920, **11:**368, *373n*, 437–38, 439–40n; indemnity imposed by Germany, **10:**88; "November Insurrection," 1830–31, **4:**499n; workers from, **7:**45, **8:**34, 215, 216n, 388, 459–60
police: interrogation by ("third degree"), **8:**147, 211, 239–40; organization of, **11:**75n, 145–46, 146–47n
—strike/lockout: 1919 (Boston), **11:**145–46, *146–*47n, 318, 319n
political action. *See* American Federation of Labor (AFL): National Non-Partisan Political Campaign Committee; American Federation of Labor (AFL): Political Program; elections in United States, national; Socialist Labor party (SLP); Socialist Party of America; socialists; trade unions: non-partisan political action by; trade unions: partisan political action by
political candidates, AFL reports on legislative records of, **6:**47–48, 492–93, 493n, **7:**16, 16n, 19, 58, 69,

72–84, 94–95, 99, 105–6, 333, 346–47, 347n, 391, 416, **8:**131–32, 387n, 395–96, **9:**165, **12:**34–35, 160–61, 169, 187, 436–37, 487–88
political prisoners, wartime, amnesty for, **11:**398n, 449–50n, 532, 533n, **12:**254; AFL and, **11:**91, 93n, 318, 318–19n, 397–98, **12:**90, 91n
Polk, Frank L., **10:**45n, 90n, **11:**91, *93n; wire from,* **11:**99–102
Polk, Leonidas L., **3:**263n
Polkinhorn, Henry A., **8:**470, *471n,* 498
Pollner, William C., **1:***, 165, *166n,* 218, 230, 235
Pollock v. *Farmers' Loan and Trust Co.,* *4:38n,* **6:**332, *340n,* **8:**264
Pomerene, Atlee, **9:**470, *472n,* **11:**157n, **12:**169, *171n*
Pomeroy, William C., **3:***, 356n, 358, *359n,* **4:***, *82n,* 241, **5:**142n, **12:**516n; at AFL conventions, **3:**423–24, 436, 438, 617–18, 651–53, 657–58, 659n, **4:**80, 82, 85, 92–93, 95–97, 268–72, 272n
Pommer, Charles, **5:**245, *245n,* **6:**90n
Poole, Ernest, **10:**160, *161n*
poor, rights of, **10:**184
Pope, George, **9:**78, *78n*
Pope, Henry M., *10:135n; letter from,* **10:**134–35
Port-au-Prince, U.S. occupation of, **9:**311n
Porter, D. Edward, **9:**168, *169n*
Porter, Edwards C., **10:**310, *312n*
Porter, James E., **4:***, *343n,* **5:***, 261, *262n; letter to,* **4:**343
Porter, John A., **6:**111n
Porter, William A., **5:**202–3, *207n*
Porter, William D., **3:**238, *241n*
Port Henry Iron Ore Co., strike/lockout, 1913, **9:**177, *178n*
Portland (Ore.) and Vicinity, Central Labor Council of, **9:**172, *172n*
Portland (Ore.) Central Labor Council, *3:371n*
Portland (Ore.) Federated Trades Assembly, *3:82n,* 371n
Portland (Ore.) Metal Trades Council, and shipbuilding workers' strike, 1917, **10:**208–9, 209n

Portland (Ore.) *Sun,* **3:**586, *587n*
Portland Oregonian, **3:**586, 587n
Portsmouth (Va.) Central Labor Union, **9:**419–22, *422n*
Portugal, uprising in, 1910, **8:**317, *320n*
Posen, **11:**49n
Post, Charles W., **6:**510, *511n,* 522, **7:**49n, 84–85, 138, 153, 245, 337–38, 401–2, 405, **8:**131n, 133, 198, 222–23, 265, 307, 309, **11:**382, 383n; *letter from,* **8:**313–14; *letter to,* **8:**315. See also *C. W. Post* v. *American Federation of Labor et al.; C. W. Post* v. *Buck's Stove and Range Co. et al.*
Post, Louis F., **9:**319, *321n,* 323, **10:**295, 296n, 303, 306, 307n, **12:**34n
Postal Telegraph and Cable Co., **8:**471n; strike/lockout, 1907, **7:**250–51, *252n;* strike/lockout, 1919, **11:**93, *94–*95n, 102–4, 104n
Post and McCord (company), strike/lockout, 1905-?, **6:**515n
Post Office Clerks, National Federation of, **7:***, 114, 115n, **11:***, 478n; and black workers, **11:**84n
Post Office Clerks of the U.S., United National Association of, **7:***, 114, 115n, **11:***
—convention: 1901 (Milwaukee), *5:391n*
Potemkin (battleship), **6:**454n
Poth, F. A., and Sons, boycott, 1902–3, *6:44–45n*
Potter, Edward W., **7:***, 345, *346n*
Potter, Henry C., **4:**304n
Potter, James K., *4:286n*
Potter-Palmer, Mrs. *See* Palmer, Bertha Honoré
potters, stoneware, organization of, **8:**47, 47n
Pottsville (Pa.) Central Labor Union, **6:**529–30, *531n*
Pouget, Emile, **8:**508, *511n*
Pouren, Jan J., extradition case, **7:**387–88, *388n*
Powderly, Terence V., **1:***, 159, *167n,* 283, 286n, 454, 466, 467n, **2:***, *22n,* 143n, 212n, 324, 340–43, 404–5, 417, 428, **3:***, *6n,* 74, 78–79, 268,

270, **4:***, *21n*, 321–22, **5:***, 266,
267n, 326–27, **6:***, *111n*, **10:***, 384,
385n, **12:***, 344, *348n;* and Bingham
House agreement, **2:**195, 198–201,
204–5, 212–13, 215, 217–19; and
Bingham House conference, 1889,
2:181; Cooper Union *address by,*
1890, **2:**332–36, 338, 338n, 339,
353–54; and eight-hour move-
ment, **1:**276–77, **2:**171; and farmers' alliances, **3:**3, 6, 6–7n, 262;
and FOTLU, **1:**161–62; and Girard
House conference, 1889, **2:**242–43;
and Home Club, **1:**402–3, 404n;
and KOL office conference, 1889,
2:230; and KOL trade assemblies,
2:49–50; *letters from,* **1:**391–92, 409–
11, 455, **2:**48–50, 132–33, 198–201,
215, 326, 328–29, 353–55, **6:**110–
11; *letters to,* **1:**167, 380, 382–84,
396, **2:**20–22, 30–32, 131–32, 199,
217–18, 228, 234, 326–27, 329–30;
and People's party, **3:**3; and reorganization of KOL, **2:**49–50; *report
of,* **1:**399–401; resignation of, **3:**414,
415n, 665–66; SG, meetings with,
2:142–43, 205, 209–10, 212, 228,
326–30, 335, 341; *Thirty Years of
Labor* (book by), **2:**227, *228n,* 247,
248n; and trade unions, **1:**284–85,
366, 380n, 383n, 385–88, 398,
425–27, 436, 438n, 463–64, **2:**17–19,
49–50
Powell, George (Arizona FOL representative), **9:**352n
Powell, George (New Castle, Pa., tin
worker), **5:***, 79, *81n*
Powell, Thomas S., *5:117n*
Powell, Walker V., **5:***, 124, *127n*
Power, Charles A., *3:6n; letter to,* **3:**6
Power, James E., **1:**447, *448n*
power network, **12:**344, 347, 348n,
376, 377n, 380–82, 382–83n
Powers, Richard, **1:***, 165, *165n*, 352,
3:*, *440n,* **4:***, 51, *51n,* **12:**375n; at
AFL convention, **3:**438, 440n; at
FOTLU conventions, **1:**211, 216,
218–19, 222, 228, 230, 282; and
FOTLU Legislative Committee,
1:228, 231–33, 234n, 235, 239, 286n
Poynton, J. F., **3:**586, 587n

Prairie Creek Coal Co., **10:**323n
Praktische Emanzipationswinke (Hill-
mann), **1:**22–43
Pratt, Clarence, **8:**52n
Pratt, Edward E., **10:**99, *102n*
Pratt, Henry W., *12:437n; letter to,*
12:435–37
Pratt, Mervyn, **4:**12, 15, *15–16n*, 57
Pray, Small, and Co.: boycott, 1894,
3:412n; strike/lockout, 1893–94,
3:411, *412n*, 460–61
*Pre Catalan v. International Federation
of Workers in the Hotel, Restaurant,
Lunch Room, Club, and Catering Industry et al.,* **11:**455, *458n*
Pree, T. J., **11:**189n
Preece, Thomas R., **12:**550, *553n*
Prenner, Johann B., **8:**198, 199n
preparedness (World War I), **9:**332n,
358–59, 359–60n, **10:**22, 34; AFL
and, **9:**344–46, 346n, 379, 383n,
524, **10:**22n, 32, 39–44; and industrial production, **10:**23–26, **12:**423;
and industrial reserve, **10:**26–28; SG
and, **9:**329–31, 346, 364–65, 374–82,
384, **10:**7, 17–20, 36–38, **12:**121
Presbyterian Church in the U.S. of
America: Department of Church
and Labor of, **7:**10, 10n; General
Assembly meeting, 1906 (Des
Moines, Iowa), **7:**10, *10n*
Prescott, William B., **3:***, *169n*, 430,
512n, **4:***, *97n*, 370, **5:***, *380n*,
8:*, 120, *121n*, **12:***, 305–6, *309n;*
at AFL conventions, **3:**434n, 609,
611n, 662, **4:**95, 97n, 272, 272n; *letters to,* **3:**168–69, **5:**379–80
president and vice-president of
United States, direct election of,
9:125, **12:**487, 511
President's Industrial Conference. *See*
Industrial Conference, First, 1919
(Washington, D.C.)
President's Mediation Commission,
10:126n, 186n, 189n, 194–95, *195n,*
205, 223–24, 225n, 248, 262, 280n,
295–96, 297n, 299, 301–3, 305,
306n, 321, 337–39, 388n, 468–69
press, freedom of the, **9:**124, **11:**8n,
18n, 70n, 159, 176, 247, 311, 562–
64, **12:**454, 487, 510

Press Association, National Reform, 3:24n
Pressed Steel Car Co., 8:475–76, 10:77
Pressmen's Union 1, Job (Denver), 5:395, 396n
Preston, Veryl, 5:387, *388n*
prevailing rate of wages, 8:383
Price, Oscar A., 10:366, *367n*
Price, William, 3:47, *48n*
Price of Freedom, The (Coolidge), 12:510, *513n*
Prida, Charles, 6:293, 293n
Priestersbach, August, 4:413, *414n*, 6:365, *368n*, 501, 503n
Prieto Laurens, Jorge, 12:391, *392n*
Primrose, Archibald P. *See* Rosebery, Lord
Prince, Alfred, *6:414n; letter from,* 6:413–14
Prince, Mary, 3:141, 143n
Prince, Samuel, 3:*, 141, *143n*, 5:148n; *letters to,* 5:147–48, 429, 7:371–72
Prince of Wales's Fund, 9:196
Princip, Gavrilo, 9:160n
printers, and George mayoral campaign, 1:431
Printers' Union, New York, *1:362n*
Printers' Union, New York German, *1:260n*
Printing Pressmen's and Assistants' Union of North America, International, 4:*, 5:*, 341n, 6:*, 129, 129n, 7:*, 338n, 8:144n, 9:*, 348n, 10:*, 262n, 12:*, 52n, 446n
—locals: local 7 (Chicago), 9:74n; local 14 (Denver), 5:393, 395, 396n; local 99 (Elizabeth, N.J.), 7:337
—strikes/lockouts: 1901 (Chicago), 5:340, *342n;* 1912-? (Chicago), 9:74n
Printing Pressmen's Union of North America, International, 4:*, 97n, 5:*, 6:*, 7:*, 9:*, 10:*, 12:*; injunctions against, 3:125–27, 128n, 129–31, 139, 263–64
—local: local 13 (Pittsburgh), 3:125–27, 128n, 129–31, 139, 263–64
—strike/lockout: 1891–92 (Pittsburgh), 3:125–27, *128n,* 129–31, 139, 263–64

printing trades councils, allied, 4:414, 5:519, 6:492; in Chicago, 5:342n; label of, 4:414, 5:12, 63n, 406, 477–78, 7:337, 377, 8:168; in New York City, 9:72, 74n, 89, 153n
Prinz, Henry, 9:19, *21n*
Pritchard, Jeter C., *6:48n;* legislative record of, 6:47–48
Proctor, Fletcher D., 3:271, *271n*
Proctor, Redfield, 3:271, *271n,* 5:458n
production, 11:386–87; improvement in processes of, SG and, 3:190, 229, 348, 393, 556, 573, 586; limitation of, 2:153, 10:116, 340, 340n. *See also* mechanization
Proebstle, Joseph, 7:*, 208–9, *210n,* 8:*, 91, *92n,* 148n, 283, 286n, 9:*, 30, *34n; letter from,* 7:221–22
Profintern. *See* Red International of Labor Unions (Profintern)
profiteering, wartime and postwar, 10:26, 42, 122, 174, 211–12, 11:18n, 120n, 233–34, 302, 423, 443–44, 542, 12:25, 28–30, 413, 424
profit sharing, 8:23–24, 24–25n, 9:45, 46n, 397–98, 11:242, 333–34
Progress (trade union journal), *1:248*
Progress and Poverty (George), 1:429, 12:33, 34n
Progressive Alliance, and election of 1906 (Illinois), 7:110n
Progressive Labor party (New York), *1:430, 2:45, 11:9
Progressive party of Germany. *See* Fortschrittspartei
Progressive party (U.S.): platform of, 1912, 8:386n, 409, 477–78, 494, 9:77
—convention: 1916 (Chicago), 9:430n
Progress Society, 4:18
Prohibition, 2:323–25, 8:423, 424n, 10:236, 291n, AFL and, 11:79–81, 81n, 12:270, 271n, 273–74n, 454; SG and, 2:321–23, 325, 8:38n, 92–94, 9:179, 406, 408n, 10:289–91, 363n, 11:79, 81, 81–82n, 183–85, 12:206, 429. *See also* U.S. Constitution: Eighteenth Amendment
Prohibition party, 4:15n; and election of 1908, 7:397–98, 399n
proletariat, 1:22, 44n
Pronk, David, 1:414, *414n*

Pross, William L., *10:129n; wire to,*
10:128–29
Prosser, Rees W., **2:**414, *415n*
Protection or Free Trade? (George),
12:34n
Protocol Agreement, 1913, **8:**439–40,
440n, 442n
"Protocol of Peace," 1910, *8:114n,*
440n, **9:**403n, **12:**529
Proudhon, Pierre Joseph, **1:**23, *43n*
Prouty, Solomon F., **8:**377, *381n*
Providence, R.I., Central Federated
Union, *12:39n*
Provincial Workmen's Association,
10:308n
Provisional Committee of Duma
Members for the Restoration of Order, **10:**45n
Pryor, Roger A., **1:***, 109, *111*–12n,
2:*, 184, *184n*
*Psychological Examining in the United
States Army* (Yerkes, ed.), **12:**168,
168n
Public Education and Child Labor Association of Pennsylvania, and AFL
Permanent Conference for Abolition of Child Labor, **12:**82n
public employees. *See* government employees
public interest, and labor controver-
sies, **12:**178
public ownership. *See* government
ownership
public schools. *See* education
public works programs, **4:**326, **9:**123,
11:475, 476n, 497, 498n, **12:**213–14,
454
Publishing House of the Evangelical
Association, **2:**319n
Puebla, Mexico, strike at, 1907,
9:307n
Pueblo Courier, **5:**97
Pueblo (Colo.) Trades and Labor Assembly, **5:**90, *93n*
Pueblo (Colo.) Workers' Industrial
and Educational Union, **6:**447,
449n
Puerto Rican workers: organization
of, **9:**533–34, 534n; and Panama Canal, **6:**382–83, 383n
Puerto Rico: annexation of, **5:**22;
cigarmakers' joint advisory board
in, **8:**19–20, 21n; conditions in,
5:24–25, 279–81, 281n, **6:**245–57,
423–28, 429n, 470, **8:**20, 87–89,
10:313–14, 315n, 436–37, 438n;
and Spain, **6:**250; and statehood,
6:256, 258n; and suffrage, **5:**139;
U.S. Industrial Relations Commission hearings on, **9:**256–58, 258n,
280, 312. *See also* Iglesias Pantín,
Santiago
—strikes/lockouts: 1900 (general
strike), **5:**415n, 423–24, 425n; 1905
(longshoremen), **6:**470, *470–71n;*
1905 (sugar plantation workers),
6:424–25, 427–28, *429n;* 1906
(sugar plantation workers), **7:**51–
52, *52n;* 1916 (sugar plantation
workers), *9:411n;* 1918 (sugar plantation workers), **10:**314, *315–16n,*
437; 1923, **12:**201
Puerto Rico Sugar Co., strike/lock-
out, 1905, **6:**424–25, 427–28, *429n*
Puget Sound Traction, Light, and
Power Co., strike/lockout, 1917,
10:154, *155n*
Pugh, James, **11:**326n
Pugh, James L., **1:**294–356 passim,
327n
Pugh, Judge, **7:**438–39
Pullman, George M., **3:***, 524, 527–29,
531, *532n,* 537, 555–56, 559, 580,
582, **5:**174, 176n
Pullman Palace Car Co., **3:**521–23,
525, 537, 579n
Pullman strike, 1894, **3:**366, *521–25,
526n,* 632, **4:**105, **7:**24; AFL Executive Council and, **3:**523–25, 532–38,
562–69, 573, 625, 659n; arrests
during, **3:**523–25, 561n; financial
support of, **3:**562–63, 567; general
strike (threatened), **3:**523–25, 526n,
534–38, 565–69, 579n, 625, 659n,
11:250–51; injunctions, **3:**186, 523–
25, 526n, 530, 531n, 538, 559–60,
561n, 563n, 639; and KOL, **3:**526n;
SG and, **3:**523–25, 527–33, 535–39,
548–49, 562–82, 587, 604, 625,
659n, **4:**389, **6:**432, **7:**402–3, **8:**99,
251, **11:**330; and sympathy strikes,
3:524, 526n, 534, 564

—Briggs House conference, **3**:523–24, 548, 564–69, 579n; *news account of,* **3**:533–35; *statement of,* **3**:535–38, 567; *wire from,* **3**:532–33

Pulp, Sulphite, and Paper Mill Workers, International Brotherhood of, **6**:*, **7**:*, 151n, **10**:*, 262n, **12**:446n; jurisdiction of, **7**:150–51, 151–52n, 202–4, 204n
—convention: 1907 (Northampton, Mass.), **7**:151–52n, 204n
—local: local 1 (Fort Edward, N.Y.), **7**:204, 204n

Pumphrey, Aquilla J., **8**:232–33, 234n

Punch Press Operators:
—local: local 224 (Schenectady, N.Y.), **6**:447, 449n

Purdy, Thomas, *letter to,* **2**:95–96

Pusey and Jones Co., **4**:499n

Putrich, Antonia, **9**:26, 28n

Putrich, Steve, **9**:26, 28n

Pyke, Lewis Eleazar, **1**:7, *7n*

Quaker Oats Co., antitrust case against, **10**:322, 323n; strike/lockout, 1917, *10:369n*

Quarrymen's National Union of the U.S. of America, **2**:*, 288n
—strike/lockout: 1892, *3:165–66n*

quarry workers, **2**:287

Quarry Workers' International Union of North America, **6**:*, 439, 439n, **10**:502n, **11**:28n, 85n, **12**:*, 129n, 223; and black workers, **11**:84n; and industrial unionism, **12**:395–98; jurisdiction of, **12**:394–98, 398n
—locals: local 73 (Rockland, Maine), **6**:399, 400n, 439, 440n; local 74 (Stonington, Maine), **6**:439, 440n; local 78 (Mt. Waldo, Maine), **6**:439, 439–40n
—strike/lockout: 1921-?, **12**:127, *129n*

Quebec City, National Trades and Labor Council of, **9**:14–15, *15n*

Quebec City Trades and Labor Council, **9**:14, *15n*

Quelch, Tom, *9:230n; letter to,* **9**:229–30

Quesse, William F., **11**:*, *450n; letter to,* **11**:450

Quick, Humphrey, **9**:26, 28n

Quick, Leon W., **6**:*, 199, *204n*

Quinlan, Patrick, **8**:503n

Quinn, James E., **1**:*, 402, *403n*, 405, **2**:*, 53, 55, *55n*, 62

Rabinowitz, Hyman, **6**:276, *278n*

Racine (Wis.) Trades and Labor Council, lawsuit against, **7**:157, *158n*

Rae, John B., **3**:*, 31, *32n*, 58, **4**:359n

Rae, Robert (British prohibitionist), **2**:324, *325n*

Rae, Robert (Phelps-Dodge auditor), **10**:337, *339n*

Railroad Brakemen, Brotherhood of, **2**:*, 108n, 218, 220n, **3**:*, **4**:*, **8**:*, **10**:*, **11**:*

railroad brotherhoods, **4**:126, **10**:22n, 123, 319–20, 320–21n, **11**:13, 130, 131n, 281n, 347–49, **12**:3; and Adamson Act, **10**:15; affiliation of, with AFL, **5**:124, **8**:249–52, **10**:249–51, **11**:78n, 308–9, 309n, 328–32, 345; and AFL Permanent Conference for Abolition of Child Labor, **12**:82n; and black workers, **11**:393–94; and election of 1924, **12**:479; and Industrial Conference, 1919, **11**:128n, 158; and Kansas Court of Industrial Relations, **11**:347n; *letter from,* **11**:238–39, 239n; and People's Legislative Service, **11**:468–71, 471n; and Transportation Act of 1920, **11**:238–39, 239n, 271, 332n; and workmen's compensation legislation, **8**:443–46, 457
—conferences: Dec. 29, 1919 (Washington, D.C.), **11**:241, *241n;* Feb. 1920 (Washington, D.C.), **11**:249–58, *258–59n;* Feb. 1921 (Washington, D.C.), **11**:426n; Apr. 1921 (Washington, D.C.), **11**:460–61, *461n,* 462; Oct. 1922 (Washington, D.C.), **12**:152–55, *155n,* 159. *See also* labor conferences
—strikes/lockouts: 1917 (threatened), **11**:251–52, *259n;* 1920 (threatened), **11**:249–58, *258–59n;* 1921 (threatened), **11**:504, 536, *539n*

Railroad Cattle Damage Case. See *Central*

Loan and Trust Co. v. *Campbell Commission Co.*
Railroad Employees, Canadian Brotherhood of, **12:***, 20, 21n, 439–42, 442n
Railroad Engineers, Amalgamated, **2:**339
Railroad Labor Board, **11:**274–75n, 536–38, 539–40n, **12:**3, 27–29, 86–87n, 103, 105, 106–7n, 108–10, 112–16, 136, 137n, 203, 481, 486–87, 510; injunction against, **12:**27, 30n, 109, 115
railroad labor disputes, negotiation of, **12:**26–28
railroads: government ownership of (*see* government ownership: of railroads); government wartime control of, **10:**320n, 341, 368, **11:**131–32n, 214n, 235, 238–39, 239n, 241n, 274n, 320, 473, 475n; land grants to, **1:**226, 285, 286n; private operation of, **11:**131n, 157n, 195n, 216n, 238–39, 239n
railroad shop craft workers, **9:**48–49, **10:**384–85, **11:**309, 344, **12:**30n; and Industrial Conference, 1919, **11:**128n; *letter from,* **11:**238–39, 239n; and People's Legislative Service, **11:**469, 471n; and Transportation Act of 1920, **11:**238–39, 239n, 271
—conferences: Feb.–Aug. 1917 (Washington, D.C.), **10:**18–19, *21n;* Dec. 1919 (Washington, D.C.), **11:**241, *241n;* Feb. 1920 (Washington, D.C.), **11:**249–58, *258–59n,* Apr. 1921 (Washington, D.C.), **11:**460–61, 461n, 462–63. *See also* labor conferences
—strikes/lockouts: 1910 (Pennsylvania), *8:190n;* 1911 (Philadelphia), **8:**228–29, *230n;* 1911–15, **8:**321–22, *322–23n;* 1919 (threatened), **11:**118–19, 119–*20n;* 1920 (threatened), **11:**259n; 1922-? (*see* railroad shopmen's strike, 1922-?)
railroad shopmen's strike, 1922-?, **12:**86, *86–87n,* 102–6, 106n, 107, 107n, 108–10, 112n, 113–21, 126–28, 130–31, 140, 202–5, 206n, 285, 300, 341, 373–74n, 412, 414n; in-

junction against, *12:87n,* 133–36, 137n, 147, 147n, 152–55, 158–59, 161, 167, 248, 486
Railroad Signalmen of America, Brotherhood of, **11:***, 344, 345n, 475n
railroad system boards of adjustment, **11:**489, 492n. *See also* Southern Lines System Board of Adjustment
railroad system federations, **11:**105
Railroad Telegraphers of North America, Order of, **4:***, 273, 275n, **5:***, 127n, **7:***, 143n, 252n, **8:***, 295n, **9:***, 342–43n, **11:***, 103, 104n, 131n, 344, 475n; affiliation of, with AFL, **5:**124–25, 127n; and black workers, **9:**342, **11:**315
—strike/lockout: 1900, **5:**295–96, *307n*
Railroad Trainmen, Brotherhood of, **2:***, **3:***, 93, 94n, 215n, 442n, 511, **4:***, 127, 127n, 273, **8:***, 114n, 457, **10:***, 251n, **11:***, 46n, 131n, 249–50, 539n; and black workers, **8:**244, 244–45n, **11:**42–43, 286, 393–94, 394n, 400, 400n; jurisdiction of, **8:**251–52, 253n, **10:**250, **11:**42–46, 46n
—strikes/lockouts: 1910, **8:**112–13, *114–15n;* 1920 (threatened), **11:**252, 254–55, 257–58, *258–59n*
Railroad Trainmen in America, Protective Order of, **11:**46n, 394n, 400
Railroad Wage Commission, **10:**319, *320n*
Railway, Big Four, **4:**168, 168n; superintendent of, *letter to,* **4:**168
Railway and Steamship Clerks, Freight Handlers, Express and Station Employes, Brotherhood of, **9:***, **10:***, **11:***, 84n, 131n, 344, 475n, **12:***, 21n, 87n, 97n, 439–40, 442, 446n; and black workers, **11:**46n, 83n, 182–83, 313–16, 316–17n, 488–91, 491–92n, 501–2, 502n, 550–52, 552n, **12:**111–12, 112n, 129–30; jurisdiction of, **11:**105; and women workers, **12:**371n
—convention: 1922 (Dallas), **11:**492n, 552, *552n*
Railway Boards of Adjustment, **10:**321n
Railway Carmen of America, Brotherhood of, **5:***, 222n, **8:***, 189n, 292n,

296, **9:***, 157n, 343n, **10:**502n, **11:***, 28n, 85n, 99n, 131n, 344, 475n, **12:***, 148n; and black workers, **11:**46n, 119–20, 478n, 564–65, 565n, **12:**148, 343n; and railroad shopmen's strike, 1919 (threatened), **11:**120n
—lodge: lodge 23 (Fort Worth, Tex.), **5:**221
Railway Clerks, Brotherhood of, **9:***, 342, 343n, **10:***, 468n, **11:***, **12:***
Railway Conductors, Brotherhood of, **3:**247n
Railway Conductors of America, Order of, **2:***, 335, 338n, **3:***, 93, 94n, 215n, 246, 247n, 442n, 511, 547n, **4:***, 273, 275n, **8:***, 114n, **10:***, 320n, **11:***, 131n, 539n, **12:***, 348n; jurisdiction of, **11:**78, 78n
—strike/lockout: 1910, **8:**112–13, *114–15n*
Railway Employees, United Brotherhood of, **6:***, 265n, 444, 447, 462
—division: division 24 (San Antonio), **6:**264, *265n*
Railway Employes, Brotherhood of Federated, **9:**48–49, *50n*
—strike/lockout: 1914 (Pennsylvania), *9:50n*
Railway Expressmen of America, Brotherhood of, **6:***, 287, 289n
railway labor adjustment boards (proposed), **11:**157n, 216n, 274n
Railway Mail Association, **12:***, 430n
Railway Mechanics, Brotherhood of, **8:**188–89, *190n*
Railwaymen, National Union of, **9:**377, 382n
—strike/lockout: 1919 (Great Britain), **11:**164, *167n*
Railway Servants, Amalgamated Society of, **6:**83–*84n*, **8:**74; injunction against, **6:**74, 78, 83, 83–84n, **8:**74
—strike/lockout: 1900, **6:**74, 78, *83n*
Railway Shop Laborers' Union, International (proposed), **11:**105–6, 106n
Railway Trackmen of America, Brotherhood of, **4:***, 127, 127n, **5:***, 177, 178n, **9:***, **11:***
Railway Train Porters' Protective Association, **11:**46n

Railway Yardmen, National Association of, **9:**341–42, 342–43n
Rainey, Henry T., **7:**96, *98n*, **12:**40, *41n*
Rainey, John W., **11:**276, *278n*, 281
Raker, John, **10:**471n
Raleigh, J., **2:**332
Ralston, Jackson H., **4:**292–93, *294n*, **5:**211n, 244n, **7:**253, 312, 441, 457, **8:**240–41, 323n, 491, **9:**3–4, 90–91, 141, 153, **11:**336, 338n, 471n, **12:**208, 317; *letters to,* **7:**453–54, **8:**160–64
Ralston, Samuel, **12:**427n
Ramos, Domingo, **9:**429n, 467, *468n*
Ramsdell, Walter L., **4:**307, *308n*
Randall, Beverly, **9:**282n
Randall, Harvey N., **6:**107n, 109, *110n*, 193, *8:386n; letter to,* **8:**385
Randolph, Asa Philip, **12:***, *289n; letter to,* **12:**288–89
Rand Revolt, 1922, **12:**43, *47n*
Rand School of Social Science, **8:**397–98, *398n*, **12:**388, 389n
Rankin, Alexander C., **1:***, 216, *217n*, 221–22; and FOTLU Legislative Committee, **1:**228, 231–35, 243
Rankin, Jeannette, **10:**163n, 319–20, *320n*
Rankin wire mill, strike/lockout, 1913, **8:**391n, 453, *455n*
Ransburg, Karl, **4:**219n
Ransome, Arthur M., **12:**231, *233n*
Rantoul, Lois B., **11:**134, *135n*
Raphael, Michael, *3:472n,* **4:**12, 15, 108n; *letter to,* **3:**471–72
Rappaport, Leo M., **8:**232n
Ratchford, Michael D., **4:***, *345n*, 370, 503, **5:***, 266–67, *267n*, **9:***, 336, *341n;* at AFL convention, **4:**407, 409n, 412–13; *letter from,* **4:**344; *letters to,* **4:**344–45, 348–52; and miners' strike, 1897, **4:**344–46, 348–52, 356–57, 359n, 363n, 364–65, 378
Rathenau, Walther, **12:**15n
Ratigan, James H., **4:**190, *191n*
Rau, Charles, **8:**159, *160n*
Raum, Green B., **1:**125, *125–26n,* 208
Rausch, William E., **4:***, 457–58, *460n; letter to,* **4:**456–60
Rauschenbusch, Walter, **12:**250n
Raushenbush, Paul, **12:**250n
Ravola, Alfonso A., **9:**467, *468n*

Ray, George W., **7:**80, 84, *90–91n*, **8:**183
Raynes, Edward, **7:**77, 90n
Reading, Lord (Rufus D. Isaacs), **10:**520, *524n*
Reading (Pa.) Federated Trades Council, **6:**262–63, *264n*, 270n
Reames, Clarence L., **10:**399, *400n*
Reardon, John, **9:**390n
Reardon, Thomas, **2:**332, *337n*
Reaves, Eugene, *4:400n; letter to,* **4:**399–400
recall, **8:**413, **9:**124
reconstruction, postwar, **10:**566, **11:**3–5, 17n, 31–34, 52n. *See also* American Federation of Labor (AFL): postwar reconstruction program of; Labour party (of Great Britain): postwar reconstruction program of
"Red, White, and Blue Special," *10:241n*
Redding, L. D., **8:**7, *9n*
Redfield, William C., **10:**78, *79n*, 99, 101, 102n, 274, **11:**191
Red International of Labor Unions (Profintern), **11:**561n, **12:**225, 235, 253, 267; congress, 1921 (Moscow), **11:**487, *488n*
"Red Special," **7:**375, 402, 425
Reece, Thomas, **5:**66, 69n
Reed, Allen, *letter from,* **10:**459–60
Reed, David G., **4:**167, *168n*
Reed, James A., **10:**409, *410n*, 412
Reed, John S., **8:**503n, **11:**428, *432n*, **12:**232n
Reed, Stuart F., **12:**346, *349n*
Reed, Thomas B., **3:**19, *19n*, **5:**41, 42n, **8:**183; AFL Executive Council, meeting with, **4:**327–29; *letter to,* **4:**487–88
Reed, Verner, **10:**195n
Reed, Willis E., **10:**252, *254n*
Reeder, William A., **7:**94, *95n*
Reese, S. B., **7:**379
Reese, S. B., Lumber Co., strike/lockout, 1908, **7:**378–80
Reeves, Bert C., **5:**393, 395, *395n*
Reeves, Ransom L., **12:**23, *21n*
referendum, **4:**235, **6:**303–6, 308n, **8:**282–85, 286n, 382, 384n, 397, 413, 415, 417, 420, **9:**124, **11:**422

Regional Federation of the Workers of Puerto Rico. *See* Federación Regional de los Trabajadores de Puerto Rico
Reibetanz, Frederick, *letter from,* **1:**171
Reichers, Charles F., **3:***, 107, *108n*, 299, 381, 383, **4:***, 147, *149n;* at AFL convention, **3:**437, 440n; *letter from,* **3:**453–54; *letter to,* **4:**198–99; and mediation of clothing cutters' strike, 1893, **3:**305–6, 313–17, 319–21, 324, 326, 333
Reid, Alexander, **5:**165, *168n*
Reid, James J., **7:**482n, **8:***, 11, *12n*, 16, 137–38, **9:***, *38n*
Reid, James P., **4:***, 251n, 335, *335n*
Reid, Mary, **6:**399, 400n
Reid, Nell, **6:**399, 400n
Reid, Stuart, *5:48n, 6:145n,* 399–400n, 404n, **7:**48, 48n, 102, 121, 461n; at AFL convention, **5:**46, 48n, 51; *letters from,* **6:**142–45, 397–99, 402–4, 435–39, **7:**99–100; *letters to,* **7:**57–58, 126
Reid, W. P., **5:**439n
Reilly, A. J., **5:**316n
Reilly, John, **2:**332
Reinemeyer, Frank P., **11:***, 106, *106n*
Reinhardt, Ernst, **2:**172, *173n*
Reinhart, Julius, *4:291n; letter from,* **4:**289–90
Reinstein, Boris, **11:**428, *432n*
Reiss, George, *7:338n; letter to,* **7:**337–38
Reitzel, F., **5:**271n
religious organizations, fraternal delegates from, AFL and, **9:**212–13, 213–14n
Remick, Charles E., **1:**361, *362n*
Remington Arms Co., strike/lockout, 1915, *9:305n*
Remington Cartridge Co., strike/lockout, 1915, *9:305n*
replacement workers. *See* strikebreakers
Reorganized United Mine Workers of America, **11:**482n
Report on Economic Conditions in Russia with Special Reference to Famine of 1921–1922 and Agriculture (League of Nations), **12:**232, *233n*

representation: proportional, **9:**124–25; right to, **11:**159, 162–63, 168, 177–78. *See also* World War I: labor representation, on U.S. agencies and boards

Republican party, **6:**36, **7:**420–21, **8:**179, **10:**227, **12:**41; AFL demands of, 1908, **7:**309–10, 310n, 348, 348n, 349, 351–52, 369, 370n, 372, 372n, **12:**459; AFL demands of, 1920, **11:**310–13, 313n, 330, **12:**269; AFL demands of, 1924, **12:**453–56, 458, 458n, 459–60; and election of 1906, **7:**89n, 99, 107n, 108; and election of 1908, **7:**309, 310n, 328, 341, 348, 348n, 349, 351–52, 369, 370n, 371–72, 372n, 380–82, 389, 397–98, 398n, 410–11; and election of 1912, **8:**386n, 409, **9:**4, 77, 111; and election of 1924, **12:**453–55, 455n, 456–57, 457n, 458, 458n, 459–60, 462–63, 467n, 472, 472n, 473, 481, 484, 486–87, 491–92, 501, 505–6, 508–11, 513, 518–19. *See also under* elections in United States, national
—conventions, national: 1868 (Chicago), **5:**159, *160n;* 1888, **7:**79; 1900, **5:**211, 211n; 1908 (Chicago), *7:310n,* 348–49, 351–52, 369, 389, 410; 1916 (Chicago), **9:**430n; 1920, **12:**269; 1924 (Cleveland), **12:**456, *458n,* 459, 462–63, 481, 484, 486–87, 501, 519
—convention, state: 1908, **7:**348

Republican party, New York Seventh Senatorial District, Committee of Notification of, *letter to,* **2:**245–47

Republican Party of Puerto Rico. *See* Partido Republicanó de Puerto Rico

"Resistencia, La," **8:**25, *26n,* 104
—strike/lockout: 1901 (Tampa, Fla.), **8:**25, *26n*

Retail Merchants' Association (Palestine, Tex.), **11:**189

Reuter, M. P., **6:**181, *182n*

Reveira, N., **1:**414

Reynolds, DeElbert A., **7:**406n; *letter to,* **7:**405–6

Reynolds, James B., **7:**245, *247n,* 388, 388n

Reynolds, Louis, **5:**387n; *letter to,* **5:**386–87

Reynolds, Mary, **11:**413, 415, 417–19, *420n*

Reynolds, Patrick, **2:**332, *338n*

Reynolds, R. J., Tobacco Co., **6:**401, *402n*

Reynolds, S. M., **12:**197n

Rheims, **11:**56; destruction of cathedral at, **9:**192, 194n, 195

Rheinpfallzer Maennerchor, **2:**250

Rhine, Jacob, **12:**304, *308n*

Rhode Island Granite Works, **3:**341

Rhode Island State Federation of Labor, *12:38n*

Rhodes, Clarence W., **4:**196, *197n,* **6:**15, 18–*19n*

Ribot, Alexandre, **10:**71, *72n*

Ricardo, David, **1:**44n

Rice, Columbus S., **5:**221, *222n*

Rice, David, **1:**58, *59n*

Rice, E. P., **1:**85

Rice, Estill Lee, **12:**540, *540n,* 541; *memorandum by,* **12:**542

Rice, Garrett, **11:**326, *327n*

Rice, Gordon, **6:**308n

Rice, Henry, **4:**203n; *letters to,* **4:**202–3, 226–27

Rice, Joseph M., **4:**387, *388n*

Rich, Albert, **9:**529n

Richards, John K., **6:**11–12, *12n*

Richards, Thomas, **12:**197n

Richardson, Charles L., **4:**468, *468n*

Richardson, George J., **12:***, 247, *247n*

Richardson, James D., **3:**137, *138n,* **7:**80

Richardson, Patrick F., **8:***, 296, 297n

Richardson, William, *6:182n;* letter *from,* **6:**181–82

Richberg, Donald R., **12:**152–55, *155n,* 373; *letter to,* **12:**317–18

Richie, Joseph, **10:**219n

Richmond, Cora V., **2:**62n

Richmond, Daniel W., **11:***, 326, *327n*

Richmond (Va.) Central Labor Union, **5:**431, *432n,* 460–62

Richmond (Va.) Central Trades and Labor Council, **5:**430, *432n,* 462

Ricker, Allen W., **10:**181, *182n*

Ricker, B. O., **2:**194

Rickert, Thomas A., **7:***, 97, *98n,* **9:***,

203, *205n,* 227, 393, **10:***, *151n,*
334n, 407, **11:***, 128n, 345, *345n,*
404n, **12:***, *117n,* 163n, 406, 408n,
443; at AFL Executive Council
meetings, **12:**493, 514; election
of, as AFL vice-president, **10:**475,
11:93n, 321, 321n, 482, **12:**97n,
338n; and election of SG's succes-
sor, **12:**555–60; *letter from,* **10:**150;
wire to, **9:**406
Ricks, Augustus J., **3:**293, *294n,* 295,
299, 302, 559, 576, **11:**330
Rico, Juan, **12:**524–26, *526n,* 537,
538n
Riddle, William, **8:**135n
Ridgely, Edwin, **5:**244n
Riedel, John G., **2:**403, *409n*
Rigall, Edward, **10:**93n
Riggs, James P., *3:175n,* 227; *letter from,*
3:174–75
Riggs National Bank, **7:**455, 456n
Rikhoff, Herman F., **12:**363, *364n*
Riley, J. J., **12:**332–33n
Riley, James W., **12:**550, *552n*
Riley, John, **10:**430, *432n,* **11:**326
Riley, W. H., **4:**359n
Río Blanco, Mexico, strike at, 1907,
9:306, 307n
Riordan, Daniel J., **5:**196, *198n*
Riordan, John, **6:**461, 463, *464n*
Riordan, William J., **9:**354, 356n
risk, assumption of, **8:**32, 181, 317–18,
9:7, 9n, **12:**4
Rist, Frank L., **2:***, *408n,* **3:***, 14n,
199n, 356n, **4:**123, *124n,* **5:**129,
138n, 374; at AFL conventions,
2:391, **4:**242n; *letters to,* **3:**197–98,
355–56
Rivera, Esteban, **6:**253, 258n
Rivera, Luis Muñoz, **8:**88, *89n*
Rivera Martínez, Prudencio, **9:**257–58,
258n, 280
Riverside Cotton Mills, strike/lockout,
1901, *5:336n*
Roach, James, **4:**20, *21n*
Roach, James E., **7:**346, 347n, **9:**44n,
46, 47n, 65, **11:***, *37n,* 140n, 525–
26; *letter from,* **11:**36–37
Roach, John, **6:**13n
Roan, Jack, **9:**283n
Roanoke (steamship), **7:**42, 43n

Robbins, Hayes, **10:**140, *142n*
Roberts, Flournoy C., **10:**314–15, *315n*
Roberts, George, **4:**368n
Roberts, George H., **10:**520, *524n*
Roberts, Horace W., *11:409n; letter to,*
11:408–9
Roberts, James C., **2:**357, *358n*
Roberts, James H., *letter to,* **12:**207
Roberts, Johnson, and Rand Shoe
Co., **8:**102, 103n
Roberts, M., **10:**244
Roberts, William, **12:**383n
Roberts, William B., *12:283n;* SG,
meeting with, **12:**282–83
Roberts, William C., **4:**380, *381n,*
11:401, *403n,* **12:**202n, 212n, 356,
383n, 507, 517; and AFL Women's
Department, considered, **12:**445n;
and election of 1924, **12:**184n, 433n,
456, 460, 461n, 467n, 472n, 483n;
and SG, death of, **12:**541, 543
Roberts, William T., **2:***, 267, *268n*
Roberts, William W., *11:106n; letter
from,* **11:**105–6
Robertson, Gideon D., *10:308n,*
11:76n; *letter from,* **10:**307–8; *wire
from,* **11:**74–75
Robertson, Robert, **4:**294n
Robertson v. *Baldwin,* **4:**293, *294n,* **5:**8,
24, 62, 304–6, **6:**148, **7:**7n
Robins, Lucy F., **11:**297, *299n,* 358n
Robins, Margaret Dreier, **8:**456n,
9:22n, *235n,* **10:**218, **11:**132, 134,
525n; *letter from,* **9:**302–3; *letters to,*
9:234–35, 318–21, **11:**523–24
Robins, Mrs. Raymond. *See* Robins,
Margaret Dreier
Robins, Raymond, **10:**509–10, *512n*
Robinson, Douglas, **8:**204n
Robinson, Elmer F., *7:50n; letter from,*
7:49–50
Robinson, George S., **6:**276, *278n*
Robinson, Henry, **11:**523n
Robinson, Herman, **4:**230n, **5:***,
453–54, *454n,* **6:***, 129, *129n,* 381n,
473–74, 474n, 516n, **7:**69, 70n, 97,
396, 449, 469–70, 471n, 482n, 492,
8:*, 36, *38n;* at AFL convention,
6:496, 497n; *letter from,* **6:**521; *letters to,* **6:**309–10, 475–76, 516–19,
7:373–74

Robinson, Judd K., **5**:*, *115n; letter to,* **5**:114–15
Robinson, Lucius, **1**:100, *102n*
Roca, Pedro, **5**:184–85, 188n
Rochdale system, **11**:233, *238n*
Rochelle, Edyth, **12**:427n
Rochester (N.Y.) and Vicinity, Central Trades and Labor Council of, **11**:456, *458*–59n
Rochester (N.Y.) Boot and Shoe Manufacturers' Association, **3**:20–21
Rochester (N.Y.) Brewing Co., **4**:332
Rochester, N.Y., clothing manufacturers, boycott, 1903–8, **6**:297n
Rochester (N.Y.) Shoe Council, **3**:20–21
Rochester (N.Y.) Trades Assembly, *3:23n*, **4**:187
Rochester Herald, strike/lockout, 1897, **4**:332, *333n*
Rockefeller, John D., **8**:274, *277n*, **9**:218
Rockefeller, John D., Jr., **9**:210–11, *211n*, 282, 283n, 301, 302n, 328–29, 399, 400n, **11**:523n
Rockefeller Foundation, **12**:185
Rocker, Charles, *letter to,* **6**:522–23
Rock Island (Ill.) Arsenal, strike/lockout, 1899, **6**:215, *215–16n*
Rockland and Rockport Lime Co., **6**:435, 439n; strike/lockout, 1905, **6**:436–39, *439n*
Rockland (Maine) Central Labor Union, **6**:404, *404n*, 438, 439n
Rockwell, E. Benjamin, **6**:92
Rocky Mountain Fuel Co., strike/lockout, 1913–14, **9**:23, *24n*, 210–11, 211n, 242, 301, 399, 400n. *See also* Ludlow, Colo., massacre
Rocky Mountain Paper Mills, **6**:131, 131n, 132
Rodarte, Fernando, **12**:359n
Rodgers, Charles P., **2**:332, *337n*
Rodgers, George, **1**:*, 165, *166n*
Rodgers, W. H., **10**:126n
Rodriguez, William E., **8**:410, *412n*
Rodriian, Henry W., *6:263n; letter from,* **6**:262–63; *letter to,* **6**:268–69
Roe, Albert A., **8**:457, *459n*
Roebuck, Joseph, *9:244n; letter to,* **9**:240–44

Roesch, George F., **2**:250, *251n; letter to,* **3**:158
Rogalino, Mrs., **3**:141
Rogalino, Netty, **3**:141
Rogers, Daniel, **1**:219, *220n*
Rogers, G. W., *letter to,* **4**:114
Rogers, J. H., *letter from,* **7**:219–20
Rogers, James E. T., **2**:206, *206n*, **5**:303, 309n, **6**:80
Rogers, Jordan, **11**:489, 491, *492n*
Rogers, Louis W., **4**:*, *114n,* **5**:*, 60, *61n*
Rogers, Thorold. *See* Rogers, James E. T.
Rogers et al. v. Evarts et al., *5:244n*
Rohner, Louis P., **1**:*, 68, *69n*
Rojas, Luis Manuel, **9**:433n
Rolland, Modesto, **9**:433n
Romania: mission of, to United States, **10**:72n; workers from, **7**:45
Rome, fall of, **4**:26, 35, **5**:26, **8**:263–64
Roncovieri, Alfred, **8**:282
Ronemus, Frank L., **5**:*, *222n; letter to,* **5**:221–22
Roney, Frank, **1**:*, 458, *460n,* **2**:*, *16n; letter to,* **2**:15
Rood, Moses Isayes, **1**:*, 7, *7n*
Rood, Sarah. *See* Gompers, Sarah Rood
Rooney, T. J., **7**:23–25
Roosevelt, Franklin D., **10**:53, *54n,* 222–23, 361, 363n, **12**:11n; and Shipbuilding Labor Adjustment Board, **10**:207n, 234
Roosevelt, Theodore, **1**:263n, 430, 431n, 443, *443n,* **3**:120n, **4**:490, **5**:82n, 406n, 425, **6**:206, 207n, 216n, 425, 510–11, **7**:24, 25n, 88, 229n, 244, 251, **8**:204n, 385, 442n, 511, **9**:202, 323, 514, **11**:9, 90, **12**:85, 436, 507, 509; and arbitration treaties, **6**:378n; and Cannon, **7**:97n; and Chinese immigration, **6**:513, 513n, 525, 527n, **7**:93; and coal strike, 1902, **6**:13–14n, 40, 40n, 45, 46n; and conservation conference, **7**:322, 322n; and deficiency bill, **6**:525–26, 526n, 527–28; and eight-hour law, **7**:6n, 76, 90n; and election of 1908, **7**:397, 398n, 413–14, 414–15n; executive orders of, **7**:5,

7n, 76, 90n, 114; and Gentlemen's Agreement, **7:**147, 148n; and Gold-field, Nev., miners, **7:**286n; and government employees, petitioning by, **7:**5, 7n, 114; and injunctions, **6:**510, 511n, 513, **7:**415n; *letters from,* **4:**395–96, **6:**378–79; *letters to,* **6:**215, **7:**3–6, 195–97, 322, 387–88; and Littlefield, **7:**96, 97n; message to Congress of, **6:**509–11, 511n, 512–13, 513n, 525, 527n; and National Civic Federation, **6:**378–79, 380n; and open shop, **7:**192; and Panama Canal, hours of labor, **6:**525; and Pouren extradition, **7:**388n; and Powderly, **6:**110, 111n; SG and, **5:**405, 416n, 423, 457, 499, **10:**129–33, 138, 139n, 142; and Sherman Antitrust Act, **7:**322n

Roosevelt, Theodore, Jr., **12:**200, *202n;* SG, meeting with, **12:**202n

Root, Elihu, **5:**437, *438n,* **6:**14n, 215, 216n, 490, **7:**245, 388n, **8:**371, 488, **9:**92, **10:**89n, 219n, 240, **12:**13, 69; mission of, to Russia, **10:**70–71, *71–72n,* 89–90n, 120–21, 121n, 186, 191–92, 261, 311

"rope of sand," **2:**335, **8:**141, **11:**570, 572n

Rosebery, Lord, **3:**565, *580n,* 640

Rosebury, Aaron, *8:368n; letter to,* **8:**363–68

Rosemund, Charles L., **11:***, 435, *435n,* 466, **12:***, 246, *247n,* 347

Rosenbaum, Adolph, **1:**414, *414n*

Rosenberg, Abraham, **6:***, 276–77, *278n,* **8:***, *114n,* **12:***, 528, *532n; letter from,* **8:**501; *letter to,* **8:**109–13

Rosenberg, B., *1:133n,* 134, 247–48, 255–56; *letter from,* **1:**132–33

Rosenberg (delegate), **3:**85n

Rosenberg, Edward, *5:292n,* 406–7, 468, 518, *6:4–5n,* 86, 87n, 101; at AFL conventions, **5:**288, 292n, **6:**60, 499, 499n; *letter from,* **6:**4; trip to Asia, **6:**5n, 111–12, *112n*

Rosenfelder, Christian, **2:**367, 370n

Rosenkranz, Charles, **3:**196n, 298

Rosensohn, Samuel J., **10:**365, *365n*

Rosenstein, Nathan, **3:**141, *142n*

Rosenstein, Rachel, **3:**141, 142n

Rosenthal, Mr. (New York City employer), and Gompers, Abraham J., work for, **4:**198

Rosenthal Brothers, **1:**178–81, *181n,* 199

Rosenwald, Julius, **10:**21n, 310, *312n,* **11:**523n

Rosko, George, **11:**142n

Rosonski, M., **5:**283, 286n

Ross, Charles, **10:**277, *279n,* 411, 412n

Ross, David, **2:**256n, 267, *268n*

Ross, Samuel, **4:***, 426, *427n,* 430–31, 432n, 434, 439n, 477; *letter to,* **4:**427–29

Rossdale, Albert B., **12:**164, *166n*

Roswog, Alexander, *1:369n; report of,* **1:**368–69

Rothschild, Sir Anthony, *1:13n*

Rotterdam (passenger liner), **11:**40n

Roubik, Joseph, **3:**150, *153n*

Rouse, Arthur B., **12:**184, *184n*

Routt, John L., **3:**43, *44n*

Rowe, John H., *1:151n; report of,* **1:**140–51

Rowe, Louis M., **4:**133, *137n,* 138

Rowe, Thomas W., **6:***, 448, *450n,* **9:***, 31, *34n*

Rowell, Chester, **8:**261, *276n*

Rowland, D. P., **4:**99, *99n,* 123

Royal Commission on Labour (Great Britain), **3:**92–93, *94n*

Rubber Workers' Union of America, Amalgamated, **6:***, 260n; AFL financial support of, **6:**258–60, 260n; label of, **6:**260n

—local: local 4 (Trenton, N.J.), **6:**260n

—strike/lockout: 1904 (Trenton, N.J.), **6:**258–60, *260n*

Rubin, William B., *8:459n,* **9:**354, **10:**47, **11:**451–52; *letters to,* **8:**457–58, **12:**149–50

Rucker, Atterson W., *8:331n; letter to,* **8:**329–31

Rucker, Edgar P., **4:**362–63, *363n*

Rucker, Nancy, **11:**460, *460n*

Rucker, Robert E., **11:**460, *460n*

Rucker, William W., **6:**529n, **8:**447, *448n*

Rucker and Witten Tobacco Co., boycott, 1903, **6:**214, 214–15n
Ruckman, John, **10:**326n
Rudge, J. H., **3:**637
Ruef, Maurice, **1:**204, *206n*
Ruehrwein, William, **4:**459, *461n*
Ruhe, C. H. William, **4:***, 398, *399n*
Ruhle, Theodore F., **2:**245, *247n*
Ruiz, Rufus M., **7:**224, *225n*
"rule of reason," **12:**85, *85n*
Rummel, Jacob, **7:**130, 142n
Rumsey, Thomas, **8:***, 293, *293n*
Runyon, Walter C., *11:543n; letter to,* **11:**542
Russanowska, Margaret, **11:**20n
Russ, Witten B., **12:**540, *540n*, 542
Russell, Agnes, **6:**238, *238n*
Russell, Charles E., **9:**378, *382–83n*, **10:**181, 228n, 261, 311, **11:**18n, **12:**11, *11n*
Russell, Wesley, **7:***, 251, *252n*
Russell, William E., **3:**137, *138n*
Russi, Charles F., Jr., *8:316n*
Russia: American Alliance for Labor and Democracy mission to, **10:**237, *238n;* American League to Aid and Cooperate with, **10:**313n, 507–12; assassinations in, **6:**321, 326n; blockade of, **11:**86, 87n, 318, 318n, 371; Bolsheviks in, **10:**275, 279n, 342–44, 507–10, 512n, **11:**150, 318; conditions in, **4:**40–41, **10:**120–21, 342, **11:**369–72, 426–31, 432n; Constituent Assembly of, **10:**507–8, 512n; February 1917 Revolution in, **10:**45, *45n;* mission of, to United States, **10:**72n, 128n, 129–30; 1905 Revolution in, **6:**422, 454, 454n, 490–91, *491n*, 492, **7:**46; October 1917 Revolution in, **10:**274, *279n*, **12:**13; police in, **6:**415; and Pouren extradition, **7:**387–88, 388n; Provisional Government of, **10:**45, 45n, **10:**279n, 292; recognition of government of, **11:**86, 87n, 150, 317–18, 318n, 371, 441–42, 478–79; trade unions in, **1:**345; trade with, **11:**317, 318n, 440–42, 443n; treaty of Brest Litovsk with Germany, **10:**344–45n, 353, 355n, 564; U.S.

mission to (Root mission, 1917), **9:**383n, **10:**70–71, *71–72n*, 89–90n, 120–21, 121n, 186, 191–92, 261, 311; Western troops in, **11:**86, 87n, 318n; workers from, **7:**45, **8:**388; workers in, **7:**45, 297–98, **8:**388; and World War I, **9:**160n, 163n, 174, **10:**88–89, 310–12, 559, 564. *See also* Soviet Union
Russo-American extradition treaty, 1887, **3:**346–47, *347n*
Russo-Japanese War, **6:**454n, **7:**267
Russo-Polish War, 1920, **11:**368, *373n;* International Federation of Trade Unions and, **11:**437–38, 439–40n
Rust, Frank A., **11:**217, *217–18n*
Ruthenberg, Charles E., **12:**132n, 403n, 431–32, *434n*, 490; *wire from,* **12:**484–85
Ryan, Daniel, **7:**256, *257n*
Ryan, Edwin S., **10:**370
Ryan, F. J., **10:**370
Ryan, Frank M., **7:***, *13n,* **8:***, 30, *31n,* 149–50, 151n, 231n, 336n, **10:***, *371n; letter from,* **10:**369–71; *letter to,* **8:**209; and McNamara case, **8:**235–37
Ryan, John, **7:**235
Ryan, John A., **11:**154, *155n,* **12:**82n, 265n
Ryan, John C., **6:**276, *278n*
Ryan, John D., **9:**270–71, *275n*
Ryan, John J., **4:**51, *52n,* 157
Ryan, Joseph J., *letter from,* **12:**8–9
Ryan, Joseph P., **12:***, *8n*
Ryan, M., **2:**332
Ryan, Martin F., **8:***, 322, *323n,* **9:***, 49, *50n,* **10:**333n, **11:***, 120, *121n,* 478n, 560n, 565n, **12:***, 128n, 324, *324n,* 345, 348n, 461n, 467n, 493; election of, as AFL vice-president, **12:**338n; and election of SG's successor, **12:**555, 557–60; and SG, death of, **12:**541
Ryan, William D., **5:***287n,* **6:***, *503n,* **7:***, *270n,* 347n; at AFL conventions, **5:**286, 287n, **6:**502, 503n, **7:**269n, 270, 270n; *letter to,* **7:**346–47
Ryan et al. v. U.S., *8:336n*
Rybicki, Valentine T., **10:**127, *128n*

Sabath, Adolph J., **8:**342, 344, *346n*
sabotage, **8:**509, **10:**155n, **12:**196n
Sacco, Nicola, *11:550n*, **12:**90, 91n
Sacco-Vanzetti case, **11:**549, *550n*,
   12:90, 91n, 320, 321n
Sacramento (Calif.) Federated Trades
   Council, **3:**474, *477n*
Sadler, Frank P., **11:**452, *454n*
Sadler, Samuel, **10:**400n, **11:**113
Sailors' and Firemen's Union, Inter-
   national Amalgamated, **3:***, 117,
   120n
Sailors' and Firemen's Union of Great
   Britain and Ireland, National,
   9:474–76, 477n, **10:**549, 554n
Sailors' Union of the Pacific, **5:***,
   339n, **7:***, 43n, 116; injunction
   against, **7:**117, 118n
—strike/lockout: 1906 (San Fran-
   cisco), **7:**93, *93n*, 116, 118n
*Sailors' Union of the Pacific et al. v. Ham-
   mond Lumber Co.*, *7:118n*
Saint-Mihiel, **11:**47, *49n*
Saks, Andrew, **4:**296, *297n*
Saks, Isadore, **4:**296, *297n*
Saks and Co., **4:**297n
Salem, Mass., fire, 1914, **11:**31, *34n*
sales tax, **11:**542, 543n, **12:**25–26, 26n,
   38, 39–40n, 169, 344, 454
Salt Lake City Federation of Labor,
   6:368–69n
Salvation Army, **12:**360
Salvatore, Siepto, **3:**513
Salvidge, A. T. J., **10:**520, *523n*
Sam, Vilbrun Guillaume, **9:**311n
Sampson, William T., **5:**4, *11n*
Samuel, Sam O., *11:247n*
Samuel, Sampson, **1:**13, *13n*
*Samuel Gompers, Frank Morrison, and
   John Mitchell v. Buck's Stove and Range
   Co.*, *7:249–50n*. *See also* Buck's Stove
   and Range Co. cases: contempt case
Samuel Gompers Fellowship, **12:**530,
   533n
*Samuel Gompers on the Kansas Court
   of Industrial Relations Law* (SG),
   11:290n
Samuels, Aaron, **1:**114, *115n*
Samuels, Arthur S., *letter to*, **11:**509
San Antonio Trades Council, *5:439n*

Sánchez, Eugenio López, **6:**253, 258n,
   425, 429n
Sanchez, José Maria, **12:**526n
Sánchez, Sandalio, **6:**253–54, 258n
Sandeman, George, **9:**518n
Sanders, William S., **10:**554, *556n*
San Diego Federated Trades and Labor Council, **11:**533–34, *534n*
Sandusky, Mrs. J., **3:**141
San Francisco: building trades dispute
   in, 1901–10, **6:**4, *5n;* earthquake
   and fire, 1906, **7:**17, *17n*, 32, 42–43,
   43n, **11:**31; election of 1908, **7:**381–
   82; Japanese students in, **7:**147,
   148n, 195; trade and labor unions
   of, *letter to*, **2:**121–22
San Francisco Building Trades Coun-
   cil, **5:**338, *339n*, 475, **6:**4, 5n, **9:**39n
San Francisco Call, boycott, 1909,
   8:142–43, *144n*
San Francisco Central Trades and Labor Alliance, *4:172n*
San Francisco Examiner, editorial in,
   7:93, 93n
San Francisco exhibition, 1915. *See*
   Panama-Pacific International Exposition, 1915
San Francisco Federated Trades
   Council, **3:**30
San Francisco Labor Council, **4:**171,
   172n, **5:**338, 339n, 475, *475n*, **6:**5n,
   102, 233, 234n, 241, **7:**43n, 220,
   220n, **8:**122n, 142–43, 144n, 175n,
   185, 188n, **9:**39n, 40, 40n; injunc-
   tion against, **6:**440–41, 442n
San Francisco minor league baseball
   team, boycott, 1901, *5:339n*
San Francisco Newspaper Publishers'
   Association, **8:**144n
San Francisco preparedness parade,
   bombing of, 1916, **9:**517, *517n*
San Francisco Steam Ship Association,
   strike/lockout, 1906, **7:**93, *93n;* injunction, **7:**93n
San Francisco Trades and Labor
   Council, *4:172n*
Sanger, Margaret H., *11:540n; letter to,*
   11:540
Sangree, Allen, **7:**256, *257n*
Sanial, Lucien D., **2:***, 368–69, *371n*,
   418–20, 426, 428, **3:***, 12, *14n*, 16,

78n, 84, 85n, 199n, **4:***, 70n, 103, *106n,* 135; 368, 368n, **5:***, 429, *430n;* at AFL convention, **2:**192, 384–91, 395, 398–99, 406; *editorial by,* **2:**421–23

San Pedro (Calif.) and Wilmington Central Labor Council, **12:**389, *390n*

Santiago, Cuba, naval battle at, 1898, **9:**197, *198n*

Saqui, Alexander, **1:**91–92, *92n, letter to,* **4:**138

Sarah Knisley v. *Pascal P. Pratt et al.,* **9:**7, *9n*

Sarfaty, Joseph, **3:**141, *142n*

Sarfaty, Mrs. Joseph, **3:**141

Sargent, Frank P., **1:***, *391n,* **2:***, 181, *182n,* 219, **4:***, 125, *127n,* 359n, **5:***, 311, *311n,* 388n, 464n, 494–96, **6:***, 195, *195n; letters from,* **5:**387–90; *letters to,* **2:**361–62, **4:**292–94

Sargent, Sumner B., **7:**186n

Sassenbach, Johann, **8:***, 241, *242n,* 393, **9:***, 107, *107n,* **12:**369n

Satō, Aimaro, **10:**193n

Saturday half-holiday, **6:**479

Saul, A., **5:**439n

Sauls, Thomas C., **8:**278, 279n

Saunders, Robert C., **11:**217, *218n*

Sauter, George, **11:**95n

Savage, Thomas J., **10:**19, *21n,* 410n; *wire to,* **10:**409–10

Savanarola, Girolamo, **12:**548, *552n*

Saxton, Charles T., **3:**26n, 29; *letter to,* **3:**25–26

Sayewiz, A., **5:**29n

Saylor, John C., *12:373n; letter to,* **12:**372–73

Sayre, Francis B., **12:**208, *209n,* 317

Sayward, William H., **5:**353, *355n,* 367–68

scabs. *See* strikebreakers

Scaife, William, **5:***, *494n; letter from,* **5:**492–94

Scalemen and Weighers' Association (New Orleans), **5:**261

Scannel, Philip J., **1:**360, *361n*

Scarlett, James A., **4:**444, *446n*

Scersey, Benjamin, **7:**379

Schaefer, Frederick, **3:**404n, **4:**237, 238n, 239

Schaefer, William C., **1:***, *151n; report of,* **1:**140–51

Schaener, Henry E., *8:35n*

Schäfer, John, **1:***, *59n,* 83, 86, 88–89; *letter from,* **1:**87–88; *report of,* **1:**56–58

Schaffer (socialist), **3:**380–81

Schamel, Harvey, **5:**115, *116n,* 149, 396n; *letter from,* **5:**393–95

Scharrenberg, Paul, **8:***, *408n,* **9:***, *206n,* 514–15, 515n, **10:***, 191–92, *193n,* **11:**128n; at AFL conventions, **8:**407, 408n, **9:**38n, 220–21, 223–24n; *wire to,* **9:**206

Schaverin, Oscar, **7:**499

Scheibel, Louis, **6:**277, *278n*

Schelling, Henry, **2:**375, *375n*

Schenectady (N.Y.) Metal Trades Council, **11:**411

Schenectady (N.Y.) Trades Assembly, **6:**176n, 179, *179n,* **7:**41n, **8:**195

Schertzinger, August, *letter from,* **7:**224–25

Scheuermann, Edward W., **11:**484, *486n*

Schieffelin, William J., **12:**529, *532n*

Schiff, Jacob H., **9:**253, *254n*

Schilling, George A., **2:***, 60, 62, *62n,* **3:**359n, **4:***, 191, *191n*

Schilling, Robert, **2:***, 341, *343n*

Schimkowitz, Samuel, **1:***, 247–48, *254n,* 255, 265–66, 273; *letter from,* **1:**256–57

Schlesinger, Benjamin, **6:***, 155, *156n,* 276–77, **10:***, *380n,* **11:***, *449n,* 455–57; at AFL convention, **10:**469–70, 471n; *letters from,* **10:**379–80, **11:**448–49

Schley, Winfield S., **5:**4, *11n,* **9:**197

Schloerb, R. W., *letter to,* **9:**254–55

Schlossberg, Joseph, **9:***, 227, *228n,* **10:***, 138, *139n*

Schlüter, Hermann, **3:**10n, **4:***, 137n, 154, *155n,* **5:***, 72–73, *73–74n*

Schmidt, Ernst, **2:**409n

Schmidt, Frederick D. "Gus," **10:**403–4, *404n*

Schmitz, Eugene E., **6:**13n, *67n,* **7:**93n

Schmuck, Thomas K., **10:**436, *436n*

Schneider, George, **12:**433n

Schneiderman, Rose, **11:***, 134, *135n,* **12:***, 406, *408n*

Schoeller, Charles, **6:**448, *450n*
Schofield, Andrew B., **3:**119, *120n*
Schonemann, Charles P. R., **1:**206, *207n*
Schonfarber, Jacob G., **5:**153, *154n*
Schrader, Levi P., *4:337n; letter to,* **4:**336–37
Schram, Louis B., **9:**200n, **10:**52n, 55, *56n*
Schrick, Andrew W., **3:**350, 351n
Schroeder, Louis, *letter to,* **3:**459–60
Schulenburg, Charles, **2:**60
Schulteis, Hermann J., **3:**94, *95n; letter to,* **3:**291–92
Schultz, Henry A., **2:**68
Schultz, Otto B., bakery, boycott, 1905–6, *7:158n*
Schulze-Delitzsch, Hermann, **1:**44n
Schurz, Carl, **1:**444, *444–45n*
Schussler, John H., **5:**395, *396n*
Schütz, Fritz, **1:**86, 87n, 88
Schwab, Charles M., **5:**358–60, *361n,* 384n, 387, 410–11, 411n, 464n, 478–80, **8:**43, 44n
Schwab, Michael, **1:***, *462n,* **2:***, 53, *55n,* 56, 59, **3:***, 350, *350n,* 358
Schwab, Peter, **4:**399–400, 400n, 401, 404
Schwanhauser, William, **5:**372, *372n*
"schwanz politics," **4:**68, *70n*
Schwartz, Dmitri A., *11:431–32n; testimony of,* **11:**426–31
Schwartz, Maude, **12:**247n, 418n
Schwartz and Jaffee v. *Hillman et al.,* **11:**455, *458n*
Schwarzschild and Sulzberger (company), strike/lockout, 1904, **6:**313–14, 314–15n
Schweitzer, Johann Baptist von, **1:**43n, **3:**639
scientific management, **9:**187–89, 189n, 228–29, 398, **12:**142, 420. *See also* Taylor system
Scientific Management and Labor (Hoxie), *9:189n*
Scott, Alice, **10:**467, *468n*
Scott, Charles F., **7:**94, *95n*
Scott, Dred, **6:**340n
Scott, Emmett J., **10:**331, *331n,* 345, 421, 426–27, 462
Scott, Henry S., **7:**278, *280n*

Scott, Henry T., **5:**433n
Scott, Hugh L., **10:**30, *38n,* 191–92
Scott, Hugh S., **7:***25n*
Scott, Irving M., **5:**483, *484n*
Scott, John (printer), **1:**457, *459n*
Scott, John (railway carman), **11:***, 190, *191n,* **12:***, 158–59, *159n*
Scott, Leroy, **10:**160, *161n*
Scott, Melinda, **9:**108, *110n,* **10:**333n, 543, 544n, **11:**20n, 240n, 275n, **12:**38n, 406, 408n; at AFL convention, **10:**467, 467n; *letter to,* **9:**258–59
Scott, Thomas H., **7:**379, *381n*
Scott, William L., **3:**490n
Scott Saxton, Mrs., **3:**34, *41n*
Scranton (Pa.) Central Labor Union, *4:263n,* **7:**96
Scranton, Pa., trade unionism in, **4:**260–63
Scranton Declaration, **5:**543–44, 544n, **8:**105, *106n,* 407–8, 408n, **12:**102, 102n, 126
"scrap of paper" (Belgian neutrality treaty), *9:296n,* 373, **10:**192, 201, 220, 564
Screwmen's Benevolent Association 1 (New Orleans), **5:**261
Screwmen's Benevolent Association 2 (New Orleans), **5:**261
Scribner's Sons, Charles, *letter to,* **4:**396–97
Scully, Christopher, **7:**224, *225n*
Scully, Mary P., **9:**98, *99n,* **12:**427n
Seager, Henry R., **8:**25n
Seal, William E., **5:**430–31, *432n*
seamen: conscription of, **4:**113, **7:**73, 171–72, 174–76; protection of, in Versailles Treaty, **11:**70, 89–90, 92n. *See also under* legislation, U.S.
Seamen's Benevolent Association of Chicago, Lake, **1:***, 161, 165, 166n
Seamen's Union, Atlantic Coast, **7:***, 498n, **8:**22
Seamen's Union of America, International, **3:***, **4:***, 99, 99n, 294n, **5:***, 39n, **6:***, 5n, 126, 128n, **7:***, 43n, **8:***, 139n, **9:***, 213n, **10:***, 204, 208n, 502n, **11:***, 28n, 85n, 153n; and black workers, **11:**84n; German intrigues with, **9:**304, 305n; jurisdiction of, **6:**51, 52n, 53–55, 373–76,

377n, 497–99, 499n, 502, **7:**270,
   11:42, 46n
—convention: 1916 (New York City),
   9:476, *477n,* 487
Seamen's Union of America, Na-
   tional, **3:***, 281n, 496, **4:***, **5:***, **6:***,
   7:*, **8:***, **9:***, **10:***, **11:***
—convention: 1893 (New Orleans),
   3:280–81, *281n*
Searles, Ellis, **12:**264, *265n*
Seattle: conditions in, **11:**224–25; general strike, 1919, **11:**61, *62–63n,* 94
Seattle and Vicinity, Central Labor
   Council of, **9:**171, 221, **10:**398,
   400n, **11:**6, 7n, 63n, 218n, 373n,
   488n, **12:**272–75, 336; AFL Executive Council and, **12:**223–25,
   233–41, 252–55, 266–71, 271n,
   274n, 322–26, 326n, 340n; *letters
   from,* **12:**233–41, 266–71; *letters
   to,* **12:**223–25, 252–55; *and Seattle
   Union Record,* **12:**257–59, 259n; SG
   and, **11:**487, **12:**223–25, 233–41,
   252–55, 266–71, 271n, 274n, 322–
   26, 326n, 340n
Seattle Brewing and Malting Co.,
   6:442n; injunction, **6:**442n
Seattle Building Trades Council,
   12:274
Seattle Metal Trades Council, **11:**62,
   63n, **12:**266, 272
Seattle Union Record (labor journal),
   12:257–59, 259n, 388, 389n; raid on
   offices of, **11:**216–17, *217–18n*
Sébastiani, Horace François Bastien,
   4:499n
Sebring, William H., **4:**40–41, *42n*
Second Employers' Liability Cases,
   10:147n
Second International, **2:**105. *See also
   under* labor conferences, interna-
   tional
Sedan, battle of, **5:**10, *11n,* 27
Seddon, James A., **10:***, 522, *524n*
Segar, Joseph, **10:**167, *169n*
Segenfeld and Kalin v. *Friedman,* **12:**302,
   303n
Seibertz, William, **7:**234–35, *236n*
Seibold, George C., **7:**447, *447n*
Seidel, Oscar G., **2:***, *233n; letter to,*
   2:232–33

Seidenberg and Co., strike/lockout,
   1898, **4:**474, *476n*
Seifert, Albert E., **2:**100, *101n,* **4:**18
Seldner, Enrique, **12:**391, *392n*
Self-Preservation and Loyalty League
   (Bogalusa, La.), **11:**366n
Sellars, W. Carroll, *12:53n; letter to,*
   12:52–53
Selleck, C. W., **6:**287
Sellers, Col. Mulberry, **8:**496, *497n*
Sellers, William, **5:**202, 205, *207n*
Sellins, Frances M., **11:**122, *123n*
Selz, Schwab, and Co., strike/lockout,
   1892, **3:**155, *155n*
Semple, Helen M., **10:**99, *102n*
Semprevivo, Samuel, **12:**255, *256n*
senators of the United States, direct
   election of, **3:**52–53, **6:**536–37,
   537n, **8:**413
Senft, Eveline, **3:**140
Senner, Joseph H., **3:**513, *514n*
Serbia: indemnity, **10:**88; mission of,
   to United States, **10:**72n; and out-
   break of World War I, **9:**160n, 163n,
   10:559
Serr, Franz, **1:**204–5, *206n*
Service Employees' International
   Union, Building, **11:***, 450n
—convention: 1921 (Washington,
   D.C.), **11:**450, *450n*
Seubert, William, *3:485n; letter to,*
   3:484–85
Sewell, William J., **5:**455, *456n*
sewing girls, **1:**313
Sexton, James, **11:**12, *17n*
Sexton, Sehon Rollin "Rolla," *11:20n;
   letter from,* **11:**18–20
Sexton, William A., **8:**9, *10n*
Seymour, Horatio, **5:**159, *160n*
Shackleton, David J., **7:***, 288, *289n,*
   489, 490n, **8:***, 116, *117n,* **9:**476
Shaffer, Theodore J., **5:***, *56n,* 384n,
   385, 385n, 388n, 411n, 464n, **6:***,
   57n, **7:***, 120–21, *122n;* at AFL conventions, **5:**54, 56n, **6:**55–56, 61,
   67–68, 70n; charges against Mitchell, **6:**104n; charges against SG,
   6:55–56, 57n, 60–61, 67–68, 70n,
   103, 104n; *letter from,* **5:**384; *letters to,*
   5:387–90
Shafroth, John F., **11:**219, *220n*

Shafter, William R., **5:**4, *11n,* 21
Shaheen, Joseph, **8:**502n
Shakespeare, William, **6:**345, 350n, **12:**33, 34n, 71, 74n, 76, 136, 137n
Shalkop, Daniel M., **5:**341, *342n*
Shamp, Chauncey L., **5:***, *171n,* 394, **6:**102–3n, **7:***, 210, *210n;* at AFL conventions, **5:**162n, 169–71, 171n, 286, 287n
Shanessy, James C., **12:***, *478n; letter to,* **12:**476–78
Shankland, David, **6:**340n
Shanks v. Delaware, Lackawanna, and Western Railroad Co., **10:**143, *147n*
Shannon, Richard C., **4:**343n
Shannon Copper Co., strike/lockout, 1915–16, **9:**351–52, *352n,* 425
Shapiro, Sarah, **10:**258–59, 261, *262n*
Sharp, Charles H., **1:***, 390, *391n*
Sharp, J. C., *letter to,* **11:**464
Sharp, J. H., **6:**114, 115n
Sharts, Joseph, **10:**528, 529n
Shattuck, John S., **1:**215, *217n*
Shaw, Albert, **6:**513, *513n*
Shaw, Anna Howard, **6:**532, *532n*
Shaw, David, **5:**316n
Shaw, Guy L., **12:**34, *38n*
Shaw, Quincy A., Jr., **9:**211, *211n*
Shaw, William, **11:**326n
Shay, Charles C., **11:***, 80–81, *82n*
Shea, Cornelius P., **6:***, *368n,* 453n, **7:***, 98n, 104n, 429, *430n;* at AFL conventions, **6:**365–66, 496, 497n, 502
Shea, John B., **1:**446, *447n*
Shea, Mary, **2:**332
Shea, Timothy, **11:**249, *259n*
Shealy, Calvin S., *8:48*–49n; *letter from,* **8:**48
Shealy, Tillman, **8:**48
Shearin, John, **11:**189n, 286n
Shearton, Charles, **8:**103, *104n*
Sheehan, John F., **4:**118n; *letter to,* **4:**117–18
Sheet Metal Workers' International Alliance, Amalgamated, **8:***, 323n, **9:***, 73n, **10:***, 21n, **11:***, 28n, 85n, 131n, 344, 345n, 475n, **12:***, 148n, and AFL Building Trades Department, **8:**151n, 295, **9:**73n; and black workers, **12:**148, 343n; and

Chicago building trades arbitration case, **11:**496n; jurisdiction of, **8:**151n, 295, **9:**70, 73n, **10:**406n, **11:**545n, **12:**73, 163n, 400, 401n; and railroad shopmen's strike, 1919 (threatened), **11:**120n
—locals: local 5 (Youngstown, Ohio), **7:**41n; local 39 (Youngstown, Ohio), **7:**42n; local 41 (Indianapolis), **12:**363, 364n; local 246 (Maywood, Ill.), **6:**245n; local 263 (Cedar Rapids, Iowa), **10:**368, 369n
—strike/lockout: 1904 (Maywood, Ill.), *6:245n*
Sheets, Henry, **9:**451n
Shelby Steel Tube Co., **4:**483–85; boycott, 1898–99, *4:485n*
Shelepina, Evgenia P., **12:**233n
Shepard, Seth, **8:**161, *164*–65n, 491
Shepetuk, Peter, **11:**353, *354n*
Shepherd, William, **12:**427n
Sheppard, Frank, **10:**445–46, *447n*
Sheppard, Lucius E., **9:***, *523n,* **11:***, *349n,* 472n, **12:***, 212n, 345, *348n,* 467n, 479; at AFL convention, **9:**521, 523n, 527; *letter from,* **11:**460–61; *letters to,* **11:**347–49, 462–63
Sheppard, Morris, *8:424n,* **10:**291n
Sheridan, John P., **6:**55, *57n,* 68, 70n
Sheridan, Philip H., **2:**214, *215n*
Sherman, Charles O., **5:***, *441n,* **6:***, 407–8, *408n,* **7:***, 44, 45n; at AFL convention, **5:**440, 441n; and IWW, **6:**443–44, 452, 455, 457, 459, 461, 463–67
Sherman, H. W., **5:**327–28n, **6:**299n, 473n
Sherman, James S., **7:**96–97, *98n,* 410, 412n
Sherman, John, **3:**373, *375n,* 387, 615, **8:**463, **12:**511
Sherman, Robert M., *7:180n; letter to,* **7:**179–80
Sherman, W. T., **12:**131n; *letter from,* **12:**130–31
Sherwood, Isaac R., **8:**100, *101n*
Shevitch, Sergius, **1:**430, **2:***, 48n, 184n, 277, *278n,* **3:***, 10, *10n,* **4:***, 152, *155n;* debate with George, **2:**398, *408n*
Shibley, George H., *6:307–8n*

Shields, Albert S., **6**:6–7, *8n*
Shields, John A., **7**:388, *388n*
Shields, John K., **9**:194, *195n,* 409–10, 410n
Shields, William E., **3**:119, *120n,* 126, 129n, 135, 138n
Shields, William J., **2**:*, *173n,* **3**:14n; at AFL conventions, **2**:171, 267, 390–91, 414, **3**:126, 129n
Shientag, Bernard L., **12**:550, *553n*
Shillady, John R., **10**:345, *350n,* 421, 429, 462
Shingle Weavers' Union of America, International, **7**:*, 112n, **9**:*, **10**:*, 253n, 375, **12**:*, 66n; and IWW, **7**:111
—strike/lockout: 1917 (Pacific Northwest), **10**:154, *155n,* 182
Shinn, Dexter L., **1**:167, *167n*
Ship, Dock, and River Workers, International Federation of, **4**:249n, **6**:*
Shipbuilding Labor Adjustment Board, *10:207n,* 208, 209n, 221n, 360–61, 362–63n; Atlantic and Gulf Coast wage scale of, **10**:318n; and Carpenters, **10**:317–18, 318–19n; creation of, **10**:204, 207n; Delaware River and Baltimore wage scale of, **10**:362n; Newport News wage scale of, **10**:318n, 410n; North Atlantic wage scale of, **10**:362n; Pacific Coast wage scale of, **10**:209n, 362n
Shipley, William B., **8**:232–34, 234n
Shipowners' Association of the Pacific Coast, **7**:93n
Shipping Federation of British Columbia, strike/lockout, 1923, **12**:442n
Shipstead, Henrik, **12**:170, *171n,* 433n
ship subsidies, **7**:73–75, 169–76, 177n. *See also under* legislation, U.S.
Shipton, George, **3**:*, 516, *517n*
Shipwrights, Associated Society of (Great Britain), **3**:640, *660n*
Shipwrights, Joiners, and Caulkers of America, International Union of, **6**:*, 377n, **7**:*
Shipwrights, Joiners, Caulkers, Boat Builders, and Ship Cabinet Makers of America, International Union of, **6**:*, **7**:*, 243n; jurisdiction of, **7**:242–43, 243n

Shiras, George, Jr., **6**:332, *340n,* **8**:264
Shirt Ironers' Union, Philadelphia, **3**:220
Shirtmakers of New York City, Co-operative, **2**:337n
shirtwaist and dress makers:
—strikes/lockouts: 1909–10 (New York City), **8**:39, *40n;* 1909–10 (Philadelphia), *8:56n,* 269
Shoe Makers, Western Union of:
—convention: 1893 (Chicago), **3**:411–12, 412n
Shoe Manufacturers' Association of St. Louis, **8**:103
Shoe Operators' Protective Union (Chicago), **3**:154
Shoe Salesmen's Protective Union of New York, United, **1**:461, *462n*
Shonts, Theodore P., **9**:492, *493n*
Shop Assistants' Union, United, **4**:207, *209n,* 216
shop benefit associations, **7**:339–40, **8**:157. *See also* company benefits system
shop committees, **10**:455–56, 456n, **11**:107, 389–90; in Great Britain, **11**:173, 176n, 244
"Shop Management" (Taylor), **8**:202, 209–10, 212n
Shop Stewards' and Workers' Committee Movement, in Great Britain, **11**:166n, 173, *176n,* 244
Short, James A., **8**:149, *151n,* 235, 237, **9**:44n, 46, 47n, 65
Short, William H., *8:208n,* **10**:178; *letter to,* **8**:205–8; *wire to,* **11**:212
Short, William M., **10**:*, 333n, *400n,* **11**:*, *7n,* 113n, 224–25, 488n, **12**:*, *225n; letters from,* **10**:397–400, **11**:6–7, 61–62, **12**:257–59, 272–73, 273–74n; *letter to,* **11**:487; and Seattle Central Labor Council, **12**:225, 237, 257–59, 259n, 272–73, 273–74n, 274–75, 323–24; *wire from,* **11**:216–17
Shotwell, James T., **11**:110, *111n*
Should a Political Labor Party Be Formed? (SG), **11**:8–16, 17n, 24–25, 25n, **12**:188, *189n,* 437
Shultz, W. M., **1**:390
Shurtleff, Wade, **11**:489, 491, *492n;*

letter from, **11:**551–52; *letter to,* **11:**550–51
Shuster, George N., *9:302n; letter to,* **9:**300–302
Sibley, Joseph, **6:**232n
sick benefits, **1:**39, 71–72, 103–4, 122, 135–38, 139n, 156–57, 157n, 158, 158n, **5:**112n, 240–41, **7:**365, **12:**6
Siddons, Frederick L., **4:**292–93, *294n,* **7:**253, 441, 457; *letter to,* **7:**453–54
Siegel, Isaac, **12:**164, *166n*
Siegel and Co., **1:**110, *112n*
Sieverman, Frank A., **2:**427n, **3:**20, *22n,* **4:**186–87, *188–89n*
Sigley, Mr. (Paterson, N.J., worker), SG remarks about, **2:**214
Sigman, Morris S., **12:***, 320, *321n,* 405, 407, 408n, 550; *address by,* **12:**526–32, 534
"Significant Straw, A" (*Journal of United Labor*), **2:**194–95, *195n,* 198–200, 204
Sign Writers of America, International Association of, *5:428n;* jurisdiction of, **5:**427–28, 428–29n, 518
Silberstein, Bernard, **2:**365n
Silberstein and Bondy, *2:365n*
Silver, William S., **4:**282, *282n*
Silver Bow Trades and Labor Assembly, **6:**285n
Silver Bow Trades and Labor Council of Butte, Mont., *12:330n;* AFL Executive Council and, **12:**326n; AFL 1923 convention and, **12:**338–39 (*see also* Dunne, William F., at AFL 1923 convention); SG and, **12:**326n
silver question: AFL and, **3:**440, 613–15, **4:**85, 92–93, 188n, 195–96, 205, 205n, 247, 255, 276–81, 281n, **5:**35–36; SG and, **3:**373–74, 387, 546, 609, **4:**40–42, 71–72, 191, 195–96, 205, 205n, 209–10, 217, 217n, 233, 235, 247, 276–77
"silver roll" employees, in Canal Zone, **11:**392–93n, 433–34, 435n, **12:**386, 386n, 410–11, 412n
Silverstein, David, **8:**491, *493n*
Silverthau and Co., **1:**190–91, *192n,* 199
Silzer, George, **12:**206n
Simmons, William H. G., **4:**285, *286n*

Simon Brothers, **1:**112, *115n,* 191–92, *192n,* 199
Simons, Algie M., **6:**443, *445n,* 449, 452, **10:**181, 228n, 493n
Simpson, Charles C., *7:25n*
Simpson, James, **7:**267, *268n*
Sims, Robert T., **10:**215–17, *218*–19n, **11:**189n
Sims, Thetus, **11:**131n
Simsrott, William A., **2:***, 181, *182n,* 219
Sinclair, Bartlett, *5:98n*
Sinclair, Harry F., **12:**228n
Sinclair, Upton, **10:**160, *161n,* 181, 228n
Singer Sewing Machine Co., **5:**99
single tax, *1:430,* **2:**47, **12:**33
Single Tax Review (periodical), **12:**32–33, 34n
Sing Sing Prison, **2:**320, 363
Sinn, Jacob, **4:**72, *75n*
Sinn Féin, **11:**89, *92n*
Sino-American treaty, 1894, *3:372n,* 488–89, *489–90n*
Sino-Japanese War, **4:**38n, 52, *53n*
Sinsheimer, Levenson, and Co., **3:**453–54; boycott, 1893, *3:296n;* strike/lockout, 1893, *3:296n*
Sirino, Severo, **6:**253, 258n
Sisson, Edgar G., **10:**495–96, *496n,* 498
Sisson, Thomas U., **4:**41, *42n,* **10:**439n
Six Centuries of Work and Wages (Rogers), **2:**206, *206n,* **5:**303, 309n, **6:**80
Skarda, Frank, **1:**108n
Skeffington, Henry J., **2:***, 18, *209n,* 228, 336, 427n, **3:***, *22n,* 151, 155, 411–12, 412n, 430, 461, 461n, 496, **7:***, 376, 377–*78n,* 396, 400n; at AFL conventions, **2:**269, 400, 412, **3:**126, 128n, 131, 135, 251, 253n, 434n; *letter from,* **3:**20–22; *letters to,* **2:**208–9, **3:**180–81
Skemp, Joseph C., **6:***, 470, *471n,* **7:***, 139, *142n,* **8:***, *279n,* **10:**44n; at AFL convention, **7:**134, 142n; *letter to,* **8:**278–79
Skinner, J. Herbert, **7:***, 419, *422n*
Skis, Stanley, **11:**42n
Skowhegan (Maine) Central Labor Union, **7:**184–85, *186n*

Slater, George H., **10:***, 390, 391–*92n*

Slaton, John M., *9:278*–79n; *letter to,* **9:**278

Slaughter, Eugene, **7:**379

Slaughter, Ralph E., *11:528n; letter to,* **11:**527

slavery, **3:**630, 633–34, 641, **8:**69, **11:**70n, 92n

Slavic immigrants, **8:**102, **12:**415

Slayton, John W., **5:**282, *286n*, **6:**67–68, *70n*, 209, 210n

Slimp (city marshal), **1:**115n

Slobodin, Henry L., **9:**378–79, *383n*, **10:**237–38, 310

Slocum, John, **5:***, *517n*, **6:***, 186, 188, *189n; letter from,* **5:**516

SLP. *See* Socialist Labor party (SLP)

Small, L. Linn, **3:**460, *461n*

Small, Lennington, **7:**359, *361n*

Small, Sylvester J. "Sam," **7:***, 250–52, *252n*

Small, W. L., **10:**156–57n

Smart, David C., **11:**478–79, *480n*

Smead, Franklin H., **3:**134, *138n*

Smiley (foreman), **4:**485

Smillie, Robert, **11:***, 357, *358n*

Smith, Alexander R., **7:**169–71, 176, *177n*

Smith, Alfred E., **8:**301n, 472, *472n*, **9:**359, 359n, **12:**316, 316n, 485n, 529; and election of 1922, **12:**169, 170n; and election of 1924, **12:**467n; and giant power, **12:**380–81, 382n; *letter to,* **12:**380–81; and railroad shopmen's strike, 1922–?, **12:**206n; and SG, funeral of, **12:**546, 550

Smith, Andrew J., **3:**382, *383n*

Smith, Charles B., **8:**404, *406n*

Smith, Charles D., **5:**395, 396n

Smith, Charles J., **1:**447, *448n*

Smith, Charles S., *5:82n*, 351, 355n; *letter to,* **5:**81–82

Smith, Charlotte, **1:**283n

Smith, Christian W., *1:151n; report of,* **1:**140–51

Smith, Clarence, **6:***, 233, *234n*, 285n, 384, 385n, 408, 455

Smith, Edward A., **7:**186n

Smith, Ellison D., *9:103n; letter to,* **9:**100–102

Smith, Ethel M., **11:**18, *20n*, **12:**246–47, 247n; *letter from,* **11:**505–6, 507n

Smith, Frank C., *letter to,* **11:**382–83

Smith (garment workers' representative), and arbitration of clothing cutters' strike, 1893, **3:**334–35

Smith, George M., **7:**120, *120n*

Smith, Hoke, **9:**10n

Smith (Indianapolis tailor), **4:**208–9

Smith, J., **10:**292

Smith, J. E., **10:**213–14, *218n*

Smith, James, **4:**433

Smith, James W., **1:***, 454, *455n*, 469–70, **2:***, 27, *28n; letter to,* **2:**56

Smith, John (of Brooklyn, N.Y., Mutual Union), **1:**361, *362n*

Smith, John (boilermakers' helper), **11:**326n

Smith, John W., **10:**439n

Smith, Joseph (Michigan State FOL representative), **8:**290n

Smith, Joseph (miner), **5:**91

Smith, Joseph (railroad worker), **11:**551, 551n, 553

Smith, Matthias M., **1:**116, *117n*, 118, 121–24

Smith, Oliver, *statement of,* **1:**446–47

Smith, Oliver P., *3:146n*, **7:**198, *199n*, **8:**8, 10n; *letters to,* **3:**145–46, 582–84

Smith, Paul J., *11:213n*, **12:**126, 149, 295, 340n, 431, 433n; *letter from,* **12:**326–27; *memorandum by,* **12:**427–28; *wire from,* **11:**212

Smith, Peter, **5:***, 164, *168n*, **7:**177n

Smith, Reginald H., **12:**73n

Smith, Robert M., *12:41n; letter to,* **12:**40–41

Smith, Walter L., **5:**244n

Smith, Walter T., **1:**111, *112n*, 113–14

Smith, William A., *8:369n; letter to,* **8:**369

Smith, William F., *5:240n; letters to,* **5:**239–40, 261

Smith, William J., **1:***, 458, *459n*, **4:***, 472, *473n*

Smith, William S., **6:**365, *368n; letter from,* **6:**414–16

Smoot, Reed, **12:**40n

Smyth, Arthur B., **2:**216, *217n*

Smyth, J. A., **10:**189n

Smyth, Nathan A., **11:**110–11, *111n*

Snapp, Howard M., **7:**346–47, *347n*
Snell, William B., **1:**372, *373n*
Snellings, Milton, **11:**63n
Snowden, Ethel Annakin, **11:**28, *30n*, 372, **12:**231
Snowden, Philip, **11:**372, *373n*
Snowden-Porter, Joanna C., *12:83–* 84n; *letter from,* **12:**83
Snyder, Charles A., **6:**142, *145n*
Snyder, Edgar, **10:**155n
Snyder, John, **8:**230
Snyder, Peter F., *12:166n; letter to,* **12:**164–66
Snyder, William A., **3:**51, *55n*
Social Darwinism, *2:110n*
Social Democracy of America, *4:342n*, 379n, **5:**342n; SG and, **4:**341, 360– 62, 377–78; and SLP, **4:**392, 393n
—convention: 1897 (Chicago), **4:**341, *342n*, 360
Social Democratic Federation, **2:**399, *408n*
Social Democratic Party of Germany. *See* Sozialdemokratische Partei Deutschlands
Social Democratic Party of Germany, Independent. *See* Sozialdemokratische Partei Deutschlands, Unabhängige
Social Democratic Party of Switzerland. *See* Sozialdemokratische Partei der Schweiz
Social Democratic Party of the U.S., **5:**340, *342n*, **7:**66
Social Democratic Workingmen's party (German). *See* Sozialdemokratische Arbeiterpartei
Social Democratic Workingmen's Party of North America, *1:84n*, 203n
Social-Demokrat (New York City labor journal), *1:203n*
Socialism (Spargo), **7:**239, *240n*
Socialist Cooperative Publishing Association, **5:**73, 74n
Socialist Labor Federation of Brooklyn, N.Y., **4:**98n, 105, *106n*
Socialist Labor party (SLP), *1:83*, 97, **2:**306–7, **3:**445, 480, 491, 562, **4:**15n, 18, **5:**73, 265, 267n, 340, 430n, **9:**112–13; and AFL, **2:**384– 408, 417, 422–24, **3:**13, 15, 90, 110,

197–98, 419, 440–41, 626, 650, 652–56, 665, **4:**97, 98n, 368, 368n, **5:**51–53, 53n; and Freight Handlers, **7:**44; and General Electric Co., **7:**41n; and Hat and Cap Makers, **7:**19n; and KOL, **4:**98n; and "new trade unionism," **3:**78n, 181; SG and, **2:**407, 418–19, 423–26, **3:**10n, 15–17, 83–84, 90, 121, 181–82, 353, 397–99, 440–41, 503, 626, **4:**11–15, 68, **5:**18, 125–26, **6:**36–37, **7:**40; and Social Democracy of America, **4:**392, 393n; and Socialist Trade and Labor Alliance, **4:**97–98n, 135; and United Hebrew Trades, **3:**354, 355n; and United Labor party, **1:**430, **2:**45, 369, 371n, 400
—branches: branch 8 (New York City), **3:**355n; branch 17 (New York City), **3:**355n
—conventions: 1894 (Syracuse, N.Y.), **4:**11–12, *15n;* 1896 (New York City), **4:**156, *157n,* 186, 188n
Socialist Labor party, American Section (New York City), and New York City Central Labor Federation, **2:**192, 363, 367–70, 378, 387, 394, **3:**8, 11, 65–66, 83–84, 114
Socialist Labor party, German Section (Baltimore), **2:**388
Socialist Labor Party of Germany. *See* Sozialistische Arbeiterpartei Deutschlands
Socialist Labor Party of Puerto Rico. *See* Partido Obrero Socialista de Puerto Rico
Socialist Party of America, *6:204n*, **8:**91–92, **11:**13–14; AFL and, **7:**422, **8:**403, 405, 409–10, **9:**36n; Berger, barred from U.S. House of Representatives, **11:**248, 248–49n; and Communist party, **11:**427–28, 432n; and election of 1902, **6:**285n; and election of 1906, **7:**110n; and election of 1908, **7:**374–75, 375n, 401–5, 425, 427n, 486n; and election of 1916, **9:**462, 462n; and election of 1924, **12:**508; and Legion, **8:**412n; members of, barred from New York State Assembly, **11:**260–61, 262n; and miners' strike, 1912–13 (West

Virginia), **8:**518, 519n; platform of, 1912, **8:**409–10; SG and, **6:**202, **9:**4, 112–15, 124, 126, 130, **10:**523, **11:**260–61, 276, **12:**40; and World War I, **9:**378–79, 383n, 462n, **10:**181, 225, 228n, 276, 510–11, **12:**452n
—conventions: 1904 (Chicago), **6:**356, *360n;* 1917 (St. Louis), *10:228n,* 261
socialists: at AFL conventions, **4:**80–82, 92–99, 102, **5:**44–45, 49–53, 53n, 54–56, 72, 162n, 281–84, 286n, 439, 441–43, 444n, 445–46, 449, **6:**58–60, 69, 196–97, 197n, 198–204, 205n, 209, 211–12, 355–59, 359–60n, 360–64, 369–70, 491–92, 493n, **7:**129–41, 269, 269n, 270, 280, 418–19, 425–26, 427n, **8:**3–4, 282–90, 403–5, 409–12, 415, 416n, **9:**7, 9n, 34–36, 36n, 212–13, 348–50, 524, 527–29, **10:**258–62, 463, 469–70, 471n, 475, **12:**94–96, 332–33 (*see also individual socialists*); and Boot and Shoe Workers, **4:**95, 99, 185–88, 340–41; and Carpenters, **4:**341; and Cigar Makers, **1:**247–48, 250–54, 258–60, 262, **4:**341, **8:**172, 396–97, 417–22; and election of 1912, **8:**409–11; Fabian, **4:**50n; and FOTLU, **1:**213, 216; and German workers, **1:**21, 247–48, 259–60, 274n; and industrial unionism, **6:**264, **8:**412; and Iron Molders, **4:**341; and IWW, **6:**444, 449, 455, 458–60, 466–68; and KOL, **1:**404n; and National Civic Federation, **5:**351–53, 491, **6:**394–96, 396–97n, **7:**244–45, **8:**170, 195–99, 286–90, 290n, 421, 422n; and New York City Central Labor Union, **1:**379n; SG and, **1:**21–22, 83, 216–18, 239, 245n, 345–47, **2:**415–16, 427, **3:**416, **4:**44, 66, 70–71, 75–76, 77n, 96–97, 158, 237, 436–39, 463–64, 473–76, **5:**54–55, 72–73, 284, 340–41, 352–53, 449, 512–13, 514n, **6:**199–204, 208, 262–65, 268–69, 357–59, 369–72, 394–96, 396–97n, 433–34, 453n, 510, 518, **7:**137–41, 238–40, 425, 427n, 479, **8:**171–73, 173n, 282, 284, 286, 290, 410, **9:**4–5, 112–35, 138–39, 245–46, 334, 461–62, 512,

10:94, 260–64, 392–95, **11:**260–61, **12:**387–88; and Street Railway Employes, **4:**118–19; and Textile Workers, **4:**341; in United States, antiwar, **10:**93, 93n, 94, 138, 225, 228n, 260–62, 392–94, 528–29, 529n; in United States, prowar, **10:**157n, 160–62n, 170n, 181, 182n, 210, 225–27, 228n, 261, 493. *See also* Socialist Labor party (SLP); Socialist Party of America; Socialist Trade and Labor Alliance; *entries under specific countries*
Socialist Trade and Labor Alliance, *4:97–98n,* **5:**430n; Barnes and, **10:**261, 264; founding of, **4:**96, 97–98n, 102–5; and IWW, **4:**98n, **6:**447, 449, 468; and KOL, **4:**104–5, 106n, 135; and New York City Central Labor Federation, **2:**192, **4:**97n; Schlüter and, **5:**72–73, 74n; and Textile Workers, **4:**335, 335n, 439n, **7:**184; and trade unions, **4:**135, 189n, **5:**56n, 491, **6:**202, 396, **7:**18; and United Hebrew Trades, **3:**355n, **4:**97n
—convention: 1896 (New York City), **4:**156, *157n,* 171, **5:**56n
—district alliances (DAs): DA 2 (United Hebrew Trades, New York City), *3:355n;* DA 3 (Brooklyn, N.Y.), *4:106n;* DA 4 (Newark, N.J.), *4:106n;* DA 7, *4:106n;* DA 11 (Chicago), **5:**101, *102n*
—local alliance (LA): LA 141 (New York City), **4:**474, 476n
Socialist Workers' and Trades Union Congress, International, 1896 (London), **4:**93, *94n,* 96, 130, 474
Social Reform Club of New York, **4:**55, *57n,* **5:**74–76
social reform clubs, AFL and, **4:**57n
Sociedad de Torcedores de Tabaco de Tampa y Sus Cercanías, La, **8:**25, *26n*
—strike/lockout: 1901, **8:**25, *26n*
Society of Equity, **8:**276n
Society of Interior Decorators, strike/lockout, 1920–21, *11:358n*
Sodekson, Nathan, **5:**475–76
Södra Spårvägspersonalens Fackförening, **5:**308n
Solidarity (IWW journal), **9:**245

Solkey, Charles, **1**:257, *257n*, 266; *letter to*, **1**:263–64
Solomon, Charles, **11**:262n
Solomons, Adolphus S., **3**:375, *376n*
Solomons, Catherine, **1**:17
Some Reasons for Chinese Exclusion. Meat vs. Rice (Gutstadt), *5:407n*, **12**:419, *419n*
Somers, Perry G., **1**:221, 227, *229n*
Sommer, B., **6**:276, *278n*
"Song of the Shirt" (Hood), **2**:80, *80n*, 83, 323
Sonneborn, Henry, and Co., **10**:91–92
Sonora, governor of, **9**:427n
Sorenson, Anna, *6:50n; letter from*, **6**:49–50
Sorge, Friedrich A., **1**:22n, **3**:*, *121n*, **4**:*, 339, *339n; letter to*, **3**:120–21
Sotock, Mike, **3**:240
South Africa, strike in, 1922 (Rand Revolt), **12**:43, *47n*
South African Republic, **5**:122, 122n
South Carolina, and alien contract labor law, **7**:156n, 195
South Carolina State Federation of Labor, **5**:313, *313n*
South Dakota Alliance, **3**:24n
Southeimer, Sol, **8**:303, *304n*
"Southern Alliance." *See* Farmers' Alliance and Co-operative Union of America, National ("Southern Alliance")
Southern California Brewers' Association, **8**:148n
Southern Economist and Trade Unionist (New Orleans labor journal), **4**:343
Southern Illinois Coal Co., strike/lockout, 1922, **12**:99n
Southern Industrial Convention: —meeting: 1900 (Chattanooga, Tenn.), **5**:303, *308n*
Southern Lines System Board of Adjustment, **11**:550–51, *551n*, 552–54, 559
Southern Pacific Co. v. Jensen, **10**:144–45, *147n*
Southern Pacific Railroad, **7**:116; strike/lockout, 1894, **3**:632, *659n;* strike/lockout, 1911–15, **8**:321–22, *322–23n*
Southern Railway Co., **8**:253n, **11**:501, 551n

Southern Streetcar Co. Employees' Union, Stockholm. *See* Södra Spårvägspersonalens Fackförening
Southwestern Coal Operators' Association, strike/lockout, 1921, **11**:482n
Sovereign, James R., **3**:*, 3, *442n*, 526n, 579n, **4**:*, 345n, *353n*, 369–70, **5**:*, 96–97, *98n; letter to*, **3**:441–42; and miners' strike, 1897, **4**:352–53, 356–57, 359n, 363n, 365, 372
Soviet Russia Pictorial, **11**:561n
Soviet Union: aid to, **12**:13–14, 15n; Bolsheviks in, **12**:288n, 290, 293; British recognition of, **12**:15n; communism in, **12**:287; conditions in, **12**:286–87, 290–92; German recognition of, **12**:15n; New Economic Policy in, **12**:287, 288n, 290; U.S. recognition of, **12**:12–14, 15n, 96–97, 97n, 98, 223–24, 234–35, 253, 267, 270, 272, 286–88, 290–94, 452n. *See also* Russia
Sozialdemokratische Arbeiterpartei, **1**:22–24, 28–29, 31, 33–37, 40, *43n*, **2**:159n
Sozialdemokratische Partei der Schweiz, **6**:364n
Sozialdemokratische Partei Deutschlands, **2**:159n, *371n*, **4**:90, 91n, 134, 306, **9**:379, 475, **10**:269, 276, **11**:11
Sozialdemokratische Partei Deutschlands, Unabhängige, **10**:342–44, 344n
Sozialistische Arbeiterpartei Deutschlands, *1:43n*, **2**:159, 371n, **4**:70n
—conference: 1893 (Cologne), **3**:469, 642, *660n*
Spaeter, Henry J., *3:410n; letter to*, **3**:409
Spain, workers from, **1**:51
Spalding, John, **6**:14n
Spangler, Jackson, **10**:195n
Spanish-American War, **4**:464–65, *465–66n*, 469–70, 482, **9**:291, 534, 534n, **10**:200, 559; and U.S. territorial expansion, **4**:405, 405n, 466n, 487–88, 488–89, **5**:xv–xvi, 3–11, 20–29, 32–35, 35n, 43–46, 48n, 61–64, 64n, 65, 136, 139–40
Spargo, John, *7:240n*, **10**:157n, *160n*, 181, 228n, 261, 389n, 492, 493n; *letters from*, **10**:159–60, 235–38; *letter*

to, **10**:388–89; *Socialism* (book by), **7**:239, *240n*

Sparks, John, **7**:286n

Spartacus, **9**:387, *387n*

Spartacus League (Spartakusbund), **10**:342–44, 344n

Spatz, John J., **6**:142–43, *145n*

Spaulding Iron and Nail Co., strike/ lockout, 1887–88, **2**:340, *343n*

Spears, Carl L., **11**:510–11, 512n

Specht, Charles A., **4**:236, *237n*

Speculator Mine disaster, 1917 (Butte, Mont.), *10:126n*

speech, freedom of, **5**:404, **9**:124, **11**:8n, 18n, 70n, 159, 163, 176, 247, 311, 562–64, **12**:264, 454, 487, 510

Speer, Wilbur F., **4**:57, *57n*

Spelling, Thomas C., **6**:527n, **7**:253, *254n*, 300, **9**:279, 280n, 323

Speltz, John, **11**:565n

Spencer, Herbert, **2**:109, *110n*, 196, **9**:17; works presented to SG, **4**:9

Spencer, William J., **6**:*, 143, *145n*, 414n, **7**:*, 368, *368n*, 443, 481, **8**:*, 151n, 213, *213n*, 237, 257, 350, **9**:157n, **10**:*, 19, *21n*, 412n, **11**:*, 22, *23n*, 392, 401, 434, **12**:*, 383n, *401n;* at AFL conventions, **6**:205, 206n, 207, **11**:475n; election of, as AFL vice-president, **6**:209, 376n; *letters from,* **10**:136–37, **12**:399–401; *letter to,* **10**:83–84

Sperry, Mark L., **5**:212–13, *213n*

Speyer, Carl, **2**:*, 384, *385n*

Speyer, George J., **3**:133, *134n*

Spiegel, Frank, **6**:85, *87n*

Spies, August, **1**:*, 277, *462n*, **2**:*, 53, *55n*, 56, 59

Spiess, Louis, **1**:113, *115n*

Spight, Thomas, *7:177n; letter to,* **7**:169–76

Spinners' Association, Amalgamated Mule, **1**:*, 329, 353n

Spinners' Association of America, National Cotton Mule, **1**:*, **4**:*, 99, 99n, 428, 429n, 476–78

—convention: 1898 (Boston), *4:478n*

—strike/lockout: 1890–91 (Newark, N.J.), *3:56n*

spinners' union (New Bedford, Mass.), **4**:476–77, *478n*

spinning jenny, **12**:304

Spitalfields district (East London), **10**:524n

Spohn, Milford, **4**:285, *286n*

Sprague, Norman C., **12**:347, *349n*

Spread the Light Club. *See* Knights of Labor (KOL): local assemblies (LAs): LA 1562 (Spread the Light Club, Brooklyn, N.Y.)

Sprecht, Gus, **2**:340, 343n

Spreckels, John D., **7**:239, *240n*

Spring, Abraham, **3**:51, *55n*, 116n; *letters to,* **3**:115–16, 193–94

Spring, George F., **9**:277–78n

Springfield (Ill.) Consolidated Railway Co., strike/lockout, 1917–18, *10:263n*

Springfield (Mass.) Central Labor Union, injunction against, **12**:10n

spruce, production of, **10**:245, 246n, 295–96, 296–97n, 299–300

Spruce Production Division, U.S. Army, *10:246n*, 297n

Spry, William, **9**:343, *344n*

"Spurlos Versenkt," **10**:325, *326n*

Square Deal (periodical), *8:314n*, **10**:390

Squire, John R. M., **1**:444, *444n*

Squire, Watson, **4**:147n

St. Bernard Coal Co., **5**:322n

St. John, Vincent, **9**:150n

St. Louis Brewers' Association, **3**:346n

St. Louis Central Labor Union, **1**:166n

St. Louis Central Trades and Labor Union, *1:166n*, **3**:205, *206n*, 249, 343–45, **4**:123n, **5**:491, **7**:154n, **8**:128, 130n; and election of 1908, **7**:373

St. Louis Founders' Association, strike/lockout, 1904, *6:245n*

St. Louis Metal Trades Association, **5**:278n

St. Louis Trades Assembly, **1**:165, *166n*

St. Louis Transit Co., strike/lockout, 1900, *5:250n*

St. Paul Coal Co., **8**:9n

St. Paul (Minn.) Building Trades Council, injunction against, **10**:252, 253–54n

Stachelberg, M., and Co., **1**:4; strike/ lockout, 1877, **1**:95, 106, 108

Stafford, William H., **9**:4–6, *9n*

Stage Employees, International Association of Colored, **11**:546

Stahl, John M., *8:45n; letter to,* **8**:44–45

Stair Builders, United Order of American, **3**:150, 153n

stairbuilders' union (New York City), **2**:332

Stallings, Jesse F., **6**:293, *294n*

Standard (Henry George journal), *1:430,* 438n

Standard Oil Co., **7**:398n, 473n, **9**:279, 301

Standard Oil Co. of New Jersey, **8**:153, 155n, 264, 276n

Standard Oil Co. of New Jersey v. *U.S.,* **8**:153, *155n,* 264, *276n, 12:85n*

Star and Western breweries, boycott, 1904–?, **6**:369n

Starr, Ellen Gates, *9:371n; letters from,* **9**:370–71, 391; *letters to,* **9**:385–87, 392–95

Starr, Joseph G., **2**:102–3, *103n*

Starzeleski, John, **11**:122, *123n*

State, City, and Town Employees' Unions, National Federation of, **7**:*, 313–14, 314–15n

—convention: 1908 (Brockton, Mass.), **7**:314, *315n*

Statement of the Seattle Central Labor Council Relative to Its Controversy with the Executive Council of the American Federation of Labor (Seattle Central Labor Council), **12**:266, *271n*

State of Nebraska v. *Employers of Labor et al.,* **10**:252–53, *254n*

state police: in New Jersey, **8**:357–58, 358n; in Pennsylvania, **8**:44n, 52n, 357–58, 358n

State v. *Holden,* **5**:114, *115n*

Stationary Engineers, National Association of, **8**:313, *314n*

Stauffer, Henry, *3:501n; letter from,* **3**:506–7; *letter to,* **3**:500–501

Stead, Francis H., **10**:523, *525n,* **12**:222n

Stead, William T., **3**:543, *547n*

Steam, Hot Water, and Power Pipe Fitters and Helpers, International Association of, **6**:*, 496n, **7**:*, 158n, **8**:*, 151n, 159–60; and AFL Building Trades Department, **8**:149–50, 151n, 296; and AFL charter, **6**:493–96, 496n; jurisdiction of, **6**:342, 343n, 496n, **7**:272, **8**:151n, 296, 399–402, 402n, 413, 414n, **12**:68–69, 72–73, 73n

Steam and Hot Water Fitters and Helpers of America, National Association of, **6**:*, **7**:*, **8**:*

—locals: local 18 (Milwaukee), **3**:494, 497, 498n; local 24 (Milwaukee), **3**:494, 497, 498n

Steam and Operating Engineers, International Union of, **5**:*, **6**:*, **7**:*, **9**:205n, **10**:502n, **11**:28n, 62, 85n; and black workers, **9**:281, 282n, 497, 497n, **11**:84n; German intrigues with, **9**:305n; jurisdiction of, **12**:394–98, 398n

—convention: 1916 (Newark, N.J.), **9**:492n

—locals: local 40 (Seattle), **11**:62, 63n; local 69 (Chicago), **9**:203, 205n; local 77 (Washington, D.C.), **9**:281, 282n; local 94 (Washington, D.C.), **9**:497, 497n; local 103 (Indianapolis), **12**:363, 364n; local 379 (New York City), **10**:381–82n; local 569 (Chicago), **9**:205n; local 754 (Lawrence, Mass.), **11**:351, 352n

steamboat hands, **1**:308–9

Steam Engineers, International Union of, **5**:*, 79n, 446, **6**:*, 135n, **7**:*, 36n, **8**:148n; injunction against, **5**:516n; jurisdiction of, **5**:161, 162n, 170–71, 172n, 290, 292n, 433–34, 503, 503–4n, 514–15, 515–16n, **6**:9–10, 10–11n, 88–89, 89–90n, 133–34, 135–36n, 208, 223–28, 228n, 297–99, 299n, 352n, 365–67, 368n, 452, 453n, 500–502, 502–3n, **7**:32–35, 36–37n, 152, 152–53n, 199–201, 201–2n, 208–10, 210–11n, 272–74, 274n, 317–18, 451–52; members of, *letter to,* **7**:217–19

—convention: 1908 (Philadelphia), *7:219n*

—locals: local 1 (Denver), **5**:393–94, 396n; local 2 (Chicago), **6**:342, 343n; local 2 (St. Louis), **6**:367, 369n; local 13 (Belleville, Ill.), **6**:367, 369n; local 18 (Cincinnati), **5**:501–3, 503n, 514–15, 516n; local 20 (New York City), **7**:373, 374n; lo-

cal 35 (Philadelphia), **6:**503n; local 56A (New York City), **7:**219n; local 138 (Butte, Mont.), **6:**352n; local 184 (New York City), **7:**150n
—strikes/lockouts: 1903 (St. Louis), **6:**367, *369n*, 500, 502; 1904 (Belleville, Ill.), **6:**367, *369n*
Steamfitters' Protective Association of Chicago. *See* Steam Engineers, International Union of: locals: local 2 (Chicago)
Steam Shovel and Dredge Men, International Brotherhood of, **9:**74n, **10:**502n, **11:**28n, 85n
Steckler, Alfred, **2:**140, *141n*
Stedman, Seymour, **10:**528, 529n, **11:**263, *265n*
Steele, John, *6:129n; letter to,* **6:**128–29
Steel Industry, Executive Council of National and International Organizations for Organizing the, **12:**281n; SG, meeting with, **12:**278–81
steel strike, 1919–20, *11:126n*, 193–94, 228–29, 253, 269–70, 359, **12:**279–80, 281n; AFL Executive Council and, **11:**151–55, 155n; AFL organizers and, **11:**154, 155n, 206, 206n; and black workers, **11:**196–97, 283–86, 286n; impending, **11:**126, 128–29, 129n, 140–41, 141n, 142, 142n, 143, 144n, 147–48; and Industrial Conference, 1919, **11:**158, 160n, 161–66, 166n, 167, 169; SG and, **11:**140–42, 144n, 147–48, 155n, 161–66, 170–71; violence in, **11:**141–42, 142n, 206, 206n
steelworkers' organizing campaigns: 1909–10, **7:**472–73, 473n, 480, **8:**12, 12n, 27–30, 31n, 44, 44n, 55; 1912–13, **8:**389–91, 391n, 453–54, 473–76; 1918, **10:**477–79, 479–80n, 500–502, **12:**279, 281n; 1919, **11:**26–27, 27–28n, 84–85, 85n, 98–99, 124–25, 125–26n, 128–29, 129n, 151–52, 359–65, 365n; 1923–24, **12:**278–81, 281n
Steenerson, Halvor, **12:**187, *189n*
Steer, William F., **4:**12–15, *16n*
Steers et al. v. *U.S.,* **8:**276–77n
Steghagen, Emma, **9:**302–3, *303n; letters from,* **9:**332, 452; *wire from,* **10:**81–82

Steinbach, L., *letter to,* **1:**391–92
Steinbach, Mrs., **4:**136, 193
Steinbiss, Herman W., **4:***, 416, *417n*
Stelle, John P., **3:**262, *263n*
Stelzle, Charles M., **7:**9–10, *10n*, 267, **8:**93, 94n
Stemburgh, Henry A., **7:***, 444, *445n; letter to,* **7:**443–45
Stephen, James F., **9:**244, *245n*
Stephens, Luther P., **2:**143, *144n*
Stephens, Uriah S., **4:***, 104, *106n*
Stephens, William D., **10:**93n, 387–88n, *397n*, 507n, 534, **11:**7, 7n, 87n, **12:**90, 91n; *letter to,* **10:**506; *wire to,* **10:**396–97
Stephenson, George, **11:**33–34, *34n*
Stepic, Stanko, **9:**28n
Stereotypers' and Electrotypers' Union of North America, International, **8:**144n, **11:***, 317n; and black workers, **11:**84n
—local: local 30 (Indianapolis), **12:**363
Stereotypers' Association, New York, **1:**458, 460n; *letter to,* **2:**90–92
Sterling, Henry, **11:**18, *20n*, 338n; *letter from,* **11:**18–20
Sterling, John, **7:**329n, **8:**459n, **9:**450n
Sterling, Thomas, **11:**260n
Sterling, W. R., **3:**656
Sterne, Simon, **6:**267, *268n*
Stetson, John B., Co., **4:**388, *389n*
Stetten, DeWitt, *12:457n*
Stettler, Frank C., **9:**317n
Stettler v. *O'Hara et al.,* **9:**316, *317*–18n
Steunenberg, Frank, **5:**93n, 97, *98*–99n, 132, **7:**24, 25n, 146n
Stevens, Daniel W., **12:**334, *337n*
Stevens, John, *12:250n; letter to,* **12:**248–50
Stevens, John F., **10:**310, *312n*
Stevenson, Adlai E., *3:489n*, **7:**361–62, *362n*, 363, 416–17, 417n; *letter from,* **4:**146; *letters to,* **3:**488–89, **4:**146
Stevenson, Letitia Green, **7:**361, 362n
Stevic, James O., *11:290n; letter to,* **11:**289–90
Steward, Ira, **1:***, 83, 315, 317, *327n*, **2:***, 426, *428n,* **3:***, 640, *660n*
Steward, Luther C., **11:***, 335, *337n*, 435, **12:***, 89n, 383n, 445, *446n*
Steward, Samuel, **9:**155n

Stewart (delegate), **3**:380
Stewart, Joseph, **8**:495, 496n
Stewart, William M., **8**:463, *468n*
"Stick to Your Union" (West), **5**:71, *71n*
Stiebeling, George C., *1:203n*
Stillman, Charles B., **9**:*, 418, *419n,*
    11:*, *396*–97n; *letter to,* **11**:395–96
Stillwagon, William C., **3**:139, *140n,*
    263
Stimac, John, **9**:26, 28n
Stimson, Frederic J., **4**:232
Stimson, Henry L., **10**:170, *170n*
"stints," **10**:116
"Stockholm" movement, **10**:342–43,
    355, 356n, 445, 465, 472
Stockton (Calif.) Federated Trades
    Council, **6**:39, *40n,* 151n
Stockyards Labor Council (Chicago),
    10:280n, 302
Stodart, Henrietta H., **3**:141, *142n*
Stoddard, Isaac T., **7**:25n
Stoddart, Thomas, **6**:93, *100n*
Stokes, J. G. Phelps, **10**:157n, 181,
    182n, 228n, 236, 261
Stokes, William H., *4:220n; letter to,*
    4:220
Stoltz, Peter, **1**:414, *414n*
Stone, Lewis P., **6**:15, *19n*
Stone, Melville, **10**:89–90n
Stone, W. W., *statement of,* **1**:446–47
Stone, Warren S., **6**:408n, **9**:*, 49,
    50n, **10**:*, 52n, 250, *252n,* **11**:*, 78,
    78n, 188n, 227, 447, 460–62, 470,
    472n, **12**:*, 467n, 468, *470n;* at AFL
    convention, **9**:521–22, 523n, 527;
    letters from, **11**:241, 308–9; *letters to,*
    9:449–50, 463, **11**:328–32, 344–45;
    wire to, **11**:187
Stone, William, **6**:14n
Stone, Winthrop E., *8:399n; letter to,*
    8:398–99
Stone Cutters' Association of North
    America, Journeymen, **4**:*, 286n,
    8:*, 151n, **9**:*, 71, 73n; injunction
    against, **12**:398n; jurisdiction of,
    9:73n
Stone Masons' International Union 1
    (Denver), **3**:79, 80n
Stone Masons' Local Protective and
    Benevolent Union 1 (Syracuse,
    N.Y.), **2**:96n

stone masons' union (Great Britain),
    3:639, 660n
Storer, José, **6**:425, *429n*
Storey, Moorfield, **9**:434n
Storrow, James J., **6**:76, *84n*
Story, Arthur B., **7**:170, 177n
Story, William, **3**:34, *41n*
Stout, Harry H., **10**:337, *339n*
Stove Founders' National Defense As-
    sociation, **7**:154, *155n,* 245, **8**:201
Stove Manufacturers' Association,
    1:402n
Stove Mounters' and Steel Range
    Workers' International Union of
    North America, **5**:*, 277n, **8**:*, **10**:*
Stove Mounters' International
    Union of North America, **5**:*, **8**:*,
    200, 201n, **10**:*, 449n; injunction
    against, **10**:449n
—local: local 1 (Detroit), **10**:449n
—strike/lockout: 1918–19 (Detroit),
    10:447–49, *449n*
Stove Mounters' Union, Interna-
    tional, **4**:*, 227–28, 229n, **5**:*, **8**:*,
    10:*
—local: local 1 (Detroit), **4**:227–28,
    229n
—strike/lockout: 1896 (Detroit),
    4:227–28, *229n*
Stove Pattern Makers, **5**:323
Stover, Charles B., **5**:74–76, *76n*
Straiton and Storm, **1**:75, *76n,* 115n,
    365, 378; boycott, 1885, **1**:365
Strasser, Adolph, **1**:*, *68n,* 84n, 106n,
    287, 365, 451, **2**:*, 23n, 25, *26n,*
    130, 130n, 226, 360, 361n, **3**:*, 77n,
    4:*, *15n,* 136, 149–50, 193, 247–48,
    5:*, 251, *252n,* **6**:*, 30, *31n,* **7**:*,
    464, *464n;* at AFL conventions,
    1:457, 460, 470, **3**:613, 616n, 619,
    621, 627, 630–31, 634–35, 639–41,
    4:10; and AFL Legislative Com-
    mittee, **4**:113n; and Cigar Mak-
    ers, reform of, **1**:71–72, 158n; and
    Cigar Makers' local 144, **1**:46, 68,
    77, 79, 247–48, 251, 254–57, 260n,
    264, 373–74; and cigarmakers'
    strike, 1877, **1**:94–96, 98, 100, 108,
    110–11, 114, 116, 119; and Dampf
    embezzlement, **4**:18n, 54; and juris-
    dictional disputes, **6**:44n, 219, 502n;

and KOL, **1:**380, 380n, 382, 385–86, 389–90, 395–96, 409, 425–26, 463–65; *letters from,* **1:**73–74, 126–27, 254, 373–74, 380, 382, 389–90, 395–96, 425–26, **2:**229; *letter to,* **4:**54; and tenement-house campaign, **1:**125–27, 169, 207, 210n, 254n, 262; and United Cigarmakers, **1:**46, 50n, 73–74

Straus, David, **1:**68, *69n*

Straus, Isidor, *3:506n*, **6:**381n; *letter to,* **3:**505–6

Straus, Oscar S., **6:**235–36, *236n,* 381n, **7:**195, 197n, 251, **10:**310, 313n; *letters to,* **6:**380–81, **11:**58–59

Strauss, William, **8:**334, *334n*, **9:**80n

Stream, John, *7:25n; letter from,* **7:**23–25

Streat, Harrison S., **1:**211, *212n*, 242

Street and Electric Car Barn Men, United Association of, **7:**242n

Street and Electric Railway Employes of America, Amalgamated Association of, **3:***, **4:***, **5:***, **6:***, **7:***, 70n, **8:***, 52n, **9:***, 34n, 191n, 251, **11:***, 21n, **12:***, 23n, 223; and black workers, **11:**84n; injunctions against, **9:**206–7, 208n, 220, **12:**21–23, 24n; jurisdiction of, **7:**240–41, **9:**388–90, 390n, **11:**78, 78n, 308–9, 309n, 328–29; and Puerto Rican workers, **9:**533–34, 534n

—convention: 1921 (Atlanta), **11:**532, *532n*

—divisions: division 192 (Oakland, Calif.), **11:**431, 431n; division 241 (Chicago), **7:**342n; division 268 (Cleveland), **7:**342n, **11:**19, 20–21n; division 308 (Chicago), **9:**390n; division 477 (Philadelphia), **8:**51, 52n, 69–70; division 587 (Seattle), **10:**155n; division 589 (Boston), **9:**390n; division 758 (Tacoma, Wash.), **10:**155n; division 761 (Springfield, Ill.), **10:**263n; division 764 (Kansas City, Mo.), **11:**21n; division 867 (Brooklyn, N.Y.), **11:**358n; division 879 (Brooklyn, N.Y.), **11:**358n; division 918 (Brooklyn, N.Y.), **11:**358n

—strikes/lockouts: 1908 (Chicago), **7:**342, *342n;* 1908 (Cleveland), **7:**342, *342n;* 1910 (Philadelphia), **8:***52n*, 69–70; 1916 (New York City), **9:**490–92, *492n,* **12:**23n; 1917 (Seattle), **10:**154, *155n;* 1917 (Tacoma, Wash.), **10:**154, *155n;* 1917–18 (Springfield, Ill.), **10:**259, *263n;* 1918 (Cleveland), **11:**19, *20–21n;* 1918 (Indianapolis), **12:**24n; 1918 (New York City), **12:**23–24n; 1918–19 (Kansas City, Mo.), **11:**20, *21n;* 1920 (Brooklyn, N.Y.), **11:**356, *358n*

Street-car Conductors, Motormen, and Car-drivers, Brotherhood of:
—strike/lockout: 1892 (Indianapolis), **3:**154, *154n*

Streeter, A. J., **2:**62n

Street Railway Employes of America, Amalgamated Association of, **3:***, 225–28, 229n, 359, **4:***, 94n, **5:***, 169n, **6:***, 145n, **7:***, **8:***, **9:***, **11:***, **12:***; AFL financial support of, **4:**167n, **5:**250, 251n; injunctions against, **6:**194, **7:**342n, **12:**24n; and mail, transportation of, in street cars, **4:**91–92; organizing in Chicago, **6:**12, 13n; organizing in Los Angeles, **6:**414–16, 416n; organizing in South, **5:**377–78

—conventions: 1892 (Indianapolis), **3:**174, *175n*, 225–28, **11:**532; 1901 (Buffalo, N.Y.), **5:**346, *347n*, 361n; 1905 (Chicago), **6:**475–76, *476n*

—divisions: division 15 (Milwaukee), **4:**166–67n; division 51 (Dayton, Ohio), **5:**379n; division 86 (Waco, Tex.), **6:**194n; division 131 (St. Louis), **5:**250, 250n; division 132 (Troy, N.Y.), **5:**361n; division 148 (Albany, N.Y.), **5:**361n; division 161 (Washington, D.C.), **5:**263, 263n; division 188 (Jamestown, N.Y.), **5:**379n; division 194 (New Orleans), **5:**378, 379n; division 203 (Los Angeles), **6:**415, 416n; division 205 (San Francisco), **6:**13n, 233; division 241 (Chicago), **6:**13n; division 260 (Chicago), **6:**13n; division 308 (Chicago), **6:**475, 476n; division 332 (New York City), **6:**408n; division in Pottsville, Pa., **6:**529–30

—strikes/lockouts: 1894 (Toledo, Ohio), *12:24n;* 1895 (Philadelphia), **4:**115, *115–16n,* 118; 1896 (Milwaukee), **4:**166, *166–67n,* 182–83; 1900 (St. Louis), **5:**250, *250n;* 1901 (Albany, N.Y.), **5:**360, *361n;* 1901 (Troy, N.Y.), **5:**360, *361n;* 1901–2 (Jamestown, N.Y.), **5:**378, *379n;* 1901–4 (Dayton, Ohio), **5:**378, *379n,* **6:**142–44, *145n;* 1902 (San Francisco), **6:**12, *13n;* 1903 (Los Angeles), **6:**415, *416n;* 1903 (Waco, Tex.), **6:**193–94, *194n;* 1905 (New York City), **6:**407, *408n,* 452, 521n

Streifler, Henry E., **8:**475, *476n,* **12:**221n; *letter from,* **12:**219–21

Strickland, C. A., **11:**87n, 93n

Strigel, John, **3:**133, *134n,* 136–37

strike, right to, **1:**343, **2:**379–82, **3:**568, **4:**28, 38, **5:**304–6, **6:**330, **7:**490, **8:**64–65, 268–69, 313, 348–49, 465, 481, 483, 490–91, **11:**156–57, 230–32, 254–55, 290n, 293, 304–6, 311, 422, **12:**108–10, 115, 181, 486–87, 510; in wartime, **10:**59–60, 60n, 61, 65–66, 129, 171, 171n, 174, 261, 282, 285n, 408n, 414, 432–33, 500

strike benefits, **1:**47, 56–57, 122, 146–47, **5:**112n, 240–41, **7:**365, 365n. *See also specific unions*

strikebreakers, **1:**297–301, **8:**422–23; black workers as, **5:**30n, 44, 322n, **10:**109, **12:**289; Japanese workers as, **12:**119–20; KOL and, **1:**395, 397–98, 406–7, 409–11, **2:**234n; Mexican workers as, **7:**93n, **9:**438–39, **11:**285, 495. *See also specific strikes*

strikes and lockouts: German intrigues in, **9:**303–4, 305n, 366n; "snowballing," **12:**75, 80n; statistics on, **1:**336–37, **10:**xiv, xxi–xxii, **11:**xv, **12:**4–5, 6–7n; strategy of, **1:**335–38, 343, **2:**34, 87, 89, 281–82, 378–82, **3:**37–38, 100–101, 546, 568–73, 578, 600–601, 605, **4:**47–48, 162–64, 474–76, **5:**284, 296–301, 506–9, **6:**78, 345, 420, **9:**84–85, **12:**177–83. *See also specific strikes*

—AFL and: appropriations for, **3:**79, 169, 250–53, **5:**xiii–xiv, 235n, 237, 253n, 256, 256n, **6:**355n, 407n, 409–10, 410n, 484n, 492, **7:**455n; assessments for, **2:**75–77, 165–67, 268–72, 283, 293–94, **3:**21–22, 23n, 168, **5:**233–35, 235n, 236–39, 251–52, 253n, 255–56, 256n, 432, **6:**350n, 354–55, 355n, **7:**455–56n, 486n, **8:**12, 12n, **9:**48n, 65–66, **11:**566; federal labor unions, support for, **6:**243–44, 244n, **8:**33–35, 35n; financial appeals for, **2:**114–15, 115n, 203, 203n, 220–21, 242, **3:**461n, **4:**167n, **5:**149–50, 151n, 250, 251n, 253n, 255, 256n, 273, 274n, 335–36, 336n, **6:**22–23, 297n, 347, 350n, 405–6, 407n, 484n, **7:**12–13, 251, 252n, 473n, **8:**12n, 27–30, 31n, 122, 123n, 136, 136n, 146–48, 517, 518n, **9:**11–13, 14n, 48n, 65, 171n, 191n, 352n, **11:**126n, 154, 155n, **12:**127–28, 129n; loans for, **3:**169, 266–67, 268n, 461, 461n, 470–71, 471n, **9:**48n; local unions, directly affiliated, support for, **3:**149, **6:**310, 489, 489n, **7:**51, 52–53n, **8:**298n, **9:**29–33, 33n; support for, refused, **3:**23n, 461n, **5:**253n, **6:**228–31, 231n, 258–60, 260n, **9:**27–28, 28n. *See also* American Federation of Labor (AFL): Defense Fund

—actors: 1906 (New York City), **6:**516–17, *517–18n*

—agricultural workers. *See* strikes and lockouts: farm workers; strikes and lockouts: sugar plantation workers

—bakers: 1880 (New York City), **2:**241; 1889 (New York City and Brooklyn, N.Y.), **2:**240–41, *242n,* 417n; 1891 (Rochester, N.Y.), *3:105n;* 1900 (Cuba), **5:**180; 1923–24, **12:**406, *408n*

—barbers: 1913 (Brooklyn, N.Y., and New York City), **8:**501–2, *503n*

—bicycle workers: 1898 (Dayton, Ohio), **4:**457–60, *460n*

—blacksmiths: 1899–1900 (Philadelphia), **5:**124, *126n,* 205–6; 1909–10 (Galeton, Pa.), *8:35n;* 1920–21 (Mobile, Ala.), **11:**484–85, *486n;* 1920–21 (Springfield, Mass.), **12:**8–9, *9n*

—blast furnace workers: 1901 (Buffalo, N.Y.), **5:**383, *383–84n;* 1903 (Buffalo, N.Y.), **6:**168, *168n,* 169, *169n,* 170, 170n

—boilermakers: 1899–1900 (Philadelphia), **5:**124, *126n,* 205–6; 1909–10 (Galeton, Pa.), *8:35n;* 1920–21 (Mobile, Ala.), **11:**484–85, *486n*

—boot and shoe workers. *See* strikes and lockouts: shoe workers

—brewery workers: 1886–87 (Philadelphia), **2:**38, *38–39n,* 42; 1888–1902 (New York City), **2:**100–101, *101n,* 107, 113–15, 203n, 341; 1900 (Kansas City, Mo.), **5:**260n; 1902 (Cincinnati), *5:503n,* 516n; 1905 (Seattle), *6:442n;* 1907 (Columbus, Ohio), **7:**209–10, *210n;* 1907–8 (New Orleans), *7:498n;* 1910–11 (Los Angeles), **8:**147, *148n*

—brick workers: 1914 (Chicago), **12:**353, *355–56n*

—building trades workers: 1892 (New York City), **3:**152, *153n;* 1900–1901 (Chicago), **5:**214–15, *215–16n,* 233; 1902 (Philadelphia), **6:**43–44, *44–45n;* 1903 (New York City), **6:**183–85, *185–86n;* 1906–7 (Lynn, Mass.), **7:**49–50, *50n;* 1910 (Gary, Ind.), **8:**159, *160n;* 1910 (Germany), **8:**198, *199n;* 1918 (Norfolk, Va.), **10:**409–10, *410n,* 411; 1919 (Winnipeg, Man.), **11:**75n; 1921–22 (Chicago), *11:496–97n,* **12:**57–58

—butchers. *See* strikes and lockouts: packinghouse workers

—button workers: 1911–12 (Muscatine, Iowa), **8:**297–98, *298n*

—cabinetmakers: Feb. 1892 (New York City), **3:**152, *153n;* Apr.–July 1892 (New York City), **3:**267, *268n*

—can workers: 1904 (Maywood, Ill.), *6:245n*

—carpenters: 1890 (Chicago), **2:**295, *296n,* 306; 1890 (Indianapolis), *2:299n;* 1891 (Newark, N.J.), **3:**70, *70n;* 1899–1900 (Philadelphia), **5:**124, *126n,* 205–6; 1902 (Philadelphia), **6:**43–44, *44–45n;* 1903–? (Schenectady, N.Y.), **6:**175–76, *176n,* 178–79; 1906–7 (Lynn, Mass.), **7:**49–50, *50n;* 1909 (New Britain, Conn.), **7:**460, *461n;* 1917 (threatened), **10:**171, 171–72n; 1918 (Baltimore), **10:**359–60, *362n;* 1918 (Beaumont and Orange,

Tex.), **10:**317–18, *318n;* 1918 (Norfolk, Va.), **10:**409–10, *410n,* 411; 1918 (Staten Island, N.Y.), **10:**359–60, *362n;* 1920–21 (Mobile, Ala.), **11:**484–85, *486n*

—cereal mill workers: 1917 (Cedar Rapids, Iowa), *10:369n*

—chair makers: 1907 (Tell City, Ind.), **7:**227–29, *229n,* 234–35

—chandelier workers: 1904 (Chicago), **6:**443, *445–46n*

—chorus singers: 1906 (New York City), **6:**516–17, *517–18n*

—cigarmakers: 1870 (New York City), **1:**49, *50n;* 1873 (New York City), **1:**66; 1874 (New York City), **1:**56–57; 1877 (New York City), *1:95–96,* 106–14, 116–21, 123, 207; 1881 (Milwaukee), **1:**297–99, *327n;* 1883 (Chicago), **3:**640; 1883 (New York City), **1:**357–58; 1885–86 (Syracuse, N.Y.), *2:13n,* 340; 1886 (Buffalo, N.Y.), **1:**411–12, *412n;* 1886 (New York City), *1:365–66,* 375–79, 382–84, 407–8, 422–24, 465, **2:**340–41; 1888 (Boston), **2:**208, *208n;* 1890 (Binghamton, N.Y.), **3:**26, *26n,* 148, **5:**241, *244n;* 1894 (Philadelphia), **4:**72–73, *75n;* 1895–96 (Detroit), **4:**176, *177n;* 1896–97 (St. Louis), **4:**340, *340n;* 1898 (New York City), **4:**474, *476n;* 1899 (Ottumwa, Iowa), **5:**128, *129n;* 1900 (Cuba), **5:**180–84, *188n;* 1900–1901 (New York City), **5:**234, *236n,* 240–43, 243–44n, 251–52, 253n, 255–56, 256n; 1901 (Tampa, Fla.), **8:**25, *26n;* 1902 (New Orleans), **6:**30–31, *31n;* 1902 (Tampa, Fla.), **6:**70, *71n;* 1903–4 (Mobile, Ala.), **6:**293, *293n;* 1907 (Havana), **7:**220–21, *221n;* 1918 (Benton Harbor, Mich.), **12:**133n; 1920–21 (Tampa, Fla.), **11:**567, *571n*

—clay miners: 1904 (Midvale, Ohio), *6:245n*

—cloakmakers: 1890 (New York City), **2:**192, 348–49, *349n;* 1898 (Chicago), **5:**101, *102n;* 1910 (New York City), **8:**109–13, *114n,* 218, 219n, 229, 269, 450; 1921 (Chicago), **11:**567, *571n;* 1921 (Philadelphia),

11:567, *571n;* 1921–22 (New York City), 11:567, *571n*

—clothing cutters: 1886 (New York City), 1:466, *467n;* 1891 (Rochester, N.Y.), 3:299, *300n;* 1893 (New York City), 3:295–96, *296–97n,* 297–300, 300–301n, 302, 304–41

—clothing workers: 1915 (Chicago), 9:354, *355–56n,* 356–57, 370–71, 371n, 386–87, 391; 1917 (New York City), *10:336n;* 1918 (New York City), 10:335, *336n*

—collar and cuff workers: 1886 (Troy, N.Y.), 1:466, *467n;* 1891–92 (Troy, N.Y.), 3:109, *109n;* 1905–6 (Troy, N.Y.), *6:483–84n,* 492

—compositors. *See* strikes and lockouts: printers

—cooks. *See* strikes and lockouts: hotel and restaurant workers

—coopers: 1899 (Milwaukee), 5:106–7, *107n,* 151; 1903–4 (Poplar Bluff, Mo.), 6:222, *223n*

—copper miners: 1903 (Arizona), 7:24, *25n;* 1913–14 (Northern Michigan), 8:512, *512–13n,* 9:11–13, 13–14n, 25–28, 28n, 43–44, 44n, 46–47, 47–48n, 51–52, 52n, 64–67, 68n, 96n, 177, 181–83, 210, 211n, 301; 1915–16 (Arizona), 9:351–52, *352n,* 425; 1917 (Arizona), 10:125, *126n,* 148–49, 167–68, 259, 262, 301, 321, 323–24n, 336–39; 1917 (New Mexico), *10:167, 169n*

—cotton mill workers. *See* strikes and lockouts: textile workers

—dockworkers: 1889 (London), 2:279–80, *281n,* 325, 3:78n, 504; 1901 (Cuba), 7:162, *164n*

—dyers' helpers: 1902 (Paterson and Lodi, N.J.), *6:29n*

—electrical workers: 1892? (St. Louis), 3:260; 1902 (New Orleans), 6:31, *31–32n;* 1913–14 (San Francisco), 9:38, 38–*39n;* 1914 (Toledo, Ohio), 9:99, *99n;* 1919 (Palestine, Tex.), 11:189–90, *191n;* 1919 (threatened), 11:95n; 1920–21 (Mobile, Ala.), 11:484–85, *486n*

—farm workers: 1903 (Oxnard, Calif.), 6:150, *151n*

—featherworkers: 1889 (New York City), *2:155n*

—firemen, stationary: 1901 (Cincinnati), 5:374–75, *375n;* 1901 (Pennsylvania), 5:381, *382n;* 1904–? (Belleville, Ill.), 6:367, *369n*

—fishermen: 1896 (Astoria, Ore.), 4:364, *364n*

—flint glass workers: 1887–88, 2:134, 197

—foundry workers: 1904 (St. Louis), 6:244, *245n;* 1906 (Troy, N.Y.), 7:53–54, *54n;* 1916 (Chicago), 9:438, *443n,* 452

—freight handlers: 1882 (New York City), 1:296–97, *327n,* 335; 1898–99 (Ludington, Mich.), 5:58–59, *59n,* 60–61; 1900 (Buffalo, N.Y.), 5:247, *247n*

—furniture workers: Feb. 1892 (New York City), 3:152, *153n;* Apr.–July 1892 (New York City), 3:267, *268n*

—garment workers: 1892 (Boston), *3:180n;* 1893 (New York City), 3:295–96, *296–97n,* 297–300, 300–301n, 302, 304–41; 1894 (Brooklyn, N.Y., New York City, and Newark, N.J.), 3:587–88, *589n,* 4:20; 1896 (New York City), 4:206, *206n,* 207, *207n;* 1902 (Chicago), 6:50n; 1903–8 (Rochester, N.Y.), *6:297n;* 1904 (New York City), 6:294–96, *297n,* 313; 1904 (Philadelphia), *6:297n;* 1904–5 (Chicago), 6:405–6, *406–7n,* 409–10, 410n; 1910–11 (Chicago), 8:269, *277n;* 1913 (New York City), 8:452, 453n

—general strikes: 1892 (New Orleans), 3:185–86, 241–42, *243n,* 252, 295n, 5:344, 346n; 1894 (threatened), 3:523–25, 526n, 534–38, 565–69, 579n, 625, 659n, 11:250–51; 1899 (Cuba), 5:180, 185–86, *187n,* 232n; 1900 (Puerto Rico), 5:415n, 423–24, 425n; 1902 (Denver), *6:18n;* 1906 (Havana), 7:162, *164n;* 1909 (Sweden), 7:484, *486n;* 1914 (miners, threatened), 9:97, *98n;* 1915 (New York City, threatened), 9:269; 1916 (Mexico City), 9:426n, 499–500, 500–*501n;* 1916 (New York City),

9:490–91, *492n;* 1917 (agricultural workers, threatened), **10:**176n; 1917 (metal miners, threatened), **10:**176n; 1918 (Germany, anti-war), **10:**342, *344–45n,* 353; 1918 (Mooney, on behalf of, threatened), **10:**387, 396, 420, 420n; 1919 (Boston, threatened), **11:**146n; 1919 (Mooney, on behalf of, threatened), **11:**6, 7n, 86, 87n, 94; 1919 (Seattle), **11:**61, *62–63n,* 94; 1919 (Tacoma, Wash.), **11:**49–50, *50n;* 1919 (threatened), **11:**207, 215; 1919 (Winnipeg, Man.), **11:**74–75, *75n,* 94, 380; 1920 (Europe, threatened), **11:**437–38, *439–40n;* 1920 (France), **11:**438, *440n;* 1920 (threatened), **11:**368–69, 372, 373n; 1922 (Rand Revolt, South Africa), **12:**43, *47n;* 1922 (threatened), **12:**133–34, 136–37, 137n, 147

—glassworkers: 1895 (Carmaux, France), **4:**76, *77n;* 1899 (Bridgeton, N.J.), **5:**283, *286n;* 1900 (Bridgeton, N.J.), **5:**246

—glove makers: 1914 (New York City), **9:**191n; 1920–21 (Chicago), **12:**451, *451n*

—granite cutters: 1892, **3:**165, *165–66n;* 1900, *5:235n,* 237; 1921-?, **12:**127, *129n*

—granite polishers: 1890 (Barre, Vt.), **2:**281–82, *282n*

—harbor workers: 1918 (New York Harbor, threatened), **10:**380–81, *381–82n,* 432–33, 434n

—hat and cap makers: 1903–4 (New York City and New Jersey), **7:**18, *19n;* 1904–5 (New York City and New Jersey), **6:**405–6, *407n,* 409–10, 410n, **7:**207; 1905–6 (Detroit), **7:**18, *19n,* 184, 186n; 1905–6 (New York City), **7:**18, *18n,* 184

—hatters: 1893–94 (Danbury, Conn.), **4:**105, *106n;* 1902 (Danbury, Conn.), *6:177n;* 1909 (Connecticut, New York, and New Jersey), **7:**454–55, *455–56n,* **8:**77

—hop field workers: 1913, 1914 (California), **9:**504, *507n,* **10:**247

—horse car drivers: 1880 (New York City), *1:327n,* 335

—hotel and restaurant workers: 1893 (Brooklyn, N.Y.), *3:485–86n;* 1913 (Albany, N.Y.), **8:**448–49, *452n;* 1913 (New York City), **8:**449, *452–53n,* **9:**489n

—house wreckers: 1920 (New York City), **11:**353

—iron and steel workers: 1882 (Pittsburgh), **1:**272, *272n,* 339–40, *353n;* 1883 (Bethlehem, Pa.), **4:**490–91, *499n;* 1887 (Mingo Junction, Ohio), **2:**24, *24n,* 40, 339–40; 1887–88 (Brilliant, Ohio), **2:**340, *343n;* 1888, **2:**134, *135n,* 197; 1892 (Beaver Falls, Pa.), *3:234n,* 238; 1892 (Homestead, Pa.; *see* Homestead strike, 1892); 1892–93 (Union Mills, Pittsburgh), *3:234n,* 238; 1901, **5:**384, *384n,* 385, *385n,* 386–88, 388n, 389–90, 411, 411n, 479, **6:**104n; 1909–10, **7:**472, *473n,* 480, **8:**7, 9n, 12, 12n, 27–30, 54–55; 1910 (So. Bethlehem, Pa.), **8:**43, *44n;* 1913 (Chicago Heights, Ill.), **8:**391n; 1913 (Rankin and Braddock, Pa.), **8:**391n, 453, *455n;* 1916 (Pittsburgh), **9:**504, *507n,* **10:**247; 1917 (Yorkville, Ohio), **10:**79, *79n;* 1919–20 (*see* steel strike, 1919–20)

—iron molders: 1896 (Chattanooga, Tenn.), **4:**315, *317n,* 318; 1897 (Sheboygan, Wis.), **4:**325, *325n;* 1905–6? (Racine, Wis.), **7:**158n; 1906 (St. Louis), **7:**153, *155n;* 1906 (Troy, N.Y.), **7:**53–54, *54n;* 1916 (Chicago), **9:**438, *443n,* 452

—iron ore miners: 1913 (Mineville, N.Y.), **9:**177, *178n;* 1916 (Mesabi Range), **9:**488, *489–90n,* 504–5, **10:**247

—janitors: 1917 (Chicago), **10:**216, *218n*

—jute mill workers: 1893 (Dundee, Scotland), *3:542n;* 1895 (Dundee, Scotland), *3:542n*

—knife grinders: 1892, **3:**197, 197n

—laborers: 1916 (Buffalo, N.Y.), *9:406n*

—ladies' garment workers: 1903 (Chicago), **6:**155, *156n;* 1909–10 (New York City), **8:**39, *40n;* 1909–10 (Phil-

adelphia), *8:56n,* 269; 1910 (New
York City), **8:**109–13, *114n,* 218,
219n, 229, 269, 450, **12:**528–29, 531;
1913 (New York City), *8:442n,* 450,
9:98; 1917 (New York City), **10:**61,
62n; 1921 (Chicago), **11:**567, *571n;*
1921 (Philadelphia), **11:**567, *571n;*
1921–22 (New York City), **11:**567,
571n; 1924 (Chicago), **12:**427–28,
428n
—lasters. *See* strikes and lockouts:
shoe workers
—lathers: 1903–6 (Philadelphia),
6:292, *292n;* 1919 (Toronto), **11:**72
—laundry workers. *See* strikes and
lockouts: collar and cuff workers
—leather workers: 1905-? (Cincinnati), **7:**11n; 1910, *8:148n;* 1910–12
(Los Angeles), **8:**147, *148n;* 1919–
20 (Indianapolis), **11:**569, *571n;*
1920 (Boston), **11:**569, *571n;* 1920
(St. Louis), **11:**569, *571n;* 1920–22
(Chicago), **11:**569, *571n;* 1921 (Peabody, Mass.), **11:**569, *571n*
—lime workers: 1905 (Rockland,
Maine), **6:**436–39, *439n*
—locomotive engineers. *See* strikes
and lockouts: railroad workers
—locomotive firemen. *See* strikes and
lockouts: railroad workers
—longshoremen: 1903 (Brunswick,
Ga.), **7:**187, *190n;* 1905 (Puerto
Rico), **6:**470, *470–71n;* 1907 (Brunswick, Ga.), **7:**187–89, *190n;* 1907
(Havana), **7:**163, *165n;* 1917 (Seattle, threatened), **10:**137, 137–38n;
1920 (Galveston, Tex.), **11:**426n;
1923 (Vancouver, B.C.), **12:**442n
—lumber workers: 1903–6? (Fort
Bragg, Calif.), **6:**170, *171n,* 241–44
—machinists: 1896 (Cleveland),
4:177, *178n;* 1899 (Rock Island
and Moline, Ill., and Davenport,
Iowa), **6:**215, *215–16n;* 1899–1900
(Philadelphia), **5:**124, *126n,* 205–6;
1900 (Chicago), **5:**214, *216n;* 1900
(Cleveland, Detroit, Philadelphia,
and Paterson, N.J.), *5:216n,* 233;
1901–2, *5:333–34n,* 367–69, 369n,
372; 1901–2 (Denver), **6:**15, *18n;*
1903–5 (Elmira, N.Y.), **6:**152, *152n;*

1906 (Troy, N.Y.), **7:**53–54, *54n;*
1906–7 (Lynn, Mass.), **7:**50, *50–51n;*
1907 (Houston), **7:**222, *222n;*
1909–10 (Galeton, Pa.), *8:35n;* 1915
(Bridgeport, Conn.), **9:**304, *305n;*
1917 (Michigan Central Railroad,
threatened), **10:**187–88, *189n;*
1920–21 (Mobile, Ala.), **11:**484–85,
486n
—maintenance of way employees.
See strikes and lockouts: railroad
workers
—marine cooks and stewards: 1906
(San Francisco), **7:**93, *93n,* 118n
—marine firemen: 1906 (San Francisco), **7:**93, *93n,* 118n
—masons: 1877–78 (London), **3:**639,
660n; 1899 (Cuba), *5:187n;* 1903
(Schenectady, N.Y.), **6:**175–76
—meat cutters. *See* strikes and lockouts: packinghouse workers
—metal mechanics. *See* strikes and
lockouts: metal trades workers
—metal miners: 1892 (Coeur d'Alene,
Idaho), **3:**185–86, 213, *214n,*
251–52, 255, 293–94, 420, **5:**93n,
6:452; 1896–97 (Leadville, Colo.; *see*
Leadville, Colo., strike, 1896–97);
1917 (Butte, Mont.), **10:**126, *126–
27n;* 1917 (general, threatened),
10:176n
—metal polishers: 1893 (Chicago),
3:356n; 1896 (Detroit), **4:**227–28,
229n; 1901–2 (Dayton, Ohio),
5:364–65, *366–67n,* 460n, 489–90;
1904 (Chicago), **6:**443, *445–46n;*
1906 (St. Louis), **7:**153, *154n*
—metal trades workers: 1898 (Dayton, Ohio), **4:**457–60, *460n;*
1901–2 (Dayton, Ohio), **5:**364–65,
366–67n, 460n, 489–90; 1901–2
(San Francisco), **5:**432, *432–33n;*
1904 (Maywood, Ill.), **6:**245n; 1906
(Schenectady, N.Y.), **7:**41n; 1906
(Youngstown, Ohio), *7:41–42n;*
1910–12 (Los Angeles), **8:**121–22,
122–23n, 136, 147, 221; 1918 (Birmingham, Ala.), **10:**376–77, *378n,*
385–86, 440–44, 516–18, 518n; 1919
(Toronto), **11:**72–73, *74n;* 1919
(Winnipeg, Man.), **11:**75n

—mine and smelter workers: 1899 (Denver and Pueblo, Colo.), **5:**114, *115n;* 1899 (Wardner, Idaho), **5:**90, *92–93n,* 95–97, 101n, 114, 129–36, 148–50, 151n, 231, 232n, **7:**24, 25n; 1903–4 (Colorado), **6:**279–81, *282–83n,* 343–44, 344n, 361–62, 452, 504–6, 509n, **7:**24, 25n

—mineral mine workers: 1896–97 (Norway, Mich.), *4:165n*

—miners: 1882 (western Maryland), **1:**284, *286n;* 1884–85 (Hocking Valley, Ohio), **1:**426, *426n,* **9:**86–87; 1887–88 (Pennsylvania), **2:**91, *92n,* 107; 1889 (Illinois and Indiana), **2:**220–21, *221–22n;* 1890–91 (Alabama), **2:**414, *414n;* 1890–91 (Vancouver Island, B.C.), *3:56n;* 1891 (Connellsville, Pa.), **3:**56–58, *58*–59n, 64n, 66, 66n, 67–68, 68n, 73–74; 1891 (Iowa), **3:**69, *70n;* 1891 (Tennessee), *3:215n;* 1892 (Tennessee), **3:**185–86, 213, *215n,* 220–21, 251–53, 420, **4:**40; 1893 (Great Britain), **3:**426, *429n,* 432, 565, 575; 1894, **3:**542–44, *547n;* 1894 (Pratt City, Ala.), *4:28n;* 1897 (*see* miners' strike, 1897); 1897 (Illinois), **7:**417n; 1898 (Virden, Ill.), **5:**26, *30n,* 43–44; 1898–99 (Pana, Ill.), *5:30n;* 1900 (Maryland), **5:**217–18, *218–19n;* 1900 (Pennsylvania), **5:**262, *263n,* **7:**484, **8:**229, 269, **9:**337, **11:**567, 571n; 1900–1903? (Kentucky), **5:**321, *322n;* 1901 (Pennsylvania), **5:**382n; 1902 (*see* miners' strike, 1902 [anthracite]); 1902 (Clarksburg, W.Va.), **6:**81, 84n; 1907 (Goldfield, Nev.), **7:**283, *286n;* 1909–10 (Cape Breton, Canada), **10:**307, *308n;* 1912–13 (West Virginia), **8:**518, *519n,* **9:**24, 210, 301, **11:**296n; 1913–14 (Colorado), **9:**23, *24n,* 210–11, 211n, 242, 301, 399, 400n (*see also* Ludlow, Colo., massacre); 1914 (threatened), **9:**97, 98n; 1915 (Arkansas), *11:494n;* 1917 (Alabama, threatened), **10:**287–88, *288n;* 1918 (Cape Breton, Canada, threatened), **10:**307–8, *308n;* 1919 (*see* miners'

strike, 1919); 1919 (Brackenridge, Pa.), **11:**121–22, *123n;* 1919 (Kansas), **11:**305–8; 1921 (Kansas), **11:**481–82n, 558; 1922 (*see* miners' strike, 1922); 1923, *12:315n*

—munitions workers: 1915 (Bridgeport, Conn.), **9:**304, *305n*

—news dealers: 1918 (New York City), **10:**335, *336n*

—oil field workers: 1917–18 (Texas and Louisiana), **10:**305, *306–7n*

—packinghouse workers: 1886 (Chicago), **1:**466, *467n,* **2:**22, 23n, 341, 343n; 1896 (New York City), **4:**229–30, *230n;* 1896–98 (Kansas City, Mo.), **4:**286, *287n;* 1904, **6:**313–14, *314–15n,* **7:**345, **11:**567, 571n; 1917 (Denver), **10:**214; 1917 (Kansas City, Kans.), **10:**214, 403, *404n;* 1917 (Omaha, Nebr.), **10:**214, 403, *404n;* 1917–18 (Chicago, threatened), **10:**279, *280n,* 285n, 302–3, 442, **11:**453n; 1921 (Chicago, threatened), *11:453n;* 1921–22, *11:453n,* 567, *571n*

—painters: 1900 (Augusta, Ga.), **6:**115n; 1903 (Schenectady, N.Y.), **6:**176n; 1919 (Toronto), **11:**72–73, *74n;* 1920–21 (New York City), **11:**356, *358n*

—paper bag workers: 1906 (Rumford Falls, Maine), **7:**104–5, *105n*

—paper makers: 1907 (Fort Edward, N.Y.), **7:**202–4, *204n*

—paper mill workers: 1903 (Denver), *6:131n*

—pattern makers: 1917 (Brooklyn, N.Y., threatened), **10:**52–53, 54n

—paving cutters: 1892, **3:**165, *165–66n*

—plate printers: 1900–1902 (Philadelphia), *5:318n,* 320; 1904–? (Brooklyn, N.Y.), **6:**380, *381n*

—police: 1919 (Boston), **11:**145–46, *146*–47n, 318, 319n

—printers: 1884 (Troy, N.Y.), **2:**341, *343n;* 1886 (Jacksonville, Fla.), **2:**340–41, *343n;* 1890–92, 1893–? (Los Angeles), **6:**212–13, *213n,* **8:**129, 146; 1891–92 (Pittsburgh), **3:**125–27, *128n,* 129–31, 139, 263–

64; 1892 (New York City), *3:486n;*
1897 (Rochester, N.Y.), **4:**332, *333n;*
1899–1900 (Kansas City, Mo.),
5:236n; 1899–1900 (Pittsburgh),
5:174–75, *176n,* 234; 1899–1902
(*New York Sun*), **5:**234, *236n,* 405,
406n; 1901 (Chicago), **5:**340, *342n;*
1905-? (Chicago), **7:**11n; 1905–8,
7:483, *485–86n;* 1905–8 (Philadelphia), **7:**85, *91n;* 1906 (New York
City), **7:**85, *91n;* 1906-? (Dayton,
Ohio), **7:**166, 168–*69n,* 193; 1912-?
(Chicago), **9:**74n; 1921–24, **11:**566–
67, *570–71n*
—printing pressmen. *See* strikes and
lockouts: printers
—quarry workers: 1892, *3:165–66n;*
1921-?, **12:**127, *129n. See also* strikes
and lockouts: granite cutters
—railroad shopmen: 1900 (Buffalo,
N.Y.), **5:**247, *247n;* 1909–10 (Galeton, Pa.), **8:**33–35, *35n;* 1910 (Pennsylvania), *8:190n;* 1911 (Philadelphia), **8:**228–29, *230n;* 1911–15,
8:321–22, *322–23n;* 1919 (threatened), **11:**118–19, 119–*20n;* 1920
(threatened), **11:**259n; 1922-? (*see*
railroad shopmen's strike, 1922-?)
—railroad telegraphers: 1900, **5:**295–
96, *307n*
—railroad workers: 1877, *1:95,* 98–99,
102, **3:**190, **11:**250; 1882 (Southwest,
threatened), **1:**343, *353–54n;* 1885
(Southwest), **1:**399–400, *402n,* 409–
10; 1886 (Southwest), **1:**101n, *402n,*
2:341; 1887–88 (Philadelphia and
Reading Railroad), **2:**92n, 108n;
1888–89 (Chicago, Burlington, and
Quincy Railroad), **2:**107, *108n,* 341,
11:330; 1890 (New York Central
Railroad), **2:**378–79, *382n,* 399,
11:330; 1892 (Buffalo, N.Y.), **3:**185–
86, 213, *214–15n,* 219, 222, 420,
4:105; 1893 (Lehigh Valley Railroad), **3:**432, *434n;* 1893 (Toledo,
Ann Arbor, and Northern Michigan
Railroad), *3:294n,* 329–31, **11:**330;
1894 (American Railway Union, *see*
Pullman strike, 1894); 1894 (Columbus, Hocking Valley, and Toledo Railroad), **4:**4–5; 1894 (Great

Northern Railroad), **3:**521, 544,
547n; 1894 (Northern Pacific Railroad), **3:**561n; 1894 (Southern and
Central Pacific Railroads), **3:**632,
659n; 1900 (Atchison, Topeka, and
Santa Fe Railway), **5:**295–96, *307n;*
1900 (Wales), **6:**74, 78, *83n;* 1905
(New York City), **6:**407, *408n,* 452,
521n; 1910 (Grand Trunk Railway),
8:112–13, *114–15n;* 1914 (Pennsylvania), *9:50n;* 1916 (Cuba), *9:534n;*
1916 (threatened), *9:450n,* 463,
495n, 529n, **12:**499; 1917 (threatened), **11:**251–52, *259n;* 1919
(Great Britain), **11:**164, *167n;* 1920
(threatened), **11:**249–58, *258–59n;*
1921 (threatened), **11:**504, 536,
539n; 1921–23 (Harrison, Ark.),
12:192–95, *196–*97n; 1922 (Chicago,
St. Paul, Minneapolis, and Omaha
Railway Co.), **12:**373n
—rubber workers: 1904 (Trenton,
N.J.), **6:**258–60, *260n*
—sailors: 1906 (San Francisco), **7:**93,
93n, 116, 118n
—sheet metal workers. *See* strikes and
lockouts: metal trades workers
—shipyard workers: 1891 (Philadelphia), **4:**491, *499n;* 1899–1900
(Philadelphia), **5:**124, *126n,*
165, 205–6; 1917 (Norfolk, Va.),
10:222–23, *223n;* 1917 (Pacific
Coast), **10:**208–9, *209n,* 259; 1918
(Beaumont and Orange, Tex.),
10:317–18, *318n;* 1918 (Norfolk,
Va.), **10:**409–10, *410n,* 411; 1920–21
(Mobile, Ala.), **11:**484–85, *486n*
—shoe workers: 1887 (Worcester
County, Mass.), **2:**24, *24n;* 1890–91
(Fairport and Rochester, N.Y.),
2:423, *427–28n,* **3:**20–21, 26; 1891–
95 (Brockton, Mass.), *3:269n;* 1892
(Chicago), **3:**155, *155n;* 1893–94
(Auburn, Maine), **3:**411, *412n,* 460–
61; 1905 (Brockton, Mass.), **7:**37,
39n; 1906–7 (Syracuse, N.Y.), **7:**185,
186n, 339
—silk workers. *See* strikes and lockouts: textile workers
—slasher tenders. *See* strikes and lockouts: textile workers

—slaters: 1889 (Pittsburgh), **2:**234n
—spinners, cotton. *See* strikes and lockouts: textile workers
—steam engineers: 1903 (St. Louis), **6:**367, *369n,* 500, 502; 1904-? (Belleville, Ill.), **6:**367, *369n*
—stone masons. *See* strikes and lockouts: masons
—stove mounters: 1884 (Troy, N.Y.), **1:**399, *402n,* **2:**8; 1896 (Detroit), **4:**227–28, *229n;* 1918–19 (Detroit), **10:**447–49, *449n*
—street railway workers: 1889 (New York City and Brooklyn, N.Y.), **2:**197, *197–98n,* 286; 1892 (Indianapolis), **3:**154, *154n;* 1894 (Toledo, Ohio), *12:24n;* 1895 (Brooklyn, N.Y.), **4:**92, *94n,* 105; 1895 (Philadelphia), **4:**115, *115–16n,* 118; 1896 (Milwaukee), **4:**166, *166–67n,* 182–83; 1900 (St. Louis), **5:**250, *250n;* 1900 (Stockholm), **5:**301, *308n;* 1901 (Albany, N.Y.), **5:**360, *361n;* 1901 (Troy, N.Y.), **5:**360, *361n;* 1901–2 (Jamestown, N.Y.), **5:**378, *379n;* 1901–4 (Dayton, Ohio), **5:**378, *379n,* **6:**142–44, *145n;* 1902 (San Francisco), **6:**12, *13n;* 1903 (Los Angeles), **6:**415, *416n;* 1903 (Waco, Tex.), **6:**193–94, *194n;* 1905 (New York City), **6:**407, *408n,* 452, 521n; 1906 (Cuba), **7:**162, *164n;* 1908 (Chicago), **7:**342, *342n;* 1908 (Cleveland), **7:**342, *342n;* 1910 (Philadelphia), *8:52n,* 69–70; 1916 (New York City), **9:**490–92, *492n,* **12:**23n; 1916–17 (Havana), **9:**534, *534n;* 1917 (Seattle), **10:**154, *155n;* 1917 (Tacoma, Wash.), **10:**154, *155n;* 1917–18 (Springfield, Ill.), **10:**259, *263n;* 1918 (Cleveland), **11:**19, *20–21n;* 1918 (Indianapolis), **12:**24n; 1918 (New York City), **12:**23–24n; 1918–19 (Kansas City, Mo.), **11:**20, *21n;* 1920 (Brooklyn, N.Y.), **11:**356, *358n*
—structural iron workers: 1905-?, **6:**514–15, *515–16n,* **7:**12–13; 1905-? (New Haven, Conn.), **6:**514, 515n; 1906-? (New York City), **6:**515n; 1915 (Bridgeport, Conn.), **9:**304, *305n*

—sugar mill workers: 1917 (Cuba), **10:**256, *257n*
—sugar plantation workers: 1905 (Puerto Rico), **6:**424–25, 427–28, *429n;* 1906 (Puerto Rico), **7:**51–52, *52n;* 1916 (Puerto Rico), *9:411n;* 1918 (Puerto Rico), **10:**314, *315–16n,* 437; 1923 (Puerto Rico), **12:**201
—suspender makers: 1904 (New York City), **6:**310, *310n*
—switchmen. *See* strikes and lockouts: railroad workers
—tailors: 1890 (Columbus, Ohio), **2:**341–42, *343n;* 1891 (New York City), **3:**125; 1892 (Boston), *3:180n;* 1894 (New York City and Newark, N.J.), **3:**587–88, *589n;* 1896 (New York City), **4:**206, *206n,* 207, *207n;* 1900, **5:**234, 235n; 1900 (Chicago), **5:**215, *216–17n*
—tanners and curriers: 1886 (Salem, Peabody, and Stoneham, Mass.), *1:471n*
—teamsters: 1902 (Boston), **5:**494–96, *496–97n;* 1905 (Chicago), **6:**452, *453n,* 469, 502; 1920 (New York City), *11:458n*
—telegraphers: 1870, **1:**343, *353n;* 1883, **1:**101n, 343, *353n;* 1907, **7:**250–51, *252n;* 1918 (threatened), **10:**481, *482n,* 485–86, 490n, 515n; 1919, **10:**515–*16n,* **11:**93, *94–*95n, 102–4, 104n
—telephone employees: 1904 (Centralia, Ill.), **6:**265–66
—telephone linemen and operators: 1919 (Palestine, Tex.), **11:**189–90, *191n;* 1919 (threatened), **11:**95n
—textile workers: 1875 (Fall River, Mass.), *1:66n;* 1880 (Cohoes, N.Y.), *1:268n;* 1882 (Cohoes, N.Y.), **1:**264, *265n,* 267–68, 293–96, **3:**318, 340n; 1882 (Lawrence, Mass.), **1:**296, *327n,* 355–56; 1889 (Kearney, N.J.), **2:**222n; 1890–91 (Newark, N.J.), *3:56n;* 1895 (Galveston, Tex.), **4:**38, *38n;* 1897–98 (Atlanta), **4:**425–27, *427n,* 428; 1898 (New England; *see* textile workers: strikes/lockouts: 1898 [New Bedford, Mass.]);

1900 (Alamance County, N.C.),
5:272–73, *274n,* 418; 1900–1903
(Knoxville, Tenn.), 6:118–19, *119n;*
1901 (Danville, Va.), 5:335, *336n,*
369–71, 6:349; 1902 (Paterson and
Lodi, N.J.), *6:29n;* 1903 (Philadelphia), 6:349, *350–51n;* 1904 (Fall
River, Mass.), 6:345–50, *350n,* 354–
55, 355n, 452, 7:237; 1907 (Skowhegan, Maine), 7:184–85, *186n;*
1907 (Veracruz), 9:306, *307n;* 1910
(New Bedford, Mass.), 8:115, *117n;*
1912 (Lawrence, Mass.), 8:324–25,
325–26n, 360, 406, 450, 501–2,
502n, 517, 518n, 9:229, 230n, 489n,
504, 10:247; 1913 (Paterson, N.J.),
8:502, *503n,* 517, 9:489n, 504–5,
10:247–48; 1914 (Atlanta), 9:170–
71, *171n,* 191n; 1919 (Columbus,
Ga.), 11:76, *76n;* 1919 (Lawrence,
Mass.), 11:65n, 350, *352n;* 1921
(North Carolina), 11:510–12, *512n;*
1922, 12:127, *128–29n,* 140
—timber workers: 1917 (Pacific
Northwest), 10:154, *155n,* 182
—tin plate workers: 1909–10, 7:472,
473n, 480, 8:7, 9n, 12, 12n, 27–30,
54–55
—tobacco strippers: 1908 (Boston),
7:308–9n, 365, 461–62
—upholsterers: 1903 (Grand Rapids,
Mich.), 6:229–30, *231n*
—waiters. *See* strikes and lockouts: hotel and restaurant workers
—watchmen and transportation workers: 1919 (Lynn, Mass., threatened),
11:186–87
—water works engineers: 1901 (Pana,
Ill.), 5:401–4, *404n*
—woodsmen and sawmill workers:
1908 (Farmers, Ky.), 7:378–80
—woodworkers: 1902 (Denver), 6:15,
17–18n
*Striking for Life: Labor's Side of the Labor
Question* (Swinton), 3:592, *593n*
Stripling, Joseph, 8:26n
Strong, Anna Louise, 12:235, *241n*
Strong, Philip, 4:*, 222–23, *223n*
Strong, Sidney D., 12:235, *241n*
Strong, William L., 4:303, *304n*
Structural Building Trades Alliance,

4:417n, 6:173–74, *174–75n,* 7:275,
276n, 278, 459–60; and Philadel-
phia Central Labor Union Building
Trades Section, 6:414, 414n
Stuermer, J. Adam, 1:397, *398n*
Stump, Herman, 4:244n
"stunts," 10:116
Sturgess, Thomas F., 5:12, *12n*
Stutz, Clara K., *10:439n; letter from,*
10:438–39
Suchanek, Joseph, *3:150n; letter to,*
3:149–50
Sudduth, Frank R., *10:110n; letter to,*
10:109–10
Sudowitz, David, 5:101–2, *102n*
Suhr, Herman, 9:507n
Suitor, Frederick W., *12:*, 398n; letter
from,* 12:394–98
Sullivan, Charles A., *8:132n; letter to,*
8:131–32
Sullivan, Denis E., 12:366, *367n,* 428n
Sullivan, Dora, *3:109n,* 176–77, 177n;
letters to, 3:108–9, 163–64
Sullivan (gas worker), 6:101
Sullivan, James H., 4:*, 83, *83–84n,*
357, 359n, 455, 5:39n
Sullivan, James W., 1:*, *438n,* 3:*,
472, *472n,* 4:*, 247–48, *249n,* 7:*,
481, *482n,* 9:*, 124, *136n,* 139, 10:*,
73n, 142n, 305; at AFL convention,
3:631–32, 659n; and Committee
on Labor, Council of National Defense, 10:73, 73n, 79n, 97, 139–41;
and European affairs, 9:192, 207,
468–69, 470n; and KOL, 1:438; *letters to,* 9:468–69, 10:139–41
Sullivan, Jere L., 5:*, 140–41, *142n,*
6:*, 10n, 16, *19n,* 8:*, *44n,* 92–93,
452n, 9:*, *246n,* 10:*, *180n,* 11:*,
46n, 12:*, *265n;* at AFL conventions, 8:145–46, 12:97n; *letters from,*
6:390–92, 11:42–46; *letters to,* 6:285–
86, 8:43–44, 448–52, 9:245–46,
12:265
Sullivan, John, 10:127, *128n,* 12:*,
461n, 524, *526n*
Sullivan, John J., 2:332, *337n*
Sullivan, Michael, 11:416, *420n*
Sullivan, Miss, 2:332
Sullivan, Olive M., *10:82n,* 11:20n; *wire
from,* 10:81–82

Sulzer, William, **8:**94, 98, *100n,* 333n, 426–27, 427n, 439n, 448; *letter to,* **8:**438–39
Sumner, Charles, **3:**633, *659–60n*
Sumner, Charles A., **11:***, 315–16, *317n*
Sunday, William A. "Billy," **12:**207, *207n*
Sunderland, Gordon, *11:248n; letter to,* **11:**248
Supreme Court of the District of Columbia, **7:**247–48, 249–50n, 253, 287, 289, 430, 440, 453–54, 465, **8:**12n, 161, 164n, 216–17
Survey (periodical), **8:**341, **10:**388, 389n, 415
Suter, George J., *2:136n; letter to,* **2:**135–36
Sutherland, George, *8:438n,* 448n
Sutherland, Howard, **12:**169, *171n,* 250
Sutro and Newmark, **1:**108, *109n,* 193, *198n,* 199, 384, 418
Suzuki, Bunji, **9:***, 327, *328n,* 513, 515, 515n
Svenska Arbetsgivareföreningen, **7:**486n
Svenska Landsorganisationen, general strike, 1909, **7:**484, *486n*
Svenson, Hilda, **11:**132, *135n*
Svindseth, N. J., *4:292n; letter to,* **4:**291–92
Swain, Albert, **12:**240, *241n,* 270
Swaine, Philip B., *11:187n; letter to,* **11:**186–87
Swales, Alonzo B., **12:***, 526, *526n,* 534
Swansey, John P., **7:**58, *58n,* 89n
Swanson, Claude, **8:**519n
sweatshops, **3:**103, 103n, 587, *589n,* **4:**19, 22, 27, 36, 40, **10:**204
Sweden, strikes/lockouts: 1900 (street railway workers), **5:**301, *308n;* 1909 (general strike), **7:**484, *486n*
Swedish Employers' Federation. *See* Svenska Arbetsgivareföreningen
Sweeney, Charles P., **11:**472n
Sweeney, Frank, **3:**215n
Sweeney, John J., **8:**188, *190n*
Sweeney, John W., **7:**384, *385n*
Sweeney, Thomas, **3:**148, *148n*
Sweet, Thaddeus C., **11:**261, *262n*

Sweetwater County (Wyo.) Trades and Labor Council, **10:**151, *152n*
Swem, Charles L., **11:**398, *398n*
Swick, Clarence, **8:**279n
Swift, James, **8:**502n
Swift, John, *4:166n,* 194, 195n; *letter to,* **4:**166
Swift and Co. v. U.S., **12:**302–3, *303n*
Swift meatpacking company, **5:**100, **10:**152n; strike/lockout, 1904, **6:**313–14, 314–15n; strike/lockout, 1921–22, *11:571n*
Swinton, John, **1:***, 200, *203n,* 288, **2:***, *39n,* 51, 429, **3:***, 298, *300n,* 592, 593n, **4:**249n, **12:**34n. See also *John Swinton's Paper*
Swiss Federal Council, **2:**157n
Swiss Trades Union Congress. *See* Union syndical suisse
Switchmen's Mutual Aid Association of the U.S. of America, **2:***, 108n, 182n, 218, **3:***, 93, 94n
—lodge: lodge 39 (Buffalo, N.Y.), **3:**185, 214n
—strike/lockout: 1892 (Buffalo, N.Y.), **3:**185–86, 213, *214–15n,* 219, 222, 420, **4:**105
Switchmen's Union of North America, **2:***, **3:***, **7:***, 424n, **8:***, 120n, **9:***, 34n, **10:***, 251n, 429, **11:***, 28n, 85n, 254, 260n, 344, 475n, 539n; and black workers, **8:**244, 244–45n, 246–47, 247n, **10:**491–92, 492n; jurisdiction of, **8:**251–52, 253n, **10:**250
—convention: 1911 (St. Paul, Minn.), **8:**247, *247n*
Switzerland, militia in, **6:**361, 364n
Swope, Gerard, **12:**550, *552n*
Sykes, Edward, **3:**400, *401n*
Sylvester, William, **11:**489, 491
sympathy strikes, **2:**382n, **3:**166n, 215n, 234n, 238, 250–51, 268n, 524, 526n, 534, 564, **4:**93, 229n, **5:**114, 340, 342n, 375, 433n, 495–96, 497n, 503n, **6:**25–29, 44n, 151–52, 175–76, 176n, 179, 184–85, 186n, 266, 369n, 407n, 470n, 518n, **7:**54n, **8:**52n, 140–41, 141n, 143, 253n, **9:**273, **10:**214, **11:**23n, 74n, 250, **12:**134. *See also* general strikes; strikes and lockouts

Syndical Chambers of France, United.
See Union des chambres syndicales
Syndicalist League of North America,
8:261n
Syndikale Kommissie van Belgie,
11:57n
Syracuse (N.Y.) Central Trades and
Labor Assembly, 5:376, *377n*
Szegedy, Henry W., 5:*, 157, *158n*

Taber, Esther, 6:520, *520n*
Tacoma, Wash.: general strike, 1919,
11:49–50, *50n;* labor situation in,
11:224–25
Tacoma (Wash.) Building Trades Alliance, 11:50n
Tacoma (Wash.) Central Labor Council, 11:49–50, *50n*, 51, 12:237, 326n,
339, 340n
Tacoma (Wash.) Railway and Power
Co., strike/lockout, 1917, 10:154,
155n
Tacoma (Wash.) Trades Council,
5:469, *470n*, 11:50n
Taff Vale case, 6:74, 78, 83, *83–84n,*
7:24, 289n, 310, 326, 421, 8:74
Taft, Charles, 8:204n
Taft, William H., 6:382–83, *383n,* 490,
490n, 7:244, 458n, 473n, 8:67, 76n,
270, 277n, 385, 9:3, 112n, 274n,
10:166n, 179n, 11:330, 12:69, 250;
and Bethlehem Steel Co., 8:102;
and Department of Labor bill,
8:470; and eight-hour legislation,
8:371; and election of 1906, 7:103,
118–19; and election of 1908,
7:281, 281n, 362n, 369, 375, 385n,
397, 398n, 402, 410–11, 413, 414n,
415–16, 416n; and German submarine warfare, 9:253, 254n; and
immigration bill, 9:80–81, 82–83n;
and injunctions, 3:293, 294n, 295,
299, 302, 559, 576, 7:87, 91–92n,
118–19, 251, 252n, 281, 379, 398n,
410, 8:152–54, 478, 487; and National War Labor Board, 10:440–41,
444; and Prohibition legislation,
8:424n; and sundry civil appropriation bills, 8:461, 468n, 469, 478–79,
484–85, 487–88, 9:81–82, 82n, 353;
and U.S. Commission on Industrial

Relations, 8:329, 455–56; and U.S.-
Mexican relations, 8:192, 193n; and
U.S. Steel Corp. investigation, 8:53,
54n; and War Labor Conference
Board, 10:334n, 407
Tagle, Manuel Vázquez, 9:306, *307n*
tailoresses, 1:303–4
Tailors, United Brotherhood of,
3:379, 4:137n
—strike/lockout: 1896 (New York
City), 4:206, *206n,* 207, *207n*
Tailors' Industrial Union, 1:*, 2:*, 3:*,
4:*, 5:*, 6:*, 7:*, 8:*, 9:*, 73n, 235–
36, 236n, 10:*, 12:*, 260–61, 261n;
and industrial unionism, 9:71, 74n;
jurisdiction of, 9:74n; label of,
9:74n, 261n
—locals: local 2 (San Francisco),
9:236; local 161 (Chicago), 9:356n
Tailors' National Union, Progressive,
1:*, 461, 462n
Tailors' National Union of the U.S.,
Journeymen, 1:*, 390, 391n, 2:*,
80n, 118, 235, 3:*, 4:*, 5:*, 6:*, 7:*,
8:*, 9:*, 10:*, 12:*
—local: local 27 (Columbus, Ohio),
2:341, 343n
—strike/lockout: 1890 (Columbus,
Ohio), 2:341–42, *343n*
Tailors' Protective and Benevolent
Union, Journeymen (San Fran-
cisco), 4:171, *172n,* 6:447, *449n,* 462
Tailors' Union, Operative (New York
City), 3:379
Tailors' Union of America, Journeymen, 1:*, 2:*, 3:*, 108n, 587, 4:*,
82n, 99, 5:*, 235n, 238, 6:*, 50n,
62n, 7:*, 424n, 8:*, 475, 476n, 9:*,
354, 10:*, 267, 267n, 12:*, 98n;
AFL financial support of, 6:189–90,
191n; and black workers, 11:84n; jurisdiction of, 6:189–90, 191n, 9:74n;
label of, 4:208–9, 6:389–90, 7:140
—convention: 1905 (Bloomington,
Ill.), 6:389–90, *390n*
—locals: local 5 (Chicago), 5:216n; local 12 (Boston), 3:179, 180n; local
23 (Brooklyn, N.Y.), 3:379, 382n;
local 102 (Pueblo, Colo.), 6:447–48,
449n, 462; local 157 (Indianapolis),
4:209n; local 161 (Chicago), 9:356n

—strikes/lockouts: 1892 (Boston), *3:180n;* 1894 (New York City and Newark, N.J.), **3:**587–88, *589n;* 1900, **5:**234, 235n; 1900 (Chicago), **5:**215, *216–17n*

Takano, Fusataro, **3:***, *473n*, **4:***, *53n*, 203–4; *letters to,* **3:**472–73, **4:**52–53

Talbot, Thomas (governor), **1:**269, *270n*

Talbot, Thomas W., **2:***, *297n*, **3:***, 406, *407n; letter to,* **2:**296–97

Talbott, Nicholas B., **2:**69, *71n*

Talley, Benjamin C., **3:**583, *584n*

Talleyrand-Périgord, Charles-Maurice de, **5:**159, *160n*

Tammany Hall, **1:**430, 439n, 448, **4:**153

Tampa (Fla.) Central Trades and Labor Assembly, **6:**70, *71n*, **7:**355

Tampa, Fla., deportations from, **8:**26, 26n

Tampico, Mexico, incident, 1914, **9:**95, *95–96n*

Tanner, Charles H., **9:**43, *44n*

Tanner, John R., **5:**30n

Tanners and Curriers of America, United Brotherhood of, **3:***, 493, 495, 498n

—locals: local 1 (Milwaukee), **3:**492–95, 497, 497n; local 3 (Milwaukee), **3:**494, 497, 498n

Tanners' and Curriers' Union, National, **1:**161, 165, 165n, **3:***

Tanquary, Lee A., **6:**61, *62n*, 67–68, 196, 197n, **8:**8, 10n

Tansey, James, **5:***, 418, *419n*, **6:***, 358, *360n*, **12:***, 251–52, *252n*

Tansill, R. W., **1:**393

Tarbell, Ida M., **6:**482n, *8:39n; letter to,* **8:**39

tariff commission, non-partisan, **9:**365, 366n

tariffs, **1:**212–13, 221, 226–28, 241–42, **4:**234–35, 281. *See also under* legislation, U.S.

Taunton (Mass.) Central Labor Union, *9:166n*

Tawney, James, **8:**132n

Tawney, Richard H., **12:**191, *192n*

taxes: on cigars, **2:**130n; excess profit, **10:**189–90, 190n, **11:**542, 543n,

12:25, 424; income, **4:**36, 38n, **6:**332, 340n, **8:**264, **12:**454; inheritance, **12:**454; progressive, **11:**8n; sales, **11:**542, 543n, **12:**25–26, 26n, 38, 39–40n, 169, 344, 454. *See also* single tax

Taylor, Charles F., **2:**172, *173n*

Taylor, Charles G., **7:**96, *97n*, 102n

Taylor, Charles P., **10:**245, *246n*, *11:113n; wire from,* **11:**112–13

Taylor, Claude O., **9:***, 65, *68n*

Taylor, E. E., and Co., strike/lockout, 1905, **7:**37, *39n*

Taylor, Frederick W., **8:**202, *202–3n*, 209–11, 212n, **12:**142

Taylor, Henry E., **5:**321, *322n*

Taylor, Howard, **4:**371n

Taylor, James A., **9:***, 214–16, 223–*24n*, **10:**472n

Taylor, Louis H., **7:**460, *461n*

Taylor, Perry D., *letter to,* **3:**183

Taylor, Thomas W., **1:**215, *217n*

Taylor, William S., *7:102n; letter to,* **7:**101–2

Taylor system, **8:**202, 202–3n, 209–12, 215–16, **9:**228. *See also* scientific management

Tazelaar, Jacob, **6:**174, *175n*, **7:**100, 104, 345–46, 347n, 445n, **8:**44n

teachers: and Chicago Board of Education, **9:**419n; and Cleveland Board of Education, **9:**137, 137–38n, 418; in Mexico, **9:**465; minimum wage for, **10:**438–39, 439–40n; organization of, **9:**137, 137–38n, 418–19, 419n, 429

Teachers, American Federation of, **9:***, 418–19, 419n, 429, **11:***, 395–96, 396n; and black workers, **11:**84n

—locals: local 5 (New York City), **10:**395n; local 8 (Washington, D.C.), **9:**466n; local 16 (Washington, D.C.), **10:**439n

Teall, Oliver S., *3:418n; letter to,* **3:**418

Team Drivers' International Union, **5:***, 391n, **6:***, **7:***, **9:***, **10:***, **11:***, **12:***; benefits of, **5:**391; dues of, **5:**391, 409–10, 410n; injunction against, **5:**497n; jurisdiction of, **5:**290, 292n, 501–3, 503–4n

—convention: 1901 (Chicago), **5:**390–91, *391n*, 409–10, 410n

—local: local 25 (Boston), **5:**409, 410n, 496–97n
—strike/lockout: 1902 (Boston), **5:**494–96, *496–97n*
Teamsters, Chauffeurs, Stablemen, and Helpers of America, International Brotherhood of, **5:***, **6:***, **7:***, **8:**302–3n, **9:***, 36n, **10:***, 60n, **11:***, 93n, 263, **12:***, 88, 89n; and black workers, **10:**135, **11:**84n; Chicago joint council of, **9:**267n; and industrial unionism, **9:**149; injunctions against, **10:**252–53, 254n, **11:**455, 458n; jurisdiction of, **9:**143–45, 145n, 146, 146n, 147–49; secession movement in, **9:**357n
—locals: local 156 (Lawrence, Mass.), **11:**351, 352n; local 211 (Omaha, Nebr.), **10:**252–53, 254n; local 273 (New York City), **11:**455, 458n; local 393 (Lawrence, Mass.), **11:**351, 352n; local 496 (Bisbee, Ariz.), **10:**169n; local 632 (Lawrence, Mass.), **11:**351, 352n
—strike/lockout: 1920 (New York City), *11:458n*
Teamsters, International Brotherhood of, **5:***, **6:***, 223n, 407n, **7:***, 98n, 364, **9:***, **10:***, **11:***, **12:***; injunction against, **7:**98n; jurisdiction of, **6:**365–67, 367–68n, 500–502, **7:**36n, 199–201, 201–2n, 272–74, 274n, 317–18, 493–97; secession movements in, **7:**97, 98n, 364, 429–30, 430n
—conventions: 1904, **6:**367n; 1905 (Philadelphia), **6:**469, *469n;* 1906, **7:**98n; 1907 (Boston), **7:**235, *236n*
—locals: local 701 (New Orleans), **7:**495–96, 498n; local 704 (Chicago), **7:**97, 98n; local in Tell City, Ind., **7:**235
—strike/lockout: 1905 (Chicago), **6:**452, *453n,* 469, 502
Teamsters' and Helpers' Union, Chicago, **7:**430n; jurisdiction of, **7:**429
Teamsters' and Loaders' Benevolent Association (New Orleans), **5:**261
Teamsters of America, United, **7:**97, *98n,* 364, 429–30, 430n
Tea Operatives' and General Labourers' Association, *5:69n*

—strike/lockout: 1889 (London), **2:**279–80, *281n,* 325, **3:**78n, 504
Teapot Dome scandal, **12:**228, *228n*
Technical Engineers', Architects', and Draftsmen's Unions, International Federation of, **11:***, 435n
Teigan, Henry G., **12:**431, *434n*
Teitelbaum, Minnie, **10:**467, *468n*
Tekulsky, Solomon, **12:**550, *552n*
Telegraphers' Protective League, **1:**353n
Telegraphers' Union of America, Commercial, **7:***, 250, 252n, **8:***, 406n, **10:***, 482n, **11:***, 94n; AFL financial support of, **7:**251, 252n
—strikes/lockouts: 1907, **7:**250–51, *252n;* 1918 (threatened), **10:**481, *482n,* 485–86, 490n, 515n; 1919, **10:**515–*16n,* **11:**93, *94–*95n, 102–4, 104n
telegraph system: government ownership of, **1:**227, 288, **3:**258–59, 260n, 401, 635, **9:**494, **10:**341, 515; government wartime control of, **10:**482n
telephone system: government ownership of, **3:**258–60, 260n, 401, **10:**341, 515; government wartime control of, **10:**482n
Tell City, Ind., floods in, 1907, **7:**227, 229n; injunction against workers in, **7:**234
Teller, Henry M., **4:**205n
Temperance Congress, National, 1890, **2:**321–25, 349–51
temperance movement, **2:**321–25, 349–51, **3:**598, **4:**414, **8:**38n, 92–94, 94n, **9:**179. *See also* drinking; Prohibition
Tenement House Manufacturers' Association, **1:**358n
tenements, cigar production in, **1:**45–47, 50–54, 56–58, 67, 73–75, 102–3, 107, 110–11, 113, 115n, 124–25, 129–31, 151–52, 169–210, 250–51, 260–62, 291–93, 365, 373, 381, 408, **2:**6–7, 124–25, 216, **3:**76–77, 77n, **7:**307, 308n, **9:**222–23; campaign against, **1:**47, 50, 58, 67, 79, 102–3, 119, 124–27, 129–31, 151–52, 169–210, 230, 242, 250–51, 258, 260–62,

292–93, 448 (*see also under* legislation, states and territories)

Teney, Charles W., **5**:*, 106, *108n*

Tennessee: organizing in, **6**:3, 119; statehood centennial of, 1896, **4**:181, 182n

Tennessee Coal, Iron, and Railroad Co., **3**:215n, **4**:28n; strike/lockout, 1891, *3:215n;* strike/lockout, 1892, *3:215n;* strike/lockout, 1894, *4:28n;* strike/lockout, 1918, **10**:376–77, *378n,* 385–86, 440–41

Tennessee State Federation of Labor, *12:31n*

Tennyson, Alfred Lord, **8**:330, *332n,* **10**:36, 39n

Tenorio, Juan, **5**:185, *188n*

Terrell, Ben, *3:263n; letter from,* 3:262–63

Terry, William E., **7**:383, *384n,* **8**:356, **9**:83n

Terry, Winfield C., **12**:551, *554n*

Testerman, Cabell, **11**:296n

Texas, election of 1908, **7**:385–86

Texas and Pacific Coal Co., **5**:505n

Texas State Federation of Labor, **6**:387–88, *388n,* **10**:390, 391n, **11**:341

—conventions: 1904 (Galveston), **6**:388, *389n;* 1918 (San Antonio), *10:392n*

Text Book of Labor's Political Demands (AFL), **8**:385, *386n*

Textile Operatives, American Federation of, **5**:274n, 419n, **11**:352n, **12**:251–52

—conferences: 1901 (Boston), *5:274n;* 1901 (Washington, D.C.), *5:274n,* 418–19, *419n*

—convention: 1900 (Washington, D.C.), **5**:274n, 418, *419n*

textile workers: AFL financial support of, **5**:273, 274n, 335–36, 336n; foreign-born workers among, **8**:345; jurisdiction of, **4**:431, 432n, 447–49, 449n; organization of, **4**:101, 101n, 130, 167–68, 250–51, 251n, **7**:183, **8**:48, 49n, **12**:251–52; unions, amalgamation of, **5**:271–72, 274n, 418–19, 419–20n; unions, dissension among, **4**:431, 447–49, 449n;

unions, dues of, **4**:447–48, **5**:419, 419–20n

—conferences: 1898 (Boston), **4**:431, *432n,* 448; 1899, **5**:274n; 1900 (Washington, D.C.), **5**:274n; 1901 (Boston), *5:274n;* 1901 (Washington, D.C.), *5:274n,* 418–19, *419–*20n; 1921, **11**:525–26

—strikes/lockouts: 1898 (New Bedford, Mass.), **4**:426, 428–29, *429n,* 430, 430n, 431–39, 473, 476–78, 478n; 1910 (New Bedford, Mass.), **8**:115, *117n;* 1912 (Lawrence, Mass.), **8**:324–25, *325–26n,* 360, 406, 450, 501–2, 502n, 517, 518n, **9**:229, 230n, 489n, 504, **10**:247; 1913 (Paterson, N.J.), **8**:502, *503n,* 517, **9**:489n, 504–5, **10**:247–48. *See also specific textile workers' unions' strikes*

Textile Workers, International Union of, **4**:*, **5**:*, 274n, 418, 419n, **6**:*, **7**:*, **8**:*, **9**:*, **11**:*, **12**:*; AFL financial support of, **5**:273, 274n, 335–36, 336n

—conferences: 1901 (Boston), *5:274n;* 1901 (Washington, D.C.), *5:274n,* 418–19, *419n*

—convention: 1900, **5**:336n

—locals: local 134 (Alamance County, N.C.), **5**:274n; local 150 (Danville, Va.), **5**:335, 336n; local 169 (Alamance County, N.C.), **5**:274n; local 175 (Alamance County, N.C.), **5**:274n; local 198 (Alamance County, N.C.), **5**:274n; local 203 (Alamance County, N.C.), **5**:274n

—strikes/lockouts: 1900 (Alamance County, N.C.), **5**:272–73, *274n,* 418; 1901 (Danville, Va.), **5**:335, *336n,* 369–71, **6**:349

Textile Workers, National Industrial Union of, **8**:115–16, *117n*

Textile Workers of America, Amalgamated, **11**:350, *351–*52n, **12**:128n

Textile Workers of America, National Union of, **4**:*, 250, 251n, 476, **5**:*, 52, 53n, **6**:*, **7**:*, **8**:*, **9**:*, **11**:*, **12**:*; and black workers, **4**:427n

—conference: 1899, **5**:274n

—convention: 1897 (Philadelphia), **4**:335, *335n,* 341

—locals: local 2 (Lawrence, Mass.),
4:448, 449n; local 122 (Atlanta),
4:425–26, 427n, 428
—strike/lockout: 1897–98 (Atlanta),
4:425–27, *427n,* 428
Textile Workers of America, United,
4:*, 431, 432n, 448, 5:*, 274n, 419n,
6:*, 119n, 357, 7:*, 185n, 8:*, 117n,
9:*, 171n, 11:*, 97n, 12:*, 54n, 62,
404, 406, 408n, 446n; AFL financial
support of, 6:347, 350n, 354–55,
355n, 8:518n, 9:171n, 191n; and
black workers, 11:84n; and Canadian textile workers, 7:236–37; injunctions against, 9:262–63n; and
IWW, 7:184–85, 8:115–16, 117n,
9:170, 11:350; organizing in South,
6:11, 11:512, 512n, 525–26, 526n
—locals: local 1 (Fall River, Mass.),
6:350n; local 23 (Fall River, Mass.),
6:350n; local 32 (Fall River, Mass.),
6:350n; local 35 (Fall River, Mass.),
6:350n; local 51 (Fall River, Mass.),
6:350n; local 178 (Warrenville,
S.C.), 8:48, 48n; local 607 (Paterson, N.J.), 8:116, 117n; local 720
(Ludlow, Mass.), 8:215, 216n; local
900 (Reading, Pa.), 9:262, 263n; local 909 (Lenoir City, Tenn.), 9:262,
262–63n; local 1124 (Columbus,
Ga.), 11:76, 76n
—strikes/lockouts: 1903 (Philadelphia), 6:349, *350–51n;* 1904 (Fall
River, Mass.), 6:345–50, *350n,*
354–55, 355n, 452, 7:237; 1912
(Lawrence, Mass.), 8:324–25,
325–26n, 360, 406, 517, 518n; 1914
(Atlanta), 9:170–71, *171n,* 191n;
1919 (Columbus, Ga.), 11:76, *76n;*
1919 (Lawrence, Mass.), 11:65n,
350, *352n;* 1921 (North Carolina),
11:510–12, *512n;* 1922, 12:127,
128–29n, 140
Textile Workers of Canada, Federation of, 7:236, *237n*
Textile Workers of Philadelphia and
Vicinity, Central Union of, 6:350n
Textile Workers' Progressive Union of
America, 2:*, 74, 76n
—convention: 1889 (New York City),
2:232, *233n*

Thayer, Walter N., 1:*, 360, *361n,* 2:*,
8, *11n*
Theatrical Protective Union 1 (New
York City), 6:518n
Theatrical Stage Employes and Mov-
ing Picture Machine Operators of
the U.S. and Canada, International
Alliance of, 3:*, 4:*, 5:*, 6:*, 11:*,
82n, 520, 520n; and black workers,
11:546, 547n
Theatrical Stage Employes of the U.S.,
National Alliance of, 3:*, 520n, 4:*,
122n, 5:*, 6:*, 11:*; jurisdiction of,
4:121–22, 122–23n
—conventions: 1894 (Chicago),
3:518–20, *520n;* 1896 (Detroit),
4:122, *123n*
—local: local 6 (St. Louis), 4:123n
Theatrical Stage Employes of the U.S.
and Canada, International Alliance
of, 3:*, 4:*, 5:*, 6:*, 509n, 11:*; and
Miners, Western Federation of,
6:505
—local: local 16 (San Francisco),
6:234, 234n
Theatrical Stage Employes of the U.S.
and Canada, National Alliance of,
3:*, 4:*, 5:*, 451n, 6:*, 11:*
—local: local 7 (Denver), 5:394, 396n,
451n
Theis, Edward H., 5:*, *460n,* 6:*, 239,
240n; injunction secured by, 5:459,
460n; *letter to,* 5:459–60
Theiss Music Hall, boycott, 1886, *1:430n*
Theobald, Henry, Jr., 4:460, *461n*
Thiel detective agency, 12:132n
Third Avenue Railway Co.: strike/
lockout, 1916, 12:23n; strike/lock-
out, 1918, 12:23–24n; strike injunction, 12:21–23, *24n*
*Third Avenue Railway Co. v. Patrick J.
Shea et al.,* 12:21–23, *24n*
Third (Communist) International
(Comintern), 11:432n, 12:253, 267
—congresses: second, 1920 (Petrograd and Moscow), 11:427–29,
432n; third, 1921 (Moscow), 11:487,
488n; fourth, 1922 (Petrograd and
Moscow), 12:293, *294n*
Thirty Years of Labor (Powderly), 2:227,
228n, 247, 248n

Thirty Years' War, **9:**264, *266n*

Thomas, A. A. (general counsel, National Cash Register), **5:**364, *367n*

Thomas, Albert A. (French socialist), **11:***, *406n,* **12:***, 189–90, *190–*91n, 232n; *letters to,* **11:**404–6, **12:**231–32

Thomas, Arthur L., **3:**43, *44n*

Thomas, Charles C., *letter to,* **2:**222–23

Thomas, Charles S., **9:**194, *195n,* **11:**220, 221n

Thomas (delegate), **3:**381

Thomas, Eben, **5:**411n

Thomas, Frank, **8:**157

Thomas, Harry D., **6:**153–54, *154n,* 492, 493n, **7:**281–82

Thomas, Hiram W., **3:**424–25, *425n*

Thomas, James D., **12:**552

Thomas, James H., **10:***, 71, *72n,* 492, 537, 551, **11:***, 29, *30n*

Thomas, John L., **2:**323–25, *325n,* 349–51, *4:446n; letter to,* **4:**446

Thomas, Llewelyn E., **5:**394, *396n*

Thomas, Llewelyn R., **4:***, 346, *347n,* 359n, **5:***, 214, *216n,* 275, 382, 382n; at AFL convention, **5:**284–85, 287n; *letter from,* **5:**276

Thomas, Norman M., *12:452n; letter to,* **12:**452

Thomas, Orion: *letter from,* **8:**280–81; *letter to,* **8:**281–82

Thomas, Percy, **7:**250–51, *252n,* **10:***, *515n,* **11:***, 103, *104n; letter from,* **10:**514–15

Thomas, Philip J., *4:263n; letter from,* **4:**259–63

Thompson, Carl, **7:**130, 142n

Thompson, Charles C., *7:447n; letter to,* **7:**446–47

Thompson, Edward D., *10:372n; letter from,* **10:**371–72

Thompson, J. Edgar, steelworks, **9:**507n

Thompson, Joseph F., **9:**510, *510n*

Thompson, Miss, **12:**461, 462n

Thompson, Thomas, **1:**165, *166n*

Thompson, W. E., **10:**187

Thompson, William B., **10:**310, *312–*13n, 512n

Thompson, William H., **11:**453, *454n*

Thompson, William O., **9:**83–85, *88n,* 112, *10:139n; letter from,* **10:**138

Thomson-Houston works (St. Louis), strike/lockout, 1892?, **3:**260

Thornburgh, William, *4:485n; letter to,* **4:**483–85

Thorne, Florence C., **8:**493n, **9:***, *433n,* **11:***, 18, *20n,* **12:***, *365n,* 378n, 433n; and AFL Women's Department, considered, **12:**404, 408n, 445n, 447–49; *letter from,* **11:**68; *letter to,* **12:**447–49; *memorandum by,* **9:**430–33; and SG, death of, **12:**541, 543; and SG, memoirs of, **11:**68, 68n, **12:**322n, 365, 385n

Thorne, William J., **3:***, *33–*34n, **5:***, 68, *70n; letter to,* **3:**32–33

Thornton, William T., **3:**98, *102n*

Thorpe, John J., **7:**241, *242n*

Threat, Eugene, **12:**341, 342n

Throckmorton, Harry S., *5:428–*29n; *letter from,* **5:**426–28

Thum, Otto F., **5:***, 90, *93n*

Thurber, Francis B., *3:375n,* **4:**351, 351n, **5:**13, *15n; letters to,* **3:**373–74, **4:**209–11, **5:**32–35

Thurman, Allen G., *letter to,* **10:**94–96

Thurston, John, **5:**244n

Tighe, Michael F., **10:**69–70n, **11:***, 128–29n, 141–42, *142n,* 151–52, 361–64, 532n, **12:***, 278–79, *281n,* 550; *letters from,* **11:**143–44, 269–70, 270n; *letter to,* **11:**147–48

Tight-Barrel Machine Workers (Milwaukee), **5:**82–83, *84n*

Tijan, Alois, **9:**26, 28n

Tilden, Laurin W., **6:***, *472n,* **7:***, 15, *15n; letter from,* **7:**47–48; *letter to,* **6:**471–72

Tile Layers' and Helpers' International Union, Ceramic, Mosaic, and Encaustic, **5:***, 453, 454n

—local: local 29 (New York City), **5:**453, 454n

Tile Layers and Trade National Union, Mosaic and Encaustic, **3:***, 429n, **5:***

Tillett, Benjamin, **2:***, 352, *353n,* 399, 407, **3:***, 16, *18n,* 516, **4:***, *249n,* **5:***, *69n,* **9:***, *197n,* 337, **10:***, 522, *524n; letter from,* **9:**195–97; *letters to,* **4:**246–49, **5:**66–69

Tillett, Jane Tompkins, **4:**249n

Tillett, Jeanette, **4:**249n
Tillett, Mabel M., **4:**249n
Tillman, James F., *3:104n,* 262; *letter to,* **3:**104
Tilton, Clint C., **7:**359–60, *361n*
Tilton, Elizabeth, **1:**100, 102n
timber workers, in Pacific Northwest, **10:**245–46, 295–96, 299–301, 375–76, 416–18, 486–89, 503
Timber Workers, International Union of, **7:***, **9:***, 453, 454n, **10:***, 154n, **12:***, 66n, 234; and black workers, **11:**366n; and industrial unionism, **12:**62; organizing activities of, **10:**375, 417–18, 418n, 486, 488, 503, **11:**366n
—local: local 116 (Bogalusa, La.), **11:**366
—strike/lockout: 1917 (Pacific Northwest), **10:**154, *155n,* 182
Times (London), **9:**289n
Timothée, Pedro, **6:**253–54, 258n
Tin, Sheet Iron, and Cornice Workers' International Association, **2:***, 110–11, 111n, 115–16, **3:***, 235, 236n, **8:***, **9:***, **10:***, **11:***, **12:***
—local: local 36 (St. Louis), **4:**147, 148n
Tin and Sheet-Iron Workers' Protective and Benevolent Association, United (New York City), *4:110n*
Tin-Plate Workers' International Protective Association of America, **5:***, 81n, **8:***, 9n, 56n; merger of, with Iron and Steel Workers, **7:**473n
—strike/lockout: 1909–10, **7:**472, *473n,* 480, **8:**7, 9n, 12, 12n, 27–30, 54–55
Titanic (passenger liner), sinking of, **8:**369, *369n,* **9:**201
Titus, Herman F., **7:**146n
Tobacco Manufacturers, Trade Mark Association of, **4:**148, 149n
tobacco strippers' conference, 1921 (New York City), *11:419n; minutes of,* **11:**412–19
Tobacco Strippers' Union, Amalgamated, **11:**419n
tobacco trust. *See* American Tobacco Co.; Continental Tobacco Co.

Tobacco Workers' International Union, **4:***, **5:***, 119n, **6:***, 214–15n; label of, **5:**118; and tobacco trust, **5:**117–19, 119n; wages of, **5:**462, 463n
—locals: local 12 (Richmond, Va.), **5:**430–31, 432n; local 40 (Richmond, Va.), **5:**430–31, 432n; local 76 (Danville, Va.), **5:**462, 463n
Tobacco Workers' Union of America, National, **4:***, 99, 99n, 395n, **5:***, **6:***
Tobin, Daniel J., **7:***, *430n,* **9:***, *36n,* 267n, 357n, **10:***, 44n, *60n,* **11:***, *25n,* 211n, 268, 345, **12:***, *89n,* 163n, 295; at AFL conventions, **9:**35, **11:**91, 473, 476–77, **12:**88; at AFL Executive Council meeting, **11:**387; and AFL, mission of, to Europe, summer 1919, **11:**111n; and AFL, mission of, to Mexico, 1921, **11:**404n; and election of 1924, **12:**461n, 489, 491–93; election of, as AFL treasurer, **10:**475, **11:**93n, 321, 321n, 482, **12:**97n, 338n; election of, as AFL vice-president, **10:**266–67; and election of SG's successor, **12:**555, 558–60; and Industrial Conference, 1919, **11:**128n, 390; *letters from,* **7:**429–30, **9:**146–49, **10:**59–60, **11:**262–64, 514–15; *letters to,* **9:**143–45, 356–57, **10:**65–67, **11:**24–25, 518–19; resignation of, from AFL Executive Council, **11:**514–15, 515n, 518–19; and SG, illness of, 1924, **12:**471n, 503n; and steel strike, 1919–20, **11:**152; *wire from,* **9:**52
Tobin, John F., **3:***, *659n,* **4:***, *94n,* 96, 103, 341, 432n, **5:***, *53n,* 410n, 491, **6:***, *360n,* **7:***, *340n,* **8:***, *103n,* 174, 175n, 325, **11:***, 64, *65n;* at AFL conventions, **3:**622–26, 657, 659n, **4:**93, 94n, 99, 280, 281n, 411, 411n, **5:**50, 53, 53n, **6:**358, 360n; *letters from,* **7:**339–40, **8:**102–3, 157
Tobin, William, **5:**89, *92n*
Tocsin (Philadelphia labor journal), **1:**427n
Todd, A. M., **7:**406n
Todd, G. Carroll, **9:**74n

Todd, Sullivan, and Baldwin, boycott, 1891, **3:**107, *108n*

Todd, William V., **1:***, *140n; letter from,* **1:**136–37; *report of,* **1:**140–51

Todd, Wilmer L., **10:**459, *460n*

Todtenhausen, August A., **3:**135, *138n,* 220–21, 251, 253n

Toledo, Ann Arbor, and Northern Michigan Railroad: boycott, 1893, *3:294n;* court case, *3:294n,* **7:**91–92n, **8:**487; injunction, **3:**294n, 295–96, 559, 576, **8:**487; strike/lockout, 1893, *3:294n,* 329–31, **11:**330

Toledo (Ohio) and Vicinity, Central Labor Union of, **3:**124, *124n*

Toledo (Ohio) Central Labor Union, **9:**99n

Toledo Electric Street Railway Co., strike/lockout, 1894, *12:24n*

Toliver, Lena, *11:326n; letter to,* **11:**325–26

Tompkins Square demonstration, 1874, **2:**57, *58n*

Tomson, William E., **1:***, 371, *371n*

Toney, Sterling B., **2:**308, *314n*

Tonsing, John F., *4:451n; letter to,* **4:**449–51

Topeka (Kans.) Industrial Council, *11:290n*

Toronto: labor situation in, **11:**380–81; lathers' strike, 1919, **11:**72; metal trades strike, 1919, **11:**72–73, *74n;* painters' strike, 1919, **11:**72–73, *74n*

Toronto District Labor Council, **9:**409n, **11:**72, *74n,* 380–81

Torpey, James J., **5:**393, 395, *396n*

Torres, Reynaldo C., *12:359n*

Tossy, L. E., *8:103n*

Towner, Horace M., **12:**200, *202n*

Townley, Arthur, **9:**424n

Townsend, Charles, **8:**132n

Tozier, Albert, **3:**82, *83n*

Tracy, Edward J., *12:424n,* 433n, 517, *517n,* 541

Tracy, George A., **7:***, 383, *385n,* 413, 414n

Tracy, Roger S., **1:**201–3, *203n,* 204, 206n, **2:**216, 217n

Tracy, Thomas F., **3:***, *664n,* **4:***, *83n,*

190, 432n, 479, **5:***, *49n,* 357n, 384n, 398n, **6:***, 4, *5n,* 11, 12n, 237–38, 519–20, **7:***, *238n,* 287–88, 311, 347n, 395, 458n, 481, **8:***, 158, *159n,* 173n, 237, 257, 325, **9:***, 157n, 479, *479n,* **12:**517n; at AFL conventions, **3:**662, **4:**83, 83n, **5:**47, 49n, 171, 172n, 434, **6:**69, 70n; *letter from,* **7:**237–38; *letters to,* **4:**169–70, **5:**356–57, 392, 455–56, **6:**33–35

Trade Press Publishing Co. et al. v. *Milwaukee Typographical Union No. 23 et al.,* **12:**302, *303n*

trade schools, **2:**182–83, *183n,* **3:**375–76, 557, **7:**14–15, 15n, 426, 427n

Trades Union Congress of Great Britain, **1:***, 164, 211, 212n, 235, 275, 281, **2:***, 105, 135n, 158, 399, 408n, **3:***, **4:***, **5:**69n, **7:**130, **8:**186, **11:**11–12, 223, 569, **12:**521; and eight-hour movement, **3:**223, 224n; Parliamentary Committee of, **1:**164, **3:**612, **11:**11, 38–39, 40n; and political action, independent, **3:**419, 619–20, 622, 625–26, 636–37; socialism, endorsement of, **3:**635–38, 640; Women's Bureau of, **12:**376; and women workers, **12:**361n, 376

—meetings: 1889 (Dundee), **3:**636, *660n;* 1891 (Newcastle-upon-Tyne), **3:**223, *224n;* 1892 (Glasgow), **3:**223–24, *224n,* 348–49; 1893 (Belfast), **3:**619–20, 635–36, 640, *659n;* 1894 (Norwich), **3:**516, *517n,* 588, 636–37, **4:**85–87, *91n;* 1895 (Cardiff), **3:**664, *665n,* **4:**50, *50n,* 53, 55, 58–60, 66, 66n, 85–91, 368, 508, **10:**525, 527n; 1896 (Edinburgh), **4:**193, *194n;* 1898 (Bristol), *4:509n;* 1899 (Plymouth), *5:113n;* 1900 (Huddersfield), *5:211n;* 1906 (Liverpool), *7:68n;* 1908, **7:**401n; 1909 (Ipswich), **7:**401n, 489–90, *490n,* 491, **10:**525, 527n; 1913 (Manchester), **8:**415, *416n,* 518; 1914 (Portsmouth), **9:**162–63, *163n;* 1915 (Bristol), **9:**404, *406n;* 1916 (Birmingham), **9:**469, *470n,* 476, 484; 1918 (Derby), **10:**504, *505n,* 521–22, 525–27, **11:**11, 13; 1921 (Cardiff), **12:**18, *20n*

Trade Union Educational League, **8**:261n, *11:561n*, **12**:44–47, 47n, 64, 126n, 311, 403; raid on Chicago office of, **12**:131, 132n

Trade Unionist (Washington, D.C., labor journal), **4**:174, *175n*

trade unions: affiliation of, with city central labor unions, **4**:189–91, 191n, 380–81, **5**:261, 440, **6**:273–75, **7**:353–55, **8**:141–42, 142n, **12**:88, 89n; affiliation of, with national unions, **4**:189–91, 191n, 380–81, **5**:79n, 440; affiliation of, with state labor federations, **8**:327, **12**:88; benefit system of, **1**:28, 30, 37, 39, 41, 71, 341–42, **2**:34–35, 144–46, 146n, **4**:448, **5**:110–11, 112n, 240–41, 416–17, **7**:365, 365n, **8**:419, 421, 422n; as class movement, **2**:28, 32–33, 118, 153, 196, 262, 425, **3**:9, 36–37, 75, **4**:60, 264, 361–62, 366–68, 468, **7**:474–75; constitutions, SG critiques of, **4**:127–28, **5**:19–20, 207–9, 399, **6**:218–19, **7**:123–25, **8**:46, **9**:267–68, 419, 419n, 420–22; democracy in, **8**:262, 363–66, **9**:392–93; dues of, **1**:61–62, 72, 80, 91, 104, 134, 136, 145, 148–49, 258, 272, **2**:33, 133–34, 284, **3**:417, **4**:89, 100–101, 447–48, 468, **5**:57, 110–11, 112n, 323, 391, 409–10, 410n, 419, 419–20n, **7**:123–24, 268n, **8**:419, 421, 422n, **9**:268, 452; federation of, **1**:26, 36, 40, 100, 159, 161, 164–65, 211–14, 220–22, 232–37, 275, 279–81, 435–54, 450–51, 456–58, 461, **2**:118, 260–62, 361–62, **3**:144–45, 166–67, 280–81, 301, 405–7, 466–68, 498–99, 499n, 518–20, 572, **4**:117, 119–21, 212, 214–15, 308–9, 311–12, **7**:476–77; Hillmann on, **1**:27–28, 31, 34–42; incorporation of, **1**:218, 225, 287, 351–52, 354n, 361, **2**:6, 11n, 140, **6**:71–83, 147–48, **12**:36, 38n; industrial agreements of, **5**:216n, 275–77, 297–98, 310, 321, 322n, 328, 329n, 334, 341, 342n, 354, 431, **7**:293, 302–4, 485 (*see also* miners and mine operators, conferences of; Murray Hill Agreement; Protocol Agreement, 1913; "Protocol of Peace," 1910); jurisdiction of, **5**:323, **6**:158n, 297–99, 493–96, 496n, **7**:221–22, 222n, 268, 269n, **8**:296–97n, **9**:224–25, 502, 526, **10**:474, 474–75n (*see also* jurisdictional disputes); and KOL, **1**:159–63, 385–89, 395–98, 401–3, 404n, 406–9, 425–27, 436–40, 453–55, 460–62, 466–69, **2**:17–22, 22n, 24, 30–31, 33–35, 39–40, 49, 102, 194–95, 195n, 198, 204, 207–9, 212, 292–93, **3**:416, 516; leadership of, **2**:72, 235, **3**:248, 332, 400, **4**:100, 164, 265–66, **6**:294–97, 297n, **7**:463–64, 464n, **11**:64, 498–99; membership of, **6**:77–78, 83, 99, 319–20, 422–23, 423n, **8**:418, 423, **12**:3, 69–70, 306–7; non-partisan political action by, **2**:9, **3**:99, 143, 201, 203–4, 419, 421, 442n, 590–91, 593, 611–12, **4**:32–33, 264–65, 310–11, 415–16, **5**:12, 162n, 265, 282–84, 286n, **6**:35–36, 492–93, 493n, **7**:311, 404–5, **9**:165–66, 423–24, 471–72, **10**:258, 419, **11**:8n; objectives of, **2**:144, 196–97, 262, 273, **3**:95–102, 354, 388–96, 431–33, 510–11, 577–79, 669–70, **4**:47–49, 378, **5**:40–42, 132, 136–38, 142–43, **7**:326, **8**:73, 93, 96, 178, 262–63, 266–68, 271, 318–20, 353–55, 367, **9**:127–30, 333–34, 339, 447–48, 536, **12**:178, 180–81, 210; officers of, *letter to,* **4**:353–54; organization of, **2**:86–88, 117–19, 121–22, 147, **3**:183, 194, 280, 473, 531, **4**:28, 37, 100, 111, 483–84, **5**:136–38, 199, 262–63, 486–88, **6**:95–96, 98, 125, 172, 339, **9**:501–3, **10**:198, **11**:531–32; and "outsiders," **4**:49, **8**:438, **9**:277, 392–93, 420–21, 431, 459–62, 512, **10**:106–7, 160, 465, 527, **11**:470, **12**:309–10, 372; partisan political action by, **1**:26–34, 38–40, 71, 83, 84n, 85–90, 97, 139, 215, 235, 248, 250–54, 272–73, 360, 429–33, 439, 441–43, 446–49, 453–54, 467, **2**:9, 45–48, 121, 160–62, 364–65, 424, 427–29, **3**:4, 6, 17–18, 23–24, 77–78, 78n, 99, 134–35, 181, 200–204, 380, 403, 421, 444–45, 479–81, 491, 504, 585–86, 588, 608, 612, **4**:9–13, 27,

32–33, 60, 183–85, 238, 264–65, **5:**68, 265–66, 282–84, 286n, 412, **6:**68–70, 234, **9:**34–36, 36n, 165–66, 245, 327, **11:**8–16, 17n, 24–25, 262–65, 265n, 266–69, 275–78, 281–83, **12:**235–36; regulation of, judicial, **12:**68–72, 74; regulation of, legislative, **11:**232–33, **12:**74, 76; and religion, **3:**99, 154, 170, 353–54, 378, 408, 475–76, 500–501, 506–7, **4:**62, 200–202, **8:**440–41, 442n, **9:**16–17, 458–59 (*see also* Catholic Church)

Trade Unions, Their Origin and Objects, Influence and Efficacy (Trant), **2:**205–6, *206n,* **3:**102n

Trade Union Unity League, **11:**561n

Training School for Active Workers in the Labor Movement, **9:**332, *333n*

Training School for Women Organizers, **9:**332, *333n*

Traiser, H., and Co., strike/lockout, 1908, *7:308–9n,* 365, 461–62

tramps, **1:**258, 260n, 341–42

Trans-Mississippi Congress, *5:168n*
—convention: 1899 (Wichita, Kans.), **5:**164, *168n*

Trans-Missouri Freight Association, **4:**338n

transportation systems, government ownership of. *See* government ownership: of railroads; government ownership: of transportation system

Transport Workers' Federation, International, **6:***, 157, 158n

Transvaal. *See* South African Republic

Trant, William, *2:206n,* **3:**97–98, 102n; *letter to,* **2:**205–6

Trapper, Herman F., *5:19n; letter to,* **5:**18–19

Trautmann, William E., **5:***, 374, *375n,* **6:***, *384n,* **7:**42n, **8:**326n, 502n; and IWW, **6:**384, 385n, 449, 452, 459–61, 463, 466, 468

traveling benefits, **1:**72, 103, 147–48, 158, 341, **5:**240–41

Travis, Claude C., *9:400n; letter to,* **9:**399–400

Treaty of Guadalupe Hidalgo, **9:**431–32, *434n*

Treaty of Paris, 1898, *4:466n,* **5:**64n, 72, *73n*

Treaty of Rapallo, *12:15n*

Treaty of Riga, **11:**373n

Treaty of Versailles. *See* Versailles Treaty

Treder, Oscar F. R., **12:**551, *554n*

Treitschke, Heinrich von, **9:**192, *194n*

Trenton (N.J.) Central Labor Union, **8:**134–35, *135n*

Tresca, Carlo, **8:**452n, 503n, **9:**488–89, *489n*

Treviño, Ricardo, *12:515n,* 524–26; *letter to,* **12:**515

Triangle Shirtwaist Co., **8:**296, 297n

Triangle Shirtwaist fire, 1911, **8:**218, *219n,* 296, 301n; investigation of, **8:**243–44

Tribune of Labor and Trades Unionist (Chattanooga, Tenn., labor journal), *4:316n*

Tri-City Central Trades Council et al. v. American Steel Foundries, **10:**252, *253n*

Tri-City Central Trades Council of Granite City, Madison, and Venice, Ill., **10:**134–35, *136n;* injunction against, **10:**252, 253n

"Triple Alliance" (in New Orleans), **3:**243n

"Triple Alliance" (in Washington state), **11:**217, *218n*

Trobitz, Charles T., *10:505n; letter from,* **10:**505

Trotsky, Leon, **10:**508–10, *512n,* **11:**112, 369–70, 427–28, **12:**64, 96, 98, 233n, 293

Trowbridge, Lydia J., *10:83n; wire from,* **10:**81–82

Troy Daily Times, strike/lockout, 1884, **2:**341, *343n*

Troy, N.Y., labor convention, 1888, **2:**151, *152n*

Truax, Edna, *12:419n; letter to,* **12:**418–19

Truax, William, **12:**93n

Truax et al. v. Bisbee Local No. 380, Cooks' and Waiters' Union et al., *12:94n*

Truax et al. v. Corrigan et al., *12:93–94n*

truck system, **1:**225–26, 336–37, 361

Truesdale, William H., **8:**118, *120n*

Trump, William D., **5:**60–61, *61n*

trusts: AFL and, **5:**50–51, 281–82,

6:359n, 7:325; as 1906 campaign issue, 7:62, 79–81, 85, 87–88, 103, 108; as 1908 campaign issue, 7:408–9; National Civic Federation and, 5:217, 218n, 464, 7:245, 246n, 258–65, 320–21, 321–22n; SG and, 3:101, 4:26, 35, 37, 44, 5:28, 98, 136, 142–46, 227, 358–61, 7:258–65, 352. *See also under* legislation, states and territories; legislation, U.S.; *and under names of specific trusts*
Truth (New York City newspaper), 12:34n
Truth about Soviet Russia and Bolshevism, The (SG), 11:372
tuberculosis, 6:203, 385–86, 485–86, 486n, 7:212, 8:207
TUC. *See* Trades Union Congress of Great Britain
Tucker, Edward L., 12:347, *349n*
Tucker, Gideon J., *3:550n; letter to,* 3:549–50
Tumulty, Joseph P., 9:203n, 10:3, *4n,* 53, 221n, 291n, 387, 391n, 11:93n, 126n, 129n, 182n, 239n, 300, 398n; *letter to,* 10:390–91; *wire from,* 11:140–41
Tunnel and Subway Constructors' International Union: and black workers, 11:84n; jurisdiction of, 9:347, 347–48n
Turati, Filippo, 10:552, *555n*
Turk, Samuel, 6:155, 156n
Turk Brothers, strike/lockout, 1903, 6:155, *156n*
Turkey, 10:568n
Turley, Edward L., 6:*, *223n; letter to,* 6:222–23
Turner, Edmund, 11:84n, 326n
Turner, Frederick, 1:*, *394n,* 466, 2:*, 18, 342, *343n,* 4:*, 140, *141n; letter from,* 1:409–11; *letter to,* 1:392–94; *report of,* 1:399–401
Turner, James K., 8:50, *52n*
Turner, John, 4:*, 207, *209n,* 216–17
Turner, W. H., 4:375, 376n
Tuttle, Charles, *letter to,* 3:229–30
Tveitmoe, Olaf A., 6:*, *273n,* 7:*, *148n,* 383, 8:*, 151n, 235, *238n; letters to,* 6:271–73, 7:147–48

Tweed, William M., 1:172, *173n,* 3:373n
Twentieth Century Fund, 7:462n
Tyler, Emily, 10:546n
Typographers, French Federation of. *See* Fédération française des travailleurs du livre
Typographia, German-American, 1:*, 258, 260n, 275, 390, 391n, 2:*, 37, 37n, 5:*, 510–11, 511n; and *Morgen Journal* arbitration case, 2:372–73
—locals: local 1 (Philadelphia), 2:25–26n; local 7 (New York City), 1:260n, 2:371–74, 3:115n, 379, 484, 486n, 6:396, 397n; local 10 (Milwaukee), 3:493–94, 498n; local 12 (Louisville, Ky.), 2:213, 213n
—strike/lockout: 1892 (New York City), *3:486n*
Typographical Union, International, 1:*, 159, 161, 165, 166n, 385–86, 2:*, 26n, 36n, 40, 67, 165, 235, 335, 339, 3:*, 68, 69n, 137, 627, 629, 4:*, 79, 80n, 95, 98–99, 5:*, 18, 19n, 234, 6:*, 129, 129n, 7:*, 142n, 8:*, 5, 6n, 144n, 303n, 9:*, 36n, 537, 10:*, 229, 231n, 11:*, 84n, 333, 12:*, 127, 223; AFL financial support of, 3:168–69, 7:486n; and black workers, 11:84n; and eight-hour movement, 2:213, 213n, 3:162, 9:120; and election of 1908, 7:383–84, 384n; and industrial unionism, 5:291, 9:502, 12:62, 66n; injunctions against, 3:125–27, 128n, 129–31, 139, 263–64, 7:11–12n; jurisdiction of, 3:457, 5:103–4, 104–5n, 112–13, 113n, 172–76, 288–92, 292n, 445, 6:339n; and mechanization, 4:392, 5:83, 291, 12:305–6; and *Morgen Journal* arbitration case, 2:372–73; and National Cash Register Co., 7:166–68, 168n, 195n; retirement home of (*see* Childs-Drexel Home for Union Printers); and strikebreakers, 1:389; and women workers, 9:315, 11:505
—conventions: 1887 (Buffalo, N.Y.), 2:36, 37n; 1889 (Denver), 2:213, 213n; 1892 (Philadelphia), 3:162,

163n, 168–69, 245; 1894 (Louisville, Ky.), **3:**618; 1896 (Colorado Springs, Colo.), *4:371n;* 1898 (Syracuse, N.Y.), **5:**18, *19n,* 104n; 1899 (Detroit), **5:**112, *113n;* 1900 (Milwaukee), **5:**257, *260n;* 1914 (Providence, R.I.), **9:**168, *168n*
—locals: local 1 (Indianapolis), **6:**523, **12:**363; local 2 (Philadelphia), **6:**210n, **7:**85, 91n; local 3 (Cincinnati), **7:**403, 405n; local 6 (New York City), **1:**361n, 362n, 438, **2:**371–74, **3:**379, **5:**236n, 405–6, 406n, **7:**91n; local 7 (Pittsburgh), **3:**125–27, 128n, **5:**176n; local 8 (St. Louis), **1:**220n, **8:**222; local 15 (Rochester, N.Y.), **4:**333n; local 16 (Chicago), **1:**211, 212n, **5:**342n, **7:**11–12n, **11:**333; local 23 (Milwaukee), **3:**494–97, 498n, **7:**130, 142n; local 49 (Denver), **5:**393, 395, 395n, **6:**131n; local 57 (Dayton, Ohio), **7:**168–69, 192, 194n; local 80 (Kansas City, Mo.), **5:**236n; local 83 (New York City), **7:**297, 298n; local 101 (Washington, D.C.), **2:**70, 71n, **4:**174; local 101 (Washington, D.C.), *letter to,* **6:**47; local 120 (Lynn, Mass.), **4:**187, 189n; local 162 (Jacksonville, Fla.), **2:**343n; local 174 (Los Angeles), **6:**212–13, 213n, **8:**221, **9:**436; local 202 (Seattle), **5:**470n; local 215 (Decatur, Ill.), **3:**362n; local 220 (Columbus, Ga.), **4:**250; local 271 (Boise, Idaho), **5:**97, 99n; local 276 (New Bedford, Mass.), **3:**362n; local 286 (Marion, Ind.), **7:**407, 408n; local 317 (New York City), **3:**379, 382n; local 348 (Girard, Kans.), **6:**221, 222n
—strikes/lockouts: 1886 (Jacksonville, Fla.), **2:**340–41, *343n;* 1890–92, 1893-? (Los Angeles), **6:**212–13, *213n,* **8:**129, 146; 1891–92 (Pittsburgh), **3:**125–27, *128n,* 129–31, 139, 263–64; 1897 (Rochester, N.Y.), **4:**332, *333n;* 1899–1900 (Kansas City, Mo.), *5:236n;* 1899–1900 (Pittsburgh), **5:**174–75, *176n,* 234; 1899–1902 (New York City), **5:**234,

236n, 405–6, 406n; 1905-? (Chicago), **7:**11n; 1905–8, **7:**483, *485–86n;* 1905–8 (Philadelphia), **7:**85, *91n;* 1906 (New York City), **7:**85, *91n;* 1906-? (Dayton, Ohio), **7:**166, 168–*69n,* 193; 1921–24, **11:**566–67, *570–71n*

Ulrich, Henry A., **5:**269–70, *271n*
Underwood, Oscar W., **8:**493n, **9:**148n, 65, *68n,* 98n, **12:**215–17
unemployment: AFL and, **11:**8n, 51, 208, 363–64, 423, **12:**454; Foster and, **12:**63; Hoover and, **11:**386–87; SG and, **2:**86, 153, **3:**229–30, 288, 366n, 377–78, 431, **4:**25, 34–36, 46, 243, **5:**87–88, **7:**491, **9:**123, **10:**290, **11:**32–33, 387, 411, 444, 494, 498n, 517, 555, **12:**32–33, 34n, 37, 52, 61, 125, 213–16, 242, 284
unemployment insurance, **9:**175n, 193n, **11:**475, 476n, **12:**17–20, 213–15, 215n
Unemployment Conference, 1921 (Washington, D.C.), **11:**515n, 530, *532n,* **12:**143, 297, 413
"unfair list." *See* "We Don't Patronize List" (AFL)
Union Advocate (AFL journal), **2:**29, *29n,* 75, 96, 107
Union Co-operative Laundry (Philadelphia), **3:**161n
Union County (N.J.) Trades Council, **7:**337–38, *338n*
Union des chambres syndicales, *2:108n,* **3:**369
Union for Practical Progress, **3:**468, *469n*
Union Furnace Co., strike/lockout, 1903, **6:**168, *168–69n,* 169–70, 170n
Union Horse Nail Co., **5:**31
Union Iron Works, **5:**433n, 483
union label: AFL and, **5:**373, 374n, 412, 413n, **7:**314, **8:**8, **12:**87–88, 88n; Allied Printing Trades, **4:**414, **5:**12, 63n, 406, 477–78, **7:**337, 377, **8:**168 (*see also* printing trades councils, allied); anti-Chinese, **1:**115n, 125, 126n; Blacksmiths, **6:**188–89; Boot and Shoe Workers, **5:**112n,

6:203, 395; Brewery Workmen, **5:**375n, **6:**88–89, 90n, 503n, **7:**36–37n, 201, 494; Carpenters, **6:**181; Cigar Makers, **1:**293, *327n,* 370, 374, 388, 392–94, 398, 400–401, 409–10, 413–14, 417, 449, **2:**124, **5:**434, **6:**203, 395, **7:**462, **8:**422n, **10:**261, 264; Eliot and, **6:**423n; farmers, **5:**120, 121n; Flour and Cereal Mill Employes, **7:**303–4; glove workers, **5:**373; Hatters, **7:**455–56n, **8:**74; International Laborers' Union, **6:**436; IWW, **6:**451, 457; KOL, **1:**366, 380, *380n,* 381–82, 384, 393–94, *394n,* 395, 397, 400, 405n, 408, 410–11, 420, 435; Ladies' Garment Workers, **6:**276, **12:**529; Meat Cutters, **5:**78, 79n; Metal Mechanics, **6:**239, 240n; Paper Makers, **6:**131–32, 203, 395; Rubber Workers, **6:**260n; SG and, **4:**113, 208–9, 218, 218n, **5:**31, 183, 350, **6:**180, 218–19, 263, 389–90, **7:**139–40, **8:**487, **9:**297–98, **12:**4; Tailors, **4:**208–9, **6:**389–90, **7:**140, **9:**74n, 261n; Tobacco Workers, **5:**118; Wood-Workers, **5:**269–70

Union Labor party, and election of 1908, **7:**382, 382n, 383–84, 384n

union leagues, **3:**380, *382–83n*

Union Lumber Co., strike/lockout, 1903–6?, **6:**170, *171n,* 241–44

Unión Obrera de Panameños, **11:**391, 393n, 434

Union Pacific Railroad, **3:**551, 552n; strike/lockout, 1911–15, **8:**321–22, *322–23n*

union shop. *See* closed shop

Union Shop and Its Antithesis, The (AFL), **12:**216, *217n*

Union Switch and Signal Co., **6:**137

Union syndical suisse, congress of, 1913 (Zurich), *8:506n*

Union Traction Co., **6:**13n; strike/lockout, 1895, **4:**115, *115–16n,* 118

United Brethren Benefit Society, **2:**117n

United Hebrew Trades, **3:**353–54, *355n,* 378, 381, **4:**97n, 105, **8:**40n, **9:**57–60, **11:**298, 531

United Labor Council of America, **11:**549, *550n*

—convention: 1922 (New York City), **11:**549, *550n*

United Labor party:
—1882 (New York), *1:248*
—1886 (Chicago), **2:**60, *409n*
—1887 (New York), *1:430,* **2:**45–47, *48n;* convention (Syracuse), **2:**45, *48n,* 369, 371n; and socialists, **2:**45, 369, 371n, 400
—1902, **6:**37n
—1906 (Pennsylvania), **7:**122n

United Manufacturers' and Merchants' Association, **8:**453n

United Mine Workers' Journal (trade union journal), *letter to,* **9:**335–40

United Mine Workers of America, Dist. No. 17, et al. v. Chafin et al., **12:**265n

United Mine Workers of America et al. v. Coronado Coal Co. et al., **10:**322, *323n,* **12:**93n

United Mine Workers of America et al. v. Pennsylvania Mining Co., **11:**492, *494n*

United Railways of San Francisco, strike/lockout, 1902, **6:**13n

United Shipping and Transportation Association, **7:**116

United Shoe Machinery Co., antitrust case against, **10:**322, 323n

United States Tobacco Journal, **1:**404, 418n

United Syndical Chambers of France. *See* Union des chambres syndicales

United Traction Co., strike/lockout, 1901, **5:**360, *361n*

United Typothetae, **11:**570n; and printers' strike, 1905–8, **7:**483, *485–86n*

University Settlement (New York City), *3:458n*

unskilled workers, **1:**160, **2:**73–74, 315, **4:**117–18, 118n, **5:**57, 79–80, **6:**119, **7:**148–49, 150n, 202–4, 240–41, 242n, 262, 306–8, 308n, 343–44, **8:**7–9, 9–10n, 339, 360, 390, 391n, 517–18, **9:**142, 143n, 172, 251–52, 530–31, **10:**415–16, **12:**165

Untermann, Ernest, **6:**443, *445n*

Untermyer, Samuel, **11:**154, *155n,* 399n, **12:**80n, 153; interrogation of SG by, **12:**68–80; *letter from,* **12:**166–67; *letters to,* **11:**399, 445–46

Upham, William H., **4:**167n
upholsterers, organization of, **8:**47, 47n
Upholsterers' International Union of North America, **6:***, 231n; AFL financial support of, **6:**228–31, 231n; and black workers, **11:**84n; injunction against, **6:**229–30
—convention: 1903 (St. Louis), *6:229*
—local: local 26 (Grand Rapids, Mich.), **6:**229–30, 231n
—strike/lockout: 1903 (Grand Rapids, Mich.), **6:**229–30, *231n*
Urban, William, **2:**60, *63n*
Urick, Ambrose L., **5:**86, *87n,* **7:***, *10n,* **8:**17n; *letter to,* **7:**9–10
Urquidi, Francisco, **9:**307n
Uruguay, and civil war in Mexico, **9:**363n
U.S. Army Base Hospital No. 37 (Dartford, Kent), SG visit to, **10:**520, 524n
U.S. Bituminous Coal Commission, **11:**192n
U.S. Bureau of Engraving and Printing, **5:**411n, **10:**229
U.S. Bureau of Insular Affairs, **12:**200
U.S. Bureau of Internal Revenue, **1:**125, 125n, 126, 126n, 129, 131, 169
U.S. Bureau of Labor (in Department of Commerce and Labor), **8:**44n, 95, 100n, 331, 341
U.S. Bureau of Labor (in Department of Interior), *2:127n,* 129, **8:**95
U.S. Bureau of Labor Statistics, **1:**219, 226, 281, 287–88, 352
U.S. Census Office, **4:**220n
U.S. Chamber of Commerce, **11:**72n, 127, **12:**301
U.S. Coal Commission, **12:**48n
U.S. Commission on Industrial Relations, **8:**329–31, *331–32n,* 455–56, 456n, **9:**9, **10:**106, 107n, **12:**42; AFL and, **9:**464n; hearings of, **9:**83–88, 90, 112–38, 138n, 139, 139–40n, 171–72, 172n, 188, 189n, 224n, 256–58, 258n, 279–80, 280n, 282, 283n, 284, 285n, 322; and minimum wage, **9:**316–17; *reports of,* **9:**311, 312n, 321–23, 324n; and scientific management, **9:**187–89,

189n. *See also* Committee on Industrial Relations; legislation, U.S.: Industrial Relations Commission
U.S. Constitution: amendment of, **9:**125, **12:**91, 93; amendment curbing veto power of Supreme Court, **12:**91, 94–95, 208, 209n, 230, 247n, 454, 487, 510, 512; amendment prohibiting child labor, **12:**81, 82–83n, 91, 208, 276, 343, 346, 348n, 374, 453–54, 455n, 486–87, 510–11; amendment on rights of trade unions, **12:**208, 209n; equal rights amendment, **12:**31, *31n,* 37, 39n, 372
—Thirteenth Amendment, **5:**303–4, **12:**110
—Fourteenth Amendment, **12:**282
—Fifteenth Amendment, **12:**282
—Eighteenth Amendment, **10:**289–91, *291n,* **11:**79, **12:**206
—Nineteenth Amendment, **3:**25n, *10:402n,* **12:**248
U.S. Department of Commerce and Labor, **6:**110, 111n, **7:**77, **8:**95, 100n; and alien contract labor law, **7:**155, 156n, 195–96, 197n; and iron and steel industry, **7:**473n. *See also under* legislation, U.S.
U.S. Department of Industry and Commerce (proposed), **5:**13–14. *See also under* legislation, U.S.
U.S. Department of Labor, **1:**288, *2:127n,* **3:**478n, **8:**100n, 332–33n, **11:**123n; AFL and, **2:**127, 129, 131–33, **4:**267, 268n; and Canadian workers, immigration of, **11:**341n; and Mexican workers, immigration of, **11:**338–39, 341n, 494–95, 495–96n; SG and, **3:**477–78, **5:**13–14, 432, **8:**94–99, 331, **9:**8, **11:**22, 160. *See also under* legislation, U.S.
—Bureau of Labor Statistics, **12:**249
—Children's Bureau, and AFL Permanent Conference for Abolition of Child Labor, **12:**82n
—Division of Negro Economics, **10:**327, *327n,* 366–67, 367n
—Training and Dilution Service, **11:**36, *36n*
—U.S. Training Service, *11:36n*

—Woman in Industry Service, **11**:36, *36n*

—Women's Bureau, and AFL Permanent Conference for Abolition of Child Labor, **12**:82n

—Working Conditions Service, **11**:36, *36n*, 68

U.S. Export Association, *5:35n*

U.S. ex rel. Abern v. *Wallis, 12:278n*

U.S. Food Administration, **10**:313–14, *315n*

U.S. Fuel Administration, *10:288n*

U.S. Government Printing Office, **10**:229

U.S. House of Representatives:

—Committee on Agriculture, **10**:111

—Committee on District of Columbia, **8**:377–79, **12**:346

—Committee on Foreign Affairs, **5**:466, **11**:432n, **12**:286, 288n, 291

—Committee on Immigration and Naturalization, **3**:512–13, 514n, **8**:339–45, **11**:503–4n, **12**:348n, 417n

—Committee on Insular Affairs, **12**:200

—Committee on Interstate and Foreign Commerce, **9**:526n, **10**:15, 17n, 123–24, **11**:156, 157n

—Committee on Judiciary, **5**:211, 211n, 316n, 326, **6**:231, 232n, 237, 537–45, **7**:84, **8**:317–20, 361, 373–75, 431, 442–47, 448n, 457, **9**:40, 40n, 52n, 106n, 140, **10**:63, 64n, **12**:82n, 147, 147n, 208

—Committee on Labor, **5**:189–97, 197–98n, 201–7, 207n, 212–13, 222–30, 230n, 478–82, 482n, 497–500, **6**:231, 232n, 476–77, **7**:26–32, 43, 43n, 77, **8**:94–99, 209–12, 374, 377; chair of, **8**:183–84, 184n. *See also* Wilson, William B.

—Committee on Merchant Marine and Fisheries, **7**:72, 78, 90n, 171, 177n, **9**:111, 112n

—Committee on Military Affairs, **5**:231, 232n, **10**:63, 64n, **12**:423, 424n

—Committee on Mines and Mining, **9**:48n, 302n

—Committee on Pacific Railroads, **3**:552n

—Committee on Post Office and Post Roads, **3**:471n, **8**:40, 42n

—Committee on Rules, **8**:374–75, 381n, **12**:346

—Committee on Ways and Means, **8**:330

—Select Committee on Importation of Contract Laborers, Convicts, Paupers, etc., **2**:142, *143n*

—Select Committee on Lobbying, **9**:3–8, 229, 230n

U.S. Immigration Commission, **3**:271, 271n, 361, **8**:330

U.S. Industrial Commission, *4:505n*, **6**:340n; SG and, **4**:503–4, 505n, **5**:142–46, 214–15, 216n, 226, 266–67, 358–60, 361n, **6**:334, **8**:329–30

U.S. Marine Corps Band, **4**:180–81, 395–96

U.S.-Mexican Joint Commission, **9**:426n, 431–32, *434n*, 482–84, 498

U.S. Navy Department, **10**:207n, **12**:200; and Ansonia case, **10**:284n; and Pacific Coast shipbuilding workers' strike, 1917, **10**:209n; and wages, **10**:52–53, 86–87, 87n, 222–23, 223n

U.S. Projectile Co., **5**:207n

U.S. Railroad Administration, **10**:320n, 366, 382n, 494, 505n, **11**:61n, 120n, 183

U.S. Railroad Labor Board et al. v. *Pennsylvania Railroad Co., 12:30n*

U.S. Reduction and Refining Co., strike/lockout, 1903–4, *6:282n*

U.S. Secret Service, **2**:224, *224n*

U.S. Senate:

—Committee on Agriculture and Forestry, **8**:79, 80n

—Committee on Commerce, **8**:369n, **10**:340, 340n

—Committee on Education and Labor, **5**:248, 325, 498, **6**:231, 232n, 526, **7**:26–27, **8**:370–71, 374–75, 395, **11**:31–34, 296–97n, **12**:279, 281n; hearings on relations between labor and capital, **1**:287–356, **8**:330, 332n; hearings on steel strike, 1919–20, **11**:85n, 123n, 152, *153n*, 154; subcommittee, hearings on eight-hour bill, **4**:489–99, 499n, 500–501

—Committee on Foreign Affairs, **9**:111, 112n

—Committee on Immigration, **5:**466–67, 470–74, 474n, **12:**348
—Committee on Insular Affairs, **12:**200
—Committee on Interstate Commerce, **8:**362, 363n, **9:**92, 526n
—Committee on Judiciary, **8:**361–62, 363n, 374, 430–37, 438n, 445, 463, 491, **9:**92, 300, **12:**208
—Committee on Military Affairs, **10:**64n, 513
U.S. Shipping Board, **10:**204, 207–*8n*, 220–21, 221n, 234, 318, 381n, 412, 452–53, 526, **11:**52n
U.S. Steel Corp., **5:***335n*, 359–60, 480, **8:**153, 454, **10:**51, **12:**140; antitrust case against, **10:**322, 323n; and Birmingham (Ala.) metal trades strike, 1918, **10:**378n, 385–86, 441; congressional investigation of, **8:**12, 12n, 30, 53, 54n; hostility of, toward unions, **5:**334, **6:**514–15, 515n, **7:**473n, **8:**189, 272, 291, 434, **9:**279, **10:**377, 391, **11:**230, 362–63, 399n; and immigration, **8:**345, **9:**81; and National Committee for Organizing Iron and Steel Workers, **11:**98, 124–25, 129, 129n, 144, 147–48, 161–63; pension plan of, **11:**333; profit-sharing plan of, **8:**23–24, 24–25n, **9:**45, 46n; strike/lockout, 1901, **5:***384–85n*, 385–88, 388n, 389–90, 479; strike/lockout, 1909–10, **8:**7, 9n, 12, 12n, 27–30, 31n, 54–55; strike/lockout, 1919–20, **11:***126n*, 171, 194 (*see also* steel strike, 1919–20)
U.S. Strike Commission, **3:**571, *579n*, **5:**308n; SG, *testimony before*, **3:**563–79
U.S. Supreme Court, amendment to curb veto power of, **12:**91, 94–95, 208, 209n, 230, 247n, 454, 487, 510, 512
U.S. Telegraph and Telephone Administration, **10:**515n
U.S. v. A. Haines et al., **9:***83n*
U.S. v. American Tobacco Co., **8:**153, *154n*
U.S. v. Armstrong et al., **11:***196n*
U.S. v. Bricklayers', Masons', and Plasterers' International Union, **12:***80n*
U.S. v. Cpl. John Washington et al., **10:***326n*

U.S. v. Cpl. Robert Tillman et al., **10:***326n*
U.S. v. E. J. Ray et al., **8:***182n*, 265, 466
U.S. v. Frank J. Hayes et al., **11:***196n*
U.S. v. Ollinger, **4:**336, *337n*
U.S. v. Press Publishing Co., **8:***204n*
U.S. v. Railway Employees' Department of American Federation of Labor et al., **12:***87n*
U.S. v. Sgt. William Nesbit et al., **10:***326n*
U.S. v. Steers et al., **8:**265, *276n*
U.S. v. Trans-Missouri Freight Association, **4:**337, *338n*
U.S. v. Wells et al., **10:**397–400, *400n*
U.S. v. Wheeler et al., **10:***324n*
Utah Board of Pardons, **9:**344n
Utah State Federation of Labor, **6:**262, 262n, *368–69n*
—convention: 1904 (Salt Lake City), **6:**262, *262n*
utilities: government ownership of (*see* government ownership: of utilities); mayors' conference on, 1914, **9:**206–7, *208n;* National Civic Federation model bill to regulate, **9:**163–64, 164n

Vaccarelli, F. Paul A., *10:381n*, 432; *letter to*, **10:**380–81
Vahey, James H., **12:**21–23, *24n*
Vail, J. M., **5:**275, **6:***, 448, *450n*
Vail, Theodore N., **10:**515, *515n*
Valentine, Joseph F., **3:***, *664n*, **5:***, *176n*, **7:***, *7n*, 32–33, 111n, 155n, **8:***, *125n*, 202n, 389n, 503–4, **9:***, *14n*, **10:***, *475n*, **11:***, *148n*, 313n, 345, 364, **12:***, *117n*, 461n; at AFL conventions, **3:**662, 664n, **5:**175, 176n, **11:**475, 476n; at AFL Executive Council meetings, **8:**379, **9:**271–73, 436, **11:**389; election of, as AFL vice-president, **6:**509n, **7:**281n, 427n, **8:**18n, 295, **9:**38n, 226n, 348n, **10:**475, **11:**93n, 321, 321n, 482, **12:**97n, 338n; and Industrial Conference, 1919, **11:**128n; *letters from*, **7:**53–54, **8:**387–89; and steel strike, 1919–20, **11:**148, 152
Valentino, John G., **12:***, 336, *337n*
Valesh, Eva McDonald, **3:***, *132n*, 419, **4:***, *82n*, 106n, 428, **5:***, 330, *330n*, 356, **6:***, 161, *163n*, 238, **8:***,

39, *40n;* at AFL conventions, **3:**131, 132n, **4:**81; *letters to,* **3:**143–44, 591–93, **4:**159–61, 193–94

Valesh, Frank, *3:128n,* 265, 591–92, **4:**81, 159–60, 194, 195n, **5:**325, 325n; at AFL conventions, **3:**126, 128n, 130, 251, 253n, 259

Valesh, Frank, Jr., **3:**592, *4:161n*

Van Cleave, James W., *7:155n,* 245, 246n, 273; and alleged National Association of Manufacturers' bribery attempt of SG, **7:**257–58n, 271; and Buck's Stove and Range Co., **7:**153–54, 154–55n, 250n, **8:**162, 204n; and Buck's Stove and Range Co. cases, **7:**253, 263, 426; and election of 1908, **7:**369, 370n; SG and, **7:**251, 401–2, 405, **8:**50, 70, **11:**382

Vancouver (B.C.) and District Waterfront Workers' Association, **12:**440–41, *442n*

Van Deman, Ralph H., *10:436n; letter from,* **10:**434–36

Vanderbilt, Cornelius, **2:**399, *409n,* **3:**481, **8:**274, **9:**218

Vanderbilt, William H., **1:**99, *101n,* 432

Vanderburgh, Joseph, **1:**262, *263n*

Vanderlip, Frank A., **10:**310, *312n*

Vanderpoorten, Abraham, **1:**107, *108n*

Vanderveer, George F., **12:**257–58, *259n*

Vandervelde, Emile G., **11:**29, *30n*

Vandervoort, John R., **4:**174–75, *175–*76n, 199, 206

Van Devanter, Willis, **8:**152–53, *154n*

Van Dornes, Gus C., **10:**19, *21n*

Vanetta, David, **8:**297, *298n*

Van Etten, Ida M., **2:***, *155n,* 289n, 415–16, **3:***, 29, *29n,* 133, 136; *letters to,* **2:**154–55, 288–89

Van Gülpen, George W., *letter to,* **3:**551

Van Holland, Henry, *letter from,* **4:**229–30

Van Horn, R. S., **12:**447n

Van Kennen, George, **12:**382n

Van Kleeck, Mary A., *10:484n; letter from,* **10:**482–83

Van Lear, Thomas, **9:**347, *348n,* 350n

Van Owners' Association of Greater New York, injunction, **11:**458n

Van Patten, Simon P., **3:***, 15, *18n*

Van Siclen, George W., *5:122n; letter to,* **5:**122

Van Siclen, James C., **11:**455, *458n,* **12:**71, 74n

Van Winkle, J. Q., **4:**168, *168n*

Vanzetti, Bartolomeo, *11:550n,* **12:**90, 91n

Vare, William S., **9:**19, *22n*

Vargas, Canuto A., **11:**300, *341n,* 391, **12:**359n, 525; *letter from,* **11:**338–41

Vargas, Hermogenes, **9:**411n

Varley, William, *11:74n; letter from,* **11:**72–74

Varnishers of New York and Vicinity, United, **1:**361, 362n

Vaughan, John D., **2:**263, 268, *268n,* 288

Vaughen, R. E., *letter to,* **6:**265–66

Veal, Philip, **6:**447, *450n*

Veblen, Thorstein, **8:**514, *517n*

Vega, José, **6:**30, *31n*

Veiller, Lawrence T., *5:254n; letter to,* **5:**253–54

Venable Bros., **6:**116

Venezuelan boundary dispute, **4:**108–9, *110n*

Veracruz, Mexico: and Tampico incident, **9:**95, *95–96n;* textile workers strike in, 1907, **9:**306, *307n*

Verbanac, Nick, **9:**182, 184n, 190–91, 191n

Verband der deutschen Gewerkvereine, **1:**33–34, *44n*

Verdun, battle of, *9:426n,* **11:**49n

Vermont Marble Co., **3:**271

Versailles Treaty:
—Covenant of the League of Nations, **11:**58, 59n
—labor clauses, **11:**41n, 69–70, 70–71n, 88–91, 92–93n, 99–102, 108–10, 135–37, 166, 236–37, 367, 405, **12:**561; AFL convention debate on, **11:**88–91; drafting of, **11:**41n, 69–70; text of, **11:**70–71n, 92–93n, 99–102
—ratification, **11:**58, 108–9, 109n, 110, 129n, 194, 212, 235–37, 404–5
—U.S. peace commissioners, *11:41n,* 52n; meetings with AFL peace delegation, **11:**39–40, 48, 55, 58n

vestibules (on street cars), **5:**347, *347n*

vestibule schools, **10:**483, *484n*

veterans, **11:**8n, 118, 148–49, 277–78, 278n; and Centralia, Wash., Armistice Day affair, 1919, **11:**217n; and Kansas coal strike, 1919, **11:**307–8; rehabilitation of, **12:**454; and Winnipeg, Man., general strike, 1919, **11:**75n

Victor-American Fuel Co., **10:**169n; strike/lockout, 1913–14, **9:**23, *24n*, 210–11, 211n, 242, 301, 399, 400n. *See also* Ludlow, Colo., massacre

Victor (Colo.) Trades Assembly, **4:**173–74

Victor Emmanuel III, **10:**550, *554n*, 563

Victor y Victor, Luis Alejandro, **11:**391, *392n*

Vigouroux, Louis, **3:**368, *370n*

Villa, Francisco "Pancho," **9:**211, *212n*, 306, 307n, 426n, 432, 437

Villalón, Jose R., **4:**132, *133n*

Villard, Ernest, **8:**343, *346n*

Villard, Oswald G., **11:**470, *472n*, **12:**43n; *letter to,* **12:**41–43

Villarreal, Antonio I., **12:**391, *392n*

Vimy Ridge, battle of, **11:**57, *58n*

Vince, Joseph, **1:**432, *433n*, 434, **3:**141

Vince, Mrs. Joseph, **3:**141

Vincens, George E., **6:**209, *210n*

"Vindex," *letter from,* **2:**214–15

Virginia State Federation of Labor, **11:**87n

Virgin Islands, conditions in, **12:**197–201

Viviani, René, **10:**72n, 563, *567n*

Vocational Association of the Middle West, **9:**353n

vocational education, **8:**79, 182, **9:**126, 355, 355n, 382. *See also under* legislation, U.S.

Vogt, Hugo, **2:***, 369–70, *371n*, **3:***, 16, *18n*, 397, **4:**135, *137n*, **5:**429, 430n

Voice (Prohibition journal), **3:**217

Volders, Jean, **3:***, 86, *87n*

Volk, Jacob, **11:**353

Volk, Lester D., **12:**25, *26n*

Volksstaat (German socialist journal), **2:**159n

Voll, John A., **10:***, *540n*, **12:**97n; *letter from,* **10:**538–40

Volstead, Andrew, **11:**338n

Volturno (steamship), sinking of, **9:**201, *203n*

"Voluntary Nature of the Labor Movement, The: A Trade Union Creed" (SG), **12:**520–23, *524n*

Von der Fehr, Frank, **3:**344, *345n*

Von Schriltz, G. A., **12:**332n

Voorhees, Daniel W., **3:**137, *138n*

Vorwärts (German socialist journal), **2:**159n

Vose, Edwin S., **7:**100, *101n*

vote, right to, **9:**184–87

Vreeland, Edward B., **8:**94, 98–99, *100n*, 210–11

Vrooman, Harry C., *3:468n; letter to,* **3:**468

Waddell, W. E., *letter to,* **9:**44–45

Waddell-Mahon Detective Agency, **8:**513n; agents as guards, **9:**11–12, 13n, 28n, 43, 182; injunction against, **9:**12, 13n

Wade, Jefferson D., *2:189n; letter to,* **2:**188–89

Wade, Martin J., **7:**387, *387n*

Wadia, B. P., **12:**234, *241n*

Wadsworth, James W., Jr., *11:294n*, 300; *letter to,* **11:**292–94

wages: AFL and, **11:**233–34, 559–60, 560n, **12:**7, 8n; of Brick and Clay Workers, **12:**353–55; of electrical workers, **10:**86–87, 87n; of garment workers, **10:**61–62, 62n; of government employees, **9:**19, 22n, 532, **10:**41, **12:**249; "iron law of," **1:**27, 31, *44n*, 87; and land, **1:**282; of longshoremen, **12:**7; in Mexico, **9:**439; National Civic Federation and, **9:**460–61, 461n; postwar reductions in, **11:**411–12, 443–44, 498n; SG on, **1:**313–15, 331–37, 339–40, **2:**83, 91–92, **3:**229–30, 274–75, **4:**21–22, 26–27, 37, 113, 433–34, **5:**87–88, **6:**347, **7:**291–94, **9:**126–27, 252, **12:**75–79, 284–85, 424; of teachers, **10:**438–39, 439–40n; of tobacco workers, **5:**462, 463n; U.S. Navy Department and, **10:**52–53, 54n, 86–87, 87n, 222–23, 223n. *See also* Board of Railroad Wages and Working Conditions; legislation,

states and territories; legislation, U.S.; living wage; minimum wage; prevailing rate of wages; Railroad Wage Commission; Shipbuilding Labor Adjustment Board; U.S. Commission on Industrial Relations
"Wages" (AFL), **11:**560, **12:**7, 8n
wage system, abolition of, **1:**86–87, 90
wage workers of the United States, *letter to,* **3:**15–18
Wagnalls, Adam W., **3:**217, *218n*
Wagner, Karl H., *letter to,* **3:**169–70
Wagner, Leopold, **1:**414, *414n,* 442; *statement of,* **1:**446–47
Wagner, Robert F., **8:**301n, 427n, 472, *472n,* **11:**18n, 459
Wagner, Theodore H., **12:**240, *241n,* 270
Wagstaff, William, **3:**196, *197n*
Wahrheit (New York City Bohemian cigarmakers' journal), **1:**274, *274n.* See also *Warheit*
Wainright, Richard, **5:**21, *29n*
Waiters' and Bartenders' National Union, **3:**:*, 89, 90n, 401n, **4:**:*, **5:**:*, **6:**:*, **7:**:*, **8:**:*, **9:**:*, **10:**:*, **11:**:*, **12:**:*
Waiters' League, Chicago, **4:**381, 382n
Waiters' Union 1 (New York City), **1:**457, 459n, **3:**379, 484, 485n
Waiters' Union of St. Louis, German Progressive, **2:**173n
Wakeman, Thaddeus B., **2:**55n, 323–25, *325n,* 429, **4:**249n
Wald, Lillian D., **12:**529, *533n*
Walder, G., **1:**73, *74n*
Waldinger, August, **2:**390, 396, *408n,* **3:**12, *14n,* 397
Waldman, Louis, **11:**262n
Waldron, John M., **11:**143n
Walker, Charles M., **7:**14, 15n, 342n
Walker, Edwin, **3:**523
Walker, Eugene, **3:**128n, 263
Walker, Harry, **5:**336, *336n,* 370–71
Walker, Henry M., *5:395n,* 452, **6:**15, 19n, **7:**385; *letter from,* **5:**393–95
Walker, John H., **7:**:*, *102n,* **8:**:*, *139n,* 279, **9:**:*, *25n,* 65, 350n, **10:**:*, 152n, *195n,* 215, **11:**:*, *82n,* 452, **12:**:*, *38n,* 409n; at AFL conventions, **7:**137, 140, 142n, 269, 273, 274n, 418–19, 422, **8:**138, 283, 287, 293, 407–8,

409n, 410, **9:**24, 25n, 27, 346, 346n, **10:**259, 262n, **11:**81, 82n, 90, **12:**337, 337n; and election of 1906, **7:**101; and election of 1908, **7:**350n, 359, 416–17; *letters from,* **7:**416–17, **10:**295–96, **11:**102–4; *letters to,* **8:**512, **9:**150–52, **12:**34–38, 186–90, 409; and President's Mediation Commission, **10:**195, 195n, 262; *wire to,* **12:**223
Walker, John P., **1:**:*, *92n; letter to,* **1:**91–92
Walker, Joseph H., **4:**419n
Walker, Meriwether, **12:**412n
Walker, Robert W., *5:505n; letter from,* **5:**504–5
Wallace (assistant manager, Battle Creek Breakfast Food Co.), **7:**302
Wallace, Edgar, *9:341n,* **10:**470n, 492, 493n, **11:**152, *153n,* 401, 512n; **12:**184n, 212n, 345, 347; and election of 1924, **12:**432–33, 433n, 456, 461n, 467n, 468, 474, 483; *letter from,* **11:**510–12; *letter to,* **9:**335–40; and SG, death of, **12:**543
Wallace, George S., **11:**295, *296n*
Wallace (Idaho) Trades and Labor Council, *9:25n*
Wallace, William, **10:**308n
Wallas, Charles, **11:**324n
Walling, William English, **6:**412, *413n,* **10:**389n, **11:**401, **12:**145, 146n, 197n; on European situation, **10:**341–44; *letter from,* **10:**356–57; *letter to,* **7:**46–47; *memorandum by,* **10:**342–44; on Russia, **10:**90n, 512n; on socialist opposition to war, **10:**181, 228n, 261
Walmsley, Herbert E., **6:**347, *350n*
Walsh, David I., *12:212*–13n
Walsh, Francis N., **1:**103–6, *106n*
Walsh, Francis P. (Frank), **8:**332n, *9:117n,* 257, 312n, 324n, 517, **10:**237–38, **11:**18n, 21n, 154, 399, 451–53, **12:**132n; and American Union against Militarism, **9:**433n; and Committee on Industrial Relations, **9:**422n; *letter from,* **9:**311–12; *letters to,* **9:**279–80, 321–23; and National Labor Defense Council, **10:**106, 107n; and packinghouse

workers, **10:**280n, 302; at U.S. Industrial Relations Commission hearings, **9:**112, 118, 124, 130, 135; and War Labor Conference Board, **10:**334n, 407

Walsh, Michael P., **1:**216, *217n*, 218, 228

Walsh, Thomas C., **3:**367, *367n*, 378, 380, 382, **4:**296n

Walsh, Thomas J., **12:**228n

Walsh v. *New York, New Haven, and Hartford Railroad Co.*, **10:**143, *147n*

Walter, Martin W., **4:**123, *124n*

Walters, A. J., **1:**237

Walters, Mrs. G., **12:**315–16, *316n; letter to*, **12:**318–19

Waltham, Mass., Chamber of Commerce, **12:**300–301

Waltham, Watertown, Newton (Mass.), and Vicinity, Central Labor Union of, *12:301n*

Walther, Herman, **1:**250, *251n*, 254n

Walton, Henry, **2:***, 181, *182n*

Walton, John C., **12:**189n

Walz, Fred C., **7:**460, *461n*

Wambaugh, Eugene, **6:**148, *149n*

Wambaugh, Sarah, **9:**270, *274n*

Wanhope, Joshua, **9:**378, *383n*

Ward, Edmond F., **6:**365, *368n*, 502, 504n

Ward, Harry F., *12:265n; letter to*, **12:**263–64

Ward, William E., Jr., **4:***, 83, *84n*

Ward Baking Co., strike/lockout, 1923–24, **12:**406, *408n*

Warder, George W., **5:**105n

Ward steamship line, strike/lockout, 1901, **7:**162, *164n*

Ware, Fred J., **3:**51, *55n*

Warfield, S. Davies, **12:**87n

Warfield, Solomon D., **12:**204, *206n*

Warheit (New York City socialist journal), *9:405n*, **10:**157n. See also *Wahrheit*

War Industries Board, *10:21n*, 75n, 411, *412n*, **12:**423, 424n

Warinner, Allen W., **12:**409, *409n*

War Labor Conference Board, *10:334n*, 408; creation of, **10:**307n, 333–34, 334n, 407, 412n; statement of principles, **10:**490n

War Labor Policies Board, **10:**527, *527n*

Warner, George, **2:**332, *337n*

Warner, George H., *4:272n, 5:168n, 6:377n;* at AFL conventions, **4:**268–69, 272n, 274, 278n, 411, 412n, **5:**165, 168n, 170–71, 174–75, 288, 292n, **6:**376, 377n, **7:**141, 143n

Warner, John D., **4:**304n

Warner, William, **8:**363n

Warner, William M., **4:**346, *347n*

Warren, Francis E., *11:199n; letter to*, **11:**199

Warren District Trades Assembly (Bisbee, Ariz.), *10:150n*, 224

Wartheimer-Swarts Shoe Co., **8:**102

Washburn, Joseph, *letter to*, **11:**411–12

Washburn, William B., **1:**270n

Washburn-Crosby Milling Co., boycott, **6:**430n

Washington, Booker T., **4:**406–7, *408*–9n, **5:**345, 346n, **8:**166n, 337n, **9:**383, **10:**331, 348, 358, 425; *letter from*, **8:**165; *letter to*, **8:**336–37

Washington, D.C.: free lectures in, **6:**267–68, 268n; home rule for, **7:**315–16; housing of black workers in, **7:**255; race riot in, *11:116n*

Washington, D.C., Building Trades Council, **4:**175n

Washington, D.C., Central Labor Union, *1:229n, 2:71n,* **4:**170, *171n*, 175n, 197, **5:**199n, 411n, **6:**35n, **11:**195, 220, **12:**245, 247n

Washington, D.C., Federation of Labor, **1:**222, *229n*, 286, **2:**18, 69–71, *71n*, 75, 189, 189n, **4:**170

Washington (D.C.) Normal School, **10:**439n

Washington, George, **6:**332–33, **8:**74, 85

Washington, Horace L., **11:**38, *41n*

Washington, Mr. (New York City employer?), proposal of, to provide work to unemployed, **3:**450

Washington and British Columbia, District Building Trades Council of, *3:55n*

Washington Association of New Jersey, **9:**254n

Washington Brewery Co., and brewery workers' dispute, **7:**152–53n

Washington County (N.Y.) Agricultural Society, **6:**339n
Washington Electric and Traction Co., **5:**262–63, 263n
Washington Evening Star: criticism of SG in, **5:**243n; editor of, *letter to,* **5:**240–43
Washington Herald, editor of, *letter to,* **9:**76–78
Washington Post, editor of, *letters to,* **7:**315–16, **12:**192–96
Washington Star, editor of, *wire to,* **11:**77
Washington (state): Democratic state convention, 1906 (Seattle), **7:**108, *109n;* election of 1906, **7:**108, 109n; election of 1908, **7:**414, 414n
Washington (state) Farmers' Alliance, **3:**55n
Washington State Federation of Industrial Organizations, **3:**55n
Washington State Federation of Labor, *5:450n,* 468, **10:**398, **11:**113n, 218n, **12:**224, 237, 325
—conventions: 1918 (Aberdeen), **10:**488, *490n;* 1919 (Bellingham), **11:**112–13, **12:**270, *271n;* 1922 (Bremerton), **12:**237, *241n;* 1923 (Bellingham), **12:**273, *274n*
Washington State Labor Congress, **5:**449, *450n,* 467–68. *See also* Washington State Federation of Labor
—convention: 1902 (Tacoma), **5:**467–68, *470n*
Washington Times, editor of, *letter to,* **11:**366–68, 368n
Washington Union Label League, **12:**247n
Waste in Industry (Committee on Elimination of Waste in Industry), **12:**142–43, *146n,* 297
Watchorn, Robert, **3:***, 277, *279n,* **4:***, 57, *58n*
Waterloo, battle of, **5:**27
Waterman, Homer F., **9:***, 27, *28n,* 47n
Waters, Harry B., **5:**395, *396n*
Watkins, David, *letter to,* **3:**356–57
Watkins, Thomas, **6:**14n
Watson, Colley, **8:**48
Watson, David K., **4:**268n
Watson, James E., **7:**97n, **12:**348n

Watson, Thomas E., *7:371n; letter from,* **7:**371
Watt, Richard M., **10:**222–23, 223n
Watters, James, **9:**409n
Watts, John T., *5:152n; letter to,* **5:**152
Wayland, Julius A., **6:**220–21, *222n*
Wayman, James C., *6:149n; letter to,* **6:**147–49
Weaver, James B., **3:**4, 277, *277n; letter to,* **3:**593
Weaver, John, **6:**6–7, *8n*
Weaver, John G., **2:***, 293, *293n*
Weavers' Protective Association, **1:**66n
Webb, Beatrice, **12:**377n
Webb, Edwin Y., **8:**442, 445, *448n,* **10:**64n
Webb, George R., **5:**312–13, 313n, **8:**48, *49n*
Webb, Martha B. Potter, **8:**303, *304n*
Webb, Sidney J., **8:**303, *304n,* **10:**112, 116, 118
Webb, William, **5:**453n
Weber, Frank J., **3:***, 496, *498n,* **4:***, *183n,* 348, 350, 352, 366, 386–87, **5:***, *151n,* **7:**130, 142n; *letters to,* **4:**182–83, 375, **5:**148–51
Weber, John, **6:**53, *57n,* **7:**281n
Weber, John B., **3:**196, *271n; letter to,* **3:**271
Weber, Joseph, **8:**12n
Weber, Robert E., **1:**218, *220n,* 230
Webster, Daniel, **7:**88, 92n
Webster, James B., **7:***, *449n; letter from,* **7:**447–48
Webster, John S., *11:157n; letter to,* **11:**156–57
Webster, Marion M., **5:**157, *158n,* **8:**62n, **10:**280n; *letter from,* **8:**297; *letters to,* **8:**56–61, 125–26
Wecker, Der (trade union journal), **7:**297, *298n*
"We Don't Patronize List" (AFL), **4:**21n, 84, 117n, 145n, 229n, 231n, 340n, 395n, 404n, 485n, 501n, **5:**107, 108n, 118, 236n, 271n, 379n, **6:**89, 118, 119n, 223n, 292n, 381n, 440, 516n, **7:**33, 53–54, 54n, 154, 154n, 167–68, 168n, 178–79, 179n, 186n, 193, 194–95, 249n, 287, 289, 295–96, 296n, 430, 434–35; discontinuation of, **7:**312–13, 313n, 330–31

Weed, Parsons, and Co., *2:11n*
Weekly Index (Massachusetts KOL journal), **3:**269
Weeks, Edwin W., **9:***, *157n; letter from,* **9:**156–57
Weeks, John W., *11:521n,* **12:**383n, 410–11, 412n; *letter to,* **11:**520–21
Weeks, Joseph D., **3:**602, *606n*
Weeks, Louis W., **4:**432n, 433, *435n*
Weeks, Walter S., **7:**170, 176, *177n*
Wefald, Knud, **12:**432, 433–*34n*
Wehle, Louis B., *10:119n,* 207n, 230, 232–34; *letter from,* **10:**119
Wehyle (delegate), **4:**12, 15
Weidman Dyeing Works, strike/lockout, 1902, **6:**29n
Weihe, William, **1:***, 385–86, 390, *390n,* 451, 458, 463–64, **3:***, 189n, *191n,* 199n, 206, 219n, 231, 239–40, 401; at AFL convention, **3:**250, 253n; *letters from,* **1:**395–96, 425–26; *letters to,* **3:**191, 218–19
Weikel, Frank, **12:**543, *544n*
Weil, Jean, **1:***, 98, *101n*
Weinberg, Israel, **9:**517–18n
Weinhard, Henry, brewery of, **3:**82, 83n
Weinstein, Gregory, **1:**429, *2:94n; letter to,* **2:**94
Weinstock, Anna, **10:**467, *468n*
Weinstock, Harris, *9:285n,* 312n; *letter to,* **9:**284–85
Weisendanger, Ulrich, **12:**551, *554n*
Weismann, Henry, **3:***, 111–12, *114n,* 353, 419, 430, 445, 480, **4:***, 18, *18–19n,* 106n; at AFL conventions, **3:**250, 252, 253n, 256, 436, 609–10, 611n, 621–22, 624, 641–44, 654, **4:**82, 92–93, 269–71, 272n, 274, 279–82; and compulsory arbitration, **3:**259, 427–28; and depression of 1893, **3:**367, 380–84
Welch, Maurice R. "Mike," **8:***, 244–45n, *247n,* **10:***, *492n; letters from,* **8:**246–47, **10:**491–92
Wellington collieries, boycott, 1891, **3:**53, 56n
Wells, Hulet M., **10:**397–400, *400n,* **11:**112, 488n, **12:**224, 234–35
Wells, William E., **7:**106, *107n*
Welsh, Bertha, *letter from,* **6:**153–54
Welsh (carpenter?), **2:**28
Welter, John M., **2:***, 248, *248n*

Welty, John, **7:**107n
Wendelken, Harry J., **6:**501, *503n*
Werner, Louis, **4:**377, *379n*
West, Edwin H., **12:**550, *554n*
West, George P., **9:**430–31, *433n,* **10:**192, 193n, **11:**472n, **12:**41–43
West, Thomas H., *5:71n; letter to,* **5:**71
West, Walter, **7:***, *451n; letter from,* **7:**449–51
West Coast Furniture Co., **5:**339n
Western Agricultural Contracting Co., strike/lockout, 1903, **6:**150, *151n*
Western Central Labor Union (Seattle), *3:55n,* **5:**469, *470n, 10:400n*
Western Iron Association of Manufacturers, **2:**135n
Western Labor Conference (of Canada), **11:**75n
Western Labor Union, *4:452–53n,* **5:**393–95, **6:**9, **7:**404; and AFL, **4:**452, 462–63, **5:**396n, 446–47, 450–52, 468–69, 517, **6:**15–17, 17n, 23n, **10:**260, 264; and Miners, Western Federation of, **4:**253, 452–53n, 486, **5:**151n. *See also* American Labor Union
—conventions: 1898 (Salt Lake City), **4:**257, 452, *452n,* 462, 486–87; 1899 (Salt Lake City), **5:**91, *93n,* 114; 1902 (Denver), **6:**17n
Western Union Employees, Association (variously Associated), **10:**481, 482n
Western Union Telegraph Co., **1:**287, 306, 354–55, 433n; pension plan of, **11:**334; strike/lockout, 1870, **1:**343, *353n;* strike/lockout, 1883, **1:**343, *353n;* strike/lockout, 1907, **7:**250–51, *252n;* strike/lockout, 1918 (threatened), **10:**481, *482n,* 485–86, 490n; strike/lockout, 1919, **10:**515–16n, **11:**93, *94–*95n, 102–4, 104n
Western Wheel Co.: boycott, 1893, **3:**356n; strike/lockout, 1893, **3:**356n
West Indian workers, in Canal Zone, **9:**496, **12:**410–11
Westinghouse, George, **6:**121–22, *122n; letter from,* **6:**136–39
Westinghouse Air Brake Co., **6:**136
Westinghouse Electric and Manufac-

turing Co., **6:**121–22, 123n, 136–39; strike/lockout, 1916, **9:**504, *507n*
Westinghouse Machine Co., **6:**137
West London Social Guild, **5:**315–16n
Westminster conference, 1917, *10:309n;* statement of war aims, **10:**309, 309–10n, 353, 356n
Westoby, Thomas, **6:**376, *377n*
Weston, C. E., **7:**354, 356n
West Virginia: American Civil Liberties Union activities in, **12:**264, 265n, 309; congressional investigation of 1913 strike in, *8:519n,* **9:**23, 51; Guyan coalfield, tactics of coal operators in, **11:**297n; and Matewan incident, **11:**294–96, *296*–97n; Mingo County, tactics of coal operators in, **11:**296n; socialist investigation of conditions in, **8:**518, *519n*
Weyand, Louis, **11:**107n
Weyl, Walter E., *8:361n; letter from,* **8:**360–61
Weyler y Nicolau, Valeriano, *4:470n*
Whalen, John S., **7:**257, *257n*
Wharton, Arthur O., **10:***, 19, *21n,* 385n, 427, **11:***, 538, 539–*40n*
"What Does Labor Want?" (SG), **3:**388–96
Wheaton, Calvin S., **2:***, 181, *182n*
Wheeler, "brother," **10:**245
Wheeler, Burton K., *12:468n;* and election of 1924, **12:**389n, 409n, 467–68n, 470n, 475–76n, 482, 484n, 487–89, 492–93, 505–6, 513
Wheeler, Fred C., *6:150n; letter from,* **6:**149–50
Wheeler, Harry A., **11:**168, *169n,* 172, 176–77
Wheeler, Harry C., **10:**126n, 324n, 337, *339n*
Wheeler, Joseph, **5:**21, *29n*
Wheeler-Holder Tie Co., strike/lockout, 1908, **7:**378–80
Wheeler Syndicate, **12:**365
Wheeling and Lake Erie Railway, **4:**359–60n
Wheeling Steel and Iron Co., strike/lockout, 1917, **10:**79, *79n*
"Wheel of Fortune," *6:445n,* 450, 454–55, 458–61, 463, 522
Whipple, Leonidas R., **10:**484, *485n*

Whistler-Scersey Lumber Co., strike/lockout, 1908, **7:**378–80
Whitcomb, William A., **7:**202–4, *204n*
White, A. Robert, **9:**383
White, Charles L., *3:533n; wire from,* **3:**532–33
White, Edward D., **6:**421, 423n, **8:**152–53, *154n*
White, Frank A., **6:**20, *20n*
White, Harry, **3:**51, *55n*
White, Henry (diplomat), **11:**41n, 48, *49n,* 58n
White, Henry (garment worker), **3:***, 111, *115n,* 260, 261n, 381–83, 421, **4:***, 57, *57n,* 206, **5:***, *102n,* 311, 464n, 482, 483n, **6:***, *4n,* 190, 235, 297n, 313; at AFL conventions, **4:**274, 275n, **6:**198, 202, 204n; *letters from,* **5:**387–90; *letters to,* **4:**296, 397–98, **5:**101–2, 404–5, **6:**3–4, 294–97; and mediation of clothing cutters' strike, 1893, **3:**305, 313–14, 319–22, 326, 333, 338
White, Henry M., **10:**154, *155n*
White, Jacob, **10:**143
White, James E., **3:**413, *414n*
White, John, **4:**274, 275n
White, John P., **6:**270, 271n, **8:***, *280n,* **9:***, 39–40, *40n,* 67, 68n, 98n, 422n, **10:***, *23n;* and AFL vice-presidency, **9:**38n, 41–42, 42–43n; *letters from,* **8:**279–80, **9:**41–42, **10:**22; *wires to,* **9:**64, 97
White, Rufus A., **3:**424, *425n*
White, W. P., **2:**50
White, W. W., **8:**106n
Whitefield, William, **9:**487, 488n
Whitehead, James, **5:***, 418, *419n*
Whitehead, Myrtle, **9:**332, *333n*
Whiteley, Joshua C., *12:339n; wire from,* **12:**338–39
Whiteman, Clement L. V., **11:**525, *526n*
White Rats Actors' Union, **9:**292n
Whitfield, Smith A., **1:**208, *210n*
Whitin, Ernest S., **10:**450, *451n*
Whitlam, Harry J., **7:**137, *142n*
Whitley, John H., *11:166n*
Whitley Plan. *See* industrial councils, in Great Britain
Whitlock, Brand, **11:**56, *58n*
Whitman, Charles, **10:**77n

Whitney, C. E., **9:**450n, 464n

Whitney, F. Stacy, *5:470n,* **6:**16; *letter from,* **5:**467–70

Whitty, Richard P., **11:**53, *54n*

Wholesale Clothiers' Exchange of Chicago, **7:**178, 179n

"Why Affiliate with the Federation" (SG), **5:**363, *363n*

Whyte, Joseph C., *7:447n; letter to,* **7:**446–47

Whyte, William P., **1:**207, *210n*

Wickersham, George W., **7:**473n, **8:**53, *54n,* 470, 490, **9:**250, 295–96n, 319, 323, 324n; *letter to,* **9:**292–95

Wickes, Thomas H., **3:**522

Wiedfeldt, Otto, **8:**198, *199n*

Wiener, Joseph, **1:**204–5, *206n*

Wiener, Julius, **1:***, 457, *459n*

Wight, Fred C., **7:**76, *90n*

Wigmore, John H., **10:**450, *451n*

Wilcox, Ella Wheeler, **6:**482n

Wild, Mark, **4:**5, 7–8n, 81

Wiley, Louis, **12:**550, *554n*

Wilhelm II, **2:**157n, 289, 289n, **4:**154, *155n,* **5:**14, 15n, **10:**199, 268–71, 275, 527

Wilkerson, A. B., **7:**240, *242n*

Wilkerson, James H., **12:**87n, 137n, 152–54, *155n,* 158

Wilkes-Barre (Pa.) Central Labor Union, *5:123n*

Wilkie, Alexander, **5:***, 154, *154n,* 166

Wilkie, John E., **7:**393n

Wilkins, Charles, **4:**359n

Wilkinson, I. B., **5:**370, *371n*

Wilkinson, Joseph, **2:***, 79, *80n*

Wilkinson, Stephen E., **2:***, 181, *182n*

Willard, Cyrus F., **3:**415, *415n*

Willard, Daniel, **10:**21n, *79n,* **11:**259n, 347–48, 349n, **12:**87n, 204, 206n, 412, 414n, 499; *letter from,* **10:**112–13; *letters to,* **10:**77–79, 115–18

Willard, Frances E. C., **3:**598–99, *599n,* **4:**32

Willard, John F., **2:**417, *417n*

Willcox, William R., **9:**163, *164n,* **10:**320n

Willert, Arthur, **10:**332, *333n*

Willey, Norman B., **3:**214n

William D. Haywood et al. v. *U.S.,* **10:**243n

Williams, Alexander S., **2:**331, *336n*

Williams, Charles, **9:**422n

Williams, Charles F., *6:20n; letter from,* **6:**19–20

Williams, David U., **6:**107n, *109n; letter to,* **6:**108–9

Williams, E. C., **7:**286n

Williams, H. H., **10:**277, *279n*

Williams, Henry W., **3:**559, *561n,* 576

Williams, Herbert M., *10:185n*

Williams, Isabel, **11:**395, *396n*

Williams, J. W., **6:**106, 107n

Williams, James H., **4:**57, *58n*

Williams, John, **5:***, *384n,* **8:***, *31n,* **10:***, 69–70n, 77–79, *79n,* 266n; *letter from,* **5:**384

Williams, John E., **10:**280n, 302–3, *304n*

Williams, John S., **7:**130, *142n*

Williams, Mrs. J. A., **5:**264

Williams, Owen A., **3:**125–28, *128n,* 134, 137

Williams, Thomas, **9:**157n, 261n

Williams, Timothy S., **2:**320, 320n

Williams, Victor, **3:**139, *140n*

Williams, Wayne C., **9:**457, *457n*

Williams Cooperage Co.: boycott, 1903–5, *6:223n;* strike/lockout, 1903–4, **6:**222, *223n*

Williamson, Henry, **3:**540, *542n*

Williams v. *Great Southern Lumber Co.,* **11:***366n*

Willis, Frank, **9:**283n

Willis, H., **4:**123

Willis, W. S., **4:**258n

Willison, W. M., **7:**379

Williston, Martin L., **3:**424, 426n

"Will Labor Lead?" (West), **12:**42

Wills, Herman E., **11:**241, *241n,* 348, 468

Wilmington (Del.) and Vicinity, United Labor League of, **5:**387, *387n,* **12:***373n*

Wilmington (Del.) Central Labor Union, **12:**372, *373n*

Wilson, Agnes Williamson, **8:**184, 184n

Wilson, Charles F., **3:**397, *399n*

Wilson, D. Douglas, **4:***, 157, *159n,* **5:***, 116, *117n,* 368; *letter to,* **4:**178

Wilson, Edith Bolling, **11:**239n, **12:**11, *11n*

Wilson, Francis, **6:**238n
Wilson, Frank, **11:**228, *229n*
Wilson, Frederick (Cleveland auto mechanic), **11:**325, *326n*
Wilson, Frederick (of Milwaukee Federated Trades Council), **9:**213n
Wilson, Hugh, *letter to,* **11:**242
Wilson, J. B., **5:**402–3
Wilson, J. Havelock, **9:***, *477n,* **10:***, 492, *493n,* 521; *letter from,* **9:**473–76; *letter to,* **9:**484–87
Wilson, James, **2:**320
Wilson, James A., **8:***, *122n,* **9:***, *34n,* **10:***, *54n,* 333n, 446, 464, **11:***, 18, *20n,* **12:***, *562n;* at AFL conventions, **9:**32, **10:**467n, 475; and election of SG's successor, **12:**555, 557, 559–60; *letters from,* **8:**121–22, **10:**52–53
Wilson, James H., **10:**424, *431n*
Wilson, John, **6:**14n
Wilson, John T., **5:***, *178n; letter from,* **5:**177–78
Wilson, Thomas Woodrow, *8:135n,* 255–56, 256n, **9:**106n, 203n, 354, 435, 476, **10:**193n, 258, 264, 371n, 391–92n, 526, 545, **11:**239n, 336, **12:**10–11, 122, 499, 509, 547–48; and AFL conventions, **9:**519–20, **10:**255, 255n, 283–84, 464, **11:**210; AFL Executive Council, meetings with, **9:**9, 10n, **10:**31–34; AFL office building, dedication of, **9:**276n, 444–45, 448n; and American entry into World War I, **10:**3–4, 4n, 33, 38n, 49n, 200, 206, 210, 260, 273–74; and Austrian peace proposal, **10:**564, 567n; and Borland amendment, **10:**455n; and Brandeis, **6:**83n, **9:**409, 410n; and carpenters' strike, 1918, **10:**360, 362n; and Clayton Act, **9:**91–92, 140–41, 197, 200–201, 446, 455; Committee on Labor, Council of National Defense, meeting with, **10:**101, 102n, 282; and conscription, **10:**514n; and deportations, Bisbee, Ariz., **10:**150n, 168; and deportations, Gallup, N.Mex., **10:**168; and eight-hour day, **10:**281–82, 286; and election of 1910, **8:**135; and election of 1912, **8:**386, 386n, **12:**511; and election of

1916, **9:**518, **12:**492; European views of, **10:**292–93, 563–64; and German peace proposal, **10:**543, 544n; and Hill, execution of, **9:**343, 344n; and Houston mutineers, **10:**327n; and immigration bills, **9:**103n, 405n, **10:**166n; and Industrial Conference, 1919, **11:**127, 158, 169, 172, 177, 179–80, 182, 182n; and International Labor Conference, 1919, **11:**136, 138n; labor record of, SG on, **9:**473, 487, 488n; and labor standards, wartime maintenance of, **10:**101, 124, 125n, 174, 204, 282; *letter from,* **11:**127; *letters to,* **8:**460–68, 477–92, **9:**200–203, 324–26, 410–11, **10:**123–25, 148–49, 172–75, 220–21, 255, 287–91, 341, 436–37, 497–99, 513–14, **11:**3–5, 183–85, 238–39, 239n, 397–98; and Little, murder of, **10:**163n; and meatpackers' strike, 1917 (threatened), **10:**280n, 442; and Mexico, U.S. relations with, **9:**96n, 307n, 324–27, 361, 363n, 426n, 432–33, 434n, 437; and miners' strike, 1913–14 (Colorado), **9:**24n, 95n, 98n, 210, 211n; and miners' strike, 1917 (Alabama, threatened), **10:**288n; and miners' strike, 1919, **11:**192n, 195; and Mooney-Billings case, **10:**93n, 387, 388n, 395–96, 397n, 534, **11:**7n; and National War Labor Board, **10:**408n; nomination of labor secretary, **8:**333n, 425; Obregón, *letter from,* **11:**300, 303n; and Overman bill, **10:**412; at Paris Peace Conference, **11:**5n, 39, 40–41n, 58–59n, 69–70; and police, organization of, **11:**145; and postwar economic readjustment, **11:**52n; and President's Mediation Commission, creation of, **10:**126n, 195n, 205; and Puerto Rico, **9:**410–11, 411n, **10:**438n; and railroad shopmen's strike, 1919 (threatened), **11:**120n; and railroad strike, 1916 (threatened), **9:**450n; and railroad strike, 1920 (threatened), **11:**259n; and Root mission to Russia, **10:**71–72n; SG, meetings with, **8:**386, 424–25, **9:**358–59, 360n, 432–33, 434n, **10:**194–95, 195n,

205, 221n, 262, 371n, 387, 395–96, 497–98, 499n, **11:**39–40, 41n, 47, 55, 125, 125–26n; and Shipbuilding Labor Adjustment Board, **10:**207n; and shipbuilding workers' strike, 1917 (Pacific Coast), **10:**209n; and steel strike, 1919–20, **11:**124–25, 125–26n, 128–29, 129n, 140–41, 144, 144n, 147, 162–63; stroke, **11:**129n, 182n; and sundry civil appropriation bills, **8:**468n, 469–70, 494–95, 495n; and telegraphers' strike, 1918 (threatened), **10:**482n, 485–86, 515, 515n; and telegraphers' strike, 1919, **11:**95n, 104n; and Transportation Act of 1920, **11:**271; and Versailles Treaty, labor clauses in, **11:**87–88, 92n; and Versailles Treaty, ratification of, **11:**129, 129n; and vocational education, **9:**353, 353n, **10:**47–48, 49n; and war aims (*see* Fourteen Points); and war Industries Board, **10:**412n; and war labor program, **10:**333, 334n; *wire from,* **11:**99–102; *wires to,* **10:**568, **11:**121–23, 128–29

Wilson, William, **1:**217–18, *220n*

Wilson, William B., **6:***, *22n,* 165, **7:***, 113, *113n,* 130, 322n, 357, **8:***, *89n,* 496n, **9:***, 9, *10n,* 112n, 359, 431–32, 435, **10:***, *38n,* 78, 101, 104, 274, 286, **11:**72n, 128n, 191, 193, 206n, 209, 259n, 336, **12:***, 217, *218n,* 493, 502, 503n; and AFL conventions, **6:**55, 57n, 66, 67n, 69, 506–7, 509n, **7:**131–33, 142n, **8:**289, 293; AFL Executive Council, meetings with, **9:**396, 396n, **10:**31–34; and American Alliance for Labor and Democracy, financial support of, **10:**498; appointment of, as secretary of labor, **8:**333n, 425; *cable from,* **10:**546n; as chair of House Committee on Labor, **8:**183–84, 184n, 209, 374; and Clayton Act, **9:**319, 321n, 323; and Committee on Labor, Council of National Defense, **10:**52n; and copper miners' strike, 1913–14 (Northern Michigan), **9:**44, 44n; and deportations from Bisbee, Ariz., **10:**168; and Division of Negro Economics, **10:**366–67;

and election of 1924, **12:**495–501; and garment workers, wages of, **10:**62n; and immigrant workers, **10:**166n; and labor legislation, **8:**100, 101n, 257, 258n, 374, 377, 379, 470; and Labor Loyalty Week, **10:**313n; and labor standards, maintenance of, **10:**55, 56n; *letters from,* **6:**22, **10:**154, 333–34, **12:**495–98; *letters to,* **6:**23, **8:**87–89, **10:**164–66, 194–95, 327, 395–97, **11:**135–37, **12:**498–501; and longshoremen's strike, 1917 (threatened), **10:**137, 137n; and meatpackers' strike, 1917 (threatened), **10:**280n, 442; *memorandum by,* **10:**304–6; and Mexican immigration, **11:**342n; and mine and smelter workers' strike, 1915–16 (Arizona), **9:**352n; and miners' strike, 1917, **10:**126; and miners' strike, 1917 (Alabama, threatened), **10:**288n; and oil field workers' strike, 1917–18, **10:**306n; and organizers, harassment of, **10:**69–70n, 404n, 519n; and pattern makers' strike, 1917 (threatened), **10:**53; and Puerto Rico, conditions in, **10:**314; and Root mission to Russia, **10:**72n; and Russia, conditions in, **10:**512n; and Sadie Gompers, death of, **10:**546n; and SG trip to Europe, **10:**473; and steel strike, 1917, **10:**79; and steel strike, 1919, **12:**279–80; and steelworkers' organizing campaign and strike, 1919, **11:**28n; and telegraphers' strike, 1918 (threatened), **10:**482n, 485; and telegraphers' strike, 1919, **11:**95n, 103, 104n; as War Labor Administrator, **10:**334n, 407, 408n, 411, 412n, 527n

Wilson, William J., **7:**355, *356n*

Wilson, William W., **11:**276, *278n,* 281

Wilson meatpacking company, strike, 1921–22, *11:571n*

Wilson v. New et al., **9:***450n,* **10:***17n,* **11:**251, *259n,* 331, **12:**497, 498n, 499

Wimsett, C. A., **6:**71n

Winders, John R., **1:**457, *459n,* 471

Windom, William, **3:**119, *120n*

Window Glass Workers, National, **9:***, 83n, **10:**22n

Window Glass Workers of America, Amalgamated, **9:***; dissolution of, **9:**82, *83n*

Wines, Abner G., **4:***, 275–76, *278n*

Winfield, Charles W., **12:**132, *133n*

Winkel, Mrs. Abraham, **3:**141, *142n*

Winkler, John, **1:***, *257n; letter from,* **1:**256–57

Winkler, Joseph, **8:**12n

Winn, William H., **4:**167, *168n,* 251n; *letter to,* **4:**334–35

Winnick, Henry, **3:**141, *142n*

Winnick, Mrs. Henry, **3:**141

Winnipeg, Man.: building trades strike, 1919, **11:**75n; general strike, 1919, **11:**74–75, *75n,* 94, 380; metal trades strike, 1919, **11:**75n

Winnipeg (Man.) Trades and Labour Council, **11:**75n

Winship, Blanton, **10:**284n

Winship, North, **10:**555n

Winslow, Charles H., **9:**54–55, *57n*

Winston, Robert, **4:**109, *110n*

Winter, Ernst G., **1:***, 110, *112n*

Winthrop, Beekman, **6:**382–83, *383n,* 424–26, 428, 429n

Wire Weavers' Protective Association, American, **10:***, 429, 431n

Wirt, William A., **9:**429, *430n*

Wischnewetzky, Florence Kelley. *See* Kelley, Florence

Wischnewetsky, Lazare, **2:**148–49, *149n,* 156

Wisconsin, election of 1906, **7:**64–67, 130–31, 139, 143n

Wisconsin State Federation of Labor, **3:**496, *498n,* **7:**157; *letter from,* **7:**64–67

—convention: 1906 (Madison), *7:67n,* 157

Wisconsin Vorwärts (Milwaukee, Wis., socialist journal), **3:**490, 492–94, 498n

Wisdom, Thomas J., **3:***, 356, *356n*

Wise, Morris S., *1:263n*

Wise, Peter, **3:**67, *68n*

Wise, Stephen S., **10:**546n, **11:**154, *155n,* **12:**82n; eulogy for SG, **12:**545, 547–49

Wisler, Russell I., **6:**218, *219n,* 234n, 341n; *letter from,* **6:**233–34

Wismar, William, **1:**414, *414n*

Witherbee, Sherman, and Co., strike/lockout, 1913, **9:**177, *178n*

Withers, Pauline M., **6:**237, *238n*

Witte, Sergey Yulyevich, *6:491n; letter to,* **6:**490–91

Witter, Martin R. H., **1:***, 385, *396n; letter from,* **1:**396

Witzel, John, **6:**214, *215n*

Wodika, Josef, **4:**219n

Wolder, Louis, **3:**141, *142n,* 381, 383n

Wolders, George, **1:**134, *134n*

Wolf, E., **3:**403n

Wolf, Jacob, **1:**418, *418n*

Wolf, Morris, **10:**528, 529n

Wolf, Robert B., **11:**384–85, 390, *391n,* **12:**413

Wolfe, James H., *12:310n; letter to,* **12:**309–10

Wolfson, Louis, **3:**615, *616n,* 633, 641

Woll, Matthew, **8:***, 258, *259n,* **9:***, *93n,* **10:***, *48n,* 358n, **11:***, 67, *67n,* 140n, 211n, 345, 426, 456, 459n, 472n, **12:***, 51, *52n,* 93n, 126, 190, 294, 312, 315n, 388; and AFL committee on wages, **11:**559, 560n; and AFL conventions, **10:**259, 261, 262n, 266, **11:**81n, 88–89, 92–93n, 474–75, 479, **12:**87, 94–95, 333, 334n; and AFL demands of Democratic and Republican parties, **11:**313n; at AFL Executive Council meeting, **11:**390; and AFL National Non-Partisan Political Campaign, **11:**275n, 283n; and Clayton Act, **9:**89, 93, 153n, 168, 323, 324n; and coal strike, 1919, **11:**195, 198n, 200–203; and election of 1924, **12:**456, 458n, 459, 461n, 465–66, 467n, 468–69, 470n, 471–72, 472n, 473, 473n, 474–75, 478–83, 483n, 489, 504–5, 507n; election of, as AFL vice-president, **11:**93n, 321, 321n, 482, **12:**97n, 338n; and election of SG's successor, **12:**555, 559–60; as fraternal delegate to TUC, **9:**162–63, 469, 485; and freight handlers' conference, **11:**488, 491; and Hearst papers, attack by, **11:**366–67, 447; and Industrial Conference, 1919, **11:**128n,

177; and International Federation
of Trade Unions, **11:**224n, 440n;
and International Labor Conference, 1919, **11:**110–11, 111n; *letters from,* **10:**46–48, **12:**468–69,
473–75, 478–80; *letters to,* **10:**178–79,
11:335–37, 522–23, **12:**208, 226–27,
472–73n; and National Women's
Trade Union League, **11:**132, 135n;
and open shop campaign, AFL
response to, **11:**401; and People's
Legislative Service, **11:**468, 470–71;
and Plumb Plan, **11:**130, 131n; and
railway shopmen's strike, 1922-?,
12:106n; and SG, death of, **12:**541;
and SG, memoirs of, **12:**385n, 533,
535n; and southern textile organizing campaign, **11:**525–26; and
Unemployment Conference, 1921,
11:532n; *wires to,* **12:**218, 378
woman and child labor, international
conferences on: 1890 (Berlin),
2:157n, 289, *289n;* 1890 (Switzerland), **2:**156, *157n*
Woman's Christian Temperance
Union, **3:**598, *599n,* **4:**414, 416n
—convention: 1894 (Cleveland),
3:598, *599n*
Woman's International Union Label
League, **7:***299n*
Woman's Peace party, **9:**231, 232n,
274n
Woman's Suffrage League, **9:**36n
Woman's Temperance Crusade, **3:**599
Woman's Trade Union League, *6:483–*
84n
—conventions: 1905 (Chicago),
6:484n; 1905 (New York City),
6:484n; 1905 (Pittsburgh; can-
celled), **6:**483, *484n*
woman suffrage: AFL and, **3:**25, 428,
5:139–40, 140n, 158–60, 160n, **6:**511,
512n, 532, 533n, **8:**146, **9:**36, 124,
10:469, 471n; Oregon referendum
on, **6:**532, 533n; SG and, **3:**40, 159,
428, **4:**32, **5:**139–40, **6:**216–17, 217n,
511–12, 512n, 532, 533n, **9:**185–87,
12:426–27. *See also* U.S. Constitution:
Nineteenth Amendment
Woman Suffrage Association, American, **3:**25n

Woman Suffrage Association, Na-
tional, **3:**25n
Woman Suffrage Association, Na-
tional American, *3:25n*
—conventions: 1904 (Washington,
D.C.), *6:216;* 1906 (Baltimore),
6:511, 512n
Women Machine Wood Workers'
Union (Oshkosh, Wis.), **9:**332, *333n*
Women's Committee for Industrial
Equality, **11:**506
Women's Committee for Recognition
of Russia, **12:**293, *294n*
Women's International League
for Peace and Freedom, **9:**274n,
12:294n
Women's National Labor League,
1:282, *283n*
Women's Protective and Provident
League. *See* Women's Trade Union
League (English)
Women's Temperance League, **12:**360
Women's Trade Union and Provident
League. *See* Women's Trade Union
League (English)
Women's Trade Union League (English), **6:**483, *484n*
—convention: 1905 (Hanley, England), **6:**483, *484n*
Women's Trade Union League, National. *See* National Women's Trade
Union League
women workers: AFL and, **3:**133, 136,
428, **4:**323, 324n, **5:**36–38, 39n, 431,
9:20, 22n, 38, 38n, 142, 214–15,
223–24n, **10:**467, 469, 470–71n,
11:476–77, 478n, 505–6, 507n,
12:30–31, 89, 89n, 249–50, 337n,
370–71, 371n; AFL Permanent Conference for Protection of Rights
and Interests of Women Wage Earners and, **12:**246–47; AFL Women's
Department and, **12:**277, 360–61,
361–62n, 404–7, 408n, 417–18,
418n, 443–45, 445–47n, 448–49,
449n, 450–51, 451n; Allgemeiner
Deutscher Gewerkschaftsbund and,
12:361n; Barbers and, **12:**237–39,
241n, 267–68, 334–37, 476–78,
478n; and Battle Creek Breakfast
Food Co., **7:**302–3; bottle caners,

7:219–20, 220n; and Cannelton, Ind., cotton mills, 7:228, 234; can workers, 6:244, 245n; cash girls, 1:304–5; cereal mill employees, 10:368–69; cigarmakers, 1:45–46, 50, 53, 66, 102, 107, 110, 122, 304, 5:129n, 7:365, 11:412–19, 419n (*see also under* cigarmakers; Cigar Makers' International Union of America); and Cleveland Street Railway Co., 11:18–19, 20–21n; Council of National Defense and, 10:57n, 81, 82n, 96–98, 98n, 108, 108–9n, 11:35–36; education of, 12:449, 449n; Electrical Workers and, 4:323, 324n, 9:99, 99n, 12:371n; and "equal pay for equal work," 4:31, 5:200, 8:262, 382–83, 10:43, 107–8, 108n, 467, 477, 483, 11:8n, 18n, 71n, 100, 159, 477; Federal Employees and, 12:371n; Garment Workers and, 6:49–50, 50n, 12:371n; in Great Britain, 5:314, 10:27, 81; hat trimmers, 7:197–99, 230–31; hours and working conditions of, 2:48, 80, 83, 289, 289n, 4:100, 491, 8:345, 9:22n, 214–15, 223–24n, 10:57n, 99–101; and inspection of workplaces, 2:176, 288–89, 289–90n; and Kansas City (Mo.) Railways Co., 11:19–20, 21n; KOL and, 3:133; laundry workers, 3:122, 284; Meat Cutters and, 5:17; Mine Workers, United, and, 4:60; Molders and, 8:387–89, 389n; net stringers, 6:153–54, 154n; organization of, 2:80, 3:102–3, 133, 136, 155, 428, 4:31–32, 314, 323, 324n, 5:36–38, 39n, 200, 431, 6:218, 520, 8:360, 9:38, 38n, 142, 186, 234, 235n, 332, 333n, 10:219, 12:30–31, 244–46, 249–50, 337n, 370–71, 371n, 376 (*see also under* American Federation of Labor [AFL]: organizers); Railway and Steamship Clerks and, 12:371n; sewing girls, 1:313; SG *articles on,* 6:480–82, 8:513–17; Tailors and, 6:49–50, 50n; telephone operators, 6:32–33, 265–66; Trades Union Congress of Great Britain and, 12:361n, 376; Typographical Union

and, 9:315, 11:505; wages of (*see under* legislation, states and territories; legislation, U.S.; minimum wage); waitresses, 7:239, 240n; and war effort, 10:27–28, 98–102, 107–8, 108n, 219, 219n, 401–2, 467, 469, 477, 482–83; watch workers, 3:347–48, 5:30. *See also specific unions, and under* legislation, states and territories; legislation, U.S.
Wood, F. W., 5:225, 230n
Wood, Francis N., *3:362n; letter to,* 3:361–62
Wood, Isaac, 2:57, *58n*
Wood, James, 4:*, 76, *77n*, 348, 353
Wood, James D., 5:321, *322n*
Wood, James E., *letter to,* 12:429
Wood, Joseph W., *3:463n,* 6:502, *504n; letter from,* 3:462
Wood, Leonard, 4:133n, 5:183–84, 186, *188n,* 7:162–64, 164–65n, *9:331*–32n, 363n, 10:37–38; *letter to,* 9:329–31
Wood, Wire, and Metal Lathers' International Union, 6:*, 292n, 8:*, 416n
—local: local 53 (Philadelphia), 6:292, 292n
—strikes/lockouts: 1903–6 (Philadelphia), 6:292, *292n;* 1919 (Toronto), 11:72
Woodbridge, Alice L., *3:452n; letter to,* 3:452
Woodbury, Oliver E., 4:270, *272n,* 5:174, *176n*
Wood Carvers' Association of North America, International, 5:*, 162n; jurisdiction of, 5:161, 162n
Woodland, Thomas P., 10:459–60, *460n*
Woodman, Con W., 6:264–65, *265n,* 7:301, 385
Woodrow Wilson Foundation, 12:10–11, *11n*
Woods, Master Workman, 2:332
Woods, Samuel, 3:*, 596–97, *597n,* 4:*, 53, *53n,* 248
Woods, W. G., 3:362
Woods, William A., 3:523, 526n, 531n, 559, *561n,* 563n, 576, 632
Woodsmen and Sawmill Workers, In-

ternational Brotherhood of, **7**:*, 112n; injunction against, **7**:378–79; and IWW, **7**:111
—locals: local 17 (Fields Landing, Calif.), **7**:111, 112n; local 26 (Farmers, Ky.), **7**:378–80, 381n
—strike/lockout: 1908 (Farmers, Ky.), **7**:378–80
Woodstock Prison, **4**:64, 65n
Woodward, Stanley D., **4**:443–44, *446n*
Wood-Workers' International Union of America, Amalgamated, **3**:*, **4**:*, 270, 272n, 381, 382n, **5**:*, 107, 108n, 162n, **6**:*, 53n, **7**:*, 272n; jurisdiction of, **5**:161, 162n, 421–22, 422–23n, **6**:51, 52–53n, 64–66, 66–67n, 165–67, 167n, 181, 211, 211n, 500, 503n, **7**:272; label of, **5**:269–70
—locals: local 3 (Denver), **6**:15, 17–18n; local 6 (Baltimore), **5**:269–71, 271n; local 99 (Colorado Springs, Colo.), **6**:15, 17n
—strike/lockout: 1902 (Denver), **6**:15, *17–18n*
Wood Workers' International Union of America, Machine, **3**:*, 533n, **4**:*, 270, 272n, **5**:*, **6**:*, **7**:*
Woolley, Robert W., *9:473n; wire to,* **9**:473
Woonsocket (R.I.) Central Labor Union, *11:248n*
Wootton, Harry E., **10**:224, 225n
Worden, S. F., **3**:659n
work, **6**:345–46, 348; right to, SG and, **4**:26, 35; specialization of, **5**:30–31, **6**:338–39
workers: as class, **1**:23–25, 26n, 29–31, 33–34, 36, 59, 86, 213, **2**:90–91, 121–22, 153, 196, **3**:229; European and American, SG comparisons of, **4**:61–64, 67–68, 70–71, 87, 89, 99–100, **5**:191–92; SG on depictions of, **7**:442–43
"Workers, The" (Wyckoff), **4**:396–97, *397n*
workers' committees, **10**:455–56, 456n, **11**:107, 389–90; in Great Britain, **11**:173, 176n, 244
Workers' Council of the U.S., **11**:549n
Workers' Education Bureau of America, **11**:500n, *12:157n,* 191, 226, 227n, 382, 383n, 387–88, 389n
Workers' Federation of the Republic of Panama. *See* Federación Obrera de la República de Panamá
Workers' International Industrial Union, **9**:150n
Workers' Monthly (American Communist party journal), **11**:561n
Workers of America, Association of United, *1:84n*
Workers' (Communist) Party of America, **11**:550n
Workers' Party of America, **11**:549, *550n,* **12**:172–73, 296n, 309, 403; and election of 1924, **12**:296n, 409, 431–32, 433n, 463, 484–85, 485n; program of, **12**:172, 173n
—conventions: 1921 (New York City), **11**:549, 549–*50n;* 1922 (New York City), **12**:172, *173n,* 403, 403–4n
Workers' Party of Canada:
—convention: 1922 (Toronto), **12**:48n
workingmen's associations, European, **1**:23–25, 26n, 30–40, 61
"Workingmen's Estate" (Arbeiterstand), *1:44n*
Workingmen's Party of the U.S., **1**:71, *83,* 85, 97, 203n; New York American Section, **1**:83, *84n,* 85; New York German Section, **1**:83, 86–89
Workingmen's Political League (Md.), **7**:120n
Workmen's Advocate (New York City socialist journal), **2**:191, *3:14n*
workmen's compensation, **8**:31–33, 191, 413, 448n, **12**:454; legislation on, **9**:75–76n, 200n, **10**:147–48n, **11**:8n, 312, **12**:4 (*see also under* legislation, foreign; legislation, states and territories; legislation, U.S.); National Civic Federation-AFL model bill and, **9**:200n; SG and, **8**:443–47, 457–58, **9**:6–7, 75, 198–200, **10**:143–47
Workmen's Council for the Maintenance of Labor's Rights, **10**:157n
"Work or Fight" draft provision, **10**:450, 451n, 513–14, 514n, 538–39, 540n

workplace safety, **3:**559, **6:**96, 479,
8:317–18. *See also under* legislation,
states and territories; legislation,
U.S.; mines: and safety legislation
workplace sanitation, **6:**479, **8:**318,
487
World Court, **12:**209, *210n*, 455
World Court Congress, 1915 (Cleveland), **9:**269, *274n*
World Power Conference, 1924 (London), **12:**347, 348–*49n;* American
Committee of, **12:**347, 348n
World's Congress Auxiliary, **3:**224n
World's Fair, 1892, New York City as
site for, **2:**233, 233n, 257
World's Fair, 1893. *See* Columbian Exposition, World's, 1893 (Chicago)
World War I: AFL and, **9:**226, 226n,
231, 232n, 265, 291, 292n, 381, 485,
525n, **10:**309, 353, 355n, 472–73,
473–74n, 531, 551; AFL Executive
Council and, **9:**231, 232n; armistice, **10:**568, *568n;* atrocities during, **9:**192, 193–94n, 195; economic
impact of, **9:**190; labor in United
States, and war effort, **11:**255,
444, 521, 521n; labor representation, on U.S. agencies and boards,
9:358–59, 360n, **10:**43, 116, 121–22,
205, 212, 319, 320–21n, **11:**18n
(*see also specific agencies and boards*);
labor standards in United States,
maintenance of, **10:**40–42, 54–56,
56–57n, 57–58, 58n, 59–60, 60n,
65–67, 74, 80, 83–84, 84n, 85–86,
91–93, 95, 98–102, 108, 109n, 123,
142, 174, 193n, 203, 211, 230, 239,
282–83, 285n, 363–65, 458; mediation, continuous, between bellig-
erents, **9:**274n; "no annexations,
no indemnities," as peace terms,
10:88–89, 90n, 93, 93n, 344, 345n;
outbreak of, **9:**160n, 163n, 173, 192,
193n; outbreak of, SG and, **9:**160,
162–63, 166–67, 168n, 175n, 372;
and reconstruction (*see* reconstruction, postwar); U.S. involvement
in, **9:**253–54, 286–87, 290–91, 447,
12:452n. *See also* peace movement;
entries under specific countries

—U.S. entry into: AFL and, **11:**88,
92n; opposition to, **10:**5, 22, 33–35;
SG and, **10:**3–4, 4n, 49, 536; Wilson
and, **10:**3–4, 4n, 33, 38n, 49n, 200,
206, 210, 273–74
Worthey, James W., **11:**326, *326n*,
489, 491, 501–2, 502n, 550–51,
551n; *letter from,* **11:**558–59; *letter to,*
11:552–54
Worthington, Nicholas E., **3:**572–75,
579n
Worth-While Revolution, A (SG), **12:**420,
421n
Woytisek, Vincent W., **1:***, 250, *251n,*
358, **3:**15, *18n*
Wright, Alexander W., **2:***, 230, *232n,*
243, 332–36, 343, **3:**3
Wright, Carroll D., **1:***, 291, *327n,*
329, 342, **2:**127n, 129, 132–33, **3:***,
288, *291n,* 477, 564, 567–71, 578,
579n, 602, 606n, **4:***, 45n, *132n,*
295, **6:**13–14n; *letter to,* **4:**131–32
Wright, Charles H., **4:**187, *189n*
Wright, Chester M., **10:***, *142n,* 181,
225, 236, 544, 546n, **11:***, *29–30n,*
93n, 274, **12:***, 184n, 199, *202n,*
359n; and AFL mission to Europe,
spring 1918, **10:**333n; and American Alliance for Labor and Democracy, **10:**157n, 162, 163n, 497n;
and election of 1924, **12:**431, 433n,
461n, 467n, 468, 470n, 471, 474,
478–80, 502, 504; *letters from,* **11:**28–
29, **12:**478–80; *letter to,* **10:**142; and
Russia, conditions in, **10:**512n; and
SG, death of, **12:**541
Wright, Daniel T., **7:**249–50n, 430–31,
434–38, *438n,* 440, 465, 478, 492n,
8:12n, 161–62, 204n, 217, 240–41,
270–71, 292–93, 335, 428, **9:**105,
106n, **11:**85, 85n, **12:**155, 156n
Wright, Donald H., **11:**381, *381n*
Wright, Edwin R., **7:***, 360, *361n,* 363
Wright, George P., **7:**108, *109n*
Wright, Hendrick B., **3:**448, *451n*
Wright, John H., **2:**36, *36n*
Wright, Julian L., **1:**454, *455n*
Wright, Marshall E., *10:137n;* wire
from, **10:**137
Wunch, Edward, **6:**339n

Wunch v. *Shankland,* **6:**330, *339–40n*
Wyatt, Calvin, **4:**373, *375n,* **6:**141n, **7:**96, *98n,* 107n, 121–22, 122n, 346, 347n, **8:**189n, 227n; *letter from,* **7:**378–80; *letter to,* **11:**517
Wyckoff, Walter A., **4:**396–97, *397n*
Wyoming State Federation of Labor, **12:**191, *192n*

Yager, Arthur, **9:**72, *74n,* 79–80, 80n, 411, 411n, **10:**313–14, 436–37
Yarnell, Samuel, *4:272n;* at AFL conventions, **4:**271, 272n, 274, 280–81, 407, 409n, 413, 416
Yates, Rose A., **10:**467, *468n,* **11:**18. *See also* Forrester, Rose Yates
Yates, William, **8:**502n
yellow-dog contracts, **1:**354–55, **11:**174–75, 507–8, **12:**8–9, 9–10n
Yerkes, Robert M., *12:168n*
Yiddish, trade union publications in, **7:**297–98, 298n
Yonkers (N.Y.) Federation of Labor, *11:317n,* **12:**551
York Manufacturing Co., **9:**347n
Young, Albert, **7:***, 97, *98n*
Young, C. Bethuel, *10:406n; letter from,* **10:**405–6
Young, Charles O., **7:**109n, *268n,* **10:***, 186n, *246n,* 417, **12:***, *225n,* 339–40n; at AFL convention, **7:**267, 268n; *letters from,* **10:**485–90, **12:**274–75; *letter to,* **10:**245–46; and Seattle Central Labor Council, **12:**224–25, 237, 253, 259n, 273–74, 274n, 275, 324; *wire to,* **10:**245
Young, Eugene J., *12:230n; letter to,* **12:**230
Young, George B., *9:56n; letter to,* **9:**54–56
Young, John R., **7:**248, 357
Young, Lucien, **5:**231, *232n*
Young, Maurice de, **9:**63n
Young, Owen D., **11:**523n, **12:**550, *552n*
Young, Samuel B. M., *9:451n; letter to,* **9:**451
Young Communist League, **12:**277n
Young Communist League of the U.S., **12:**277n
Younger, Maud, **7:**46, *47n;* "The Di-

ary of an Amateur Waitress" (article by), **7:**239, *240n; letters to,* **7:**238–40, **8:**382–84
Young Men's Christian Association, and AFL Permanent Conference for Abolition of Child Labor, **12:**82n
Young Women's Christian Association, **12:**360; and AFL Permanent Conference for Abolition of Child Labor, **12:**82n
Young Workers' Communist League of America, **12:**277n
Young Workers' League of America, *12:277n;* SG, meeting with representatives of, **12:**275–77
Yūaikai, **9:**513, 515n
Yucatán, governor of, **9:**427n
Yudico, Samuel O., *9:426n,* **12:**359n; *letter to,* **9:**425–26

Zacharias, Benjamin, *3:340n;* and mediation of clothing cutters' strike, 1893, **3:**306
Zahniser, Charles R., **11:**154, *155n*
Zanesville (Ohio) Chamber of Commerce, **11:**342–43
Zapata, Emiliano, **9:**212n, 306, *307n*
Zaranko, William, **11:**323–24, *324–25n,* 378; *letter from,* **11:**352–53
Zaring, John, **6:**361, *364n*
Zaritsky, Max, **11:***, 498, *499n*
"Zehn Philosophen, Die," *1:83*
Ziesing, August, **6:**515n
Zilliox, Truman M., *letter to,* **10:**103–4
Zimmerman, William H., **8:**232–34, 234n
Zimmermann, Arthur, **10:**34, 38n
Zimmermann telegram, **10:**34, *38n*
Zinoviev, Grigory Y., **11:**428, *432n,* **12:**293, 294n
Zionism, **9:**405n; SG and, **9:**60, 403–5, 405n
Zoatzer, Henry, **1:**431
Zoercher, Jacob, **7:**227, *229n*
Zolezzi, Norman A., **9:**341, *342n*
Zorn, Julius, **5:***, *56n,* 375n, 453n, **6:***, *10n,* **8:***, *92n;* at AFL conventions, **5:**53, 56n, 171, 172n; *letters from,* **6:**8–10, **8:**91–92; *letter to,* **5:**374–75

Zubarán Capmany, Rafael, *9:159n,*
425, 498, 500n; *letter to,* **9:**158–59
Zuber, John J., *3:340n;* and mediation
of clothing cutters' strike, 1893,
3:305–6, 314, 326–27, 332
Zuckerman, Max, **6:***, 406, *407n,* **7:***,

18–19n, 142n, **9:***, *110n,* **11:***, *499n;*
The Deceit of the I.W.W. (book by);
7:19n; letters from, **7:**17–18, 207–8,
9:107–10; *letter to,* **11:**498–99
Zukowski, Walter J., **10:**215, *218n*
Zwerling, T., **6:**276, *278n*

University of Illinois Press
1325 South Oak Street   Champaign, IL 61820-6903
www.press.uillinois.edu